"Fond of liquor, dancing and gaming"

New-York Runaways, 1769-1783

Compiled by
Joseph Lee Boyle

CLEARFIELD

Copyright © 2020 by
Joseph Lee Boyle

All Rights Reserved.

Published for Clearfield Company by
Genealogical Publishing Company
Baltimore, Maryland
2020

ISBN 9780806359113

INTRODUCTION

The majority of the individuals in this compilation are runaway servants and slaves, but a number are runaway apprentices, both men and women, military deserters, with horse thieves, counterfeiters, burglars, jail breakers, an occasional murderer, enemies of the United States, and other lowlifes are represented. Many more military deserters for this period appear in this writer's two volume *"He loves a good deal of rum..." Military Desertion During the American Revolution, 1775-1783*, published in 2009, by Clearfield Company, Baltimore, Maryland.

Tracking an individual by name may often lead to a dead end as multiple names were common, and middle names were not often used at this time. Peter Provost advertised for an Irish boy named John Foshy, who also called himself John Green. Indented servant Lawrence Gojion, used the alias John Johnston. Williams Gibbbs/Gibs creatively used the name John Smith.

Some of the runaway Negroes also used multiple names such Quash, "but frequently calls himself George." Oliver apparently decided to call himself Joe, and a man once known as Caesar, "calls himself Julius Caesar."

Some runaway ladies used multiple names such as the "noted whore" Mary Arnold, who went by Mary Newbergh and ran off with John Reese. Mary Pontenner, alias Mary Morris, alias Black, alias Mary Sharp, alias Mary Hancock, married one Richard Watkins, and left him after robbing and plundering him. In 1774 Peter Garson advertised for a "servant girl, whose name cannot be well known, she has assumed so many names at different times and places; she has called herself Hannah Swinburn, Hutcheson, Nancy Ring, &c."

Some of the multiple names that appear are likely due to spelling or pronunciation errors such as Hubs/Hubbs, Conary/Conray/Conroy, and Thorpe/Thorpp. Names not common in English may have been quite creatively spelled by the advertisers. There are also nicknames such as a "Negro Man named JACOB, belonging to *Henry Brasier*, and formerly known in this City, by the Name of the Fu-Fu Negro, or MONEY-DIGGERs." John McGay, a native of Ireland was commonly called Limerick.

Multiple spellings of names sometimes appear in the same ad such as Gibbs/Gibs. When ads are published in different newspapers or even in the same paper, discrepancies in the ads sometimes appear. If the variations are substantial, the separate ads are included. For example John Foster advertises in five papers in 1773 for Negro Cush. The reader should be prepared for phonetic spellings of people they are interested in such as Enslee/Inslee and of course Jonson/Johnston/Johnson is always a challenge. In a few cases letters were indistinct and thus appear in brackets.

Some of the runaways were well skilled. Butchers, bakers, coopers, carpenters, blacksmiths, shoemakers and taylors (tailors) are represented. Skills of others might today be questionable such as that of a black man named Richmon who was advertised by Captain Cunningham, the British Provost Marshall, as being "the Common HANGMAN."

Advertisers often questioned the supposed skills of people. Sheriff Henry Rosekrans advertised suspected counterfeiter Joseph Spragge, who "pretends to be a doctor, silversmith and brassfounder; is a artful cunning fellow, and no doubt will change his name." William Thompson, "pretends to understand Basket-making, Masonry and Farming." Some skills such as that of a ditcher, fuller, and wool comber no longer exist, and have you lately heard of a tinker or netmaker or pot-ash boiler. In many ads privateers and privateering are mentioned indicating skills at sailing.

It is impossible to know how many runaways there really were. No newspapers were published in Delaware for the entire period covered. The American Revolution found New York City and adjacent areas occupied by the British forces from August 1776, until November 25, 1783. While newspapers were published in the city and state, the turmoil of the era may have caused many omissions.

Also printed handbills were often circulated, and some masters may have only advertised with them. Given that so many of the servants appear to be scapegraces, one wonders why their masters spent money to advertise for them, let alone pay a reward for their return. Masters were likely to ignore those who left for a few days of dissipation, particularly planters during the agricultural slow season. Why ads were often delayed can only be guessed at. Patrick Clark waited until 1783, to advertise for David who had runaway the previous November. In July 1776, Joseph Rodman advertised for William who ran away "about three Years ago."

Some masters may have not wanted to pay the cost of the ads. Those masters whose servants absconded from more remote parts of the colony may not have bothered to advertise them. Subscribers who waited lengthy periods to advertise must have greatly reduced the chance of capturing the rogue. Several ads seem to have been intended to let the runaway know how little the master thought of them as very low rewards were posted. Daniel Sickles offered only "a pair of OLD SHOES" as a reward for returning runaway apprentice John Leverage. One wonders why John J. Van Rensselaer bothered to advertiser for Rob who "has done very little work for the 3 last years, as he was inclined to a consumption, but laterly feigned himself so." Green-Bush, near Albany, June 30, 1783.

Indented servant Ezekiel Hams was described by Jesse Fairchild as "much addicted to drunkenness; very talkative when intoxicated; an abominable liar, horrible swearer, and the most ungrateful, profligate wretch existing; he is, in fact, a nuisance to society and disgrace to humanity." A hundred dollar reward was offered for Remember Baker and Zimrie Allen who "are notorious for blasphemous expressions in conversation, and ridiculing every thing sacred."

Some of the escapees were rather agile despite physical problems and restraints. Ann McDonald with remarkable red hair, had no trouble leaving Thomas Harrison though she "walks rather lame." Negro "has lost the first joints of three of his small toes on the left foot; he walks limping with one foot turned outward."

Advertisements by men whose spouses "eloped" from them are usually not included as there is rarely much detail included. Men never appeared in advertisements for having left from their ladies.

Some enchanting ladies are included such as Parnel Humphrevil, whose husband David had proof she was still married to William Saunders when he married her and warned the public not to trust her on his account, as he would pay none of the debts of the "adulterous Contemner of the Laws of God, Government, and Society." Sarah Bolton advertised for her husband William, and "a notorious woman, named Mary Bradey, a common prostitute; whore, bawd, and thief...as far as I am informed they practise nothing but thieving through the county, as she is known to be a notorious thief, and pretends to be his wife." Zachariah Neer on the other hand ran away with another man's wife. A woman to catch the eye was Ann Miller, "of a swarthy complexion, black hair, and a black beard on her upper lip."

A charming fellow was the thief James McIntire who "pretends to be a pedlar, and is an ignorant, impudent, talkative, drunken, lying fellow, besides being a thief, described by George Connolly in 1772. Jeremiah McGoun "whose look won't recommend him to the favour of many," was a barber. James McIntire was an "is an ignorant, impudent, talkative, drunken, lying fellow, besides being a thief," according to George Connolly. In 1769 Orange County sheriff Jesse Woodhull advertised for jail breaker "Claudius Smith, alias, James Reed, alias, John Wright, he is a great bully, and will fight where ever he goes, being very conceited of his strength...he is a remarkable thief. He was confined for debt, theft, and rioting.—He is a noted horse stealer."

This work also includes individuals with New York connections who did not run away from that colony/state. An "artful and cunning" eighteen year old negro boy named Cato ran away from Jonathan Moulton in New Hampshire, but was born at New York. John Webb ran away from Philadelphia but "served part of his time with Gilbert Ash, in New York."

The outbreak of the American Revolution was not welcomed by everyone. A reward was offered in May 1776, by Dutchess County for John Underhill, "a person notoriously disaffected to the liberties of America...having left his place of residence, with a design to join the ministerial armies; and having also persuaded others, even servants to go with him." Benjamin Moril and William Slack broke jail in Exeter, New Hampshire, having brought from New York as "notorious enemies to American Liberty....'Tis imagined the above persons absconded with a view to join and give intelligence to the ministerial forces."

This compilation lists all individuals mentioned. If an individual is listed with more than one name, all the names appear in the index. While many of the Negroes and some Indians are listed as slaves, many are not, so they may have been paid servants. People described as mixed Indian and Negroe blood such as "a Negro man named Stephen...is part Indian" who was advertised by Roswell Hopkins in 1768, and "a servant Fellow, part Negro and part Indian, named James" advertised by Jacob Balding of Fish Kills, are indexed by both races. Those designated as "Mustees" are also listed separately as they were of unspecified mixed races. In one confusing ad in *Rivington's New-York Gazette, and Universal Advertiser*, on December 24, 1783, the runaway boy is listed as an Indian, and then as a Negro. Two blue eyed brothers, mulatto slaves were described as "remarkably white" when advertised in September 1776. Charles Broadhead advertised for a "Mulatto Negro Man named TOM.—It is thought he will try to pass for a white or free Man, as he is of the whitest Sort of Mulattoes, his Father being a white Man"

I have retained the original spelling, punctuation, and capitalization of the ads. Illegible words or letters are in brackets. Sometimes the ads in different papers are very similar and only the ad which occurs first in time is included, with references to the later ones. Minor differences in the advertisements are considered to be capitalization, spellings such as trousers/trowsers and 7/seven. If the ads are substantially different, each appears at the time it is first run. The majority are advertised in only one paper, many in two.

Newspapers Consulted:

It should be noted that none of these newspapers had a complete run for the period. Some, such as *The Censor* (Boston) were published less than one year. Also, there were no newspapers published in Delaware, and few for New Jersey, where ads for New-York runaways might have appeared. Newspapers from south of Maryland were not consulted.

The American Gazette, or the Constitutional Journal
The American Journal and General Advertiser
The Boston Chronicle
The Boston Evening Post
The Boston Evening Post, and the General Advertiser
The Boston Gazette, and Country Journal
The Boston News-Letter
The Boston Post-Boy
The Censor
The Connecticut Courant; and the Weekly Advertiser
The Connecticut Journal, and the New-Haven Post Boy
The Constitutional Gazette
The Continental Journal, and Weekly Advertiser
Dunlap's Maryland Gazette, or The Baltimore General Advertiser
Dunlap's Pennsylvania Packet or, the General Advertiser
Essex Gazette
Essex Journal
Exeter Journal
Freeman's Journal, or New-Hampshire Gazette
Freeman's Journal; or the North American Intelligencer
The Independent Chronicle
Independent Gazetteer
The Independent Journal
The Independent Ledger
The Independent New-York Gazette
The Maryland Gazette, and Baltimore Journal
The Maryland Journal
The Massachusetts Gazette
The Massachusetts Gazette, and Boston News-Letter
The Massachusetts Spy Or, Thomas's Boston Journal
The New-Hampshire Gazette,
The New-England Chronicle, or The Essex Gazette
The New-Hampshire Gazette, and Historical Chronicle
The New-Jersey Gazette
The Newport Gazette
The Newport Mercury

The New-York Chronicle
The New-York Gazette, and Weekly Mercury
The New-York Gazette: or, The Weekly Post-Boy
The New-York Gazette, or Northern Intelligencer
The New-York Journal; or The General Advertiser
The New-York Mercury
The New-York Morning Post
The New-York Packet and the American Advertiser
The Norwich Packet and the Connecticut, Massachusetts, New-Hampshire and Rhode-Island Weekly Advertiser,
The Pennsylvania Chronicle, and Universal Advertiser
The Pennsylvania Evening Post
The Pennsylvania Gazette
The Pennsylvania Journal, and Weekly Advertiser
The Pennsylvania Ledger: or the Virginia, Maryland, Pennsylvania, and New-Jersey Weekly Advertiser
The Pennsylvania Packet; and the General Advertiser
The Providence Gazette; And Country Journal
Rivington's New-York Gazetteer, or the Connecticut, New-Jersey, Hudson's River, and Quebec Weekly Advertiser
Rivington's New-York Loyal Gazette
The Royal American Gazette
The Royal Gazette
The Royal Pennsylvania Gazette
The Salem Gazette
Spooner's Vermont Journal
Story and Humphrey's Pennsylvania Mercury
The Vermont Gazette
Der Wöchentliche Pennsylvanische Staatsbote, (Philadelphia)

1769

FOUR DOLLARS Reward.

RUN-away last Night, from the Subscribers, a Servant Man, named James Johnson, but may probably change his Name. He was born in Holyhead, in Wales, and says he was brought up to the Farming Business: He is about 5 Feet 8 Inches high, thin Visage, darkish Complexion, black curl'd Hair; had on when he went away, a half-worn blue Jacket, with white Flannel Lining; blue Coating Trowsers, a new Oznabrigs Shirt, a pair of half-worn Shoes, and a round Felt Hat, with black Binding. Whoever apprehends said Servant, or brings him to the Keeper of Bridewell, or to his Master, shall receive the above Reward, and all reasonable Charges,
          paid by   William Dobbs, and James Taylor.
The New-York Gazette; and the Weekly Mercury, January 23, 1769; January 30, 1769.

FORTY SHILLINGS *Reward.*

RUN-away, about three Weeks ago, from on board the Ship Phoenix, a Servant Man named James White, by Trade a Weaver, about 5 Feet 7 Inches high: Had on when he went away, a short Jacket, Check Shirt, blue Shag Breeches, Yarn Stockings, and a Pair of good Shoes. Whoever apprehends said Fellow, and brings him to Thompson and Alexander, shall have the above Reward.
The New-York Gazette; and the Weekly Mercury, January 23, 1769; January 30, 1769; February 6, 1769; February 13, 1769; February 20, 1769.

New-York, January 31*st,* 1769.

RUN-away, on Sunday last, the 29th instant, from the subscriber, living in Flushing, on Long-Island, an Irish servant lad, named James Lawson, about 21 years old, his nose pretty long, a little pitted with the small-pox, short black hair, and of a dark complexion, pretty slender, and about 5 feet 10 inches high: Had on, and took with him, when he went away, an old brown under waistcoat, the back parts of different colours, with two slips of velvet behind; a close brown kersey upper waistcoat, with breeches of the same; white stockings, half worn shoes, and an old hat. Whoever takes up and secures the said run-away, so that he may be had again, shall receive Forty Shillings reward, and all reasonable charges,
          paid by   ABRAHAM LAWRENCE.
The New-York Journal; or, the General Advertiser, February 2, 1769; February 9, 1769; February 16, 1769. See *The New-York Gazette; and the Weekly Mercury,* September 12, 1768.

Five Dollars Reward,
BROKE out of Kingston Goal, in Esopus, Ulster County, about the latter End of November last, a Convict, named Robert Graham, he is about Forty Years of Age, about 5 Feet 8 Inches high, of a dark Complexion, and wears his own black Hair, and is very timorous in the Night Time: Whoever takes up and secures the above Person, in any of his Majesty's Goals, so that he may be brought to Justice, shall receive the above Reward with all reasonable Charges, paid by the Sheriff.
DANIEL GRAHAM.
The New-York Gazette; and the Weekly Mercury, February 6, 1769; February 13, 1769; February 20, 1769. See *The New-York Gazette; and the Weekly Mercury*, May 1, 1769; May 8, 1769.

RUN-away from his Master last Thursday, the 23d of Feb. Inst. a German Servant Lad, named Valentine Reuter, about 15 Years old, well-set, about 5 feet high, brown Hair, smooth faced, and of a florid Complexion:—Had on when he went away, a old brown napt Coat. Whoever takes up and secures the said Run-away, so that he may be had again, shall receive Four Dollars Reward, and reasonable Charges,
from   JOHN W. POLLEMAN.
The New-York Gazette; and the Weekly Mercury, February 27, 1769; March 6, 1769; March 13, 1769.

RUN away the 20th instant, Feb. from the subscriber, a little apprentice boy, named Philip Sparling, about four feet [sic] high, much pitted with the small-pox: Had on when he went away, a pair of good buckskin breeches, but much soiled, and no coat, waistcoat, nor hat; looks to be old. All masters of vessels are desired to take notice, that any person who either takes away, or harbours the said apprentice, will be proceeded against as the law directs; and any person who shall bring the said apprentice, to me, in the city of New-York, living near the Baptist meeting house, shall have Two Dollars reward, and all reasonable costs and charges
paid, by   CHARLES MILLER.
The New-York Journal; or, General Advertiser, March 2, 1769; March 16, 1769; March 23, 1769. See *The New-York Mercury*, June 24, 1765, and *The New-York Gazette; and the Weekly Mercury*, April 10, 1769.

RUN-away from Mrs. Horsmanden, on Thursday the second Instant March, a young Negro Wench, named *Dido*, about 17 or 18 Years of Age: She is a tall, thin, likely Negro Girl; Had on when she went away, a new Check short Gown and Pettycoat, a new scarlet trimmed Cloak, a Chip Hat, and very good under Cloathing, Whoever will bring her to her Master, shall

have Twenty Shillings Reward, and all reasonable Charges. All Masters of Vessels are warned from carrying her off, and all Persons against entertaining her, as they will answer the same at their Peril.
The New-York Gazette; and the Weekly Mercury, March 6, 1769; March 13, 1769.

New-York, February 25, 1769.
ON Monday Night the 20th Instant, made his Escape, or was taken off from one of the Island called the *Two Brothers*, near *Hell Gate*; a Negro Man named JACOB, belonging to *Henry Brasier*, and formerly known in this City, by the Name of the Fu-Fu Negro, or MONEY-DIGGER: He is between 40 and 50 Years of Age, full Face, large flat Nose, with a small Scar on the lower Part of it:—His Eyes very full, as if they were starting out of his Head; he had on a red Duffils Jacket, with blue Lining, blue Breeches, a Felt Hat, and common Shoes and Stockings. He speaks both *English* and *Dutch*, and was born and brought up in the *Jersies*, a little above *Brunswick*.—Whoever takes up said Negro, and brings him to his Master, on the *North Brother Island*, shall have FORTY SHILLINGS Reward, and all reasonable Charges,
   paid by HENRY BRASIER.
The New-York Gazette or the Weekly Post-Boy, March 6, 1769; March 13, 1769.

Twenty Shillings Reward,
RUN-AWAY from the Subscriber, on Wednesday the 22d, inst. an IRISH Servant Lad, named WILLIAM BROWN, 'twixt fifteen and sixteen years of Age, about five Feet high, talks tolerable good English, has straight brown Hair, a DOWN-LOOK and LAZY-WALK.—Had on when he went away, a Felt Hat, cock'd up behind, Brown Jacket, Green Vest, Check Shirt, Black Everlasting Breeches, tore at the Knees, Blue Stockings, and old Shoes with Pinchbeck-Buckles.—Whoever takes up and secures said RUN-AWAY so that I may have him again, shall have the above REWARD, by applying to me at the *NEWEST PRINTING-OFFICE* in *Broad-Street.*
   JAMES ROBERTSON.
☞ All Masters of Vessels and others, are forbid to carry off or harbour him at their Peril.
The New-York Journal; or, the General Advertiser, March 23, 1769.

RUN-away from me the Subscriber, a Mulatto Fellow, named Dick, it is likely he will try to get to Sea, as he has been two Voyages to Lisbon: he speaks good English, was born in New-England, and it is supposed he will go that Way; he is about five Feet seven Inches high, very broad

shouldered, a little bandy leg'd, and very flat Nose, and has lost one of his under Teeth: Had on when he went away, a grey Jacket and Trowsers, but it is supposed he will change his Clothes: Whoever takes him up in this City, shall have Three Dollars, and if out, shall have Five Dollars Reward, and all reasonable Charges
    paid by me SUSANNA M'DONALD.

N. B. All Masters of Vessels and others, are forbid to carry off or harbour him at their Peril.   *New-York, March* 23d. 1769.

The New-York Journal; or, the General Advertiser, March 30, 1769; April 6, 1769; April 20, 1769. See *The New-York Gazette; and the Weekly Mercury*, April 10, 1769.

RUN-AWAY on Thursday the 30th March last, from the subscriber living in New-York, an apprentice lad named James Mc. Pherson: He is about 5 feet high, of a slender make, blue eyes, with a scar in his forehead, somewhat pock mark'd, and dark hair tied. Had on when he went away, a brown knap waistcoat, double breasted, with gilt buttons and lined with green baze; a light colour'd pair of cloth breeches, with gilt buttons; blue stockings, long quartered pumps, with square brass buckles, a half worn beaver hat, and a check shirt. Whoever takes up and secures the said apprentice in any of his Majesty's goals, or brings him to his master, shall receive Twenty Shillings reward, and all reasonable charges,
    paid by BARTHOLOMEW COXETTER.

N. B. He is supposed to have gone for Philadelphia, as he crossed the North River ferry.

The New-York Gazette; and the Weekly Mercury, April 3, 1769; April 10, 1769; April 17, 1769; May 8, 1769.

RUN-away from Capt. M'Donald, a mulato fellow, named Dick, about 5 feet 7 inches high, broad shoulder'd, bandy leg'd, and has lost one of his under teeth: Had on when he went away, a brown jacket and ozenbrigs trowsers, but it is said he is gone towards New-England, in an India dress. Whoever said fellow, so that his master may have him again, shall receive three dollars reward if taken in this city, and five dollars if taken out, and all reasonable charges,
    paid by me SUSANAH M'DONALD.

N. B. All masters of vessels and others, are forbid to carry off or harbour him at their peril.

The New-York Journal; or, the General Advertiser, March 30, 1769; April 6, 1769; April 20, 1769. See *The New-York Gazette; and the Weekly Mercury*, April 10, 1769.

RUN away from the subscriber, living on Goshen-Hill, a servant boy named Philip Sparling, about 4 feet high, [sic] and much pitted with the small pox: Had on when he went away a coat of black frize, much worn, and a waistcoat, buckskin breeches much soiled and broke in the crotch, a pair of blue-grey stockings, old shoes, and a sailors blue cap. He is an artful rogue, having taken up near 30l. due to his master; therefore all captains of vessels, and others, are forewarned not to carry off or harbour him, upon pain of being dealt with as the law directs, and whoever will bring him to his said master, shall receive two dollars reward, and all reasonable charges,
                paid by me   CHARLES MILLER.
The New-York Gazette; and the Weekly Mercury, April 10, 1769; May 8, 1769. See *The New-York Mercury*, June 24, 1765, and *The New-York Journal; or, General Advertiser*, March 2, 1769.

                    FIFTEEN DOLLARS Reward,
RUN away from Jacob Starn, living on Change Water Iron-Works, in Sussex county, West New-Jersey, some time in March in the year 1768.— An Irish servant man named Thomas Murphy, about five feet eight inches high, well set, black curl'd hair, a shoemaker by trade, which he undoubtedly now follows, as he was a middling good workman at the same, he is about 19 years of age, he work'd at his trade from the time he run away, till about the middle or latter or end of June, along the North River, near Kinderhock, Claverack and Livingston's Mannor, and there chang'd his name from Thomas Murphy to Thomas Newman, and pass'd by the name of the New-England Shoemaker, and from thence it is said he went to New-England:—Whoever shall apprehend and secure said servant, in any of his Majesty's goals, so that his master may have him again, or bring him to Dirck Brinckerhoff, of the city of New-York, merchant, shall have the above FIFTEEN DOLLARS reward, and reasonable charges
                paid by   JACOB STARN,
                    or DIRCK BRINCKERHOFF.
The New-York Gazette or the Weekly Post-Boy, April 10, 1769; April 17, 1769; April 24, 1769; May 1, 1769; May 15, 1769: May 29, 1769; June 5, 1769; June 19, 1769; *The New-York Gazette; and the Weekly Mercury*, April 10, 1769; April 17, 1769; April 24, 1769; May 8, 1769. Minor differences between the papers. See *The New-York Journal; or, the General Advertiser*, April 7, 1768, and *The New-York Journal; or, the General Advertiser*, May 19, 1768.

FIFTY DOLLARS Reward.

BROKE out of goal on Saturday the 15th of last April, from the subscriber, being high sheriff of the county of Orange, one Claudius Smith, alias, James Reed, alias, John Wright, about 5 feet 8 inches high, straight and well built, and pale complexion, very light short hair, and white beard; he has had four or five grains of powder blown in under his right eye; he has short white teeth, and seldom shows them when he laughs; he is a great bully, and will fight where ever he goes, being very conceited of his strength: He had on very bad cloaths when he went away, but it is supposed he will not wear them long, as he is a remarkable thief. He was confined for debt, theft, and rioting.—He is a noted horse stealer. Any person who takes up and secures the said run-away, so that he may be had again, shall receive the above reward, and all reasonable charges paid, by Jesse Woodhull, high sheriff of the county of Orange, or by Jeremiah Colman, deputy sheriff of the said county.

The New-York Gazette; and the Weekly Mercury, May 1, 1769; May 8, 1769; May 15, 1769; *The Boston Gazette, and Country Journal,* May 15, 1769. Minor differences between the papers.

RUN-away the 26th ultimo, from James Varian, a High Dutch Servant Man, named Jacob Raline, 30 Years old, about 5 Feet 9 Inches high, black Hair, thick set, round shoulder'd, a large Scar on his right Jaw: He had on a brown homespun Jacket, blackish Colour Flannel Lining, with Brass Buttons, blue Coating Trowsers, Felt Hat, blue Stockings, unknown what Shirt he had on, as he took with him two with Flannel Shirts, one Tow Shirt, one speckle Linen. Whoever takes up the said Servant, and returns him to his Master, shall have 40s. Reward, if taken in this Government; and if out of it 3l. and all reasonable Charges,
    paid by me, JAMES VARIAN.

The New-York Gazette; and the Weekly Mercury, May 1, 1769; May 8, 1769; May 15, 1769; May 22, 1769.

Five Pounds Reward.

BROKE goal in Kingston, in Ulster county, one Robert Graham, who was committed for murder. He is about 5 feet 8 inches high, a well set fellow, black curl'd hair, and black eyes, and is a great coward at night, aged 40 Years. This is to require all officers and others, to exert themselves in apprehending of him, that he may be brought to justice; and for their encouragement for so doing they shall be paid the above reward, and all reasonable charges,
    by me DANIEL GRAHAM.

The New-York Gazette; and the Weekly Mercury, May 1, 1769; May 8, 1769. See *The New-York Gazette; and the Weekly Mercury,* February 6, 1769.

RUN-away from the Subscriber, in the Clove, in Orange county, on Thursday 13th Instant, a hired labourer, who called himself John Nellson, about 5 feet 7 inches and an half high, thick well set, of a fresh complexion, he wears his own short black hair, bushy behind; he has a scar on the left side of his head, and when he went away he had on an old brown cloth coat, with a jacket of the same much patched on the breast, and old leather breeches. He stole away with him a blue broad cloth coat full trim'd, not much wore; a light coloured velvet jacket, the backs of light broad cloth; a whitish coloured cloth jacket, with a green coloured pocket book with a brass clasp, with two promissory notes, and several writings, with a wallet and handkerchief in it. Whoever takes him up, or secures him that the things may be had again, shall receive Five Pounds reward,
    paid by WILLIAM BELL.
The New-York Gazette; and the Weekly Mercury, May 1, 1769; May 8, 1769.

RUN away from the Subscriber, living near the Fishkills Landing, in Dutches-County, on Sunday Night last, the 7th of May Instant, Two Servant Men, bought from Philadelphia, viz. William Thomas, a Welch Man, about 21 Years of Age, 5 Feet 4 Inches high, fair Complexion, fresh coloured, small black Eyes, sandy colour'd curl'd Hair, well set, speaks not very good English, and is somewhat hard of hearing.—is by Trade a Mason, but has sometime been employ'd in farming Business; one of his Great Toes has been lately mash'd, so that he has lost the End of it, with the Nail, and the Wound is supposed to be not quite heal'd yet, the other Great Toe has been out of Joint, and does not stand in the natural Order: He had on an old Beaver Hat, which had been a Millar's, and was white with the Meal, a snuff colour'd Broad-Cloth Coat, pretty much soil'd with Grease, Tar, &c. a pair of old Buckskin Breeches, a dark cloth sailors short Jacket, had several Shirts with him of white Linen and check'd Flannel, the rest of his dress forgot.

  Benjamin Taylor, about 18 Years of Age, an Englishman, about 5 Feet 4 Inches, well set, but slenderer than the other, freckled and somewhat hard favour'd, very red long Hair, had been employ'd in the farming Business, has a bashful Behaviour: Had on a Felt Hat, a brown Camblet Coat, and a snuff colour'd homespun Jacket and Breeches. They had, and it is supposed took with them, a small Pocket Compass and a Pocket Pistol.—Whoever takes up and returns the said Servants, or either of them, or secures them in

Gaol, giving me Notice, shall receive Twenty Shillings New-York Money Reward, for each, besides all reasonable Charges.
    JOHN HALSTEAD.
 The New-York Journal; or, The General Advertiser, May 11, 1769; May 18, 1769; May 25, 1769; June 1, 1769.

RUN-away from the subscriber, the first day of May inst. a negro man aged about 23 years, of a yellow complexion, middle stature, this country born, speaks good English, and plays on the fiddle, tho' but poorly: Had on when he went away, a brown homespun waistcoat and breeches, a tow shirt, felt hat, woollen stockings, thick shoes with strings in. Whoever will take up said negro and bring him to the subscriber, living in Westchester, or secure him further that he may get him again, shall have 40s. reward, and all reasonable charges
   paid by me. STEPHEN HUNT.
 The New-York Gazette; and the Weekly Mercury, May 15, 1769; May 22, 1769; May 29, 1769; June 5, 1769; June 12, 1769; June 19, 1769.

AB*sconded from his bail, some time in April last, John Holyoake, by trade a shoe-maker; said when he went away he was going to Philadelphia,, where 'tis supposed he has altered his name to English: He is a well-set man, full fac'd, grey eyes, and long chin, has lost several of his fore teeth, and speaks rather hasty.—Had on when he went away, light brown bearskin coat, with a surtout of the same colour, and a brown camblet cloak lined with green baize over the same, buckskin breeches and half spatterdashes, and wore a queut whig, which 'tis thought he will leave off as his hair under it was pretty long. Whoever secures, &c. the said John Holyoake, and will give immediate notice to James Ettredge, sadler, in New-York, shall receive Five Pounds reward.*
 'Tis hoped, as he is a very great impostor, the printers of the other news-papers will insert the above for the good of the public.
 The New-York Gazette; and the Weekly Mercury, May 29, 1769; June 5, 1769; June 12, 1769; June 19, 1769; June 26, 1769; July 3, 1769.

            Easton, June 23, 1769.
WAS committed to the goal of this county, a man, who calls himself JAMES CLARK, *he was sent here on suspicion of being a run-away servant; his right name is supposed to be* EVAN DAVIS, *who was advertised lately in Maryland, by Jonathan Roberts, and Samuel Blunt; he is about 5 feet 7 or 8 inches high, sandy complexion, his dress very indifferent. Whoever has any right to this man, is desired to come and take him away, in 6 weeks time, or else he will be discharged.*

ALSO a man, who calls himself JAMES M'KINSEY, *is about 5 feet 9 or 10 inches high, full faced, of a blackish complexion; he says he is a servant belonging to John Abbot, on the east side of the North River, in New-York government. His master is desired to come and take him away, in 6 weeks time, or else he will be discharged,*
     by   JACOB BACHMAN, Goaler.
The Pennsylvania Gazette, June 29, 1769.

MADE his escape from two men, ordered by the Constable to have the charge of him, a Negro man named JACK, 27 years of age, about 5 feet 9 inches high, a very black fellow; had on a linen shirt and trowsers, an old hat, a brownish jacket without sleeves, no stockings, a pair of shoes not blacked. The said fellow was taken into custody on suspicion of murdering a Negro man, belonging to Ichabud Smith, of this place: All persons are desired to apprehend said Negro, and confine him to goal, giving notice to the Subscriber, that he may be brought to justice; the above-named Negro was born in the county, and belongs to Mr. Isaac Ketcham, of this town.
    TIM. CONCKING, Constable.
                Huntington, July 6, 1766. [*sic*]
 N. B. It is supposed that one SAMUEL TITUS, a cooper, (who has not followed that business for some time past) has carried him off with an intention to sell him. Titus is a man about 5 feet 7 inches high, a thin fac'd slender fellow; had on when he went off, a brown coat, but as we understand he had other clothes, he will no doubt change his dress. Whoever takes up said Titus, and the above described Negro, and secures them or either of them, so that they may be brought to justice, shall have twenty shillings reward for each, and all reasonable charges paid.
 The New-York Gazette; and the Weekly Mercury, July 24, 1769; July 31, 1769; August 7, 1769.

                 New York, July 10, 1769.
       TWENTY DOLLARS Reward.
ABSCONDED from his Place of Abode, a certain Hamilton Ballantine, about 22 or 23 Years of Age, is very talkative, brags greatly of his Learning, and is a noted Liar; he professes to be a Schoolmaster, and is likely to have gone to Pennsylvania, as he said he taught School in that province. Whoever takes up said Ballantine, and secures him in any of his Majesty's Goals, shall have the above Reward, and reasonable Charges,
     paid by me   BENJAMIN CRAIGE.
 The Pennsylvania Gazette, July 27, 1769.

New-York, August 4, 1769.
FIVE POUNDS, Reward.
ABSCONDED from his Bail, on Tuesday the 1st Instant, a certain John Lidle, about 16 or 17 Years of Age, and 5 Feet 4 Inches high; a well-set Man, fair Complexion, sandy Hair hanging loose, which perhaps he may cut off; has a Mole a little below his Left Ear, walks very upright, and is by Trade a Cooper: He had on, when he went away, a short blue Coat, which does not reach to his Knees, and has a white Lining; had with him a brown Jacket with Pockets like a Coat, generally wears white Stockings, but it is probable he may change his Dress. He has been at Sea, and made several Voyages to London; so that it is apprehended he may offer to ship himself as a Seaman, therefore, all Masters of Vessels and others, are hereby warned and desired not to carry him off, as they will answer it at their Peril. And whoever takes up and returns the said John Lidle, or secures him in any of his Majesty's Gaols, so that the Subscriber may get him again, shall upon due Information by Letter or otherwise, receive the above Reward, of FIVE POUNDS, New-York Money, and all reasonable Charges, of the Subscriber, Cooper, near Peck's Slip.
JOHN CARNES.
The New-York Journal; or, The General Advertiser, August 10, 1769; August 17, 1769; August 24, 1769.

RUN away about three weeks ago, an Irish indented servant named Sarah Frasier, belonging to Mrs. Henry, opposite the New Dutch church; had on when she went away, a dirty white short gown, an old crimson quilted petticoat, she is under 20 years of age, fresh colour'd, mark'd with the small-pox, rather fat, not tall, has been seen lurking about the Barracks. Whoever harbours or detains her will be prosecuted as the law directs; and whoever will secure her, and give notice to the Printer, shall when produced, receive a handsome reward; she has not been more than five months in America.—
The New-York Journal; or, the General Advertiser, August 17, 1769; August 24, 1769; August 31, 1769; September 7, 1769.

Philadelphia, August 24, 1769.
FIFTY SHILLINGS Reward.
RUN away, the 15th instant, from the Subscriber, an English servant man, named Christopher Hanns, by trade a Painter, about 26 years of age, of a dark complexion, black hair, about 5 feet high; had on, when he went away, a dark coloured cloth jacket, with sleeves, buckskin breeches, worsted hose, and a check shirt. It is supposed he is gone towards the Jerseys, with a man,

named Cunningham, late of New-York. All masters of vessels are forbid to carry him off at their peril. Whoever secures said Hanns in any of his Majesty's goals, or brings him to his master, living in Philadelphia, shall receive the above reward, and reasonable charges,
     paid by WILLIAM TOD.

The Pennsylvania Gazette, August 24, 1769; September 15, 1769. See *The New-York Gazette; and the Weekly Mercury,* September 4, 1769, and *The Pennsylvania Chronicle, and Universal Advertiser,* From Monday August 28, to Monday, September 4, 1769.

THREE POUNDS Reward.

RUN-away the 15th of August last, from the subscriber, living in Philadelphia, an English servant man, named Christopher Hanns, by trade a painter, about 26 years of age, of a dark complexion, black hair, about 5 feet high: Had on when he went away, a dark coloured cloth jacket with sleeves, buckskin breeches, worsted hose, and a check shirt; it is supposed he is gone towards New-York, with a man named Cunningham, a painter, late of New-York. Whoever secures said Hanns in any of his Majesty's goals, or brings him to his master, shall receive the above reward, and reasonable charges,   paid, by WILLIAM TOD.
N. B. All masters of vessels are forbid to carry him off at their peril.

The New-York Gazette; and the Weekly Mercury, September 4, 1769; September 11, 1769; September 18, 1769; September 25, 1769. See *The Pennsylvania Gazette,* August 24, 1769, and *The Pennsylvania Chronicle, and Universal Advertiser,* From Monday August 28, to Monday, September 4, 1769.

Five Pounds Reward.

R*AN away the 15th instant, from the subscriber, an English servant man, named Christopher Hanns, by trade a painter, about 26 years of age, of a dark complexion, black hair, about five feet high; had on, when he went away, a dark coloured cloth jacket, with sleeves, buckskin breeches, worsted hose, and a check shirt. It is supposed he is gone towards the Jerseys, with a man, named Cunningham, late of New York. All masters of vessels and others are forbid to carry him off at their peril. Whoever secures said Hanns in any of his Majesty's goals, or brings him to his master, living in Philadelphia, shall receive the above reward, and reasonable charges,*
    paid by *WILLIAM TOD.*

The Pennsylvania Chronicle, and Universal Advertiser, From Monday August 28, to Monday, September 4, 1769; From Monday September 4, to Monday, September 11, 1769; From Monday September 18, to

Monday, September 25, 1769. See *The Pennsylvania Gazette*, August 24, 1769, and *The New-York Gazette; and the Weekly Mercury*, September 4, 1769.

STOLEN,

ON Thursday the 24th Instant, between the Hours of four and five in the Afternoon from my Bleach-field at Blooming-dale, 12 ½ Yards of Yd. wide Linnen, not fully bleach'd by a young Fellow about five Feet three Inches high, of brown Complexion, and something pitted with the Small-Pox; he has on red Plush Jacket with strip'd Linnen Backs, mixt colour'd Breeches, pale blue Stockings, old Shoes worn out at the Toes, and square Regimental Buckles: All Persons are desire to stop said Linnen, should it be offered for Sale, and whoever takes up said Thief and secures him in any of his Majesty's Goals, so that he may be brought to Justice shall have ten Shillings Reward and reasonable Charges
          paid, by   GARRET COZINE.

The New-York Chronicle, From Thursday August 31, to Thursday September 7, 1769.

New-York, Sept. 13, 1769.

RUN-away from his lodgings at the house of the subscriber, rigger and corker, at the Ship-yards in this city, a man, who called himself John Gibbs, and said he was a doctor. He stole from the subscriber and carried off with him, a sailor's new cotton red and white jacket with sleeves, a pair of blue and white striped trowsers, check shirt, and a considerable sum of money. He is a very tall smooth faced man, has a fair complexion, dark brown hair, long nose, full eye, speaks thick, and broad Scotch; had on a black waistcoat, white thread stockings, and a blue surtout coat, and had much the appearance of a gentleman.—Whoever takes up and delivers him, or secures the said thief, shall be handsomely rewarded for their trouble.
          JOHN JOSEPH.

The New-York Journal; or, The General Advertiser, September 14, 1769; September 21, 1769; September 28, 1769; October 5, 1769. The last ad does not have the date and location at the top.

RUN-away from the Subscriber, on Sunday Evening last, the 10th Instant, a Servant Man, named Robert Tarbitt, born in Paisley in Scotland, and speaks much with the Accent of that Country, and has only been about 18 Months in America. He is about 22 Years of Age, 5 Feet 5 Inches high, fair Complexion, light brown Hair, which he generally has tied behind, and by trade a Taylor; he carried several Suits of Clothes with him, particularly a short blue Coat, and a light Sagathie Coat, and black Stocking Breeches:—

Also an Apprentice Lad, named Christopher Angele, born in this City, about 18 Years of Age, short brow curled Hair, pretty much pitted with the Small-Pox, and about 5 Feet 5 Inches high; carried with him a short blue Coat, and a Purple Suit of Clothes, and is by trade a Taylor.—Whoever apprehends either of them and secures them or either of them, so that I may have him again, shall receive Three Pounds Reward for each, besides all reasonable Charges.—And I hereby forewarn all Persons from carrying off, harbouring, or concealing the aforesaid two Servants, or they must expect to answer it as the Law directs.
    JOHN LABOYTEAUX.   *New-York, Sept.* 12.
 The New-York Journal; or, The General Advertiser, September 14, 1769; September 21, 1769; September 28, 1769.

RUN-away on the 11th instant of September, from the subscriber, a servant man named John Walker, an Englishman, lately arrived in the Dutchess of Gordon: He is about 23 years of age, 5 feet 5 inches high, slender made, fair complection, much pitted with the small-pox, is a great talker, and is by Trade a Bricklayer. He had on when he went away, or took with him, one white and one check'd shirt, buckskin breeches, blue ribb'd stockings, new shoes, a blue broad cloth coat and waistcoat, about half worn, and a felt hat which he generally wore flopped.—Whoever shall take up and secure the said runaway, so that I may get him again, shall have Forty Shillings reward and all reasonable charges
    paid by JOHN BESSONET.
 All masters of vessels and others are warned not to harbour, conceal or carry off said servant, as they will answer it in the law.
 The New-York Journal; or, The General Advertiser, September 14, 1769; September 21, 1769. See *The New-York Journal; or, The General Advertiser*, October 5, 1769.

BROKE out of the work-house, on Saturday night the 9th of September, a negro fellow named Roger, (some times goes by the name of John) a noted villain, that was burnt in the hand the last supreme court. He has made an attempt to rob the house of the subscriber, on Sunday evening the 10th. It will be esteemed a favour of all good people that shall try to secure him either in town or country, that he may be brought to justice.—Whoever secures him in any of his Majesty's goals, shall meet with a handsome reward, by applying to
    ENNIS GRAHAM.
 The New-York Gazette; and the Weekly Mercury, September 18, 1769.

FIVE DOLLARS REWARD.
RUN-AWAY the 10th instant, from the subscriber, living in New-York, a German servant man and his wife, their name is George Enger, and Elizabeth his wife, he pretends to be a shoemaker, and miner by trade; the man is about five feet four inches high: Had on when he wet away, an old green waistcoat, and check trowsers, he has short white hair, thick lips, snuffs a great deal; he is about 45 years old. Whoever secures said servants, or either of them, in any of his Majesty's gaols, or brings them to me the subscriber, shall receive the above reward, and all necessary charges, by me
HENRY HORNEFFER.
N. B. All masters of vessels are forbid to carry him off, at their peril.
The New-York Journal; or, The General Advertiser, September 21, 1769; September 28, 1769; October 5, 1769; October 12, 1769.

BROKE out of the Work-House of this City, on Saturday Night the 9th Instant, a Negro Fellow, named GEORGE, about 30 Years old, a little of the Mulatto Complexion, the Property of Captain Provost, of Peramus, in New-Jersey; and in all Probability, will endeavour to get on board some Vessel, in order to escape to the West-Indies. Whoever takes up said Fellow, and secures him, so that he may be had again shall receive Forty Shillings Reward, in New-York,
from   GEORGE LUDLOW.
The New-York Gazette; and the Weekly Mercury, September 25, 1769.

FIVE POUNDS Reward.
RUN-AWAY from John Thomas Esq; of West-Chester County, and province of New-York, on the 19th instant; an Indian slave, called Abraham, will pretend to be free born, 26 years of age, about 5 feet 5 inches high, well set, long black hair, something curled, one of his fore teeth in his under jaw broke off: Had on when he went away, a redish brown lappelled jacket, with slash sleeves, breeches of the same, a dark brown under jacket, without skirts, all with metal buttons; and a new felt hat.—It is likely he will change his name and dress, cut off his hair, and strive to get among the Indians.—Whoever takes up and returns the said slave, or secures him in any of his Majesty's gaols so that his master may have him again, shall receive the above reward, and all reasonable charges paid,
by me   JOHN THOMAS.
N. B. All masters of vessels and others are forbid to carry him off, harbour or entertain him.
Rye, in West-Chester County, 25th Sept. 1769.

The New-York Journal; or, The General Advertiser, September 28, 1769; October 5, 1769; October 12, 1769; October 19, 1769. See *The New-York Journal; or The General Advertiser*, October 22, 1767.

RUN away on the 24th ult. *from the subscriber, a servant man named John Walker, an Englishman, late arrived in the Dutchess of Gordon: He is about 23 years of age, 5 feet 5 inches high, slender made, fair complexion, much pitted with the small pox, is a great talker, and is by trade a Bricklayer. He had on when he went away, or took with him, one white and one check'd shirt, buckskin breeches, blue ribb'd stockings, new shoes, a blue broadcloth coat and waistcoat, about half worn, and a felt hat which he generally wore flopped. He went off in company with one William Pitcher, who had formerly been a soldier: Had on a blue coat lined with red, and brass buttons, also a blue watchcoat and a sailor's jacket with lace over the seams; he is a well set man, about 38 years of age, and has a wife in Shrewsbury.—Whoever shall take up said runaway, so that I may get him again, shall have 40s. reward, and all reasonable charges*
        paid by   JOHN BESSONET.

All masters of vessels and others are warned not to harbour, conceal or carry off said servant, as they will answer it in the law.

The New-York Journal; or, The General Advertiser, October 5, 1769; October 12, 1769; October 19, 1769; October 23, 1769; October 26, 1769; *The New-York Mercury*, October 9, 1769; October 16, 1769; October 23, 1769. Minor differences between the papers. See *The New-York Journal; or, The General Advertiser*, September 14, 1769.

RUN-away on Saturday Night the 23d Inst. from Jurry Emigh, of Beekman's Precinct, in Dutchess County, a negro man named CUFF, about 5 Feet high, pretty well set, and is middling black, speaks tolerable good English, and generally wore his Hair (or Wool) tied behind: Had with him when he went away, a light coloured Broadcloth Coat, somewhat on the short Fashion, and pretty old; a dark blue figur'd Everlasting Jacket with red Lining, and a light colour'd Thickset Breeches, a Pair of Tow Linen Trowsers, and perhaps some other Cloathing unknown. There is a Supposition that he hath a Pass to travel. Whoever takes up said Negro, and brings him to his said Master, shall have Forty Shillings Reward, and all reasonable Charges paid,
        by me   JURRY EMIGH.

The New-York Gazette; and the Weekly Mercury, October 23, 1769; November 6, 1769.

New-York, 20th of October, 1769.
RUN-away yesterday from the subscriber, now in the city of York, an Irish servant man, named Daniel Collins, 29 years of age, 5 feet 7 inches high, fair complection and well faced, his hair fair, and cut short round, speaks the West country dialect, and fast: Had on a light coloured short lapelled coat, half worn, a red callimanco jacket, double breasted, coarse trowsers, good shoes, and square metal buckles, but it is supposed he will change his name and clothes. Whoever secures said servant in any gaol, so that his master may have him again, shall have Forty Shillings,
   and reasonable charges,
    paid by JAMES CRAWFORD.
 N. B. All masters of vessels or others, are forbid to harbour or carry him off, at their peril.
The New-York Journal; or, The General Advertiser, October 26, 1769; November 2, 1769; November 16, 1769.

RUN away on Thursday the 8th Instant, November, from the Subscriber then at New-York, a Scotch indented Servant Man, named John Southerland, about 27 Years of Age, 5 Feet 7 Inches high, short brown Hair, pale yellow Complexion, occasioned by Sickness he lately had in the West-Indies; has been a Soldier and wounded in the Thigh with a Ball, the Scar of which may be seen; is much addicted to Drink, has lived 4 or 5 Years in the Jersies, employed in the Farming Business;—had on when he went away, a check'd Shirt, a Pair of Russia Drab Breeches or Oznaburg Trowsers, black Stockings English made Shoes, Pinchbeck Buckles, an oldish brown under Waistcoat, a short blue one lined with white Flannel over it, and a narrow brimm'd Boy's Felt Hat. He also carried off with him the following Clothes, with which he was sent to a Washerwoman, viz. Two check'd Linen Handkerchiefs, two or three Pairs of white Cotton Stockings, one or two Pairs of Oznaburg and two Pair check'd Trowsers, one or two white Frocks, two or three check'd, and four ruffled Shirts, one of two of which were marked on the Flap with the Letters L. G. in a yellow Stain.— All Persons to whom any of the said Goods may be offer'd for Sale, or who may afterwards discover them, are desired to stop them, and the said Servant, and whoever delivers him to Mr. William Milner, at the Exchange in New-York, shall receive four Dollars Reward, and all reasonable Charges. All Masters of Vessels and others, are hereby warn'd not to carry off, harbour or conceal the said Servant, as they will answer it at their Peril.
    LEMUEL GUSTINE, junr.
The New-York Journal; or, The General Advertiser, November 16, 1769; November 23, 1769; November 30, 1769; December 7, 1769.

See *The New-York Journal; or, The General Advertiser*, March 1, 1770.

RUN away from his special Bail Thomas Dunlap, a chelsea pensioner from the 17th Regiment of Foot.—Had on when he went away, a Blue Coat and Jacket, Leather Breeches, pretty much wore, Thread Stockings and bad Shoes; he was born in Ireland, is about Five Feet high, Brown Hair and Fair Complexion, he is a Weaver by Trade and very much adicted to Liquor, he resided since his being discharged from the Army two Years upon Staten-Island where he work'd at his Business, he has given three false Orders to the Subscriber on three different Men upon Staten-Island to the amount of £. 18 : 18 : 00 N. C. which Orders were refused as the men were not indebted to him One Copper.

Whoever apprehends the said Dunlap, and secures him in any of his Majesty's Gaols, shall have FIVE DOLLARS Reward, and all reasonable Charges paid by ALEXANDER M'DONALD.

New-York, Nov. 20, 1769.

The New-York Chronicle, From Monday November 13, to Monday November 20, 1769; From Monday November 20, to Thursday November 23, 1769; From Monday November 23, to Thursday November 30, 1769.

Four Dollars Reward.

FOR any person who shall apprehend and deliver to John Harris Cruger, a sailor negro man, the property of Capt. Jones, of the ship Francis, from whom the said negro absconded the last week; by the name of Pompey, slender made, about five feet eight inches tall, his face very black and smooth.

The New-York Gazette; and the Weekly Mercury, November 20, 1769; November 27, 1769; December 4, 1769.

Five Dollars Reward.

RUN-away from the subscriber last Wednesday, an Indian man, named John Andress, a stout well made man, about 20 years of age, formerly a servant to Captain Giles, at the North-River, and afterwards a servant to Mr. Palmer, who lives in the country; he was born at Point-Judith, close by Rhode-Island, and was some time ago purchased of Mr. Dobs, keeper of the bridewell; he is well known in this town: Had on when he went away a blue jacket, frock and trowsers. Whoever takes up said run-away, and brings him to me the subscriber, shall have the above reward, and all reasonable charges paid, by   JAMES PRINCE.

The New-York Gazette; and the Weekly Mercury, November 20, 1769; November 27, 1769; December 4, 1769; December 11, 1769; December 18, 1769.

Five Dollars Reward.
RUN-away from the subscriber at Kingston in Ulster County, the 20th day of September last, a servant man, named Daniel M'Coy, about 30 years old, 5 feet and a half high, a taylor by trade, and a smart workman, is pretty much marked with the small pox, long black hair, a Highlander born, and speaks pretty much with the Highland accent: Had on when he went away, a superfine blue broad cloth coat and jacket, with other cloathing and cloth not made up, with six or seven pounds in money, and is a lover of liquor. Whoever secures the said servant in any of his Majesty's goals, or brings him to his master, shall receive the above reward and reasonable charges paid, by JAMES RICHEY.
The New-York Gazette; and the Weekly Mercury, November 20, 1769; December 4, 1769.

Lancaster Goal, November 14, 1769.
WAS committed to my custody, on the 25th of October, on suspicion of being a run away servant, a certain John Davis, as he calls himself, is a Welshman, and says he served his time out with Jacob Roara, of Conegocheague, in Maryland; he is 5 feet 7 or 8 inches high, black complexion, near 35 years of age; had on, when committed, a blanket coat, a red spotted flannel jacket, tow trowsers, good hat, shoes and stockings. Also was committed to my custody, on the 6th inst. on suspicion of being a run away servant, a certain John Gorman, as he calls himself, about 5 feet 9 or 10 inches high, short black hair; had on, when committed, a old short brown jacket, an old blue one, breeches the colour of the jacket, old shoes and stockings, an old shirt, and hat; on his own confession, says he did belong to the Niger Frigate, of New York, Captain Wilkinson, commander. Their masters, if any they have, are desired to come and pay their said servants charges, and take them away, otherwise they will be sold out for their fees, in three weeks from the date hereof, by
GEORGE EBERLY, Goaler.
The Pennsylvania Gazette, November 23, 1769.

RUN-away, last Wednesday, from the Subscriber, living at Goshen, in the County of Orange, and Apprentice Lad named Joshua Drake, about 19 Years of Age, brown Complexion, squints with one of his Eyes, black Hair, generally tied behind, about 5 Feet 6 Inches high, well set, but uncertain what Clothes he had on: He took with him a bay Mare, about 14 Hands

high, with a long Tail, and generally trots, but can pace. Whoever takes up said Run-away with the Mare, so that they may be both had again, shall receive Forty Shillings Reward,
   paid by SAMUEL CARPENTER.
The New-York Gazette; and the Weekly Mercury, December 11, 1769; December 18, 1769; December 25, 1769; January 1, 1770; January 8, 1770; January 15, 1770; January 22, 1770; January 29, 1770.

RUN-away from the Subscriber, living at Westchester, on the first of October last, a Negro Fellow named HANNIBAL: He is a short thick Fellow, of a yellow Complexion, big Forehead, and thick Lips, has a Scar under his Chin that sometimes runs, and commonly wears a Worsted Cap.—Had on when he went away, a Mouse coloured Jacket, Deerskin Breeches, and Tow Shirt and Trowsers. He absented himself about a Year ago, obtained a Pass, and went by the name of Free Tom; and it is very probable that he may have one now. Whoever apprehends said Negro, and delivers him to the Subscriber, shall receive Five Pounds Reward, and all reasonable Charges,
   paid by PHEBE HADDEN.
The New-York Gazette; and the Weekly Mercury, December 18, 1769; December 25, 1769; January 1, 1770; January 8, 1770; January 15, 1770; January 22, 1770.

RUN-away from the Subscriber, living at the White-plains, in the Manor of Cortlandt, the twenty-fourth of November last, a Mustee Wench, Servant to John Underhill, named Lucey; she is very well set and pretty fat: Had on when she went away, a long Gown with ruffled Cuffs, and several striped Pettycoats, and a black Hat. Whoever takes up the said Wench, and brings her to the Subscriber, shall receive Forty Shillings Reward, and all reasonable Charges,
   paid by JOHN UNDERHILL.
The New-York Gazette; and the Weekly Mercury, December 18, 1769; December 25, 1769; January 22, 1770; January 29, 1770.

RAN-AWAY from the Subscriber, at South-Hampton on Long-Island, about 3 Weeks past, a light coloured INDIAN SERVANT, named JACOB WOOLY, of a middle Stature, reads and writes well; whoever will secure said Indian, in any of his Majesty's Jails, and give Notice thereof, or deliver him to the Subscriber at South-Hampton, shall receive THREE DOLLARS REWARD, and all necessary Charges,
   paid by JOSEPH JACOB.   Dec. 11, 1769.
The Newport Mercury, December 25, 1769.

RUN-away, from his Bail living at Fresh-Water in the City of New-York, in Saturday the 8th Instant, a certain John Wilmington, a Sawyer by Trade, he is about 5 Feet 4 Inches high, short black curled Hair, full-faced, thick and well set: Had on when he went away, a mixed coloured broad Cloth Coat, with a slash Sleeve, lately turned, and has got a brown Coat and Jacket since. Whoever takes up the said Wilmington, and will bring him to the Subscriber, or lodge him in any Goal so that he may be had again, shall receive Five Pounds Reward
                    paid by   BENJAMIN BETTS.

The New-York Gazette; and the Weekly Mercury, December 25, 1769; January 1, 1770; January 8, 1770; January 15, 1770; January 22, 1770; January 29, 1770; February 12, 1770.

PHILADELPHIA, *December* 18.

Last Saturday night was committed to Goal of this city, on suspicion of counterfeiting paper money, a Low Dutchman, who goes by the name of Rosey Grant; he is about 60 years old, rather corpulent; about 5 feet 10 inches high, say that he was born in New-York government, and that he lived some time in Eusopus. He was detected by Robert Taggart, a Shopkeeper in Market-street, whom he endeavoured to deceive, in the dusk of the Evening. The bill not appearing regularly printed, Mr. Taggart went and shewed it to several Gentlemen, who also doubted the legality of the bill; but when he returned to his shop, the man was gone, and had left the goods behind him. Mr. Taggart immediately searched after him in several Taverns, and at found him at one in Strawberry Alley. Upon searching him, 68 three pound bills were found in his breeches.

The New-York Gazette or the Weekly Post-Boy, December 25, 1769; *The New-York Journal; or, The General Advertiser*, December 28, 1769. Minor differences between the papers.

1770

Albany, December 29, 1769.
Five Pounds Reward.
STolen in the Night preceding the 28th Instant, from Col. Bradstreet, a strong well made black HORSE, fifteen Hands high, with a good Saddle and Bridle, and supposed to be taken by a dark Mulatto or Negro Man, who made his Escape out of the Goal a Day or two before, where he was confined for running away from his Master Mr. Nathaniel Richards, of Newark, in New-Jersey. Said Mulatto or Negro, is about 5 Feet 10 Inches high, thin made, large flat Nose, with curled Hair down each Cheek, had on a long grey Surtout Coat. Whoever takes up said Horse, with or without the

Negro, shall have the above Reward, with reasonable Charges, on bringing him to Col. Bradstreet, or securing him, and sending Word thereof, and if the Negro is taken it is requested that he be secured in some Goal, and Information thereof, given to Col. Bradstreet His Name is said to be Ben, and that he has changed it to BON or BOND.

N. B. An Irishman commonly called TOBY QUIT, absconded the same Night from Albany, and perhaps might have taken the Horse; He is about 5 Feet 9 Inches high, fair short Hair, tied behind, had on an old Hat, with a blue half worn Surtout Coat, with brass Buttons on each Side, and a double Cape.

The New-York Gazette or the Weekly Post-Boy, January 8, 1770; January 15, 1770; January 22, 1770; January 29, 1770; February 5, 1770; February 12, 1770; February 19, 1770. See *The New-York Gazette or the Weekly Post-Boy*, February 26, 1770.

RUN-away, from the Ship Henry, Capt. Hunter, on Thursday the 4th Instant, the two following Apprentice Lads, viz, Barney Gannon, and Patrick Mc. Elvey; the former is about eighteen Years old, has short black Hair, sore Eyes, stout and well made: Had on when he went away, a grey Ratteen Jacket, short Trowsers, and black Stockings. The latter is about eighteen Years old also, long dark brown Hair tied behind, a slender Lad, and squinted much: Had on a brown Coat and Breeches. Whoever takes up and secures the above mentioned Runaways, so that they may be had again, shall receive Forty Shillings Reward for each, and reasonable Charges,

        paid by   Thompson and Alexander, in New-York.

The New-York Gazette; and the Weekly Mercury, January 8, 1770; January 15, 1770; January 22, 1770; January 29, 1770.

RUN away, Wednesday Night, from John De Lancey, of the Borough-Town of West-Chester, a likely young Mulatto Portuguese Fellow, who speaks bad English, some five Feet eight or nine Inches high; he took off with him a Beaver Hat half worn, a Sailor's Cap, a double breasted Coat of fine blue Broad Cloth with Mohair Buttons, a red Duffel great Coat, brown Breeches, three shirts one of striped Flannel, one of check'd, one of Plain Linen, one Pair of fine bluish worsted and one pair of coarse wollen Stocking. Whoever will secure said Fellow so that his Master gets him again, or bring him to the subscriber, shall have Forty Shillings Reward, and all reasonable Charges

        paid by   JOHN DE LANCEY.   Jan. 15, 1770.

The New-York Journal; or, The General Advertiser, January 18, 1770; January 25, 1770; February 1, 1770; February 8, 1770. See *The New-York Gazette; and the Weekly Mercury*, February 5, 1770.

Forty Shillings Reward.

RUN-away on the night of the 4th inst. from on board the brig Free Mason, Capt. John Sample, from Newry, a certain Joseph Rodgers, a redemptioner, aged about 21 yearsold, 5 feet 7 or 8 inches high, by trade a block-maker: Had on a mix'd blue coat, a brown waistcoat and green breeches, but may change his cloathing having stole sundry sorts of apparel from on board the vessel; he is a native of New-London, in Connecticut, and will probably travel that way. Whoever apprehends and returns him will be entitled to the above-mentioned reward,
    by applying to Capt. Sample, or William Neilson.

The New-York Gazette; and the Weekly Mercury, January 22, 1770; January 29, 1770.

WHEREAS about the 19th of December last, a certain Person who called himself Schuyler, or Cuyler and said he was Brother in-Law to Col. Cortlandt, came to the House of the Subscriber, living at Stanford, in Connecticut, and hired a Horse, as he said, to ride to the said Col. Cortlandt's, and was to have returned in two or three Days, but has never been since heard of, and is supposed to be an Impostor: Had on when he went away, a Claret-coloured Surtout Coat, a mixed-coloured Under-Coat, and Vest, bound with black, and lappelled, black Breeches, light Stockings, Pinchbeck Buckles, had a Gold Loop and Button to his Hat, with a Cockade in the same; said he was an officer, and that he was cast away near Placentia, with the Surveyor-General; had a Draught of the said Bay with him, which he said he drew himself; and is about 5 Feet 8 or 9 Inches high. The Horse is a bright Sorrell, about 14 Hands high, 4 Years old, has crooked large Legs, and is apt to cut behind. Whoever takes up said Fellow, with the Horse, so that he may be brought to Justice, and the subscriber get his Horse, shall receive Five Dollars Reward,
    paid by MUNSON JARVIS.

The New-York Gazette; and the Weekly Mercury, January 22, 1770; January 29, 1770. See *The Massachusetts Gazette: and the Boston Weekly News-Letter*, March 1, 1770.

THREE POUNDS Reward.

RUN-AWAY from the Subscriber, at Hunterdon County, in New-Jersey, an Apprentice, named DAVID COX, about Twenty Years of Age, a Carpenter and Joiner by Trade, but its likely he may pass for a Mill-Wright, as he has two Brothers of that Trade, that works near Albany.—He is about 5 Feet 10 Inches high, large bon'd, knock knee'd, of a dark Complexion, down Look, black Eyes, black Hair, and wears it tied. Had on when he went away, a

grey coloured Coat and Jacket, pretty much worn, with Horn Buttons on them, new Leather Breeches, with black Horn Buttons, Russia Shirt, black Yarn Stockings, new Shoes, also a rusty Castor Hat, wears it cock'd: It is also suspected he has stole his Indentures, and will very likely show them for a Pass, as he is near of Age. Whoever apprehends said Apprentice, and secures him in any Goal, so that his Master may have Notice thereof, shall have the above Reward,
     paid by me JAMES TAYLOR.
 N. B. Perhaps he may change his Cloaths, that he may not be discovered.
 The New-York Gazette, or the Weekly Post-Boy, January 29, 1770; February 12, 1770; February 19, 1770.

RUN-away from the subscriber, living in this City, the 24th Inst. a Negro Wench named Nan, late the Property of John Barres, Baker of this Place: She carried with her a Female Child of a Year old: The Wench is of a Mulatto Colour, pretty tall, and born on Long-Island: Had on when she went away, a homespun Pettycoat, a Jacket, and a large red Bearskin Cloak, and always wears her Shoes down in the Heels. Any Person that takes up the said Wench in the Street, shall receive Twenty Dollars Reward, or Five Dollars if they can discover any Person that conceals her, as she has been persuaded by some bad People to run away. All Persons whatsoever are cautioned against harbouring the said Wench, or Masters of Vessels from carrying her off, as they will answer the same to
    ALEXANDER LESLIE.
 The New-York Gazette; and the Weekly Mercury, January 29, 1770; February 5, 1770; February 12, 1770.

RUN-away, *the 17th ultimo, from John De Lancey, of the Borough-Town of West-Chester, a likely young Mulatto Portuguese Fellow, who speaks bad English, about five feet eight or nine Inches high; he took off with him a Beaver hat half worn, a Sailor's Cap, a double breasted Coat of fine blue road* [sic] *Cloth with Mohair Buttons, a red Duffel great Coat, brown breeches, three Shirts, one of striped Flannel, one of check'd, one of Plain Linen, one Pair of fine bluish worsted and one Pair of coarse wollen Stockings. Whoever will secure said Fellow so that his Master gets him again, or bring him to the subscriber, shall have Forty Shillings Reward, and all reasonable Charges*
    paid by *JOHN DE LANCEY.*
 The New-York Gazette; and the Weekly Mercury, February 5, 1770; February 12, 1770; February 26, 1770; March 12, 1770; March 26,

1770. See *The New-York Journal; or, The General Advertiser*, January 18, 1770.

RUN-away on Tuesday the 20th Inst. at Night, from the Subscriber, a Negro Fellow named Waverage: He is of a middle Size, and very black; not this Country born, but talks middling good English, and is a very complaisant Fellow; Had on when he went away, a new Wool Hat, a brown Great Coat, and a light brown short Coat, and brown Jacket, pale blue Breeches and Stockings. Whoever takes up and secures said Negro Fellow, so that his Master may have him again, shall be well rewarded, and all reasonable Charges
    paid, by JOSEPH CORNWELL.
 N. B. All Masters of Vessels and others, are forbid to carry off said Fellow, or harbour him.
 The New-York Gazette; and the Weekly Mercury, February 26, 1770; March 5, 1770; March 26, 1770.

RUN away the 17th of September last, from Nathaniel Richards of Newark in New-Jersey, a dark Mulatto or Negro Man named Ben, who appears to have been taken up at Albany and committed to Goal there, and to have escaped out of the Goal, the Night of the 27th of December, and is supposed to have stole a Horse, Saddle and Bridle, from Col. Bradstreet; for which he has been advertised by the Colonel: He is about 5 Feet 10 Inches high, thin made, a large flat Nose, with curld Hair down each Cheek, and had on a long grey surtout Coat. Whoever shall take up said Mulatto, and secure him, so that his Master may have him again, shall have FIVE POUNDS Reward, and all reasonable Charges.
 N. B. An Irishman commonly called TOBY QUIT, absconded the same Night from Albany, and appears to be the same person who went off with him from Newark, and perhaps might have taken the Horse: He is about 5 Feet 9 Inches high, fair short Hair, tied behind, had on an old Hat, with a blue half worn Surtout Coat, with brass Buttons on each Side, and a double Cape.
 The New-York Gazette or the Weekly Post-Boy, February 26, 1770; March 5, 1770; March 12, 1770; March 19, 1770; April 2, 1770; April 16, 1770. See *The New-York Gazette or the Weekly Post-Boy,* January 8, 1770.

NEW-YORK, February 14.

WHEREAS about the 19th of December last, a certain Person who called himself Schuyler, or Cuyler and said he was Brother in-Law to Col. Cortlandt, came to the House of the Subscriber, living at Stanford, in

Connecticut, and hired a Horse, as he said, to ride to the said Col. Cortlandt's, and was to have returned in two or three Days, but has never been since heard of, and is supposed to be an Impostor: Had on when he went away, a Claret-coloured Surtout Coat, a mixed-coloured Under-Coat, and Vest, bound with black, and lappelled, black Breeches, light Stockings, Pinchbeck Buckles, had a Gold Loop and Button to his Hat, with a Cockade in the same; said he was an officer, and that he was cast away near Placentia, with the Surveyor-General; had a Draught of the said Bay with him, which he said he drew himself; and is about 5 Feet 8 or 9 Inches high. The Horse is a bright Sorrell, about 14 Hands high, 4 Years old, has crooked large Legs, and is apt to cut behind. Whoever takes up said Fellow, with the Horse, so that he may be brought to Justice, and the subscriber get his Horse, shall receive FIVE DOLLARS Reward, paid by MUNSON JARVIS.

The Person advertised in this Paper the 22d of this Month, by the Name of Schuyler, or Cuyler, and that runaway with a Horse from Mr. Munson Jarvis, of Stanford, in Connecticut, seems to be a knowing Hand, and have a thorough Knowledge of the Country; for, on the 19th Instant, he made his Appearance at the House of Mr. William Crook, at Rariton, where he spent 4 or 5 Days, passed there by the Name of Harmanus Ten Eyck, Son of Jacob H. Ten Eyck, Esq; Member for the County of Albany; that he himself kept a Store in Albany, that his Clerk had robbed him of a Sum of Money, and that he was going to Philadelphia in Pursuit of him; that being scarce of Cash, he borrowed £.9-15-0, from Mr. Crook, a Pair of Saddle Bags, and some clean Linnen, and gave a Draft on Mr. Anthony Ten Eyck, of this City for the same, who he said was his Cousin, and then took his Leave.—He had the Sorrel Horse with him mentioned in the Advertisement, and is certainly the same Person. His real Name is imagined to be Bratt, and the very Man that was punished in this City for robbing Mr. Bennet, the Jeweller.

(It is probable the above Fellow is the same that imposed upon Mr. Bardin, by the Name of Depeyster, advertised some Weeks ago in this Paper.)

The Massachusetts Gazette: and the Boston Weekly News-Letter, March 1, 1770. See The New-York Gazette; and the Weekly Mercury, January 22, 1770.

Twenty Dollars Reward.
RUN-away on Thursday the 8th of November, 1769, from the subscriber, then at New-York, a Scotch indented servant man, named John Southerland, about 27 years of age, 5 feet 7 inches high, short brown hair, pale yellow complection, occasioned by sickness he lately had in the West-

Indies; has been a soldier and wounded in the thigh with a ball, the scar of which may be seen; is much addicted to drink, has lived 4 or 5 years in the Jersies, employed in the farming business:—Had on when he went away, a check'd Shirt, a Pair of Russia drab breeches or oznaburg trowsers, black stockings English made shoes, pinchbeck buckles, an oldish brown under waistcoat, a short blue one lined with white flannel, over it, and a narrow brimm'd boy's felt hat. He also carried off with him the following clothes, with which he was sent to a washerwoman, viz. Two check'd linen handkerchiefs, two or three pairs of white cotton stockings, one or two pairs of oznaburg, and two pair check'd trowsers, one or two white frocks, two or three check'd, and four ruffled shirts, one of two of which were marked on the flap, with the letters L. G. in a yellow stain.—All persons to whom any of the said goods may be offer'd for sale, or who may afterwards discover them, are desired to stop them, and the said servant; and whoever delivers him to Mr. William Milner, at the Exchange in New-York, shall receive Twenty Dollars reward, and all reasonable charges. All masters of vessels and others, are hereby warn'd not to carry off, harbour or conceal the said servant, as they will answer it at their peril.
     LEMUEL GUSTINE, jun.

The New-York Journal; or, The General Advertiser, March 1, 1770; March 8, 1770; March 15, 1770; March 22, 1770; March 29, 1770; April 5, 1770; April 12, 1770; April 19, 1770; May 3, 1770; May 10, 1770. See *The New-York Journal; or, The General Advertiser*, November 16, 1769.

RUN-away from the Subscriber, about 10 Days since, living at the Nine-Partners, in Dutchess County, and Province of New-York, near Mr. *Samuel Mabbit's*, a certain JOHN HICKLEN, about 5 Feet 10 Inches high: Had on when he went away, a dark brown Surtout Coat, a light brown Broadcloth Coat, a Jacket, the Colour uncertain, and a Pair of black Breeches; wears his own Hair, which is short and curled. Whoever takes up the said Run-away, so that he may be had again, shall receive Forty Shillings Reward, and all reasonable Charges,
    paid by SAMSON VEAL.

The New-York Gazette; and the Weekly Mercury, March 5, 1770; March 12, 1770; March 26, 1770.

BRoke Gaol and made their Escape, on Tuesday Night, the sixth Instant; John Barnes, John Lawton and James Cunningham, three Prisoners confined for Debt: Barnes is a Man about six Feet high of a meagre Visage, pitted with the Small-Pox, wears his own dark brown Hair, has a great Impediment in his Speech, was born in the County of West-Chester:

Lawton is a Man about 5 Feet 7 Inches high, wears a Piss-burn'd Wig, is very talkative, pitted with the Small Pox, and a Native of Ireland: Cunningham is a Man of about six Feet high, is a most notorious Cheat, and well known in this City as such; he wears his own hair of a dark Colour, mark'd with the Small Pox, and is a Native of the City of New-York. Whoever takes up and secures any of the said Prisoners, so that they may be had again, shall have a Reward of Five Pounds if taken within this County, and Ten Pounds if taken in any other County or out of the Province, with all reasonable Charges
        paid by   John Roberts Sheriff, or
                     James Mills, Gaoler.   *N. York*, 7th *March* 1770.
The New-York Journal; or, The General Advertiser, March 8, 1770; March 15, 1770; March 22, 1770.

                            Fifty Dollars Reward.
WHEREAS the sloop Three Friends, burthen about Fifty Tons, Carpenters Tonnage. Was on the Night of the 12th Instant taken out of the Great Dock, and carried away, supposed by Capt. Ephraim Goldsmith, who was formerly Part Owner and Master of her, which Vessel said Goldsmith, had given a Bill of Sale for, to the Subscriber, for Barratry, committed by him in a late Voyage to be performed from New-York, to the Bay of Chaluers, in the Gulf of St. Lawrence.—The Perpetrators of the Robbery got themselves possessed of the Key of the Stores, where the Sails and Rigging lay housed, from whence they took them, with some Provisions.
    The Sloop is remarkable for having been a Coaster to Rhode-Island, under the Command of Capt. Lawton: Is payed well on the in Side, with Spanish Brown and Tar, and the Heads of the Timbers with Red Lead; her Quarter Deck, which was lengthened last Summer, runs over the after Part of her Main Deck; her Mouldings painted yellow, with black Sides and Stem;—is pretty full built, and of an easy Draft of Water.
    Ephraim Goldsmith, who formerly commanded her, is a Person about 6 Feet high, raw bon'd, and appears to be about 42 or 43 Years of Age, wears his own Hair, of a sandy Colour, and commonly wears a flapt Hat, has a heavy down Look, stoops much in walking, and has a Family in New-Haven.—Whoever secures the Vessel, and the said Goldsmith, so as to convict him, shall receive the above Reward, or Twenty Dollars for the Sloop and Thirty Dollars for the said Goldsmith.
                  SAMUEL BAYARD, jun.
The New-York Journal; or, The General Advertiser, March 15, 1770.

RUN-away from the subscriber, on Friday the 23d instant, a negro lad, named Tom, about 20 years of age, 5 feet 5 inches high, well set, of a yellowish complexion, pock mark'd about the nose, speaks good Dutch and English: Had on when he went away, a blue watchcoat, a brown pea waistcoat, brown cloth breeches, and stockings new footed with a different colour, and a pair of old double soled shoes. Whoever takes up the said negro, and brings him to Nicholas Anthony, tanner, in Broad-street, New-York, shall have 20s. reward.

All masters of vessels are hereby forbid to carry said negro off, as they shall answer it at their peril.

The New-York Gazette; and the Weekly Mercury, March 26, 1770.

STOLEN from the Subscriber, living in Smith's-Clove, in Orange County, on Monday the 16th last, by a Person who called himself ALEXANDER, a BROWN HORSE, 14 Hands high, 10 Years old, could both pace and trot. ALEXANDER loves Liquor, and is very talkative, of a rudy Complexion, 23 Years old, with dark-coloured Hair, about 5 Feet 8 Inches high: Had on a pale blue short lapelled Coat, a Swanskin Jacket, and Leather Breeches. Whoever takes up and secures the Thief, and the Horse, shall have Forty Shillings Reward, and reasonable Charges,
              paid by   GARRET MILLER.

The New-York Gazette; and the Weekly Mercury, April 23, 1770; April 30, 1770.

A THEFT.

STOLEN on Friday night last, the 13th April instant, from the house of Moses Owens, on the White Plains in West Chester County, the following goods, viz. a coat and 1 pair of Breeches, of dark blue sagathy, the coat lined with tammie of the same colour; 1 lightish colour'd mix'd broad cloth coat and waistcoat, the coat lined with shaloon, the buttons upon both the coat and waistcoat of yellow metal. One black velvet waistcoat, 1 pair of brownish colour'd worsted stockings, and one and a half pair of threat stockings, (one stocking of the two pair, being droped just without the window) The said goods were stolen by one William Townsend, (a hired servant to the said Moses Owens) Townsend calls himself an Englishman, is about 28 years of age, about 5 feet 10 inches high, slim made especially about the legs and thighs, thin face, brown hair, has been a regular in the army for some years, and said he was lately come from Canada. Had on, a coarse shirt, old blue Breeches, much patched, a blue and white waistcoat, striped cross wise, and a short blanket coat, and an old felt hat. He went off with another man, who called himself John Wright, is an Irish man, about 25 or 26 years of age, near 6 feet high, brown complexion, black curl'd hair, much pock broken; had on a lightish colour'd coarse cloth jacket, a check woolen shirt and tow cloth trowsers, pretty much worn, and an old

felt hat. As they were heard in private conversation together, just before the robbery, and both went off together, it is not doubted, but they were confederates, Therefore who ever will apprehend them, or either of them, and confine them in gaol or deliver them to the subscribers, with the above goods, or such of them as can be found upon the said thieves, shall receive Twenty Shillings reward for each, besides all reasonable charges.
    MOSES OWENS. NATHANIEL ADAMS.
The New-York Journal; or, The General Advertiser, April 19, 1770; April 26, 1770; May 3, 1770; May 10, 1770.

WHEREAS *PARNEL my Wife, hath three sundry Times eloped from my Bed and Board, without any just Reason; and whereas she was married on the 2d Day of August, 1769, by the Name of Parnel Butler, (which was her Maiden Name) to one William Saunders, Silver-Smith, now living in this City, it appears by a Certificate, which I have from the Rev. Lumbertus De Reade: Therefore I would caution and warn every Person from trusting her on my Account, as I will pay no Debts of her contracting; and would earnestly recommend it to all the Modest and Virtuous, to shun and avoid her as an adulterous Contemner of the Laws of God, Government, and Society.*
    DAVID HUMPHREVIL. *New-York, April* 12, 1770.
The New-York Journal; or, The General Advertiser, April 19, 1770.

RUN-away on the 14th Ult. from Tappan, in Orange County, a Negro Man Slave named JIM; he is about 5 Feet 6 Inches high, of a very black Complexion, about 20 Years of Age, a little bandy legged, Guinea born, but speaks good English: He had on a light grey Sailor's Jacket, and blue Duffils Trowsers, without a Hat. Any Person who takes up and secures the said Runaway, that he may be had again, shall have Five Dollars Reward, and all reasonable Charges paid by Archibald M'Vicker, in New-York, or Daniel Hughes, at Frederick's Town County, in Maryland;
    or William and Taylor, in Philadelphia.
The New-York Gazette; and the Weekly Mercury, April 30, 1770; May 7, 1770; May 14, 1770.

             New-York, 2*d May*, 1770.
RUN-AWAY from the Subscriber, living in Broad-Street, on Saturday the 28th of April last, a yellow Skin Negro Wench, named Bellow, born in Barbados, about 23 *Years of Age, of a middle Stature: Had on when she went away, a blue striped Homespun Petticoat, a blue Coating Waistcoat, lined with Oznabrugs, a blue Cotton Romall Handkerchief tied about her Head, and a red and white cross-bar'd Handkerchief round her Neck,*

without Shoes or Stockings. Whoever will apprehend and bring the said Negro Wench to her Master, shall have Five Dollars, Reward; and whoever harbours or conceals her, may rest fully assured of having the Severity of the Law put in force against them.
RICHARD HARRIS.

The New-York Journal; or, The General Advertiser, May 3, 1770; May 17, 1770; May 24, 1770; June 21, 1770; June 28, 1770; July 5, 1770; June 14, 1770; *The New-York Gazette; and the Weekly Mercury*, May 7, 1770; May 14, 1770; May 21, 1770; May 28, 1770; June 11, 1770; June 25, 1770. Minor differences between the papers. The *Mercury* does not have the location and date at the top. Name is also spelled Bella in later versions.

RUN-away on the 14th of April last, from the subscriber living at Red-Hook, in Dutchess County, an indented servant man named Michael Greenfield, by trade a nailer, about 40 years of age, 5 feet 7 inches high, of a dark complexion, dark brown hair, smooth faced: He had on when he went away, a white cloth coat and jacket, leather breeches, and black stockings. He hath lived two years in New-York, and is supposed to be still in or about that city. Whoever takes up and secures the said run-away, so that he may be had again, shall receive six dollars reward, and all reasonable charges
paid, by   HERMON HOFFMAN.

The New-York Gazette; and the Weekly Mercury, May 14, 1770; May 21, 1770; May 28, 1770; June 11, 1770.

WENT away on the 25th of April last, a Man aged 42 Years, named John Van Der Veer, about 5 Feet 6 Inches high, dark brown curled Hair, by Trade a Weaver; he speaks Low Dutch as his Mother Tongue, and broken English: Had on when he went away, a whitish homespun Linsey Woolsey Coat, and old Jacket of the same, Buckskin Breeches, blue Woollen Stockings, and Brass Buckles in his Shoes.—He is not in his Senses, and talks very little; has been seen the Day after he went away on Staten-Island. Whoever takes up and brings him to his Mother at Flatbush, in King's County, shall have a reward of 40*s*. Any Person discovering where he is, who shou'd not choose to go to that Trouble of bringing him Home, is hereby kindly requested to send a few Lines to his Mother, and for so doing shall be liberally rewarded
by   BELIRJE VAN DER VEER.

The New-York Gazette; and the Weekly Mercury, May 14, 1770.

Four Pounds Reward.

RUN-away from Henry Allen, at Great-Neck, on Long-Island, a Mulatto Fellow named Peter, about 5 Feet 9 Inches high, a well set likely Fellow, has a Mark from his Wrist to the Elbow of his left Arm, occasioned by a Scald; and a Scar of Inoculation just under his right Knee; he is about thirty-five Years old, wears his own Hair queed up: Had on when he went away, a new brown coloured Sirtout Coat made very long, a brown Jacket, Leather Breeches, striped Trousers, and a Beaver Hat, with a good Pair of Shoes and Stockings; it is supposed he will try to get off by Water: All Masters of Vessels are forbid carrying him off. Whoever takes up said Fellow and secures him in any of his Majesty's Goals, so that his Master may have him again, shall have the above Reward,
          paid by   Henry Allen, at Great-Neck, or
                 Jeremiah Allen, Gunsmith, in New-York.
The New-York Gazette; and the Weekly Mercury, May 14, 1770; May 21, 1770; June 11, 1770; June 25, 1770.

RUN-away from his bail, and with another man's wife, a certain high-dutch man named Zachariah Neer, of a middle size, black short hair, black beard, has lost two of his fore teeth, can speak good English, and is a joiner by trade: Had on when he went away, a mist blue coat and waistcoat, lapel'd, bound with blue binding. She is low-dutch, of a middle size, full fac'd, blue eyes, double chin, was born in Albany, and is named Angle: Had on a dark chinze gown, with blue and yellow spots, and a long blue camblet cloak; and took with her a hair trunk mark'd W. H. Whoever apprehends the said Zachariah Neer, shall have Five Pounds reward, and all reasonable charges, by applying to the printer hereof, Witness our hands.
          EBNER ROBERTS, RALPH WATSON.
Albany, May 7, 1770.
The New-York Gazette; and the Weekly Mercury, May 28, 1770; June 4, 1770; June 11, 1770; June 25, 1770.

New-York, 28th May, 1770.
RUN away from the subscriber in New-York, an indented servant man, a sailor by trade, named Robert Mathews, about 5 feet 10 inches high, dark brown hair, of a fair complexion, blew eyes, well built, and much pitted with the small-pox, knock kneed, was born in Philadelphia; had on when he went away, a brown forest cloth coat, green waistcoat, blue and white striped lining, coarse trowsers, with buttons on them marked 16. Whoever takes up the said run away, and secures him in any of his majesty's goals, or brings him to his master, shall have Four Dollars, and all reasonable
          charges paid by HENRY USTICK.

The New-York Journal; or, The General Advertiser, May 31, 1770; June 7, 1770; June 14, 1770; June 21, 1770.

BROKE Suffolk county goal, and made their Escape on Tuesday night the 19th ult. Thomas Robinson, Jun, confined for debt; and Benjamin Davis, for horse stealing; Davis is a young man, of middling stature, fair complexion, born at Smith-Town, in Suffolk county; a notorious villain,—every person's aid is desired to apprehend him. Robinson is about six feet high, meagre swarthy visage, short black and grey hair, between forty and fifty years of age. Whoever takes up and secures him so that he may be had again, shall have Five Pounds reward, and all reasonable charges
   paid by, GEORGE MURRISON, Sheriff, or,
     BENAJAH EDWARDS, Goaler.
The New-York Gazette; and the Weekly Mercury, June 4, 1770; June 11, 1770.

RUN-AWAY, *on Saturday the second Instant, June, a Negro Boy, named CATO: a Sweep-Chimney, about 12 Years of Age, very black, smooth faced Guiney born, and speaks good English: Had on, when he went away, an Ozinbrigs Shirt and Trowsers, pretty much worn, a white Frock Coat, he formerly belonged to Capt. Goodridge of the Packet. Whoever takes up and secures the said Negro, so that he may be had again, shall have Twenty Shillings Reward, and all reasonable Charges*
   paid, by NICHOLAS FLETCHER, *near the New-Goal.*
The New-York Gazette; and the Weekly Mercury, June 11, 1770; June 18, 1770; June 25, 1770; July 23, 1770.

RAN away on the 10th of April last past from Daniel Cook, of Long-Island, a Negro Woman, about 20 years old, speaks good English, born on Long-Island, about middling stature, she is a likely wench, had a large pack of cloaths, strip'd short gown, and several callico gowns; has chang'd her dress for man's cloaths, and was seen to have a blue broadcloth coat, and the remainder of her cloaths appears to be man's as she had about 3 or 4 pounds in money—had rings in her ears.
  Whoever will take up said Negro, and secure her in any of his Majesty's goals, so that I can receive said negro, shall have a reward of FOUR POUNDS, and all necessary charge
   paid by me, DANIEL COOK.
New-London, May 14, 1770.
The New-London Gazette, June 15, 1770; June 22, 1770.

New-Rochel, (in Westchester County), June 7.
Three Pounds Reward.
RUN-AWAY from the Subscriber, living in New-Rochel, a Mulato Slave, name JAMES, about 26 Years of Age, 5 Feet 10 Inches high, slender set, wears his own short black Hair, speaks good English and Dutch, with a Scar on his Forehead just within the Hair, one of his Legs smaller than the other, occasioned by a Wound, and a Scar by a Ball on one of his Knees. Had on when he went away, a dark brown homespun Waistcoat, Tow Shirt, and long Tow Trowsers, good Shoes and Stockings, an old Felt Hat, Whoever takes up said Servant, and secures him in any Goal, or brings him to his Master, shall have the above Reward, and necessary Charges
         paid by me   BENJAMIN STEVENSON.
The New-York Gazette; and the Weekly Mercury, June 25, 1770; July 2, 1770; July 9, 1770; July 16, 1770; July 23, 1770; August 6, 1770.

RUN-AWAY from the Subscriber hereof, an Irish Servant Man, about 25 or 26 Years of Age, and near 6 Feet high, very much pitted with the Small-pox, named Nicholas Fitzgerald, speaks much on the Brogue, is a talkative boasting Fellow. Had on when he went away, a white Jacket with Sleeves, a Pair of long white Trowsers, Check Shirt, and a good Hat with a large Brim. Whoever takes up said Servant, and brings him to the Subscriber, or secures him in any of his Majesty's Goals, shall have Fifty Shillings Reward, and reasonable Charges
         paid, by   SAMUEL HENRY.
N. B. He run-away last August, and went by the Name of Thomas Kelly; it is imagin'd he has chang'd his Cloths, and thought to be gone off with one John McIntosh, a Ditcher.
The New-York Gazette; and the Weekly Mercury, June 25, 1770; July 2, 1770; July 9, 1770; July 23, 1770; August 6, 1770.

                                     New-York, June 21, 1770.
RUN away, on Friday last, from the subscriber, living in New-York, an apprentice lad, named James Pall, a baker by trade; had on when he went away, a beaver hat, a tow-cloth jacket and trowsers, wore no stockings, had brass carved buckles in his shoes, and a scar under his right eye.—Whoever secures and brings him to his master, shall have a dollar reward, and all reasonable charges,
         paid by   JOHN STAGG.
The New-York Journal; or, The General Advertiser, June 21, 1770; June 28, 1770; July 5, 1770; July 12, 1770.

New-York, June 27.
RAN away on Sunday the 24th instant from the subscriber, an indented servant boy named Belcher Preston, born in the province of New-Jersey, about seventeen years of age, five feet seven inches high, well set, fair complexion, brown short hair, greyish eyes, his upper teeth projecting; had on when he went away, a blue jacket and waistcoat, leather breeches lately cleaned, with a patch between the legs, white thread stockings new, a pair shoes almost new, and a pair plain metal buckles, supposed to be gone into Chester county or Philadelphia. Whoever apprehends or secures the said indented servant boy in any of his Majesty's goals, or otherwise give notice to the printer hereof, shall receive Five Dollars reward and all reasonable expences paid, by   RICHARD BOLTON.
N. B. All masters of vessels are forwarned carrying him away at their peril.
The New-York Journal; or, The General Advertiser, June 28, 1770; July 5, 1770; July 12, 1770; July 19, 1770.

WHEREAS on Friday the 6th instant, was stolen from Jeremiah French, of Dover, in Dutchess County, a white Roan Stallion, by Joseph and Israel Hodges, which horse they sold to Broughton Reynolds, at Brooklyn Ferry, on Long-Island, Tuesday the 11th, for the Sum of 6l. and are since absconded, and supposed to be gone towards Peek's-Kill. Israel is about 24 Years old, 5 Feet 9 Inches high, pretty well set, and wore his own black curled Hair: Had on a blue Jacket, without sleeves, check Shirt, and long Tow Cloth Trowsers. Joseph is about 5 Feet 8 Inches high, pretty slim, and wore his own Hair, black and curled: Had on a short blue Coat, Tow Cloth Shirt, and striped Homespun Trowsers. Whoever takes up and secures he above mentioned Persons, shall have 40*s*. Reward, and all reasonable Charges, paid by JEREMIAH FRENCH.
BROUGHTON RAYNOLDS.
The New-York Gazette; and the Weekly Mercury, July 16, 1770; July 23, 1770; July 30, 1770.

RUN-away from the Subscriber, living at Newtown, on Long-Island, on Sunday the 8th Instant, a Negro Man named CATO, about 25 Years old, 5 Feet 7 Inches high, or thereabouts, pretty well set, and not very black. Had on when he went away a Homespun striped Jacket, and Tow Cloth Trowsers. Whoever takes up and secures said Fellow, so that he may be had again, shall receive 40*s*. Reward, and have all reasonable Charges paid by   NICHOLAS WICKHOFF.
The New-York Gazette; and the Weekly Mercury, July 16, 1770; July 23, 1770; July 30, 1770; August 6, 1770; August 13, 1770; August 27, 1770; September 10, 1770; September 17, 1770; September 24, 1770.

Twenty Five Pounds Reward,
WHEREAS on Thursday Night last, John Harrison Vinton, otherwise called John Vinton, did feloniously cut the Sloop Sally, of about Eighty or Ninety Town Burthen, from the Dock, and carried her off; and whereas I am two Thirds Owner of the said Sloop, and the said Vinton is considerably in my Debt. I do hereby offer the above Reward of Twenty Five Pounds, New-York Currency, to any Person or Persons whosoever, who shall apprehend the said John Vinton, confine him in any of his Majesty's Goals, so that he may be brought to condign Punishment, and Seize the said Sloop, so that she may be brought again to the Harbour of New-York.
Given under my Hand in the City of New-York, the 30th July 1770.
GEORGE JOHNSON.
The New-York Journal; or, The General Advertiser, August 9, 1770; August 16, 1770; August 23, 1770.

WHEREAS on Monday afternoon the 6th instant, a young man who came to town about a week ago with Capt. Collard from Newport, lodged at Mr Milner's near the Exchange, called himself Lee, pretended to be the son of Col. Lee, of Marblehead, (a Gentlemen of worth and fortune) well known to the subscriber, who having when in company of the said pretended person, received a sum of money, which he could not conveniently carry to his lodgings, did on the offer of the said Lee or carry it in his pocket book, did entrust him with it for that purpose; as he has not since return'd to his lodgings, nor been seen or heard of by the subscriber, he is apprehensive that the said Lee is an imposture and cheat, and hereby offers a reward of 4 dollars, besides all reasonable expences, to any person who shall apprehend the said Lee, and carry him before a Magistrate, (giving me or my attorney notice) so that he may be dealt with as the law directs.
The said person is a young man, about 25 years of age, and 5 feet 7 inches high, middle size, stoops a little, very swarthy complexion, looks like a Portuguese, short black hair, not long enough to curl, but stands high in a thick bunch before; he is very talkative, and has something of a lisp or impediment in his speech: He had on a blue broadcloth coat, leather breeches, remarkably yellow, or a pair of black stocking breeches, and wears his hat flop'd behind, and cock'd before, over one eye.
If the said Lee should be taken up after my Departure, notice is desired to be given to Capt. Smith of the Boston Packet, and if he should be departed, to Mr. William Milner, near the Exchange.
SIMEON FREEMAN,
Master of the sloop Betsy, from Jamaica, bound to Boston.
The New-York Journal; or, The General Advertiser, August 9, 1770; August 16, 1770; August 23, 1770; August 30, 1770.

Dover, July 28, 1770.

RUN-AWAY from *Jeremiah French*, of Dover, in Dutchess County, and Province of New York, A Swarthy Complexion Man, with large gray Eyes, his little finger upon his Right Hand smaller than Common, about twenty five Years of Age, had on an old Beaver Hatt, with a hole in the Crown, a check'd woolen Shirt, a white flanuel Jacket, with black specks in it, short, wide Tow Trowsers and bare Legged:—Whosover shall take up said Man, and secure him, or bring him home to me, shall have FIVE DOLLARS Reward, and all necessary charges paid,
    by me JEREMIAH FRENCH.
N. B. *His Names* [sic] *is* Jabez Herrenton.

 The Connecticut Courant, And Hartford Weekly Intelligencer, August 20, 1770; September 3, 1770; *The Massachusetts Gazette: and the Boston Weekly News-Letter*, August 30, 1770. Minor differences between the papers. The *Gazette* does not have the location and date at the top.

RUN-away from the subscriber, living in Ball-Town, in the patent of Kayaderosseras, alias, Queen's Borough, in the county of Albany, on the twenty-sixth ult. a negro man named Ishmael, about 6 feet 3 inches high, about 30 years of age: Had on when he went away, a blue sagothy coat, a blue flower'd camblet jacket, a pair of blue camblet breeches, a white tow shirt, a pair of double soal'd shoes without buckles; carried with him besides, two woolen check shirts, one tow shirt, one check linen shirt, one holland shirt, likewise a short gun, a fiddle with a red fiddle bag, and plays on the fiddle. Said negro formerly belonged to Capt. Samuel Richards, of Norwalk, in Connecticut. Whoever takes up and secures said negro, so that his master gets him again, shall have 5 dollars reward, and all reasonable
    charges, paid by ELIPHELET KELLOG.

 The New-York Gazette; and the Weekly Mercury, September 3, 1770; September 10, 1770; September 17, 1770; October 1, 1770; October 8, 1770; October 29, 1770; November 5, 1770. See *The New-York Gazette; and the Weekly Mercury*, April 29, 1771.

      Five Dollars Reward.
RUN-AWAY, *on Wednesday evening the 10th inst. from on board the sloop Speedwell, lately arrived from Boston, a negro man named Will, about 5 feet 6 inches high, a healthy strong well-set fellow of yellowish complexion, born at Bermuda, the property of Mr. Paul Bascome, of that Island: Had on when he went away, an old green jacket, a pair of oznaburgs trowsers, a woollen shirt, and grey yarn stockings. Whoever takes up said negro, and brings him to the subscriber on board the sloop*

Speedwell, lying at Bookman's-slip, or to Mr. Anthony Griffiths, on Rotten-Row, shall receive five dollars reward, if taken up in town, or ten if taken up in the country, and all reasonable charges
      paid by PASCHAL N. SMITH.
 N. B. *All masters of vessels and others are forwarned carrying off or harbouring said negro, as they may expect to answer it to the utmost rigour of the law.*
 The New-York Gazette; and the Weekly Mercury, October 15, 1770; October 22, 1770.

RUN away from John Anthony, of the city of New-York, cordwainer, an apprentice lad, named Ezekiel Johnston, about 18 years of age, about five feet four inches high, short dark hair; had on when he went away, a chocolate coloured coat double breasted, blue German serge waistcoat and breeches, grey ribb'd stockings, and a good castor hat; was seen going through New-Rochelle, on monday at noon, and intends for Rhode-Island or Boston. Whoever takes up said apprentice, and send him to his master, shall have Four Pounds reward, and all reasonable charges, paid by his said master.
 The New-York Journal; or, The General Advertiser, October 18, 1770; October 25, 1770; November 1, 1770.

TAKEN up by the subscriber, living in Newburgh, Ulster-County, a negro man named *Tom*, about 23 years of age, short stature, speaks very broken English, and one of his hands rather smaller than the other, and the fingers crooked, occasioned by a fall out of a tree; is very meanly cloathed having neither cap or hat, shoes or stockings: He has told different stories in regard to his master, but as near as I can find out by the negroes talk, his masters name is Samuel Pese Lising, lives in New-England, in Middletown. Whoever appears with a proper claim and title, paying the cost, may have him again, by applying to
    JOSEPH ALBERTSON.
 The New-York Gazette; and the Weekly Mercury, October 29, 1770; November 5, 1770; November 12, 1770.

RUN-away on Saturday morning October the 27th, 1770, from the subscriber, living in New-York, a negro wench named LILL, was born on Long-Island, and late the property of Mr. Jecamiah Mitchell, of Flushing, boatman: She is a tall thin wench, about seventeen years of age, rather upon the yellowish or tawny black, than otherwise; she had on when she went away, a thick coarse woollen jacket and pettycoat, of an iron or russet colour; a blue cloth cloak with a hood to it, made of coarse knap; tho' she may change her dress, as she took with her a strip'd homespun jacket and pettycoat, and sundry other things. Any person that secures the said wench, so that her master may have her again, shall have TWENTY SHILLINGS reward, and all reasonable charges paid; and all persons are hereby forewarned from harbouring or secreting the said wench, or detaining her from her from her said master, as they may depend upon being prosecuted to the utmost severity of the law, for so doing.

The New-York Gazette; and the Weekly Mercury, November 5, 1770.

RUN-away the 27th of Octo. 1770, from Joseph Drake, of Goshen, in the county of Orange, in the province of New-York, a negro man named DICK, about twenty two years old, of a black complexion, speaks good English and Spanish, about five feet eight inches high, a well set likely fellow: Had on and took with him, two homespun shirts, one fine the other coarse; one close bodied homespun light colour'd coat with flat pewter buttons; one grey jacket of the same cloth, double breasted, with round pewter buttons; a pair of buckskin breeches, with Philadelphia buttons; and one pair tow cloth trowsers, three pair yarn stockings, two grey, one blue; one felt hat, a gun with a curl'd maple stock, mended with brass at the britch; a bay horse about eleven years old, marked with a swallow fork on his right Ear. It is supposed the said negro will endeavour to get to the back parts of Boston government. Whoever takes up and secures the said run-away, and brings him to his said master, or secures him again, shall receive FORTY SHILLINGS reward, and all reasonable charges
   paid, by said JOSEPH DRAKE.

The New-York Gazette; and the Weekly Mercury, November 5, 1770; November 12, 1770; November 26, 1770; December 3, 1770. See *The New-York Gazette; and the Weekly Mercury,* May 27, 1771, and *The New-York Gazette; and the Weekly Mercury,* June 8, 1772.

FORTY SHILLINGS Reward.

RAN AWAY from Peter Huggeford, of the White Plain, in the County of West Chester, a negro man called ABRAHAM, a short well set Indian looking fellow, about 24 years of age, curled hair, one tooth in the under jaw before, broke off: Had on when he went away, a dark brown broadcloth jacket, almost new, with an old light coloured homespun jacket over it, a pair of light coloured breeches of the same, with a pair of tow trowsers over them, white yarn stockings and old shoes: he took with him a tow and a fine linen shirt, and wore a checked handkerchief about his neck; it is supposed he will attempt to get among the Indians, as he has done twice before: Any person who will return said negro to his master, or secure him

in any of his Majesty's goals, so that his master may have him again, shall receive the above reward, and all reasonable charges,
        paid by   PETER HUGGEFORD.
The New-York Journal; or, The General Advertiser, November 15, 1770; November 22, 1770; November 29, 1770; December 6, 1770; *The New-York Gazette; and the Weekly Mercury*, November 19, 1770; November 26, 1770. Minor differences between the papers.

        Forty Shillings Reward.
RUN-AWAY *from the snow James and Mary, a certain William Kennedy, an indented servant, about five feet seven or eight inches high, full fac'd, black hair: Had on when he went away, a black coat and jacket, blue grey stockings, pretends to cawl* [sic] *or net making, had made many needles for this purpose; he was formerly a soldier in Yorkshire in Old England; it is supposed he took with him a large black dog Newfoundland breed. Whoever takes up said servant, and will bring him to the subscriber, shall have the above reward, and all reasonable charges,*
        paid by   ARCHIBALD M'VICKER.
The New-York Gazette; and the Weekly Mercury, December 3, 1770; December 10, 1770; December 17, 1770.

RUN away from the subscriber, living at Rynbeck, in the province of New-York, a mulatto fellow named KANE, about 28 years old, about 5 feet 8 inches high, and speaks Dutch and English:—Had on when he went away, a light coloured French coat. Whoever takes up the said run away, so that he may be had again, shall receive FORTY SHILLINGS reward, and all reasonable charges
        paid, by   JACOB SCHERMERHORN.
The New-York Gazette; and the Weekly Mercury, December 3, 1770; December 10, 1770.

        TWENTY DOLLARS Reward.
STOLEN out of the pasture of Gabriel Briggs, of the Manor of Corlandt, a dark brown HORSE, with white fet-locks on his hind feet, the under side of his mane cut short, paces and trots, is a high mettled horse, about 15 hands and a half high, neither mark'd nor branded; also a hunting saddle, with a blue house, bound with leather: Supposed to be stolen by one Richard Pendergast, a short, well set man, a native of Ireland, a ditcher, in good apparel and much given to laughing loud, who absconded at the same time, and is supposed to be gone to Philadelphia. Whoever secures the horse and saddle, or horse alone, shall have Six Pounds reward, or Eight Pounds with the thief, and all reasonable charges,

paid by   GABRIEL BRIGGS.   *Dated Nov. 1st.* 1770.
The New-York Journal; or, The General Advertiser, December 6, 1770; December 13, 1770; December 20, 1770; December 27, 1770.

RUNAWAY from me the Subscriber, a Negro Boy, named SPIER; had on when he went away a blue Cloth Coat, with another short white Ditto under it, old knit yellow Breeches, Shoes and Stockings, and his Hat sewed up all round. He is about Fifteen Years of Age, is remarkably black, large Nose, with Guinea Cuts on his Cheeks, has to very large Lubs near each Ear, is pretty well set, and a little knock knee'd, very apt to smile when spoken too. If taken up Town One Dollars Reward, and if out of Town Two Dollars, and all reasonable Charges, will be
paid by   JOHN SLIDELL.
N. B. I do forewarn all Persons from harbouring, concealing, or carrying off said Slave, at their Peril. He took with him a large white Blanket.   New-York, Nov. 16, 1770.
The New-York Gazette or the Weekly Post-Boy, December 10, 1770; December 17, 1770.

RUN-away from Zacheus Newcomb, Charjotte precinct, in Duchess county, an INDIAN BOY, named Jeffery, of 18 years old, about 5 feet 4 inches high, with black curled hair:—Had on when he went away, a short brown coat, and worsted vest without sleeves, woollen breeches; born on Long-Island, and stole from his master, one new coat and vest, home made, mix'd colours of a deep and pale blue, plain made, with Philadelphia buttons; one castor hat, and two silk handkerchiefs. Whoever takes up the said servant, and brings him to his said master, or secures him in any of his majesty's goals, so that he may have him again, shall have Three Pounds reward, and all reasonable charges
paid by me,   ZACHEUS NEWCOMB.   Dec. 12, 1770.
The New-York Gazette; and the Weekly Mercury, December 17, 1770; December 24, 1770; December 31, 1770; January 7, 1771.

Five Dollars Reward.
WHEREAS the sloop Phoebe, from Horse-Neck, Greenwich, was robbed on Thursday night the 13th instant, by a person who calls himself John White, of sundry articles, amongst whom was between nine and ten pounds in cash, in silver and paper; a pair of new shoes, with pinchbeck buckles: He is an Irishman, about 5 feet 6 inches high, and supposed to be about 35 years of age, a thick pretty well-sett fellow, with yellowish hair, a little pock-pitted, speaks English tolerably well, and calls himself a Scotchman. Whoever takes up and secures the said villain, so that the things may be had

again, shall receive the above reward from me, on board the said sloop Phoebe, lying at Peck's-slip.
JOHN ADDINGTON.
The New-York Gazette; and the Weekly Mercury, December 17, 1770; December 24, 1770; December 31, 1770; January 7, 1771; Janary 14, 1771.

FORTY SHILLINGS Reward.
RAN-away from the Subscriber on Friday the 23d ult. a servant Fellow, part Negro and part Indian, named James; he is about 5 Feet 9 Inches high, well set, has a large bushy Head of Hair, he is Lame with a Sore on his left Heel: Had on when he went away, a light colour'd Vest with a blue Lining, a striped under Vest, a new Felt Hat, a wooling Check Shirt, tow and line Trowsers. Whoever takes up said Servant and secures him, so that his Master may have him again, shall have the above Reward and all reasonable Charges paid,
   by me JACOB BALDING.
Fish Kills, Dutchess County, Nov. 27, 1770.
The New-York Gazette; and the Weekly Mercury, December 17, 1770; December 24, 1770; January 7, 1771; January 14, 1771. Only the first ad has the location and date at the bottom.

1771

SIX DOLLARS Reward.

RUN away, the 2d day of January, 1771, from the subscriber, in Philadelphia, a certain JOHN WEBB, born in Amboy, served part of his time with Gilbert Ash, in New York, and lately carried on the Joiner's business in this City; he is fond of liquor, dancing and gaming, addicted to lying, and by his misconduct is become a servant; he is about 5 feet 9 or 10 inches high, 22 years of age, fair complexion, light curled hair, fresh coloured, full faced, well set, likely fellow, lost one of his under fore teeth, a great boaster, talks much of his bringing up, and pretends he has something depending in Amboy; had on, and took with him, a new castor hat, a new brown broadcloth coat, a white swanskin jacket, with red spots, ticken breeches, white and check shirts, white neckcloths, or borrowed others, as it was his practice when he was his own master; he has been seen in different dresses in this city, since he went away. Whoever takes up said servant, and brings him to me, or secures him in any goal, so that his master may have him again, shall have the above reward, and reasonable charges,
   paid by JOSEPH BOLTON.

N. B. All masters of vessels, and others, are forbid to carry him off, or harbour him, at their peril.
The Pennsylvania Gazette, January 10, 1771.

THREE DOLLARS REWARD.

RUNAWAY the 31st day of October last from Peter Overpaw, of the Cat's Kill, in the county of Albany in the province of New York, (and was the next day brought by the subscriber, of Enfield) a negro man, about 30 years of age, 5 feet 4 or 5 inches high, one of his hands considerably smaller than the other, and has been about 3 years in the country. Whoever takes up or secures the said negro, so that the subscriber may get him again, shall receive the above reward, besides all reasonable charges.
This 7th January 1771.   JOHN M'LISTER.
Enfield, Jan. 7, 1771.
The New-York Journal; or, The General Advertiser, January 17, 1771; January 24, 1771, February 7, 1771.

Flushing, Queen's County, Long-Island, Dec. 30, 1770.
RUN-away from the subscriber hereof, a Negro man, named WILL, aged about 50 years, a middle sized fellow, not very black, talks both English and Dutch, his teeth is black by smoking. Had on when he went away, a light colour'd great coat, with metal buttons, a light colour'd close body coat with metal buttons, black horse-skin breeches, black stockings, shoes with strings in them, and an old castor hat. Whoever takes up the said Negro, and secures him, so as his master may have him again, shall have Twenty Shillings reward, and all reasonable charges
paid, by me   JOHN VANLIEU.
The New-York Gazette; and the Weekly Mercury, January 21, 1771; January 28, 1771; February 4, 1771; February 11, 1771.

Five Pounds Reward.
RUN-away from the subscriber, friday evening, January 25th, a negro fellow named John Poleet, about 5 feet 9 inches high, is well made; and has the letters L. G. marked on his left arm: Had on when he went away, a blue great coat, with buttons of the same, and a long pair of trowsers. Whoever will apprehend the said fellow so that his master may have him again, shall receive the above reward, and all reasonable charges paid by me.
N. B. The above fellow talks French, and understands dressing hair.
MAXIMILIAN JACOBS.
The New-York Gazette; and the Weekly Mercury, January 28, 1771; February 4, 1771; *The New-York Journal; or, The General Advertiser*,

January 31, 1771. The *Journal* has "Apply to the Printer." at the bottom.

RUN-AWAY from the Subscriber, on Tuesday the 4th Instant, living at Fredericksburgh, Dutchess County, an indented Servant Boy, about 12 Years of Age, named DONALD M'KENZIE, pretty big of his Age, brown Hair, and brown Eyes. Whoever takes up the said Runaway, and sends him to his Master, or to Captain Alexander Kidd, on Mr. Cruger's Wharf, New-York, shall have 20s. Reward, and all reasonable Charges paid, &c.
    JOHN Mc.ARTHUR.
The New-York Gazette; and the Weekly Mercury, March 4, 1771; March 11, 1771.

RUN away on Thursday the 7th of March, from Peter Low, a mulatto slave, named *Syme* or *Symon* (half Indian breed) aged about 24 years, is a chimney sweeper, had on when he went, an old thicksett coat, an old blue watch coat, an old beaver hat, and other old clothes, has his utensils for sweeping with him,—he is short and well set, has a heavy walk, speaks slow and thick, both Dutch and English, has short but strait Indian like hair, and generally smiles when spoken to; 'tis likely he lurks about town, perhaps he may pretend to be free. Masters of vessels or others are cautioned against carrying him off.

 Whoever takes up the said negro or secures him so that his master may have him again, shall have Ten Shillings, if taken out of the City with reasonable charges,
   paid by PETER LOW.
The New-York Journal; or, The General Advertiser, March 14, 1771; March 21, 1771; March 28, 1771; April 11, 1771. See *The New-York Gazette; and the Weekly Mercury*, March 18, 1771.

RUN-away on Thursday the 7th of March, from Peter Low, a mulatto slave named Syme, or Symon, (half negro and half Indian breed) about 24 years old, is a chimney sweeper; Had on when he went, an old thickset coat, an old beaver hat, an old watch coat, and other old cloaths; had his utensils for sweeping with him. He is short and well set, walks heavy, speaks slow and thick, both Dutch and English, has short but strait Indian like hair, and generally smiles when spoken to; as he may perhaps pretend to be a free man, masters of vessels and others, are forewarn'd from carrying him off; and whoever takes up the said slave, and secures him so that his master may have him again, shall have Two Dollars, and if taken out of the city of New-York, Four Dollars reward, with all reasonable charges,
   paid by PETER LOW.

The New-York Gazette; and the Weekly Mercury, March 18, 1771; March 25, 1771; April 1, 1771. See *The New-York Journal; or, The General Advertiser*, March 14, 1771

Orange Town, March 16, 1771.

RUN-AWAY *from the subscriber, on Sunday the 24th instant, a negro man named TOM, aged about 30 years, a well built, square shoulder'd fellow, of a swarthy colour, thick lips, speaks good Low-Dutch, about 5 feet 6 inches high: Had on when he went off, a grey homespun coat and breeches, and streaked vest, bluish stockings and half worn shoes, and a felt hat; carried off with him two tow shirts; and it is supposed he is gone off in company with one Isaac Delamator, a lad of about 19 years of age. Whoever apprehends the said negro man, and secures him in any of his majesty's goals, or brings him home, so that his master may have him again, shall have 40s. reward, besides all reasonable charges,*
by applying to JOHN HARING.

The New-York Gazette; and the Weekly Mercury, April 1, 1771; April 15, 1771. See *The New-York Gazette; and the Weekly Mercury*, August 5, 1771.

RAN-away from the subscriber of Claverack, on the 1st day of instant April, a negro man named Harry, about 5 feet high, had on when he went away, a greyish coloured coat, a pair of buckskin breeches, green Indian stockings, large brim'd beaver hatt, something worn.—
Whoever shall take up said Negro, and convey him to Col. John Ashley of Sheffield, or confine him in any of his Majesty's goals, and send word to the subscriber, shall have Three Dollars reward, and all necessary charges paid, by   JOHN UPHAM.
Claverack, April 10, 1771.

The Connecticut Courant, and Hartford Weekly Intelligencer, From April 9, to April 16, 1771; From April 16, to April 23, 1771; From April 23, to April 30, 1771.

WILLIAM LAWSON,
(Shoemaker at the Sign of the Boot and Star,
near Peck's Slip in New-York)
....

RUN AWAY from the said LAWSON, on the 14th inst. April, an Apprentice Boy, named DAVID SANFORD, about 16 years of age, of a brown complexion, 5 feet 6 inches high, had on, or took with him when he went away, a homespun blue and white Wilton coat, a blue callimanco jacket, leather breeches, three checked shirts, a pair of blue and a pair of grey woolen stockings, a furr hat half worn, and a striped jacket and trowsers. It is supposed he is gone towards Newark. Whoever takes up and secures the said Run away, giving proper notice, so that his master may get him again, shall receive THREE DOLLARS Reward, besides all reasonable charges from me,   WILLIAM LAWSON.

N. B. All persons are hereby forwarned, not to employ, harbour, conceal, entertain, or carry away the said apprentice, as they will be prosecuted according to law.

The New-York Journal; or, The General Advertiser, April 25, 1771; May 11, 1771; May 23, 1771.

RUN-AWAY from the Subscriber living in Ball-town, in the Patent of Kayaderosseros, alias Queensborough, in the County of Albany, on the 26th of August last, a Negro Man named ISHMAEL, about 6 Feet 3 Inches high, about 30 Years of Age: Had on when he went away a blue Sagothee Coat, a blue flower'd Camblet Jacket, a Pair of blue Camblet Breeches, a white Tow Shirt, a Pair of double-soal'd Shoes without Buckles, and carried with him besides two Woollen check Shirts, one Shirt a check Linen and a Holland Shirt a short Gun, a Fiddle which he carried in a red Bag, and a small Hand-Trunk where he kept his Rosin; he plays on the Fiddle, and is supposed to have got a forged Pass, and is remarkable for the largeness of his Feet: said negro formerly belonged to Capt. Samuel Richards, of Norwalk, in Connecticut. Whoever takes up and secures the said Negro, so that his Master may have him again, shall receive 10 Dollars Reward, and all reasonable Charges,
            paid by   ELIPHELET KELLOG.
If taken up, the Person is requested to acquaint the Printer hereof.

The New-York Gazette; and the Weekly Mercury, April 29, 1771; May 6, 1771; May 13, 1771; May 27, 1771. See *The New-York Gazette; and the Weekly Mercury*, September 3, 1770.

Five Dollars Reward.
RUN-AWAY *from his master, William Bergett, an indented servant; he is a Frenchman, speaks very little English, is about 20 years of age, thin fac'd, and slender, about 5 feet 5 inches high: Had on when he went off. a blue coat with gilt buttons, scarlet waistcoat laced with narrow silver lace, and lined with yellow; a new hat with a gold loop and button, which clothes are the property of his master; he has also a short green jacket, is by trade a peruke-maker and hair dresser: It is supposed he is gone either to Boston or Philadelphia. Whoever will give information of him to the printer, so that he may be apprehended, shall receive five dollars reward.*

The New-York Gazette; and the Weekly Mercury, May 13, 1771; May 20, 1771; May 27, 1771.

Forty Shillings Reward.

RUN-away from the Subscriber, two Slaves, one an Indian Boy, about 18 Years of Age, named JACK, with long black Hair, 5 Feet 1 or 2 Inches high: Had on a blue Cloth Coat, with white metal Buttons, white Flannel Jacket, and black Manchester Velvet Breeches: The other lately belonged to Doctor Chovet, named BRUTUS, near 5 Feet 8 Inches high, about the same Age: Had on a black short Jacket, with an under yellow one, and Buckskin Breeches, with old Shoes and Stockings, can read and write, and probably may forge a Pass. Whoever secures them both, or brings them to the Subscriber, shall have the above Reward, and reasonable Charges, or for either, TWENTY SHILLINGS,
WM. BROWNEJOHN, jun.
The New-York Gazette; and the Weekly Mercury, May 13, 1771; May 20, 1771; June 3, 1771.

RUN-away from Joseph Drake, near Goshen, in Orange county, a negro fellow, about 24 years old, 5 feet seven inches high, very black, speaks good Spanish and English: Had on a wool hat, a grey home made coat, and jacket (patch'd) with pewter buttons; and old tow shirt, old buckskin breeches, grey stockings, and took with him two pair of shoes; also a sorrel horse, about 15 hands high, 5 years old, branded with the letters **I. D.** on the near buttock. Five dollars reward and all reasonable charges will be paid to any person that secures the same so as the owner may have them again.
The New-York Gazette; and the Weekly Mercury, May 27, 1771; June 3, 1771; June 17, 1771. See *The New-York Gazette; and the Weekly Mercury*, November 5, 1770, and *The New-York Gazette; and the Weekly Mercury*, June 8, 1772.

RUN-away, from the Subscriber, living at Oysterbay, in Queen's County, on Long-Island, on Sunday Evening the 28th ult. A Negro Fellow, named JACK, about 35 Years old, 5 Feet 8 Inches high, his Ancles very big, small Toes, and walks stooping: Had on when he went away, a blue Coat, and Buckskin Breeches, but 'tis imagined he would change his Dress, and he took several Clothes with him; he had plenty of Money, and may have a forged Pass. Whoever takes up and secures said Fellow, so that he may be had again, shall receive Forty Shillings Reward, and all reasonable Charges paid by   JOHN HULET.
The New-York Gazette; and the Weekly Mercury, June 3, 1771; June 17, 1771.

Five Dollars Reward,

WILL *be given to any Person, that shall take up and secure a Negro Boy named Thom, a very likely Fellow; about five Feet six or seven Inches high, slender made, long Visage, smooth Face and very black, has lost one of his foremost Teeth; he is about 23 Years of Age. Had on a brown Coat, Waistcoat and Breeches, white Metal Buttons, and Linnen Trowsers, a Silver Loop in his Hat; he has been seen in different Parts of the Town; the above Reward will be paid by his Master,*
DAVID CLARKSON.
The New-York Gazette; and the Weekly Mercury, June 3, 1771.

Five Pounds Reward,

RUN AWAY from the Subscriber living in Flushing on Long-Island, a Lad of about 14 or 16 Years of Age, named THOMAS FARRINGTON, (supposed to be inticed away by his Brother Daniel Farrington); he is of a middling fair Complexion with lightish brown Hair; had on when he went away, a wool Hat with a Button and Loop, a brown homespun Coat, a Linen Vest, Velvet Breeches, and a Pair of Shoes above half worn. Whoever takes up said Lad and returns him to his Master, shall be intitled to the above Reward, and all reasonable Charges
        paid by   MATTHEW FRANKLIN.   June 3.
N. B. He took with him a red and white Dog, partly of the Hound Breed.
The New-York Journal; or, The General Advertiser, June 6, 1771; June 20, 1771; June 27, 1771.

Twenty Shillings Reward.

RAN-away, on Wednesday night last from the subscriber, living in Oyster-bay, in Queen's county, a mulatto slave named Aser (tho' he may alter his name). He is about eighteen years old, five feet six inches high, middling stocky, black curl'd hair, and a fresh look, having had the small pox, tho' shews it not much:—Carried of with him, a bearskin red great coat, a kersey blue tight body'd coat, a blue broad cloth jacket, and a new castor hat; he had also a frock and trowsers, and two pair of shoes. Whoever takes up said slave, and secures him in any of his majesty's goals, so that his master may get him again, shall be entitled to the above reward of Twenty Shillings, and all reasonable charges
        paid by me   GEORGE WEEKES.
The New-York Gazette; and the Weekly Mercury, June 17, 1771; July 1, 1771; July 8, 1771; July 15, 1771.

FIVE DOLLARS REWARD.
RUN-away from Joseph Greswold's farm on the north side of Hempstead-Plains, on the 26th of May last, a negro man named Waybridge, had on when he went away, an old hat cock'd up with pins, a grey homespun over jacket with yellow brass buttons, an under red jacket, an old homespun shirt, buckskin breeches, old broken shoes and stockings, about 5 feet 7 inches high, very black, and has three scars or marks on each side of his face: He is supposed to be lurking on Long-Island, and harboured by negroes or ill disposed persons, as he has been seen sundry times since he run-away, and is well known to be a run-away. Whoever secures the said negro, so that his master may have him again, shall be paid the above reward, by   JOSEPH GRESWOLD.
N. B. No greater reward will be offer'd; and whoever harbours or conceals the said negro, shall be prosecuted with the utmost rigour of the law.
The New-York Gazette; and the Weekly Mercury, June 17, 1771; June 24, 1771; July 1, 1771; July 15, 1771; July 29, 1771; August 19, 1771.

New-York, June 19, 1771.
WHEREAS a certain Elizabeth Allen, robbed me the Subscriber, of four handsome Gold Rings, with sundry fine Lace Head Clothes, Ruffles, Aprons, Handkerchiefs, two fine short Gowns and Petticoats, one of them of fine Muslin, and the other flower'd Lawn, and several full-trim'd Mens Shirts, with different Pieces of new Linen Cloth, and many other Articles.—She is a low thin Woman, about 34 Years of Age, wants her fore-Teeth; jet black Hair twisted down her Cheeks; of a brownish Complexion; speaks very bad English; came lately from Holland; her right-Arm is thicker than her left, and wore when she went away, a Wax Necklace with a large red Stone in the Middle, and a Silver-ston'd Hair Pin. Any Person who will secure her, so that the Things may be had again, shall receive Five Dollars Reward; and all Persons are requested to stop these Articles if they are to be sold or pledged.
ROSAMOND GLASFORD.
The New-York Journal; or, The General Advertiser, June 20, 1771; June 27, 1771; July 4, 1771; July 11, 1771.

New-York, June 13, 1771.
R*UN away, about eight Days since, from his Master, William Bayard, Esq; a Mulatto Slave, named Charles; he is about 5 Feet 8 Inches high, much Pock-broken, about 40 Years of Age, and is just growing grey, speaks very good English, understands all Kinds of Business in the Farming and Gardening Way, as well as tending on a Gentleman; is a good Coachman,*

and rather light made: He carried of with him a large Bundle of Cloaths. Ten Dollars Reward will be paid, and all reasonable Charges, to any Person or Persons who shall apprehend and secure him in the nearest Goal where he may be taken, provided Notice thereof is given to his Master, or the Subscriber, in Newport, to that his Master may have him again. All masters of vessels and others are forbid to carry him off.
    SAMUEL HART.

The Providence Gazette; And Country Journal, From June 15, to June 22, 1771; From June 29, to July 5, 1771. See *The New-York Gazette; and the Weekly Mercury*, July 8, 1771.

Three DOLLARS Reward.

RUN away on Tuesday the 18th inst. from the pot-ash works at Freshwater, an indented servant man named Richard Smith, about 24 years old, he was born in the west of England, and came over to America, in Capt. Holmes, from Bristol: He had on when he went away a blue jacket, a white shirt, 2 tow trowsers, stockings and shoes: he is got a wart in the left corner of his mouth, which may be easily discerned, and has also got an impediment in his speech, and talks much upon the west country tongue. Whoever secures said servant, and delivers him to the subscriber, at the pot-ash works, shall have three dollars reward, and all reasonable charges
    paid by JAMES CARGILL.
N. B. It is likely he may change his name.

The New-York Gazette; and the Weekly Mercury, June 24, 1771; July 1, 1771; July 15, 1771; July 29, 1771.

RUN-away from Mr. Isaac Guion's house, at New Rochelle, on Tuesday the 11th inst. at night, an Irish young man, about 22 or 23 years of age, whom Mr. Guion had hired a month ago to do his farming business; and has stole from the said Mr. Guion that same night, a dark brown trotting horse, and a new brible; [*sic*] a silver watch, and a pair of plain silver buckles, one silver spoon, a blue and white wilton coat, one check and one white shirt, with several other things too tedious to mention. The horse is mark'd with a small star on his forehead, and is galded a little on his left side of the saddle shirt; the watch has a small bruise on the out side of the case; the spoon is mark'd with the letters I. M. G. This young man went by the name of Samuel Johnston when here, told Mr. Guion he came from Philadelphia; talks good English, is stout made, 5 feet some inches high, and wears his own short dark brown hair, inclining to curl: Had on when he went away, a striped jacket without sleeves, a fine white shirt, a pair of Ruffia drab breeches, white Stockings, and new shoes. Whoever takes up said thief,

with the things stolen, and will secure and bring them to this government, shall have FIVE POUNDS reward,
    from ISAAC GUION.
The New-York Gazette; and the Weekly Mercury, June 24, 1771; July 1, 1771; July 8, 1771; July 15, 1771; July 29, 1771.

RUN away on the 23d Instant, from the Subscriber, an indented Servant Man, named Barry Conner, born in Ireland, 25 years of age, and about 5 Feet 3 Inches high, fair fac'd, a little freckled, redish Hair: Had on when he went away, a blue Camblet Coat, a white Nankeen Waist Coat, a Pair of good Fustian Breeches; has been some Time in the Army, in the 26th Regiment, now lying in New-York. Whoever takes up and secures said Servant, so that his Master may have him again, shall have FORTY SHILLINGS Reward, and all reasonable Charges
    paid, by MATTHIAS HEYER,
    Baker, in New-York.
The New-York Journal; or, The General Advertiser, June 27, 1771; July 4, 1771; July 11, 1771; July 18, 1771; *The New-York Gazette; and the Weekly Mercury*, July 1, 1771; July 8, 1771; July 15, 1771; July 29, 1771; August 19, 1771. Minor differences between the papers.

RUN-away some time ago from Daniel and Israel Lewis, of Charlotte precinct, Dutchess county, a negro man named ISAAC, a well made fellow, about 35 years old, 5 feet 8 inches high, middling black, and is well set: Had on when he went off a felt hat, brown jacket, check shirt, leather breeches, tow trowsers, and shoes and stockings. Whoever will take up said negro and secure him in any of his majesty's goals, so that the subscriber may have him again, shall have Forty Shillings reward,
    paid by DANIEL LEWIS, ISRAEL LEWIS.
The New-York Gazette; and the Weekly Mercury, July 1, 1771; July 8, 1771; July 15, 1771. See *The Connecticut Courant*, From June 25, to July 2, 1771.

RUN away from Daniel & Israel Lewis of Charlotte Precinct, in Dutches county, province of New York, a Negro man named ISAAC, between 30 and 40 years of age, had on when he went away, a brown vest, and check shirt, a pair leather breeches, and a small pack of other cloaths, any person that shalll take up said negro and cofine him so that the owners may have him again, or return him to said owners, shall receive twenty shillings reward and all necessary charges
    paid by us. DANIEL LEWIS, ISRAEL LEWIS.

Charlotte Precinct, June 17, 1771.
The Connecticut Courant, and Hartford Weekly Intelligencer, From June 25, to July 2, 1771. See *The New-York Gazette; and the Weekly Mercury*, July 1, 1771.

New-York, June 14, 1771.
RUN-AWAY from William Bayard's farm, Hoobock, opposite the city of New-York, a mulatto servant man, named CHARLES, about 40 years o age, 5 feet 7 or 8 inches high, much pock-broken, his head partley grey, wears a cap sometimes; speaks good English, rather thin, understands all kinds of farming business, is a good coachman and gardner, and tends well on a Gentleman; has carried a number of cloths with him, so that he cannot well be described, as to what he wears; passes, it is said, for a freeman, and has a forged pass with him. All masters of vessels are forbid to carry him off; and all taverns, and other houses from entertaining him. Whoever will secure the said fellow in the nearest goal where he is taken up, and give the earliest intelligence to his master, shall have TEN DOLLARS reward, and al reasonable charges,
   paid by WILLIAM BAYARD.
The New-York Gazette; and the Weekly Mercury, July 8, 1771; July 15, 1771; July 29, 1771; August 19, 1771. See *The Providence Gazette; And Country Journal*, From June 15, to June 22, 1771.

Great-Barrington, June 26, 1771.
This day escaped from me the subscriber in this place, a negro man named Harry about 24 years of age speaks good English, had on a red coat, cuff'd and lappel'd with green velvet, suppos'd to be an old coat of his masters, Sir John Johnson, Knt. on Mohawk river, said negro is about 5 feet 9 inches high, well built, a pleasant countenance, shows his teeth much when he laughs—has bushy hair behind and cut off before. Whoever will take up said negro man, and secure him in any of his Majesty's goals, so that Sir John may have notice of him, or to me at Schenectady, shall have Three Dollars reward and all necessary charges
   paid, by me CALEB GLEASON.
The Connecticut Courant, From July 2, to July 9, 1771.

RUN-AWAY from the Subscribers living in New-York, the 16th Instant, three Apprentice Boys: JOHN CHRISTEY, about 5 Feet 1 Inch high, fair Complexion, light streight Hair, a Baker by Trade. CHRISTOPER FISHER, by Trade a Barber, 15 Years of Age, about 4 Feet and ½ high, short brown Hair, a Scar over his right Eye. Also DANIEL CHRISTEY, about 5 Feet high, fair Complexion, streight light Hair, a Blacksmith by Trade, and is a

good Nailer. Whoever takes up and secures said Apprentices, so that their Masters may have them again, shall receive Two Dollars Reward for each of said Apprentices, and all reasonable Charges,
     paid by WALTER QUAKENBOS,
       DAVID BARCLAY, JOHN SEGER.
 N. B. All Masters of Vessels and others are forbid to harbour or take them off at their Peril; it is thought needless to describer their Clothes as they may change them; but 'tis imagined they are gone towards Philadelphia.
 The New-York Gazette; and the Weekly Mercury, July 29, 1771; August 5, 1771; August 19, 1771; September 2, 1771.

      FORTY SHILLNGS Reward.
RUN-AWAY from the Subscriber, living in Orange-Town, on Saturday the 17th of July, a Negro Man named TOM, about 30 Years of Age, a well-built, square-shouldered Fellow, of a swarthy Complexion, thick Lips, speaks good Low-Dutch and some English; is about 5 Feet 6 Inches high: It is uncertain what Cloaths he had on and took with him. Whoever apprehends the said Negro Man, and secures him in any of his Majesty's Goals, or brings him home to his Master, shall have the above Reward, and all reasonable Charges,
    paid, by FREDERICK HARING.
 The New-York Gazette; and the Weekly Mercury, August 5, 1771; August 12, 1771; August 19, 1771; September 2, 1771; September 9, 1771. See *The New-York Gazette; and the Weekly Mercury*, April 1, 1771.

 RUN-AWAY *from the subscriber, living at Eastchester, Westchester County, on or about the 1st of May last, a negro boy, named FIL, about 16 years of age, 5 feet 6 inches high, or thereabout. Had on when he went away, a purple homespun jacket and tow trowsers, striped homespun shirt; he speaks not very plain English, has very long feet, and knocks very much in walking, and is supposed to be carried off by some white person to make sale of. Whoever takes up and secures him, so that his master may have him again, shall have Five Dollars reward, and all reasonable charges,*
    paid by me, *SAMUEL TREDWELL.*
 The New-York Gazette; and the Weekly Mercury, August 5, 1771; August 12, 1771; August 26, 1771; September 2, 1771.

      FIVE DOLLARS Reward.
RUN *AWAY from the Subscriber, from on board his Sloop Speedwell, lying at Beekman's-Slip, last Sunday Evening the 4th Inst. an Apprentice Boy*

named *JONATHAN FRIEND CHILD,* 17 *Years of Age, about 5 Feet 3 Inches high, lusty, strong built, round shoulder'd, and short light brown Hair: Had on when he went away, a striped worsted Jacket, Check Shirt, Nankeen Breeches, light worsted rib'd Stockings, a Pair of thin Pumps, a new red and white Silk Handkerchief, a Dutch Cap, Pinchbeck Shoe and Silver Knee Buckles,—he also took with him, a Pair of oznaburg Trowsers, and a Pair of coarse blue kersey Breeches. Whoever takes up said Apprentice and delivers him either to Mr. Anthony Griffiths of this City, Mr. Henry Smith, of Boston, or the Subscriber, shall receive the above Reward, and all reasonable Charges*
     paid by PASCHAL N. SMITH.
 N. B. All Masters of Vessels and others are forewarn'd from harbouring, concealing or carrying off said Apprentice, if they would avoid the Penalty of the Law.   *New-York, Aug.* 8. 1771.
 The *New-York Journal; or, The General Advertiser,* August 8, 1771; August 15, 1771; August 22, 1771; September 5, 1771; *The New-York Gazette; and the Weekly Mercury,* August 12, 1771; August 19, 1771; August 26, 1771; September 2, 1771. The *Mercury* does not have the date and location at the bottom.

       FIVE POUNDS REWARD.
DESERTED from Capt. Gordon's Company of the XXVIth Regt. quartered in the city of New-York, WILLIAM ORAM, Serjeant, a stout able-bodied man, about 5 feet 11 inches high, aged 36 years, born in the north of Ireland, by trade a shoemaker, has light colour'd hair, inclinable to red, blue eyes, and a round full face: Had on when he deserted, his regimental coat, white linen waistcoat and breeches, white thread stockings, and a silver lac'd hat.—As the above deserter has been guilty of a breach of trust, and many frauds, it is supposed no person will conceal him, or afford him any assistance in making his escape; and whoever apprehends and secures him, so that he may be brought to the regiment, shall (over any above his Majesty's allowance for apprehending deserters) receive
     FIVE POUNDS reward, from
    A. GORDON, Capt. 26th. Regiment.
 The *New-York Journal; or, The General Advertiser,* August 8, 1771; August 15, 1771; August 22, 1771; August 29, 1771; *The New-York Gazette; and the Weekly Mercury,* August 12, 1771; August 19, 1771; August 26, 1771; September 2, 1772. Minor differences between the papers.

TWENTY SHILLINGS Reward.

RUN away last Night from the Subscriber, living on Long-Island, at the Wallabaugh, a Negro Man named NEWPORT, about four or five and twenty Years old, about five Feet and a half high, a well set Fellow, Guinea born, but speaks good English, and is a great talker, he formerly belonged to one Joseph Robertson, living on the East End of Long-Island; he is branded on the Breast with three Letters: Had on when he went away, a light colour'd Cloth Jacket, Tow Cloth Shirt and Trowsers, almost new. Whoever takes up the said negro, shall receive the above Reward, and all reasonable Charges,
    paid by me ARIS REMSEN.

N. B. All Masters of Vessels and others, are hereby forewarned not to harbour or carry him off at their Peril.

The New-York Journal; or, The General Advertiser, August 8, 1771; August 15, 1771; August 22, 1771; September 5, 1771.

TWENTY SHILLINGS Reward.

RUN-away from the subscriber a servant lad of about 16 years of age, a short thick fellow, mark'd with the small pox, short black hair, named Michael O'Niel of a sulky down look, took with him a dark grey jacket, and a new ozenbrig jacket and trowsers, a check shirt and 2 check trowsers, and a half worn beaver Hat. Any person that will apprehend the said Lad, and brings him to the subscriber, or secure him, in any of his Majesty's Goals so that he may be had again, shall be entitled to the above reward from Alexander Stewart, in New-York, and all reasonable charges
  By MARTHA VERNON.   Albany, July 29, 1771.

N. B. All Masters of Vessels are forewarned to carry him off at their Peril.

The New-York Gazette; and the Weekly Mercury, August 12, 1771.

DESERTED *from his Majesty's 29th Regiment of Foot; JAMES GORDON, labourer, aged 21 years; he is 6 feet high, of a swarthy complexion, dark brown hair, hazle eyes, pitted with the small pox, round small visage, straight and well made, born in Enniskillen, Ireland, And,*

  JOHN LOVELL, labourer, aged 27 years, 5 feet 10 ¼ inches high, of a brown complexion, brown hair, light grey eyes, a little pitted with the small pox, long and full visage, a little stoop in the shoulders, stout made. Whoever secures either of the above deserters, and lodges them in any of his Majesty's goals, shall receive Eight Dollars *reward, on applying to the Commanding Officers of the 29th regiment at Perth-Amboy, Brunswick, or Elizabeth-Town; 21st regiment at Philadelphia, of 26th regiment at New-York.*

N. B. *The publick are cautioned not to harbour the above deserters, as they are of infamous characters.*
Gordon is an old deserter, and was in the Royal Americans.
The New-York Gazette; and the Weekly Mercury, August 12, 1771.

WHEREAS on Sunday the 4th inst, a man who called himself Robert Williams, came and agreed for lodgings at my house, where he (together with his wife, a brother and a sister of hers) stayed until Monday the 12th instant, when pretending he should return at night, he with the rest went clandestinely off, taking with them, as I some time after discovered, on my property, 4 silver tea spoons marked S B 1 large plain gold ring, 1 heart and hand gold ring, 1 gold ring with 12 small garnets set round a white mocoa stone, 1 black Barcelona handkerchief, of which a small piece is burnt out of one corner, a boy's black beaver hat with a white lining and a broad loop; also half a guinea, two half dollars, two English shillings and some other money not particularly remembered. Williams is a small well looking man, about 30 years of age, born in Wales, has short curl'd brown hair, usually wore a snuff-coloured coat and linen waistcoat with work'd green flowers. His wife wore a round furr'd beaver hat, with a gold band round the crown. She, her brother and sister, were all of a remarkably brown complection, had black eyes, and very black long curl'd hair, and from their appearances, and pretending to tell fortunes, are supposed to be of the people called Gypsies: They had a variety of clothes, and Williams and his wife were seen to have plenty of money both gold and silver. Any person to whom any of the said goods may be offered for sale, or who may otherwise discover them, are desired to stop them and the persons who have them in their possession. Also if any of the above described persons are seen, to stop and search them; and if any of the said goods are found in their possession, or otherwise, notice is left for me at the Printing-Office on Hunter's Quay, the favour will be thankfully and properly acknowledged.
M. BROWN.
The New-York Journal; or, The General Advertiser, August 15, 1771; August 22, 1771; September 12, 1771; September 19, 1771.

BROKE gaol from Queen's county, last Sunday night, the 25th inst. Levy Moses, and Theodorus Benjamin, who have been confined for some years past. Moses, is a lusty Man, about 5 feet 10 inches high; Benjamin is a thin Man, of about 5 Feet 7 or 8 Inches high; they are both Jews, and are supposed to be in New-York. All masters of vessels and others, are forwarned to carry them off at their peril.
THOMAS WILLETT, Sheriff.
Queen's County, August 27, 1771.

The New-York Journal; or, The General Advertiser, August 29, 1771; September 5, 1771; September 12, 1771; September 19, 1771. See *The New-York Gazette; and the Weekly Mercury*, September 2, 1771.

BROKE Goal, from Queen's County, on Sunday Night, the 25th of August last, Levy Moses and Dorus Benjamin, who have been confined for some Years past; Moses is a lusty Man, about 5 Feet 10 Inches high; Benjamin is a thin Man, of about 5 Feet 7 or 8 Inches high; they are both Jews, and are supposed to be in New-York. All Masters of Vessels, and others, are forwarned to carry them off at their Peril.
    THOMAS WILLETT, Sheriff.
The New-York Gazette; and the Weekly Mercury, September 2, 1771; September 9, 1771; September 16, 1771; September 23, 1771. See *The New-York Journal; or, The General Advertiser*, August 29, 1771.

RUN-away on Tuesday the 30th of July, from the subscriber, living in New-York, a negro man named *CATO*, about 45 years old, 5 feet 6 inches high, of a yellow complexion: Had on when he went away, a striped homespun jacket, a pair of buckskin breeches, an old tow shirt, a pair of blue yarn stockings, and an old coarse hat;—he can talk Low-dutch and English. Whoever takes up and secures the said negro, so that he may be had again, shall receive *Forty Shillings* reward, and all reasonable charges,
    paid by JACOB ARDEN.
The New-York Gazette; and the Weekly Mercury, September 2, 1771; September 9, 1771; September 16, 1771; September 23, 1771; September 30, 1771.

             New-York, August 12, 1771.
    TWENTY DOLLARS Reward.
    DESERTED from his Majesty's
  29th Regiment, 29th July last,
  JAMES GORDON, Labourer, aged 21 *Years,* 6 *Feet high, swarthy Complexion, dark brown Hair, hazle Eyes, pitted with the Small Pox, round and small Visage, straight and well made; born in Inniskillen, in Ireland.*
    29th July, 1771.
  JOHN LOVELL, Labourer, aged 27 *Years,* 5 *Feet* 10¼ *Inches high, brown Complexion, brown Hair, light grey Eyes, a little stoop shouldered and well made.*
    22d July, 1771.
  JOHN GIBBONS, Carver and Gilder, aged 27 *Years,* 5 *Feet* 11¾ *Inches high, ruddy Complexion, brown Hair, light grey Eyes, thin Visage, and much carbuncled, straight and light made.*

30th August, 1771.

THOMAS JONES, Cabinet-Maker, aged 21 Years, 6 Feet ¼ Inches high ,fresh Complexion, dark brown Hair, light grey Eyes, long Visage, a Scar over the Right Eye, a large Mole on the Left Cheek, heavily limbed, a little in-kneed, turns in his Toes when he walks, and a little pitted with the Small-Pox, well made; born in the Town of Buvissakane, and County of Tipperary, in Ireland.

30th August, 1771.

JOHN HART, Weaver, aged 25 Years, 5 Feet 10¼ Inches high, pale Complexion, light brown Hair, inclined to curl, dark brown Eyes, thin but round Visage, straight and well made, was born in the City of Limerick, in Ireland.

Whoever secures any of the above Deserters, and lodges them in any of his Majesty's Goals, shall receive the above Reward for each, by applying to the Commanding Officers of the 29th Regiment, Perth-Amboy, Brunswick, Elizabeth Town, or to the Commanding Officer of the 21st Regiment, at Philadelphia, or to the Commanding Officer of the 26th Regiment, at New-York.

N. B. The Public are cautioned not to harbour the above Deserters, as they are of infamous Characters, and have robbed their Captain, and their Comrades of several Valuables.

GORDON is an old Deserter, and was flogged out of the Royal Americans.

The New-York Journal; or The General Advertiser, September 5, 1771; September 12, 1771; September 19, 1771; September 26, 1771; October 3, 1771; September 10, 1771; The New-York Gazette; and the Weekly Mercury, September 9, 1771; September 23, 1771; September 30, 1771; October 14, 1771; October 21, 1771; October 28, 1771; November 4, 1771; November 21, 1771. Minor differences between the papers.

RUN-away from John Strickland, of the city of New-York, cordwainer, an apprentice lad, named Nathaniel Plumsted, 18 years old, 5 feet 5 inches high, black curl'd hair, and is supposed to be entertained by his friends at Peek's Kill: Had on when he went away, a blue cloth coat, drilling breeches, and a good castor hat. Whoever takes up the said run-away, and will bring him to his master, shall receive Five Dollars reward, and all reasonable charges,

paid by   JOHN STRICKLAND.

The New-York Gazette; and the Weekly Mercury, September 9, 1771; September 23, 1771; September 30, 1771.

RUN-away, from the subscriber, on Monday the 26th ultimo, an apprentice Lad, named Lawrence Verwy, about 18 years of age, and about five feet high, is lame in his left foot, and has a sullen look: had on when he went away, a speckled striped short, and oznabrigs trowsers, a yellow strip'd waistcoat without sleeves, by trade a gunsmith, speaks both English and Dutch. Whoever takes up said apprentice, and will bring him to his master, shall have TWO DOLLARS reward, paid by COLLIN VAN GELDER. N. B. All persons are forbid to harbour said apprentice, and all masters of vessels are forewarned from carrying him off at their peril.
The New-York Gazette; and the Weekly Mercury, September 9, 1771; September 16, 1771; September 23, 1771; September 30, 1771.

RUN-AWAY from Jeremiah Brower, on King's County, on Long-Island, on Tuesday the 2d inst. a Negro Man named FRANK, 30 Years old, about 5 Feet 10 Inches high, not very black, and may say he is free: Had on when he went away a Tow Shirt and Trowsers, a homespun Jacket, and Wooll Hat, without either Shoes or Stockings, and understands to take Care of a Mill.—Whoever takes up and secures the said Run-away, so that his Master may have him again, shall receive FIVE DOLLARS Reward, and all reasonable Charges, paid by Jeremiah Brower, jun. in New-York, or at Long-Island by JEREMIAH BROWER.
The New-York Gazette; and the Weekly Mercury, September 9, 1771.

FORTY SHILLINGS Reward.
RUN-away from the subscriber, at Albany, a likely negro fellow named BEN, about 17 or 18 years old, about 4 ½ [sic] feet high is sprightly and well built: Had on when he went away, a brown waistcoat, ozenbrig shirt and trowsers, and a large pair of shoes. It is thought he is gone to New-York, as he had formerly lived with James De Lancey, Esq; in the Bowery, and has still his mother living in New-York, and it is probably will keep lurking about that place. Whoever takes up and secures the said negro, so that his master may have him again, shall have the above reward, and a reasonable charges, paid by the subscriber in Albany,
or by Van Vienck and Kip, in New-York.
WESSEL VAN SCHAICK.
The New-York Gazette; and the Weekly Mercury, September 16, 1771.

RUN-*away from the subscriber last night, an indented servant man named Jacob Lewis, about 19 years old, about 5 feet 4 or 5 inches high, well-set, long black hair: had on when he went away a homespun grey mixed coat an jacket, tow shirt not whited (the collar of which was made, too small, and has a piece of white cloth sewed on one side) a pair of tow trowsers;*

likewise took with him a pair of leather breeches, a light coloured broad cloth coat, a pair of shoes that is capt, a pair of yarn stockings that is newly footed, an old felt hat. Any person that will apprehend the said servant, and bring him to his master, or secure him so that he may have him again, shall have a reasonable reward for their trouble.
     DANIEL COLEMAN. *Blooming Grove, Sept.* 14, 1771.
 The New-York Gazette; and the Weekly Mercury, September 23, 1771; September 30, 1771; October 7, 1771.

                Dutchess County, Sept. 7, 1771.
BROKE our of goal last night, one JOSEPH SPRAGGE, lately confined for suspicion of counterfeiting and passing dollars made of base metal. A man about thirty five years of age, fair complexion, and round faced, about 5 feet 10 inches high; he pretends to be a doctor, silversmith and brassfounder; is a artful cunning fellow, and no doubt will charge his name. Also one HUGH KENNEDY, confined for debt, about 5 feet 6 inches high, yellow hair, about thirty years of age; 'tis supposed they travel together. Whoever takes them up, and returns them to the Court-House in Dutchess County, shall have FIVE POUNDS for Spragge, and SIX DOLLARS reward for Kennedy; with all reasonable charges,
    paid by HENRY ROSEKRANS, Jun, sheriff.
 The New-York Gazette; and the Weekly Mercury, September 23, 1771; September 30, 1771; October 7, 1771; October 14, 1771.

RUN AWAY from the subscriber living in Harlem, on Sunday the 24th of September, a negro man named TOM, about 26 years of age, 5 feet 8 or 9 inches high, thin visage, very thick lips, and remarkably black; had on when he went away, a blue cloth jacket and breeches, homespun shirt and trowsers, and a half worn felt hat. Whoever takes up and secures the said negro in any of his Majesty's gaols, so that his master may have him again, shall receive Thirty Shillings reward, and all reasonable charges,
    paid by SAMSON BENSON, Jun.
 The New-York Journal; or, The General Advertiser, September 26, 1771; October 3, 1771. See *The New-York Gazette; and the Weekly Mercury*, August 10, 1772.

RAN away from the Schooner Fair-American, in the Harbour of Newport, William Augustus Peck Master, a tall slim Fellow, named William Barnes, belonging to Long-Island, as he says, wears his own black hair; had on when he went away a short blue waistcoat, homespun striped trowsers and small flapt hat; whosover takes up said Run-away and returns him on board

the said Schooner shall have two Dollars reward, and all necessary charges,
               paid by   WILLIAM AUGUSTUS PECK.
N. B. It is suspected he went across the Island, towards Portsmouth.
    The Newport Mercury, September 30, 1771.

RUN away from *Peter Provost*, gunsmith in New York, about 5 weeks ago, an Irish servant boy named *John Foshy*, he some times calls himself *John Green*, about 5 feet 3 inches high, light complexion, sandy coloured hair, longer over his ears than behind, about 19 years of age, no beard. Had on when he went away, a little round hat, black neckcloth, blue cloth coat, with striped waistcoat, black knit breeches, white thread stockings, brass buckles in his shoes a little knock kneed, ancles fall in more than common, very talkative about his trade. Whoever secures said boy in any of his Majesty's goals, or conveys him to New York, so that his master may get him again, shall have FORTY SHILLINGS reward, and all necessary charges
               paid by   PETER PROVOST,   September 7, 1771.
               living just opposite the old slip market.
N. B. Said boy was seen in Hartford since he left his master.
    The Connecticut Courant, And Hartford Weekly Intelligencer, From October 1, to October 8, 1771; From October 8, to October 15, 1771.

Run away from me the subscriber, a negro man, named TOM, a little on the molatto colour, aged 19 *years, speaks good English, and low Dutch, has a blemish in one eye. Had on when he went away, a light blue coat, white Philadelphia buttons, and vest of the same colour. Whoever takes up said negro, and brings him to me, shall have five dollars reward, and all reasonable charges*
               paid by me,   JOHN DELAMETTER.
Dutchess County, Armenia, Oblong, Oct. 25, 1771.
    The Connecticut Courant, From October 8, to October 15, 1771.

RAN away on Saturday the 12th instant, from the subscriber, living at the Ship-yards, an indented servant girl, named CATHERINE BEASLEY, about 15 years of age, fair complexion, smooth faced, of a middling stature, blue ey'd; had on a callico gown, blue quilted petticoat, and took with her several other clothes. Whoever takes up and returns the said servant girl, to me the subscriber, shall be handsomely rewarded for their trouble, and any person, who keeps, or entertains her, shall be prosecuted as the law directs,
               by   JAMES DICKSON.
    The New-York Journal; or, The General Advertiser, October 17, 1771; October 24, 1771; October 31, 1771; November 7, 1771.

RAN away last Monday the 14th, instant, from the subscriber living in Irish-street: a high Dutch servant girl named Catherine Araway Gustan, about 16 years of age, short and well made, brown hair and pretty much mark'd with the small-pox, had on when she went away, 1 black and white stuff petticoat, 1 red and white callico do. 1 oznabrugs short gown, 1 red short cloak, black bonnett, a pair of stockings and shoes. Whoever takes up and secures said servant so that her master may have her again, shall have two Dollars reward if taken in the city and 20*S*. if taken out of the city, and other reasonable charges paid by me,
     GEORGE CAMPBELL, or the Printer hereof.
 N. B. All masters of vessels and others are forewarned not to harbour, or carry off the said girl, as they shall answer it at their peril.
 The New-York Journal; or, The General Advertiser, October 17, 1771; October 24, 1771; October 31, 1771; November 7, 1771. See *The New-York Gazette; and the Weekly Mercury*, October 21, 1771.

RUN-away on Monday the 14th Instant, from the Subscriber, living in Irish-Street, a High Dutch Servant Girl named Catherine Araway Gustan, about 16 Years of Age, short and well made, brown Hair and is pretty much marked with the Small-Pox: Had on when she went away, a black and white Stuff Petty-coat, and a red and white do. rather long for her, an Ozenbrigs short Gown, a short red Cloak, a black Bonnet, and Shoes and Stockings. She ran away once before, and was harboured at Jamaica, on Long-Island. Whoever takes up the said Run-away, so that her Master may have her again shall have 20s. if taken in the City, and 3 Dollars if out of the same
    paid by GEORGE CAMPBELL.
 The New-York Gazette; and the Weekly Mercury, October 21, 1771. See *The New-York Journal; or, The General Advertiser*, October 17, 1771.

FORTY SHILLINGS REWARD.

RUN-AWAY from me the Subscriber, about the latter end of April last, a Negro Man named John Baptist, between 40 and 50 Years of Age, a thick clumsy Fellow, 5 Feet 3 or 4 Inches high, has a large flat Nose, and much Pock-mark'd; his little Finger of his left Hand broke, and quite streight; he speaks French and English, but the latter very badly. Whoever secures the said Negro, so that his Master may have him again, shall have the above Reward, and all reasonable Charges,
    paid by me WILLIAM DARLINGTON.
 The New-York Gazette; and the Weekly Mercury, October 21, 1771; November 4, 1771; *The New-York Journal; or, The General*

Advertiser, October 31, 1771; November 7, 1771; November 14, 1771; November 21, 1771.

New-York, Nov. 13, 1771.
WHEREAS one Joseph Lowe, this morning went from his lodgings, in the house of the subscriber, at the Slip-Market, and had robbed him of about Nine Pounds in cash, and the following goods. viz.

One pair of blue, and one pair of sky-blue breeches, one blue velvet and one green shag jacket, one thickset coat, one pair of pumps, the straps lined with red leather; one pair of square silver buckles, marked M S, one silver watch, made in Gosport, with a leather string, to which hung a silver seal, a silver bevil, square and compass.

The said Lowe in an Englishman about 17 or 18 years of age, and 5 feet 6 inches high, wore his own black hair a little curled, stoops a little in his walk, speaks very broad, has an impediment in his speech, and a little winking with his eyes when he talks fast: He is by trade a Nail-maker, and probably wears some of the clothes above-mentioned. Whoever takes up the said thief, so that he may be brought to justice, shall have Three Pounds York-money Reward, and all reasonable charges
paid by   JOHN SEGER.
The New-York Journal; or, The General Advertiser, November 14, 1771; November 21, 1771; November 28, 1771; December 5, 1771.

Ten Dollars Reward.
RUN-AWAY from me the subscriber, living in Pearl-street, New-York, a few days ago, a negro man named GEORGE, about 25 years of age, a likely well-made fellow, about 5 feet 10 inches high, smooth face: Had on when he went off, a green ratteen waistcoat, with several large stains cross the back and other parts; pretends to be free; he speaks good English, but has a sulky way in his speech. Whoever takes up and secures him, so that his master may have him again, shall receive the above reward, and all
expences paid, by   JACOB MOSES.
The New-York Gazette; and the Weekly Mercury, November 18, 1771; November 25, 1771; December 2, 1771; December 9, 1771; December 16, 1771; December 23, 1771; January 6, 1772; January 20, 1772.

1772

FIVE POUNDS Reward.
RUN-AWAY from Samuel Banks, of North-Castle, Middle-Patent, in the county of West-Chester, on the 14th day of November last past, a negro

man named WILL, 5 feet 6 inches high, about 24 years of age, of a yellowish complexion; had on when he went away, a felt hat and grey jacket, a pair of buckskin breeches, somewhat old, has a mark on the back of his right hand: He is a sprightly smart fellow, speaks good English, and somewhat fast.—It is supposed he has a forged pass, and is harboured or lurking about the city of New-York.—Whoever does apprehend and take up the said negro man, and brings him to his master, or to Alexander Montgomery, near Peck's-Slip, in New-York, or lodges him in any of his Majesty's goals, to that his master may have him again, shall receive the above reward, and all reasonable charges
paid, by   SAMUEL BANKS.

All masters of vessels are forbid carrying off or concealing said negro, and all persons are forwarned to harbour him, as they may expect to be dealt with as the law directs.

The New-York Gazette; and the Weekly Mercury, January 13, 1772; January 20, 1772; January 27, 1772; February 10, 1772; February 17, 1772; February 24, 1772; *The New-York Journal; or, The General Advertiser*, January 23, 1772; January 30, 1772; February 6, 1772. Minor differences between the papers.

Hartford, January 27, 1772.

Broke out of the County Goal in this town, the last evening, one JOHN SMITH, who came into this colony a few years since, supposed from the province of New-York, and has resided chiefly at Suffield, where he married a wife, and where, as it is supposed, his principal business has been (with sundry others) counterfeiting money, chiefly the New-Jersey and New-York new Bills, for which he was convicted before the honourable Superior Court sitting in this place, but had not received his punishment, he was a likely prompt looked youngerly man, somewhat short of stature, wears his own hair.—Also, escaped at the same time, one Obadiah Mathers of New-Cambridge in Farmington, who was committed on an execution of 50l. now recovered against him at said Court, by a young woman for defamation.—Also, on Jechaniah Holcomb of Simsbury, one Jonas Case of Hebron, and one John Swaney a transient person, last from Chatham, all for debt.—Also, one George Tryon, belonging to Farmington, a young lad committed for want of bail, on a young woman's swearing a child upon him.—Whoever shall take up the said John Smith, and return him to the goal from whence he escaped, shall have a reward of Six Pounds, Lawful Money, and for the said Mathers, Forty Shillings, and for either of the others, Thirty Shillings.
per   EZEKIEL WILLIAMS, Sheriff.

The Connecticut Courant, From January 21, to January 28, 1772; From January 28, to February 4, 1772.

FIVE DOLLARS Reward.

RUN-away from the subscriber hereof, a negro fellow named Frank, aged about twenty years, well built only his legs a little crooked and a piece off one of his thumbs, occasioned by an accident; had on a wooll hat, a homespun coat and jacket, of a light brown colour, dusted with meal, and a buckskin breeches. Whoever takes him up and secures him, so that his master may have him again, shall receive the above reward and reasonable charges, by   JEREMIAH BROWER.
All masters of vessels are forbid to carry him off at their peril.

The New-York Gazette; and the Weekly Mercury, February 3, 1772; February 10, 1772.

RUN-AWAY from his bail in New-York, a certain Abraham Barew, a Jew, but cannot be distinguished from a christian by his eating beef, pork, or any other kind of victuals; he is about 5 feet 6 inches high, of a pale complexion, light hair, tied behind: Had on a suit of brown broad cloth cloaths, and a reddish coloured surtout coat; he pretends to be a trader and lately lived in Philadelphia, where he kept a mill for grinding ginger and medicines for apothecaries. Whoever takes up and secures him in any of his majesty's goals, so that he may be had again, shall receive Forty Shillings reward, and all reasonable charges,
    paid by   George Starkey, goaler, at New-Brunswick,
        or John Bridgewater, tavern-keeper, in New-York.

The New-York Gazette; and the Weekly Mercury, February 10, 1772; February 17, 1772.

RUN-AWAY on Sunday the 8th Instant, from the Subscriber, living on Potbakers Hill, an Irish Servant Girl named Mary Cartay, speaks bad English, about twenty Years of Age, short and well made, black hair, pretty much marked with the Small-pox: Had on when she went away, a brown Silk Gown or yellow and red mixt Stuff do. an old red Pettycoat, a black Satten Cloak lined with blue, a black Silk Bonnet, with Boys Shoes and blue Stockings. Whoever takes up the said Runaway, so that her Master may have her again, shall have Twenty Shillings, if taken in this City, or Three Dollars if out of the same,
        paid by   JOHN MIFORD.

The New-York Gazette; and the Weekly Mercury, March 16, 1772; March 23, 1772; March 30, 1772; April 6, 1772; April 13, 1772.

Four DOLLARS Reward.

RUN-away from Joseph Lewis, living at Huntington, on Long-Island, a Negro Boy named BEN, about 18 Years of Age, small of Stature, yellow Complexion, very much mark'd with the Small-pox, has a Blemish in one of his Eyes, lost one Joint of one of his Fingers, and much bandy-leg'd: Had on when he went away, a dark brown Coat, a light double-breasted jacket, a Pair of dark dyed Buckskin Breeches, a red Duffles Waistcoat, a Felt Hat, and a new Pair of Pumps. Whoever takes up and secures said Boy, by applying to his aforesaid Master, or to Thomas Tucker, in New-York, shall receive the above Reward, with all reasonable Charges.

N. B. The above Boy has been seen in New-York about ten Days ago: This therefore is to forewarn all Masters of Vessels, and others, from harbouring or carrying off said Boy, as they will answer it at their Peril. He had also with him a pretended Pass, with the Widow Tucker's Name inserted therein.

The New-York Gazette; and the Weekly Mercury, March 23, 1772; March 30, 1772; April 20, 1772; May 4, 1772; May 11, 1772; May 18, 1772.

RUN *away from the subscriber, living in Newburgh, Ulster county, and province of New-York, an apprentice (to the carpenter's business) named* PATRICK M'GUIRE, *about 22 years of age, about 5 feet 10 inches high, dark colour'd hair, tied behind; took with him a bay horse 15 hands high, branded with a* **P** *on the near buttick, paces and trots well; and also a small silver watch with a large chain: Had on when he went away a snuff coloured upper jacket, and a patched pair of black breeches. He was born in Ireland; run away the third of April last, and 'tis supposed went towards the Jersies; may probably change his name and clothes. Whoever secures said thief and horse, with the watch, shall have* Five Dollars *reward, and all reasonable charges paid, or for the thief* Three Dollars,

        by me   JOSHUA MILLS.

The New-York Gazette; and the Weekly Mercury, April 20, 1772; April 27, 1772.

EIGHT DOLLARS Reward.

R*UN away from the subscriber, living in the township of Greenwich, Gloucester county, and province of West New-Jersey, on Monday, the 20th day of April, at night, an indented servant man, named* WILLIAM BUTLER, *but very likely he may change his name, and forge a pass, as he is an artful grand rogue, and can write a middling good hand, says he was born in New-York government, and served his time there, a Taylor by trade, a slim, thin visage, about 5 feet 9 or 10 inches high, wore his own dark*

hair, tied behind, and long locks over his ears, and turned up before, but very likely he may have cut it off; he has several, blue specks under his left eye, which he says was marked with powder, has a large bottle nose; had on, when he went away, a reddish brown coat, very much pieced in the side seams, and on the shoulders, and the lining patched in the fore skirts with new shaloon, darker than the old lining, a fine beaver hat, a good deal wore, an old pair of dirty leather breeches, pale blue woollen stockings, footed with yarn paler than the legs, old shoes, tied with strings, a coarse ozenbrigs shirt, very much worn about the wristbands; stole and took with him a lightish coloured coat, about half made, one striped Bengal jacket, only cut out, one half thicks jacket, new made up, but too small for him, lined with red, with metal buttons, one superfine scarlet jacket, very much worn, and has been turned. Whoever secures said servant, in any of his Majesty's goals, so that his master may get him again, shall have the above reward, and if brought home TEN DOLLARS,
         paid by me   THOMAS HEWETT.

N. B. All masters of vessels, or others, are forbid to harbour or carry off said servant, at their peril.

The Pennsylvania Gazette, April 30, 1772.

RUN-away from the subscriber in Albany, the 21st day of April, 1772, a mulatto negro man, named Harry, about twenty five years old, about five feet 9 inches high, well set, broad shoulders, born in New-England, speaks nothing but English, a cut on one of his legs with an ax, large great toe joints; had on when he went away, a long strait bodied coat greyish colour, a blue jacket of camblet, a check linen shirt, leather breeches, with turtle shell buttons, copper eyes, with silver tops, blue rib'd stockings, with his hair cut on the top of his head. Whoever will secure said negro, in any of his Majesty's goals, so that I can have him alive, shall have forty shillings reward, and all reasonable charges
         paid by   ELISHA BENEDICT.

N. B. This is to desire and forbid all Captains of vessels not to take said negro on board of their ships or boats.

The New-York Gazette; and the Weekly Mercury, May 4, 1772; May 11, 1772; May 18, 1772.

WHEREAS Catharina Margarita Schick, otherwise Lilith, wife of me Christian Schick, of John's-Town, in the county of Albany, and province of New-York, black-smith, hath repeatedly and for a great length of time, behaved herself in so unbecoming and bad a manner to me, and so disaffectionately to her children, that I find it wou'd not be consistent, with prudence to myself, or justice to my children, to live, or cohabit with her

any longer. Therefore to prevent her running me in debt, which must render me less able to provide for such children, and may otherwise hurt me: I hereby caution all persons whatsoever, not to credit her in any manner, or on any (except her own) account, as I am determined not to pay any debt, even to the smallest amount, which she may contract, tho' I am always willing to take and provide for my children, as far as I am able.
     CHRISTIAN SCHICK.
The New-York Gazette; and the Weekly Mercury, May 4, 1772; May 18, 1772.

RUN-away on the 11th of May Inst, from William Field, of Phillips's manor, Westchester county, an Indian boy named CHARLES, about 20 years of age, black straight hair, about 5 feet 8 or 9 inches high. He has taken away with him a good grey homespun great coat, two jackets near the same colour, a pair of new sheepskin breeches, two with flannel homespun shirts, a good felt hat this country make. It is supposed he will pass for a free man; all masters of vessels are forbid to carry him off at their peril; and whoever will bring the said servant to his master, or secure him in any of his Majesty's goals, so that he may have him again, shall receive twenty shillings reward, and all reasonable charges
    paid, by WILLIAM FIELD.
The New-York Gazette; and the Weekly Mercury, May 18, 1772; May 25, 1772; June 1, 1772; June 8, 1772.

     FIVE POUNDS REWARD.
RAN away from his bail on Monday last, one JACOB VAN DERVOORT, of King's county, Nassau-Island, a shoemaker by trade, of a middling stature, black hair, much pitted by the small-pox in his face, and one of his legs much thicker than the other; when he went off he had on a blue cloth coat, nankeen waistcoat and breeches, and took with him his working tools. Whoever will secure the said JACOB VAN DERVOORT, and bring him to the subscribers, or one of them, or give information so that he may be apprehended, shall have the reward of FIVE POUNDS, besides all reasonable charges and expences, paid by the said subscriber,
     JAQUES DENYSE, Junr.
     RUTGERT VAN BRUNT, sheriff.
The New-York Journal; or, The General Advertiser, May 28, 1772; June 11, 1772; June 18, 1772; *The New-York Gazette; and the Weekly Mercury*, June 8, 1772; June 15, 1772. Minor differences between the papers.

WHEREAS a Person who calls himself by the Name of Robert Craige, of Norwich, in the Colony of Connecticut, was taken into Custody by me Braddock Cory of Southampton, Constable, and was convicted before three of His Majesty's Justices of the Peace for said Township, for passing Counterfeit Bills of the Currency of New York; but in carrying the said Prisoner to Goal, he made his Escape. He appears to be between 30 and 40 Years of Age, near Six Foot high, wears his own Hair; had on when he went away a blue Broad cloth Coat and brown Velvet Waistcoat and Breeches, white sale worsted Stockings, and shag Beaver Hat.—Any Person or Persons who will apprehend and secure the said Prisoner to any of His Majesty's Goals, shall receive Ten Dollars Reward, and all reasonable Charges to be paid by me
   BRADDOCK CORY, Constable. Southampton, May 7, 1772,
The New-London Gazette, May 29, 1772.

RUN-AWAY from the subscriber, living at Fish-kills, Dutchess County, the 11th of May, an apprentice lad named David Berkins, about 16 year of age; had on when he went away, a brown serge coat, a striped red and white silk waistcoat, a pair of buckskin breeches, a pair of blue yarn stockings, an old beaver hat: He is about 5 feet high, well featur'd, dark eyes and black hair, and commonly wears it club'd; had a smooth fair skin. The said lad understands the taylors trade, and it is supposed he will apply for work, all masters are therefore requested to be cautious how they employ him; and commanders of vessels are desired not to carry him off at their peril. A reward of TEN DOLLARS, and all reasonable charges, will be given to any person who will take up and secure the said lad, so that the subscriber may have him again. STEPHEN BATES.
The New-York Gazette; and the Weekly Mercury, June 8, 1772; June 15, 1772; June 22, 1772.

RUN-away from the subscriber, at Goshen, on the 25th day of May, a negro man named DICK, about 24 years of age, is very black, speaks good English and Spanish, is about 5 feet 7 inches high: Had on and took with him when he went away, a great coat of a grey colour, with large flat metal buttons, a grey jacket with sleeves, and old grey waistcoat with blue patches in it, a good woollen shirt and tow shirt, a pair of old leather breeches with pewter buttons, an old pair of grey stockings, and a pair of new shoes, and an old pair of do.—Likewise an old wooll hat: It is supposed he has a pass.—Whoever takes up the said run-away negro, and secures him and the pass, if any he has, so that the subscriber may have him again, shall have 4 dollars reward, and all reasonable charges
   paid by me JOSEPH DRAKE.

The New-York Gazette; and the Weekly Mercury, June 8, 1772; June 15, 1772; June 22, 1772; June 29, 1772. See *The New-York Gazette; and the Weekly Mercury*, November 5, 1770, and *The New-York Gazette; and the Weekly Mercury*, May 27, 1771.

RUN-away from the subscriber, on the 8th of this inst. a negro man named ABEL, about 30 years of age, of a yellowish cast: Had on when he went away, a green plush jacket without sleeves, cloth breeches and tow shirt, and an old hat. Whoever takes up said negro and brings him to his said master, shall have FORTY SHILLINGS reward, and all reasonable charges,
   paid by ZEPHENIAH PLATT.   11th June 1772.
The New-York Gazette; and the Weekly Mercury, June 22, 1772; June 29, 1772; July 6, 1772; July 13, 1772.

RUN-away from Michael Ganter, gunsmith in the city of New-York, on the 24th inst. an indented servant man named ANTHONY COSTEKIN, a native of I\reland, about 5 feet 7 inches high, has a large scar in his upper lip, and short black hair: Had on when he went away, a lightish brown coat and waistcoat, and a pair of dirty leather breeches. Whoever takes up and secures said run-away, so that his master may have him again, shall receive Forty Shillings reward,
   paid by MICHAEL GANTER.
The New-York Gazette; and the Weekly Mercury, June 29, 1772; July 6, 1772; July 13, 1772.

RUN-away from the subscriber, living in Schenectady, on the 23rd of May last, a negro lad named CATO, about seventeen years of age, five feet and a half high: Had on when he went off, a wooll hat, homespun jacket, buckskin breeches, and woollen stockings. He is supposed to be taken away by one John Messel, who absconded with his wife, at the same time. Whoever takes up and secures the said negro, so that his master may have him again, shall have the third part of is value.
   PHILIP VAN PETTA.
The New-York Gazette; and the Weekly Mercury, June 29, 1772; July 6, 1772; July 13, 1772.

      FIFTEEN POUNDS Reward.
BROKE Jail in the county of West-Chester, on Monday the 22d instant, the three following persons, viz. Philip Pinkney, about 28 or 30 years of Age, 5 feet 8 or 10 inches high, well set, and light brown hair. Oliver Killock, 23 or 24 years of age, six feet high or better, can work at the shoemakers or coopers trade, has black hair intermixt with grey; and Nathan Purdie, about

5 feet 6 or 8 inches high, about 60 years of age, a cooper by trade, his hair somewhat grey. Whoever takes up the said persons, and returns them to the gaol keeper of the county of West-Chester, shall have the above reward, or five pounds for either of them, June 29, 1772.
paid by   JAMES DE LANCEY, sheriff
The New-York Journal; or, The General Advertiser, July 2, 1772; July 9, 1772; July 16, 1772; July 23, 1772; *The New-York Gazette; and the Weekly Mercury*, July 6, 1772; July 13, 1772; July 20, 1772; July 27, 1772; August 10, 1772.

RAN away from the subscriber, on Wednesday the 8th instant, a negro man named Squire, about 19 or 20 years of age, five and an half feet high, slim made, long visage, large eyes, down look, remarkable thick lips, and is slow of speech; he was born in Guinea, but speaks good English: Had on an oznaburg or check shirt, oznaburg trowsers, a broad striped blue and white waistcoat, and is supposed to have taken with him an old coarse brown cloth pea jacket, lined with green baise, a pair of old shoes and an old hat. He was seen on board of a boat, and it is supposed is gone towards Philadelphia: He was heard to say that he would endeavour to get some white man to travel with him as his master, and it is therefore not improbable that some such evil minded person may be with him, and pretend to own him. Whoever takes up, and returns the said negro to men, near Burling's Slip, in New-York, shall have five pounds reward, besides all reasonable charges.
J. WYNANT VAN ZANT.   New-York, July 12, 1772.
The New-York Journal; or, The General Advertiser, July 16, 1772.

Twenty Shillings Reward.
RUN-away the 17th inst. July, from Adam Gilchrist, taylor, in New-York, a negro man nam'd Timbo, a likely fellow in the face, and stout made, but very bandy leg'd, his knees laps over one another: Had on an old homespun shirt and trowsers, and left word he was going to wash himself Whoever brings the said negro man to Adam Gilchrist, shall receive the above reward. N. B. This therefore is to forewarn all masters of vessels to harbour him at their peril.
The New-York Gazette; and the Weekly Mercury, July 20, 1772; July 27, 1772; August 3, 1772; August 10, 1772; September 7, 1772.

TEN DOLLARS Reward.
RUN AWAY the 11th of this Instant, from the Subscriber, Charles Broadhead, of the Wallkill, in the County of Ulster, and Province of New-York, a Mulatto Negro Man named TOM, about 30 Years of Age, very

lusty and well built, of a smiling Countenance, talks both English and Low-Dutch very well, is very handy, understands all sorts of Farmers Work, and is a middling good Shoemaker: Had on and took with him when he went away, a lightish colour'd home made Cloth Coat, with flower'd Brass Buttons, a whiteish-colour'd Durant Lining, and a blackish Coat of French Cotton, pretty much wore, one Pair of Check Trowsers, one Pair of mist blue and white coarse Stockings, a Pair of Pumps, a Pair of Brass Buckles not fellows.—It is thought he will try to pass for a white or free Man, as he is of the whitest Sort of Muattoes, his Father being a white Man, and it is imagined he will call himself Thomas Car.—Whoever takes up the said Negro and secures him, so that his said Master may have him again, or brings him to his said Master, shall have the above Reward, and
Charges, paid by me   CHARLES BROADHEAD.
N. B. All Masters of Vessels, and others, are forbid carrying him off, as they will be accountable for the same.

The New-York Gazette; and the Weekly Mercury, July 20, 1772; July 27, 1772; August 3, 1772; August 10, 1772; August 24, 1772.

FIVE DOLLARS REWARD.

RUN away from the subscriber, near the New Dutch-church, New-York, two Irish servant women, the one named Ann Miller, of a swarthy complexion, black hair, and a black beard on her upper lip, about twenty five or thirty years old: had on when she went away, a black petticoat, and a flowered linen bed gown, with the flowers wash'd almost white, a white linen handkerchief about her neck, and took with her a blue and white small striped linen gown, a blue and white broad striped homespun petticoat, blue worsted stockings, and old leather shoes.—The other Elizabeth Curry, about eighteen years old, of a fair complexion, freckled in the face, fair hair, had on a broad blue and white homespun petticoat, and a cotton bed gown, of a red ground, a dimond figure, a dark checkered silk handkerchief about her neck, no cloak, hat, or cap on her head; and took with her a common Indian linen gown, black and redish brown spotted figure with small check aprons each, leather shoes and some other things. 'Tis supposed they went off with Mr. Henry Usticks two nailers, that went off the same time towards Kingsbridge, or the iron works in the Jerseys. Any person that will apprehend the said runaways, shall have the above reward, and all reasonable charges paid them; and all persons are forewarned not to harbour or conceal them, or any master of vessels to carry them off, at their peril.
ALEXANDER LESLIE.

The New-York Journal; or, The General Advertiser, July 30, 1772; August 6, 1772; August 13, 1772; August 20, 1772.

FORTY SHILLINGS Reward.

RUN-AWAY away from the Subscriber, living in New-York, on the Morning of Tuesday, the 28th Instant, an apprentice boy, named JOHN MARKLAND, between 16 and 17 Years old, about 5 Feet 7 Inches high, black curled Hair, and of a pale Complexion: He was seen on board the Snow Lord Stanley, Capt. Strickland, the Morning he absented himself, and as he has not been since seen in this City, 'tis imagined is gone in the said Vessel to the Island of Jamaica, where he will endeavour no doubt to work at the Printing Business, to which he has been brought up: He is a sly artful Fellow: He had on when he went away, a blue Jacket and Trowsers, but took with him a Suit of blue Broad-Cloth. The Subscriber will be much obliged to all the Printers in America, to publish this Advertisement in their Papers, and transmit the same to Jamaica, as soon as convenient, with a Request that the Printers there may publish the same. The above Reward will be paid by HUGH GAINE.

The New-York Journal; or, The General Advertiser, July 30, 1772; August 6, 1772; August 13, 1772; August 20, 1772. See *The Pennsylvania Journal, and the Weekly Advertiser*, August 5, 1772, *The New-York Gazette; and the Weekly Mercury*, August 3, 1772, and *The Pennsylvania Gazette*, August 12, 1772. The same ad with very minor differences also appears in numerous issues of *The Connecicut Journal and the New-Haven Post Boy*, *The Massachusetts Spy*, *The New-Hampshire Gazette, and Historical Chronicle*, *The New-London Gazette*, and *The Newport Mercury*, in August into September 1772.

RUN *away from the subscriber, living at Harrison's Purchase, in the township of Rye, and county of West-Chester, on the 19th day of July instant, a negro man named PLATO, about twenty-eight years old, a black, short, thick fellow; has had the small-pox: Had on and took with him, a homespun blue and white coat, a new felt hat and an old one, two new tow shirts, a pair of new long tow trowsers, and two pair of old shoes. Whoever takes up said negro, and secures him so that his master may have him again, shall receive Twenty Shillings reward, and all reasonable charges,*
paid by me NATHAN FIELD.

The New-York Journal; or, The General Advertiser, July 30, 1772; August 6, 1772; August 13, 1772; August 20, 1772; *The New-York Gazette; and the Weekly Mercury*, August 3, 1772, August 10, 1772; August 24, 1772.

NEW-LONDON, July 31.

Last Saturday Two Men were committed to Jail in this Town of Suspicion of stealing a Watch out of the Shop of Mr. Robert Douglass,

Jun'r, of this Town: They say they cane from Smith's Manor; and call their Names Thomas Wilkinson, and John Vinderburg; the former is about 23 Years old, about 5 Feet 7 Inches high; has light brown Hair and pitted with the Small Pox; the latter 22 Years of Age; about the same Stature of the first mention'd has dark brown Hair, well Set, and has a large Scar from his Forehead to his under Lip.—They appears to be Villains; and there is Reason to suspect they've been concerned in breaking open and robbing a Sloop in the North River.

The New-London Gazette, July 31, 1772.

Run away from the subscriber, a prisoner named *George Gordon*, alias *Hamlinton*, a Scotchman, about five feet ten inches high, short brown hair, long favor'd, a high forehead, a very long Nose, a remarkable scar across his left cheek, had on a blue double breasted waistcoat, a check shirt, long white trowsers and a beaver hat about half worn.

Whoever will take up and deliver said prisoner to me, shall have *Five Dollars* reward and all necessary charges paid by me,
Fenner Palmer,   Constable of Dover.
Dover (Dutchess County) July 29, 1772.

The Connecticut Courant, And Hartford Weekly Intelligencer, From July 28, to August 5, 1772; From August 11, to August 18, 1772; From August 18, to August 25, 1772.

RUN-AWAY from the Subscriber, living at Goshen, in Orange County, on Tuesday Night last, a Negro Fellow named STEPHEN, about 5 Feet 8 Inches high: Had on a Homespun Jacket, Tow Trowsers, and an old Hat.— Whoever takes up the said Negro, so that his Master may have him again, shall have THIRTY POUNDS Reward, and all reasonable Charges,
paid by   SILAS HORTON.

The New-York Gazette; and the Weekly Mercury, August 3, 1772; August 10, 1772; August 17, 1772; August 24, 1772; September 7, 1772.

FIFTY DOLLARS Reward.

RUN-AWAY from the subscriber, living in New-York, on the Morning of Tuesday, the 28th ult. an Apprentice Boy, named JOHN MARKLAND, between 16 and 17 Years old, about 5 Feet 7 Inches high, black curled Hair, of a pale Complexion, knock-knee'd, and thick Legs: He was seen on board the Snow Lord Stanley, the Morning he absented himself, and as he has not been since seen in this City, 'tis imagined is gone in the said Vessel to the Island of Jamaica, where he will endeavour no doubt to work at the Printing Business, to which he has been brought up: He is a sly artful Fellow: Had

on when he went away, a blue Jacket and Trowsers, but took with him a suit of blue Broad-Cloth. The Subscriber will be much obliged to all the Printers in America, to publish this advertisement in their Papers, and transmit the same to Jamaica, as soon as convenient, with a Request that the Printers there may publish the same. The above reward will be
     paid by HUGH GAINE.

The New-York Gazette; and the Weekly Mercury, August 3, 1772; August 10, 1772; August 17, 1772; August 24, 1772; August 31, 1772; September 7, 1772; September 14, 1772; October 5, 1772; October 19, 1772; October 26, 1772; November 2, 1772. See *The New-York Journal; or, The General Advertiser*, July 30, 1772, *The Pennsylvania Journal, and the Weekly Advertiser*, August 5, 1772, and *The Pennsylvania Gazette*, August 12, 1772.

                New-York, July 27, 1772.
W*ENT off with my husband, William Bolton, a notorious woman, named Mary Bradey, a common prostitute; whore, bawd, and thief; which can be proved against her by several in this city; of riding through this city on a cart, and afterwards was severely whipped at the public whipping post, and is likewise with child by another man: She is about five feet two inches high, square built, lightish coloured hair, and has a child with her, and a boy about 6 or 7 years of age. The said Bolton pretends to be a school master, is about 5 feet 2 inches high, of a fair complexion, lightish coloured hair, tied: Had on a lightish coloured cloth coat, and a red plush jacket—as far as I am informed they practise nothing but thieving through the county, as she is known to be a notorious thief, and pretends to be his wife; which I can prove to the contrary, as I was lawfully married to him by parson Johnson, of Albany, by the consent of his Colonel, as he was then a soldier:—She stole of Capt. Sherren, seven miles this side of Stanford, a pocket-book—the people pursued after them, but could not find them;—and likewise stole 35 yards of linen between Bedford and Cassell, in New-England. And likewise stole from Mr. Samuel Odgen, of Horse-Neck the 7th of last June, several other things. Whoever apprehends the said William Bolton and the said Mary Bradey, and delivers them to the goal keeper here, shall have eleven dollars reward, and all reasonable charges,*
     paid by SARAH BOLTON.

  N. B. Whoever apprehends them and secures them in any of his Majesty's gaols, and directs to me at the widow Douglas's, back of the New-Goal, near the Barracks, shall be intituled to the above reward.

  The New-York Journal; or, The General Advertiser, August 6, 1772; August 13, 1772.

WHEREAS my wife, HANNAH FREDERICK, did, on the 3d of June last, elope from my bed and board, from Fish Kills, in Duchess County, in New-York government, with a certain ABRAHAM HUDSON, who left New-York on the 15th ult. and proceeded to Elizabeth-Town, and from Thence to Philadelphia. Her maiden name was Hannah Coleman, and served her time with John Taylor, at Tinicum-Island, and as I am apprehensive she will contract debts on my account, these are therefore to forewarn all persons from trusting her on my account, as I shall pay no debts of her contracting after the date hereof. Philadelphia, July 29, 1772.
——— FREDERICK.

The Pennsylvania Chronicle, and Universal Advertiser, From Saturday, July 25, to Saturday, August 1, 1772; From Saturday, August 1, to Saturday, August 8, 1772; From Saturday, August 8, to Saturday, August 15, 1772.

FORTY SHILLINGS Reward.

RUN-AWAY away from the Subscriber, living in New York, on the Morning of Tuesday, the 28th ult. an apprentice boy, named JOHN MARKLAND, between 16 and 17 years old, about 5 Feet 7 Inches high, black curled Hair, of a pale Complexion, knock-kne'd, and thick Legs: He was seen on board the Snow Lord Stanley, the Morning he absented himself, and as he has not been since seen in this City, 'tis imagined is gone in the said Vessel to the Island of Jamaica, where he will endeavour no doubt to work at the Printing Business, to which he has been brought up: He is a sly artful fellow: Had on when he went away, a blue Jacket and Trowsers, but took with him a Suit of blue Broad-Cloth. The Subscriber will be much obliged to all the Printers in America, to publish this Advertisement in their Papers, and transmit the same to Jamaica, as soon as convenient, with a Request that the Printers there may publish the same. The above Reward will be
paid by HUGH GAINE.

The Pennsylvania Journal, and the Weekly Advertiser, August 5, 1772; August 12, 1772; August 26, 1772; *The Pennsylvania Chronicle, and Universal Advertiser,* From Saturday, August 1, to Saturday, August 8, 1772; From Saturday, August 8, to Saturday, August 15, 1772; From Saturday, August 15, to Saturday, August 22, 1772; *The Pennsylvania Packet; and the General Advertiser,* August 10, 1772; August 24, 1772. Minor differences between the papers. The *Chronicle* states he has "thick Lips." See *The New-York Journal; or, The General Advertiser,* July 30, 1772, *The New-York Gazette; and* the *Weekly Mercury*, August 10, 1772, and *The Pennsylvania Gazette*, August 12, 1772.

RUN-AWAY from the Subscriber, living at Harlem, the 2d inst. a Negro Man named TOM: Had on when he went away, a Tow Shirt and Trowsers, Homespun Jacket lined with green, and an old Hat; walks upright, very thick Lips, about 5 Feet 9 Inches high, and very black. Whoever takes up the said Negro, and brings him to his Master, or secures him in any of his Majesty's Goals, shall have THIRTY SHILLINGS Reward, and all reasonable Charges, paid by the Subscriber.
    SAMSON BENSON, jun.
The New-York Gazette; and the Weekly Mercury, August 10, 1772; August 17, 1772; August 24, 1772. See *The New-York Journal; or, The General Advertiser*, September 26, 1771.

    FORTY SHILLINGS Reward.
RUN away from the subscriber, living in New York, on the morning of Tuesday, the 28th ult. an apprentice boy, named JOHN MARKLAND, between 16 and 17 years old, about 5 feet 7 inches high, black curled hair, of a pale complexion, knock-kneed, and thick legs; he was seen on board the snow Lord Stanley, the morning he absented himself, and as he has not been since seen in this city, it is imagined is gone in the said vessel to the Island of Jamaica, where he will endeavour no doubt to work at the Printing Business, to which he has been brought up; he is a sly artful fellow; had on, when he went away, a blue jacket and trowsers, but took with him a suit of blue broadcloth. The subscriber will be much obliged to all the Printers in America, to publish this advertisement in their papers, and transmit the same to Jamaica, as soon as convenient, with a request that the Printers there may publish the same. The above reward will be
   paid by HUGH GAINE.
The Pennsylvania Gazette, August 12, 1772; *The Boston News-Letter*, August 13, 1772. Minor differences between the papers. See *The Pennsylvania Journal, and the Weekly Advertiser*, *The New-York Journal; or, The General Advertiser*, July 30, 1772, and *The New-York Gazette; and the Weekly Mercury*, August 3, 1772.

    FORTY SHILLINGS Reward.
RUN-away the 2d inst. from the subscriber, living in Albany, EZEKIEL HAMS, an indented servant; he is upwards of thirty years of age, about 5 feet 8 inches high, has short black hair, and a swarthy complexion; he professes to be a blacksmith, is much addicted to drunkenness; very talkative when intoxicated; an abominable liar, horrible swearer, and the

most ungrateful, profligate wretch existing; he is, in fact, a nuisance to society and disgrace to humanity. He had on when he went off, a dark wilton coat, a snuff coloured jacket, check trowsers, a pair of new shoes, cast steel buckles, one of them broke, and a felt hat. His master offers the above reward more with a view that he may be brought back and forced to give satisfaction to those he has imposed on in this place, than any self-interested motive, the vagabond not being intrinsically worth One Shilling; however, any person that will apprehend and secure him in any of his Majesty's goals, or return him to his master, shall be intitled to the above reward, and all reasonable charges
     paid by JESSE FAIRCHILD.
The New-York Gazette; and the Weekly Mercury, August 17, 1772; August 24, 1772; August 31, 1772; September 7, 1772.

BROKE out of the Goal in this Town the Night after the 10th Instant, and made their Escape.... John Morris, a transient Person, formerly of Albany, is about 5 Feet 2 or 3 inches high, wears black Hair, committed for Horse Stealing....Whoever shall take up John Grant, William Hurlbut, and John Morris, or either of them, shall have Forty Shillings reward for each...
     paid by ELY WARNER, Goaler
             Hartford, August 13, 1772.
The Connecticut Courant, And Hartford Weekly Intelligencer, From August 11, to August 18, 1772.

RUN-AWAY *from the subscriber, living in New-York, on Saturday morning, the 8th inst. a negro man named CATO, of about 22 years old, and about 5 feet 9 inches high; he is very black, streight, and well limb'd, looks grum, speaks pretty good English, a little lisping. Three months ago he belonged to Charles Tooker, of the borough of Elizabeth, county of Essex, in the province of New-Jersey: It is supposed he is gone that way: Had on an ozenbrigs shirt, jacket, and trowsers, a new felt hat, shoes and stockings, he likewise took with him an ozenbrigs shirt, jacket and trowsers, and almost a new beaver hat, and a blue waistcoat half worn. Whoever takes up the said negro man, so that his master may have him again, shall receive 20s. reward, if on this island, and 40s. if taken elsewhere, and all reasonable charges,*
     paid by JOHN DE PEYSTER, jun.
The New-York Gazette; and the Weekly Mercury, August 24, 1772; August 31, 1772; September 7, 1772; September 28, 1772; October 12, 1772; October 19, 1772. See *The New-York Gazette; and the Weekly Mercury,* December 7, 1772.

FIVE POUNDS Reward.

RUN away the morning of the 22d of August, 1772, from the subscriber, living in Fourth-street, Philadelphia, a servant LAD, named ANDREW GUFFEN, about 16 or 17 years of age, lusty and well grown for his age, smooth faced, and fresh coloured, short curly hair, of a lightish colour, large mouth, and speaks much on the north of Ireland dialect, of which country he is; he had on, when he went away, a grey superfine broadcloth coat, with a scarlet collar, and carved silver washed buttons, striped waistcoat with sleeves of a different colour, black breeches, and white thread stockings, ribbed, a half-worn hat, and old shoes, 2 pretty good coarse shirts; he will be apt to talk of pot-ash making, as he has worked at that business for these 6 months past, and will very likely go towards New-York, as his father, 2 brothers, and a sister, are in that government. Whoever takes up and secures said servant , so that his master may have him again, shall have the above reward, and all reasonable charges,
    paid by me WILLIAM HENDERSON.

N. B. If he will return of his own accord, he shall be forgiven all charges, and no punishment inflicted on him.

The Pennsylvania Gazette, August 26, 1772.

RUN-away, an apprentice boy, WILLIAM PRYOR, by trade a painter, about 5 feet 4 inches high, dark hair tied behind, large dark eyebrows, and not a very fair complexion: He took with him a light cloth colour short jacket lapel'd, black horn buttons, and lined with green bays; tow cloth trowsers, a white thickset frock which has been turn'd, a clouded knit waistcoat, and buckskin breeches not much soil'd. He went off on Sunday the 23d ult. and was seen the same day about the 17 mile stone on the Boston road, in company with three other run-aways, one of them a taylor, about 5 feet high, red hair tied, and freckled face; Had on a short blue coat, and a claret colour'd Bath coating frock in his bundle, and speaks very quick. Any person that will apprehend the said boys, and give notice to Thomas and James Barrow, painters, in Broad-street, or to Mr. John King, taylor, in ditto, shall have Four Dollars reward for each of them, and reasonable charges.

If the apprehender will put them on board a vessel for New-York, and send them to the above Barrow, or King, all charges shall be paid. One of the boys (a pewterer) has parents in New-London, which may probably induce them to go that way.

The New-York Gazette; and the Weekly Mercury, August 31, 1772; September 7, 1772; September 14, 1772.

RUN-AWAY from the subscriber, living in New-York, about the 20th of August, an apprentice lad named Hugh Gorman, about 20 years of age, 5 feet 8 inches high, of a sandy complexion, much freckled, and reddish hair: Had on when he went away, a blue jacket and long trowsers. Whoever takes up and secures the said run-away, and will deliver him to Messieurs Walter and Thomas Buchanan, merchants in New-York, shall have FORTY SHILLINGS reward,
        paid by   ALEXANDER STEWART.
The New-York Gazette; and the Weekly Mercury, September 7, 1772; September 14, 1772; October 5, 1772.

RUN-away from the subscriber, living at the Nine-Partners, in Dutchess county, on Friday the twenty eighth day of August last, one Lawrence Gojion, alias John Johnston, an indented servant man; he is about 5 feet 8 or 9 inches high, well built, full faced, has a very remarkable long crooked nose, ruddy complexion, light sandy coloured hair, with a reddish beard, speaks good English, is a native of Philadelphia, and by trade a carpenter: Had on when he run-away, an old white broad cloth coat, and ozenbrigs shirt and trowsers. He will undoubtedly change his name as he has done before. He has two brothers living at the Wallkill, in Ulster county, and is supposed to be gone there. Any person that takes up said run-away and confines him in any of his Majesty's goals, or brings him to Poughkeepsie, in Dutchess county, so that his master may have him again, shall receive Three Pounds reward, and all reasonable charges.
        JACOB LAWRENCE.
The New-York Gazette; and the Weekly Mercury, September 7, 1772; September 14, 1772; September 21, 1772.

RUN-away from the subscriber, living at Westchester, a negro lad named CLAUS, about 18 years old, and 5 feet 7 or 8 inches high: Had on when he went away, a white hat about half worn, a brown jacket without lining, tow shirt and trowsers, and an old pair of shoes: He speaks good English and Dutch. Whoever takes up the said negro and secures him, so that he may be had again, or delivered to his master, shall have Forty Dollars reward, and all reasonable charges,
        paid by   ISAAC LIGGETT.
The New-York Gazette; and the Weekly Mercury, September 14, 1772; September 21, 1772; October 5, 1772; October 12, 1772.

              THREE POUNDS REWARD.
RAN away, on sunday the 20th instant, (from the subscriber) a negro man, named Manuel; he is about 6 feet high, pretty well set, 22 or 23 years of

age, speaks slow, tho' very good English, and is a complete hand at farming business: Had on when he went away a white flannel jacket with leather buttons, a blue Cloth over his jacket, an old wool hat, and tarr'd tow trousers. 'Tis supposed he is gone to Connecticut from whence he was lately purchased, or to Long Island where he is well acquainted, having tarried there some time, when he absented himself from his former master. Whoever will take up said negro and bring him to me the subscriber, in New-York, or secure him in any of his Majesty's goals, so that I may have him again, shall be intituled to the sum of THREE POUNDS, and all reasonable charges
paid by   THOMAS IVERS.

N. B. It's probable said negro may be gone towards Albany, as he was once back among the Indians. New-York, September 23, 1772.

The New-York Journal; or, The General Advertiser, September 24, 1772; October 1, 1772; October 8, 1772; October 15, 1772.

TEN POUNDS REWARD.

WHEREAS *on the Morning of Tuesday the 22d Instant, the House of Sampson Benson, of Harlem, in the Out-Ward of this City, was, broke open and robbed by two Villains, of about 70l. in Silver, York Bills, and Jersey Money. One of the Rogues is named William Thompson, has a striped Jacket, and is an Englishman. The other named John Burn, a Razor-Grinder by Trade, a lusty well set likely Man, about 5 Feet 8 Inches high, of a fresh Complexion, and a well-looking Fellow: Had on a light drab colour'd Jacket and has taken sundry other Cloaths with him, among them a Green Coat and Breeches, and a red Jacket. Whoever takes up the said Villains, so they may be brought to Justice, shall have the above Reward,*
paid by   SAMPSON BENSON.

The New-York Gazette; and the Weekly Mercury, September 28, October 5, 1772. See below for a different ad about this robbery. See *The Connecticut Journal, and the New-Haven Post-Boy*, October 16, 1772.

FIFTEEN POUNDS REWARD.

WHEREAS *the House of Sampson Benson, at Harlem, in the Out-Ward of the City of New-York, was on Tuesday Morning the 22d Day of September 1772, broke open by two Villains, and robbed of about £.70 in Silver, New-York, and New-Jersey Money Bills, and sundry Articles of Goods, among which were the following, viz. A green Silk Purse, a Silver Watch, to which was fastened a Silver Chain, a Compass Seal, the Face of which appeared very dull and obscure, &c. The Person suspected to be the Principal in the above Robbery, called himself William Thompson, appeared to be about 24*

or 25 Years of Age, a well made Man, about 5 Feet 7 Inches high, fresh Complexion, short curled black or dark brown Hair, has a down bashful Look, speaks slow, and like an English Man, but said he was born in New-Jersey, and that he served his time to a Miller, but pretends to understand Basket-making, Masonry and Farming; had on a light colour'd Cloth Coat, pretty much worn, a short Jacket striped cross wise, and narrow striped Trowsers: The other Villain supposed to be concerned in the above Robbery, is a Razor Grinder, who called himself John Burn, is a lusty well set likely Man, about 5 Feet 8 Inches high, of a fresh Complexion; had on a light drab colour'd Jacket but has taken sundry other Cloaths with him, among which was a Green Coat and Breeches, and a red Jacket.—Whoever takes up and secures one or both the said Villains, so that he or they be brought to Justice, and convicted of being concerned in the Robbery aforesaid, shall receive for Thompson Ten Pounds, and for Burn, Five Pounds current Money of New-York, Reward,
     paid by SAMPSON BENSON.

The New-York Gazette; and the Weekly Mercury, October 5, 1772; The New-York Journal; or, The General Advertiser, October 8, 1772; October 15, 1772. Minor differences between the papers. The *Journal* spells the advertiser's first name as Samson. See above for a different ad about this robbery

                September 30, 1772.
RAN-AWAY from the Subscriber (of Bedford, in the County of West-Chester, and Province of New-York,) on the Night after the 24th of September, Instant, a Negro Man named STEPH, about 6 Feet high, about 30 Years old, this Country born, has two Scars on his Head, his Cloathing can't be particularly described as he took with him various Kinds; he speaks good English, loves strong Drink, and is very noisy, and is supposed to have a forg'd Pass. Whoever shall take up said Servant, and return him to his Master, or secure him in Gaol, so that I may have him again, shall have Three Dollars reward, and all necessary charges
     paid, by   ELIJAH HUNTER.

The Connecticut Journal, and the New-Haven Post-Boy, October 2, 1772; October 9, 1772; October 16, 1772; October 23, 1772. See *The New-York Gazette; and the Weekly Mercury*, October 12, 1772.

RUN-AWAY from the subscriber, at Bedford, the twenty-fourth ult. a negro man named STEVE, about 6 feet high, and has two scars on his head, one near his forehead, by the edge of his hair, the other the back part of his head: Took with him when he went away, a large bundle of cloaths, a red great coat, two tight bodied coats, one dark and the other light-coloured

brown, two pair of breeches, one blue and the other black, a pair of brown trowsers, two shirts, one check and the other white, with many other things, which makes it uncertain what dress he may have on. Whoever takes up and secures said negro, so that his master may have him again, shall have Three Dollars reward, and reasonable charges,
    paid by ELIJAH HUNTER.
The New-York Gazette; and the Weekly Mercury, October 12, 1772; October 19, 1772. See *The Connecticut Journal, and the New-Haven Post-Boy*, October 2, 1772.

Last Saturday, were apprehended here William Thompson and John Burn, for robbing the house of Mr. Samson Benson in New-York: They were sent off for New-York yesterday.
The Connecticut Journal, and the New-Haven Post-Boy, October 16, 1772. See *The New-York Gazette; and the Weekly Mercury*, September 28, October 5, 1772, and *The New-York Gazette; and the Weekly Mercury*, October 5, 1772.

          New-York, October 18, 1772.
    THREE DOLLARS Reward.
RUN away from Caleb Morgan, living in East-Chester, a Negro man, named SAM, about 5 feet 9 or 10 inches high, well set, of a yellowish complexion, the end of his forefinger on his righthand is almost mashed off:—Had on when he went away, a blue broad cloth coat, a pair of buckskin breeches, a beaver hat half worn, and a pair of new shoes, two shirts, &c.—Whoever takes up said Negro, and secures him again, shall be intituled to the above reward, and all necessary charges
    paid by CALEB MORGAN.
N. B. All masters of vessels and others are forewarned not to harbour or carry off said Negro at their peril.
The New-York Journal; or, The General Advertiser, October 22, 1772; October 29, 1772; November 5, 1772; November 12, 1772; November 19, 1772.

RUN-away from the Subscriber, living at Huntington on Long-Island, an Indian Fellow named Peter, better that [*sic*] 5 Feet high, and middling well set, has two white Spots upon the right Side of his Head: Took with him a Felt Hat, a red tight-bodied Coat, a brown Jacket, striped Trowsers, and a Gun: Whoever takes up the said Fellow and secures him, so that he may be had again, or delivers him to his Master, shall have Two Pounds Reward, and all reasonable Charges,
    paid by GILBERT FLEET.

The New-York Gazette; and the Weekly Mercury, October 26, 1772; November 2, 1772; November 16, 1772; November 30, 1772; December 7, 1772.

Six Pounds Reward.

RUN-away from Caleb Morgan, in East-Chester, the eighteenth day of October last, a negro man named Sambo, about 25 years of age, about five feet nine inches high, of a yellow complexion, pretty slim built, a sober looking fellow: Had on when he went away, a blue broad cloth coat, with red lining; a black Manchester velvet jacket without sleeves, a pair of buckskin breeches, and blue stockings, a good pair of thick shoes, two shirts, and an old felt hat; one of his fore fingers (the tip end) is bruised off, so that the skin grows fast to the bone; the other hand the middle finger is something crooked, so that he cannot open it so straight as the others. He talks very good English, and I believe he can talk Dutch, he being brought up among the Dutch the west side of the north river. It is mistrusted that a white man has carried him away in order to make sale of him, or has given him a pass; the mans name that is mistrusted is John Norris, about 30 years of age, often goes down to the Jerseys; perhaps he may have changed his named, he is a lusty man. If any person does discover any white man with the negro, and they have made sale, or does offer to make sale of him, and takes up the white man with the negro, and secures them in any in any of his Majesty's goals, so that I can come at my negro again, and the white man brought to justice, shall have the above reward, or Five Pounds, and reasonable charges, for the negro alone;
        paid by   CALEB MORGAN.

The New-York Gazette; and the Weekly Mercury, October 26, 1772; November 2, 1772; November 16, 1772; November 30, 1772; December 7, 1772.

DESERTED from the Schooner Rachel, Thomas Euins, a short thick Sailor, about 5 Feet 6 inches high, short black Hair, Pock-broken, speaks thick: Also Zoessennah Young, a slender Man, about 5 Feet 10 Inches high, short black Hair, pale Face, black Eyes, born in New-York Government. Whoever shall apprehend the above Deserters, and secure them in his Majesty's Jail, shall have TWO DOLLARS Reward,
        paid by   ESTES HOWE,
                near Christ-Church, N. End. Oct. 30, 1772.

The Boston Gazette, and Country Journal, November 2, 1772; November 16, 1772.

RUN away from the subscriber, in New-York, on Monday the 26th of October, and was seen at King's Bridge on Wednesday the 28th, an Irish servant girl about eighteen years old, of a fair complexion, freckled, smooth faced, light brown hair, not above two or three inches long; had on a broad blue and white striped homespun petticoat, and a small striped blue and white jacket, no cap on, an old round black hat, no ribband to the crown, a course dowlas apron; was bare footed, had no shoes, smooth tongued, and a very great liar; was seen to pass the old bridge in the above dress, in company with a man in a red or reddish coat or waistcoat; she had no other clothes with her, and cannot easily alter her dress; is supposed to have gone the Albany road. Any person that will secure the said runaway, shall have TWO POUNDS reward, and TWENTY SHILLINGS if they can secure the fellow that carried her off, so that he can be brought to justice, and all reasonable charges paid them. All master of vessels are forbid harbouring or carrying her off as they will answer the same to
                  ALEXANDER LESLIE.

The New-York Journal; or, The General Advertiser, November 12, 1772; November 19, 1772; November 26, 1772; December 3, 1772.
The second, third and fourth ads show her as an Irish servant girl "named ELIZABETH CURRIE".

Philadelphia, November 16, 1772.
              FIVE POUNDS REWARD.
RAN AWAY from on board the ship Wolfe, Richard Hunter, master, from Londonderry, a redemptioner named COLLIN M'DONALD, born in the Highlands of Scotland, and will be easily known by his accent; about 36 years of age, a taylor by trade, about six feet high, with black short hair; had on a blue coat and red waistcoat; said he had a wife near Albany, and is supposed to have gone that way. Whoever apprehends the same, and brings him to the subscribers, shall have THREE POUNDS reward, if taken in this province, and if out of it, shall be intitled to the above reward, and all reasonable charges,
            paid by   GRAY, FLETCHER, and Co.

The Pennsylvania Packet; and the General Advertiser, November 16, 1772; November 23, 1762; November 30, 1762. See *The Pennsylvania Gazette*, November 18, 1772, and *The New-York Gazette; and the Weekly Mercury*, November 23, 1772.

                        Philadelphia, November 18, 1772.
                FIVE POUNDS Reward.
RUN AWAY from on board the ship Wolfe, Richard Hunter, master, from Londonderry, a redemptioner, named COLIN M'DONALD, born in the

Highlands of Scotland, and will be easily known by his accent; about 36 years of age, a Taylor by trade, about six feet high, with black short hair; had on a blue coat and red waistcoat; said he had a wife near Albany, and is supposed to have gone that way. Whoever apprehends the same, and brings him to the subscribers, shall have THREE POUNDS reward, if taken in this province, and if out of it, shall be intitled to the above reward, and all reasonable charges,
    paid by GRAY, FLETCHER, AND Co.

The Pennsylvania Gazette, November 18, 1772; November 25, 1772. See *The Pennsylvania Packet; and the General Advertiser*, November 16, 1772, and *The New-York Gazette; and the Weekly Mercury*, November 23, 1772.

              Philadelphia, Nov. 16, 1772.
        FIVE POUNDS Reward.

RUN-AWAY from on board the Ship Wolfe, Richard Hunter, Master, from Londonderry, a Redemptioner named COLLIN Mc. DONALD, born in the High-Lands of Scotland, and will be easily known by his Accent; He is about 36 years of Age, a Taylor by trade, 6 Feet high, with black short Hair: Had on a blue Coat and red Waistcoat, said he had a Wife near Albany, and is supposed to have gone that way. Whoever apprehends him and brings him to the Subscribers, shall have the above Reward, and all reasonable Charges,
    paid by GRAY, FLETCHER, and Co.

The New-York Gazette; and the Weekly Mercury, November 23, 1772; December 7, 1772. See *The Pennsylvania Packet; and the General Advertiser*, November 16, 1772, and *The Pennsylvania Gazette*, November 18, 1772.

         FIVE POUNDS Reward.

RUN-AWAY from Lewis Morris, of Morrisiania, in the County of Westchester, a Negro Man named Jack, about 28 Years of Age, 5 Feet 11 Inches high, has a remarkable thick Neck, is something in-kneed, and is a stout Black, has a Scar on his Chin: Had on when he went away, a brown Cloth Great Coat, a brown Knap Coat, a short Jacket of Kearsey Homespun, a Pair of Leather Breeches dyed purple, a Pair of Homespun black and white Stockings. Whoever apprehends said Fellow, and brings him to his Master, or secures him in any public Goal, shall be entitled to the above Reward, and all reasonable Charges.

The New-York Gazette; and the Weekly Mercury, November 23, 1772; November 30, 1772; December 7, 1772; December 21, 1772; December 28, 1772.

Taken up, and confined in goal in New-London, a Negro Man, about six feet high, well built, of a whitish cast, has a large scar from his chin inclining to his throat, another scar on his left cheek, and very much scarified on his back with whipping. Had on when taken, a dark cloth colour'd or redish ratteen close bodied coat, trim'd with horn button, and not lined, the sleeves too short for him, a homespun kersey jacket pretty much worn, a black Barcelona handkerchief, an old drab great coat, cloth colour'd, much worn, and looks to have belonged to a gentleman; had a pack with one pair buckskin brreches, one pair dark colour'd leather ditto, and sold another pair of new buckskin breeches this day, two pair yarn stockings, one white, the other dark colour'd, two pair shoes, a pair serge breeches almost new, a pair dark stockings, and a pair pinchbeck buckles in his shoes—Says he came from Bucks County in Pennsylvania, and that he waited of Governor Penn, the Duchess of Gordon, William Bayard, Esq; John Watts Esq: and many other gentlemen both in New-York, and Philadelphia, and pretends to be a good butcher, coachman, and table tender, &c. His master may have him again, by applying to the Goaler in New London and paying charge.

New-London, Nov. 23. 1772.

The New-London Gazette, November 27, 1772.

RUN-AWAY from the snow Freeholder, John Ton, master, a boy about 17 years of age, named JOHN EDWARDS, 5 feet 4 inches high, or thereabouts, has streight black hair: Had on when he went away, a blue jacket, flannel under waistcoat, and a round hat. Whoever apprehends the said boy, and brings him to Thomas Durham, shall have a reward of Twenty Shillings.

The New-York Gazette; and the Weekly Mercury, November 30, 1772; December 7, 1772; December 14, 1772; December 21, 1772.

FIVE DOLLARS REWARD,

RUN-away from Samuel Ogden, of Boontown, in the County of Morris, and Province of New-Jersey, on Sunday the 16th of October last: A Negro Man named Mingo or Tim, he is about 30 Years of Age, has a Scar either on his Nose or one of his Cheeks; is about 5 Feet 7 or 8 Inches high, plays on the Violin, speaks good Dutch and English, and is much addicted to Strong drink: Had on when he went away a dark brown broad cloth Coat, with brass Philadelphia Buttons, a Pair of red coating Trowsers, an ozenbrig Shirt and wool Hat. He was formerly the property of Isaac Wilkins, Esq; of West-Chester, about which place it is not unlikely he may be lurking. Whoever apprehends said Negro and returns him to his Master, or secures

him in any of his Majesty's Goals, shall be paid the above Reward, and all reasonable Charges
> by   SAMUEL OGDEN.

The New-York Gazette; and the Weekly Mercury, November 30, 1772; December 7, 1772; December 14, 1772; December 28, 1772; January 4, 1773.

RUN-AWAY from the subscriber, living in New-York, on the 8th day of August last, a negro man named CATO, of about 22 years old, and about 5 feet 9 inches high: He is very black, streight, and well-limb'd, looks grum, speaks pretty good English, a little lisping: Had on an ozenbrigs shirt, jacket, and trowsers, a felt hat, shoes and stockings. He likewise took with him an ozenbrigs shirt, jacket and trowsers, and almost a new beaver hat, and a blue great coat half worn. Whoever takes up the said negro man, so that his master may have him again, shall receive FIVE POUNDS reward, and all reasonable charges,
> paid by   JOHN DE PEYSTER, jun.

The New-York Gazette; and the Weekly Mercury, December 7, 1772; December 14, 1772; December 21, 1772. See *The New-York Gazette; and the Weekly Mercury*, August 24, 1772.

New-York, December 23, 1772.
EIGHT DOLLARS REWARD.

RAN away, about a fortnight ago, from his master, living in the Bowery, near New-York, ROBERT M'FALL about 6 feet high, pitted with the small-pox, short light curled hair, and speaks slow, with the Scotch accent; had on when he went off, a blue short coat, with breeches of the same, brown yarn stockings, and tow shirt, shoes half worn, with odd brass buckles; carried with him a long brown homespun coat and breeches, the warp yellow linen, and filling brown worsted, and the breeches patched with a different Cloth; one pair of half worn shoes and some other clothes. Whoever brings the above run-away to PETER STUYVESANT, in the Bowery, near New-York, or to PATRICK M'DAVITT, merchant, in New-York, shall be paid the above reward.

☞ This Runaway was born in the North of Ireland.

The New-York Journal; or, The General Advertiser, December 24, 1772; December 31, 1772; January 7, 1773; January 14, 1773; *The New-York Gazette; and the Weekly Mercury*, December 28, 1772; January 4, 1773; January 11, 1773; February 1, 1773; February 15, 1773. The *Gazette* does not have the final line.

THIRTY DOLLARS REWARD.

BROKE Gaol and made their Escape from the County of Morris, in East New-Jersey, on Monday Night the Seventh of this Instant, the following Prisoners; namely JOHN NORRIS, about Twenty Eight Years of Age, near Six Feet high, a stout sturdy Fellow, charged with stealing a Negro Man from one Morgan of East-Chester, in the Province of New-York, who says he has a Wife and Brother in that County. GEORGE HALL, a West-countryman, about Twenty Five Years of Age, near Five Feet, Ten Inches high, slim built, has a brown Broad-cloth Coat and Vest, and a Pair of old Leather Breeches on. GEORGE CAMPBELL, an Irishman, about Twenty Four Years of Age, near Five Feet Six Inches high, thick set, well built, walks a little lame, having all his Toes froze off. DANIEL M'CURDY, about Twenty Four Years of Age, near Five Feet, Ten Inches high, slim built, has remarkable large white Eyes, and was brought up to Suckersunny in this County. JAMES DOUGLAS, about Twenty three Years of Age, near Five Feet, Eight Inches high, well built, had on a Homespun Wilton blue and white Coat, Vest and Breeches, and is a profane swearer, and much addicted to Gaming and excessive Drinking.

Whoever apprehends, and secures the above Persons in any of his Majesty's Goals, so that the Subscriber may have them again, shall be entitled to the above Reward, or Ten Dollars for Norris, and Five for each of the other Four,
    paid by me, JONATHAN STILES, Sheriff.
    Morris County, Dec. 8, 1772

The New-York Gazette; and the Weekly Mercury, December 28, 1772; January 4, 1773.

1773

RUN away from the subscriber, the 1st instant, an Irish servant man named Lawrence Kelly, a baker by trade, has a down look, short black hair, and knock kneed; had on when he went away, a brown knap jacket and a white under one, blue Breeches, good stockings and shoes. Whoever will take him up or secure him in any of his Majesty's Goals so that his master may have him again, shall have three dollars reward and other reasonable charges
    paid by RICHARD TEN EYCK.

N. B. All masters of vessels and others are hereby forwarned not to conceal of carry off said runaway, or they will be dealt with according to law.

The New-York Journal; or, The General Advertiser, January 7, 1773; January 14, 1773; January 21, 1773; January 28, 1773.

SOME time ago, a man who called himself KENNEDY, hired a pettiauger from Wm. M'KIM, in order to go oystering, but has not since been seen. Any person securing said KENNEDY, so that he may be brought to justice, shall have FOUR POUNDS reward: he is a middle sized man, has brown hair and full face; the pettiaguer will carry about three cord of wood, open-stern'd, and half-deck'd. The above reward will be paid at the North river,
    by REBECCAH WATSON.
The New-York Gazette; and the Weekly Mercury, January 11, 1773.

      TWENTY SHILLINGS Reward.
ABSENTED himself from his Master, living in Hanover-Square, the 2d Inst. a Negro Man called Dick, aged 19 Years. He had on when he went away, a Beaver Hat, smartly cocked, a new light coloured Coat and Waistcoat, with Metal Buttons, green Linings, the Collar and Cuffs of the Coat turned up with Green; new Buckskin Breeches, a Pair of ribbed Stockings of a mixed Colour, and Silver Buckles in his Shoes. He is a likely, well-made Fellow, and speaks both English and Dutch. It is supposed he has been seduced by bad Company during the late Holydays; and that he is lurking somewhere in the City, or its Environs. Whoever secures the said Negro, so that the Subscriber may have him again, shall receive Twenty Shillings Reward,
    from CHARLES INGLIS.
The New-York Gazette; and the Weekly Mercury, January 11, 1773; January 18, 1773; January 25, 1773.

RUN-AWAY from the Subscriber, on Sunday Evening the 27th Day of December last, a Negro Man named JACK, about 33 Years old, a short spare Fellow: Had on when he went away, a brown double-breasted short Forrest Cloth Jacket, with plain Brass Buttons, lined with red Baze; a red Baize under Jacket, Leather Breeches, and blue Yarn Stockings. He took with him a light Coat much wore of fine twilled Frize, the knap wore off, and a new blue Watch-coat of Coating, with white plated Buttons, He was purchased from Hendrick Emons, of Rockey-Hill, in New-Jersey, about 9 Years ago, and it is supposed he is either gone that Way, where he has a Mother, or else to Anthony Van Eyck's, at Albany, where he has a Wife.— Any Person that will take up said Negro and secure him, so that his Master may have him again, shall have Forty Shillings Reward, and all reasonable
    Charges, paid by PETER KETELTAS.
The New-York Gazette; and the Weekly Mercury, January 11, 1773; January 18, 1773; January 25, 1773; February 1, 1773; February 8, 1773; February 15, 1773.

RUN-away from the subscriber, a negro man called Singo, about thirty years of age, five feet seven inches high, talks good English, he's a stout made clumsy fellow, small limb'd, walks with the inside of his feet foremost, thick lip'd, has a scar above one of his eye-brows, wants a good many of his double teeth: Had on when he run-away, an ash colour'd homespun coat, lined with a light blue colour'd linsey, with round top'd white metal buttons, with a green knap'd jacket double breasted, lin'd with light coloured thick cloth, a pair of blue everlasting breeches, a new wool hat, and check woollen shirt. Any person that apprehends said negro, and confines him in any of his Majesty's goals, so as the subscriber may have word thereof, shall have FORTY SHILLINGS Reward, and all reasonable charges; and if brought to the subscriber near Goshen, in Ulster-county, province of New-York, and precinct of Wall-Kill, shall have FIVE POUNDS and all reasonable charges
    paid by me ARCHIBALD M'CURDY.

He is supposed to be carried to Newport, in Rhode-Island, by negro jockeys, being brought out of said place about ten or eleven years ago.
The New-York Gazette; and the Weekly Mercury, January 18, 1773; January 25, 1773; February 1, 1773.

FIVE DOLLARS REWARD.

RUN AWAY from the house of the subscriber in North-Castle, one JACOB WHITMAN, a likely well looking man, about 5 feet 9 inches high, black hair and is a taylor by trade; had on when he went away, a blue broad cloth coat (which had been turned, as appeared by the button holes, &c.) with silver washed buttons; a new blue broad cloth waistcoat, and a new pair of leather breeches. He stole and carried off with him, a silk cross-barred waistcoat and a castor hat; and rode a small sorrel horse, who carries his tail much erect, and has lost his ears, which are cut off slope wise. Whoever takes up and secures the said runaway in any of his Majesty's gaols, shall receive the above reward,
    by applying to JOSIAH HUNT.
The New-York Journal; or, The General Advertiser, January 21, 1773; January 28, 1773. See *The New-York Gazette; and the Weekly Mercury*, February 22, 1773.

FIVE POUNDS REWARD,
NEW-YORK CURRENCY REWARD.

RAN away from John De Peyster, living in New-York, on the 8th day of August last, a negro man named CATO, about 22 years old, and about 5 feet 9 inches high; he is very black, straight and well limb'd; looks grim, speaks pretty good English, a little lisping; had on, when he went away, an

oznabrigs shirt, jacket and trowsers, a felt hat, shoes and stockings; a great coat, half worn, and almost new beaver hat with him; said negro man is now at or about Rhode-Island: Whoever will take up said fellow & deliver him either to the Capts. Webster, Johnson, St. Croix, or to the subscriber, or confine him in any of his Majesty's gaols and give notice thereof to any of the forementioned persons, shall receive five pounds, New-York currency, reward and all necessary charges
paid by LEMUEL WYATT.
The Newport Mercury, January 25, 1773.

RUN-AWAY from the subscriber on the 29th of August last, a negro man named SAM, aged about 26 years, is about 5 feet 10 or 11 inches high, has black smooth skin, streight built, and well limb'd; has a scar on one of his knees, can speak both English and Dutch, but sounds mostly on the latter: He is very strong and nimble, and does not want for wit; is very ingenious, and understands farming very well; he can play well on the violin, and is fond of company: It is likely he may have forged pass, and pretend to be free. All masters of vessels and others, are hereby forbid to harbour or carry off the said slave, or any wife to assist him. Whoever apprehends him, and delivers him to the subscriber, in the Manor of Cortlandt, shall receive a reward of FIVE DOLLARS, with reasonable charges, if taken in Westchester County; and if taken out of said county, THREE POUNDS, with charges as above,
paid by JOHN BRYAN.
The New-York Gazette; and the Weekly Mercury, February 8, 1773; February 15, 1773; February 22, 1773; May 3, 1773.

RODE away with from Albany, about the 27th of Jan. last, by one John Sullivan Baldhead, a German, (who undertook to deliver it at the Blue Bell, at Harlem) a red roan Gelding, about 5 Years old, fifteen Hands high, a Blaze down his Forehead, hind Legs white, Main and Tail a mixture of white, red, and black,—Whoever will stop the Man and Horse, that the one may be prosecuted, and the Horse returned to the Owner, shall be suitably rewarded by Jacob Moore, at the Bell at Harlem, or Blaze Moore, Tobacconist, facing the College, New-York.
The New-York Gazette; and the Weekly Mercury, February 8, 1773; February 15, 1773.

John Sydelman, is a Man about 46 years of age, of low stature, bald headed, his hair of a lightish colour, and combs it backwards; he is a High Dutchman or Hanoverian; speaks tolerable good English; has carried off an Horse given to him in charge to deliver at New-York. It is thought he has

taken his course to some part of New-England. The horse is between 5 and 6 years old, between 14 and 15 hands high, between a bay and mouse colour, a large white blaze in his forehead, some of his feet white, a switch tail, both trots and paces.—Any person who will apprehend the said Sydelman, and secure the horse so that the owner may have him again shall receive TEN DOLLARS reward, and all reasonable charges
paid by HENRY WILLIAMS, in Beaver street,
New York, and JOHN SMITH.
The New-London Gazette, February, 19, 1773.

Forty Shillings Reward.
RUN-away from the subscriber, living in North-Castle, Westchester county, a man named Jacob Whitman, born on Long-Island, and talks much after the Yankee tone, is about 5 feet 9 inches high, a likely fellow, with black hair a little curled; he is much given to drink, and when intoxicated is excessive noisy and much for playing his favourite game of husselcap, at which he is something dextrous in cheating. Had on a blue broad cloth coat turn'd, with silver wash'd buttons, buckskin breeches, large square brass buckles, and a castor hat; took likewise a silver cross bar'd vest, and another castor hat, which he stole from the subscriber. He is both taylor and weaver by trade, but following the tayloring mostly; one of his legs is ulcerated on the shin, round which he commonly wears a handkerchief. Rode away a small sorrel horse with a bushy tail, and is very remarkable for having both ears cut off sloping, is 12 hand high. Whoever takes up the said Whitman, and secures him in any goal, shall have the above reward
from   JOSIAH HUNT.
The New-York Gazette; and the Weekly Mercury, February 22, 1773; March 1, 1773. See *The New-York Journal; or, The General Advertiser*, January 21, 1773.

THREE POUNDS REWARD.
RUN-away the first of this instant March, in the evening of the same day, a servant man named John Willis, Taylor by trade, (he says) born in Boston, New-England, about five feet seven or eight inches high, a very lively walk, close kneed, brown hair and eyes, a pert look, high nose, especially in the middle there is a bump, and perhaps the scar or redness may be seen, occasioned by a blow last winter, he is very talkative, loves company, and sometimes will get drunk: Had on when he went away a new suit of blue broad cloth cloaths, trim'd with the same colour. Whoever takes up said servant and secures him in any of his majesty's goals or returns him to his said master, shall receive the above reward.
JOHN BAINBRIDGE.

The New-York Gazette; and the Weekly Mercury, March 22, 1773; March 29, 1773; April 12, 1773; March 19, 1773; March 26, 1773; April 19, 1773; April 26, 1773.

RUN-away on Tuesday night the 5th of January: A negro man about 5 feet 7 inches high, a well set fellow, not very black but something upon the yellow, aged about thirty-one years, his name is Ned: had on when he went away, a blue duffles watch coat about half worn, and much faded, a wool hat half worn, with a pewter button, light coloured vest of homespun, with pewter buttons, light coloured broad cloth breeches, sheeps black stockings. Whoever takes up the said negro and secures him, or brings him home, so that his master may have him again, shall receive FIVE POUNDS reward, with all reasonable charges paid by the subscriber at Cortlandt's Manor, in the county of Westchester.
        SIMON MABEE.
The New-York Gazette; and the Weekly Mercury, March 22, 1773; March 29, 1773.

RUN-away from the subscriber, living at South-Hampton, on Long-Island, about three months ago, a negro fellow named CUSH, about 5 feet 9 inches high, between 28 and 30 years of age: Had on when he went away, a sailor's blue jacket, a red baise shirt, with a check shirt over it; and a pair of woolen trowsers; he is slender made, has lost two fore teeth, and has a scar or seam on one ear; supposed to have a pass. Whoever can secure the pass so that the author of it may be brought to justice, shall have TEN POUNDS reward for their trouble, and TEN DOLLARS for apprehending the negro, and all reasonable charges
        paid by   JOHN FOSTER.
The New-York Gazette; and the Weekly Mercury, April 12, 1773. See *The New-London Gazette,* April 30, 1773, *The Boston Gazette,* May 3, 1773, *The New-York Journal; or, The General Advertiser,* May 13, 1773, and *The Newport Mercury,* May 17, 1773.

TAKEN *up in January last, by Benjamin Hopkins, and James Tripp, a negro man named Scotland, who says he is a free fellow, and came from the West-Indies to Philadelphia. He was lately taken up in Connecticut, but upon receiving information that he was free, gave him a pass: He is a trim built fellow, of a shining black countenance, about 5 feet 8 inches high, 22 years of age, has a scar under his right eye, and some curious marks on his back, that leads down diminishing from each shoulder: Had on when taken up a red duffles coat, and blue duffles trowsers. Whoever owns the said*

negro, can readily get him by applying to the subscribers in North Castle, Westchester county, York government.
BENJAMIN HOPKINS,   JAMES TRIPP.
The New-York Gazette; and the Weekly Mercury, April 12, 1773.

THIRTY POUNDS REWARD.
BROKE goal on Thursday the 15th inst. the three following persons, Thomas Smith, about 28 years of age, 5 feet 8 or 9 inches high, thin made, very active, and speaks very quick. Zephaniah Hubbs, about 30 years old, 6 feet high, and thin made. Abraham Miller, jun. of a very dark complexion, about 5 feet 9 or 10 inches high, with a mould just below one of his eyes. Whoever takes up and secures the said run-aways, and will deliver them to the goaler of the county of West-chester, shall have 10l. for each, or the above reward for the whole,
paid by   JAMES DE LANCEY, jun. sheriff.
The New-York Gazette; and the Weekly Mercury, April 19, 1773; April 26, 1773; May 24, 1773. See *The New-York Gazette; and the Weekly Mercury*, October 30, 1775, for Hubs/Hubbs

FORTY SHILLINGS Reward.
RUN-away from me the subscriber, at the Fishkills, in Dutchess county, a negro fellow named JAMES, 30 years of age, about 5 feet 9 inches high, clumsy built, his legs bow out, and may easily pass for an Indian. It is supposed he is somewhere on Long-Island, as he formerly lived there: Had on when he went away, a castor hat, blue great coat, light-coloured tight bodied do. and vest, and a pair of leather breeches. He took with him a pair of cloth breeches and a bundle of clothes. Whoever will take up said runaway, and secure him, so that his master may have him again, shall be entitled to the above reward, and all reasonable charges,
paid by   JOSHUA CARMAN, jun.
The New-York Gazette; and the Weekly Mercury, April 19, 1773; April 26, 1773.

100 *Dollars Reward.*
EScaped out of the custody of me the subscriber at Salisbury, on the night after the 19th day of April instant, Remember Baker of Arlington, in Charlotte county, and province of New-York, and Zimrie Allen of said Salisbury, being each of them under an arrest for blasphemy, committed in said Salisbury, on or about the 28th day of March last. Said Baker is about 5 feet 9 or 10 inches high, pretty well sett, something freckled in his face. Said Allen is near 6 feet high, slim built, goes something stooping, dark hair; each of said fellows being arm'd with sword and pistol, and are

notorious for blasphemous expressions in conversation, and ridiculing every thing sacred. Whoever will apprehend said fellows and deliver them to the custody of the subscriber, so that they may be brought to justice, shall have thirty Pounds lawful money reward, for both, and fifteen pounds for either,
   paid by NATHANIEL BUELL, *Constable of Salisbury.*
The Connecticut Courant, And Hartford Weekly Intelligencer, From April 20, to April 27, 1773; From April 27, to May 4, 1773; From May 4, to May 11, 1773.

TEN DOLLARS Reward.

RUN AWAY, *on the 12th day of this inst. April, from the subscriber, living in Forks township, Northampton county, a servant man, named Abraham Fitched, or Fisher, born in Long Island, of English descent, about 34 years old, dark hair, 5 feet 8 inches high, ruddy complexion, small faced, redish beard, several powder spots in his face, by the flash of a gun, speaks English, and sometimes broken Low Dutch; had on a half- worn Five Shilling felt hat, a new coarse tow shirt, one new fine Irish linen ditto, with a heart, and I think the subscriber's name on it, a green or almost snuff coloured coat, a fulled linsey half-worn double breasted jacket, white breeches, of country cloth, blue and white yarn stockings, half-worn Dutch pumps, with a pair of large buckles, of Bethlehem make. Whoever takes up said servant, and brings him home, or secures him in any of his Majesty's goals, shall have the above reward, and reasonable charges,*
   paid by JOHN VAN ETTEN.
N. B. All masters of vessels are forbid to carry him off, at their peril.
The Pennsylvania Gazette, April 28, 1773; May 12, 1773; June 9, 1773. See *The New-York Gazette; and the Weekly Mercury,* May 10, 1773, *The Pennsylvania Gazette,* November 3, 1773, and *The Pennsylvania Gazette,* October 12, 1774.

Ran-away from the Subscriber, about three Months since, a Negro Man, named *CUSH,* about 26 Years old, was born in Stonington, is about 5 Feet 9 Inches high, rather slim built, is a strait likely Fellow, not very black; has one or two of his fore Teeth out, and a Scar on one of his Ears; had on when he went away, a red Bayse Shirt, blue outside Jacket and a blue mill'd Cap; has with him a forg'd Pass. Any Person that will secure said Negro in any of his Majesty's Goals, so that his Master may have Word, shall have *Ten Dollars* Reward, and all necessary Charges
   paid. JOHN FOSTER. *Southampton, April* 19, 1773.
The New-London Gazette, April 30, 1773; May 7, 1773; May 14, 1773; *The Connecticut Journal, and the New-Haven Post Boy,* May 7, 1773; May 14, 1773; May 21, 1773; May 28, 1773. Minor differences between the papers.

The *Journal* adds "N. B. It is supposed the Fellow stole a Boat and got over from the West End of Long-Island to the Main." See *The New-York Gazette; and the Weekly Mercury*, April 12, 1773, *The Boston Gazette*, May 3, 1773, *The New-York Journal; or, The General Advertiser*, May 13, 1773, and *The Newport Mercury*, May 17, 1773.

RAN-AWAY from his Master John Foster, on Long-Island, about three Months since a Negro-Man Named Cush, about five Feet Nine Inches high, his Complection not very black, one of two of his fore Teeth out, a Scar upon one of his Ears, Speaks good English, has Forg'd a Pass; had on when he went away a blue Mill'd Cap, a blue outside Jacket, and a red Bays Shirt.—It is likely he may have chang'd his Dress, and he has broke open his Master's Store, and Stole to the value of 100 Dollars in Cash and Goods.

Whoever shall apprehend said Negro and commit him to any of his Majesty's Goals, shall have 10 Dollars Reward, and all necessary Charges paid; and for securing the Pass 10 Dollars, if it can be prov'd who was the Forger of it,
     Paid by me JOHN FOSTER.

All Masters of Vessels and others are hereby Cautioned against harbouring, concealing or carrying off said Servant as they would avoid the Penalty of the Law.   *East Hampton, April* 28, 1773.

The Boston Gazette, May 3, 1773, May 10, 1773. See *The New-York Gazette; and the Weekly Mercury*, April 12, 1773, *The New-London Gazette*, April 30, 1773, *The New-York Journal; or, The General Advertiser*, May 13, 1773, and *The Newport Mercury*, May 17, 1773.

TWENTY DOLLARS Reward.

WHEREAS Frederick Shonnard, of the city of New-York, shop-keeper, did, on the 8th of March last, let a certain *James Thompson*, have a small schooner about twenty tons burthen, to go to Blue Point; and as the said Thompson, nor schooner, has since been heard of either at Blue Point, or in this city, it is imagined that the said Thompson had fraudulently carried her off to some other part. The schooner was quick sheer'd, with a new stern without lights, her frame live oak, her bottom plank'd with pine, her hold cieled with inch pine boards, with two or three new beams at or near the hatches, also her sails new, with one old and one new shroud at each side of the foremast, the new shroud rather too large for such a vessel. Whoever apprehends the said James Thompson, and delivers him together with the vessel, unto Frederick Shonnard, in New-York, shall have the above reward.

The New-York Gazette; and the Weekly Mercury, May 3, 1773; May 10, 1773; May 24, 1773; May 31, 1773.

TEN DOLLARS Reward.

RUN-AWAY on the 12th of April, from the subscriber, living in Fork's township, Northampton county, a servant man named ABRAHAM FITCHED or FISHER, born on Long-Island, of English descent, about 34 years old, dark hair, 5 feet 8 inches high, ruddy complexion, small faced, redish beard, several powder spots in his face by the flash of a gun, speaks English, and sometimes broken Low Dutch: Had on a half-worn Five Shilling felt hat, a new coarse tow shirt, one new fine Irish linen do. with a heart, and I think the subscriber's name on it, a green or almost snuff coloured coat, a fulled linsey half-worn double-breasted jacket, white stockings, half-worn Dutch pumps, with a pair of large buckles of Bethlehem make. Whoever takes up said servant, and brings him home, or secures him in any of his Majesty's goals, shall have the above reward, and reasonable charges,
        paid by   JOHN VAN ETTEN.

The New-York Gazette; and the Weekly Mercury, May 10, 1773; May 17, 1773; May 24, 1773. See *The Pennsylvania Gazette,* April 28, 1773, *The Pennsylvania Gazette,* November 3, 1773, and *The Pennsylvania Gazette,* October 12, 1774.

RUN *away from John Foster, of Southampton, on Long-Island, some Time in February last, a Negro Man, named CUSH, about 5 Feet 9 Inches high, this Country born, not very black; has lost some of his Fore Teeth; has a Scar on one of his Ears, and slim built; is a very plausible Fellow, and it is probably he has a forged Pass with him. He had on when he went away, a red Baize Shirt, blue mill'd Cap, and a blue Outside Jacket. As he stole several Articles of European Goods, and some Money from his Master, it is desired, in case any are offered for Sale they may be stopt. Ten Dollars Reward will be given for securing the said Fellow in any Goal, with all reasonable Charges, upon Information given to his said Master, in Southampton, or the Subscriber in New-York.*
        DANIEL PHOENIX.

The New-York Journal; or, The General Advertiser, May 13, 1773; May 20, 1773; May 27, 1773; June 3, 1773; June 10, 1773; June 17, 1773; June 24, 1773. See *The New-York Gazette; and the Weekly Mercury,* April 12, 1773, *The New-London Gazette,* April 30, 1773, *The Boston Gazette,* May 3, 1773, and *The Newport Mercury,* May 17, 1773.

RAN away from his master John Foster, on Long-Island, about three Months since a Negro man named Cush, about five feet nine inches high, his complection not very black, one of two of his fore teeth out, a scar upon one of his ears, speaks good English, has a forged pass; had on when he went away a blue mill'd cap, a blue outside jacket, and a red baize shirt.

Whoever shall apprehend said negro and commit him to any of his Majesty's gaols, shall have ten dollars reward, and necessary charges paid; and for securing the pass, 20 dollars, if it can be prov'd who was the forger of it, paid by me, JOHN FOSTER.

All masters of vessels and others are hereby cautioned against harbouring, concealing or carrying off, said servant, as they would avoid the Penalty of the law. *South-Hampton, April* 28, 1773.

The Newport Mercury, May 17, 1773; May 31, 1773; June 7, 1773; June 14, 1773. See *The Boston Gazette*, May 3, 1773, *The New-York Gazette; and the Weekly Mercury*, April 12, 1773, *The New-London Gazette*, April 30, 1773, and *The New-York Journal; or, The General Advertiser*, May 13, 1773.

RUN-away from the Subscriber, living at Stirling Ironworks, an indented Irish Servant Man, named William Derwin, about 5 Feet 8 Inches high, dark Complexion, dark brown Hair, a thick well set Fellow, has a Scar on his left Eyebrow, made by the Blow of a Shovel, speaks good English: Had on when he went away, a striped blue and white Linsey jacket, and a green Cloth Waistcoat, with a Piece of Black Cloth put in the back to make it wider, a Pair of Buckskin Breeches, or perhaps a Pair of Oznabrigs Trowsers, and it is likely he may have a blue Broad-Cloth Coat; he is supposed to have gone with one Thomas Butler, a coarse thick set Irishman, very much pitted with the Small-Pox; also it is very likely he may be in Company with another Irishman, named Edward Hefferman, a stout thick well made Man, who went away at the same Time—Whoever takes up and secures said Runaway, in any of his Majesty's Gaols, so that his Master may have him again, shall have Three Pounds Reward, and all reasonable Charges paid. And all Persons and Masters of Vessels in particular, are forbid to harbour, conceal, or carry him away, as they will answer it at their Peril. ABEL NOBLE. Stirling, April 21st, 1773.

The New-York Journal; or, The General Advertiser, May 17, 1773.

Ran away from the Subscriber last Night, a Negro Woman named LETTICE, she's of a very sprightly make, of midling height, and slender built, born upon Long-Island, speaks good English, carried with her a coarse purple and white chintz Gown, a strip'd linnen, and a brown worsted Ditto, three strip'd Petticoats, a red tammy Quilt, two new towcloth Shifts,

a red broadcloth Cloak, a pair blue cloth Shoes, a black Bonnet, and sundry other articles. Whoever will return said Negro to the Subscriber in Norwich, shall have two Dollars Reward, and all necessary Charges
          paid by me   THOMAS TRUMAN.
Norwich, May 27, 1773.
The New-London Gazette, May 28, 1773; June 4, 1773; June 11, 1773.

BROKE goal at Goshen, in Orange county, and province of New-York, on Monday night the seventeenth of May, inst. two prisoners, one named William Lee, or Grove, about 28 or 30 years of age, small stature, streight and likely, has black curled hair, black beard, dark grey eyes, and is a talkative drunken fellow, by occupation a pot-ash boiler. He broke open a store, and took a quantity of goods, and is strongly suspected of being gone towards New-Haven, in company with one Alexander Flaningham, a young man, born at Goshen, has a very red face, near 6 feet high, stoops, and by occupation a labourer. Had on an old blue cloth coat, and vest without sleeves. Lee had on an old black coat, and the remainder of both their other apparel was very mean and dirty. The other prisoner named Justice Bennit, committed for horse stealing, about 21 or 22 years of age, pale fac'd, light brown hair, down look, country born, and about 5 feet 8 or 9 inches high: Had on good cloaths, but the particulars are not known, as he was a very short time under confinement. Whoever apprehends said prisoners, so that the subscriber may have them again, shall have Thirty Pounds reward for both, or Ten Pounds for either,
          paid by   JEREMIAH COLMAN, Sub-sheriff.
The New-York Gazette; and the Weekly Mercury, May 31, 1773; June 7, 1773; June 14, 1773; June 21, 1773.

                    EIGHT DOLLARS Reward.
RUN away, the 19th of April last, from the subscriber, living in Nottingham, Chester county, a servant lad, named WILLIAM ROOKER, says he was born in New York, about 5 feet high, thick and well made, lisps a little in his speech, sour look, lightish yellow hair, curls a little; had on, when he went away, a short coat, of a redish brown colour, lined with striped linsey, striped linsey jacket, without sleeves, old leather breeches, old grey ribbed stockings, old check shirt, felt hat, about half worn, good shoes, lately soaled; took with him a silver Watch, with a china face, steel chain and seal, a small piece cracked out of the face, has been mended where the swivel goes in the case. Whoever takes up said servant, and brings him home, or secures him so that I may get him again, shall have the above reward, and reasonable charges,

paid by   JOSEPH LACEY.
The Pennsylvania Gazette, June 2, 1773; June 9, 1773; June 16, 1773.

RUN AWAY from John Garnsey of Amenia Precinct in Dutchess County, on the 29th of May last, a Negro man named Sambo, a large well set fellow, pitted with the small pox, talks very broken, had with him a grey great coat, a light coloured vest, a pair of leather breeches, two pair stockings. Whoever shall take up said negro and bring him to me, shall have two dollars reward, and all necessary charges
paid by me,   John Garnsey.   June 1st, 1773.
The Connecticut Courant, From June 1, to June 8, 1773; from June 8, to June 15, 1773; From June 15, to June 22, 1773.

Cumberland County, Pennsylvania, May 31, 1773.
LAST week was committed to the goal of said county, a certain JAMES SMITH *(as he calls himself) however, he is the identical man that left a stolen horse at John Trindle's, in said county, last fall; the horse was afterwards proved to be the property of Jacob Ryder, of the Manor of Philipsbourgh, in the county of West Chester, and province of New York; he had with him, when committed, a likely black horse, about 14 1/2 hands high, supposed to be stolen, as it is reported he is a notorious horse thief, and has been in several goals before, and broke out of them all; he is a middle sized man, fair haired, pitted with the smallpox, about 5 feet 9 inches high, says he was born in the Jerseys. Therefore I request the said* Jacob Ryder *to come, or send for the said prisoner, as soon as possible.*

Runaway from his bail, last March, a certain HENRY KERR, *about 26 years of age, 5 feet 6 inches high, thin faced, black hair, tied, is much addicted to drinking, served his time in Chester county; it is supposed he has gone there. Any person or persons securing said KERR in any goal, shall have* THIRTY SHILLINGS *reward, and reasonable charges,*
paid by   ROBERT SEMPLE, *Goaler.*
The Pennsylvania Gazette, June 9, 1773.

RUN away from the Subscriber, James Heagan, an Irishman, he is about 5 feet 8 inches high, thin visage, black hair, and eye-brows, and some red spots under his eye, one of his shoulders higher than the other, small legs, and walks parrot-toed, his ankle out of joint, and a remarkable lump on his breast, his right wrist is broke with a lump on it, which he says he got by accident, by being ship-wrecked in the West-Indies, he has on when he went off, a whitish coat, a blue jacket, and a white twill'd pair of breeches, passes for a Wine-Cooper, and was redeemed out of New York Goal,
by   SAMUEL PAGE.

Any Person securing the said fellow shall be intitled to the sum of Three Pounds to be paid by the Subscriber at the Fresh-Water.
Rivington's New-York Gazetteer, June 10, 1773; June 24, 1773.

FIVE POUNDS Reward.

RUN-AWAY *from the subscriber, on Tuesday the first of this inst.* an Irish servant man named WILLIAM LEONARD, *by trade a taylor; he is about 25 years of age, about 5 feet high, has long black hair, which he generally wears clubb'd, black beard, is well-set, and speaks good English; he has a sly look, and is an artful fellow: Had on when he left his master's service, a blue coat, with basket buttons, a brown cloth waistcoat, a pair of large denim breeches, white shirt, a pair of brown worsted stockings, a beaver hat, and black silk handkerchief, but took other cloaths with him, and it is probable he may change his dress. Whoever apprehends said servant, and secures him, or returns him to his master living in Princes-street, New-York, shall have the above reward, and all reasonable charges,*
fromJAMES M'KENNEY.

N. B. It is requested that all masters of vessels, and others, will pay some attention to the above advertisement, and not harbour or carry off said fellow, as they may expect to answer is at their peril.
The New-York Gazette; and the Weekly Mercury, June 14, 1773; June 21, 1773.

Fifteen Dollars Reward.

RUN-AWAY from the subscriber of Hebron, on the evening after the 10th instant, a negro man named TONEY, about 6 feet high, very black talkative and of a sprightly countenance, about 24 or 25 years old—carried away with him 1 brown loose coat, yellow binding, 1 coat and vest, mix'd red and white, no lining, one sleeveless vest brown plaincloth, 2 striped tow shirts, 2 white holland ditto, 1 pair leather breeches, 1 pair check trowsers and 1 check shirt, 3 pair of stockings, 2 pair boots, 1 pair shoes, and a felt hat. Also supposed to be in company with said Negro, one Samuel Gilbert of New Canaan, in the province of New-York, hired man to the subscriber, about 19 years of age, dark brown hair and eyes, about 5 feet and 8 inches high, had with him a gray serge coat, dark brown broad cloth lapel'd vest, 2 short jackets for every day, blewish colour, 1 pair leather breeches, 1 pair sagathy ditto, 1 pair black rib'd stockings, 1 pair blue ditto, bever hat, 2 woolen shirts, 2 white holland ditto, one frock, tow cloth—sundry of the above articles were stolen by one or both of the above described fellows. Whoever shall take up said negro servant and return him to his master, or shall confine him in any of his majesty's goals, shall have ten dollars

reward, and all necessary charges paid. For the said Gilbert, five dollars reward, and all necessary charges paid,
    by me *Samuel Gilbert,* jun.

 N. B. All masters of vessels and others, are forbid carrying off said negro, on the penalty of the law.   *Hebron, June* 11, 1773.

 The Connecticut Courant, From June 8, to June 15, 1773; From June 15, to June 22, 1773; From June 22, to June 29, 1773.

FIVE POUNDS REWARD.
A Rogue! A Rogue! A Rogue!

WHEREAS an atrocious villain, known by the name of Isaac Vander Velden, has within a few days past imported on several persons in this city, with bills of exchange, which he has forged in the name of Mr. Paul Hogstrasser, of Albany: He, the said Vander Velden is a German, but speaks good English, with a little of his own country accent, talks fast, and affects a good deal of propriety in his conversation, has a very good address, and appears capable of executing any artful piece of fraud. He is about five feet eight inches high, remarkably well set, fair complexion, and wears his own hair: He is known both in Philadelphia and Albany, and pretends to have large rights in lands on the Missisippi. Every friend to the public is therefore requested to secure the above impostor in any of his Majesty's jails, so that he may be brought to justice, and the above reward, with reasonable charges, will be paid by application to the Printer hereof.

N. B. He is supposed to be gone toward Philadelphia.
      New-York, June 16, 1773.
 Rivington's New-York Gazetteer, June 17, 1773.

 RUN-away from the brig Peter and John. John Simons, Master, an Irish servant named JOSEPH FORESTER, about 24 years old, 5 feet 5 inches high, hazel eyes, brown complexion, wears his own hair tied behind, and has a cut under his chin. Had on a green jacket, a red and white striped waistcoat, blue shag breeches, grey rib'd stockings, with pewter buckles in his shoes. Any person who shall apprehend, or bring the said Joseph Forester to Greg, Cunningham, and Co. merchants in New-York, or to said Simons, on board said vessel, shall receive a reward of Five Pounds.
      JOHN SIMONS.

 The New-York Gazette; and the Weekly Mercury, June 21, 1773; June 28, 1773; July 5, 1773; August 2, 1773; August 9, 1773; August 16, 1773; August 23, 1773; August 30, 1773; September 6, 1773.

Hartford, June 26, 1773.
TAKEN up, and now in the custody of the subscriber, a Negro man, who calls, his name PETER, is about 50 years of age, about 6 feet high, speaks good English—says he belongs to Abraham Van Vlack, of the new City, about Albany. He has on a pair old leather Breeches, and a brown waistcoat, lin'd with red baize. Whoever owns said Negro, may have him, proving his property and paying charges.
Apply to Samuel Turner.
The Connecticut Courant, From June 22, to June 29, 1773.

New-York, June 28.
RAN away, from the Subscriber, an Apprentice Boy, named JAMES JONES; had on when he went absented himself, a light coloured Cloth Coat, called Parson's Grey, a striped red and white worsted jacket, and thread stockings; also, he has taken sundry wearing Apparel from his said Master. Whoever takes up the said Apprentice, and delivers him to his Master, in New-York, shall receive TWO DOLLARS Reward,
paid by, PETER ARELL.
N. B. All Masters of Vessels are forbid harbouring or carrying the said Apprentice off, at their Peril.
The New-York Journal; or, The General Advertiser, July 1, 1773; July 8, 1773; July 15, 1773.

Goshen township, Chester County, July 5, 1773.
RUN away from the subscriber, on the 4th instant, an indented servant girl, named ELIZABETH CLARK, born in England, and speaks in the North of England dialect, of a middle size, black hair, dark eyes, and brown complexion; had on, when she went away, a striped linen short gown, a yellow stuff petticoat, blue yarn stockings, high heeled leather shoes, tied with strings; she also took with her a pattern of a gown, of yellow stuff, the same of her petticoat. She has a sister living in New-York, and it is likely she may make that way. Whoever takes up and secures said servant, so that her master may get her again, shall have FOUR DOLLARS reward, and reasonable charges,
paid by EDWARD HICKS.
The Pennsylvania Gazette, July 7, 1773; July 21, 1773; August 4, 1773.

Ran away from me the Subscriber, of *East-Hampton*, on *Long Island*, the 11th of *June* last, a NEGRO Man Slave named *PRINCE*, but has since called himself by sundry different Names: He lived Six Years with Mr. *Daniel Deniso*n, at *Stonington*, in *New-London* County; is about 28 Years old, of midling Stature and Bigness, and straight limed; tells various Stores to prevent his being taken for a Runaway. Had on a Kersey Waistcoat of a redish cast, with Cuffs, striped Towcloth Trousers, with a Patch on one or both Knees, whited Towcloth Shirt, and a Castor Hat with a white Loop.

Whoever will take up said Slave and return him to me the Subscriber in *East Hampton*, or secure him in any of his Majesty's Goals, so that I may have him again, shall receive THREE DOLLARS Reward, and all necessary Charges

    paid by me JOHN MULFORD. July 5, 1773.

The New-London Gazette, July 9, 1773; July 16, 1773; July 23, 1773.

Five Dollars Reward,

RUN away on Thursday last from on board the Brig Hannah, Capt. Henderson, an Indian Fellow, called Jack, about 22 years of age, thick and well set, about 5 feet high, streight black hair, which he generally wears tied behind; had on when he went away a green jacket, oznaburg trowsers, a check shirt, a new pair of shoes, a sailor's hat; he has since been seen at the Ferry on Long Island. Whoever apprehends the said Indian, and secures, or returns him, to his master in New-York, shall have the above reward, and all reasonable charges paid them by

    WALTER and T. BUCHANAN, and Co.

N. B. It is requested, that no master of vessels, or others, will harbour, or carry off said Indian, otherwise they may depend on being prosecuted.

Rivington's New-York Gazetteer, July 15, 1773.

RUN-away from Robert Davis, lately arrived from Ireland, in the ship Robert, Matthew Russell, commander, an indented servant man named *Richard Henderson,* about 25 years of age, about five feet, nine inches high, slow in speech, short black hair, cut before, pock marked; had on a new felt hat, a dark grey county cloth coat and waistcoat, leather breeches, grey yarn stockings, new shoes, and white metal buckles. Whoever apprehends the said servant, and brings him to Capt. Matthew Russell, shall have *ten shillings* reward if took in town, and *twenty shillings* if in the country, and all reasonable charges

    paid by ROBERT DAVIS.

The New-York Gazette; and the Weekly Mercury, July 19, 1773; July 26, 1773; August 2, 1773; August 16, 1773.

ON Wednesday the 7th of July, inst. the house of Mr. Isaac Valantine, of Westchester, was broke open and robbed of some wearing apparel, viz. A deep blue broad cloth coat with gilt buttons, lined with white durant; a jacket near the same colour of the coat; a pair of black knit breeches, lined

with white linen and pieced about the pockets with coarse pale blue cloth; and one black silk handkerchief, fring'd and whip'd. 'Tis supposed the villain that committed this robbery is gone towards Philadelphia: He is a stout built fellow, a little round shoulder'd, very dark complexion, and pretty thick lips; had on a snuff colour'd coat much faded, and striped trowsers. Whoever secures him so that the owner may have the above articles again, shall receive a reward of FORTY SHILLINGS,
          paid by   ISAAC VALINTINE.
The New-York Gazette; and the Weekly Mercury, July 26, 1773.

RUN-away from the Brig Mercury, John Trimingham, master, belonging to Bermuda, on Thursday the 15th inst. a negro fellow named POMPEY, about five feet ten inches high; speaks but indifferent English: Had on a blue jacket and trowsers; his hair a little grey, has lost part of one of his toes. Whoever apprehends the said fellow, and brings him to Mr. John Harris Cruger, merchant, in New-York, shall receive THIRTY SHILLINGS reward, and all reasonable charges.
    The New-York Gazette; and the Weekly Mercury, July 26, 1773; August 2, 1773; August 9, 1773; August 30, 1773.

RUN AWAY
From the ship Robert, Capt. Russel, lately arrived from Newry, JAMES M'CUW, an indented Servant to JOHN STEPHENSON, a low man about 25 years of age, round and ruddy visage, full eyes, he wears his own hair, pale brown cutt short, or a fair coloured wig with one buckle, a blue nap coat with white metal buttons, a felt hat and brown thicksett breeches,— Whoever brings him again to the said JOHN STEPHENSON at the printer's, shall receive, if taken in the City, One Guinea reward, or if taken in the country, a reward of Five Pounds currency, with reasonable charges.
    Rivington's New-York Gazetteer, July 29, 1773; August 5, 1773. See *The New-York Gazette; and the Weekly Mercury*, August 2, 1773. The ad in the *Mercury* said he was "bald headed"

RUN-away from the ship Robert, Capt. Russel, lately arrived from Newry, JAMES M'CUW, an indented Servant to John Stephenson; a low man about 25 years of age, round and ruddy visage, full eyed, is bald headed, and wears a pale brown cut, or a fair coloured wig with one buckle: Had on a blue coat and waistcoat, with white metal buttons; brown thickset breeches, and a felt hat; also took with him a white linen waistcoat. Whoever brings him to said John Stephenson, shall receive (if taken in the city) ONE GUINEA reward, or if in the country, a reward of FIVE POUNDS currency, with reasonable charges.

Enquire of H. Gaine.
The New-York Gazette; and the Weekly Mercury, August 2, 1773;
August 9, 1773; August 16, 1773; August 30, 1773. See *Rivington's New-York Gazetteer*, July 29, 1773.

RUN-AWAY *on Sunday morning the 25th ult. from on board the ship Robert, Matthew Russell, commander, a redemptioner named ROBERT BLACK, about 30 years old, 5 feet 8 inches high, black hair, and of a swarthy complexion: Had on when he went away, a brown twilled linen coat; his other cloaths uncertain. 'Tis imagined he is either gone to Philadelphia or Albany. Whoever takes up and secures said run-away so that he may be had again, shall have TEN DOLLARS reward,*
   paid by Messrs. Hugh and
    Alexander Wallace, or Matthew Russell.
The New-York Gazette; and the Weekly Mercury, August 2, 1773;
August 9, 1773; August 16, 1773; August 30, 1773.

    Four Dollars Reward.
RAN-AWAY from the Subscriber. at Skenesborough, on Sunday the 22th Instant, a Spanish Negro Man named NED; he is about Six Feet high, of a Robust make and dark Olive Complexion; his Breast and Body scarified after the Manner of his Country: He travels with a false Pass signed by *James M'Coy*, Captain in one of his Majesty's Regiments: Has a large Pack, with a red Jacket and long Trowsers and a blanket Coat, talks broken English. It is conjectured he will attempt to get to the Sea Coast, therefore, all Masters of Vessels are forbid to carry him off, or any other Person to harbour him at their Peril.

  Whoever shall apprehend and secure the said Negro so that the Owner may have him again, shall receive FOUR DOLLARS Reward, and all reasonable Expences
   paid by ANDREW P. SKENE. Skenesborough, July 24, 1773.
  N. B. If the said Servant be taken up near Boston, they may apply to GERSHAM BEECH, at Mr. Moore's, at the Sign of the Lamb, Boston.
  The Massachusetts Gazette: and the Boston Weekly News-Letter,
August 12, 1773.

RAN away, from the subscribers, on Sunday night, the 8th of this instant, two indented servant men; one named Joseph Jones, aged 23 years, about 5 feet 8 or 9 inches high, saucy complexion, light hair tied behind; says he was born in England, (but appears to be an Irishman, as he has the brogue) and went from there to Ireland, where he shipped as a servant for this country:—Had on when he went away, a light coloured camlet coat, black

everlasting breeches; a white shirt; blue yarn stockings, and an old felt or castor hat, with spots of tar upon the crown.—The other named John Stagg, born in England, but shipped from Ireland, as a servant also—says he was 21 years old last Christmas; has a long scar upon his chin, is about 5 feet 7 or 8 inches high, sandy complexion, short light hair: Had on when he went away a stripped under waistcoat, without sleeves, a short green outside jacket, lined with white flannel, a white shirt, stripped trowsers, a small brim felt hat, and a pair of turned pumps that have been half-soaled, with copper buckles in them; took with him also, a pair of double soaled shoes, partly worn, and a pair of plated buckles; likewise a pair of saddle-bags. Any person that will apprehend said servants, and bring them to their masters, or secure them in any of his Majesty's gaols, and give notice thereof, so that their masters may have them again, shall receive TEN DOLLARS reward, for both, or FIVE for either of them, and all reasonable charges, paid by DANIEL TUTHILL,
THOMAS EVERSON.
Blooming-Grove, in Orange-County, August 10, 1773.

The New-York Journal; or, The General Advertiser, August 12, 1773; August 19, 1773; August 26, 1773; September 2, 1773.

RUN-AWAY on Friday last from the subscriber, an Irish servant man named JAMES CARTHY, about 16 years of age, upwards of 5 feet high, of a good countenance, his hair lately cut short: He had on when he went away, a black cloth coat and breeches, a yellow and brown homespun jacket, the back white linen, and without sleeves; brown thread stockings, yellow metal buckles, a silver stock buckle, and a pair of tow cloth trowsers. He carried off with him a small box containing one twenty shilling bill, a small bag of silver, a few coppers, and several accounts. Whoever will bring the said run-away to his master, shall be amply rewarded, and all necessary charges paid. It is to be hoped that no masters of vessels, or others, will harbour or carry off the said James Carthy; it those should be the came, they may depend upon being prosecuted according to the law.
SAMUEL AUCHMUTY.

The New-York Gazette; and the Weekly Mercury, August 16, 1773; August 23, 1773; August 30, 1773; September 6, 1773.

TWENTY SHILLINGS Reward.
RUN-AWAY *on the first inst. an indented servant lad named DANIEL CONNELL, lately arrived in the brigantine Galway-Packet, Hugh Fallon, master: He is about 20 or 25 years of age, 5 feet 6 inches high. Had on a green jacket, brown breeches, and check shirt; has neither hat, shoes, or*

stockings; walks as if he was lame, speaks much on the brogue, and has short black hair: He was seen the day of his escape at Kingsbridge, and it is probable gone up the North-River, or to Connecticut. Whoever apprehends him shall have the above reward, with any reasonable charge attending his delivery in New-York,

by applying to Mrs. Lynch, in Broad-street.

The New-York Gazette; and the Weekly Mercury, August 16, 1773; August 23, 1773; August 30, 1773; September 6, 1773; September 27, 1773; October 11, 1773; October 18, 1773. See *The New-York Gazette; and the Weekly Mercury*, July 3, 1775.

FIVE DOLLARS *Reward.*

RAN away from the subscriber, living at Still-Water, Albany County, the 2d of July last, an indented Irish servant, named Enos Sline, about 18 or 19 years of age, 5 feet 6 or 7 inches high, well made, short black hair, has a scar on one of his cheeks (supposed to be on the right) Had on an outside green jacket, the lining torn out, an under striped flannel waistcoat, oznaburgs trowsers, coarse linen shirt, a pair of turned pumps, and a thick felt hat, with a red stain on the crown. 'Tis supposed that he is gone to New-York, Whoever takes up said Run away, or secures him in any of his Majesty's gaols, so that his master may have him again, shall be entitled to the above reward, and all other reasonable charges paid, either by John Jones, Tavern-keeper, near the Exchange, in New-York, or Mr. John Black, living in Still-Water.

New-York, August 23, 1773.

N. B. He has a good deal of the brogue, or Irish accent in his speech.

The New-York Journal; or, The General Advertiser, August 26, 1773; September 2, 1773; September 9, 1773; September 16, 1773.

TEN DOLLARS Reward.

RUN-AWAY from the subscriber, at Salem, in the county of Westchester, and province of New-York, on the 25th day of April last, an apprentice lad named JABEZ CLOSE, by trade a Taylor, about 19 years of age, 5 feet 6 or 7 inches high, slim built, black eyes, light streight hair, tied behind, thin face, and a fierce look: Had on and took with him, a blue and white flannel coat; with white shalloon lining, blue broad cloth vest, the backs made of black and blue flannel, with brass buttons, leather breeches, black and white ribb'd stockings, a new castor hat, and sundry other articles. He is a nimble expect lad at the needle. It is supposed he is gone towards Goshen, or some part of Albany county, and assumes the name of Reed. Whoever apprehends said lad, and conveys him to the subscriber, shall be entitled to the above reward, with reasonable charges

from JOHN BAXTER.
The New-York Gazette; and the Weekly Mercury, August 30, 1773; September 6, 1773. See *The Connecticut Journal, and the New-Haven Post Boy*, September 10, 1773.

Five Pounds Reward.

RUN AWAY on Tuesday the 31st of August last, from his master, living in Stone-street, New-York, an indented servant man, named DONALD HOLME, a native of the North Highlands of Scotland, by trade a Carpenter, about five feet two inches high, and strong made, of a florid complexion, speaks broad Scotch; had on when he went off, a red jacket, with white metal buttons, nankeen vest, ozenbrigs trowsers, a pair of good shoes, with steel buckles:—Any person who shall apprehend or bring the said Donald Holme to the printer hereof, shall receive the above reward.

Rivington's New-York Gazetteer, September 2, 1773; September 9, 1773; September 16, 1773; September 23, 1773.

TEN DOLLARS Reward.

RAN away from the Subscriber of Salem, in West Chester County, on Sunday the 25th of April last, an Apprentice Lad named JABEZ CLOSE, a Taylor by Trade, about 19 Years of Age, 5 Feet 6 or 7 Inches high, is very trim built, thin fac'd, has black Eyes, and a fierce Look, and has light brown long strait Hair tied behind; had on and took with him, a blue and white mixt Flannel Coat with light brown Shaloon Lining, blue Broadcloth for the fore Parts of his Vest, and black and blue Flannel for the back Parts, and brass Buttons, Leather Breeches, one Pair of blue Stockings, one Pair of black and seam'd Ditto, one Pair Homespun striped Linnen long Trowsers, one check'd homespun Shirt, one white Ditto, one Wooling Ditto, and a new Castor Hat. Amy Person securing the said Lad in any of his Majesty's Goals, and giving Notice, or delivering him to the Subscriber at Salem, shall have the above Reward, and reasonable Charges
    paid, by me JOHN BAXTER.
    Salem, August 24, 1773.

The Connecticut Journal, and the New-Haven Post Boy, September 10, 1773. See *The New-York Gazette; and the Weekly Mercury*, August 30, 1773.

Three Pounds Reward.

RUN away the 24th of August last, from the subscriber living in this city, three indented servant men, one of them named Thomas Humphreys, a shoe-maker by trade, about 30 years of age, black hair, and pale visage: Had on a light brown cloth waistcoat, red shag breeches, and a white shirt.

The second is named Thomas Kettey, a taylor by trade, about 18 years of age, light hair, a fresh well-looking fellow, and has a small scar in his face: Had on a green jacket, check shirt and tow trowsers. The third is named John Mahony, a shoe-maker by trade, about 17 years of age, a short swarthy fellow, and freckled face: Had on a brown coat, check shirt and trowsers. All of them came here in the Galway Packet from Cork. Whoever takes up the said servants and secures them so that the owner may have them again, shall have the above reward and reasonable charges paid, by applying to
    Mrs. Catharine Lynch, in Broad-street,
      near the Exchange; or Twenty Shillings for each.
The New-York Gazette; and the Weekly Mercury, September 13, 1773; October 11, 1773; October 18, 1773. The last two ads have "N. B. They were all lately seen at Eastchester." at the bottom.

FORTY SHILLINGS REWARD.

RUN away from the subscriber, living in Hopewel township, York county, on the 12th instant, a servant man, named THOMAS MAYFIELD, born in the province of New-York, about 5 feet 4 or 5 inches high, round faced, down look, with short black hair; had on, and took with him, a small wool hat, without lining, a light coloured homespun coat, above half worn, a double-breasted damascus jacket, the hind part linen, white drilling breeches, white ribbed thread stockings, half worn shoes; has also with him a coarse crocus shirt and trowsers; it is supposed that he will make for New-York government, as he has relations living there. Whoever takes up said servant, and secures him, so as his master may get him again, shall have the above reward,
    paid by WILLIAM SMITH. Sept. 13, 1773.
The Pennsylvania Gazette, September 22, 1773; October 6, 1773; November 10, 1773.

Ten Pounds Reward.

RUN away in the night of the 13th instant, an apprentice lad named HUGH OWEN, about 17 years of age, born in Wales, five feet five or six inches high, pale fac'd, sandy Hair, grey Eyes, a short turn-up nose, naturally passionate, writes a tollerable good hand, and has with him a forged Pass. It is supposed he will attempt to work at the Currying business, to which he was bound; had on and took with him an English beaver hat with light brown linen lining, deep in the crown, and the makers name in a round paper with these words, "Water Proof Hats;" one brown cloth coat with white flowered buttons, and waistcoat of the same, one do. with plain white metal buttons, the lining much mended and made larger in the sleeves, one surtout coat made of a darkish coloured bearskin, one pair of black knit breeches, one pair brown thread hose, a pair of white do. three pair of good shoes, one pair plated buckles, one white irish linen shirt, one Dowlas do.— Whoever takes up and secures said Apprentice so, that his master may have him again shall be entitled to the above reward, and all reasonable charges paid by me   JOHNATHAN MEREDITH.

Rivington's New-York Gazetteer, September 23, 1773; September 30, 1773; October 7, 1773; October 14, 1773.

Forty Shillings Reward.

RUN away from the subscriber, living at Westchester, on Monday last the 26th instant, an indented Indian fellow, who calls himself John Anderson, a very lusty well set fellow; had on a blue half-thick jacket, tow shirt and trowsers, and was bare foot, a new wool hat, had in his pocket a Scotch nightcap of a dull brown colour, it had been painted and it is likely he may wear it, is much pockmarked, has a very full face, short bushy hair. Whoever apprehends said fellow, so, that his Master may have him again, shall be paid the above Reward and all reasonable charges by me   MOSES WAYMAN.

Westchester, September 27, 1773.

***It is supposed he may endeavour to go to sea, as he has been bred to it.

Rivington's New-York Gazetteer, September 30, 1773; October 14, 1773.

TEN DOLLARS, Reward.

RUN-away from me the Subscriber, on Tuesday the 28th of September last, two Apprentice Lads, one of them named Matthew Divikin, a native of Ireland, a Weaver by Trade; the other named William Hickling, Country born: The former had on when he went away, a new grey Cloth Jacket lined with white Flannel, and a Pair of Buckskin Breeches: He is about 15 Years old, talks much in the Hibernian Dialect, and has short brown Hair. The latter is about 12 Years old, and had on when he went off a light coloured Cloth Coatee, a striped Jacket, an old Pair of Buckskin Breeches, and an old Beaver Hat; and has short flaxey Hair, a fair Complexion, and a remarkable shrewd and cunning Aspect. Any Person or Persons that will apprehend the said eloping Vagrants, shall be intitled to FIVE DOLLARS for each, together with a reasonable Allowance adequate to the Trouble and Expence they may have been got to in securing the same.

CORNELIUS RYAN.

N. B. All Masters of Vessels are hereby forewarned carrying off the said Apprentices, as they may expect to be prosecuted with the utmost Rigour of the Law.

The New-York Gazette; and the Weekly Mercury, October 4, 1773;
October 11, 1773; October 19, 1773; November 1, 1773.

FORTY SHILLINGS REWARD.

RUN-AWAY *from the subscriber, on Sunday the 3d inst. a negro fellow named YORK: Had on when he went away, a green pea jacket, and long tarry trowsers; he is of a black complexion. Whoever brings him to the subscriber shall be entitled to the above reward.*

THOMAS MOORE.

N. B. All masters of vessels are forbid to carry him off, or any person from harbouring him, as they may expect to answer it as the law directs.

The New-York Gazette; and the Weekly Mercury, October 4, 1773;
October 11, 1773.

New-York, October 4, 1773.

RAN AWAY from the subscriber, an indented servant man named JAMES BIRMINGHAM, by trade an upholsterer, and has followed it in Philadelphia, but since has been a dray-man in New-York: He is about five feet eight inches high, of a dark complexion, full faced, black eyes, and hair tied behind, very talkative, and chews tobacco; it is likely he will change his name, as he pretends to be an Englishman, and sometimes an Irishman, according to the company he gets into; it is needless to mention his cloaths, as he has got a chest with different suits with him. Whoever apprehends the said servant, so that his master may have him again, shall receive FIVE DOLLARS reward, and all reasonable charges, from me

M. EDEN, Brewer, on Golden-Hill, or

Capt. THOMAS ALBERSON, in Philadelphia.

The Pennsylvania Packet; and the General Advertiser, October 11, 1773.

FIVE POUNDS Reward.

RUN-AWAY on the 6th day of June last, from Alexander White, Esq; high sheriff of the county of Tryon, one JEREMIAH BOICE; he is about 25 years of age, 5 feet 9 inches high, stout made, with lightish colour'd hair; he understands all kind of farmer's business, and has lost one of his large toes: Had on when he absented himself, a blue coat, and a red waistcoat, trim'd, with brass buttons. He went off in company with one JOSHUA AGAN, an apprentice to Gilbert Tice, of Johnstown; he is about 5 feet 5 inches high, slim made, of a fair complexion, much addicted to liquor, and a profane swearing fellow. They are supposed to have gone to New-Jersey, or Egg-Harbour. Whoever takes up said fellows, and confines them in any of his

Majesty's goals, so that they may be had again, shall receive FIVE POUNDS for each, with all reasonable charges, from
ALEXANDER WHITE, GILBERT TICE.
The New-York Gazette; and the Weekly Mercury, October 18, 1773; October 25, 1773; November 1, 1773.

Ten Dollars Reward.

RAN away, on Sunday morning last, from the subscriber, in Broad-street, an apprentice lad named Matthew Pryor, by trade a Peruke-Maker, about 18 years of age, four feet ten inches high, and has brown hair. He had on, when he went away, a new suit of light cloaths, and took with him other cloaths, &c. Whoever takes up the said apprentice, and secures him in any gaol, so that his master may get him again, shall have the above reward, and all reasonable charges, October, 26, 1773.
paid by JAMES DEAS.
N. B. All masters of vessels are forwarned carrying him off.
Rivington's New-York Gazetteer, October 28, 1773; November 4, 1773; November 11, 1773.

SEVEN POUNDS Reward.

RUN-away from the subscribers living in the town of Goshen, on Wednesday the 19th ult. the two following persons, viz. One of them an apprentice lad named WILLIAM DARBY, about 19 years old, five feet five inches high, has a good many large freckles in his face, light brown hair, and of a mild soft speech; had on when he went away, a blue short coat and a short green jacket, leather breeches, a pair of blue stockings with white spots, and a white chip hat without lining: He carried with him one shirt, one pair of leather breeches, a short light coloured coat and breeches, one pair of light coloured ribbed fale stockings, and a felt hat; as said Darby has worked at the blacksmith's trade it is thought he will endeavour to get into that business. The other is named SAMUEL EVENS, who has escaped from his bail, twenty eight years old, about five feet eight inches high, well set, fresh coloured, black hair very thin on his head and somewhat curled, is very fond of drink and company, boasts greatly of his strength, speaks very thick and short, and pretends to be something of a shoe-maker and carpenter; he has but very coarse cloathing, and is country born. Whoever takes up the former and secures him so that the subscribers may have him, shall have forty shillings reward, and for the latter five pounds reward, and all reasonable charges
paid by JAMES BUTLER, RICHARD BAYLIS.
The New-York Gazette; and the Weekly Mercury, November 1, 1773; November 8, 1773; November 22, 1773.

RUN AWAY, on the 19th of October, 1773, from Trenton Ferry, in Pennsylvania, a servant man, named JOHN SMITH, born in Staffordshire, England, about 6 feet high, round shouldered, otherwise will made, has a thin visage, brown short hair; had on, when he went away, a half worn castor hat, with a small brim, blue inside jacket, without sleeves, an old brown outside jacket, tow trowsers, no stockings, half soaled shoes, and carved white metal buckles. It is thought he made towards New-York, being formerly in the service of Mr. Maslin, of that city. Whoever apprehends said servant, and secures him, so that either of the subscribers may have him again, shall have a reward of THREE POUNDS, and reasonable charges.
WILLIAM PAXSON, PATRICK COLVIL.
All masters of vessels are forbid to carry him off, at their peril.
The Pennsylvania Gazette, November 3, 1773; November 17, 1773; December 1, 1773.

SIX DOLLARS reward.
RUN away, on the 24th day of October, 1773, from the subscriber, living in the Forks township, Northampton county, a servant man, named ABRAHAM FITCHET, or FISHER, who was advertised in the Pennsylvania Gazette last April, No. 2316, born on Staten-Island, of English descent, he is about 34 years of age, 5 feet 6 inches high, of a ruddy complexion, small faced, redish beard, several powder spots in his face by the flash of a gun, and his face thin and lean, short black hair, speaks good English, and sometimes Low Dutch, is much given to liquor, and to talk of the war, as he has been out three or four campaigns last war; had on, when he went away, a half-worn felt hat, a new brown lincey jacket, with small cuffs, with metal or pewter buttons, a new under blue and white Wilton jacket, home made, with buttons of the same, a new coarse homespun linen shirt, tow and linen trowsers, a pair of new shoes, with large square carved brass buckles, black and white yarn stockings. Perhaps he may change his clothes, as he of used to do. Whoever takes up said servant, and secures him in any of his majesty's goals, so that his master may have him again, shall have the above reward, and, if brought home, reasonable charges,
paid by JOHN VAN ETTEN.
***He has been a Sailor; all masters of vessels are forbid to carry him off, at their peril.
The Pennsylvania Gazette, November 3, 1773; November 17, 1773. See The Pennsylvania Gazette, April 28, 1773, The New-York Gazette; and the Weekly Mercury, May 10, 1773, and The Pennsylvania Gazette, October 12, 1774.

FIVE DOLLARS Reward.

RUN-AWAY from the subscriber, on the 1st inst. an Irish servant man named JAMES ROSBOTTOM, by trade a weaver: He has short black hair, a down look, a blemish on his right eye, knock-knee'd, and walks stooping: Had on when he went away, a brown coat and jacket, a light-blue pair of stockings, a pair of tow trowsers, with brass buckles in his shoes: It is probable he may assume the name of Beck. Whoever takes up said servant, and secures him, so that he may be had again, shall have the above reward, and reasonable charges

from   JOHN BECK.

N. B. Masters of vessels and others, are hereby forbid to carry off said run-away, as they may expect to answer it at their peril.

The New-York Gazette; and the Weekly Mercury, November 8, 1773; November 15, 1773; November 22, 1773; December 6, 1773; December 13, 1773; December 27, 1773; January 3, 1774. See *Dunlap's Pennsylvania Packet or, the General Advertiser*, November 29, 1773.

STOLEN

Away from the subscriber, the night after the seventh day of October, a black grey Mare, with a meely nose, with a long feather each side of her neck, natural pacer, thick set, low carriage, better than 13 hands high, and 4 years old.—Also, a bridle, saddle and saddle bays, and two bushels and an half of wheat, and a very long bag; supposed to be stolen by one James Bales, as he calls himself, about middle sized man for height and bigness, short brown curled hair, pale complexion, blue eyes—had on when he went away, a brown wrap-raskel, and an old blue Jacket, striped trowsers, a felt hat, and he was a young man. Whosoever taketh up the said thief and Mare, and returns them to the owner, shall have Five Dollars reward, or half for either of them, and all necessary charges paid,

by me   SAMUEL KNAP, in the Great Nine Partners,

in Dutchess county, colony of New-York.

The Connecticut Courant, And Hartford Weekly Intelligencer, From November 2, to November 9, 1773.

A RUN-AWAY NEGRO

WAS taken up on Tuesday last the 9th inst. on the Post Road between New-York and Albany, near Col. Cortlandt's: He says he belongs to Sir William Johnson, Bart. and that he was by him sent down to New-York, to be shipt, but not liking to go to Sea, ran off. Says his Name is Dick; is a well-set Fellow: Had on a blue Coat and Jacket, Buckskin Breeches with Trowsers

over them. The Fellow is secured in the Goal of the Borough Town of Westchester: From the Goaler of which may be had further Intelligence.
The New-York Gazette; and the Weekly Mercury, November 15, 1773; November 22, 1773.

Ten Dollars
REWARD,

RUN-AWAY, on Tuesday night, from MICHAEL VARIAN, a NEGRO WENCH, named VIOLET, about eighteen years old, of a yellowish colour, about five feet high; she has a scar on her arm, where she was inoculated, about the size of a shilling, and a small blemish in one of her eyes: Before she went off, she took away a large quantity of cloaths, belonging to her mistress, consisting of chintz gowns, two black silk cloaks and hats, a red short cloak, laced caps, &c. Whosoever brings the said Wench to the Bull's-Head in the Bowery Lane, shall receive the above reward.
Rivington's New-York Gazetteer, November 18, 1773.

RUN-AWAY the 19th Instant, from on board of Capt. Henry Wendells's Sloop, an indented Mulatto Servant named Tom Saunders, born on Staten-Island, is about Twenty-two Years of Age, and near six Feet high: Had on when he went away, a white Swanskin Waistcoat and blue Duffles Trowsers. All Persons are forbid to harbour said Servant; and a Reward of Forty Shillings, with reasonable Charges, will be paid to the one that brings him to Capt. Barent Roseboom, of the Sloop Tryon, now lying at the Albany Pier;
        or to Mr. John W. Vredenburgh, living near the same.
The New-York Gazette; and the Weekly Mercury, November 22, 1773; November 29, 1773; December 6, 1773.

                      New-York, 22d November 1773.
RUNAWAY

ON Saturday the 14th inst. from the Subscriber, near the Coffee-House, an Apprentice Lad named SEEMER STOUT, between 18 and 19 Years of Age; full faced, pretty lusty, had dark brown Hair, generally tied behind; is a Shoemaker by Trade, and has about two Years to serve. He had on, a blue Coat with Brass Buttons, a white Shirt and Stock with a Brass Buckle, a Pair of Lamb Skin Breeches, grey Worsted Stockings, long quarter'd Pumps with Pinchbeck Buckles, and a Beaver Hat, made in the present Fashion. Whoever takes up and returns the said Runaway, or secures him giving Notice, so that I may get him again, shall be handsomely rewarded for their Trouble; and all Persons are hereby warned, not to carry off,

conceal, harbour, or entertain the said Apprentice, as they will answer it at their Peril.
                ABRAHAM STOUT.
The New-York Journal; or, The General Advertiser, November 25, 1773; December 2, 1773; December 9, 1773.
                FORTY SHILLINGS REWARD.
RAN AWAY from the subscriber, living in New-York, on the 1st of this inst. (November) an Irish servant man named JAMES ROSSBOUTOM, a weaver by trade, and loves drink; he is a simple down looking fellow, with a sour countenance, pitted with the small-pox, has straight black hair, a blemish on his left eye, and walks stooping and heavy footed; had on when he went away, a brown short coat and waistcoat, tow trowsers, light blue stockings, and an old wool hat: It is suspected he is in Philadelphia, and has changed his name. Whoever takes up and secures said servant, shall have the above reward, and reasonable charges paid by the subscriber, or
      JAMES RIDDLE in Philadelphia.   JOHN BECK.
Dunlap's Pennsylvania Packet or, the General Advertiser, November 29, 1773; December 20, 1773; January 24, 1774. See *The New-York Gazette; and the Weekly Mercury*, November 8, 1773.

                FOUR DOLLARS Reward.
RUN *away from the subscriber, living at Maroneck, West-Chester County, an Apprentice Boy aged about 18 years, middling well grown, light hair and light eyes, freckl'd in his face, and understands something to the shop-joiners trade. Had on when he went away, a wool hat, blue jacket, check shirt, two trowsers, and blue yarn stockings; took with him a pair of leather breeches and a sailor's frock; and was seen at New-York the 16th instant. It is supposed he will endeavour to get on board some vessel outward bound. Whoever will secure him so that his master may have him again, shall have the above reward, and all reasonable charges*
        paid by   GILL BUDD HORTON.
                          Maroneck, Nov. 20, 1773.
    N. B. All Masters of vessels and others, are forbid carrying him off, as they must expect to answer the same.
    The New-York Gazette; and the Weekly Mercury, November 29, 1773; December 6, 1773; December 13, 1773; December 27, 1773; January 3, 1774.

                    ABSCONDED
FROM the subscriber, on the 16th inst. a prisoner named GROVER KNAPP, five feet ten inches high, a little pock pitted, and light brown hair,

tied. Said Knapp stole from Samuel Titus, one hat, a rap-rascal of a blue colour, one waistcoat of a mixt blue colour, and a pocket book with five shillings in cash. Any person or persons that will apprehend said Knapp, and bring him to Goshen goal, or deliver him to either of the subscribers, shall have TEN DOLLARS reward, and all reasonable charges paid.

JOSEPH HOLLY.   SAMUEL TITUS.

Goshen, Dec. 18, 1773

The New-York Gazette; and the Weekly Mercury, December 20, 1773; December 27, 1773; January 3, 1774; January 17, 1774; January 24, 1774.

TEN DOLLARS Reward.

WHEREAS a certain William Hill, on the beginning of Sept. last, did in a fraudulent manner, obtain of the subscriber one pinchbeck watch, with a single case, winds up in the face, the hole where the key goes a little flowered: He is a well made man, about 5 feet 7 inches high, dark complexion, with short curl'd black hair, has an odd kind of speech, somewhat like the high Dutch accent, says he is an Englishman, and a gunsmith, but he has wrought at the silver-smith's business and commonly wears blue cloaths. Whoever apprehends the said William Hill, so that he may be brought to justice and the watch obtained, shall be entitled to the above reward, or for either watch or man five dollars,

paid by   BASIL FRANCIS.

Watch and clock-maker in Albany.

The New-York Gazette; and the Weekly Mercury, December 27, 1773; January 3, 1774; January 10, 1774; January 17, 1774.

TWELVE DOLLARS Reward.

RUN-AWAY on Thursday morning last, from the ship Experiment, George Robson, Master, an apprentice lad named MORGAN POWELL, of low stature, his hair of a yellow cast, smooth face, and large nose; had on when he went away a blue sailor's jacket, and coarse linen short trowsers. Also Run-away from the said ship, JAMES WALKER, a scotch lad, also apprentice to the said master, of middle stature, short black hair, freckled face; had on when he went away an old light blue sailor jacket, but as he took away other cloaths might probably change his dress. Whoever will apprehend the said lads, and bring them to Reade and Yates in New-York, shall receive for Morgan Powell ten dollars reward, and for James Walker two dollars, and all reasonable charges.

N. B. Whoever employs or harbours the said apprentices shall be prosecuted according to law.

The said Morgan Powell was seen by several people this morning, near the seven mile stone on the road the King's-bridge, and seem'd to be returning to New-York.
The New-York Gazette; and the Weekly Mercury, December 27, 1773; January 3, 1774; January 10, 1774; January 17, 1774.

1774

RUN AWAY,
From the Subscriber,
A WHITE boy, named GEORGE WILMOT, twenty years old, of a thin visage, light coloured hair, with a mole on his right cheek: Had on when he went away, a light drab jacket, blue duffil trowsers, and a hat.
All persons are hereby warned from harbouring, or giving him any credit on my account.
GEORGE POWERS.   *Butcher in the Fly-Market.*
Rivington's New-York Gazetteer, January 20, 1774; January 27, 1774.

ON Monday the 17th instant, run-away from the subscriber, an Irish servant man named JOHN M'LARMAN, who I suppose will pass by the name of JOHN GOSSLING: He had on when he went off, a short double breasted drab coloured coating jacket, a pair of blue coat trowsers, plain brass buckles, a wooll hat, streight lank brown hair, about 5 feet 10 inches high, and 23 years old; is a likely streight young fellow. All Captains and Masters of vessels are requested not to take off said servant at their peril. Whoever takes up and secures said fellow so that his master may have him again shall have FIVE DOLLARS reward, and all reasonable charges
            paid by   JEREMIAH REGAN.
The New-York Gazette; and the Weekly Mercury, January 24, 1774.

RUN-away on the 27th Instant, from the Subscriber, an Apprentice Lad, named John Kirk, about 18 Years of Age; had on when he went away a blue Kilmarnock Cap, red Watchcoat, blue Cloth Jacket and blue Duffles Trowsers. Whoever takes up and secures said Apprentice, so that his Master may have him again, shall receive Six Shillings Reward,
        by   CHRISTIAN SCHULTZ, Baker in New-York.
The New-York Gazette; and the Weekly Mercury, January 31, 1774; February 7, 1774; February 14, 1774; February 28, 1774.

RUN AWAY
LAST Night from the Brig Sparrow, Moses Sawyer, Master, two indented Servants, viz. one Indian Fellow, about 25 Years old, about 5 Feet 6 Inches

high, a thick, fat Fellow, with straight, black Hair, something of a down Look. Had on when he ran away, a brown Devonshire Kersey Jacket, lined with red Baise; a red Baise Shirt, and red Duffil Trowsers; and took with him a striped Blanket. The other a Mustee Fellow, with bushy Hair, about 5 Feet 3 or 4 Inches high, had on much the same Clothes as the Other: Took with him a Blanket and sundry other Clothes. Any Person that will secure the said Fellows, in any of his Majesty's Goals, within one Month from the Date, shall receive Ten Dollars Reward,
    by JOHN FOSTER.
  N. B. All Master's of Vessels, or other persons, are forbid carrying off, or harbouring the said Fellows, as it is supposed they are harboured in some Part of this Town.   New-York, Feb. 9, 1774.
 The New-York Journal; or, The General Advertiser, February 10, 1774.

TEN POUNDS REWARD,

ABSCONDED from his bail on Wednesday sen'night, a certain Thomas Lyon, late of Philipsburgh, in the county of West-Chester, and province of New-York, Boatman, about twenty-seven or eight years of age, of a dark complexion, short black hair, a large black beard, about five feet seven or eight inches high, of a down look; as to his dress uncertain. Whoever will apprehend the said Thomas Lyon, and commit him to any of his Majesty's gaols or bring him to the subscriber, shall receive the above reward with all reasonable charges, by applying to the subscriber
    WILLIAM COOLEY.
 Rivington's New-York Gazetteer, February 10, 1774; February 17, 1774; March 3, 1773. See The New-York Gazette; and the Weekly Mercury, February 14, 1774.

TEN POUNDS Reward.

ABSCONDED from his bail, on the second day of February instant, a certain Thomas Lyon, late of Philipsborough, in the county of Westchester, and province of New-York, boatman, about twenty seven or eight years of age, of a dark complexion, short black hair, a large black beard, about five feet seven or eight inches high, a down look, his dress uncertain, went off in company with one Timothy Cronk, of the same place. Whoever will apprehend the said Thomas Lyon, and commit him to any of his Majesty's goals or bring him to the subscriber, shall receive the above reward with all reasonable charges, by applying to
    WILLIAM COLEY.

The New-York Gazette; and the Weekly Mercury, February 14, 1774; February 21, 1774; February 28, 1774; March 7, 1774. See *Rivington's New-York Gazetteer*, February 10, 1773.

TEN DOLLARS Reward.

RUN-away from the Subscriber, an indented Servant Man, named WILLIAM LAWRENCE, about five Feet high, short brown Hair, fair Complexion, has lived with several Gentlemen, can shave and dress hair very well; had on and took with him, a light coloured or red Coat, with blue Lining, a Pair of Leather Breeches and white Stockings, with different coloured Jackets; the said William Lawrence is a Native of Ireland. Whoever takes up the said Servant, and secures him in any of his Majesty's Goals, giving Notice thereof to the Subscriber, shall be entitled to the above Reward, and all reasonable Charges paid. All Masters of Vessels and others are strictly forbid to carry off, conceal, harbour or employ said Servant, as they will answer the contrary at their Peril.

SAMUEL FRAUNCES.

The New-York Gazette; and the Weekly Mercury, April 4, 1774; April 11, 1774; April 18, 1774; April 25, 1774; May 2, 1774; May 9, 1774; May 16, 1774.

FIVE DOLLARS Reward.

RUN-away from the subscriber, living in Westchester, the 28th of March last, a servant man named John Fullanton, but has gone by the name of John Smith, slim built, about 5 feet 7 inches high, walks somewhat lame, knock-kneed, lisps in his speech, says he was born in Scotland, but speaks more upon the north of Ireland accent, sandy complexion, bushy hair, red beard; had on when he went away a long blue coating surtout, pretty much worn, a light mixt coloured coating short coat, almost new, black stocking breeches, an old white coloured waistcoat, brown yarn stockings footed, a pair of shoes almost new, tied with strings, is very talkative, and given to drink. Whoever secures said servant so that his master may have him, shall receive the above reward and reasonable charges

paid by   SAMUEL WEBB.

The New-York Gazette; and the Weekly Mercury, April 11, 1774; April 18, 1774; April 25, 1774; May 2, 1774.

Great Nine-Partners, Dutchess County,

March 30, 1774.

TEN DOLLARS REWARD.

RUN-AWAY about the 22d of March, two young Men, born in Armagh, Ireland, WILLIAM and DANIEL ROWAN, brothers, by trade weavers, and curious workmen, William is about 23 or 24 years of age, 5 feet 10 inches high, slim and active, black hair club'd, his earlocks buckled and kept in form, long visage, a little pitted with the small pocks: Had on when he went off, a light blue coat and vest trimmed with yellow gilt buttons, newly turned, without lining, and took with him a suit of claret coloured broad cloth, with a large gold twist button; his cloaths and hat floped in the present mode.—Daniel is about 21 or 22 years of age, 5 feet 6 inches high, and took with him a suit of light coloured broad cloth, with a gay silver twist button, much pitted with the small pocks, round visage, black hair, turned up at top, as his brother's. They are very fashionable, and talk quite free from the brogue; are insinuating in conversation, and when they have anything to say, speak quick, and deliver it with great earnestness; William, when in company, turns the chat upon trigonometry, navigation, surveying, and other branches of the mathematicks. They walk spry and fast, and are remarkably fopish in their gait.

The public are cautioned to beware of them, as they have taken two creatures not their property, one of which is a black mare, 6 years old, about 14 hand high, three white legs, bald faced, and a natural trotter, value about 20l. and committed several other breaches of trust.—
Whoever secures any or either of them, so as they may be brought to justice, shall receive the above reward, on application to the subscribers.
            SIMON FLAGLOR,   DANIEL HAMILL.

N. B. As it is supposed they may steer for the West-Indies, all masters of vessels are warned not to harbour or ship them, as they would avoid the penalty of the law.

Rivington's New-York Gazetteer, April 14, 1774; April 21, 1774.

TEN DOLLARS Reward.

RAN-AWAY from the Subscriber of Bedford, in the Province of New-York, on Sunday the 10th Instant, two Negro Men, one named Caesar, about 32 Years old, about 6 Feet high, knock-knee'd, has with him a grey Great Coat, two grey Jackets, and a Pair of Leather Breeches. The other named Cuff, about 28 Years old, about 5 Feet 8 Inches high, slim made, is very likely and active, and pretends to be a Sailor; had on a red Great Coat, blue Broadcloth Jacket with Metal Buttons, Swanskin Ditto, blue Duffil Trowsers, and black Breeches. 'Tis supposed they have forg'd a Pass. Whoever shall take up said Negroes, and secure them, or return them to the Subscriber, shall have Ten Dollars Reward for both, or Five Dollars for each, and all reasonable Charges
            paid by me,   LEWIS M'DONALD.

N. B. Masters of Vessels or Others, are forbid concealing or carrying off said Negroes, as they will answer the same at their Peril.

New-Haven, April 13, 1774.
The Connecticut Journal, and the New-Haven Post Boy, April 15, 1774; April 22, 1774; April 29, 1774. See *The New-York Gazette; and the Weekly Mercury*, April 18, 1774.

The following is a Description of
HUGH Mc. CANN.

HE is a native of Ireland, was born in the county of Armagh, has been in America (by his own account) upwards of four years, has practised labouring, and sometimes followed the miller's business: He is about 19 or 20 years of age, about 5 feet 3 and a half inches high, dark brown hair, wears it loose and is quite straight, very much pitted with the small-pox, of a pale complexion; left Crown-Point the 16th of January last, and on Friday the 21st took the road to Hartford in Connecticut; had with him a sorrel coloured gelding, about 15 hands high, rising 5 years old, and a grey mare rising 4 years old; he had on when he went away a light coloured surtout, a nankeen body coat, blue jacket, and brown cloth breeches.

The above Mc. Cann having eloped and feloniously carried away a large sum of money, and other value, being the produce of a stock of goods which he was employed to sell and dispose of, by the subscriber, who will give a reward of TWENTY FIVE DOLLARS, to any person or persons who will apprehend the said Hugh Mc. Cann, and lodge him in any of his Majesty's goals, so that he may be brought to justice.

JOHN WATSON.

N. B. The above reward will be paid on applying to James Wallace, Merchant, at Philadelphia, provided the said Mc. Cann be taken up at that quarter, or by the subscriber living in New-York.

The New-York Gazette; and the Weekly Mercury, April 18, 1774; April 25, 1774; May 2, 1774; May 9, 1774.

RUN away from the subscriber; living at Bedford, Westchester county, on Sunday night last, two Negro men named Caesar and Cuff; Caesar is about 30 years of age, 6 feet one inches high, had on when he went away, a grey great coat, two white jackets, one red ditto, and buckskin breeches: Cuff is about 29 years of age, 5 feet 8 inches high, had on when he went away a red duffils great coat, a blue strait coat, with white linning, a flowered flannel jacket, black everlasting breeches and white stockings. Whoever secures the said runaways, so that their master may have them again, shall have Forty Shillings reward for each, and all reasonable charges
paid by   LEWIS M'DANIEL. April 13, 1774.

The New-York Gazette; and the Weekly Mercury, April 18, 1774; April 25, 1774; May 2, 1774; May 9, 1774. See *The Connecticut Journal, and the New-Haven Post Boy*, April 15, 1774.

FIVE DOLLARS Reward.

PATT. BRYAN (alias O'BRYAN) absented himself from the subscriber on Sunday last, the 24th instant. He is an indented servant, born in Cork, from whence he came to this country last fall in the Needham, Capt. Cheevers; is about five feet four or five inches high, a smooth faced good looking lad, may be 18 or 20 years old, short black hair curled, speaks a little on the native Irish accent, had on a light coloured cloth coat and vest, with plain yellow buttons, the under part of the sleeves of the coat of a different colour, being turned; brown worsted plush breeches, good shoes, pinchbeck buckles, a half-worn beaver hat bound with velvet: He also had with him, a blue broad cloth coat and vest, a grey surtout coat, two pair of white drilling breeches, and some stript summer jackets, several fine white shirts and stocks. As he hath been a very sober orderly boy, 'tis probable he has been decoyed by some artful person, and having several acquaintance [sic] in Philadelphia and Baltimore, may be gone that way; as he can write pretty well, he may forge a pass or a receipt for his passage. Whoever will apprehend and return him to his master, or give information, if at a distance, will be entitled to the above reward,

by WILLIAM NEILSON.

Rivington's New-York Gazetteer, April 28, 1774; *Dunlap's Pennsylvania Packet or, the General Advertiser*, June 13, 1774. *Dunlap's* has "*New-York, April* 25, 1774" at the top and the last line reads "the above reward, by WILLIAM NEILSON in Philadelphia, or JAMES CALDWELL in New-York."

WHEREAS a certain person who went by the name of John Russel, lately taught school in Remsen's bush, in the county of Tryon, and province of New-York, and lodged some time in my house, and then run-away, and fraudulently took out of my house an obligation given me by Messrs. Hugh and Thomas Thompson, of West New-Jersey, for the payment of the sum of 112l. 10s. light money, on the first day of May next, witnesses are John Mehelm, and Hannah his wife; which bond he has lately tendered to said Thompson, with a forged order from me, and demanded the money, saying that all I had was consumed by fire, and that he was sent by me for the money; they suspecting the falsity of it, and the forgery of it, refused payment. In order to prevent his imposing said bond on others, the subscriber desires all persons to be cautious and not to take an assignment thereof, and it offered to any one it is requested that it may be stopped, as

the said Thompson's will pay it to no other but me, and it can be of no service to any body else.—Said Russel is a pretty tall stout fellow, wears streight light brown hair, none on his temples, little or no beard, has been wounded in his right leg, and walks with his knees bending inwardly: He is an Irishman, and has lived sometime in New-England; and when he demanded the money in the Jerseys, he went by the same of Humphrey Thompson, and probably will continue that name, or change it to another.
SAMUEL BARNHARDT.
The New-York Gazette; and the Weekly Mercury, May 2, 1774; May 9, 1774; May 16, 1774.

FIVE DOLLARS Reward.
RUN-away from the subscriber (the 27th April last) living at King's-Bridge, an elderly negro fellow named Jack, about six feet high, bald pated, Guinea mark'd, &c. speaks good English, and has a smattering both of French and Dutch, lived formerly on Staten-Island: had on when he went away, a grey homespun jacket and breeches, with a pair of coarse tow-cloth trowsers. Any person that secures the said negro, so that the owner may have him again, shall be entitled to the above reward, and all reasonable charges, paid by   L. G. TETARD.
N. B. As the fellow has formerly been a sailor, he may probably take to sea; therefore all captains of vessels are forewarned carrying him off at their peril.
The New-York Gazette; and the Weekly Mercury, May 16, 1774; May 23, 1774; June 13, 1774.

New-York, 29th May, 1774.
PATRICK Mc. DURCAN, an Irish boy, about fifteen years old, indented to the subscriber for upwards of four years to come, was sent on an errand last Thursday, about 4 o'clock in the afternoon, and has not since returned. If any person can give information where the said servant now is, or will bring him to the subscriber's house in Broad-street, will be rewarded for the trouble; and whoever carries him off, entertains or employs him after this notice, will be prosecuted; if he returns of himself, and determines to behave as in duty bound from the treatment he has and will meet with, he will this time be forgiven.

He is a well-set boy, wears his own hair which is brown and pretty short: Had on an ozenbrigs frock and trowsers, a good pair of buckskin breeches, an old livery waistcoat, green, laced with yellowish lace, and white metal buttons, a new pair of shoes with brass buckles, but may wear a pair of silver plated buckles, a check shirt, worsted stockings, and an old flapt hat.

JOHN C. KNAPP.
The New-York Gazette; and the Weekly Mercury, May 30, 1774; June 6, 1774; June 13, 1774; June 20, 1774.

RUN AWAY from the subscriber, living in West-chester county, on Tuesday the 24th ult. an indented servant man, named JOHN M'LARNAN, born in the North of Ireland, about 5 feet 11 inches high, 23 or 24 years of age, a strait likely fellow: had on and took with him, a new light coloured short broad cloth coat and jacket, a pair of half worn brown broad cloth breeches, a round wool hat, a pair of half worn shoes, and brass buckles: he took with him a young yellow dog, with a black nose, and a fife, it is very probable that he will change his name; he has several grains of gun-powder plainly to be seen in his right ear and temple, and has the capital letters J. M. C. L. on the back of his left hand. Whoever shall take up and secure said servant, so that his master shall have him again, shall receive FIVE DOLLARS reward, and all reasonable charges,
   paid by JAMES DE LANCEY.
Rivington's New-York Gazetteer, June 2, 1774; *The New-York Gazette; and the Weekly Mercury,* June 6, 1774; June 13, 1774; June 20, 1774; July 4, 1774.

Palatine District, County of Tryon, May 1st, 1774.
EIGHT DOLLARS REWARD.
RUN *away from the subscriber, on the 5th of April last, an indented servant man named Adam Vicetur, about six feet high, aged about forty years, thick and well set, sandy hair curled the wrong way, has an extraordinary red face; talks English, Low Dutch and High German. Had on a pair of deer skin breeches, a swan skin jacket, and a blanket coat. Whoever takes up the above servant, and lodges him in any of his Majesty's goals, shall receive the above reward by*
   JASPER NESTELL, *in New-York, or*
   MARTINUS NESTELL, *living in the above district.*
The New-York Gazette; and the Weekly Mercury, June 6, 1774; June 13, 1774; June 20, 1774.

RUN-*away from their bail, living in New-York, the first instant and are supposed to be gone towards Philadelphia, two Men, one of which named John David Pulby, was born in Dantzick, but talks pretty good English, is about 5 feet 4 inches high, lightish brown curled hair, and wants the little finger of his right hand. The other is named Victor Beard, a Frenchman born, but has been in America several Years, about 5 feet 10 inches high, short curled hair, is stout and well set. Whoever takes up and secures the*

said run-aways, and will lodge them in any goal so that they may be had again, shall receive 40s. *for each, and all reasonable charges,*
    paid by PETER HALL.
The New-York Gazette; and the Weekly Mercury, June 6, 1774; June 13, 1774; June 20, 1774.

Five Dollars Reward.

RAN AWAY from the subscriber living in Philadelphia, a servant man named David Foster, who since his elopement has changed his name to David Wear; he is five feet eight inches high, fair complexion, smooth faced, his hair commonly clubbed or tied; he is very fond on strong liquor, and full of talk when in drink. He was formerly an assistant to one Andrew Porter, schoolmaster in Philadelphia, and is it now thought he is teaching school at a place called Still-Water; he writes a good hand, teaches figures, and understands the Latin tongue; he has forged a pass for himself by which any person may employ him. Whoever secures said servant in any of his Majesty's gaols, so that his master may have him again, shall have the above reward, and all reasonable charges
    paid by ANDREW MOYNIHAN, JEREMIAH REILY,
         Shoemaker, in Battoe-Street, New-York
Rivington's New-York Gazetteer, June 9, 1774.

Five Dollars Reward.

RAN AWAY on the night of the 4th Instant, from Abraham Lawrence, living at Flushing, on Long-Island, a Negro Man named GEORGE, about 5 feet 8 inches high, very thin visaged, of a yellowish complexion, and has black bushy hair, which he commonly wears tied behind; had on and took with him a whitish linen coat, a grey homespun coat, blue jacket, buff-coloured half-worn velvet breeches, with some patches, black stockings, and old shoes, and most commonly wears his hat cocked; though may change his coat to a brown. Whoever takes up said run-away and returns him to his master, or secures him in any of his majesty's gaols, with giving his master notice thereof, shall have FIVE DOLLARS reward, and all reasonable charges paid by the subscriber. All masters of vessels and others, are forbid carrying off, or harbouring said run-away, as they will be dealt with according to law.
    ABRAHAM LAWRENCE. Flushing, June 6th, 1774.
N. B. He has been seen in New-York with a bundle of cloaths tied up in a handkerchief, which he stole the night before he came off. He came over Long-Island Ferry to New-York on Sunday the 5th instant, in company with a white man who paid his ferriage. It is supposed they are both gone to the Eastward.

Rivington's New-York Gazetteer, June 9, 1774; June 16, 1774; June 22, 1774. See *The New-York Gazette; and the Weekly Mercury*, June 13, 1774.

FIVE DOLLARS Reward.

RAN AWAY on the Night of the 4th Instant, from ABRAHAM LAWRENCE, living in Flushing, on Long-Island, a Negro Man named GEORGE, he is of a yellowish Complexion, has black bushy Hair, which he commonly wears tied behind; 5 feet 8 inches high; had on and took with him a whitish Linen Coat, a grey homespun Coat, blue Jacket, Buff coloured half-worn Velvet Breeches, with some Patches, black Stockings, and old Shoes, and most commonly wears his Hat cocked; tho' may change his Coat to a brown.—Whoever takes up said Run-away and returns him to his Master, or secures him in any of his Majesty's Goals, with giving his Master Notice thereof, shall have FIVE DOLLARS Reward, and all reasonable Charges paid by the Subscriber.—All Masters of Vessels and others, are forbid carrying off, or harbouring said Run-away, as they will be dealt with according to Law.

ABRAHAM LAWRENCE.   Flushing, June 6th, 1774.

The New-York Gazette; and the Weekly Mercury, June 13, 1774; June 20, 1774; June 27, 1774; July 4, 1774; July 11, 1774. See *Rivington's New-York Gazetteer*, June 9, 1774.

June 15th, 1774.

RUN AWAY from the subscriber living in Stratford, a Mulatto slave about 6 feet high, had on when he went away, a blue coat, felt hat, black lasting breeches, and had divers other clothes with him, has lost the fore finger from his left hand; he has also iniced away with him a lad of about 17 years of age, about 5 feet 3 inches high, black hair, had on a green coat and jacket. Whoever takes them up, and returns them, or either of them to me, if in New-York, or any other place out of Connecticut, shall have Ten Dollars each, and half that sum if in Connecticut, and reasonable charges paid by me   WILLIAM NICHOLS.

The New-York Journal; or, The General Advertiser, June 23, 1774; June 30, 1774; June 7, 1774; June 14, 1774.

Six Dollars Reward.

RAN AWAY an indented servant, named John Mure, lately arrived from Scotland, about 18 years of age, 5 feet 6 inches high, pale faced, just out of a fit of sickness, wears his own hair; had on when he went away, two white Swanskin jackets, one red strip'd do. one pair of wide trowsers, one pair of Check do. two pair of brown Tow-cloth do. three check shirts, one white

do. one pair of Claret coloured breeches, two pair of ribb'd stockings.—
Whoever takes up the said John Mure and brings him to Garret Rapalje, shall have *SIX DOLLARS* reward: it is expected he has shipped himself as a sailor, on board some vessel, therefore all Masters of vessels, are forbid to take him off.
   Rivington's New-York Gazetteer, June 16, 1774; June 22, 1774; July 7, 1774.

RUN away from the Subscriber on the 11th instant, an apprentice boy about 16 years of age, named William Winten; he has short straight red hair, pretty much freckled in the face, is very impudent, and much given to talking: Had on a wool hat, a check shirt, a red cloth waistcoat lined with blue baize, and a pair of cream coloured cloth breeches. It is supposed he will endeavour to travel to Major Skene's patent, beyond Albany, under a pretence of seeing a man who he calls his father. Whoever takes up and secures said boy, so that his master may get him again, shall have Ten Shillings reward, and all reasonable
   charges by me JEREMIAH WOOL.
   The New-York Gazette; and the Weekly Mercury, June 20, 1774; June 27, 1774; July 4, 1774; July 11, 1774; July 18, 1774.

FIVE DOLLARS Reward.

ELOP'D on Wednesday morning the 22d inst. an indented servant man named WILLIAM MAIN: he arrived here in the brig Commerce, Capt. Nicholls, from Glasgow, is about 5 feet 5 inches high, and of a lathy [*sic*] make; black short hair, black eyes, thin fac'd, and speaks broad Scotch: had on when he went off, a light-colour'd broad cloth coat, black vest, breeches and stockings, and took with him a vest of the same as the coat, with an old black coat and new trowsers: he says he lived four years in Glasgow, and proposes himself the occupation of a schoolmaster, altho' he writes a bad hand, but is a little acquainted with the rudiments of the latin. Whoever will please to secure him, and will bring him to H. Gaine, shall be paid the above reward, will all reasonable charges.
   The New-York Gazette; and the Weekly Mercury, June 27, 1774; July 4, 1774; July 11, 1774; July 18, 1774.

EIGHT DOLLARS Reward.

RUN-AWAY from the subscriber, living at the corner of Beekman's-slip, an apprentice boy named JEREMIAH M'GOUN, by trade a barber, a thick short fellow, about five feet three inches high, brown hair, and freckled face, whose look won't recommend him to the favour of many; had on when he went away a light coloured cloth coat, with plain silver buckles, a

pair of black stocking breeches, linen stockings, an old beaver hat. Whoever takes up and secures the said runaway so that I may have him again, shall receive the above reward, and all reasonable charges
    by JAMES THOMPSON.
Masters of vessels and others are forbid carrying him off at their peril.
 The New-York Gazette; and the Weekly Mercury, July 4, 1774; July 11, 1774; July 18, 1774.

RUN AWAY

ON *Tuesday the* 28*th ult. June, from Frederick Brideam, at Spring Gardens, New-York, an Apprentice Lad, named JOHN BURKE, born in the Province of New-York, aged about* 16 *Years, about* 5 *Feet high, thin made, and pale, black Hair and Eyes, has not had the Small-Pox; had on a Pair of homespun Trowsers, new Check Shirt, coarse whitish Waistcoat without Sleeves, and a Wool Hat: Had with him a new Nankeen Waistcoat and Breeches, took away a considerable Sum of Silver Money. Whoever takes up and returns, or secures the said Apprentice, shall receive a Reward of THIRTY SHILLINGS New-York Money.*
    FREDERICK BRIDEAM.
 The New-York Journal; or, The General Advertiser, July 7, 1774; July 14, 1774; July 21, 1774; July 28, 1774.

               New-York, June 24, 1774.
RUN-AWAY from his bail on Monday last, Samuel Gamble, born in Ireland, a middle sized brown complexioned man, about 33 years of age, he has a cast in his right eye, a cut in his nose, and a carbunkle face, it is supposed he is gone to Philadelphia. Whoever apprehends him, and puts him in prison, shall have Twenty Shillings reward, and all reasonable charges, from
    RUTH PERRY, near the Coffee-House.
 Rivington's New-York Gazetteer, July 7, 1774. See *The New-York Gazette; and the Weekly Mercury,* July 11, 1774.

RUN-*away from his bail on the* 26*th of June last, Samuel Gamble, a native of Ireland, by trade a taylor, of a middle size, brown complexion, about* 33 *years of age, has a cast in his right eye, a cut in his nose, and a carbunckle face: Had on when he went off, a light coloured coat and red jacket with black spots, black breeches, white stockings, and plated shoe buckles. It is supposed he is gone to Philadelphia. Whoever apprehends him, and puts him in prison, shall have Twenty Shillings reward, and reasonable charges,*
    From *RUTH PERRY, near the Coffee-House.*

The New-York Gazette; and the Weekly Mercury, July 11, 1774; July 25, 1774. See *Rivington's New-York Gazetteer*, July 7, 1774.

EIGHT DOLLARS REWARD.

To the person or persons who will SECURE WILLIAM BAILEY, a run-away servant, in any of his Majesty's goals, on the continent of America, on their giving notice to any of the following persons, viz. Mr. John Kennedy, merchant, in Baltimore, Maryland, Messrs. Boyle and Glen, merchants, in Philadelphia, or to his master, John Shaw, merchant, in New-York. The abovementioned run-away is about 5 feet 7 inches high, smooth complexion, and mild address, knows something of the weaving business, writes a good hand, and has kept a school for some time past, and it is probable may have a forged pass with him. He was seen in Philadelphia in May last: Had on a white coat and waistcoat, and old fustian breeches. It is supposed he is gone towards Baltimore or Lancaster: He has behaved in the most ungrateful manner to the subscriber, who will pay, exclusive of the above reward, all reasonable charges in conveying him to prison, and bringing the account
        to   JOHN SHAW, in New-York.

The Pennsylvania Journal, and the Weekly Advertiser, July 13, 1774; July 20, 1774; September 7, 1774; September 14, 1774; *Dunlap's Pennsylvania Packet or, the General Advertiser*, August 29, 1774; September 12, 1774; *The Pennsylvania Gazette*, October 12, 1774. Minor differences between the papers. See *The Pennsylvania Journal, and the Weekly Advertiser*, December 7, 1774.

TWENTY SHILLINGS Reward.

RUN-away from the subscriber, living at Ramapough, in Orange County, on Sunday the 10th instant, a negro man named Hack, about 40 years of age, 5 feet 4 inches high, not very black: Took with him a green broad cloth coat, and one white ditto, the other cloaths he had with him unknown. Whoever secures the said negro so that his master may have him again, shall receive the above reward,
        paid by me   LAWRENCE VAN BUSKIRK.

The New-York Gazette; and the Weekly Mercury, July 18, 1774; July 25, 1774.

FIVE DOLLARS REWARD.

RAN-AWAY from the subscriber the 19th instant, an indented servant man, named George Patterson, born in Perth-Shire in North-Britain, by trade a Blacksmith, about 22 years of age, pockpitted, dark complexion, down-looking, he is a thick well set fellow and arrived here in the George,

Capt. Bog, from Greenock; had on a blue lappell'd coatee with yellow buttons, blue jacket, ozenbrigs trowsers and a course [*sic*] white shirt.— Whoever takes up and secures the said servant, so that he may be had again, shall have the above reward and all reasonable charges
paid, by WILLIAM SMITH.
Rivington's New-York Gazetteer, July 21, 1774; July 28, 1774.

Broke out of Litchfield County Goal, the Night after the 25th of July instant, Philip Rollins, who was committed for Horse-stealing, is about 25 Years old, 5 Feet 9 Inches high, short black Hair, pitted with the Small Pox, wore a blue Surtout, and blue Breeches, and had a pair of old Yarn Stockings, says that he was born on Long-Island. Whoever will take up said Fellow and return him to the Goal from whence he made his Escape, shall have Thirty Shillings Reward.
WILLIAM STANTON, Goaler.   Litchfield, 26th July, 1774.
The Connecticut Courant, and Hartford Weekly Intelligencer, July 26, 1774; August 2, 1774; August 16, 1774.

WHEREAS on Tuesday the 19th instant, a person of a middle stature, something swarthy, drest in a light brown coat, white vest, and tie wig, took a black gelding from the subscriber, under pretence of going to King's Bridge, about 14 hands and an inch high, with a blaze running into his near nostril, part of one hind foot white, is something sun burnt, trots and canters well, and is about six years old; with a hunting russet saddle and bridle, not much worn; and as he has not been heard of since, though strict inquiry hath been made after him, it is more than probable he intends to go off with the horse: In order therefore that he may be detected in his evil design, the sum of Five Pounds New-York currency will be paid to any one that shall apprehend the above described person, so that he may be brought to justice, and the horse, &c. restored to the owner; and Three Pounds for the horse alone, with reasonable charges.
GARRIT PATERSON.
The New-York Gazette; and the Weekly Mercury, July 25, 1774; August 1, 1774; August 8, 1774.

New-York, July 27, 1774.
FIFTY POUNDS REWARD.
WHEREAS on the 19th of June last past, a certain JOSEPH THORP was entrusted with a considerable sum in Half Johannes, of nine penny weight, to be delivered by him at Quebec, and as he has not yet made his appearance there, with other suspicious circumstances, it is apprehended that he is gone off with the money. He is a native of England, about six feet

high, swarthy complexion, very dark keen eyes, and pitted with the small pox, of a slender make, stoops as he walks, talks rather slow, with some small impediment in his speech. He lived some time in Boston, from whence he removed to Quebec, assuming the character of a merchant in both places; he was also once in trade in New-Castle, Virginia, and has a brother settled there. It is believed he went on board Captain John F. Pruym, for Albany, and took with him a blue casimer, and a dark brown suit of cloaths.

Whoever secures the said JOSEPH THORP in any of his Majesty's gaols on this continent, shall be entitled to ten per cent, on the sum recovered, and the above reward of FIFTY POUNDS when convicted. Apply to Curson and Seton of New York, Joseph Wharton, jun. of Philadelphia, Robert Christie, of Baltimore, James Gibson, and Co. Virginia, John Bonfield, of Quebec, Melatiah Bourne, or John Rowe, of Boston. It is requested of those that may have seen this Joseph Thorp, since the 19th of June last past, or know any thing of the rout he has taken, that they convey the most early intelligence thereof to any of the above persons, which will be gratefully acknowledged.

All Masters of Vessels are forewarned from taking him off the continent.

Dunlap's Pennsylvania Packet or, the General Advertiser, August 1, 1774; September 5, 1774; September 19, 1774; *The Pennsylvania Journal, and the Weekly Advertiser*, August 3, 1774; August 17, 1774; August 31, 1774; *Rivington's New-York Gazetteer*, August 4, 1774; August 11, 1774; August 18, 1774; September 2, 1774; September 22, 1774; September 29, 1774; *The Boston Evening-Post*, August 15, 1774; August 22, 1774; *The Boston-Gazette, and Country Journal*, August 15, 1774; August 22, 1774; August 29, 1774; *The Newport Mercury*, August 15, 1774; August 22, 1774; August 29, 1774; *The Massachusetts Spy Or, Thomas's Boston Journal*, August 18, 1774; September 8, 1774; September 15, 1774; September 29, 1774; *The New-York Journal; or, The General Advertiser*, August 18, 1774; September 1, 1774; September 8, 1774; September 15, 1774; September 22, 1774; September 29, 1774; October 6, 1774; October 13, 1774; October 20, 1774; October 27, 1774; November 10, 1774; November 17, 1774; November 24, 1774; December 1, 1774; December 22, 1774; *The Connecticut Journal, and the New-Haven Post Boy*, August 19, 1774; *The Massachusetts Gazette: and the Boston Weekly News-Letter*, August 25, 1774; *The Connecticut Gazette; and the Universal Intelligencer*, August 26, 1774; *Boston News-Letter*, September 1, 1774; *The New-York Gazette; and the Weekly Mercury*, August 8, 1774; August 15, 1774; August 22, 1774;

September 5, 1774; September 12, 1774; October 3, 1774; November 14, 1774; November 21, 1774; December 5, 1774; December 12, 1774; December 19, 1774. *Minor differences between the papers. In several ads the man's name appears as Throp.* See *The New-York Gazette; and the Weekly Mercury*, October 3, 1774, and *The Boston Evening-Post*, January 9, 1775.

FOUR POUNDS Reward.

RUN-AWAY from the subscriber about the 16th ult. living on Long-Island, two Indian Men, one of them named Peter January, upwards of 5 Feet high, and has some grey Spots in his Head; the other named John Honce, about 5 Feet 7 Inches high. Whoever takes up the said Indians, and secures them in any of his Majesty's Goals, shall have the above Reward, or Forty Shillings for either of them.

RICHARD FLOYD.

The New-York Gazette; and the Weekly Mercury, August 1, 1774; August 8, 1774. See *The Newport Mercury*, September 12, 1774.

Schohary, July 17, 1774.
FIVE POUNDS Reward.

RUN away from the subscriber living in Schohary, the 6th instant, a Negro man named BRAM, he is of a yellowish complexion, much pock mark'd; about five Feet six inches high; had on when he went away, a white woollen homespun jacket, a wool hat, a woollen shirt, buckskin breeches, linen trowsers, a pair of grey stockings, a good pair of shoes, and plated buckles.

Whoever takes up said Negro, and secures him in any of his Majesty's goals, so that his master may have him again, or delivers him to Jacob C. Ten Eyck, Esq; at Albany, shall receive the above reward, with all reasonable charges.

JOHN J. BACHER.

N. B. All masters of vessels and others, are hereby forwarned not to harbour of carry off said negro.

The New-York Gazette; and the Weekly Mercury, August 1, 1774; August 8, 1774; September 5, 1774; September 12, 1774; *Rivington's New-York Gazetteer*, September 2, 1774; September 29, 1774. *Minor differences between the papers. Rivington's does not have the location and date at top, and states he ran away "the 6th of July last".*

RUN-away from Abraham Schenk, a Servant Man named James Spence, lately arrived from Scotland: Had on when he went away a blue mixed Coat, a red Jacket, and Osnabrig Trowsers. He is about 5 Feet 9 Inches high, between thirty and forty Years of Age, pretends to be a Carpenter by

Trade; one of his fore Fingers stiff, writes a good Hand, curled Hair, lately cut one of his Legs, which is not yet healed, pretends to be very Religious. Whoever takes up the said Servant and brings him to Capt. John Tanner, in New-York, near the White-Hall; or to Abraham Schenck, in New-Rochelle, or secures him in any of the Goals, shall receive THREE POUNDS Reward, and all reasonable Charges
    paid by ABRAHAM SCHENK.
The New-York Gazette; and the Weekly Mercury, August 22, 1774; August 29, 1774; September 5, 1774; September 12, 1774.

New York, August 19, 1774.
THREE DOLLARS Reward.
RUN away, some time ago, from the Subscriber, living at the upper end of Leary-street, a servant girl, whose name cannot be well known, she has assumed so many names at different times and places; she has called herself *Hannah Swinburn, Hutcheson, Nancy Ring*, &c. has sometimes said England and other times Ireland was the place of her nativity; she can speak French tolerably well, by a careful inspection, she may easily be known by her ruddy complexion, and especially by her second finger on the left hand being remarkably crooked: She had on, when she went away, a long calicoe gown, striped with red, a green petticoat, and a round hat; she was seen on Tuesday last near Princeton, on the road leading to Philadelphia, and is supposed to be gone thither, and will be very aft to associate with those of her own sex, who are of infamous characters. Whoever takes up the said servant girt, and secures her, so that her master may have her again, shall receive the above reward, and all reasonable charges,
    paid by PETER GARSON.
  N. B. All Masters of vessels and others, are forbid to harbour or carry her off at their peril.
The Pennsylvania Gazette, August 24, 1774.

Manor of St. George, August 23, 1774,
RAN away from the subscriber, at the manor of St. George on the south side of Long Island, opposite to Brookhaven, a mulatto slave, half Negro and half Indian, named DICK, about 5 feet 8 inches high, full faced, and has thick lips, bushy hair, and is about 23 years of age. He carried with him a bundle of clothes, which cannot be particularly described, except a red cloth jacket among them, and a blue cloth coat.—Also ran away, along with him, from Colonel Nathaniel Woodhull, of the same place, an Indian fellow named JOE, 20 years of age, about 5 feet 6 inches high. Whoever takes up either of the said fellows, and secures him or them in any of his Majesty's gaols, or shall bring one or both of them to their said masters, shall have

twenty shillings reward for each of them, if taken up in this colony, and five pounds for each if taken in any other colony, and all reasonable charges,
paid by   WILLIAM SMITH.

The New-York Journal; or, The General Advertiser, August 25, 1774; September 1, 1774; September 8, 1774; September 15, 1774; *The Connecticut Journal, and the New-Haven Post Boy*, September 16, 1774; September 23, 1774.

EIGHT DOLLARS REWARD.

RAN AWAY from the subscriber, a servant man named WILLIAM BAILEY, about five feet seven inches high, of a smooth complexion, mild address, knows something of the weaving business, writes a good hand, has kept a school for some time past, and 'tis probable may have a forged pass with him: Had on a white coat and waistcoat, and old fustian breeches: He was seen in Philadelphia in May last, and it is supposed is gone towards Baltimore or Lancaster. Whoever will secure said the servant in any of his Majesty's gaols, shall have the above Reward, on giving notice to Mr. JOHN KENNEDY, merchant, in Baltimore, Mr. JOHN BOYLE, merchant, in Philadelphia, or to the subscriber, merchant, of New-York, who will pay all reasonable charges to conveying him to gaol and bringing the account
in to   JOHN SHAW.

Dunlap's Pennsylvania Packet or, the General Advertiser, August 29, 1774; September 12, 1774. See *The Pennsylvania Journal, and the Weekly Advertiser*, July 13, 1774, and *The Pennsylvania Journal, and the Weekly Advertiser*, December 7, 1774.

New-York, July 5, 1774.

RAN AWAY from his security, a certain JAMES HUNT, a New-England young man, by trade a hatter, wore his own hair, smooth faced, and slender, is supposed to have gone to Philadelphia or Carolina to work at his trade. Whoever shall apprehend and take him up, and lodge him in any of his Majesty's gaols, so that his security may have him again, shall have FOUR POUNDS, New-York currency, Reward, and all reasonable charges paid, by applying to the Printer hereof, or to the subscriber living in New-York,
NESBITT DEANE.

Dunlap's Pennsylvania Packet or, the General Advertiser, August 29, 1774; September 19, 1774.

FIVE DOLLARS Reward.

RUN-AWAY from the subscriber living in Schoharie district, in the county of Albany, and province of New-York, a negro man named PRINCE: Had on when he went away, a black homespun jacket, a coarse white linen shirt,

a pair of linen breeches, an old beaver hat bound with a yellow ribbon, and a pair of old shoes. Whoever takes up said negro, so that his master may have him again, shall have the above reward, and all reasonable charges,
   paid by Jacob Van Schaick, in Albany,
       or Johannis Lawyer, jun. in Schoharie.
The New-York Gazette; and the Weekly Mercury, August 29, 1774; September 12, 1774.

       RAN AWAY,
ABOUT a four [sic] weeks ago, from the farm of Charles Aitkin, Esq; at Haerlem, a mulatto man, named PIEROT: he is about 5 feet 8 inches high, near 40 years old: he was born in the West-Indies.
 Whoever takes him up and brings him to Mr. Lawrence Kortwright, in New-York, shall have TWENTY SHILLNGS reward, and all reasonable charges paid.
Rivington's New-York Gazetteer, September 2, 1774.

RUN-away from his bail, from on board the Golden Rule, Capt. Cragg, lately arrived from the Isle of Whitehorn; a certain JOHN M'CREADY, about 30 years of age, 5 feet 10 inches high, spare fac'd, black visage, short black hair, a blacksmith and currier by trade: Had on when he went away, a light blue coat and jacket, black velvet breeches, clouded worsted stockings, and turn'd pumps, took with him a black coat and jacket; and sundry other cloaths. Whoever secures the said run-away and brings him to William M'Dougall, Merchant, New-York, shall have TWENTY SHILLINGS Reward, and all reasonable charges
   paid by PATRICK M'MIKING.
The New-York Gazette; and the Weekly Mercury, September 5, 1774; September 12, 1774.

   Four Pounds, New-York Currency, Reward.
RAN away from the subscriber, about the 16th ult. living on Long-Island, two Indian men, one of them named PETER JANUARY, upwards of 5 feet high, and has some grey spots on his head; the other named JOHN HONCE, about 5 feet 7 inches high, is a little hard of hearing. Whoever takes up the said Indians, and secures them in any of his Majesty's gaols, shall have the above reward, or forty shillings for either of them.
   RICHARD FLOYD.
The Newport Mercury, September 12, 1774; September 19, 1774; September 26, 1774. See *The New-York Gazette; and the Weekly Mercury*, August 1, 1774.

RUN-AWAY on the 8th inst. from the John and Jane, Capt. Abel Chapman, just arrived from London, three indented servants, viz. John Young, about 21 years of age, short stature, large features, and speaks the Northumberland dialect. Alexander Ross, about 19 years of age, pretty tall and thin, white faced, and speaks the Scotch dialect. Thomas Smith, about 14 years of age, short stature, round faced, and marked with the small-pox. Whoever will bring any of the aforesaid servants to Messrs. Curson and Seton, in New-York, or to Capt. Chapman, aforesaid, shall receive a reward of 20s. for each servant.

N. B. All masters of ships are hereby forewarned not to ship the above servants, for if they do they will certainly be prosecuted with the utmost rigour of the law.

The New-York Gazette; and the Weekly Mercury, September 12, 1774; September 19, 1774; October 3, 1774.

Ten Dollars Reward.

R*UN AWAY on Friday the 26th of August, from the Subscriber, living in Middle Patent, North Castle, in Westchester County, and Province of New-York, a Negro Man, named WILL, about 27 Years of Age, 5 Feet 6 Inches high, of a yellow Complexion, a spry lively Fellow, and very talkative; has Part of his right Ear cut off, and a Mark on the back Side of his Hand: Had on when he went away, a Butternut coloured Coat, Felt Hat, and Tow Trowsers. Whoever takes up said Negro, and brings him to his Master, or secures him in any Gaol, so that he may have him again, shall receive the above Reward, and all reasonable Charges*
              paid by   JAMES BANKS.

N. B. All Masters of Vessels, and others, are hereby strictly forbid not to harbour or carry off said Negro, as they must answer it at their Peril.

The New-York Journal; or, The General Advertiser, September 15, 1774; September 22, 1774; September 29, 1774; October 6, 1774. See *Rivington's New-York Gazetteer*, September 15, 1774.

TEN DOLLARS Reward.

RUN AWAY on Friday the 26th of August 1774, from the Subscriber, living in Middle-patent, North-Castle, Westchester county, and Province of New-York,

A NEGRO MAN,

Named WILL, about 27 years of age, five feet six inches high, somewhat of a yellow complexion, a spry lively fellow, and very talkative; had on when he went away, a butter-nut coloured coat, felt hat, tow cloth trowsers; he has part of his right ear cut off, and a mark on the backside of his right hand.

Whoever takes up said Negro and brings him to his master, or secures him in gaol, so that his master may have him again, shall receive the above reward and all reasonable Charges,
        paid by   JAMES BANKS.
N. B. Masters of vessels are hereby warned not to carry off the Negro.
    Rivington's New-York Gazetteer, September 15, 1774; September 22, 1774; *The New-York Gazette; and the Weekly Mercury*, September 24, 1774; October 3, 1774. Minor differences between the papers. See *The New-York Journal; or, The General Advertiser*, September 15, 1774.

TEN DOLLARS Reward.
RUN away from the subscriber, living in New-York, the 10th instant, an indented Scotch servant named JAMES CLARK,
ABOUT twenty five years of age, speaks pretty good English, of a middling stature, comely and well set, something fleshy and fresh coloured, very full faced, and thick lips, and light brown hair; had on, and with him when he went away, a light brown surtout, blue broad cloth jacket, blue plush breeches, several pair of tow cloth and check trowsers, a white jacket neatly wrought or embroidered with silk flowers on the fore parts, a felt hat, and Scotch cap, new shoes and brass buckles, and several white tow shirts, &c. Whoever takes up and secures, or conveys said servant to his master, shall receive the above reward, and reasonable charges,
        paid by   TIDDEMAN HULL.
New-York, the 12th of the 9th month (called September.)
    Rivington's New-York Gazetteer, September 15, 1774; September 22, 1774. See *The New-York Gazette; and the Weekly Mercury*, September 19, 1774.

TEN DOLLARS Reward.
RUN away from the subscriber, living in New-York, the 10th instant, an indented Scotch servant named JAMES CLARK, about 25 years of age, speaks pretty good English, of a middling stature, comely and well set something fleshy and fresh coloured, very full face, thick lips, and light brown hair: Had on and took with him when he went away, a light brown surtout coat, blue broad cloth jacket, blue plush breeches, several pair of tow cloth and check trowsers, a white jacket neatly wrought or embroidered with silk flowers on the fore parts, a felt hat and Scotch cap, new shoes and brass buckles, several white tow shirts, &c. Whoever takes up and secures or conveys said servant to his master, shall receive the above reward and reasonable charges,
        paid by   TIDDEMAN HULL.

The New-York Gazette; and the Weekly Mercury, September 19, 1774; September 26, 1774; October 3, 1774. See *Rivington's New-York Gazetteer*, September 15, 1774.

RUN-away from the subscriber living in New-York, the 10th inst. an indented Scotch servant named JAMES TAYLOR, about 19 years of age, 5 feet 6 or 7 inches high, has a down look, fresh colour, and speaks bad English: Had on when he went away, a light purple coat without flaps, and vest, a pair of corded velvet breeches, and half worn shoes with plated buckles.—Whoever takes up said servant and secures him so that his master may have him again, shall receive FIVE DOLLARS reward, and all reasonable charges,
    paid by THOMAS GARDNER.
The New-York Gazette; and the Weekly Mercury, September 19, 1774; September 26, 1774; October 3, 1774.

WHEREAS *one John M'Mahan, alias Mahony, of Heburn, a taylor by trade on the 19th of July last, took from the subscriber, at New-York, a black gelding, about six years old, with a narrow blaze that runs down into his left nostril, part of one of his hind feet white, trots and canters well, about 14 hands high, somewhat sun-burnt; with a good russet hunting saddle and snaffle bridle, half worn. And whereas the subscriber is informed the said John M'Mahan, was at work, about a fortnight ago, at Pomfret, 64 miles this side of Boston, at one Mr. Greene's, an inn-keeper, and had the horse there, but told the informer that he if he did not find it to his liking he would proceed to Boston. He wears a tie wig, a light coloured hat, and white vest, is pitted with the small pox, and very remarkable in his common discourse for swearing by the god of war. In order that he may be apprehended and brought to justice, I do hereby promise a reward of Ten Pounds to any person that shall apprehend and deliver the horse and saddle to me the owner, in New-York, and Three Pounds for the man.*
    GARRET PETERSON.
The New-York Gazette; and the Weekly Mercury, September 19, 1774; September 26, 1774; October 3, 1774.

STOLEN Out of the pasture of Richard Varian, at Fresh-Water, in the night of the 2d of September, supposed by a man who calls himself Issachar Dean, a black MARE, seven years old, half blooded; she suckled a colt when stolen, is about fourteen hands and three quarters high, a natural trotter, has a very small star in her forehead, and small fellon on the back part of her left eye; thin neck and legs, and a small tail. Whoever takes up said mare, and returns her to the owner at Fresh-Water, and secures the

thief, so that he may be brought to justice, shall have FOUR POUNDS reward, and for the mare alone FIVE DOLLARS,
paid by THOMAS ARDEN.
The New-York Gazette; and the Weekly Mercury, September 19, 1774; September 26, 1774; October 3, 1774.

TEN DOLLARS Reward.
RUN-AWAY *from the Paper-Mill at Hampstead Harbour, on Long-Island, on Sunday Morning the* 12*th Inst. an Apprentice Lad named* SAMUEL HILL, *about* 16 *Years of Age, is a well-looking Lad, and understands something of the Hatter's Business: 'Tis supposed he is gone towards Wall-Kill or Goshen, in Ulster-County, or Kinderhook, in Dutchess, where he has Relations: Those that harbour or secure him may depend on being punished as the Law directs in such Cases. And whoever takes up and secures the said Run-away, so that he may be had again, shall receive the above Reward from* HENRY ONDERDONK,
HENRY REMSEN, *or* HUGH GAINE.
The New-York Gazette; and the Weekly Mercury, September 26, 1774; October 3, 1774.

For Newbern, North-Carolina,
The Brig PRINCE of WALES,
THOMAS ALLEN, Commander,
Run away from said Brig,
An apprentice boy named William Simm, Born in Scotland, about 14 or 15 years of age, speaks the English language tolerably well, had on when he left the brig, an old sailor's jacket and trowsers, neither had hat or shoes; was some days at King's Bridge, which place he left on Tuesday last, and said he was going to New-London. Whoever takes him up, and will bring him to Capt. Allen, or to Jay and Barclay, shall receive a Guinea reward, and all reasonable charges allowed.
Rivington's New-York Gazetteer, September 29, 1774; October 6, 1774; October 13, 1774.

IT is surmised that JOSEPH THORPE, (who was formerly advertised in this and other Papers, with a Reward of £. 50, and 10 per Cent. on the Sum recovered) is still upon this Continent, and thought to be lurking in the interior Parts of the Eastern Colonies. The Public are therefore earnestly requested to keep a sharp look-out at the different Sea Ports, to prevent the Villian's escaping; and also to give whatever information they can respecting him, to any of the Persons mentioned in the Advertisement, that may be nearest to them.

It appears that his real Name is JOSEPH THORPP, a native of Litchfield, in Staffordshire.

The New-York Gazette; and the Weekly Mercury, October 3, 1774; December 5, 1774; December 12, 1774; *Rivington's New-York Gazetteer*, October 6, 1774; October 13, 1774; October 20, 1774; December 8, 1774. See *Dunlap's Pennsylvania Packet or, the General Advertiser*, August 1, 1774; and *The Boston Evening-Post*, January 9, 1775. *Rivingtons* spells the name as THROPP.

FORTY SHILLINGS REWARD.

RUN AWAY from the subscribers, two Scotch indented servants, viz. a woman about 22 years of age, named ISABEL M'ARTHUR, of a ruddy complexion, pitted with the small-pox, dark brown hair, and dark eyes; speaks very bad English: Had on when she went away, a strip'd cotton short gown, a homespun petticoat, and a black bonnet; it is very probable she may change her dress, as she took with her, a green gown, and one of Scotch plaid, with several short gowns of Scotch stuff.

The other a man, named ALEXANDER MORRISON, about 40 years of age, red hair, remarkably clumsy ancles, and crooked feet. Whoever will secure the said servants, so that their masters may have them again, shall receive the above reward, or Twenty Shillings for either,

paid by   ABRAHAM MESIER.   RALPH THURMAN.

The New-York Journal; or, The General Advertiser, October 6, 1774; October 13, 1774; October 20, 1774; October 27, 1774.

EIGHT DOLLARS REWARD.

Yesterday absented from her master, a Scotch indented servant girl, named Martha M'Loud, about 18 years of age, a likely well set person, of a fair complexion, light coloured hair, cut short; had on, when she went away, a round-ear'd cap, cross-barred charlotte gown, of brown and white colours, intermixed with green and white flowers, a blue worsted skirt, two red petticoats, one of which is fine serge, a pair of old buckskin shoes, and white worsted stockings; she lately lived with a certain Alexander Chisholm, Innkeeper, in Burlington, who assigned her to George Bartram, merchant, in Philadelphia, and was by him assigned to me, the first of this instant. Whoever apprehends said servant, and delivers her to her master, the subscriber, or secures her so as she may be had again, shall receive three pounds reward, and all reasonable charges

paid by   John Zell.

The New-York Journal; or, The General Advertiser, October 6, 1774.

October 3, 1774.
Run-away from the Subscriber,
Two Indented Scotch Servants,
THE one named John Robinson, by Trade a Carpenter, about five Feet eight Inches high, of a brown Complexion, with long black Hair cued, had on a light blue Cloth Coat and Breeches, thread Stockings, and white Shirt: the other named John M'Intoch, a Gardener by Occupation, of a brown Complexion, short dark Hair, slim made, had on a dark blue Coat, dirty Buckskin Breeches, and old Worsted Stockings.—Any Person that shall apprehend the said two Servants, or secure them in any Gaol, shall have a Reward of Ten Dollars, or forty Shillings for either of them, and with reasonable charges.   James Van Cortlandt.
Rivington's New-York Gazetteer, October 6, 1774; October 13, 1774. See *The New-York Gazette; and the Weekly Mercury*, October 10, 1774.

RUN-AWAY from the subscriber, two indented Scotch servants, one named John Robinson, by trade a carpenter, about 5 feet 8 inches high, of a brown complexion, with long black hair, queued: Had on a light blue cloth coat and breeches, thread stockings, and white shirt. The other named John M'Lintock, a gardner by occupation, of a brown complexion, short dark hair, and slim made: Had on a dark blue coat, dirty buckskin breeches, and old worsted stockings. Any person that shall apprehend the said two servants, or secures them in any goal, shall have a reward of Ten Dollars, or Forty Shillings for either of them, and with reasonable charges.
JAMES V. CORTLANDT.
The New-York Gazette; and the Weekly Mercury, October 10, 1774; October 17, 1774. See *Rivington's New-York Gazetteer*, October 6, 1774.

R*UN away, the second of October instant, from the subscriber, living in the Borough of Lancaster, an apprentice lad, named* Michael Houseal *(he says he is a son of the Rev. Mr. Houseal, Minister, in New-York) he is a slim, active, ill-natured fellow, about 5 feet 8 or 9 inches high, fair complexion, red sandy coloured hair, tied behind; had on, and took with him, a brown suit of clothes, almost new, of broadcloth, also another coat, of red and white mixed broadcloth, one short coattee, of white fustian, 4 or 5 fine shirts, some with ruffles; he is much pitted in the face with the small-pox, and a sadler by trade. Whoever takes up the said apprentice, and brings him to me, shall have One Dollars reward,* HENRY DEHUFF.
    It is suspected he is gone off with one Jacob Zeigler, an apprentice to Mr. Mendenhall, watch-maker, in Lancaster.

The Pennsylvania Gazette, October 12, 1772. See *The Pennsylvania Gazette,* October 12, 1774.

FOUR DOLLARS and FOUR PENCE Reward.

RUN away from the subscriber, in the Borough of Lancaster, the evening of the first of October instant, an apprentice lad, named JACOB ZEIGLER, about 18 years of age, 5 feet 7 or 8 inches high, palish complexion, of a sour down look, some what freckled, has dark brown hair, which he wears tied; had on a dark brown cloth coatee, striped jacket and trowsers, and a small hat, bound round with sattin ribbon, though he may vary his dress, as he has taken a quantity of cloathing with him; he is much addicted to swearing and keeping evil company; it is thought he is gone towards Baltimore, or New-York, in company with a lad named *Michael [Hershal],* pretty tall and slim, of a pale complexion, marked with the small-pox, and wears his hair tied; they were seen in company the evening *Zeigler* went off. Whoever apprehends and secures the said apprentice, so that he may be had again, shall have Four Dollars of the above reward, and reward, and reasonable charges, paid by MATTHIAS SLOUGH, his guardian, and Four Pence only,

paid by his master. THOMAS MENDENHALL.

The Pennsylvania Gazette, October 12, 1774. See *The Pennsylvania Gazette,* October 12, 1774.

TEN DOLLARS Reward.

RUN away, on the 24th day of October, 1773, [sic] from the subscriber, living in the Forks township, Northampton county, a servant man named ABRAHAM FITCHET or FISHER, born on Staten-Island, of English descent, he is about 34 years of age, 5 feet 6 inches high, of a ruddy complexion, small faced, redish beard, several powder spots in his face by the flash of a gun, and his face thin and lean, short black hair, speaks good English, and sometimes low Dutch, is much given to liquor, and to talk of the war, as he has been out three or four campaigns last war; had on, when he went away, a half-worn felt hat, a new brown lincey jacket, with small cuffs, with metal or pewter buttons, a new under blue and white Wilton jacket, home made with buttons of the same, a new coarse homespun linen shirt, tow and linen trowsers, new shoes, with large square carved brass buckles, black and white yarn stockings. Perhaps he may change his clothes, as he is used to do. Whoever takes up said servant, and secures him in any of his Majesty's goals, so that his master may get him again, shall have the above reward, and, if brought home, reasonable charges,

paid by   JOHN VAN ETTEN.

He has been a Sailor; all masters of vessels are forbid to carry him off, at their peril.   *October* 8, 1774.
The Pennsylvania Gazette, October 12, 1774. See *The Pennsylvania Gazette*, April 28, 1773, *The New-York Gazette; and the Weekly Mercury*, May 10, 1773, and *The Pennsylvania Gazette*, November 3, 1773.

Five Dollars Reward,
RUN-AWAY from on board the ship Liberty, a certain James Cullem, an indented servant, born in Ireland, about 21 years of age, five feet three inches high, fair complexion: Had on when he went away, a light blue suite of cloaths and white stockings. Whoever will bring him back, or lodge him in any of his majesty's goals, shall receive the above reward, and all reasonable charges, by applying to
TEMPLETON & STEWART.
The New-York Gazette; and the Weekly Mercury, October 13, 1774.

WESTCHESTER, Oct. 3.
Run away from the Subscriber,
A Negro Man, named CLOSS,
ABOUT five Feet seven Inches high; had on when he went away, a brown homespun jacket, coarse Tow Shirt, and stripped Trowsers, rather long; he speaks good low Dutch, and English.
Whoever takes up and secures the said Negro, so that his Master may have him again, shall have Five Dollars reward, and all reasonable Charges paid by   SAMUEL WELL.
All Masters of Vessels and others, are forwarned to harbour or carry off said Negro, as they will answer it at their peril.
The New-York Gazette; and the Weekly Mercury, October 13, 1774; October 20, 1774.

New-York, Oct. 7.
Run away the 6th Inst. from
MORICE SIMONS,
A Negro Man, named PRINCE,
ABOUT Five Feet nine Inches high, twenty Years old, had on when he went away a new Suit of brown Thick-set, wears a Silver Loop, Button, and Band on his Hat; he also wears his Hair tied behind, and a large Tupee before.
Whoever will deliver the said Servant to his Master, at Mrs. Smith's near the Fly-Market, or Mr. Stephen Rapalje, shall receive a Reward of

twenty Dollars.—All Masters of Vessels are hereby forewarned not the ship the said Servant, as he may probably attempt to pass for a Freeman.
Rivington's New-York Gazetteer, October 13, 1774; October 20, 1774. See *The New-York Journal; or, The General Advertiser*, October 20, 1774; October 27, 1774.

RUN away the 6th. instant, from Maurice Simons, a Negro man named PRINCE, about 5 feet 9 inches high, twenty years old; had on when he went away, a new suit of brown thickset, wears a silver loop, button, and hand in his hat; he also wears his hair tyed up behind, and a large tupee before. Whoever will deliver the said servant to his master at Mrs. Smith's, near the Fly-Market, or Mr. Stephen Rapalje, shall receive a reward of twenty dollars.

N. B. All masters of vessels are hereby forewarned not to ship the said servant, as he may probably attempt to pass for a free man.

New-York, October 7, 1774.

The New-York Journal; or, The General Advertiser, October 20, 1774; October 27, 1774. See *Rivington's New-York Gazetteer*, October 13, 1774.

THIRTY DOLLARS REWARD

RUN AWAY from the subscribers, on Monday evening the 23d instant, the following indented servants, viz. JAMES DOUGLASS, born in Scotland, about 5 feet 9 inches high, and about 32 years of age; a stout well set fellow, dark hair and black complexion, little pock marked with a surly visage, speaks thick and much on the Scotch dialect; by trade a Brass Founder. Had on when he went away, a light coloured ribbed thickset coat, wilton jacket, and brown breeches, a small round brim'd hat. The above is nearly a description of his dress, though he may probably alter it.

JOHN WARDROPE, about 40 years of age, 5 feet 9 inches high, thin visage, dark complection, born in Scotland, which may be known by his speech, by trade a Taylor, and had on a dark brown coat, with silver plated buttons.

ARCHIBALD SCOT, about 32 years of age, 5 feet 9 inches high, dark complection, short black hair, likewise born in Scotland, and a Taylor by trade; has on a Parson's grey coat. They may perhaps all have changed their dress: They are supposed to be still in company, and to be gone towards Philadelphia as they all crossed Powles Hook ferry together—Whoever apprehends said servants, and lodges them in any of his Majesty's gaols, so as their masters may have them again, shall, if secured in this province receive Five Dollars reward; and if in any other province, Ten Dollars reward, for each,

paid by   SAMUEL KEMPTON,
           HERCULES MULLIGAN. New-York, 26th Oct. 1774.
The New-York Journal; or, The General Advertiser, October 27, 1774; November 10, 1774; November 17, 1774; November 24, 1774.

EIGHT DOLLARS REWARD.

RAN AWAY the 8th inst. (October) from on board the ship Hill, George Marshall, master, lying at New York, an indented English servant man named WILLIAM LEE, by trade a shoemaker, about 27 years of age, 5 feet 7 or 8 inches high, well made, of a dark complexion, and long brown hair which he commonly wore tied; had on and took with him, a blue coating coat and jacket quite new, with white lining, a pair of thickset breeches, two check shirts, a new wool hat, a black silk handkerchief, one pair of blue worsted and one pair of blue yarn stockings, a pair of good shoes with small round copper buckles, and a few shoemakers tools. He was in the country before, and probably will forge a pass and change his name. Whoever takes up said servant, and brings him to the Captain on board, or to the subscriber living near the Drawbridge in Water-street, Philadelphia, will be entitled to the above Reward, and reasonable charges.
           THOMAS HARRIS.
N. B. All masters of vessels are forbid to carry him off at their peril.
Dunlap's Pennsylvania Packet or, the General Advertiser, October 31, 1774; *The New-York Gazette; and the Weekly Mercury*, December 12, 1774; December 19, 1774. Minor differences between the papers.

FORTY SHILLINGS Reward.

RUN-AWAY from the subscriber on the first instant, an indented servant man named JAMES EMERY, born in Paisley, in Scotland, by trade a weaver, aged 22 years, about 5 feet 4 inches high, bow legg'd, of a swarthy complexion, pitted with the small pox, short black hair: Had on, and 'tis supposed took with him when he went away, a good beaver fan tail hat, short green coat, blue cloth waistcoat, fustian breeches, rib'd worsted stockings, and plain pinchbeck buckles: He has also taken with him a suit of new claret coloured moreen cloaths, lined with the same, also sundry other articles. Whoever apprehends the said servant so that his master may have him again, shall have the above reward and all reasonable charges
           paid by   ALEXANDER ROBERTSON.
The New-York Gazette; and the Weekly Mercury, November 7, 1774; November 14, 1774; November 21, 1774.

Forty Shillings Reward,

RAN-away, from the subscriber, butcher, in the Fly-Market, a negro man, named Diamond, about eighteen years old, is of a dirty black colour, has thick lips, stoops a little, and has a cut on his left cheek, done the day he went off, two double breasted homespun jackets, one striped and the other plain, white oznabrig trowsers, blue stockings, and a pair of old shoes. Whoever will take up and secure said Negro, so that his master may have him again, shall receive the above reward, and all necessary charges,
     paid by DANIEL ENSLY.

N. B. All Masters of vessels, are forbid to conceal the above negro, or carry him off, at their peril.

The New-York Gazette; and the Weekly Mercury, November 7, 1774; November 14, 1774; November 21, 1774.

THOMAS LYNCH
At his Store in Broad-Street,
....

A reward of TWO POUNDS each, and all expences paid, will be given by Thomas Lynch, to any person who takes up, and lodges all or any of the following indented servants, in any of his Majesty's goals in this, or any other province, viz;

THOMAS HUMPHRY, TIMOTHY KILTY, or KEITH, JOHN MAHONY. [*sic*] The above-mentioned three Irishmen ran-away from on board the brig Galway Packet, Hugh Fallen, commander, in the month of July 1773, and took their route to the county of West-Chester, and are suspected to reside near the White Plains.

A further reward to the above of ONE POUND each, will be given on the same terms and conditions, for the apprehending of the two following indented servant women, who are also Irish, viz.

ELENOR ROACH and CATHARINE FITZGERALD.

These servants, it is said, are in or near this city, and left their place of abode in the last week.

Any person or persons who harbours any of these servants, shall be prosecuted with all the rigour of the law. Whoever apprehends any of these servants, shall be entitled to the above reward, on delivering them to the said Thomas Lynch, or lodging them in safe custody, as directed in this advertisement.

> *Rivington's New-York Gazetter,* November 10, 1774; *The New-York Gazette; and the Weekly Mercury,* November 14, 1774; November 21, 1774; November 28, 1774; December 5, 1774. Minor differences between the papers. For the missing men, the *Mercury* reads "or KEITH, and JOHN MAHONY."

ARGYLE, October 15, 1774.
Run-away from the subscriber,
A Negro Man named Gaffee,
ABOUT twenty-six years old, five feet six inches high; had on a dark brown jacket, blue frize trowsers, new shoes, and a white shirt; he also took with him, a striped linen shirt, and wore a felt hat. Any person that apprehends said Negro, and secures him, so as his master may have him again, shall receive the reward of TEN DOLLARS, and all reasonable charges paid by the subscriber,
DUNCAN M'ARTHUR.
Living in the township of Argyle, near Saratoga.
Rivington's New-York Gazetteer, November 10, 1774.

FORTY SHILLINGS REWARD.
RAN AWAY from the subscriber on the 22d day of August last, an English servant man named William Moore, brought up to husbandry, about five feet five inches high, marked with the small pox, sore eyes, and about 25 years of age. Had on when he went away, a brown snuff coloured coat, lining of the same colour, mohair buttons, superfine scarlet waistcoat, with two pockets, the flaps turning upwards, and small yellow buttons, with a cape to the same: one pair of old cloath brown breeches, one pair of white ribbed stockings, a pair of plated buckles, a white frock and trowsers, and two old check trowsers, an old sailors jacket, with canvas seams, two check shirts, and an old felt hat, stoops much in his walk, and talks the west country dialect, and was seen at Amboy ferry, enquiring for work. Whoever takes up the said servant and secures him in any of his Majesty's gaols, shall have the above reward, and all reasonable charges,
paid by   William Weston, butcher, in Philadelphia.
N. B. The said William Moore ran away from his bail.
Rivington's New-York Gazetteer, November 17, 1774.

FIVE POUNDS REWARD.
RUN-away, on Sabbath the 30th of October last, from the Subscriber, Bookseller, opposite the London Coffee-House, Front-Street, Philadelphia; a Scots Servant Man, named Andrew Ure, about five Feet five Inches High, has a long Face, is stout made, of a ruddy Complexion, has a kind of impediment in his Speech, and speaks very fast, almost unintelligible, has very thick jet black Hair, about one Inch long; and had on when he went away, a narrow brimm'd wool Hat, not cock'd, a black and white speckled Wilting cloth Coat, trimm'd with black Ferret down the Breast, and button Holes, black horse hair Buttons, a Pair of very good Buckskin Breeches, a Pair of brown and white ribb'd Stockings, black Shoe Buckles much wore,

a black Handkerchief about his Neck, a blue and white strip'd linen Shirt, one Coarse linen Shirt, and a check'd cotton Shirt in a Bundle; he is a Book-binder by Trade, and may work as a Journeyman. Whoever takes up and secures said Andrew Ure in any Goal, shall have the above Reward, and reasonable Charges

paid by ROBERT AITKEN.

The New-York Gazette; and the Weekly Mercury, November 21, 1774.

FIVE DOLLARS Reward.

RUN *away from the subscriber, on Monday Night the 14th Instant, a Negro Man named NERO, about twenty years of age, near five feet ten inches high, slim built; his fore finger on his right hand is cut of near the first joint. He had on when he went away a lead coloured homespun jacket, a flannel check shirt, a new castor hat, a pair of new shoes. He formerly belonged to Captain Nathaniel Underhill, at Westchester county. Whoever secures the said Negro in any of his Majesty's Goals, or brings him to his said Master, shall be intitled to the above reward, and all reasonable charges paid by me AMOS PINE.*

Beekman's-Precinct, in the County of Dutchess, and Province of New York, November 16, 1774.

N. B. *It is supposed the said Negro has got a forged pass.*

The New-York Gazette; and the Weekly Mercury, November 21, 1774; November 28, 1774; December 5, 1774.

New-York, November 26, 1774.

FIFTEEN DOLLARS Reward,

TO the person or persons who will secure
WILLIAM BAILEY, a runaway servant, in any of his Majesty's goals on the continent of America, on their giving notice to any of the following persons, viz. Mr. JOHN KENNEDY, Merchant, in Baltimore, Maryland. Mr. JOHN BOYLE, Merchant in Philadelphia, or to his master, JOHN SHAW, Merchant in New-York; the above mentioned runaway is about 5 feet 7 inches high, smooth complexion, and mild address, knows something of the weaving business, writes a good hand, and has kept a school for sometime past; it is probable he may have a forged pass with him; he has for some time past wrought at the copper mines, in Lancaster county, from whence he took his departure last month, and reported that he was going towards Shamokin; he has behaved in the most ungrateful manner to the subscriber, who will pay, exclusive of the above reward, all reasonable charges, on conveying him to prison, and bringing the account to
JOHN SHAW.

The Pennsylvania Journal, and the Weekly Advertiser, December 7, 1774; December 14, 1774; *The Pennsylvania Gazette*, December 14, 1774; January 25, 1775. Minor differences between the papers. See *The Pennsylvania Journal, and the Weekly Advertiser*, July 13, 1774, and *Dunlap's Pennsylvania Packet or, the General Advertiser*, August 29, 1774.

RUN AWAY

ABOUT a week ago, from the subscriber, a mulatto boy, named CHARLES HIX, 9 or 10 years of age, has a small face, stutters much in his speech, and is a chimney sweeper.

He went off in company with, and was probably seduced away by his mother, who is a dark mulatto, much spotted with the small-pox, and supposed to be between 30 and 40 years of age. Whoever returns, or secures, the said boy in any gaol, giving proper notice, shall be handsomely rewarded for their trouble, besides being paid all reasonable charges.
    HERMAN ZEDTWITZ.

The New-York Journal; or, The General Advertiser, December 8, 1774; December 15, 1774; December 22, 1774.

Ten Pounds Reward.

RUN away from the Subscriber, a Negro Slave, named John Rattan, he sometimes passes by the Name of John Manley, about thirty-three Years of Age, five Feet five or six Inches high: Had on when he went away, a light colour Cloth Coat, and blue Cloth Waistcoat and Breeches; he is a likely Fellow, speaks very good English, and is very sensible.

Whoever delivers him to Mess. Hugh and Alexander Wallace, Merchants, in New-York, shall receive the above Reward, and all reasonable Charges.
    ROBERT CATHERWOOD.

Rivington's New-York Gazetteer, December 8, 1774; December 15, 1774; December 22, 1774.

TEN DOLLARS Reward.

RUN away from the subscriber, the 10th of October, 1775, a Negro fellow named Stephen. He is thick set and well built, near 5 feet 2 inches high, and about 23 years of age; had on a brown homespun coat, check linen shirt, leather breeches, black stockings, and thin shoes. Whoever takes up the said Negro and brings him to the subscriber, living two miles below Albany, shall have the above reward, and all reasonable charges
    paid by me   ABRAHAM SLINLANG.

The New-York Gazette; and the Weekly Mercury, December 12, 1774; December 19, 1774.

THREE DOLLARS REWARD.

RUNAWAY from the subscriber, the 10th instant, two indented Mulatto boys; one named SIMEON, might be taken for a white boy; about 20 years of age, four feet [sic] two inches high; had on when he went away, a dark gray suit of kersey clothes, stockings of the same colour, shoes nailed with hob nails, supposed not to have any hat. The other named SAM, middling dark complexion, about 18 years of age, five feet 2 inches high, had on when he went away, a light gray suit of kersey clothes, a white flannel shirt, and good felt hat; supposed to have other clothes with him. Whoever returns or secures said boys, giving proper notice, so that their masters may have them again, shall be entitled to the above reward, and all reasonable charges, paid by   SAMUEL PHILIPS   WILLIAM ARTHUR.
Smith Town, Long Island, Dec. 21, 1774.

The New-York Journal; or, The General Advertiser, December 22, 1774; December 29, 1774; January 5, 1775; January 12, 1775.

Three Pounds Reward.

RUN away on Sunday the 18th of December, from on board the Julian, Captain Burke,

An Indented Irish Servant,

Named PATRICK COLEMAN, a Taylor by Trade, very slender made, about five Feet eight or nine Inches high, had on a blue Frock Coat with a red Cape, red Waistcoat, and a grey Frize Pair of Breeches; he is about his Chin full of Pimples, speaks bad English, with a long Accent, and has short black Hair: when speaking to a Person always looks frightened and scar'd; he had also a small spotted red and white Silk Handkerchief.

Whoever apprehends the said Servant, so that he may be had again, shall have the above Reward, from
   GREG, CUNNINGHAM, and Co.
New-York, December 22, 1744. [sic]

Rivington's New-York Gazetteer, December 22, 1774; December 29, 1774; January 5, 1775; January 12, 1775; January 19, 1775. See *The New-York Gazette; and the Weekly Mercury*, December 26, 1774,

THREE POUNDS Reward.

RUN-AWAY on Sunday the 18th of December, from on board the brig Julian, Capt. Burke, an indented Irish servant named Patrick Coleman, a taylor by trade, very slender made, about 5 feet 8 or 9 inches high: Had on a blue frock coat, with a red cape, red waistcoat, and a grey frize pair of

breeches; he had with him a small spotted red and white handkerchief; he is full of pimples about his chin; speaks bad English, with a long accent, and when talking to a person looks frighten'd or scar'd: He has short black hair. Whoever apprehends the said servant, so that he may be had again, shall have the above reward, from
GREG, CUNNINGHAM, and Co.

The New-York Gazette; and the Weekly Mercury, December 26, 1774; January 2, 1775; January 9, 1775. See *Rivington's New-York Gazetteer*, December 22, 1774.

FIVE DOLLARS Reward.

RUN-away from the subscriber, living in Little Dock-street, near the Coenties-Market, yesterday morning, a Scotch servant girl, named Jane M'Creddie, she is 25 years of age, about 5 foot 3 inches high, pretty much pitted with the small-pox, well set, speaks very much the Scotch Dialect, and came from Greenock in September last: She had on and took with her when she went away, a short camblet gown with green, red and yellow stripes, a green callimancoe quilted petticoat, a long gown about the same colour of the short one, a new black satten bonnet lined with blue and ribbons on the crown; what is most remarkable, she has a scar on one hand and thumb.   JOHN MYFORD.

The New-York Gazette; and the Weekly Mercury, December 26, 1774; January 2, 1775; January 16, 1775; January 23, 1775. See *Rivington's New-York Gazetteer*, January 12, 1775.

RAN AWAY on the 3d day of November instant, from the subscriber, an indented Irish servant man, (named James Tankard) from the Albany Pier, New-York. He is about twenty-four years old, five feet eight inches high, pretty well set, and thin visaged, wears his own short, strait, black hair; had on when he went away, a white linen shirt, a brown cloath coat and jacket, leather breeches, pretty much soiled and worn. Any person apprehending said servant, and securing him in any of his Majesty's gaols in North America, so that his master may have him again, shall have TEN DOLLARS reward, and all reasonable charges paid, by applying to Mr. John Keating, New-York, or to me in Tryon county.
for DAVID COX,   EDWARD WALL.

N. B. All masters of vessels and others are forbid to carry him off, at their peril, and whosoever harbours or conceals him will be prosecuted.

Rivington's New-York Gazetteer, December 29, 1774; January 5, 1775.

1775

Newtown, Bucks county, Pennsylvania, January 2, 1775.
NINE POUNDS Reward.
BROKE out of the goal of this county....*James M'Cue*, who was committed as a runaway servant, and says he belongs to Mr. John Stephenson, of New-York, he is an Irishman, is very impudent, and is very well dressed, of a sandy complexion, is about 30 years of age, about 5 feet 6 or 7 inches high, had on a half worn beaver hat, a blue coat, red vest, buckskin breeches, yarn stockings and good shoes, is a shoemaker by trade, has a kitt of tools with him, and a check wallet, and sundry articles of womens apparel. Whoever will apprehend and secure said persons in any of his Majesty's goals, so that they may be had again, shall have...the sum of Three Pounds for *M'Cue*, and all reasonable charges,
         paid by   SAMUEL BILES, Sheriff.
The Pennsylvania Gazette, January 4, 1775.

PROVIDENCE, Dec. 17.
Joseph Thorp, who in June last absconded with a large sum of money, the property of Messieurs Carton and Seton, merchants of New-York, and which he was to have delivered at Quebec, sailed from Newport about the first of July, as a passenger, on board the brig Freedom, Gideon Crawford master of this port, bound for London. Capt. Crawford landed said Thorp at Beachy, in England, and returned here from London in October last; but never saw the advertisement for apprehending him till his return.
    The Boston Evening-Post, January 9, 1775. See *Dunlap's Pennsylvania Packet or, the General Advertiser*, August 1, 1774, and *The New-York Gazette; and the Weekly Mercury*, October 3, 1774.

Five Dollars Reward.
Run-away from the Subscriber, living in Little
Dock-street, on the 22d of December last,
A Scotch Servant Girl,
Named JANE M'CREDDIE,
TWENTY-FIVE years of age, about five feet three inches high, pretty much pitted with the small-pox, well set, speaks the Scotch dialect, and came from Greenock in September last; she had on, and took with her, when she went away, a short camblet gown, with green, red and yellow stripes, a green callimancoe quilted petticoat, a long gown about the same colour of the short one, a new black sattin bonnet lined with blue, and ribbons on the crown; what is most remarkable, she has a scar on one hand and thumb. Whoever secures the above mentioned servant in any of his

Majesty's gaols, so that her master may have her again, shall be entitled to the above reward, and all reasonable charges

paid by   JOHN MYFORD.

P. S. All masters of vessels are forwarned at their peril not to carry her off the continent, or any person to harbour her.

Rivington's New-York Gazetteer, January 12, 1775; January 19, 1775; February 2, 1775; February 9, 1775. See *The New-York Gazette; and the Weekly Mercury*, December 26, 1774.

EIGHT DOLLARS Reward.

RUN-AWAY *from the subscriber, living in Philadelphia, the latter end of October last, a mulatto boy, about* 17 *or* 18 *years of age, with straight black hair, which he dresses: he is tall and slim, very much the look of an Indian, has a little blemish in one of his eyes; has lately been cured of a sore on one of his great toes, and another on his shin a little above the instep; has the marks of whipping on his back. He is a barber by trade, dresses hair very well, is fond of strong liquor, and was some time in Bristol waiting on the subscriber. He took with him all his clothes, viz. a red coat turned up with a white cape and cuffs, a black, a white, and a blue ditto, a red and white, and a black waistcoat, and white Russia breeches. It is said he went from Philadelphia to New-York, in the Swan man of war, Capt. Ayscough, commander, and was there turned on shore for some offence he had committed on board. Whoever will apprehend and bring him to Adrian Renaudet, living at Mrs. Pine's, in Maiden-Lane, New-York, or to Messrs. Fuller and Fisher, in Philadelphia; or secures him on any of his Majesty's goals so that his master can come at him, shall have the above reward and all charge, paid by either of the above named gentlemen,*

or   THOMAS BURTON.

The New-York Gazette; and the Weekly Mercury, January 16, 1775; *The Pennsylvania Packet, or the General Advertiser*, February 20, 1775; February 27, 1775.

WHEREAS *my Wife Mary has lately eloped from me, and may perhaps endeavour to run me in Debt; these are therefore to warn all Persons not to Trust or entertain her on my Account, as I will pay no Debts she may contract.   MORRIS DECAMP. This* 13*th Jan.* 1775.

The New-York Journal; or, The General Advertiser, January 19, 1775; January 26, 1775; February 2, 1775. See *The New-York Journal; or, The General Advertiser*, March 2, 1775.

RUN away from the subscriber, on the fifth day of this instant, an apprentice lad named James Russel, about five feet eight inches high, is

about nineteen years old, by trade a weaver, very much pock broken, black hair and black eyes, and is very apt to shut one eye when talking with any one: He had taken with him a blue broad cloth coat, a striped linsey jacket, a pair of large brass shoe buckles, and a felt hat near half worn, and two striped shirts.—
Whoever takes up said run-away, and delivers him to the subscriber, at Springfield, in Essex County, shall receive a reward of FIVE DOLLARS, and all reasonable chages [sic]
    by JAMES BLACK.   Springfield, January 14, 1775.
The New-York Gazette; and the Weekly Mercury, January 23, 1775; January 30, 1775.

RUN away from the subscriber, a sweep, aged 16 years, named JAMES WINTERBOTTOM, had on a grey jacket and leather trowsers; stutters very much in his language. Whoever takes up the said boy shall have Five Dollars reward, and all reasonable charges.
    H. ZEDTWITZ.
The New-York Gazette; and the Weekly Mercury, January 23, 1775; January 30, 1775. See *The New-York Journal; or, The General Advertiser*, March 2, 1775.

RUN-away from on board the ship Monimia, Capt. Morrison, a servant lad named William Samond, about 18 years, 5 feet 10 inches high, pretty well made, much pitted with the small pox: Had on when he went away, a short grey jacket, check trowsers and a round hat. Whoever takes up said lad and delivers him to Capt. Morrison, at Hallet's-wharf, shall have 40s. reward.
The New-York Gazette; and the Weekly Mercury, January 23, 1775; January 30, 1775.

    Whereas Elizabeth Corey
of Windsor, in the county of Cumberland, in the Colony of New York, who has been brought in guilty of murdering her Child, has absconded from me her Keeper, the 3d Day of January Instant; This is therefore to give Notice, that if any Person or Persons will take her up, and bring her to Cumberland County so that she may be secured, shall have TEN DOLLARS Reward, and necessary Charges
    paid by me   ALEXANDER PARMELE, Constable.
  N. B. She is about 19 Years of Age, a comely Woman, has a large blackish Eye, middle sized Person, black Hair, and low of Speech.
    Windsor, January 14th 1775.
The New-Hampshire Gazette, and Historical Chronicle, January 27, 1775; February 17, 1775.

FIVE DOLLARS Reward.
RUN AWAY on the twenty-ninth ult. WILLIAM LOUDON, a servant lad, about seventeen years of age, a Taylor by trade, of a lively countenance, speaks on the Scotch dialect, short strait hair—Had on when he went way, a suit of cloth clothes [sic] a little on the grey, good shoes, pale blue rib'd stockings, check shirt, and a white hat; rather small of his age.—Whoever brings said boy to Thomas Burling in Chapel street, New York, shall receive the above Reward, or if confined in a goal that he may be had, THREE DOLLARS.
The New-York Journal; or, The General Advertiser, February 2, 1775.

Six Dollars Reward.
RUN AWAY on the 4th instant, with a black mare, 8 years old, about 14 hands high, a natural paces, 4 white feet, one wall eye, a white stripe on her nose, one EBENEZER ALLIN, who is about 22 years of age, of a light complexion, light coloured hair; had on a light coloured strait bodied coat and surtout, a red broad cloth jacket, and a black velvet jacket, deer skin breeches, is supposed to have gone towards Philadelphia and Maryland. Whoever secures said thief in any of his Majesty's gaols, so that he may be brought to justice, shall be entitled to the above reward. And whoever can inform of said mare, shall be entitled to 3 Dollars,
    paid by me   ABIJAH PERKINS.
                  New Marlborough, Ulster County, Jan. 23, 1775.
The New-York Journal; or, The General Advertiser, February 2, 1775; February 9, 1775; February 16, 1775; February 23, 1775.

Twenty Shillings Reward
Will be paid by the Subscriber, for taking up A servant boy named ROBERT NOONAN, HE is about 14 Years of Age, rather small, has very thin white Hair, and a small Scar on his Right Cheek; had on a blue Jacket, and a very large Pair of brown Breeches; was lately imported in the Needham, Captain Cheevers, from Cork, he went off on Sunday last. The above Reward, and all reasonable Charges will be paid to any Person that will bring him to
      DANIEL M'CORMICK.   *New-York, Feb.* 2, 1775.
Rivington's New-York Gazetteer, February 2, 1775; February 9, 1775; February 23, 1775. *The New-York Gazette; and the Weekly Mercury*, February 6, 1775; February 13, 1775. Minor differences between the papers.

N. B. Run away from James Smith, Fuller, at the mills at Great Neck, Long-Island; a young negro wench, about 21 years of age, she is remarkably fat and short in stature, has lost part of her thumb on her right hand, occasioned by a felon. Whoever takes up and secures the said wench, or informs the said Smith or the subscriber where she may be had, shall receive 3 dollars reward, from the subscriber in New York. And all persons are hereby forewarned harbouring said wench, as they must expect to be treated as the law directs in such cases.
      CORNELIUS RYAN.   *New-York, Feb.* 7, 1775.
The New-York Journal; or, The General Advertiser, February 9, 1775.

RUN-AWAY from the subscriber, a negro man named Caesar, about 40 years old, 5 feet 10 inches high, stout and well-made: had on a cloth drab coloured coat, blue jacket, red duffles trowsers, and blue Kilmarnock cap; he is a very insinuating deceitful fellow, pretends he has leave to look out for a master, and probably has a counterfeit pass with him. Whoever secures the above negro in any of his Majesty's goals, or delivers him to the subscriber, at his grist-mills, near Poughkeepsie, shall be handsomely
      rewarded. JOHN BARNES.
      N. B. He speaks Dutch as well as English.
The New-York Gazette; and the Weekly Mercury, February 20, 1775.

RUN AWAY,
From on board the Brig, CHARMING PEGGY,
John Lawrence, Jun. Master
An Indented Servant Man,

Named ANDREW ANDERSON; he is about 5 feet 10 Inches high, about 23 Years of Age, of a dark swarthy Complexion, has long black Hair, and was born in Scotland. Any person who will secure the said Servant, so that his Master may have him again, shall receive twenty Shillings Reward, by applying to Mr. James Stewart.—All Masters of Vessels are wared [*sic*] against carrying him off.
    Rivington's New-York Gazetteer, February 23, 1775.

A Reward of EIGHT DOLLARS

WILL be paid from taking up a servant man named WILLIAM BATEMAN, about 25 years old, fair complexion, brown hair tied behind: had on a brown surtout coat, a beaver hat with a large cut in the brim. He was born in England, and came from London to Philadelphia in the ship Minerva, Arthur Hill, master. The said Bateman is a Jeweller and Lapidary by trade, has worked in this city with Charles Oliver Bruff, and left this town about three weeks ago, and was heard to say he would go the New-Haven, Rhode-Island or Boston, to try his business.

The above reward and all reasonable charges will be paid to any person that will bring the above servant to

    PETER BERTON.   New-York, Feb. 20, 1775.

The New-York Gazette; and the Weekly Mercury, February 27, 1775; March 6, 1775.

RUN AWAY from the subscriber on the 26th of February last, an Irish servant boy, named Thomas Folton, about 16 years of age, has a long face and nose, and a down look: came from the county of Tyrone, with Captain Cheevers; had on a half worn hat, a wilton coat, a broad cloth jacket, without sleeves, a pair of breeches of the same, a white shirt, a light pair of knit woolen stockings, a pair of single soal shoes, and plated buckles. It is suspected that he was deluded away by one of Mr. Zedwitz's sweepers, who ran away at the same time, and perhaps they are gone toward Philadelphia, as he several times said that he had a brother in Pennsylvania. Whoever takes up the said runaway, shall have Five Dollars reward, and all reasonable charges, paid by

    JOHN WETZEL, Baker, in Bayard Street.

P. S. Since inserting the foregoing, intelligence has been received, that the above runaways went off in a boat belonging to Mr. Banker, which they stole from the Exchange dock.

The New-York Journal; or, The General Advertiser, March 2, 1775; March 9, 1775; March 16, 1775.

TWO DOLLARS Reward,
Will be paid for bringing home

A *RUN AWAY apprentice lad, named JAMES WINTERBOTTOM, who is about 16 years of age, 5 feet high, thin small face, pale complection, and reddish hair; was born in Liverpool, speaks good English, but stutters much in his speech, and is by trade a Chimney Sweeper. He had on when he went away, a light coloured cloth coat, with polished steel buttons, a red plush waistcoat, and new deer skin breeches. Whoever takes up and returns the said runaway, or gives notice of any person who takes him away, harbours, conceals, or entertains him, so that the subscriber gets him again, shall receive the above reward and all reasonable charges: and any person concerned in carrying him away, or keeping him from his master, may depend upon a legal prosecution,*

    by HERMAN ZEDTWITZ.

The New-York Journal; or, The General Advertiser, March 2, 1775; March 9, 1775; March 16, 1775; March 23, 1775. See *The New-York Gazette; and the Weekly Mercury*, January 23, 1775; January 30, 1775.

WHEREAS the Store of the subscribers, was broken open and robbed, in the night of Tuesday, the 22d. instant, of a sum of money, supposed upwards of Thirty Pounds; the robbery supposed to be committed by a man who worked for Darby Doyle, on Staten Island, a year of two ago, and passes by the name of John Williams: He is a tall slim fellow, much marked with the small-pox, and has a down look; wore a brown surtout, a reddish coat and reddish waistcoat, a new pair of leather breeches, new shoes and black stockings, had a pair of Gold sleeve buttons, one tyed with thread, the link being broke. The money known to be just, is one Five Pound Bill York currency, one ditto Three Pounds Pennsylvania, new emission, parked on the back G. S. one Half Johannes, one Four Dollars Bill, Maryland money, the remainder in Pennsylvania and New-Jersey Bills, and some Silver; he wore a new hat made by John Dennis, lin'd with red, and had an old pair of greasy leather breeches and sundry other articles, tyed up in a bundle, and may have taken some other goods, not yet missed. Whoever secures said robber, or any of his associates, so that he, or they may be brought to justice, shall on conviction, receive Ten Pounds, Proclamation money, of New-Jersey, and all reasonable charges,
     from JOHNSTON and BARBERIE.
    Perth Amboy, 27th February, 1775.

The New-York Journal; or, the General Advertiser, March 2, 1775; March 9, 1775; March 23, 1775.

RUN AWAY,
From on board the Brig, CHARMING PEGGY,
John Lawrence, Jun. Master,
An Indented Servant Man,

NAmed ANDREW CARENER; he is about 5 Feet 10 Inches high, about 23 Years of Age, of a dark swarthy Complexion, has long black Hair, and was born in Scotland. Any Person who will secure the said Servant, so that his Master may have him again, shall receive twenty Shillings Reward, by applying to Mr. James Stewart.—All Masters of Vessels are wared [*sic*] against carrying him off.

Rivington's New-York Gazetteer, March 2, 1775; March 16, 1775.

A THIEF!
Twenty Dollars Reward.

STOLEN last Saturday Night from the Subscriber, living in Northcastle, Westchester County. A bright BAY MARE. ABOUT thirteen hands and a half high, a star in her forehead, her off hind foot white, is much galled on the withers by the saddle, and is three quarters English blood: She was stolen by one SAMUEL WILSON, of the same place; he is about five feet eight inches high, short black curled hair, a large mouth, and often makes use of the words *any how* in conversation. Had on, when he went away, a red great coat, half worn, a black velvet jacket, and dirty leather breeches; he was born in Ireland and pretends to be a farrier and horse jockey. Any person who delivers the thief and mare to the subscriber, shall have the above reward.
JOSEPH GOLING. Feb. 28, 1775.
Rivington's New-York Gazetteer, March 2, 1775; March 16, 1775.

THREE POUNDS Reward.
RUN away from the subscriber, the 15th instant, a bought servant man, named Hugh M'Diarmed, about 5 feet 7 or 8 inches high, and about 25 years of age, by trade a taylor, has fair hair, is thick and well made, and lame in his right knee, his right thigh thicker than the other. He is a native of the Highlands of Scotland, but speaks tolerable good English: had on when he went away a short blue cloth coat, and jacket of the same, light blue Scotch camblet breeches, a pair of Highland hose, pinchbeck buckles, and a small round wool hat. Took with him a pair of new shoes, and a pair of coarse white wollen stockings. Whoever takes up the said servant, and secures him in any of his Majesty's goals, so that his master may have him again, shall receive the above reward, and all reasonable charges,
      by me   JAMES MOORE.
Schenactady, Albany County, Feb. 16. 1775.
The New-York Gazette; and the Weekly Mercury, March 6, 1775; March 13, 1775; March 20, 1775.

Stolen from the subscriber on the evening of the 17th inst. at Little White Creek, in the county of Albany, a red roan horse 5 years old, near 15 hands high, a natural trotter, very lofty carriaged, with a long tail, shoe and toe cork'd all around, a newish saddle with a clay colour'd plush housing, and a green surcingle round the saddle and horse, with a bridle and halter on the horse,—The thief is unknown, but has been described in a blue dress, 'tis supposed the thief has steer'd for this town. Whoever will apprehend and secure the thief, and return the horse to the subscriber living at St. Chaick, in said county, shall have FIFTEEN DOLLARS reward and all necessary charges paid by   PHIPPS WALDO.

New-Haven, Feb. 22, 1775.
The Connecticut Journal, and the New-Haven Post Boy, March 8, 1775.

Four Pounds Reward.

RUN away from the subscriber, living in East Chester, on the 6th instant, a Negro man named Robin, about 5 feet 7 inches high, a well set fellow, of a yellow complexion, part Indian, a great bushy head of hair, somewhat different from a Negro, speaks good English, and can speak Dutch, no particular mark, if he can get liquor is apt to get drunk; it is imagined he has a pass, being very intimate with a Negro fellow, who can write, had on a felt hat half worn, a blue duff[il] great coat, a tann coloured over jacket, and an under one, frize, a buck skin pair of breeches, took along with him two pair of black woollen stockings, and two pair of shoes; it is imagined he has directed his course toward the North River, to get over among the Indians, he lived at Fish Kill, on Phillips's Manor, and on York Island. Whoever takes up and secures the said Negro fellow, so that his master may have him again, (in any of his Majesty's goals) shall have the above reward, if taken in this county, (five pounds, if taken in any other county) and seven pounds if taken among the Indians, with all reasonable charges
    paid by ISAAC WARD. *East Chester, March* 7, 1775.
The New-York Journal; or, The General Advertiser, March 9, 1775; March 16, 1775.

FIVE POUNDS Reward.

BROKE *gaol on the* 6th *of February,* 1772, [sic] *at the borough-town of Westchester, a certain Michael Reyer, but assumes the name of Michael M'Kelson: he is about 6 feet high, stout made, has black eyes and black hair, by trade a shoemaker. He formerly lived at Tappan, in Dutchess County, and is now supposed to be at the Fish Kills. Whoever secures him, and brings him to the said goal, shall have the above reward, from the subscriber, serjeant of the mace of the borough-town of Westchester.*
    JOHN VALENTINE.
The New-York Gazette; and the Weekly Mercury, March 20, 1775; March 27, 1775; April 17, 1775.

STOLEN,
Out of the house of Abraham Merritt, tavern-keeper, in
Collebarack, in the Manor of Cortandt, the 29th Instant:
THIRTY POUNDS and upward, in Half Johanneses and Guineas. The thief is a man about 5 feet 8 or 9 inches high, had on a claret coloured surtout coat, a red waistcoat, black breeches, blue homespun stockings, steel

buckles, a black or dark-blue tight coat, a half worn out hat; he had his head bound up with a black handkerchief, and a black patch on his nose, which he said was sore, occasioned by a fall from a horse; but that is supposed not to be true. Whoever will secure the thief, with the money, in any of his Majesty's goals, shall have Forty Shillings reward, and all reasonable charges paid by me   ABRAHAM MERRITT.
Manor of Cortlandt, March 29th, 1775.
The New-York Gazette; and the Weekly Mercury, April 3, 1775; April 10, 1775.

TEN DOLLARS Reward.

RUN-AWAY *from the subscriber, living in Newborough, in Ulster county, and the province of New-York, a Highland boy named Daniel M'Calay, about 5 feet high, and 17 years of age, is of a very dark skin, and has light coloured hair; he has two brown spots, one on his right thigh, the other on his belly: he speaks very bad English:* had on when he went away, a short coat and breeches, made of whiteish colour'd fulled linsey woolsey, a plaid jacket with three blue patches before, shoes and stockings, a pair of large ribb'd leggings, white mittens, and a check shirt.—Whoever takes up said boy and secures him, so that he may be had again, shall have the above reward, from   WILLIAM WEAR.
The New-York Gazette; and the Weekly Mercury, April 10, 1775; April 17, 1775.

TEN DOLLARS REWARD.

RAN away from the subscriber, living in Dutchess County, Nine Partners, Charlottee Precinct, on Monday night, the 2d instant, a certain Jonathan Taylor, about 35 years of age, 6 feet high, swarthy complexion; long black hair, clubbed behind, stoops in the shoulders, and speaks with a New-England accent. He wore a dark brown homespun short skirted coat, with metal buttons, a waistcoat of the same, the button holes bound with green binding; a pair of common leather breeches sometime worn, pale blue stockings, long quartered shoes, a set of round wrought silver shoe and knee buckles (which he bought at New York on Wednesday last) a check shirt, and a flapped half worn beaver hat. He was hired by the subscriber as a farmer or labourer, for 8 months, and after he had served about 3 weeks of the time, was on Monday the 22d, sent with a teem and a load of wheat to Poughkeepsie, 6 hoes to be left on the road, and an order to receive of Mr. P. Schenck, at Poughkeepsie, £.5. current money &c. Before he set out, he stole from the subscriber, a small black leather pocket book, and about 5 or £.6 in money. On the road he sold the 6 hoes for 30s. in goods, and took with him—he deliver'd the wheat, the receipt for which he carried off with him, also the £. 5. of Mr. Scenck, and left the teem at a tavern on the road. On some causes of suspicion, he was pursued, heard of at New-York, and taken at South Amboy ferry, on Friday morning, where he owned the theft, and delivered up the pocket book, with about 2 dollars in it, the rest of the money he said was in his bundle, but watching an opportunity, he sprung out of the house, fled to the woods and has not since been taken. And as there was no money in the bundle he left behind, it appears that he had, on the whole stolen from the subscriber, about £. 11. It is supposed he will make for Philadelphia, or conceal himself in some of the towns in New-Jersey.

Whoever takes him up, and secures him in any public goal, giving notice, shall be entitled to the above reward, and to all reasonable charges if brought to the goal in Poughkeepsie, paid by the subscriber.
JAMES TALMADGE. *April* 10, 1775.

The New-York Journal; or, The General Advertiser, April 13, 1775; April 20, 1775; May 4, 1775.

FORTY SHILLINGS Reward.
Stop Thief! Stop Thief!

BROKE open, and stole out of the house of the subscriber, on Sunday night the 8th instant, a SILVER WATCH, a China face, a steel chain, a small compass to it, with a very dull face; one New-York bill of 3l. two dollars, and a quantity of small silver, supposed to be near 4l. A certain straggling man, who was about the house that evening, is suspected to have committed this robbery; he is middle sized, supposed to be about thirty years of age, much pitted with the small-pox, strait black hair, which hung much about his face; had on a red coloured surtout coat, the binding little lighter than the cloth, a pair of buckskin breeches, with carved silver shoe and knee buckles, grey ribbed worsted stockings. Whoever secures said thief, so that he may be brought to justice, shall receive the above reward, and all reasonable charges paid, by NEHEMIAH SMITH.
New-Marlborough, April 9, 1775.

Rivington's New-York Gazetteer, April 13, 1775; April 27, 1775.

To the PUBLIC.

NOTICE is hereby given, that on Tuesday last there was taken up and committed to the goal of this city, a certain Anne Cain, who about two years ago was carted about this city, with one John Mitchel, for shop-lifting. There was found in her possession some cambricks, lawns, very fine tambour worked pincushions, wearing apparel, &c. supposed to be stolen; and any person who may see the goods by applying to the subscriber at the goal. Also, notice is hereby given to Abraham Merrit, of Westchester

county, that on Tuesday last the subscriber apprehended, and has now in his custody, a certain Joseph Shepherd, who answers the description in Mr. Gaine's paper, of the thief who robbed the said Merrit. Some half johannes's were found with him, which are secured by the subscriber, and Mr. Merrit is desired to take the necessary steps for having him removed to Westchester county goal.
     FRANCIS CHILD.
The New-York Gazette; and the Weekly Mercury, April 17, 1775.

FOUR POUNDS REWARD.
ON Friday the seventh inst. ran away from the Subscribers, Two servant Men lately from Ireland, the one named JAMES M'LAUGLIN, a thick short set fellow, remarkable for a down look, short hair, and a tawny complexion—He had on when he went off, a home-made coarse short coat of a brownish colour, and breeches of the same, and a coarse woollen striped shirt.—And the other, WILLIAM SHORT, a slim made fellow, black hair, had on when he went off, a blue short coat and blue jacket, a pair of old buckskin breeches, a pair of white woollen stockings; he is about five feet six inches high, they are both Weavers, and can work pretty well at Farming.—Whoever will bring said Rascals back to the Subscribers living in Hanover and New-Windsor precincts, shall have the above Reward, and reasonable charges.
    Robert Annan. William Tillford.
The New-York Journal; or, The General Advertiser, April 20, 1775; April 27, 1775; May 4, 1775; May 11, 1775.

RUN away from the subscriber, an indented servant named George Maxwell, born in the north of England, is a good groom, but a drunken fellow; about 5 feet 6 inches high, brown hair, marked with the small pox; had on brown cloaths, buckskin breeches, and a crimson coloured surtout coat. Forty Shillings reward will be paid to whoever takes him up and
     returns him to HUGH WALLACE.
The New-York Gazette; and the Weekly Mercury, April 24, 1775; May 1, 1775; May 8, 1775; May 15, 1775.

FOUR DOLLARS Reward.
RUN-AWAY from Abraham Lawrence, of Flushing, on Long-Island, Queen's county, on the 28th of March, a negro man named OLIVER, (belonging to Samuel Smith, on the north side of Staten Island) but may have changed his name, as it is said he has called himself Jerry: He is about 22 years of age, 5 feet 7 or 8 inches high, has something of a yellow cast in his colour: Had on and took with him when he went away, two old blue

coats, one long skirts, the other short, a striped jacket, a pair of old homespun breeches, a pair of striped trowsers, a pair of two trowsers, two pair of stockings, one pair deep blue, the other grey, and an old beaver hat. It is thought he has money, and likely may change his cloaths: He has been seen at Elizabeth-Town and in New-York, in company with Col. Morris's negro named Jerry. Any person that secures said negro, so that his master may have him again, shall have the above reward, and all reasonable charges, paid by Samuel Smith, on the north side of Staten Island, Abraham Lawrence, at Flushing, Jonathan I. Dayton, at Elizabeth-Town Point, or Simon Hellers, at the White-Hall, in New-York.

He is very still, having but few words to say to any body; his hair is something bushy, and it is thought he has got on board some boat or sloop belonging to the East or North River, or the Jersies.

N. B. All masters of vessels, and others, are hereby forwarned from concealing or carrying off said negro at their peril.

The New-York Gazette; and the Weekly Mercury, April 24, 1775; May 1, 1775; May 15, 1775; May 22, 1775; May 29, 1775.

ABSCONDED from his bail on Saturday the 22d instant, a certain Humfrey Thompson, who has taught school at Ramapoh, in Orange County, for 12 months past. Said Thompson is about five feet ten inches high, twenty-five years of age, fair complexion, with long fair hair tied. He had on when he went away a green coat and waistcoat, buckskin breeches, a light coloured surtout coat. Whoever takes up said Thompson and lodges him in any of his Majesty's goals, shall have Forty Shillings reward, and all reasonable
     charges paid by me LEWIS CONKLIN, jun.
     Orange County 24th April, 1775.

The New-York Gazette; and the Weekly Mercury, May 1, 1775; May 8, 1775; May 15, 1775.

RUN away from the Subscriber, JAMES WRIGHT, Engraver, about 5 Feet 7 Inches High, has a Cast in his Eyes, but particularly in One. Had on when he went away, a light coloured Coat with plated Buttons, red Jacket and white Breeches. Whoever secures him shall have the above Reward and all
    reasonable Charges of THOMAS BLOCKLEY,
    Hanover Square. *New-York*, 10th *of May*, 1775.

Rivington's New York Gazetteer, May 11, 1775; May 18, 1775.

STOLEN, from John Armstrong at Mr. Hyatt's, at Kingsbridge, by John Williams, stiling himself a silver smith,—a pale blue serge coat, a striped silk jacket, a silver watch, with a compass, seal, one shirt, a stock, two silk handkerchiefs, a new beaver hat, cut in the present fashion, two case pistols

with some cash in the jacket pocket. The above John Williams is an Englishman, about twenty three years of age, five feet seven inches high, black hair pock-marked, swarthy complection. Whoever secures him in any of his Majesty's gaols shall receive a reward of five dollars, and all reasonable charges from   JOHN ARMSTRONG.
Rivington's New York Gazetteer, May 11, 1775; May 18, 1775.

RUN-AWAY from the subscriber, on the 30th of April last, an apprentice boy named Zachariah Roberts, a shoemaker by trade: he is about 18 years of age, about 5 feet 5 inches high, has lately had the small-pox, had on when he went away, a light grey bound coat, blue waistcoat, and leather breeches. Whosoever takes up the said apprentice shall have Two Dollars reward,   paid by   JOHN WALKER.
He is supposed to be gone towards Stanford, as he was born there.
   N. B. All persons are forbid to harbour or employ him, as they will be prosecuted as the law directs.
The New-York Gazette; and the Weekly Mercury, May 15, 1775; May 22, 1775; June 19, 1775.

RUN-AWAY from his bail, on Friday the 12th inst. a certain Ambrose Sands; it is said his real name is Ambrose Bill: He is about 6 feet high, rather slim, pale face, wears his own hair, which is brown and short; he is about 23 years of age: He has been for 9 months past teaching school at Hell Gate, on Long-Island. Whoever apprehends said Sands, so that he is delivered up to his bail, shall receive Five Pounds reward, on application to Joseph Hallet, in New-York, or Jacob Blackwell, at Hell Gate, on Long Island.
The New-York Gazette; and the Weekly Mercury, May 15, 1775; May 22, 1775. See *The New-York Gazette; and the Weekly Mercury*, May 29, 1775.

New-York, 16th May, 1775.
RUN AWAY from the Subscriber, a servant lad, named WILLIAM PHILLYA, a Cordwainer by trade. he is about 5 feet 4 or 5 inches high, of a fair and fresh complection, and has short straight hair, of a lightish colour. He had on when he went away, a blue cloth coat, and took with him, a claret coloured coat, and a green double breasted waistcoat; a pair of nankeen breeches, also a pair of blue serge ditto, two new check shirts, and one white ditto; it is supposed that he is gone towards New England All persons, or masters of vessels, are forewarned not to harbour, or carry the said servant off, at their peril. Whoever takes up and secures the said servant in any of his Majesty's gaols, so that his master may have him

again, shall have Five Dollars reward, and all reasonable charges
paid by me   JOHN KING

The New-York Journal; or, The General Advertiser, May 18, 1775; May 25, 1775; June 1, 1775; June 8, 1775; June 15, 1775; June 22, 1775; June 29, 1775; July 6, 1775; July 13, 1775; July 20, 1775. All but the first ad show "Golden-Hill" after New-York and the runaway's name as "PHILLIPS."

THREE POUNDS Reward.

RUN-AWAY from the subscriber living in Morris County, East New-Jersey, a servant man bought last December, for a new comer into the country, by the name of Isaac Jones, but being sworn before sent to a doctor to be cured of the foul disease, declares his name to be Solomon Isaac, is a Jew, was born in London, came into this country ten years ago, served seven years in Virginia or Maryland, from thence came to New-York, was put in goal, had thirty lashes for stealing; then went to Philadelphia, where he was three times in goal and punished for stealing. He is about 36 years of age, about five feet four or five inches high, black complexion and black curled hair, speaks thick, and is a smart trim built fellow. Had on when he went away a half worn castor-hat, an old light coloured worsted coat without pockets, a light blue jacket, leather breeches with wooden buttons, worsted stockings, good shoes and buckles, and a white flannel shirt: took with him a small loose coat without a cape, of brown coloured homespun kersey. Whoever takes up said servant, and secures him so that his master may have him again, shall have the above reward, and all reasonable charges
paid by me   HARTSHORNE FITZ RANDOLPH.

As he is a grand villain it is very likely he will change his apparel and name, and cut of [sic] his hair. He can speak High Dutch, and is pitted with the small pox.

The New-York Gazette; and the Weekly Mercury, May 22, 1775; June 19, 1775; *The New-York Journal; or, The General Advertiser*, May 25, 1775; June 1, 1775; June 8, 1775; June 15, 1775. Minor differences between the papers. The *Journal* drops the "E" from the advertiser's first name.

New-York, May 23, 1775.

Last night run away from the subscriber, living in New-York, a certain English servant man, named WILLIAM EDWARDS, about 19 years of age, and was imported by Captain Ackland, from London, about 8 weeks ago; he is of a middle size, about 5 feet 5 or 6 inches high, black hair, and blue eyes, and a fair smooth complection; he is a tolerable good English

scholar, and writes a fair intelligible hand: Had on when he absconded, a light coloured cloth jacket, and a flannel under jacket, a half worn beaver hat, a check shirt, Oznabrugs trowsers, black worsted stockings, black shoe buckles; he also took with him two pair of blue breeches, one of cloth, and the other of sagathie, and an old checked shirt; he is remarkable for his affability and polite manner of talking to strangers. Whoever secures the said runaway in any of his Majesty's gaols in this province, shall have a reward of Two Dollars; and if taken out of this province, a reward of Three Dollars, on delivering him unto
     JOHN DEPEYSTER.
The New-York Journal; or, The General Advertiser, May 25, 1775; June 1, 1775; June 8, 1775; June 15, 1775.

RUN AWAY from Pittsfield in the county of Berkshire, and province of the Massachusetts-Bay, on the 18th day of April last, Major Israel Stoddard, a man about 5 feet 9 inches high; he had on when he absconded, a tail'd wig, is something thin favour'd talks thick and inconsistent; said Stoddard has exerted himself to the utmost of his power, to thwart and counteract the resolutions of the Continental Congress, and has been proved to have kept up a constant correspondence with General Gage. He was well acquainted with the very day the King's troops were to commence war with the Americans at Lexington and Concord, on which account he quitted his country, fled to the city of New-York, and having taken fright, is said to have fled to Long Island—Whoever shall take up said Stoddard, and secure him, or return him to Pittsfield, in the province of the Massachusetts, shall have Ten Dollars reward. All friends of American liberty are called on to secure this Catiline, they traitor and patricide.
  Signed by order of the Committee of Correspondence and Inspection for the towns of Pittsfield, Richmond, and Lenox.
    JOHN BROWN, Clerk. May 18, 1775.
The New-York Journal; or, The General Advertiser, May 25, 1775.

RUN-AWAY *from the subscriber, living in Beekman-street, in the city of New-York, the 27th May, a servant girl named Anne Cooper, born in Scotland, and came from there thirteen months ago, and is about 23 years of age, middling stature, broad shoulders, fresh complexion, (apt to turn pale when angry) long visage, marked with the small pox, small black eyes; had on and took with her when she went away, a black silk hat lined with white silk, a short holland gown, one linen and one linsey wolsey petticoat, striped blue and white, one long gown black and red sprig India callicoe, three plain muslin caps, four handkerchiefs, one a red and white speckled cotton, a gauze, a linen, and one a lawn, a lawn apron, two homespun* coarse shirts, one pair of coarse linen hose, a pair of shoes, black flesh, half worn, with one pair of pinchbeck buckles, &c.

Any person that secures said servant girl, so as her master can have her again, shall have Twenty Shillings reward if taken within this city, elsewhere forty shillings, and all reasonable charges
to be paid by   THOMAS STEELE.

All masters of vessels and others, are hereby forwarned from concealing, carrying off, or employing said servant girl at their peril.

The New-York Gazette; and the Weekly Mercury, May 29, 1775; June 5, 1775; June 12, 1775; June 19, 1775; June 26, 1775; July 24, 1775.

AMBROSE SANDS, who was advertised by Col. Blackwell, for a supposed escape from his bail in this paper on May 15th, is returned; and his absence was occasioned by neglect, and no intention to injure his friends.   JACOB BLACKWELL.

The New-York Gazette; and the Weekly Mercury, May 29, 1775; June 5, 1775; June 12, 1775. See *The New-York Gazette; and the Weekly Mercury,* May 15, 1775.

RUN away from the subscriber, living at Paquanack, in Morris County, a servant man named William Ricket, about twenty-four years of age, five feet ten or eleven inches high, black curled hair, much pock-pitted: Had on when he went away a blue country cloth coat, a nankeen waistcoat, a pair of check trowsers, brown linen stockings, and good pumps. Any person that takes up said runaway and secures him in any of his Majesty's goals so that his master may have again, shall receive TEN DOLLARS reward, and all reasonable charges
            paid by   JOHN HARRIMAN.
N. B. His father's name was John Ricket, late of Brookland-Ferry, Long-Island.

The New-York Gazette; and the Weekly Mercury, June 5, 1775; June 12, 1775; June 19, 1775; June 26, 1775.

New-York, June 6, 1775.
YESTERDAY morning Run away, from the subscriber, living in New-York, a German Servant MAN, named HENRY HARMES, about 28 years of age, a Sugar baker by trade, pretends to be a Bread baker, and says he understands Husbandry; and was imported in Capt. Ackland from London, about 3 months ago.—He is about 5 feet, 6 inches high, well made, a fair complexion and black eyes: Had on when he absconded, a brown curled whig, pompadour cloth coat, waistcoat, and breeches, with yellow metal buttons, in imitation of spangles;—took with him a brown homespun

waistcoat, 2 check and four white shirts, a worsted striped cap, and several other cloaths: Whoever secures the said Run away in any of his Majesty's Gaols shall have Three Pounds Reward, and all reasonable charge paid, by   JOHN VAN CORTLANDT.

The New-York Journal; or, The General Advertiser, June 8, 1775; June 15, 1775; June 22, 1775; June 29, 1775; *The Pennsylvania Ledger: or the Virginia, Maryland, Pennsylvania, & New-Jersey Weekly Advertiser*, August 5, 1775; August 12, 1775; August 19, 1775. Minor differences between the papers. The *Ledger* substitutes "vest" for waistcoat."

RUN-*away from the subscribers, the* 4th *inst. an indented servant man named Thomas Holmes; about 37 years old, 5 feet 7 inches high, short brown hair tied behind; and taughtschool at Haerlem: He had on when he went away, a blue coat, jacket and breeches, of German serge. Whoever takes up and secures the run-away, so that he may be had again, shall receive Four Dollars reward, and all reasonable charges, paid by*
JOHN MYERS, and   ISAAC DAY.

The New-York Gazette; and the Weekly Mercury, June 12, 1775; June 19, 1775; June 26, 1775.

STOLEN

YESTERDAY about 2 o'clock, from on board a sloop lying at Burling's Slip, 152 dollars tied up in a leather bag, by HENRY LLOYD, an English man, about 5 feet 6 inches high, of a dark complexion, short curled black hair and remarkable black eyes, a smart sensible man; had on a Sailor's short blue Jacket, and blue and white striped Trowsers.—Whoever takes up and secures said THIEF in any Gaol, with all the Money and other Effects that shall be found with, or deposited by him in other hands, shall receive FIFTEEN DOLLARS Reward, besides all reasonable Charges.
STEPHEN THORP.

The New-York Journal; or, The General Advertiser, June 15, 1775; June 22, 1775; June 29, 1775.

TEN POUNDS REWARD.

RUN-AWAY from Major Prevost, in Bergen county, East Jersey, on September 29th last, A middle aged NEGRO MAN and his WIFE. They were advertised in Mr. Holt's paper three months last fall, and have been since travelling through New-England, sometimes in an Indian dress. The man is a preacher, short, black, and well set, and speaks slow; the woman is rather lusty, has a cast in one eye, bad teeth, smooth tongued, and very artful. Their names are Mark and Jenny, which they have changed, whoever will take up the said negroes and deliver them here at New-York, either by land or water shall have the above reward and all reasonable charges, or the same sum with charges for either of them, to be paid by Thomas Clarke of this city, if delivered at New-York,

    or if at Hakinsack by Archibald Campbell.

Rivington's New-York Gazetteer, June 15, 1775; June 22, 1775.

RUNAWAY from the subscriber, on Sunday the 11th instant, an apprentice boy, named ROBERT BURNHAM, about 15 years of age, of a fair complexion; had on when he went away, a brown coat, blue waistcoat, with black binding, a pair of buckskin breeches, &c. Whoever shall take up said apprentice, so that his master may have him again, shall be intitled to a reward of 13 coppers and a half, and all reasonable charges

    paid by CHARLES WHITE,
    Copper-smith, in New-York.

N. B. All persons are forewarned not to harbour or secret the said apprentice, as they shall answer the same at their peril.

Rivington's New-York Gazetteer, June 15, 1775; June 22, 1775.

RUN-AWAY from on board the Sloop Seaflower, a young Negro Fellow named America, about 20 years old, very black, pitted with a small Pox, and his under Lip very thick: Had on a striped Short and Trowsers, red Cap, and is supposed to be be secreted in this City. Five Dollars Reward will be given to any Person who brings the said Negro to the Printer hereof,

    or JOHN SEBRING.

The New-York Gazette; and the Weekly Mercury, June 19, 1775; June 26, 1775.

RAN-away from the subscriber, in the night between the 20th and 21st instant, an English indented servant, named BENJAMIN DURANT; about 5 feet 4 or 5 inches high, well-set, but walks heavily: A round full Face, but of a dirty sallow complexion, and straight black hair. He has a scar on the left side of his forehead, in the edge of his hair; and has had the fingers and wrist of his left hand lately scalded, so that the marks are yet fresh. Is supposed to be about 22 or 23 years old, and is apt to get drunk. He carried with him two short jackets of brown cloth; two striped linen shirts pretty much worn, and a new one of white linen, without buttons on the collar; two pair of new tow trowsers; a pair of leather and an old pair of thickset breeches; a pair of thread and a pair of woolen stockings; and wears a small flopped hat, with the edges of the brim turned up.

Whoever shall return the said servant to the subscriber, or to Mr. David Seabury, in New-York, shall receive 4 Dollars reward, and reasonable charges shall be allowed.
    SAMUEL SEABURY.
The New-York Gazette; and the Weekly Mercury, June 26, 1775; July 3, 1775; July 24, 1775; August 14, 1775.

RUN away from the Subscriber, on the 18th of June, two Negro Men, one named Exeter, the other Ireland, and a Wench called Flora, with a small Child; one of the Negro Men is six Feet high, the other five Feet and nine Inches, with each of them a Gun, and poorly cloathed. Whoever will take up said Negroes and secure them so that I may have them, or bring them to me, shall receive Twenty Dollars Reward, and all necessary Charges
    paid by me. WILLIAM GILLILAND.
Willisbourge, on the West Side of Lake Champlain, 20 Miles to the Northward of Crown Point.
The New-England Chronicle, or The Essex Gazette, From June 22, to June 29, 1775; From June 29, to July 6, 1775.

    THREE POUNDS REWARD.
            New-York, June 22, 1775.
RUN away from the subscriber, a German servant man, who arrived here in the beginning of March, named JOHN HENDRICK REESE, a baker by trade, about 23 years old: He speaks bad English, is about five feet high, and has straight black hair: Had on and took with him a long blue coat, striped cotton jacket, two pair of striped trowsers, two English hats, one new and the other about half wore, five check shirts, and two white ditto; new shoes with plain plated buckles, and a pair of nankeen breeches. It is supposed he is gone off with a woman who has a husband in Pensacola; her name is Mary Arnold, but goes by the name of Mary Newbergh, her maiden name, she is a noted whore;—they will perhaps pass for man and wife: She is a tall woman, about 24 years of age, black eyes and hair, and likely built. Whoever takes up and secures said servant, in any of his Majesty's gaols that his master may have him again, shall have the above reward, and all reasonable charges paid by
    CHRISTIAN VAN PHULL, Baker, in Partition-Street.
The New-York Journal; or, The General Advertiser, June 29, 1775; July 6, 1775; July 13, 1775; July 20, 1775. See *The Pennsylvania Gazette*, July 5, 1775.

            New York, June 28th, 1775.
    FORTY SHILLINGS Reward.

RUN-AWAY from the Subscriber last Friday, an indented servant woman named Ann Hill, said she was born in Philadelphia, has been in Ireland and England, and is about thirty years of age; took with her, 1 purple sprigged new callico gown, 1 red sprigged old ditto, 1 green moreen ditto, 1 black sattin cloak edged with ermine, 1 black mode hat, with blue lining, and narrow lace; 1 black bonnet, 1 green moreen, 1 small purple sprigged callico, 1 homespun, and 1 much worn quilted petticoats; 1 fine, and 2 coarse new shirts; 1 flowered bordered kenting, 1 white linen, and 1 muslin aprons. It is supposed that she is gone to Horseneck, and probably may have changed her name as she went after a butcher, named William Howard, (an apprentice to Mr. Bogart) who said he had married her the night before. She went off with the wife of one Lindsey, a Tanner, who is a servant, and it is said has inlisted in the Connecticut Forces, under General Wooster— Whoever takes up and returns, or secures the said woman servant, shall be entitled to the above reward, besides all reasonable charges.
          JAMES BARROW.
The New-York Journal; or, The General Advertiser, June 29, 1775; July 6, 1775.

A reward of Forty Shillings each will be given by the subscriber, to any person or persons who will apprehend the following indented Irish servants, viz. Peggy Fitzgerald, who for some time past lived at Mr. William Lupton's, in this city. She is short in her person and full faced: She absconded about fourteen days past, and is said to be gone to Philadelphia.
    Catharine Fitzgerald, who formerly lived with Daniel Sickelles, shoe-maker, of this city. She absconded last October, and is said to reside in some of the house of ill fame in the suburbs of this city.
          ....
    All the above-mentioned servants came in the brig Galway Packet, Hugh Fallen, commander, from Cork. A particular description of them is unnecessary, as on speaking to any of them will be sufficient to give all the necessary information that can be required....The above-mentioned different rewards will be paid by
          THOMAS LYNCH, in Duke Street, New-York.
The New-York Gazette; and the Weekly Mercury, July 3, 1775; July 24, 1775.

    A reward of Four Pounds each will be given for the apprehending the following mentioned Irish servants, to wit: Daniel Connell, John Hease, John Brophill, John Mahony, by trade a shoe-maker, Timothy Kilty, by trade a taylor.

All the above-mentioned servants came in the brig Galway Packet, Hugh Fallen, commander, from Cork. A particular description of them is unnecessary, as on speaking to any of them will be sufficient to give all the necessary information that can be required. Those last mentioned men servants are said to be gone towards New-England, and have absconded since the years 1772 and 1773. The above-mentioned different rewards
will be paid by THOMAS LYNCH,
in Duke Street, New-York.
The New-York Gazette; and the Weekly Mercury, July 3, 1775; July 24, 1775. See *The New-York Gazette; and the Weekly Mercury*, August 16, 1773, for Connell.

NEW YORK, June 22, 1775.
RUN away from the subscriber, a German servant man, named *John Hendrick Reese*, he speaks bad English, is about 5 feet high, and has straight black hair; had on and took with him a long blue coat, striped cotton jacket, two pair of striped trowsers, two English hats, one new and the other about half wore, five check shirts, and two white ditto; new shoes, with plain plated buckles, and a pair of nankeen breeches. It is supposed he is gone off with a woman who has a husband in Pensacola; her name is *Mary Arnold*, but goes by the name of *Mary Newbergh*; they will perhaps pass for man and wife; she is a tall woman, about 24 years of age, and likely built. Whoever takes up and secures said servant shall have Five Dollars reward, if taken up in this province, and if out of the same, Ten Dollars, and all reasonable charges paid by
CHRISTIAN VAN PHULL, Baker, in Partition street.
***The above servant is a Baker by trade.
The Pennsylvania Gazette, July 5, 1775. See *The New-York Journal; or, The General Advertiser*, June 29, 1775.

New-York, June 28th, 1775.
THREE DOLLARS REWARD.
RUN-AWAY from the Subscriber, in Maiden-lane, opposite the Oswego market, a servant lad named ROBERT MATHESON, about 5 feet 2 inches high, talks broad Scotch, he is fresh coloured, broad face, rather a down look, long straight hair; he is very sly; by trade a cooper. Had on when he went away, a blue coat and jacket, a pair of leather breeches, about half worn, a beaver hat; about half worn, a pair of large shoes, with pinchbeck buckles in them: took with him three fine shirts: he is supposed to be going towards Albany. Whoever takes up said servant shall receive the above reward, and all reasonable charges
paid by   ROBERT BRACE, Baker.

All masters of vessels are forbid to carry him off at their peril.

N. B. Said ROBERT BRACE undertakes to bake all sorts of pyes and meat at any hour in the day; likewise best ginger bread and ginger bread nuts.

Rivington's New-York Gazetteer, July 6, 1775; July 13, 1775; July 21, 1775.

RUN away, on Saturday night the 24th of June, from the subscriber, a Flushing on Long-Island, a Negro man, named CATO, about 30 years old, much addicted to strong liquor, and when drunk, talks much; he is about five feet ten inches high, had on when he went away, and old beaver hat, tow shirt and trowsers, and some woollen cloaths, with white yarn stockings. He is gone to New-York by water, in a small craft that rows with tow oars, with a small square sail, and was seen to land at New-York. Whoever takes up said Negro, and secures him so that his master may get him again, shall be entitled to TWENTY SHILLINGS reward, and all reasonable charges

paid by me   STEPHEN LAWRENCE.

Rivington's New-York Gazetteer, July 6, 1775.

FIVE DOLLARS Reward.

RUN-AWAY from the subscriber living in the city of Albany, the 4th of June last, a negro man named CATO: He had on when he went away, an old ozenbrigs waistcoat, an old pair of patched tow-cloth trowsers, and an ozenbrigs shirt: He took with him a mix-colour'd homespun cloth coat, with white metal buttons on it, a nankeen pair of breeches, 2 pair of stockings, one of them thread, the other white cotton, with a square cut out of the top of each of them to take out the former mark; and a new ozenbrigs shirt. He is about 25 or 26 years of age, 5 feet 6 inches high, tall, thin and raw-bon'd; he has remarkable white teeth, of a low slow speech, and shews his upper teeth when he smiles. Whoever takes him up and secures him, so that his mistress may have him again, shall have the above reward, and all reasonable charges,

paid by me   FRANCES HOLLAND.

The New-York Gazette; and the Weekly Mercury, July 10, 1775; July 24, 1775.

New-York, July 8, 1775.

THREE DOLLARS REWARD.

RUN AWAY from the Subscriber, an indented Scotch servant lad, named Robert Marshall, about 5 feet 2 inches high, talks broad Scotch, fresh coloured smooth face, fair hair cut very short; is in conversation very sly and plausible, may pretend to a knowledge in the tobacco cutting business—Had on when he went away, or took with him, a dark grey cloth coat and waistcoat, velvet breeches, worsted stockings, canvas and striped cotton trowsers, shoes with yellow metal buckles, round felt hat.

Whoever takes up said servant, and brings him to me in Wall Street, shall receive the above reward, and all reasonable charges.

WILLIAM MAXWELL.

The New-York Journal; or, The General Advertiser, July 13, 1775; July 20, 1775; August 3, 1775.

Sop [sic] Thief! Stop Thief!

STOLEN on Tuesday morning last, out of the house of Abraham Bond, 30l. in cash, by an Englishman of middle size, about five feet six inches high, dark complexion, and has a large scar on his right cheek occasioned by the Small pox: Had on a blue and white Wilton coat, striped yellow and white double breasted vest, black breeches, brown rib'd stockings, large silver shoe buckles, close work, wore a small hat bound with black ribbon, short black curled hair, and one of his upper fore teeth out.—Whoever takes up said Thief and brings him to the subscriber, living in New-York, or secures him in any of his Majesty's Goals, so that he may be brought to justice shall have TEN DOLLARS Reward, and all reasonable charges

paid by ABRAHAM BOND.

The New-York Journal; or, The General Advertiser, July 13, 1775; July 20, 1775.

TWENTY-FIVE POUNDS Reward.

WHEREAS on or about the 20th of June last past, a certain *Nathan Hoyt* was entrusted by John Canfield, Esq; of Sharon, in Connecticut, with a considerable sum in Half Johannes's, and other money, to be delivered to the subscriber, in New-York. Said *Hoyt* has been captain of a sloop from Red Hook, in Dutchess county, to New-York, for some months, and having converted some part of his cargoe into cash, which he took with him, he set out from New-York on Monday, the 26th of June, in the South-Amboy Stage-boat, and was seen in Philadelphia on the Wednesday following. *Hoyt* is about 6 feet high, rather slim built, redish curled hair, his teeth rather forward in his mouth, speaks thick and grum, has a grum look, walks upright; took with him a light Wilton suit of clothes, with other clothes unknown, a whitish beaver hat, and a cane with a sword fixed therein. Whoever secures said *Nathan Hoyt* in any of his Majesty's goals on this continent, shall be entitled to Seven per cent. on the sum recovered, and the above reward of Twenty-five Pounds when convicted, by applying to Mr. *Francis Casper Hasenclever*, Merchant, in Philadelphia, Messieurs

Nicholsons and *Kennedy*, Merchants, in Baltimore, *John Lawrence*, and Company, Merchants, in Virginia, Mr. *Alexander Gillon*, Merchant, Charles Town, South-Carolina, or the subscriber, in New-York.
                  NICHOLAS HOFFMAN.
   The Pennsylvania Gazette, July 19, 1775; *The Pennsylvania Journal and Weekly Advertiser,* July 19, 1775; July 26, 1775; September 13, 1775. Minor differences between the papers. The *Journal* has "New-York, July 10, 1775." at the bottom.

                                              New York, July 17, 1775.
                  THIRTY SHILLINGS REWARD.
RUN AWAY on the 14th instant, from the subscriber, living in the Manor of Scarsdale, in the county of Westchester, and colony of New York, an English servant lad, named JACOB PYER, about 18 years of age, about five feet three inches high: Had on when he went away, an Oznaburgs shirt, a pair of new trowsers, an old swanskin waistcoat, a pair of old shoes, a coarse felt hat, about half worn, bound with black He is a thick well set fellow, walks stooping, without moving his arms, has brown straight hair, a learing squint with his eyes, when he looks at any person; is not talkative, and has a stupid look. He has lately hurt the second and third finger from his thumb, on his left hand; the nail of the second much torn up, and the third affected; has a downy beard.
   Whoever takes up said lad, and secures him in any of his Majesty's goals, giving notice thereof, or returns him to the subscriber shall have the above-mentioned reward, and all reasonable charges paid by me
                  JONATHAN GRIFFING TOMPKINS.
   N. B. Every person or persons are forbid harbouring said servant, and all Captains of vessels are forbid carrying him off at their peril.
   The New-York Journal; or, The General Advertiser, July 20, 1775; July 27, 1775; August 3, 1775; August 10, 1775. The last three ads show the advertiser's middle name as "GRIFFIN."

                      FIVE DOLLARS Reward.
RUN AWAY the 15th of June last, from the subscriber in Albany county, a likely Molatto servant girl name DORCAS about 18 years of age, well proportioned, speaks good English, and pretends to be free. Whoever takes up and secures her again, shall have the above reward, and reasonable
            charges, paid by   BENJAMIN FRENCH.
   The New-York Journal; or, The General Advertiser, July 27, 1775; August 3, 1775; August 10, 1775; August 17, 1775; August 24, 1775.

RUN AWAY from Richard Brooke, of Butternuts, in the county of Tryon, and province of New-York, JOHN M'CORMICK about 5 feet 9 inches high, pretty full faced, dark brown curled hair, a little round shouldered, and turns out his toes pretty much; had with him when he went off, a blue coat and jacket, a pair of striped coarse trowsers, but has changed his coat and jacket several times since he went off, and is suspected to have murdered one Josiah Jackson, of the same place, about three days before he ran away: He is of Irish extraction, but born in America. Whoever apprehends and confines him in any of his Majesty's gaols, so that he may be had again, shall receive Three Pounds reward,
   paid by RICHARD BROOKE, or
        GEORGE BURKS, Butcher in the Fly-Market.
The New-York Journal; or, The General Advertiser, July 27, 1775; August 3, 1775; August 10, 1775; August 17, 1775; August 24, 1775.

      THREE DOLLARS REWARD.
RUN-away the 20th inst. from the subscriber, living in Newtown, Queen's County, Long-Island, an apprentice lad named Joseph Collings, about 5 feet 9 inches high, of a light complexion, with a mark under his jaw, occasioned by the king's evil; wears his own hair tied: Had on and took with him the following clothes,—one grayish serge coat, with a sagathoy waistcoat of like colour; one light coloured cloth coat and waistcoat; three pair of breeches, one pair blue cloth, the other two nankeen; and a half worn hat cut in the fashion. The above lad is between 19 and 20 years of age, and by trade a taylor. All masters of vessels and others, are forewarned not to carry off or harbour said apprentice at their peril; and whoever apprehends and secures him, so that his master may have him again, shall have the above reward, and all reasonable charges,
   paid by ALEXANDER MEHARG.
The New-York Gazette; and the Weekly Mercury, July 31, 1775; August 7, 1775; August 14, 1775.

             New-York, July 10th, 1775.
     NEW-YORK CURRENCY.
WHEREAS or or about the 20th of June last, a certain NATHAN HOIT, was intrusted by John Canfield, Esq; of Sharon in Connecticut, with a considerable sum in Half Johannes's & other money, to be delivered to the subscriber in New-York. The said HOIT has been Capt. of a sloop from Red Hook in Dutchess county, to New-York for some months, and having converted part of a cargo into cash, which he has also taken with him, he set out from this city in the South Amboy Stageboat, on Monday the 26th of June last and was seen at Philadelphia the day following. HOIT is about 6

feet high, rather slim built, has reddish curled hair, his teeth rather forward in his mouth, speaks thick and grum, has a grum look, and walks upright.—Took with him, one light Wilton suit of clothes, and others unknown, a whitish beaver hat, and a cane with a sword fixed in it.

WHOEVER secures said *Nathan Hoit* in any of his Majesty's gaols on this Continent, shall be entitled to seven per cent, of the sim recovered, and the above reward of TWENTY-FIVE POUNDS, when convicted.

Apply to Mr. Francis Gasper Hasenclever, mercht. Philadelphia; Mr. John Kennedy, merchant, Baltimore; Messrs. John Lawrence and comp. merchants, Virginia; also to Neil Jameison, Esq; of Norfolk, Virginia; Messrs. Alexander Gillon and comp. merchants, Charlestown, South Carolina, or in New-York, to NICHOLAS HOFFMAN.

N. B. It is requested of those who may have seen this *Nathan Hoit*, since the 28th of June last, or know any thing of the rout he has taken, that they convey the most early intelligence thereof, to any of the above gentlemen, which will be gratefully acknowledged.

***All masters of vessel are forwarned not to take him off the Continent.

The Maryland Gazette, and Baltimore Journal, August 2, 1775; August 8, 1775.

RAN AWAY from the subscriber, on Lupton's Wharf, an apprentice named Peter Haley, about five feet four inches high, mark'd with the Small Pox, has a down look: He inlisted some time ago under Capt. Johnson, in the Provincial service, since which he is gone off. This is therefore to forewarn all Captains of Vessels and Others, from carrying off or harbouring said Apprentice, they must expect to be prosecuted according to law,
by WILLIAM SMITH.

The New-York Journal; or, The General Advertiser, August 3, 1775; August 10, 1775; August 17, 1775.

Forty Shillings Reward.

RUN AWAY from the subscriber, a servant man, called and known by the name of DAVID BURNS, said he was brought up at Kinderhook, about five feet four inches, well set, speaks High and Low Dutch very well, likewise a good singer; has light eyes, brown hair, and a good set of teeth: Had on a castor hat, half worn, flannel short blue cloth jacket, without sleeves, a pair of leather breeches, very dirty, and an old pair of shoes. Whoever will secure the said servant, so that his master can get him, shall have the above reward, and if brought to his house, shall likewise be paid all reasonable charges, by me,

ANDREW MOORE. Beckman's Precinct, Dutchess County, July 27, 1775.
N. B. Said servant was taken out of Poughkeepsie Gaol, and the cash paid by me for his release.
Rivington's New-York Gazetteer, August 3, 1775; August 10, 1775; August 17, 1775.

TEN DOLLARS REWARD.

Run-away from the subscriber, Hugh Montgomery, a servant man, by trade a breeches-maker. Any person that will take up said servant, and bring him to his master in New-York, shall receive the above reward. All persons are hereby forewarned not to harbour, conceal, or carry off said servant, as they may expect to be prosecuted as the law directs in such cases.

The New-York Journal; or, The General Advertiser, August 17, 1775; August 24, 1775; September 7, 1775; *The New-York Gazette; and the Weekly Mercury*, October 9, 1775; October 16, 1775; October 23, 1775; October 30, 1775; November 6, 1775.

RUNAWAY from the subscriber, about three Months ago,
AN Irish indented servant, named Gilbert Fitz Gibbons. He has been accustomed to attend horses, particularly Racers, and Hunters, and to drive carriages. He is of a size full large for an horseman, of a fresh complexion, his hair is a little grey, about 36 years old. He is very talkative, speaks and swears with the brogue. Whoever will secure this man so that he may be delivered to his master, Dr. Kearsley, at Philadelphia, shall be handsomely rewarded.

Rivington's New-York Gazetteer, August 17, 1775; August 24, 1775; September 7, 1775.

RUN-AWAY from the subscriber, at Brookland, Long Island, on Tuesday morning the 22d instant, a negro man named Prince, aged 19 years, very black, about 5 feet 9 inches high, walks stooping, one leg smaller than the other, plays on the fife; had one along with him; looks very innocent. Had on when he went away, an old outside winter coat, double breasted, with brass buckles. an under brown thread jacket, without sleeves, an old white shirt, a new pair of oznabrig trowsers and breeches, brown thread stockings, and shoes, with plated buckles, and a good beaver hat. Whoever brings the negro to me, at Brookland aforesaid, shall receive Forty Shillings reward and all reasonable charges.
CHRISTOPHER SWEEDLAND.

Rivington's New-York Gazetteer, August 24, 1775; August 31, 1775; September 7, 1775.

TEN DOLLARS Reward,

RUN-AWAY from the subscriber, on Wednesday the 6th inst. a negro fellow named FORK, but probably may change it to that of Dick, as he did when he absented at a former time: He is about 23 years of age, of a middling stature, slender made, his right knee bent inwards, a lengthy visage, yellowish complexion, a slender long nose, and has lost some of this fore-teeth.—Had on a pair of osnaburgh trowsers, and spotted flannel jacket. Whoever will take up and secure the said negro, so that his master may have him again, shall receive the above reward.

THOMAS BROOKMAN.

N. B. He was seen last Saturday sen'night in this city, and it is supposed he is lurking in or about it at present, all persons are therefore forbid to harbour said negro, and all masters of vessels are forewarned not to carry him off

The New-York Gazette; and the Weekly Mercury, September 1, 1775.

TEN DOLLARS Reward.

RUN-away from the subscriber, early on Tuesday morning the 5th instant, a negro man named TITUS, about 25 years old, and about 5 feet 8 inches high, well made and proportioned every way, and is very likely for a negroe: he had on when he went away, a short brown coat, made of coating; an old homespun blue and white striped linen jacket with sleeves, and a blue and white striped homespun trowsers, almost new. The hat he is supposed to have took with him is very remarkable, (unless since changed) having no brim round it, it is very much worn. He can play a little both on the fiddle and fife. Whoever takes up and secures said servant, so that his master may have him again, shall have the above reward if took out of the colony of Connecticut, and Eight Dollars if within the colony, and all reasonable charges

paid by   HENRY VAN DYCK.

The New-York Gazette; and the Weekly Mercury, September 11, 1775; September 18, 1775; September 25, 1775; *The New-York Journal; or, The General Advertiser,* September 14, 1775; September 21, 1775; September 28, 1775; October 5, 1775. Minor differences between the papers.

RUN-AWAY from the subscriber, a negro man slave named BEN, aged about 18 years, is about 5 feet 8 inches high, middling black, full fac'd, likely visage, streight lim'd. African born, but has been in this country since

he was five or six years of age, speaks good English and some Dutch: Had on when he went away (which was on the 10th instant) a homespun jacket, without sleeves, a tow shirt and trowsers, shoes and stockings, and a felt hat about half worn, but has been lately seen in New-York with a long brown surtout. Whoever apprehends the said slave, and will deliver him to the owner, at Poughkeepsie, in Dutchess County, or to William Martin, of the New Paltz, or will confine him in any prison, giving notice to his said master, shall receive FIVE DOLLARS reward, and all reasonable charges paid.   JOHN CONCKLIN.
The New-York Gazette; and the Weekly Mercury, September 25, 1775; October 9, 1775; October 16, 1775.

A Negro man, supposed to be a runaway, who had on a light coloured surtout coat, a red vest, striped trowsers, and a brown check handkerchief, and having with him a bundle, was seen travelling the road to North-Castle, near the house of the subscriber, who attempted to take him up, but he made his escape after dropping a bundle, which contained the following articles, viz. a beaver hat, half worn, a brown vest with white metal buttons, three linen, and one check'd shirt, one oznaburg frock, and one pair of drilling breeches. The owner of the above cloaths, may have them on proving his property, and paying charges.
    WILLIAM FORMAN.
The New-York Journal; or, The General Advertiser, October 5, 1775; October 12, 1775; October 19, 1775; October 26, 1775.

RUN AWAY,
A Negro man, named SMART; he is about 25 or 30 years of age, about 5 feet 9 inches high, and is a stout well-set fellow; he was lately sent from Philadelphia to New-York, with 40 or 50 dollars, in Continental money, with which he has run off. Whoever will apprehend said negro and bring him to the printer hereof, shall have five dollars reward, and all reasonable charges paid.
Rivington's New-York Gazetteer, October 5, 1775; October 12, 1775.

ESCAPED from Springfield Gaol, on Monday the 2d instant, JONATHAN HAMPTON, of New-York, the master carpenter, taken at the Light House Island Boston: He is about 5 feet 10 inches high, short curl'd hair, something hard of hearing; had on a blue surtout, darkish brown coat, green jacket, black breeches, a pair of mixed coloured ribbed stockings, silver shoe and knee buckles, sleeve buttons of an oval shape. Whoever shall take up said Jonathan Hampton, and convey him to me at Springfield, or secures

him in any gaol, shall have FOUR DOLLARS reward, and all necessary charges, paid by me　ABNER SMITH, Gaoler.
Springfield, October 4, 1775.

The Connecticut Journal, October 11, 1775; October 18, 1775; *The New-York Journal; or, The General Advertiser*, October 12, 1775; October 19, 1775; October 26, 1775; November 2, 1775; *Thomas's Massachusetts Spy Or, American Oracle of Liberty*, October 13, 1775; October 20, 1775; October 27. 1775; *The Connecticut Courant, and Hartford Weekly Intelligencer*, October 16, 1775. Minor differences between the papers.

RUN-AWAY on the first instant, a Negro Man, named MINGO, belonging to Benjamin Hutchinson, in Southold, Suffolk county, about 19 years of age, almost like a Mulatto, pretty round faced; a little stooping or round shouldered, looks very bashful; has on when he went away, a dark brown coat with silver plated buttons, a dirty linen jacket, blue striped trowsers, shoes, and a pair of double rimmed buckles. Any person apprehending said Negro, shall have Four Dollars reward, and all reasonable charges,
paid by　BENJAMIN HUTCHINSON.

The Constitutional Gazette, October 11, 1775; October 25, 1775. See *The New-York Gazette; and the Weekly Mercury*, November 6, 1775.

TWO DOLLARS REWARD,

RUN AWAY from the Subscriber, living in Orange County, precinct of New Cornwall, early on Monday morning the 18th ult. a Negro man named CAMBRIDGE, about 38 years of age, about five feet four inches high, thick and well made, talks like a new Negro, and when a little confused, hardly to be understood: Had on when he went away, a blue coat, green jacket faced with red, blue stockings, new shoes, and a new wool hat, home hat, a linen check shirt, took with him two old brown homespun jackets, one tow shirt, two trowsers, and one pair of blue and white striped trowsers; has a scar on the upper part of his forehead, walks crippling, toes turned out, supposed he will make for New-York, and attempt to get on board a man of war, having communicated these his intentions to one of his companions.—Whoever takes up said Negro, shall have the above Reward, and all reasonable charges
paid by　GILBERT WEEKS.

The New-York Journal; or, The General Advertiser, October 12, 1775; October 19, 1775; October 26, 1775; November 2, 1775.

RUN away the 11th instant from the subscriber, next door to the Coffee House, an apprentice lad named Garrat Sickles, 18 years of age, about five

feet and an half high, slim made, brown hair and complexion, and freckled face. Had on or took with him, several shirts white and checked, a pair buckskin breeches and a pair of tow trousers, thread and woolen stockings, a pair of round plated buckles, a new pale blue cloth coat and waistcoat, mohair buttons; a mixt homespun and a new striped jacket, a wool and a castor hat, both fashionably made. Whoever takes up and returns the said apprentice, if taken up in the county of New-York, shall receive twenty shillings, and if taken out of the county, three pounds reward, and all reasonable charges,
    paid by DANIEL SICKLES.
The New-York Journal; or, The General Advertiser, October 12, 1775, October 19, 1775; October 26, 1775; November 2, 1775.

    New-Fane, Province of New-York, October 10, 1775.
RAN away from me, in April last, an Apprentice Lad, named JOHN GILLEY; had on when he went away, a spotted jacket without Sleeves, a woollen Shirt, and tow Trowsers, about four Feet and an half high, has a Scar on one Cheek. Whoever will take up said Apprentice and convey him to Mr. Earle, Innholder in Paxton, to Mr. Jones, Innholder in Mendon, or to me in New-Fane, shall receive Five Dollars Reward, and necessary Charges
    paid by SAMUEL ROBINSON.
The Massachusetts Spy: Or, American Oracle of Liberty, October 13, 1775; October 20, 1775; October 27, 1775; *The New England Chronicle*, From October 12, to October 19, 1775; From October 19, to October 26, 1775; From October 26, to November 2, 1775; Minor differences between the papers.

RUN-AWAY the 12th of September, from the subscriber, an apprentice lad, named William Cotton, nineteen years of age, a shoe-maker by trade; has long black hair, wears it commonly club'd, is something remarkable in having very crooked legs. Any person or person, that apprehends or secures said runaway, shall receive as a reward One Shilling sterling.
    John Milldollar.
The Constitutional Gazette, October 14, 1775; October 25, 1775; October 28, 1775.

      FIFTY DOLLARS Reward.
RUN-AWAY from the subscriber, an English convict servant man, named BENJAMIN SAGERS, a blacksmith and gunsmith by trade, a very streight round fac'd fellow, about five feet eleven inches high, has a remarkable down frowning look, short light hair, and several scars on his head and face:

Had on when he went away, a white shirt, blue coat, striped trowsers, spotted stockings, new pumps, and an old beaver hat cut in the fashion: May probably forge a pass, as he writes a good hand. Whoever takes up and secures said servant in any of his Majesty's gaols, so that his master may have him again, shall have, if twenty miles from home, Forty Shillings, if forty miles, Four Pounds, if eighty miles, Eight Pounds, and if one hundred miles, the above reward, and reasonable charges, if brought home,
    paid by AWERAY RICHARDSON.

The New-York Gazette; and the Weekly Mercury, October 16, 1775; October 23, 1775; October 30, 1775; November 6, 1773; November 13, 1775; November 20, 1775; November 27, 1775; December 4, 1775; February 12, 1776; *The New-York Journal; or, The General Advertiser*, October 19, 1775; October 26. 1775. The *Journal* spells the advertiser's first name as AWBRAY.

STOLEN from the subscriber living at Rye, the beginning of August last, a bright sorrel mare, with a bald face, natural trotter, her feet white, four years old, about 14 hands high, and had a trick of heaving up her head. 'Tis supposed she was taken away by a certain Zephaniah Hubs; he is 6 feet high, slender made, and a down look, with light hair and thin beard. Whoever takes up and secures the above mentioned Hubs, so that he may be convicted of the said robbery, shall have TEN POUNDS reward, and all reasonable charges,
    paid by SAMUEL LYON.

The New-York Gazette; and the Weekly Mercury, October 30, 1775; November 6, 1775. See *The New-York Gazette; and the Weekly Mercury*, April 19, 1773 for Hubs/Hubbs.

FORTY SHILLINGS *reward, with all reasonable charges will be given to any person who will bring to JOHN DE LANCEY, in the Bowrey, or secure in the city of New-York, or county of Westchester, a Negro man who has left his mistress. He is a good looking fellow, about five feet eight or nine inches high, civil spoken, a great cockscomb, and one of the best waiters at a table in this country; plays upon the French horn, is a tolerable good cook, coachman and groom, but his vanity proving more powerful than his honesty, he fraudulently obtained a silver watch, which being discovered it is imagined occasioned his going off. He has several suits of good cloaths, was generally called Caesar, but names himself Joseph Low.*

The New-York Gazette; and the Weekly Mercury, October 30, 1775; November 6, 1775; November 13, 1775; November 20, 1775; November 27, 1775.

RUN away from the subscriber the 16th instant a NEGRO man named William about 22 years of age, five foot three inches high, had on a new wool hat, a white broad cloath coat about half worn, two brown homespun jackets, the one with sleaves, white homespun breeches, a pair of blue stockings, woollen check'd trowsers, he is a well built fellow and speaks very good English.—Whoever takes up said Negro and returns him to me in the Little Nine Partners shall have FOUR DOLLARS reward and all necessary charges
paid by   ANDREW PULVER.   Oct. 8, 1775.

The Connecticut Courant, And Hartford Weekly Intelligencer, November 6, 1775.

RUN-away from the Subscriber, a Negro Man called Mingo, 20 Years of Age, of a yellow Cast, round Face, and middling flat Nose, about five Feet two Inches high: Had on when he went away, a Felt Hat cut in the Fashion, a brown Sirtout, a homespun streaked Jacket, homespun chequered Trowsers, a Pair of blue Stockings speckled with white; carried with him a Pair of mix'd blue hone knit Stockings. Whoever takes up and secures the said Fellow, so that his Master may have him again, shall receive Four Dollars Reward, and all reasonable Charges paid by me, Benjamin Hutchinson, of Southold, Suffolk County, Long-Island.

The New-York Gazette; and the Weekly Mercury, November 6, 1775; November 27, 1775; December 4, 1775. See *The Constitutional Gazette,* October 11, 1775.

THREE DOLLARS REWARD.

RUN AWAY from me the Subscriber, living in New York, on the tenth of October last, an Apprentice lad, named MOSES BADGELY, a shoemaker by trade, about 19 years of age, five feet high, thick, well set, fresh coloured, short black curled hair; had on a blue camblet coat, strip'd silk vest, buckskin breeches, blue yarn stockings, half worn shoes—It is supposed he has gone to his father's, Joseph Badgely, in Turkey, New-Jersey.—Whoever takes up said Runaway, and secures him in Elizabeth Town goal, so that his Master may have him again, shall have the above Reward and reasonable charges.
JOHN HANCOCK.

All persons are forbid harbouring or employing said servant, as they will answer it by their peril.

The New-York Journal; or, The General Advertiser, November 9, 1775; November 23, 1775; November 30, 1775.

RUN AWAY from the Subscribers living in the townshhip of Hemsted, Long-Island, Two Negro Men, each about 19 years of age, and of a middling size, the one named MICHAEL, the other FRANK.—Michael is a handsome black fellow, wore his hair tied behind, had on and took with him a short brown and a green coat, white Russia breeches, two homespun coarse blankets, and sundry other articles of clothing.—Frank, is a thin faced fellow of a yellowish cast, had on a bearskin short coat and vest, pewter buttons and striped trowsers.—It is supposed they went off in a small craft, on Monday morning the sixth instant.—A reasonable Reward will be paid to any person who takes up and secures one or both of them, besides all charges,

paid by Capt. JOHN WOOLEY, HENRY WOOLEY.

The New-York Journal; or, The General Advertiser, November 9, 1775; November 23, 1775; November 30, 1775.

EIGHT POUNDS Reward.

RUNAWAY from the subscriber, on Sunday morning the 12th inst. two servant lads, by trade nail-makers, named JAMES MURRY and JAMES JEFFRY MURRY; the first is about 20 years of age, five feet eight inches high, dark eyes, black curled hair, swarthy complexion, speaks slow, has the Scotch accent; had on when he went away, a light coloured wilton coat, brown cloth waistcoat, light fustian breeches, blue yarn stockings, check shirt, black handkerchief, new shoes, pinchbeck buckles, new felt hat. James Jeffray [*sic*] is about 19 or 20 years of age, five feet three or four inches high, had on when he went away, a light coloured suit of fustian cloaths, brown ribbed stockings, new shoes, a pair of silver plated shoe buckles, white shirt, black handkerchief, new felt hat, brown curled hair, small blue eyes, down look, speaks broad Scotch.

Whoever takes up the said Servants, and brings them to their Master, or secures them in any of his Majesty's goals, so that their master may have them again, shall have the above reward, or FOUR POUNDS for each, and all reasonable charges

paid by   HENRY USTICK.

N. B. Masters of vessels and others, are forbid to harbour or carry them off at their peril. The above servants came to this place in the Ship Sharp, from Greenock, in Scotland, about 16 months ago.

The Constitutional Gazette, November 15, 1775; *Rivington's New-York Gazetteer*, November 16, 1775; November 23, 1775; *The New-York Gazette; and the Weekly Mercury*, November 20, 1775; November 27, 1775; December 4, 1775; December 11, 1775; December 18, 1775; December 25, 1775; January 1, 1776; January 8, 1776. Minor differences between the papers. *Rivington's* and the *New-*

York Gazette shows the last names as "Murray." *Rivington's,* and the *New-York Gazette* show the second man's middle name as "Jeffray." The later ads have "*New-York, Nov.* 13, 1775" at the bottom or top. See *The New-York Journal; or, The General Advertiser,* November 23, 1775.

FIVE DOLLARS REWARD.

RUN AWAY from the Subscriber, on the fifth day of November instant, a Servant Man, named LUCAS WINEKOOP, by trade a Gunsmith, five feet eleven inches high, marked with the small pox, lean in flesh, one thigh shorter than the other, straight brown hair and blue eyes; had on a brown coat, buckskin breeches, an old beaver hat.—Whoever takes up said servant and brings him home to his Master, or secures him in any goal, so that his Master may have him again, shall have the above Reward, and all reasonable charges paid by me

JAMES WEEKS, living in Fishkills,
Rumbouts Precinct, Dutchess County

The New-York Journal; or, The General Advertiser, November 23, 1775; November 30, 1775; December 7, 1775; December 14, 1775.

New-York, November the 13th, 1775.
EIGHT POUNDS REWARD.

RUN AWAY from the subscriber, on Sunday morning the 12th inst. two servant lads, by trade nail-makers, named JAMES MURRY and JAMES JEFFRAY MURRY; is about 20 years of age, five feet eight inches high, dark eyes, black curled hair, swarthy complexion, speaks slow, has the Scotch accent, had on when he went away, a light coloured wilton coat, brown cloth waistcoat, light fustian breeches, blue yarn stockings, check shirt, black handkerchief, new shoes pinchbeck buckles, new felt hat: James Jeffray is about 19 or 20 years of age, five feet three or four inches high, had on when he went away, a light coloured suit of fustian cloaths, brown ribbed stockings, new shoes, a pair of silver plated shoe buckles, white shirt, black handkerchief, new felt hat, brown curled hair, small blue eyes, down look, speaks broad Scotch. Whoever takes up the said servants and brings them to their master, or secures them in any of his Majesty's gaols, so that their master may have them again, shall have the above reward, or four pounds for each, and all reasonable charges

paid by   HENRY USTICK.

N. B. Masters of vessels and others, are forbid to harbour or carry them off at their peril.

The above servants came to this place in the ship Sharp, from Greenoch, in Scotland, about 16 months ago.

The New-York Journal; or, The General Advertiser, November 23, 1775; November 30, 1775; December 7, 1775; December 14, 1775. See *The Constitutional Gazette*, November 15, 1775.

FIVE DOLLARS Reward.

RUN-AWAY, a likely young negro man, named REDDING, about 5 feet 9 or 10 inches high, country born, of a very black complexion, and speaks good English: Had on when he went away, a green coat, a pair of duffles trowsers, yarn stockings, and a felt hat: He is supposed to be upon this island. Whoever apprehends said fellow, and will bring him to H. Gaine, shall receive the above reward, and have all reasonable charges paid.

The New-York Gazette; and the Weekly Mercury, November 27, 1775; December 4, 1775; December 18, 1775.

STOLEN,

OUT of the pasture of Major Zebulon Ross, of Dover, in Dutchess County, on the 19th of November, a yoke of working CATTLE, by a person who said his name was Moore, and who drove the cattle to New-Millford, and sold them to Benjamin Gaylerd.

Said Moore says he lives at Huntington, on Long-Island, is about five feet ten inches high, lusty built, of dark complexion, and dark hair, uses the Quaker language in discourse; had on a light coloured cloth coat and watch coat much worn, snuff coloured Manchester velvet jacket, and a pair of leather breeches much worn. This fellow went from New-Millford to Poughkeepsie, and from thence to New-York. TEN DOLLARS reward, and reasonable charges will be given for apprehending and securing him in any of his Majesty's goals, and notice thereof given to

ZEBULON ROSS, or BENJAMIN GAYLERD.

The New-York Gazette; and the Weekly Mercury, December 4, 1775; December 11, 1775; December 18, 1775; December 25, 1775. See *The Connecticut Journal*, January 3, 1776.

FORTY SHILLINGS Reward.

STOLEN out of the store of the subscriber, on Saturday the 16th instant, about 6 o'clock in the evening, the follow articles, viz.

    3 and three quarter yards superfine purple cloth, with a blue selvage,

    6 yards rattinet, to match ditto,

    2 and a half dozen large silver spangled buttons,

    2 and a half small ditto,

    1 yard buckram, twist, &c.

    10 and half yards fine linen,—By a person about 5 feet 6 inches high, of a sandy complexion, dark brown hair; had on a blue and white striped

jacket, with a purple under ditto, and blue trowsers. Whoever takes up and secures the thief, together with the goods, shall have the above reward paid by   THOMAS CRABB.

The New-York Gazette; and the Weekly Mercury, December 18, 1775; December 25, 1775.

FIVE DOLLARS Reward.

RUN AWAY from the subscribe, living in the Precinct of Fishkill, on the 6th instant, a Negro man, named POMP, about five feet five inches high, a handsome made fellow, very polite; had on a grey surtout, black broadcloth coat and vest, striped trowsers, and a pair of buckskin breeches under the trowsers; it is supposed he took with him sundry other clothes, unknown: He belongs to Mr. Brush, of Ulster County; said Negro has a pass which was forged. The above reward will be given, to any person who shall secure said Negro, so that his master may get him again, and all reasonable charges paid by   JOHN VAN BUNSCHOTEN.

The New-York Journal; or, The General Advertiser, December 21, 1775; December 28, 1775; January 4, 1776; January 11, 1776.

1776

RUN-AWAY from the subscriber, on the 19th of December, 1775, an apprentice lad named John Leverage, about 5 feet 9 inches high, slim built and thin visage, pock-marked and has dark brown hair. Had on when he went away a light coloured knap short fly coat, lined with green baize, brown under jacket, a pair of new buck-skin breeches, and a pair of tow trowsers, one check and one white shirt; a pair of plated buckles, and a beaver hat half worn; is by trade a shoemaker, and has a blemish in his right eye. Whoever takes up the said and brings him to Daniel Sickles, next door to the Coffee-House, in New-York, shall receive a pair of OLD SHOES reward.

The New-York Gazette; and the Weekly Mercury, January 1, 1776; February 19, 1776; February 26, 1776. See *The New-York Gazette; and the Weekly Mercury*, March 4, 1776.

STOLEN out of the pasture of Major Zebulon Ross, of Dover, in Dutchess County, on the 19th of November, a yoke of working CATTLE, by a person who said his name was Moore, and who drove the cattle to New-Milford, and sold them to Benjamin Gaylerd.

Said Moore says he lives at Huntington, on Long-Island, is about five feet high, lusty built, of dark complexion, and dark hair, uses the Quaker language in discourse; had on a light coloured cloth coat and watch coat

much worn, Snuff coloured Manchester velvet jacket and a pair of leather breeches much worn. This fellow went from New-Milford to Poughkeepsie, and from thence to New-York. TEN DOLLARS reward, and reasonable charges will be given for apprehending and securing him in any of his Majesty's goals, and notice thereof given to
    ZEBULON ROSS, or BENJAMIN GAYLERD.

THe above imposture having defrauded the subscriber, in the same way, by selling him a yoke of oxen, which he stole from Milford; and for encouragement to any one who shall take him up, so that he be brought to justice, a handsome reward, in addition to the above
  will be given by JOHN CORNWALL
    of New-Haven. January 3, 1776.

The Connecticut Journal, January 3, 1776; January 10, 1776. See *The New-York Gazette; and the Weekly Mercury,* December 4, 1775.

RAN away from the subscriber, on the 11th of November last, a likely negro man, named Harry, about five feet ten inches high, speaks good English, wore away a lightish coloured broad cloth coat and vest, a good beaver hat, large pack, with an indian wampam belt for a tump loin; a waggon maker by trade, and can work very well at the carpenter's business; heard since he went away, that he has a red great coat, likewise he, as I hear, has a counterfeit pass. Whosoever takes up said negro, and returns him to me, living on the Mohawk-River, Tryon County, shall have ten dollars reward, and all necessary charges
   paid by me, ABRAHAM HODGES.
N. B. Said Negro is about 30 years of age.

Thomas's Massachusetts Spy Or, American Oracle of Liberty, January 5, 1776; January 12, 1776; January 19, 1776. See *The Connecticut Gazette; and the Universal Intelligencer,* February 2, 1776.

     Forty Shillings Reward.
RUN AWAY from the subscriber, living in Jamaica, on Long-Island, a negro man named MINK; had on when he went away, a blue surtout coat, and brown under clothes, a strong well made fellow, about five feet ten inches high; was seen at John M. Scott's Esq; on Monday the 8th instant. Whoever secures the said negro, so as the owner may have him again, shall have the above reward, and all reasonable charges,
    paid by SAMUEL SMITH.
      Jamaica, 10th January, 1776.

The New-York Journal; or, The General Advertiser, January 11, 1776.

SIX DOLLARS Reward.

RUN-AWAY from the subscriber living near Allen's Town, an English servant man named William Newman Loxford, about 5 feet 8 inches high, full fac'd and brown complexion: Had on and took with him, a brown coat, two striped summer vests, greasy buckskin breeches, and felt hat. Whoever secures said servant, so that his master may have him again, shall have the above reward, and reasonable charges,

paid by   ROBERT WRIGHT.

The New-York Gazette; and the Weekly Mercury, January 15, 1776; January 22, 1776; February 5, 1776.

FORTY SHILLINGS Reward.

RUN-AWAY *from Col. John Reid, on Wednesday the 10th day of January, inst. a negro man named SAM, born in New-Jersey, formerly lived in Doctor Mercer's family: He is about 21 years of age, about 5 feet 5 inches high, slender made, small featured; he carried with him a blue cloth surtout coat, with yellow metal buttons, a tight-bodied blue cloth livery coat, with red cuffs and collar, and also red lining, a blue cloth coatee, with red lining, cuffs and collar, and white metal buttons, two white linen vests, a red cloth and a blue cloth vest, two hair of leather breeches, a pair of red everlasting breeches, two pair of mixed blue and white stockings, one pair of brown and one pair of blue worsted stockings, and some silk stockings, a pair of fashionable plated shoe and knee buckles, a new castor hat, some white stockings, with a pinchbeck stock buckle. He carried with him a violin, which he plays. Whoever apprehends the said run-away and secures him, so that his master may have him again, shall be paid the above reward, and all reasonable charges,*

by JOHN REID, near the Fort.

The New-York Gazette; and the Weekly Mercury, January 15, 1776; January 22, 1776; January 29, 1776; February 5, 1776; February 12, 1776; February 19, 1776.

FIFTEEN DOLLARS Reward.

RUN AWAY from Col. Jonathan Moulton of Hampton in the colony of New Hampshire, in October last, a negro boy named Cato, about 18 years old, and about 5 feet and an half high, or something more; a more likely, strait limb'd, well built and active a boy is seldom to be seen, and plays well on a fife; he is very apt to scowl, or knit his brown, and has had the small-pox by inoculation, which he shows but little in his face, but the place on his arm where he was inoculated is plain to be discovered. Since he ran way he was taken up at Durham, and in conveying him to his master he made his escape; since that he was at headquarters and offered to inlist, but not meeting with success, he went from thence to Lexington, where he offered his services to Mr. John Buckman, innholder in that town, and called himself Elijah Bartlet, and said that he was free born; Mr. Buckman suspecting him to be a runaway, which the boy perceiving, he stopped but a few days, and went off privately, which was some time in November last, and his master has had no intelligence of him since. He had on when he went away, a blue duffel round jacket, with cuffs, and without lining, a blue serge jacket, both almost new, and a pair of leather breeches, and carried with him 3 check shirts, 2 of which were cotton & woolen, and the other linen, with large checks, &c. but it appears he has exchanged some of his outside cloaths for other of another colour.

Whoever will take him said runaway and convey him to his master, or secure him in any of the colony goals, so that his master can have him again, shall have fifteen dollars, and all necessary charges
    paid by JONA. MOULTON.
        Hampton, January 1, 1776.
N. B. As the boy was born at New-York, and from some other reasons it's likely he is thence making his way; but it's more likely he will offer himself to work by the month or year, in some part of the colony of Massachusetts Bay or Connecticut, and whoever may have the opportunity of taking up said runaway is cautioned to take particular care lest he makes his escape again, as he is so artful and cunning a boy.

The New England Chronicle: or, The Essex Gazette, From January 4, to January 11, 1776; From January 11, to January 18, 1776; From January 18, to January 25, 1776.

        Gloucester Gaol, January 8, 1776.
WAS committed to my custody, on suspicion of being run-aways, the following persons. ELIAZER TRAESEY, who says he belongs to Peter Leathermount, of Tullpahocks Township, in the County of Lancaster. ABRAHAM DORCHESTER, belonging to Thomas Carmichael, of Little-Britain Township, in the County of Lancaster. JOHN M'FARLONG, belonging to Thomas Iwins, of the City of New-York. Their masters, if any they have, are desired to come and pay charges, and take them away, otherwise they will be sold for the same.
    RICHARD JOHNSON, Gaoler.
Dunlap's Pennsylvania Packet or, the General Advertiser, January 15, 1776.

      TWENTY SHILLINGS REWARD.
RUN AWAY on Monday the 13th Instant, from the Subscriber, an apprentice lad named JOHN WEBB, born in New-York, about nineteen

years of age, five feet eight inches high, fair complexion, light brown hair and eyes, by trade a blacksmith—He had on a dark dove coloured knapt coat, a pair of buckskin breeches, a pair of home-spun stockings, and a pair of new shoes.—Took with him a pair of blue shag breeches, and a claret colored coat—Whoever takes up and returns the said apprentice, or secures him in any goal, giving notice to his said master, shall receive the above
reward, JOHN BAILER, Cutler.

☞ All persons are hereby forwarned not to harbour entertain or conceal the said apprentice, as they will answer it at their peril.
N. B. He proposed going to Boston.

The New-York Journal; or, The General Advertiser, January 25, 1776; February 1, 1776; February 8, 1776; February 15, 1776.

RUN-AWAY, a fortnight ago, from the subscriber, and supposed to be lurking about the city, an English lad named JAMES BIXTON: He has been pretty regularly brought up to the apothecary's business, with a smattering knowledge of physick and surgery; a fair complexion, near sighted, and wears his hair short; his apparel when he went off, a suit of brown cloaths, that has been turned, a beaver hat, new shoes, and pinchbeck buckles: he is much addicted to drinking and keeping low company, consequently will be likely to borrow some money if he can find any persons that will trust him.—Whoever takes up the said James Bixton, and secures him in the work-house of this city, shall have Twenty Shillings paid
them, by DONALD M'LEAN.

The New-York Gazette; and the Weekly Mercury, January 29, 1776; February 5, 1776.

Ran away from me the Subscriber on the 11th of November last, a likely Negro Man, named Harry, about five feet ten inches High, speaks good English; had on when he went away, a light coloured broad cloth streight bodied Coat and Vest, a good beaver Hatt, a large Pack with an Indian Wampum Belt for a Tump loin; a Waggon maker by Trade; can work well at the Carpenter's Business; heard since, he had on a red Great Coat; likewise he (as I hear) has a counterfeit Pass. Whoever takes up said Negro and returns him to me, living on the Mohawk River, Tryon County, shall have TEN DOLLARS Reward, and all necessary Charges
paid by me, ABRAHAM HODGES.
N. B. Said Negro is about 38 years of age.

The Connecticut Gazette; and the Universal Intelligencer, February 2, 1776; February 9, 1776; February 23, 1776. See *Thomas's Massachusetts Spy Or, American Oracle of Liberty*, January 5, 1776.

Fifteen Dollars REWARD:

RUN-AWAY some time ago from Captain George Mitchel, of Onslow-County, North-Carolina, a Molatto fellow named NICK, formerly belonged to Col. Lewis Morris, of Morrisania, but he has gone by the name of JAMES DENNISON, in the Boston Camp, where he has been most of the last summer, and is supposed he is gone that way again, as he was in New-York on Monday last, in a Rifle-man's dress, with a brown wig, buckskin breeches, green leggings and a blue regimental coat, he is a straight limbed stout fellow, exceedingly smooth tongued, and very intelligible; says he is a freeman; he is of a yellow or molatto colour, capable of doing almost any kind of business.—Whoever takes up the said SLAVE and confines him in any of the public goals in America, so that his Master may have him again, shall have the above REWARD, and all reasonable charges, paid by the above George Mitchel or Ward Hunt of New-York.

The New-York Journal; or, The General Advertiser, February 8, 1776; February 15, 1776; February 22, 1776; February 29, 1776; *The Constitutional Gazette*, February 10, 1776; October 14, 1774; February 24, 1776. Minor differences between the papers.

RUN-AWAY from the subscriber, living in the city of New-York, the 13th instant, an apprentice lad named SAMUEL JOHNSON, about nineteen years of age, is tall and slim, much pock-fretted, of a dark complection, black curled hair, and is much addicted to lying and drinking; is brought up to the skinner's and breeches maker's business: took with him a new blue sagathy coat; one brown surtout; one wilton vest; one claret coloured do. lined with green; two new shirts, one white the other check; two pair of good leather breeches; one knit do. black; two pair of yarn stockings ribbed; and half worn shoes. Whoever secures the said apprentice so that his mistress may have him again, shall have FORTY SHILLINGS reward, and all reasonable charges
paid by   RACHEL GETFIELD.

The New-York Gazette; and the Weekly Mercury, February 19, 1776; February 26, 1776; March 4, 1776.

RUN away from the subscriber, February the 20th a yellow wench named Sim, about 5 feet ten inches high, had on when she went away, a narrow striped homespun short gown, a wide striped homespun petticoat, speaks good English, walks very much parrot-toed, has Indian hair, a midling likely wench; whoever brings her to JOHN RUTTER in Cherry Street, shall receive a handsome reward.

N. B. All masters of vessels and others are forbid to harbour or carry her off at their peril.

The Constitutional Gazette, February 21, 1776; February 24, 1776.

RUN-AWAY *on the 27th ult. from the subscriber, a negro man named Caesar; he formerly belonged to Cohus Degraw; he is about 5 feet 6 inches high, walks stooping, yellow thin face, his little finger on his left hand is stiff, and about half bent: Had on when he went away, a blue coat with a large cape, a Russia sheeting shirt, black breeches, no hat, but a blue cloth cap: He was seen at Jamaica, at William Forbes's, on Wednesday last. Whoever takes up said negro and secures him in Bridewell, so that his master may have him again, shall have TWO DOLLARS Reward,*
    from GEORGE BEVOISE.
    N. B. His master forewarns any person whatever from harbouring or employing him, as they may expect to answer it at their peril.
    The New-York Gazette; and the Weekly Mercury, February 26, 1776; March 4, 1776; March 11, 1776.

WHEREAS Mary my Wife, hath eloped from my Bed and Board; this is therefore to forewarn all Persons not to trust her on my Account, as I will pay no Debts of her contracting since her Elopement; and I likewise desire that no Person will entertain her, for perhaps she may leave them the Child which she has with her, as, by her own Information, she has done before, or by her hard Usage of it, may be the Occasion of its Death, as she has done one (since she has been my Wife) by her strolling about, which she will do as long as any will entertain her in their Houses.
    SETH LEE.   Hampenborough, February 5, 1776.
The New-York Gazette; and the Weekly Mercury, February 26, 1776; March 4, 1776.

FIVE DOLLARS Reward.
RUN AWAY from the subscriber, living in Fish-Kills, Dutchess County, on the 14th inst. a molatto fellow, named Sam, formerly went by the name of Top, about 5 feet 7 inches high, a well set fellow; had on a dark grey jacket, a blue broad-cloth coat, a red watch coat, striped woolen shirt, and an old wool hat.—Whoever takes up said fellow and secures him in any goal, so that his master may have him again, shall receive the above reward, and all reasonable charges
    paid by   OBADIAH COOPER.
The New-York Journal; or, The General Advertiser, February 29, 1776; March 7, 1776; March 28, 1776.

RUN-AWAY from the subscriber, on the 10th of February, 1775, [*sic*] an apprentice lad named John Leverage, about 5 feet 9 inches high, slim built and thin visage, pock-marked and has dark brown hair. Had on when he went away a light coloured knap short fly coat, linned with green baize, brown under jacket, a pair of new buck-skin breeches, and a pair of tow trowsers, one check and one white shirt; a pair of plated buckles, and a beaver hat half worn; is by trade a shoemaker, and has a blemish in his right eye. Whoever takes up the said and brings him to Daniel Sickles, next door to the Coffee-House, in New-York, shall receive a pair of OLD SHOES reward.

The New-York Gazette; and the Weekly Mercury, March 4, 1776; March 11, 1776. See *The New-York Gazette; and the Weekly Mercury*, January 1, 1776.

THREE DOLLARS Reward.

RUN AWAY from the subscriber the last evening, a negro man named WILL, supposed to be about forty years of age, country born, about five feet nine inches high, a talking noisy fellow with his intimates, thin visage and large mouth, has lost all his upper fore-teeth except one remarkable large tooth standing single; had on and took with him, a red duffle great coat, a short blue cloth coat, a light coloured serge or sagathee coarse brown double breasted jacket of velvet, and a red cloth jacket lined with white, one pair black stocking breeches, and a pair blue duffle trowsers, woolen and linen stockings, an old beaver hat, and one white wool hat, a pair thick shoes half soled, and a pair of old pumps.—Supposed to be seduced away by a man, by the name of John M'Cleane, a native of Scotland, about five feet nine or ten inches high, wore red trowsers and green lapel'd coat, with short black hair, had a hat cut in the form of a jockey's hat. Whoever takes up and secures said negro and white man, so that his master may have him, and the man brought to justice, shall have the above reward of Three Pounds, or Thirty Shillings for each, and all reasonable charges paid if taken fifty miles from home; if one hundred miles, double the sum,

paid by   JAMES HORTON, Jun.

Rye Neck, 3d March, 1776. Westchester County.

N. B. As the negro is an ingenious fellow, it is thought he will endeavour to get on board a man of war, or go to the King's forces.

The New-York Journal; or, The General Advertiser, March 7, 1776; March 14, 1776; March 21, 1776; March 28, 1776.

Five Dollars Reward.

STOLEN out of the stable of the subscriber, on the night of the 18th of January last, a brown gelding, about 14 hands and an inch high, three years old, paces fast but trots indifferently, has a white spot on his nose, the hair of his tail cut very irregular; also a good saddle, with a red hair-plush housing fringed. The thief is one John Sutten, about 5 feet 9 inches high, dark complexion, pockpitted, black hair, which he generally wears clubbed, slow of speech; has been a soldier in Capt. Heman Allen's Company, of Salisbury, last summer's campaign: Had on a red jacket, green or blue coat, red watch coat, a felt or castor hat. The thief has been seen in Salisbury since he committed the theft, and rode a pied horse, which tis probably he exchanged the one he stole for. Whoever takes up the thief and secured him so that he may be brought to justice, and the horse and saddle returned to the owner, shall have the above reward, and all necessary charges paid, and for the horse and saddle only, two dollars,

   paid by JACOB EVERSON. Dutchess-County,
   Amenia Precinct, Province of New York, Feb. 28, 1776.

The Connecticut Courant, and Hartford Weekly Intelligencer, March 11, 1776; March 18, 1776; March 25, 1776.

RUN-away last Tuesday the 5th instant, from the subscriber living at Brooklyn Ferry,—A negro man named TOM, about 23 years of age, five feet 8 inches high; had on when he went away, a blue jacket, buckskin breeches, blue and white striped stockings, a tow shirt, an old beaver hat cut small, a half worn pair of shoes, with odd buckles.—He is a likely well set fellow, understands butchering very well; was late the property of John Beck, of the city of New-York, butcher, speaks Dutch and English tolerable well. Whoever takes up and secures the said negro, so that his master may have him again, shall receive 20s. reward if taken in the city, and if taken out of the City 40s. and all reasonable charges

   paid by JOHN CARPENTER.

N. B. All masters of vessels and others, are forewarned carrying off or concealing said negro at their peril.   March 11, 1776.

The New-York Gazette; and the Weekly Mercury, March 11, 1776; March 18, 1776; March 25, 1776; April 8, 1776; *The New-York Journal; or, The General Advertiser*, March 14, 1776; March 21, 1776; March 28, 1776; April 4, 1776; *The Constitutional Gazette*, March 23, 1776; March 27, 1776. Minor differences between the papers.

      TWELVE DOLLARS Reward.

RUN-AWAY on Thursday the 7th day of March, 1776, from the subscriber, Casparus Conyn, of Claverack, in the county of Albany, a negro man named BEN; he is pretty black, about 5 feet 6 inches high, 18 or 19 years of age; had one when he went away, a white flannel shirt, with a check collar and wristbands; a light coloured great coat, an old plush breeches; a brown jacket, old shoes, black and white twisted woollen stockings. Whoever takes up said negro, and secures him, so that his master may have him again, shall receive TWELVE DOLLARS reward, and all reasonable charges

paid by me, CASPARUS CONYN.

N. B. Said negro ran away last year from John Conklin, of Poughkeepsie, and was on board the man of war.

The New-York Gazette; and the Weekly Mercury, March 18, 1776; March 25, 1776; April 8, 1776.

FIVE DOLLARS Reward.

RUN-AWAY on the 20th of March, from the subscriber, a negro wench named SARAH. She formerly belonged to Cornelius Webers, carman, of this city. She is a likely mulatto wench, and well known by the name of mulatto Sarah. Whoever takes up said wench, and brings her to her master, living in New-York, shall have the above reward.

CORNELIUS RYAN.

N. B. All persons are forwarned not to employ or harbour her at their peril.

The New-York Gazette; and the Weekly Mercury, March 25, 1776; April 1, 1776; April 8, 1776; April 15, 1776.

RUN AWAY the 7th of March and 17th of September, two apprentice lads, one named William Goodwin, before advertised, about 19 years of age, and John Knecht about seventeen, by trade a shoe-maker, the latter had on, a striped shirt, brown jacket, blue breeches and stockings, has got black hair, black eyes and brown complexion. Any person or persons that apprehends or secures said John Knecht, shall be handsomely rewarded

by JOHN MILDOLAR.

N. B. It is supposed that Goodwin has persuaded the other away, and gone and enlisted: All persons are hereby forewarned not to harbour or carry them from this place or any other at their peril.

The Constitutional Gazette, March 27, 1776.

FOUR DOLLARS REWARD,

RUN AWAY from the Subscriber, a Negro Man named JACOB, about 25 years of age, five and one-half feet high, well made, his complexion a little of the yellowish cast, his face marked with large pocks, has a down look, long black wool hair, and a coarse rough voice.—He had on when he went away, a light coloured upper jacket, with a black under one, and breeches.—He formerly lived with John Foster at Folier's meadow, and has lately been seen thereabout, and near Rockaway, and when charged with running away, says that he has been home—The Subscriber therefore

desires, that if he is discovered, he may be brought home, or confined in any goal, for which a Reward of Two Dollars, if take up in the county and of Four Dollars if out of the county, with all reasonable charges, will be paid by the Subscriber.
     JACOB FOSTER.   Rockaway, 21st March, 1776.
The New-York Journal; or, The General Advertiser, March 28, 1776; April 4, 1776; April 11, 1776; April 18, 1776.

ON the 23d of March last was committed to goal for picking of pockets the wife of John Meulin; after being committed, some of the constables were ordered to go and search the house, when finding a green pocket book, two pair of silver clasps, supposed to have been taken from some pocket book, one pair of gold Sleeve buttons one ditto of silver, one pair of gold earrings, a few silver spoons and some bars of silver. Any person who have lost any of said articles may apply to
    ABRAHAM VAN GELDER, Constable.
The Constitutional Gazette, April 10, 1776.

RAN-AWAY, a Negro Wench called Pamela, a tall thin Girl, about Twenty-two Years of Age.—Any Person that will bring her to Anthony Ford, at Gerard B. Beekman's, Beckman's-Slip, shall have Five Dollars Reward. All Persons are forbid harbouring her, and all Masters of Vessels or Boatmen from carrying her off. It is supposed she is secreted some where in Town, or in the Neighbourhood of Morrisannia.
The New-York Gazette; and the Weekly Mercury, April 15, 1776; April 22, 1776; April 29, 1776; May 6, 1776.

RUN-AWAY from the subscriber, living in New-Burgh, in Ulster county, the 14th instant, April, a mulatto slave, named SIMON, about 30 years of age, 5 foot 11 inches high; he was born at Rariton in New-Jersey; speaks good English, and middling good Low Dutch; is a pretty likely fellow, apt to drink, wears his own hair tied behind; has a scar on his upper lip, and one of his upper fore teeth out: Had on when he went away, and old blue coat lined with woolen check, the sleeves partly torn off; a new striped flannel jacket; a streaked woolen shirt, and a pair of superfine cloth breeches; mixed woolen stockings; half worn beaver hat, with a silver loop and button; and carried with him besides the above, an old coarse blue surtout coat; a pair of old leather breeches; an old pair of pale blue worsted stockings; a half worn Dutch blanket, and a double breasted swanskin waistcoat. Whoever tales up and secures the said slave in any goal in America, or bring him to me, shall have TEN DOLLARS reward, and all reasonable charges

paid by THOMAS PALMER.
The New-York Gazette; and the Weekly Mercury, April 15, 1776; April 22, 1776; April 29, 1776; May 6, 1776; May 13, 1776.

THREE DOLLARS Reward.

RUN-away from the Subscriber, living in the South-east Precinct of Dutchess County, in the Oblong, an indented Scotch servant, named ALEXANDER M'LEOD, about nineteen years of age, about five feet four inches high, dark reddish hair, very natural to curl, broad spoken, supposed to have had on when he went away, a woolen check shirt, a brown grey double breasted jacket, a light grey coat quite new, an old dark grey surtout coat, all of homespun bearskin, a pair of new wilton breeches;—took with him two pair of yarn and one pair of worsted hose.—Whoever takes up and secures said servant in any gaol, so that he may be had again, shall receive the above Reward, and all reasonable charges paid by
JOHN FIELD of Oblong, or JOSEPH HULL, jun.
near Beekman's-slip, New-York.
The New-York Journal; or, The General Advertiser, April 18, 1776; April 25, 1776; May 2, 1776; May 9, 1776.

TWENTY SHILLINGS Reward.

RAN-AWAY from the subscriber, the 24th inst. a negro man named TOM, had on when he went away, an old beaver hat, a blue homespun coat and jacket, greasy leather breeches, old grey stockings, and half worn shoes, speaks Low Dutch and English.

Whoever apprehends him on this side of Kingsbridge, shall have the above reward, and if on the other side forty shillings by me
DANIEL ENSLEE, Butcher in the Fly Market.
The Constitutional Gazette, April 27, 1776; May 1, 1776. See *The New-York Gazette; and the Weekly Mercury*, April 29, 1776; *The Constitutional Gazette*, May 25, 1776, and *The Constitutional Gazette*, June 26, 1776.

STOLEN, from the subscriber on the night of the 11th inst. out of the house of Adolph Waldron, at Horns-Hook, in New-York, 1 brown short bodied coat, the lining somewhat tore, 1 jacket of the same cloth and lining, one pair of leather breeches, 2 check shirts, 1 or 2 white ditto, 3 pair of woolen stockings, 2 pair of worsted ditto, 2 neckcloths, 1 check handkerchief, 1 stick of blackball, 1 pair of new shoes, 1 pair of half boots, somewhat wore, 1 corn bag, 1 pair of silver shoe buckles, 1 fur cap, made of beaver skin, with some gold lace on the foretop of it, a bunch of papers, accounts, newspapers and pamphlets, &c. It is supposed that Charles Smith, James Conner,

and Robert Weldon are the theives; they belonged to Capt. John DeWit's company of Dutches county, in the minute service, who were stationed at Horns Hook at the time these things were taken away; and they, after being dismissed staid in New-York, it is thought they are there disposing the stolen goods. Whoever takes up any or all three of those men and secures them so that they may be brought to justice, shall be well rewarded by me
JOHN BORTLE, Little Nine Partners,
County of Dutches, April 16, 1776.
The Constitutional Gazette, April 27, 1776.

The son of Andrew Bogie, named Thomas Bogie, about 15 years old, now in this country, and supposed to be in the Continental Army, is hereby informed, that his father resides at George Swan's, in New-Scotland, near Albany, where he would be glad to hear from him, by letter, or any other way. One James Reedy is the said Thomas's comrade, and supposed to be now with him.
Thomas's Massachusetts Spy Or, American Oracle of Liberty, April 27, 1776; May 3, 1776; May 10, 1776; May 24, 1776.

TWENTY SHILLINGS REWARD.
RAN-away from the subscriber the 23d inst. a negro man named TOM, twenty-one years old, about 5 feet 7 inches high, crooked shins, had on when he went away, an old beaver hat, a blue homespun coat and jacket, greasy leather breeches, old grey stockings, and half worn shoes, speaks Low Dutch and English. Whoever apprehends him on this side of Kingsbridge, shall have the above reward, and if on the other side forty shillings by me
DANIEL INSLEE, butcher in the Fly-market.
The New-York Gazette; and the Weekly Mercury, April 29, 1776; May 6, 1776. See *The Constitutional Gazette,* April 27, 1776, *The Constitutional Gazette,* May 25, 1776, and *The Constitutional Gazette,* June 26, 1776.

Run away from the subscriber, on the night of the 20th inst. April, a young man named Isaac Evens, about 20 years of age; said runaway had on a lead coloured double breasted coat and a light coloured double breasted jacket, a new pair of leather breeches; he is of a swarthy complexion, has very thick lips and short brown hair, talks but little, and is very apt to speak one side of the truth. He stole a pair of stockings and a pair of knee buckles: Said thief took about five pounds worth. Whoever will take up said thief and bring or convey him to the subscriber, shall have five dollars reward, and all necessary charges paid by me SOLOMON WHEELER. Amenia Precinct, Dutchess County, Province of N. York, April 20, 1776.

The Connecticut Gazette; and the Universal Intelligencer, May 6, 1776; *The Connecticut Courant, and Hartford Weekly Intelligencer,* May 13, 1776.

RUN AWAY from the subscriber, on the 2d of February last, a servant girl named Catherine Levisan, aged fourteen years, is of high Dutch extract, and is pretty short and thick. Whoever will take up and secure her, so that her master may have her again, shall receive one Dollar reward.
                    CORNELIUS RYAN.
All persons are forwarned from harbouring her, as they may expect to answer it at their peril.

The Constitutional Gazette, May 8, 1776.

SIXTEEN DOLLARS Reward.
RUN-AWAY from the Subscriber, living in Philadelphia, about ten Months since, was taken up in Albany the first Instant, and absconded again in this City the 7th of the same Month, a certain John George Spicer, by Trade a Gunsmith, about 5 Feet 6 inches high, dark Complexion, with sandy Hair, spoke bad English, and wore his Hair clubbed. Had on when he went away a Half-worn brown Coat and red Jacket, grey Wollen Stockings, Pumps and Silver Buckles; had two Blankets with him, and a grey Surtout, and his Breeches and Leggens in One, of grey Cloth. He had also a Pinchbeck Watch, and a Variety of Clothing. Whoever takes up and secures the said Run-away in any Gaol, so that he may be had again, shall have the above Reward, and reasonable Charges
             paid by   JACOB RITTER.

The New-York Gazette; and the Weekly Mercury, May 13, 1776; May 20, 1776; May 27, 1776.

TWENTY SHILLINGS REWARD.
RAN-away from the subscriber the 23d inst. a negro man named TOM, twenty-one years old, about 5 feet 7 inches high, crooked shins, had on when he went away, an old beaver hat, a blue homespun coat and jacket, greasy leather breeches, old grey stockngs, and half worn shoes, speaks Low Dutch and English. Whoever apprehends him on this side of Kingsbridge, shall have the above reward, and if on the other side forty shillings by me
             DANIEL INSLEE, butcher in the Fly-market.

The Constitutional Gazette, May 25, 1776. See *The Constitutional Gazette,* April 27, 1776, *The New-York Gazette; and the Weekly Mercury,* April 29, 1776, and *The Constitutional Gazette,* June 26, 1776. See second ad below.

New-York, May 10, 1776.
RUN AWAY *from the Subscriber, a Negro Man, named TOM, about 5 feet 7 inches high. Had on when he went away a fantail'd castor hat, a black silk handkerchief, a homespun coat and jacket greasy leather breeches, and grey stockings, and half worn shoes. Whoever apprehends him on this side King's-Bridge, and returns him to his master, shall have Twenty Shillings Reward, and if on the old side, Forty Shillings, paid by me*
DANIEL ENSLEE, Butcher in the Fly Market.
The Constitutional Gazette, May 25, 1776. See *The Constitutional Gazette,* April 27, 1776, *The New-York Gazette; and the Weekly Mercury,* April 29, 1776, and *The Constitutional Gazette,* June 26, 1776.

FIVE DOLLARS REWARD.
RUN AWAY about the beginning of April last, from the subscriber in New-York, a negro man named TOM, about 23 years of age, yellowish complexion, middling height, well set, was born in New-York, and speaks good English; has been bred to the butcher's business, and is left handed. He had on when he went away, a light greyish coat, and nankeen breeches, the other parts of his dress not remembered. Whoever takes up and returns the said negro, shall have the above reward, besides all reasonable charges.
ISAAC VARIAN.
N. B. He has been long addicted to running away, and was not long since taken up at Albany, and brought as low as Haverstraw, where he made his escape, and was lately brought home.
The New-York Journal; or, The General Advertiser, June 6, 1776; June 13, 1776; June 20, 1776; June 27, 1776.

TWO DOLLARS Reward.
AGREEABLE to a resolution of the Committee of the South East Precinct of Dutchess County, the 20th May, 1776, whereby Joseph Field and Benajah Tubbs, were ordered to pursue, apprehend, or cause to be apprehended, John Underhill, a person notoriously disaffected to the liberties of America, and who was then under bonds to the said Committee, not to leave the place without their leave, and also to attend said Committee at their call; and said UNDERHILL having left his place of residence, with a design to join the ministerial armies; and having also persuaded others,

even servants to go with him,—we the said Joseph Field, and Benajah Tubbs, do offer the above reward, and all necessary charges, to any person who shall apprehend this dangerous person, and return him the said Committee, or confine him in any gaol, so that he may be had. Said Underhill is a person about five feet eleven inches high, black straight hair, something short, brown complexion, very full mouth, and hard favoured, &c. All persons are desired to have a look out, and apprehend said villain, and shall be entitled to the above reward,
  by JOSEPH FIELD, or BENAJAH TUBBS.
The New-York Journal; or, The General Advertiser, June 6, 1776; June 13, 1776; June 20, 1776.

TWO DOLLARS REWARD.

RANAWAY from the subscriber, in New-York, a negro man called JACK, about 30 years of age, five feet eight inches high, smooth faced, thick lips, a large mouth, and stoops much in walking. He is well known in this city, and at New-Rochelle, having been formerly the property of Mr. George Traill. Whoever will be so kind as the apprehend and commit him, or return him to me, shall be welcome to the above reward.
  W. MALCOM.
The Constitutional Gazette, June 12, 1776; June 19, 1776.

RAN-AWAY from the Subscriber, on Sunday the 23d of June instant, a negro man named TOM, about 5 feet 7 inches high: Had on when he went away, a fantail'd hat, a black silk handkerchief, a plain homespun jacket without sleeves, oznabrig trowsers, and no shoes.
  Whoever apprehends him on this side of Kingsbridge, and returns him to his master, shall have Twenty Shillings reward; in on the other side Forty Shillings, paid by me
  DANIEL ENSLEE, Butcher in the Fly-Market.
The Constitutional Gazette, June 26, 1776. See *The Constitutional Gazette*, April 27, 1776; *The New-York Gazette; and the Weekly Mercury*, April 29, 1776, and *The Constitutional Gazette*, May 25, 1776.

FIVE DOLLARS REWARD.

RUN AWAY from the subscriber on the 16th instant, a negro man named PRINCE, had on when he eloped, a small round beaver hat a short white broad-cloth coat, a red jacket, a white shirt, green superfine cloth breeches, black and white worsted stockings, new shoes and buckles; he is about 25 years old, 5 feet 5 or 6 inches high, well set, very handy, and speaks good

English. Whoever secures said negro, so that his master may have him again, shall have the above reward.
                    WILLIAM CONARY, Jun.
                    Dover, Dutchess County, June 18, 1776.
    The New-York Journal; or, The General Advertiser, June 29, 1776; July 4, 1776; July 11, 1776; July 18, 1776; July 25, 1776; August 8, 1776; August 15, 1776; August 29, 1776. See *The Connecticut Courant, and Hartford Weekly Intelligencer*, July 1, 1776, and *The New-York Gazette; and the Weekly Mercury*, July 29, 1776.

RUN AWAY from the subscriber at Dover, in Dutchess County, and Province of New-York, on the 16th inst. a Negro man named Prince, had on a round beaver hat, a short white broad cloth coat, a red inside jacket, green superfine breeches, white shirt, black and white worsted stockings, new shoes, about 25 years of age, 5 feet 5 or 6 inches high, well set, speaks good English. Whoever shall take up said Negro, and secure him so that his master may have him again shall have five dollars reward and all reasonable charges paid by me,
                    Wm. CONROY, jun.   Dover, June 20, 1776.
    The Connecticut Courant, and Hartford Weekly Intelligencer, July 1, 1776; July 8, 1776; July 22, 1776; July 29, 1776. See *The New-York Journal; or, The General Advertiser*, June 29, 1776, and *The New-York Gazette; and the Weekly Mercury*, July 29, 1776.

RUN-away from the Subscriber, living at New-Rochelle, about three Years ago, a Negro Man named WILLIAM: He has bushy Hair, speaks good Dutch and English, and plays on the Fiddle. Any person that will apprehend the said Negro, shall receive Twenty Shillings Reward, and all reasonable Charges paid by me,
                    JOSEPH RODMAN. June 24, 1776.
    The New-York Gazette; and the Weekly Mercury, July 1, 1776; July 8, 1776; July 22, 1776.

RUN-AWAY, a Negro Man named JAMES, tall and thin, the whites of his Eyes remarkably red, and his Face full of Eruptions: He is a talkative plausible Fellow, and had on when he went away an old grey Bearskin Short Coat, Check Shirt, Linen Breeches, and worsted Stockings, and is supposed to be gone towards the East End of Long-Island. Whoever takes up and secures the said Negro, so that his Master may get him again, or brings him to Doctor Samuel Bard, in New-York, shall receive TEN DOLLARS Reward, and all reasonable charges
                    paid by   SAMUEL BARD.

The New-York Gazette; and the Weekly Mercury, July 1, 1776; July 8, 1776; July 22, 1776.

EIGHT DOLLARS REWARD.

RAN away from the Subscriber in *Balstown*, in the County of *Albany*, about 5 Weeks ago; a Negro Man named CATO, about twenty-five Years of Age, about 5 feet four inches high, middling well-sett, has thick Lips and a short flat Nose; had on when he went away, a strip'd woolen Shirt, and light colour'd Jacket, without sleeves, faced with grey Homspun, one pair tow linnen Trowsers, wove with a Wale, Leather Breeches, and an old Hat.

Whoever takes up said NEGRO, and brings or conveys him to Capt. *Daniel Hubbard* of *Pittsfield*, or Mr. *Thomas Luttridge* at *Albany* Ferry, or J. GILL, Printer in Queen-Street, BOSTON, or secure him in any Goal, and gives Notice to the Subscriber, so that he may have him gain, shall have the above reward, and all necessary Charges

paid by   ANDREW MITCHEL.

N. B. The above Negro was seen one day last Week at Lanesborough, and is a sly Rogue, and whoever takes him, is desired to be careful of him.

The Continental Journal, and Weekly Advertiser, July 4, 1776; July 11, 1776; July 18, 1776.

TEN DOLLARS Reward.

RUN AWAY from the subscriber on Thursday the 20th instant, a negro man named JACK, about 35 years of age, a square well built fellow, pretty black, speaks broken English, was born in Guinea, and has his country's marks, viz. scars across the middle of his forehead, towards his nose, and has lost one of his under fore teeth. He understands something of the brass founders business, and can handle the file very well, and it is supposed will endeavour to pass for a freeman. He took with him several sorts of clothes, viz. a light coloured cloth jacket without sleeves, a blanket coat, a brown surtout coat, a short coat with sky blue lining, a pair of blue breeches, a pair of long tow trowsers, a good beaver hat, and an old ditto, a pair of black women's shoes, and plated open work round buckles. He also carried off with him his master's gun, fitted for, but without a bayonet, and a grenadiers broad sword, brass mounted. He is supposed to be sculking in the country, or among the troops, where several of his colour have been observed to be very fond of his company.—Whoever takes up the said negro and delivers him to his master in New-York, shall receive Ten Dollars reward, besides all reasonable charges; and whoever shall confine him in any gaol, giving due notice, so that his master may get him again, shall be handsomely rewarded; and all persons are hereby forewarned not to conceal, harbour, or carry him off at their peril.

JACOB WILKINS. *New-York, 29th June,* 1776.
The New-York Journal; or, The General Advertiser, July 4, 1776; July 11, 1776; July 25, 1776; August 8, 1776.

RUN-away from the Subscriber, living in King's County, Long-Island, a short Time ago, two Negro Men, one named Nathaniel, a very handy Fellow, about 5 Feet 6 Inches high, straight and well built, 24 Years old, of a yellow Complexion, with long Hair tied up with Ribbon; born at Newtown, Queen's County, and lived at Flatbush. Had on when he went away, a brown Linen Jacket, with an under one double breasted, one Side red Cloth the other Homespun; also homespun Trowsers, and a half worn Hat. The other Fellow that he went away with belonged to Jeromus Remsen, at Town, and very much like the other, being Brothers; he was very well cloathed, and went by the name of Jacob, and is a Cooper by Trade. Whoever secures the above Runaways in any Goal, so that their Masters may have them again, shall have Eight Pounds Reward, and all reasonable Charges
    paid by HENRY WYCKHOFF.
The New-York Gazette; and the Weekly Mercury, July 8, 1776; July 15, 1776; July 22, 1776; July 29, 17766; August 5, 1776; August 12, 1776.

FORTY SHILLINGS REWARD.
RAN AWAY from the Subscriber, on Monday the 1st of July instant, a negro boy named PRINCE, about twenty-one years of age, five feet seven inches high, thin made. Had on when he absconded, a blue cloth jacket, white homespun shirt and trowsers, is a butcher by trade, and it is supposed he hath entered in the Continental Army. Whoever will bring him to his master, in Rosevelt-street, near the Tea Water Pump, shall have the above reward for their trouble.
    GOODHEART SIEGLER.
The Constitutional Gazette, July 10, 1776; July 13, 1776; July 20, 1776; July 27, 1776. See *The Constitutional Gazette,* July 15, 1776.

FORTY SHILLINGS REWARD.
RUN away from the Subscriber, on Monday the first Inst. a Negro Man, about 21 Years of Age, named PRINCE, five Feet seven Inches high, thin made: Had on when he absconded, a blue Cloth Jacket, a white Homespun Shirt and Trowsers, and is a Butcher by Trade. He is supposed to have gone towards Rye, or enter'd in the Army. Whoever will bring him to his Master in Rosevelt's Street, near the Tea Water Pump, shall have the above Reward for their Trouble.

GOODHEART SIEGLER.
The Constitutional Gazette, July 15, 1776; July 22, 1776; July 29, 1776. See *The Constitutional Gazette,* July 10, 1776.

THIS is to certify, that Ann Burch, formerly Broadway, (now Ann Child) has eloped from me the subscriber, and took with her a number of pairs of breeches, the property of some of the Officers and Privates of the State's army: It is therefore requested, that she be apprehended by any person who may have any knowledge of her, so that she may be confined, until she has delivered the Gentleman's property which she has taken. She is a short woman, pock marked, flat nose, occasioned by losing the gristle, and wants two of her foremost teeth. Whoever apprehends said woman, so as she may be confined, shall by handsomely rewarded by me,
JOSEPH CHILD, Skinner.
N. B. I will pay no debts of her contracting from the date hereof.
Chatham Street, New-York, July 16, 1776.
The Constitutional Gazette, July 17, 1776; July 27, 1776.

New-York, July 17, 1776.
RAN-AWAY on Monday the 15th instant, a negro lad about 18 or 20 years of age, named YORK; had on when he went away, a home-spun jacket, linen frock, tow shirt and trowsers, an old beaver hat with a gilt button: He also took with him a light brown short coat with green cuffs and collar, speaks bad English, has a scar on the fore part of his head. Whoever brings him to me (the subscriber,) shall be handsomly rewarded.
THOMAS GRISWOLD.
The Constitutional Gazette, July 17, 1776. See *The New-York Gazette; and the Weekly Mercury,* May 12, 1777, *The New-York Gazette; and the Weekly Mercury,* June 9, 1777, and *The New-York Gazette; and the Weekly Mercury,* September 14, 1778.

FOUR DOLLARS REWARD.
RUN AWAY from the subscriber living on Great-Neck, in the township of Hemstead, a mulatto slave named DANIEL, 20 years of age, about five feet four inches high, round shouldered, has a down-look, dark curled hair, and stammers in his speech; had on when he went away, a tow shirt and trowsers, a linen jacket without sleeves, a cut felt hat, and a pair of thick shoes. All persons are hereby forewarned harbouring said slave, or assisting him in getting away, as they must expect to answer for it at their peril. Whoever takes up said slave and secures him so that the owner may have him again, shall receive the above reward, and all reasonable charges paid by JOHN MITCHEL. June 13, 1776.

The New-York Journal; or, The General Advertiser, July 25, 1776; August 8, 1776; August 15, 1776; August 29, 1776.

RUN-away from the Subscriber on the 16th Instant, a Negro Man named PRINCE, about 25 Years of age, 5 Feet 5 or 6 Inches high, well proportioned, very handy, and speaks good English: Had on a small round Beaver Hat, a short white Broad Cloth Coat, red Jacket, white Shirt, green superfine Breeches, black and white Worsted Stockings, new Shoes and Buckles. Whoever secures said Negro so that his master may have him again, shall have FIVE DOLLARS Reward, and all reasonable Charges,
    paid by me WILLIAM CONRAY, Jun.
    Dover, in *Dutchess County, June* 8, 1776.
The New-York Gazette; and the Weekly Mercury, July 29, 1776; August 12, 1776. See *The Connecticut Courant, and Hartford Weekly Intelligencer*, July 1, 1776, and *The New-York Journal; or, The General Advertiser*, June 29, 1776.

    Three Dollars Reward.

RUN-away the 20th instant, from the subscriber, in the Borough of Westchester, a Negro Fellow named CATO, about 24 Years of Age, 5 Feet 6 Inches high; he is very black, remarkable large Mouth with broad Teeth, and wrinkled Forehead; is plausible and smooth in speaking, and may pass himself for a Sailor, having been used to a boat. He took with him when he went away, a green short Coat with red Collar and Cuffs, short brown Frize Coat, one brown and one white linen Waistcoat, one brown linen breeches, two Pair homespun Throwers, Two homespun Shirts and one white ditto, and may have other Cloaths with him that is not know. Whoever takes up the said Negro and secures him, shall have the above Reward, and reasonable Charges paid them, by
    JOHN SMITH. Frog's Neck, in Westchester,
        July 22, 1776.
 He had got a Pass as a Freeman, and passes by the Name of Thomas Jackson.
 The New-York Gazette; and the Weekly Mercury, July 29, 1776.

LEFT his lodging on the 24th day of July last, Peter Guion, of New-Rochelle, in the county of West-Chester, (being disturbed in mind) he is supposed to have gone towards Albany: Had on when he went away, a brown vest, check shirt, and yarn stockings, and has long black Hair tied behind. Whoever will secure the said Peter Guion, and supply him with all kind of necessaries, until they can notify the subscriber thereof, or bring him home, shall have all costs and reasonable charges paid. And in order to let his friends know where he is with dispatch (if not convenient to bring him home) a line directed to Abraham Guion, Esq; of New-Rochelle, to the care of Caleb Hyatt, at King's Bridge, or otherwise, as is most convenient, will be very gratefully received by

          ABRAHAM GUION.   New-Rochelle, June 3d, 1776.

The New-York Gazette; and the Weekly Mercury, August 5, 1776; August 12, 1776.

RUN-AWAY from the Subscriber, on Saturday the 27th Instant, an Apprentice Lad named Abijah Clark; slender built, thin Visage, smooth Face, light brown Hair tied behind: He is about five Feet four or five Inches high; Blacksmith by Trade; had on when he went away, a claret coloured over jacket; a Pair of Plush Breeches or Oznabrig Trowsers; plated Buckles in his Shoes; is supposed to have gone towards New-York, or inlisted into some Company. Whoever takes up said Apprentice, and will bring him to the Continental Ship Yard at Poughkeepsie, shall have THIRTY SHILLINGS Reward, and reasonable Charges
        paid by me   JAMES ODELL.
                                        Poughkeepsie, 30th July, 1776.

***The Subscriber is under Contact to Work for the Public, his Apprentice's absconding causes Delay; every Friend to his Country is desired to stop him.

The New-York Gazette; and the Weekly Mercury, August 12, 1776; August 26, 1776; September 2, 1776.

ALL *true Friends in the United States of America, are desired to endeavour to apprehend and confine a certain WILLIAM OWENS, by occupation a Schoolmaster, he is about five feet six or seven inches high, middling well set, black hair, has lost his left eye, (the other is black) about 23 or 24 years old, is a native of Ireland, and speaks with something of a brogue. Had on when he went away, a small half worn beaver hat, with a yellow button and loop, a red and white mixed broadcloth coat, and took with him jackets, breeches and stockings of various sorts; rode a large sorril horse, with a blaze in his face, and is supposed to have gone to the northward, with one EBENEZER LEELY, a noted Tory. Said OWENS feloniously took away a number of BOOKS belonging to various persons, viz. the last volumes of Pope's Odyssy, three volumes of Swift's works, Atkinson's Epitome, Seaman's Daily Assistant, a Kalendar, a Mariner's Compass rectified, Love's Surveying, the Pantheon, or History of the Heathen Gods, &c.—He has lately been found out to be a grand TORY, although he usually professed WHIGGISH principles; and as a convincing proof of his wicked designs, upon opening his chest since he absconded, three dozen musket cartridges were found in it, which it is thought the said Ebenezer Leely brought from on board the men of war not lying in Hudson's river, and delivered to him with a view of his putting them into the hands of some other Rascals, in order to butcher their neighbours.*—*He left Blooming-Grove (where he was employed as a Schoolmaster) about the 16th of July last, and said he was going to Fort Montgomery.*

The Committee desires the foregoing Advertisement may be inserted in all the public papers printed in New-York, as it is thought that if the said Owens and Leely, or either of them could be apprehended, some matters of consequence might transpire.—*Said LEELY is a tall fellow, rather slender, has a red face, county born, about thirty years old.*
    In behalf of the Committee,
    ELIHU MARVEN, Chairman.
    Cornwal Precinct, Orange County, Aug. 1st.
The New-York Gazette; and the Weekly Mercury, August 12, 1776.

RUN AWAY on the 10th instant, from the Subscriber in Flushing, an Apprentice lad named SAMUEL WOOD, aged 19 years, son of the widow Day.—It is supposed he was seduced or deluded away by ill advisers, rather than his own inclination, and I am determined to prosecute any person who harbours, entertains, or employs him.—Whoever takes up and returns him, shall have a reasonable reward for their trouble.
    RICHARD LOWDEN.   New York, 14th August, 1776.
The New-York Journal; or, The General Advertiser, August 15, 1776.

    THREE DOLLARS Reward.
RUN AWAY from the subscriber, a Negro servant, named ISAAC, 22 years of age, five feet six inches high, down look, and tells a poor story: Had on when he went away, a felt hat small brimmed, a dark coloured under jacket, without sleeves, tow shirt and trowsers, and a pair of old shoes. Whoever takes up said servant, and secures him in any gaol, so that his master may have him again, shall have the above reward, and all
    charges paid by me,   JAMES ROGERS.
N. B. It is supposed he is gone to New-England.
    Huntington, Aug. 13, 1776.
The New-York Journal; or, The General Advertiser, August 15, 1776.

    FIVE DOLLARS Reward.
RAN-AWAY from the subscriber, on Tuesday, the 30th of July, 1776, a negro man, named CASTER, about five feet inches high, thin make, walks very upright, about 35 years old. Had on when he went away, a pair of white linen trowsers, tow shirt, one pair old shoes, and brass buckles; he is

of a pleasant countenance, and is well pleased and elevated when any one speaks to him about war. If taken on the island of New-York, the above reward will be paid, with all reasonable charges; and if taken out of the county of New-York, Eight Dollars reward and reasonable charges. All masters of vessels, and other, are requested not to harbour or carry the said negro off.
The New-York Gazette; and the Weekly Mercury, August 19, 1776; *The Constitutional Gazette*, August 21, 1776; August 24, 1776. Minor differences between the papers.

RUN-AWAY from the Subscriber, one JOHN LANGDEN, a Boy about Sixteen Years of Age, very Small of his Age: Had on when he went away a blue Coat and Jacket, a Pair of Trowsers and under his Trowsers a Pair of Buckskin Breeches, this Particular is mentioned, that it is probable he has flung away his Trowsers, as they were old. Whoever secures the said Boy, and brings him to me the Subscriber, Shoemaker, near the Fly-Market, New-York, shall receive Two Dollars Reward, and all reasonable Charges,
    by me DANIEL GREEN.
The New-York Gazette; and the Weekly Mercury, August 26, 1772; September 2, 1776.

FIVE DOLLARS Reward.
RUN-away from the subscriber, a negro man named Tom, about 50 years of age, five feet high, thick set, yellow complexion, lisps some little tho' hardly perceiveable: Had on when he went away, a pair of brown tow trowsers, striped woollen shirt, a felt hat about half worn, a pair of new shoes with buckles, a waistcoat with the fore parts brown, the back parts white. Whoever takes up the said negro man, and brings him to the subscriber, shall have the above reward, and all reasonable charges paid,
    by me JOHN VAIL. Cortlandt's Manor, July 1, 1776.
The New-York Gazette; and the Weekly Mercury, September 2, 1776; September 21, 1776; September 28, 1776; October 5, 1776.

TEN DOLLARS REWARD.
RUn away from the subscribers, living in Ulster county, two mulatto slaves, remarkably white, on the 22d inst. both well set, about 5 feet eight inches high, black hair, blue eyed, one of them stoop shouldered, and long chinned; one took with him a grey short coat with yellow buttons, a brown jacket, a double breasted red streaked jacket, with white homespun trowsers, a pair of speckled stockings, with a Kilmarnock cap; the other took with him, two suits, the one black wilting, and the other brown cloth, made regimental fashion, with a beaver hat, marked on his cheek with

gunpowder, and both brothers.—Whoever takes up said mulatto slaves, and secures them, so that their masters may have them again, shall be intitled to the above reward, and all reasonable charges, paid by
    Col. JAMES M'CLUGHERY, and JOSEPH HOUSTON.
    Hanover, Ulster county, Sept. 24, 1776.
The New-York Gazette; and the Weekly Mercury, September 28, 1776; October 5, 1776; October 19, 1776.

RUN-away from the Guard at Newark Goal, a Negro Man named SAM, about 5 Feet 6 inches high, formerly belonging to Mr. Lot, of Long-Island.—Had on a striped Jacket without Sleeves, and a Pair of Tow Trowsers. Whoever takes up said Negro and returns him to Newark Goal, or secures him so that he can be had by the Subscriber, shall receive Five Dollars Reward,
   paid by me JOSIAH BRYAN, Lt. Col.
The New-York Gazette; and the Weekly Mercury, October 5, 1776; October 19, 1776.

MADE his escape from Litchfield county goal in the evening after the 16th instant, Nathan Guyer, taken upon Long-Island last May, and sent by the convention of the State of New-York to be confined in this goal for treasonable practices against the American States; he is about 60 years of age, short curl'd gray hair, about 5 feet 9 inches high, thick sett, has lately been sick of a fever, had on when he went away a blue coat, striped linnen jacket and trowsers and check'd shirt, 'tis supposed he will try to get on Long-Island again. Whoever will apprehend and return him to said goal again shall receive FIVE DOLLARS reward.
    LYNDE LORD, *Sheriff*. Litchfield, Sept. 6, 1776.
The Connecticut Courant, and Hartford Weekly Intelligencer, October 7, 1776; October 14, 1776.

RUN-AWAY from the subscriber, living at Jamaica, on Long-Island, a young Negro fellow named YORK, tall and very black. He had on when he went off (which is about three weeks ago), a blue camblet waistcoat, a pair of coarse tow trowsers, and pinchbeck Buckles in his Shoes. Whoever secures the said Negro so that his master may have him again, shall receive EIGHT DOLLARS reward, and all other reasonable charges,
    paid by CHARLES ARDING.
N. B. He affects to laugh when he speaks.
    Jamaica, Long-Island, October 12, 1776.
The New-York Gazette; and the Weekly Mercury, October 14, 1776; October 21, 1776; October 28, 1776; November 4, 1776; November 11, 1776.

RUN-AWAY the third instant, a Negro lad named YORK, supposed to be lurking about the camps or shipping. Any person giving intelligence where he may be found, shall have a reward of Five Dollars, and a further reward of Five Dollars more if brought to me, the proprietor, in Wall-Street.
WILLIAM MAXWELL.

N. B. YORK is about 19 years of age, 5 feet 7 or 8 inches high, rather thinly made, had on when he eloped, an old brown cloth jacket, with plain yellow metal buttons and red cloth collar, a brown cloth waistcoat, with small yellow metal buttons, a check shirt, brown linen trowsers, shoes with yellow buckles, and no stockings, an old round hat with tarnish'd gold edging, speaks good English, and may pretend to be free.
New-York, October 12, 1776.
The New-York Gazette; and the Weekly Mercury, October 14, 1776; October 21, 1776.

Brooklyn Ferry, 16th October, 1776.
FIVE DOLLARS REWARD.

RUN AWAY on the second instant, from the Subscriber, living at Brooklyn-Ferry, on Long-Island, a Negro Boy named FEONCE, about 17 years of age, five feet, six or seven inches high, stoops in his walk, when pleased is apt to shew his teeth very much, is very fond of strong liquor: Took with him a pale blue broad cloth coat and waistcoat, a leather jockey cap, a striped yellow and blue linsey woolsey waistcoat, two pair of tow trowsers, and a pair of old shoes. If any person will take up the said Negro, and secure him so that his Master can get him again, shall have the above Reward, and all reasonable charges paid; or if they can inform his Master where he is, so that he can get him again, shall have FOUR DOLLARS Reward. JOHN RAPALJE.
The New-York Gazette; and the Weekly Mercury, October 21, 1776; October 28, 1776; November 4, 1776; November 11, 1776.

Newport, Nov. 2, 1776.

RAN away from on board the brig Dudly-Castle, a Negro fellow, named JAMES TRUDDLE, belonging to Capt. Amleton Darling of Smithtown, on Long-Island; he is about 5 feet 5 inches high, a well-set fellow, something upon the Mustee order, middling long hair:—Whoever shall take up and secure him in any of the gaols to the United States of America, so that the subscriber may have him, or return him back to his quarters at Newport, shall have a reward of 10 dollars, and all necessary charges,
paid by ROBERT ELLIOTT.
The Newport Mercury, November 11, 1776.

RUN-AWAY some time ago, from Philip Skene, Esq; of Skenesborough, a Spanish Negro man named Ned, near 6 feet high, of a yellow Complexion, about 40 years old.

He was taken a few days ago, on board the City of London, Capt. M'Fadzean, where he was in the capacity of a cook; since which time he has made his escape, supposed thro' bad advice, as he has lately been received and slept on board said ship. Yesterday he was seen in town, waiting an opportunity to get on board some vessel. It is therefore requested that no person in this city, or master of vessel will conceal said Negro, as they will answer for the consequences.

A reward of Forty Shillings will be given to any person that will take up said slave, and bring him to his master,
    at Mrs. Airy's, or to Capt. Vardill, near Burling's-Slip.
    New York, October 28, 1776.
The New-York Gazette; and the Weekly Mercury, October 28, 1776; November 4, 1776; November 11, 1776.

STOLEN on Wednesday the sixth instant (November) from the subscriber, EIGHTEEN POUNDS Currency, viz Three half Johannes and Two Guineas, the remainder in silver Dollars, by a boy, between the years of sixteen and seventeen, lately from England: Had on a striped flannel red and white jacket, a blue cloth vest, and a pair of white thickset trowsers, a pair of good shoes and stockings, his hair lately cut and lost his fore teeth; has an impediment in his speech, appears to be very quiet and peaceable. It is imagined he yet remains in town. Any person or persons who will give proper intelligence where he may be had, on will apprehend him, so that the Owner may have his property, will receive TEN DOLLARS Reward, with reasonable charges paid, by
    EDWARD WALSH, in George-street, New-York.
The New-York Gazette; and the Weekly Mercury, November 11, 1776; November 18, 1776; November 25, 1776; December 2, 1776.

MADE his escape from the county goal in Springfield in the State of Massachusetts-Bay, in the night after the 8th instant, Abraham Hait, who was sent by the committee of New-York to be confined in said goal for treasonable practices against the American States, he is about 30 years of age, 5 feet 10 inches high, of a light complexion, wore away a blue coat and leather breeches, he says he belongs to New-Castle in the State of New-York; also John Pickering, who was sent by said committee to Worcester goal and was taken sick at Springfield. Whoever will take up and return them to said goal shall receive Five Dollars reward,
    THOMAS STEBBINS, *Chairman of said committee.*

Springfield, Nov. 8. 1776.
The Connecticut Courant, and Hartford Weekly Intelligencer,
November 18, 1776; November 25, 1776; December 2, 1776; December 9, 1776.

Fifty Dollars Reward.

WHEREAS Major Christopher French, Ensign Joseph Moyland, and John Bickle, belonging to the British Army, Peter Herron, a Tory, and Capt. Jacob Smith, who was taken lately on Long Island in Arms, all escaped from Goal last Night to join the British Army....All Persons, and especially all Officers, Civil and Military, are requested to assist in pursuing and taking said Prisoners.—Whoever shall take up and return either of said Prisoners to Harford Goal shall be entitled to a premium of TEN DOLLARS, and all necessary Charges,
paid by EZEKIEL WILLIAMS, sheriff.

Hartford, Nov, 16, 1776.
The Connecticut Courant, And Hartford Weekly Intelligencer,
November 18, 1776; November 25, 1776.

ESCAPED from the Goal in Springfield, in the county of Hampshire, the night after the 16th instant, John Johnson, Joshua Ferris, Thomas Gleason, Samuel Wilson, Henry Chace, Ryner Van Rosen, six persons who were sent by the committee of the State of New-York to the goal in said Springfield, for aiding, assisting and abetting in treasonable practices against the liberties of America; also Robert Patterson and John Hamilton, both Highlanders, and Allen Soper and Bryan Cullen, marines, which were prisoners of war, confined in goal by orders from his Excellency General Washington, and by the council of the State of Massachusetts-Bay.—All persons are requested to assist in pursuing and taking up said prisoners.—Whoever shall take up and return either of the above-persons sent by the committee of the State of New-York to said goal, shall be entitled to a premium of FIVE DOLLARS; and for each of said prisoners or war, the thanks of the committee of the town of Springfield, and all necessary charges
paid by   THO'S STEBBINS,
Chairman of the Committee of Springfield,
Springfield, Nov. 17, 1776.
The Connecticut Courant, and Hartford Weekly Intelligencer,
November 18, 1776.

BROKE out of the New Goal last Friday night, three prisoners, viz. George Digman, a sailor, 5 feet 5 and 1-2 inches high, well made, and fresh

complexion, with brown hair;—Daniel Moss, black hair, pale complexion, 5 feet 7 inches high;—Elisha Tilton, 5 feet 9 inches high, slender made, and brown complexion.—Two Dollars reward will be given for each by
                Serjeant Hubert, at the New Goal.
The New-York Gazette; and the Weekly Mercury, November 25, 1776; December 9, 1776; December 16, 1776.

RUN-away from Samuel Sackett, living near the Fly-market, a negro man named Joe, about 6 feet high, about 30 years old, of a yellow complexion, stout fellow; a negro wench, with a young child about 5 months, the wench about 24 years old, of a yellowish complexion, stout and well set; likewise a negro wench middling tall and slim, middling black and pitted with the small-pox; it is thought they are all in the army. Whoever takes up said negroes, or any one of them, and delivers them safe to Samuel Sacket, or secures them in any Goal, so that he may get them again, shall have ten dollars a piece.
                SAMUEL SACKETT.
The New-York Gazette; and the Weekly Mercury, November 25, 1776; December 2, 1776; December 9, 1776.

RUN-AWAY, from the subscriber, the 19th instant, living at Brower's wharf, near the New Crane, a negro boy, named Ned, about twelve years of age; this country born, and speaks very good English: Had on when he went away, a blue under jacket, a whitish Wilton coat, a new pair blue duffle trowsers, a check shirt, a pair of new shoes and whitish stockings, Whoever secures said negro boy, so that his master may have him again, shall receive four Dollars reward, and all other reasonable charges
                paid by,   JOHN BRYSON.
The New-York Gazette; and the Weekly Mercury, November 25, 1776; December 2, 1776; December 9, 1776.

                FIFTY DOLLARS Reward.
On the night after the 20th instant escaped from Litchfield, David Matthews, Esq; late Mayor of the city of New-York, who was some months since taken from thence, on being charged with high crimes against the American States, but on being given his parole was admitted to certain limits, which he has most basely and perfidiously deserted. He is well made, about 6 feet high, short brown hair, about 39 years old, and has a very plausible way of deceiving people. It is supposed he will endeavour to get to Long Island, where his family now reside. Whoever shall take him up, and return him to the subscriber in Litchfield, shall receive the above reward, and necessary charges

paid, by MOSES SEYMOUR.
Litchfield, Nov. 26, 1776.
The Connecticut Journal, November 27, 1776; December 3, 1776; December 11, 1776.

RUN AWAY, in the night betwixt the 10th and 11th inst. A Negro Wench, named PHOEBE; she is very well known in town; she belongs to the widow Ryder. Whoever will bring her to the subscriber, at No. 53, in Queen-street, opposite the end of Beekman-street, will receive Two Dollars Reward.
J. SMITH.
N. B. All persons are forbid harbouring or carrying her off.
The New-York Gazette; and the Weekly Mercury, December 16, 1776; December 23, 1776; December 30, 1776.

RUN-AWAY from the subscriber, living in New-York, a negro lad about 20 Years of age, goes by the name of Fortune Brookman, about 5 feet 3 inches high, squat shape, his right knee bends inwards, wants some of his fort Teeth: Had on when he went away, a red plush waistcoat, and snuff coloured long trowsers. Whoever secures said run-away shall have FOUR POUNDS reward,
paid by   THOMAS BROOKMAN.
At Mr. Nicoll's, near Coenties Market.
The New-York Gazette; and the Weekly Mercury, December 16, 1776; December 23, 1776.

EIGHT DOLLARS REWARD.

RUN-away on Monday the 22d of December, a negro man named CAESAR, about 30 years of age, very short, well-set, bandy leg'd, of a grave countenance, speaks civilly, and wants some of his fore teeth, wears commonly a dirty looking cloth coat with buttons of the same colour, a new round hat with a high crown, and a set of silver shoe and knee buckles of open work; in wet weather commonly wears boots, and has a variety of cloaths. He passes himself for a free man and a glazier by trade. Whoever takes him up and secures him in any Goal so that his master gets him again, shall receive Eight Dollars reward, and reasonable charges, on application to the printer, or to the subscriber, at the ordnance-office in New-York, All persons are forewarned not to harbour, employ, or carry of said negro.
WILLIAM WOOD.
The New-York Gazette; and the Weekly Mercury, December 30, 1776; January 6, 1777.

RUN-away from the subscriber, at Newtown, on Long-Island, a negro man called Jack, of a yellow complexion, bushy hair, about 30 years old, rather short in stature, and well-set. Whoever takes up said negro, and delivers him to the owner, shall receive FIVE DOLLARS,
    WATERS SMITH. Newtown, Dec. 23, 1776.
The New-York Gazette; and the Weekly Mercury, December 30, 1776; January 6, 1777.

1777

A NEGRO WENCH,
RUN-AWAY, supposed to Flatbush, on Long-Island, where he was lately purchased of Cornelius Van Der Veer, jun. is about 22 years old, call'd BETTY, can speak both Dutch and English, is of a stubborn disposition, especially when she drinks spirituous liquors, which she is sometimes too fond of; is a pretty stout wench, but not tall, smooth fac'd and pretty black; 'tis probable she may be conceal'd in this city. Whoever harbours her will be prosecuted, but such as give information to Wm. Tongue, her owner, in Hanover-Square, shall receive FIVE DOLLARS with thanks. She usually wore a striped homespun pettycoat and gown.
The New-York Gazette; and the Weekly Mercury, January 6, 1777; January 13, 1777; January 20, 1777.

RUN-away from the subscriber, an apprentice man named HENRY LENT, about 5 feet ten inches high, fair complexion, short brown hair: Had on when he went away a brown over jacket, striped homespun waistcoat, blue cloth breeches and brown thread stockings. Whoever takes up said apprentice and secures him so that he may be had again, shall receive SIX PENCE New-York currency,
    paid by ABRAHAM ANDERSON.
N. B. All persons are forbid harboring said apprentice.
The New-York Gazette; and the Weekly Mercury, January 13, 1777; January 20, 1777.

RUN-away on Wednesday the first inst. from on board the ship Union, William Hamilton, master; lying at [blank] wharf, a black man named Prince, about twenty-one or twenty-two years of age, speaks good English, and formerly lived with a Mr. Lashel or Lasher, in the Broadway; is well known in this place, and had on when he went away a blue jacket and pair of fearnothing trowsers. Whoever will give intelligence of him to the printer, so that he may be secured; or brings on board the said ship, shall receive two guineas reward and every other charge.

The New-York Gazette; and the Weekly Mercury, January 13, 1777; January 20, 1777.

THREE DOLLARS Reward.

RUN AWAY from Richard Harris in Little Queen-street, next door to the Scotch meeting house, a young negro boy named *Daniel*, about nine years of age, the top part of his left ear is thicker than his right, his hair on his head very thin, and is very small for his age; had on when he went away, an old brown surtout coat, and a cotton check shirt. Whoever will bring the said negro boy home to his master, shall have the above reward.

The New-York Gazette; and the Weekly Mercury, January 20, 1777; January 27, 1777; February 3, 1777; February 17, 1777.

BROKE GOAL

ON the night of the 1st instant, in Exeter, the persons lately bro't from the State of New York, & notorious enemies to American Liberty, viz.— Benjamin Moril, of a midling stature, about 35 years of age, of a robust make; had on a red straight bodied coat and waistecoat, long blue trowsers, and a short brown Wig.— Wm. Slack, of a short stature, about 25 years of age; had on a blue short coat, brown waistcoat, old leather breeches and short brown hair.— John Lawson, of a tall slender made, about 35 years of age; had on a homespun Bengall coat, brown jacket & breeches, strait brown hair, & remarkably pitted with the small pox. 'Tis imagined the above persons absconded with a view to join and give intelligence to the ministerial forces.—All true friends to their country, are earnestly desir'd to exert themselves in endeavouring to apprehend said enemies, and confine them, and give notice to the subscriber, at Exeter, (in New Hampshire) where he or they shall be handsomely rewarded, and all charges paid by   JOSEPH STACY, Goal Keeper.

N. B. The printers in this, and the neighbouring states are desir'd to publish *the above*.

Freeman's Journal, or New-Hampshire Gazette, January 21, 1777; January 28, 1777. See *The Independent Chronicle and the Universal Advertiser*, January 23, 1777.

ON the Night of the first Instant, the County Goal in Exeter, was broke open, and three persons, lately brought from the State of New York, notorious enemies to American Liberty, made their Escape, viz.

Benjamin Morrill, of about 35 Years old, of a robust make, with a red Coat and Jacket, long blue Trowsers, short brown Wig:— *William Slack*, about 25 Years old; with a blue Coat, light brown Waistcoat, old Leather Breeches, and short of Stature, short brown Hair:— *John Lawson*, about 35

Years old, of a tall, slender make, much Pock broken, brown Hair, Homespun Bengall Coat, brown Jacket and Breeches.

It is imagined the above-described Persons have absconded, to join and give intelligence to the British Army.—All true Friends to their Country are earnestly called upon to exert themselves in apprehending said Runaways, and confine them, and give Intelligence to the Subscriber, shall be handsomely rewarded, and all charges

paid by JOSEPH STACY, Goal-Keeper.

Exeter, January 2, 1777.

All printers through the United States are desired to publish this Advertisement.

The Independent Chronicle and the Universal Advertiser, January 23, 1777. See *Freeman's Journal, or New-Hampshire Gazette*, January 21, 1777.

WENT off on Sunday the 26th. ult. from his master Archibald Hamilton, late Captain in his Majesty's 31st regt. a negro named CUFFY, a short thick-set fellow. If he applies to any officer to serve him, it is requested he will secure him; and it any other secures him they shall have two guineas reward.

The New-York Gazette; and the Weekly Mercury, February 3, 1777; February 10, 1777; February 24, 1777; March 3, 1777.

FIFTEEN DOLLARS Reward.

RUN AWAY from the subscriber, on Long-Island, a Negro Man named JAFF, who now calls himself, Jeffery Johnson, is about five feet nine inches high, yellowish complexion, and bushy hair, is a pretty forward chap, very free in his discourse, and had on when he went away, a claret coloured coat and breeches and a scarlet jacket, is supposed to be somewhere at Brunswick or Amboy. Any person who secures the said negro, so that the subscriber, his master, gets him again, shall be intitled to the above reward, and all reasonable costs and charges,

paid by   REM COUWENHOVEN, in King's County.

The New-York Gazette; and the Weekly Mercury, February 10, 1777; February 17, 1777; February 24, 1777; March 3, 1777; March 24, 1777.

Went off last THURSDAY,

FROM his master, a negro boy named CYRUS, he may probably change his name to that, of JIM, about 14 years old, his cloathing as follows: a light blue coat and waistcoat, a mint brown pair of breeches, a clouded pair of yarn stockings and white metal buckles, with a round hat and white shirt.

Whoever takes up said negro, and will bring him to the subscriber living in New-York, shall have ONE GUINEA reward,
            by   F. M'DAVITT.
The New-York Gazette; and the Weekly Mercury, February 10, 1777; February 17, 1777; February 24, 1777; March 3, 1777.

Broke out of the public Goal in New London, the Night after the First Day of February Instant, one SAMUEL GLOVER, a notorious Offender, taken up at Long-Island for accepting an infamous Commission under Gen, Howe.—He is something Tall, has black Beard and Hair, talks grum and slow; had on a long grey Surtout. Whoever will take up said Glover, and secure him to me shall have Eight Dollars Reward, and all necessary
        Charges paid by   EPHRAIM MINER, Goaler.
                                    New-London, Feb. 1, A. D. 1777.
The Connecticut Gazette; and the Universal Intelligencer, February 14, 1777.

RUN-away from George Bevoise, a negro man named FRANK, about 19 years of age, between 5 and 6 feet high, has lost two of his fore teeth, stutters in his speech and has thick lips: Had on and took with him a blue sailor's jacket, an old grey coat-tee, a pair of blue stockings, two pair of grey ditto, and three or four blankets. Whoever takes up said negro man and brings him to his said master, living near Brooklyn-ferry, shall have
                THREE DOLLARS reward.
The New-York Gazette; and the Weekly Mercury, February 17, 1777; February 24, 1777; March 3, 1777; March 10, 1777. See *The New-York Gazette; and the Weekly Mercury*, July 14, 1777.

THIS may inform the following persons, viz.— *Joseph Foster, John Smith, John Strong, Thomas Hopkins, William Cutler, Zachariah Willis, William Edwards, Arnold Darby, John Pickett, John Disko, Jacob Wherton* and *William Hilton,*—that were inlisted by John G. Frazer, at Ticonderoga, are returned over to my company at Boston or Springfield, by the 10th of March next, otherwise they will be advertised as deserters.
                NATHANIEL CUSHING, Captain.
The Connecticut Journal, and Weekly Advertiser, February 20, 1777; February 27, 1777; March 6, 1777.

BROKE out of Litchfield county goal in the evening of the 18th day of February instant, the following prisoners, viz. John Thomas, William Forbes, and Thomas Doyle....Forbes, sent to this goal by the Convention of the State of New York for treasonable practices against the American

States, is a tall slim built fellow, about 5 feet 10 inches high, black hair, clear skin, about 34 years of age....Whoever will apprehend and return them to said goal again shall have 10 dollars for Forbes,
        paid by   LYNDE LORD, Sheriff.
                            Litchfield, 19th February, 1777.
The Connecticut Courant, and Hartford Weekly Intelligencer, February 24, 1777.

                           TEN DOLLARS Reward.
RUN away, the 16th instant, a Negro man named LOUI, about 20 years of age, 5 feet 8 inches high, strait made, a gruff look, and speaks like the West India Negroes, appears a civil innocent fellow when spoken to, wears a short blue coat lapelled, with yellow metal buttons, white waistcoat and breeches, or white flannel trowsers, good shoes and stockings, white shirt and a black silk stock, and commonly wears a white cap bound with red on his head; came lately from St. Vincents with the 6th regiment. Whoever delivers him to the printer, or gives information where he may be got again, shall receive the above reward and charges paid.
    N. B. Any Person harbouring or employing said Negro, will be prosecuted, and a reward of TEN GUINEAS paid to the person that makes a discovery of his being taken out of the country.
    The New-York Gazette; and the Weekly Mercury, March 3, 1777; March 10, 1777; March 17, 1777; March 24, 1777.

                           FOUR POUNDS Reward.
A *Well set sorrel MARE with a white face and light coloured Mane and Tail, about 9 Years old, trots and hand-gallops well, paces but little, was sold to me the 15th of Jan. last, by a Person that call'd his Name Hudson; he said that the had lately mov'd from Long-Island, and now liv'd at Colchester, and said he was going into the Service. (Said Mare is since claim'd as stolen Property). Said Hudson is a well-built Man, near 30 Years of Age, about 5 Feet 9 Inches high, has a Scar under his left Eye and has had the Small-Pox, his Hair is brown and was cut very short. It's likely he chang'd his Name and Place of Abode. Therefore whoever shall discover the Cheat, and give me Information, that the Knave may be brought to Justice shall be intituled to the above Reward*
            from BEZALEEL FISK.   Middletown, Feb. 26, 1777.
    The Connecticut Gazette; and the Universal Intelligencer, March 7, 1777; March 14, 1777.

DESERTED on Friday the 7th inst. from the Watters brigantine, Joseph Jackson, master, now lying near Peck's slip. a stout well-made man, about 5

feet 6 inches high, 21 years of age, and blind of his left eye: He had on when he went away, a short blue sailors jacket, with a green vest underneath, and a pair of fearnought trowsers. He is of a swarthy complexion, and has short streight hair; his name is Isaac Watson, and was born either in Cumberland or Westmoreland, in Old England. He is an apprentice to Robert Waters, Esq; in White Haven, and is supposed to be on board some small craft in the river. Whoever will bring him on board the said brig, shall have Five Dollars reward.
The New-York Gazette; and the Weekly Mercury, March 10, 1777; March 17, 1777; March 24, 1777.

RUN-AWAY on Saturday the 8th inst. a negro man about 50 years of age, goes by the name of Joseph Thompson: He is about 5 feet 11 inches high, has a remarkable black spot under his eye. Had on when he went away, a gray watchcoat, claret coloured breeches, and plain silver buckles; he often wears boots, can play upon the violin, and work at the carpenters trade.—Whoever will bring him to Jacob Bennet, jun. at Bushwyck, or confine him, shall have Ten Dollars reward, and all expences paid.
The New-York Gazette; and the Weekly Mercury, March 17, 1777; March 24, 1777; March 31, 1777; April 7, 1777.

DESERTED from his Majesty's ship Brune, James Hurd, belonging to the detachment of marines on that ship; he was servant to the lieut. of marines, and was about the age of 23, five feet eight inches in stature, or thereabouts, of a fresh complexion, wears his hair short, with a Tyburn top: Had on when he deserted a thickset frock and waistcoat, with a red collar; red drilling breeches, with a leather cap such as the light infantry wear. Whoever apprehends the said deserter shall have what is customary on those occasions.
The New-York Gazette; and the Weekly Mercury, March 17, 1777; March 24, 1777.

THIS is to give Notice to Lewis Sylli[a], inlisted by me at Ticonderoga, in Capt. Abraham Hunt's Company—To John Stover, inlisted at Albany in said Company—And to Thomas Chilman, inlisted likewise at Albany in said Company, to repair to their Companies at Boston or Springfield by the first of April, otherwise they will be deemed and treated as Deserters.
                PHILIP ULMER, Lieut. of said Comp'y.
The Boston-Gazette, and Country Journal, March 31, 1777; April 7, 1777.

RUN-away from the Brigantine Venus, Richard Thirsby, master, George Doutherts, an indented servant lad, about 18 years of age, of slender make, about 5 feet 8 inches high, pock pitted, has black hair, and had on a brown short lapel'd waistcoat. Whoever will bring him to the said brigantine, or to Mrs. White, near the Coffee-House, shall have four dollars reward.
The New-York Gazette; and the Weekly Mercury, March 31, 1777; April 7, 1777; April 14, 1777; April 21, 1777; April 28, 1777.

FOUR DOLLARS Reward.

RUN-away from the Snow Rum-Adventure, Peter Leadbeater, Master, lying at Peck's-Slip, on Thursday the 3d Instant, an Apprentice Boy named James Sandwich, about 5 Feet high, 16 Years old, with light coloured curl'd Hair: Had on a blue Jacket, ragged long Trowsers, blue Drawers, a round Hat, and had Shoes. Whoever apprehends said Boy, so that he may be had again, shall have the above Reward,
paid by the Printer.
The New-York Gazette; and the Weekly Mercury, April 7, 1777; April 14, 1777.

RUN-away from the brigantine William, James M'Ewen, master, an apprentice boy named Antonio Flories, a Spaniard, born in Mallaga, 14 years of age, short but well made, dark complexion, and short hair. Had on when he went away, a blue jacket, white drawers, and an ozenbrigs frock by way of shirt. He is supposed to be harboured by one mother Griffiths, on Golden-Hill. Whoever takes up the said boy and brings him to Mr. Archibald Willson, merchant, in Queen-street, shall receive Three Dollars reward.

N. B. All masters of vessels, and others, are forewarned not to carry off, harbour, or conceal the said apprentice.
The New-York Gazette; and the Weekly Mercury, April 14, 1777; April 21, 1777.

RUN-away from Powles-hook, a negro Man called Osborn, about five feet four inches high, twenty-seven years of age, has a remarkable small waist and bad legs, of a plausible address, pretends to a knowledge of cookery; has a downcast look when he is spoke to by strangers, seemingly the effect of bashfulness. Had on when he went off, a brown coat, white waistcoat, breeches and stockings, and a new round hat. Whoever will secure him, or give information to the Printer, so that he may be secured, shall receive Five Dollars Reward. And 'tis requested to no person will employ him.
The New-York Gazette; and the Weekly Mercury, April 21, 1777; May 12, 1777.

DESERTED the 13th inst. from the Grand Duke victualler, at Brownjohn's wharf, an apprentice boy named Nathaniel Turvey, about 15 years of age, small stature, crooked back'd, walks lame on his right leg. Had on when he went away, a blue jacket, but has since put on a white swanskin jacket. Whoever apprehends him and brings him on board the said ship shall have Four Dollars reward.

The New-York Gazette; and the Weekly Mercury, April 28, 1777; May 5, 1777.

RUn-away from the Argo Transport, lying in the North-River, near the Eagle, George Tate, Master, the 19th of April, an Apprentice Lad named William Miller, about 16 Years old, little of his Age, wears his own brown Hair, and is clipped pretty close on his Forehead: Had on a dirty red Jacket, and dirty Trowsers and pretends in the Taylor's Trade. Five Dollars Reward will be paid for apprehending of said Lad,
               by GEORGE TATE.

The New-York Gazette; and the Weekly Mercury, April 28, 1777; May 5, 1777.

ABSENTED from the service of Thomas Mattin, the 16th inst. JOE, a negro man; he is a stout well made young fellow, about five feet nine inches high, can shave and dress hair pretty well: He had on when he went away, a green cloth coat and waistcoat, and a pair of leather breeches. Whoever apprehends and brings the said negro to his master, in Hanover-square, New-York, shall receive EIGHT DOLLARS, reward.
    N. B. It is requested that no person will employ said fellow, and all masters of vessels are desired not to suffer him in board their vessels, or carry him from this country.
If he returns voluntarily, his fault will be forgiven.

The New-York Gazette; and the Weekly Mercury, April 28, 1777; May 5, 1777; May 19, 1777; May 26, 1777.

DEserted from Capt. Sergant's Company in Col. John Crane's Battalion of Artillery, William Candull, late of New-York, aged 23, 5 feet 10 inches, dark Complexion, and black short Hair, somewhat Pock broken. William Thompson, formerly of Newport, aged 22 years, 5 feet 3 inches, dark complexion, and black long Hair. Whoever shall take up said Deserters and confine them in any of the Continental Goals, or bring them to the North Rendezvous in Boston, shall receive Six Dollars for each and all necessary
       Charges paid by   SAMUEL BASS, Lieut. (Artillery.

Boston May 4, 1777.
The Boston-Gazette and Country Journal, May 5, 1777; May 12, 1777; May 19, 1777.

RUN-AWAY from the subcrbier in the night of the 16th of April, a Negro boy named LIVERPOOL; had on a brown jacket, a blue cap, blue stockings and red vest: is a short thick fellow, about 18 years of age. Whoever will take up and secure said Negro so as his master may have him, shall have FIVE DOLLARS reward, and all reasoanble charges paid by me his master, living near Salisbury Furnace on the Oblong in Dutchess County.
    JOSHUA DAKINS. April 26, 1777.
The Connecticut Courant, and Hartford Weekly Intelligencer, May 5, 1777; May 12, 1777.

RUN-away from the Thomas and Betsey victualler, Charles Edwards, master, on the night of the 2d instant, an apprentice lad named Thomas Day, of a ruddy complexion, smooth-faced, about 5 feet 2 inches high, 16 years old, and has black hair: Took a variety of cloaths and a bed and hammock, with him. All Persons are forbid to harbour or entertain him. Whoever takes up and secures said run-away, so that he may be had again, shall receive Five Dollars reward,
   from CHARLES EDWARDS.
The New-York Gazette; and the Weekly Mercury, May 5, 1777; May 12, 1777; May 19, 1777.

DESERTED *from Stockbridge December and January, David Purdie, belonging to the Nine Partners, 23 years of age, 5 feet 10, light complection, light hair and eyes. Peter Patterson, a High Dutchman, speaks broken English, has a down look 5 feet 10, 50 years of age. Edward White of Beckit, 5 feet 4, dark complection, dark hair and eyes. Silas Fay, of Beckit, 5 feet 7, dark hair and eyes, 21 years of all, all of capt Chadwick's company, col. Brewer's regiment, at Ticonderoga. Whoever shall take up one or all of the above deserters, and return them to their regiment, or confine them in goal in any of the United States, shall receive 10 dollars reward for each, and all necessary charges paid by*
    THEOPHILUS MANSFIELD, Lieut. May 10. 1777.
The Connecticut Courant, and Hartford Weekly Intelligencer, May 12, 1777; May 19, 1777.

DESERTED from the Prince of Wales victualler, at Moore's wharf, Henry Denton, master, the 9th of May, 1777, two apprentice lads, the one named George Shaw, about 22 years old, of a brown complexion, wears his own light colour'd short hair, about 5 feet 9 inches high; and had on a dirty flannel jacket. The other named David Fairfield, about 20 years old, 5 feet 6 inches high, wears his own black hair, and is of a dark complexion; had on a blue jacket, but both of them is supposed to have changed their cloaths since. Whoever takes up and secures that said run-aways, so that they may be had again, shall receive Eight Dollars reward for each,

    from HENRY DENTON.

  N. B. All masters of vessels are forbid to harbour or entertain the said apprentices, as they will answer it at their peril.

The New-York Gazette; and the Weekly Mercury, May 12, 1777; May 19, 1777; May 26, 1777; June 2, 1777.

RUN-away from the subscriber, on the 9th of May, an apprentice boy named Robert Dougel, about 4 feet 6 inches high, fair complexion, brown hair tied behind: Had on when he went away a short lose blue jacket, leather breeches, a new check shirt, and a white stock; took away with him some money belonging to his master. Whoever takes up said apprentice and secures him, or gives information to John Barrow, baker, in King-street, No. 13, shall have Six Pence reward.

  N. B. All persons are forbid harbouring or taking off said apprentice, at their peril.

The New-York Gazette; and the Weekly Mercury, May 12, 1777; May 19, 1777; May 26, 1777; June 2, 1777.

RUN-away from the subscriber, living in Ferry-street, No. 19, a negro fellow named YORK, about 20 years of age, is short and well set; speaks broken English and is apt to stammer: Had on when he went away, a short light-colour'd brown coat with green cuffs and collars, an old pair of leather breeches, with yarn stockings and Hessian shoes. Whoever takes up or gives information of said negro, so that he may be had again, shall receive Three Dollars reward,

    by THOMAS GRESWOLD.

The New-York Gazette; and the Weekly Mercury, May 12, 1777; May 19, 1777; May 26, 1777; June 2, 1777. See *The Constitutional Gazette*, July 17, 1776, *The New-York Gazette; and the Weekly Mercury*, June 9, 1777, and *The New-York Gazette; and the Weekly Mercury*, September 14, 1778.

ABSENTED from his service, a negro man called SAM, a thick heavy made fellow, 5 feet 6 or 7 inches high, about 28 years old, the property of the late widow Hester Weyman. Whoever will bring him to the subscribers, executors to said Mrs. Weyman's estate, shall be entitled to a reward of

Five Dollars. All masters of vessels and others, are requested not to take said fellow off, as the loss will fall on orphan children,
    PETER GUELET, GABRIEL H. LUDLOW.
The New-York Gazette; and the Weekly Mercury, May 19, 1777; May 26, 1777; June 2, 1777.

                 Norwich, 8th May, 1777.
         THIRTY DOLLARS REWARD.
JAMES MASON, a Scotchman, taken in New-York, upon suspicion of Toryism, sent to Connecticut and confined in Norwich goal, being since allowed to walk abroad was in the service of the subscriber when about three weeks ago he obtained a pass from Governor Trumbull to go to the Jersies, and did on Friday last leave this place on the business of the subscriber, upon promise of returning the next day; carried with him of the subscriber's property a sorrel mare about 14 hands high, trots hard—bridle, saddle, and saddle bags, and likewise a silver watch, and seven dollars in continental bills, but hath not since been heard of. Said runaway wore away a check'd woollen jacket with sleeves, check's shirt, leather breeches and an old blue great coat, has light hair, a down guilty look, and appears at first sight to be uncommonly ill-natured.—Whoever will apprehend the runaway and return him, with the mare and watch, to the subscriber, or confine him in any goal in this State, thereby securing the above articles so that the subscriber may obtain them, shall have the above reward, and all necessary
      charges paid by   DEODAT LITTLE.
The Connecticut Gazette; and the Universal Intelligencer, May 23, 1777; May 30, 1777.

          FIVE GUINEAS Reward.
RUN-away from the Christie transport, A. Bodfield, master, now lying in the North-River, the following sailors, viz. John Williams, an Irishman about 18 years of age. Archibald M'Vickers, a Scotchman, about 25 years of age. George Rankin, a native of America, about 38 years of age. James Nicol, a Scotchman, about 21 years of age, and Alexander Banks, a Scotchman, about 20 years of age. It is to be hoped no master of a ship will harbour or carry them off, as it is a means of encouraging them and many other idlers, that are now lurking about this town, who run from ship to ship receiving a month's advance from every person that will trust them with it, without any intention of abiding in any one ship. Whoever takes up the said men and returns them to their ship, or secures them in any goal or guardhouse, on acquainting the master of the Christie thereof, shall receive the above reward, or one guinea for each of them.
    A. BODFIELD.

Dunlap's Pennsylvania Packet or, the General Advertiser, May 26, 1777; *The New-York Gazette; and the Weekly Mercury*, May 26, 1777; June 2, 1777; June 9, 1777. The *Gazette*, shows the second man's name as M'Vicker.

RUN-away, on Thursday the 15th instant, from the subscriber, living at Corlear's-Hook, a negro lad named CHESS: He us about 20 years of age, speaks thick, is fond of dressing his hair high before, has remarkable large feet, and his eyes of a redish cast; had on a blue coat and breeches, and is fond of dress. Whoever will deliver the said negro to the subscriber, or to Mrs. Yates, living at Wall-street, or lodge him where his master may have him again, shall receive HALF A JOE reward. All persons whatever are forbid harbouring him at their peril.
STEPHEN SKINNER.

The New-York Gazette; and the Weekly Mercury, May 26, 1777; June 2, 1777; June 9, 1777.

RUN-away from Thomas Harriot, living at Jamaica South, on Long-Island, a negro man named Wilkes, about 5 feet 7 inches high, well-set, smooth face, speaks bad English is apt to blunder, has remarkable large eyes, and is about 19 or 20 years old: Had on when he went away, a short gray coat with brass buttons, brown jacket, homespun trowsers, and a beaver hat cock'd. Whoever apprehends the above fellow so as his master may get him again, or delivers him to Capt. John Hitchin's, near John Wood's, Esq; shall have 4 dollars reward, and reasonable charges paid. All persons are requested not to harbour or employ him, and master of vessels are desired not to ship or carry him off. He has been bred to the sea.

The New-York Gazette; and the Weekly Mercury, May 26, 1777.

Five Dollars Reward.

RUN-away from the subscriber, the 30th of May, a negro boy named POMPY, about 17 years old, and well-made: Had on when he went away, a red jacket, ozenbrigs shirt and trowsers, shoes and stockings, with a kind of jockey cap, and is supposed to be gone in the Queen's Rangers, or some other department. Its hoped no gentlemen in the army or navy, or master of vessel will inlist or carry him off; and whoever will bring him to the subscriber, shall have the above reward, and all reasonable charges paid by   JOHN MOWATT, cabinet and chair maker,
in William-street, New-York.

The New-York Gazette; and the Weekly Mercury, June 2, 1777; June 9, 1777; June 16, 1777; June 23, 1777.

RUN-away on Saturday the 24th of May, from the subscriber, living at Brooklyn Ferry, a negro man named PETER, about 25 years of age, 5 feet 9 or 10 inches high: Had on when he went away, a grey surtout coat, woollen shirt, and tow trowsers, and is supposed to be lurking about the city. Whoever will deliver the said negro to his master, shall have 4 dollars reward.   JACOB HICKS.
The New-York Gazette; and the Weekly Mercury, June 2, 1777.

SIX POUNDS Reward.
RUN-AWAY on the first day of June instant, three NEGROES, two men and one woman, the property of George Shaw, of the city of New-York, tanner. One is about 6 feet high, or upwards, and goes by the name of JAMES RICHARDS, or RICHARDSON, the other negro named HARRY ROBBINS, of a middling stature, yellow complexion, and might complaisant in discourse, but very deceitful and given to liquor. The other a negro woman, of a coal black complexion, named ANN, very nimble and brisk on her feet, but bold and impudent behaviour, born in New-Castle county, on Delaware.

The two negro men has entered into his Majesty's service as waggon drivers, and their names are on the Commissary's books, but are my property. Whoever will take up the said negroes, and bring them to me the subscriber, shall have FORTY SHILLINGS for each, and all reasonable charges paid by   GEORGE SHAW.
The New-York Gazette; and the Weekly Mercury, June 9, 1777; June 16, 1777; June 23, 1777; June 30, 1777; July 7, 1777; July 14, 1777.

Three Pounds Reward.
RUN-AWAY from the subscriber, about four weeks ago, a negro fellow named York, about twenty years of age, is short and well set, speaks broken English, and is apt to stammer: Had on when he went away a short light brown coat, with green cuffs and collar, an old pair of leather breeches, with yarn stockings and Hessian shoes. Whoever takes up said negro and secures him, or gives information so that he may be had again, shall receive the above reward, with all reasonable charges,
From   Thomas Griswold, distiller, at No. 10, in Ferry-street, near Peck's-slip.
The New-York Gazette; and the Weekly Mercury, June 9, 1777; June 16, 1777; June 23, 1777. See *The Constitutional Gazette*, July 17, 1776, *The New-York Gazette; and the Weekly Mercury*, October 14, 1776, *The New-York Gazette; and the Weekly Mercury*, May 12, 1777, and *The New-York Gazette; and the Weekly Mercury*, September 14, 1778.

RUN-away on Saturday the 24th of May, from the subscriber, living at Brooklyn Ferry, a negro man named PETER, about 24 years of age, 5 feet 9 or 10 inches high: Had on when he went away, a gray surtout coat, woollen shirt, and new trowsers, and is supposed to be lurking about the city. Whoever will deliver the said negro to his master, shall have
                4 dollars reward.   JACOB HICKS.
The New-York Gazette; and the Weekly Mercury, June 9, 1777; June 16, 1777.

DEserted from Capt. Ely's company, Col. Douglas's regiment, some time since, one Garret Degrout, of Long Island, 5 feet 10 inches high, pock broken, about 30 years old. Four dollars reward, and all necessary charges will be paid for taking him up, and returning him to any officer in the regiment.   *Asa Lay*, Lieut. May 30 1777.
The Connecticut Journal, June 11, 1777; June 18, 1777.

WHEREAS a certain *Francis Kingston* (a native of Devonshire, who came to New-Jersey a few years since) on the 29th ultimo came into this city with a flag, in order to procure a passage to his family in England, and has not been since heard of. He is of a middling stature and thin habit, wore a blue cloth coat, and other old cloaths; is about 30 years of age, and sometimes disordered in his mind. As it is possible, that for want of knowledge of his unhappy circumstance, he may have been impressed or imprisoned, any person who will kindly give any information concerning him to Samuel Burling, merchant, at No. 36, in Wall-street, will do a humane office, and receive an adequate compensation for their trouble.
The New-York Gazette; and the Weekly Mercury, June 16, 1777.

RUN-AWAY on Sunday the 15th instant, from the Swan transport, Capt. Deal, an apprentice lad named ANDREW: He is a mulatto, was born in Honduras Bay, about 5 feet high, straight, strong, black hair; had on a blue suit of cloaths, with fashionable buttons, and long trowsers. Whoever takes up and secures the said boy, so that his master may have him again, shall receive FIVE DOLLARS reward,
            paid by   JONATHAN DEAL.
The New-York Gazette; and the Weekly Mercury, June 23, 1777; June 30, 1777; July 7, 1777; July 14, 1777.

RUN-away from the subscriber the 17th instant, a negro man named Plymouth, to which he may add the name of John, having sometimes assumed that name. He is about twenty-six years of age, fond of dressing his hair high before, has large feet and is fond of dress, of low stature,

stoops, of very black complexion, and thick lips: had on when he went away a round hat with silver loop and tussel; a thick set coat, waistcoat and breeches, but may vary his dress, having carried other cloaths with him; it is apprehended he is gone towards the army in the Jerseys, having lived with capt. Drewry, of the 63d regt. last fall and part of last winter. If any of the gentlemen of the army should meet with him, it is requested they will stop him; any other person that will deliver said negro to Mr. Thomas Lynch, merchant, in Duke-Street, New-York, to the subscriber on Staten-Island, or lodge him where his master may have him again, shall receive five dollars reward. All masters of vessels and others are forbid carrying him off, or harbouring him at their peril.
      TERRENCE KERIN.
The New-York Gazette; and the Weekly Mercury, June 23, 1777; June 30, 1777; July 7, 1777; July 21, 1777; July 28, 1777.

      TEN DOLLARS Reward.
RUN-away from the Two-Friends victualler, Thomas Jones, master, on the 25th inst. John Davison, a servant, about 20 years of age, black complexion, and wears his own hair: Had on an old blue jacket and long trowsers. Whoever will inform the said master so that he may be secured, shall on his being so, receive the above reward,
    paid by Thomas Jones, lying off the king's yard.
N. B. All masters of vessels are forbid to harbour him at their peril.
 The New-York Gazette; and the Weekly Mercury, June 30, 1777; July 7, 1777; July 14, 1777.

      Five Pounds Reward.
RUN-away from the subscriber, on Tuesday the 15th of April last, a negro man, of a yellow complexion, part Indian, well set, walks with his knees wide apart, flat nose, about five feet eight or nine inches high, forty five years of age, of thereabouts, goes by the name of Abraham: Had on when he went away, a brown homespun jacket, tow shirt, a pair of buckskin breeches, black and white yarn stockings, and a new pair of shoes.
 The said negro took with him a small mulatto wench, by the name of Moll, which he claims as his wife, and two negro children; one a boy three years old, the other a girl fire months old. The above negroes were seen on Long-Island, not long since. Whoever apprehends the said run-aways, and brings them to Thomas Bartow, in New-York, or to the subscriber, or secures them so that the owner may get them again, shall receive the above reward, or Three Pounds for the negro, and Two Pounds for the wench and children, and all reasonable charges
    paid by THOMAS PELL. Manor of Pelham, June 22, 1777.

The New-York Gazette; and the Weekly Mercury, June 30, 1777; July 7, 1777; July 14, 1777.

RUN-away on Saturday the 21st. ult. a likely negro wench, named Charity, about 19 years of age, 5 feet high. She took a child with her, about two years old, named Peter, who frequently calls the mother by name. It is probable she may endeavour to get to the White–Plains, as she was bought from doctor Graham, about ten months since, and seemed anxious to get back. Whoever apprehends said wench, and brings her to the subscriber in Chapel-Street, shall have Eight Dollars reward.
      SAMUEL PEARCE.
The New-York Gazette; and the Weekly Mercury, June 30, 1777; July 7, 1777; July 14, 1777.

LAST evening left [from] several places where they were at labour in Hartford and Wethersfield, and it is supposed with intent of making their escape (from the most agreeable confinement, if confinement can ever say to the agreeable) to Long-Island, where they were lately taken prisoners by Col. Meigs, the several persons hereafter named, viz.

  Anthony Wright, by trade a weaver, was a tall thin favoured man, something hump-shouldered, had short brownish hair, had a green coat with white button holes.

  Isaac Miner, rather tall, short strait hair, had a pair of good new check trowsers, light cloth jacket without sleves, by trade a shoemaker.

  Dennis Kelley, rather short, well set, pretty thick lips; had on a green coat and whitish cloth jacket and breeches.

  Martin Ryenson, midling of stature, rather slender, had short hair, a green coat newly turned, had something peculiar in the look or cast of his eyes, was by trade a hatter. Its probable that some others are gone with them, though not yet known.

  Whoever shall take up all or either of the said persons that have now escaped, whether described or not and convey him or them to either of the county goals in this State, will have the satisfaction of bringing one or more who may probably be exchanged, and to be the means of redeeming one or more of our poor distressed prisoners in New-York, for which purpose they were kept, and shall receive pay for their reasonable expence, from
      EZEKIEL WILLIAMS, Com. of Pris'rs.
      Hartford, July 3 1777.
The Connecticut Courant, and Hartford Weekly Intelligencer, July 7, 1777; July 14, 1777.

THREE DOLLARS Reward.

RUN-AWAY from the subscriber on the night of the 8th instant, a negro lad named FRANK, about 18 or 19 years of age; he stutters very much, has thick lips, and a great stock of impudence; has lost two of his upper fore teeth. Had on a brown coat with a cape, and old black breeches, but 'tis supposed he will alter his dress, as he has taken two check shirts and a pair of trowsers with him. It is imagined he has gone to the fleet at Staten-Island, as he stole a canoe, stretch, paddle, and oars. Whoever apprehends said negro, and returns him to his master, shall receive the above reward from   GEORGE DEBEVOISE.

The New-York Gazette; and the Weekly Mercury, July 14, 1777; July 21, 1777. See *The New-York Gazette; and the Weekly Mercury*, February 17, 1777.

TEN DOLDARS [sic] Reward.

LEFT Brigadier General De Lancey's service, from his farm at Bloomingdale, a negro fellow named HARMAN, of a yellowish colour, broad face and shoulders, hollow back, big buttocks, and remarkable strong well shaped legs, with a very large foot, is about 25 years of age, understands farming. Had on a Dutch thrumb'd cap, a blue sailors jacket, speckled or white shirt, good trowsers and shoes, with a spare buckskin breeches. This is his second elopement, and by his dress may induce masters of ships to entertain him, who are requested to deliver him to New-York goal, Whoever takes him up shall have the above reward paid by General Delancey, the printer, or Mr. Joseph Allicocke.

The New-York Gazette; and the Weekly Mercury, July 21, 1777; July 28, 1777; September 15, 1777; September 22, 1777; September 29, 1777; October 6, 1777. Ads after the first show the reward as DOLLARS.

RUN-AWAY on Saturday the 5th instant, from the subscriber, living on Long-Island, a negro lad named DUKE, (but it is thought he has changed his name to Dick) he is about 20 years of age, about 5 feet 4 inches high, has thick lips and large eyes: Had on when he went away, a white swanskin double-breasted jacket, white drilling breeches, a tow cloth shirt, and blue and white stockings. He crossed Dennis's ferry to Staten-Island, and has most likely imposed himself upon some of the gentlemen of the army for a free man.—Whoever will deliver the said negro to the subscriber, or to the printer hereof, or lodge him where his master may have him again, shall receive Five Dollars reward.—All persons whatever are forbid harbouring him at their peril.
           NICHOLAS OGDEN.

The New-York Gazette; and the Weekly Mercury, July 21, 1777; July 28, 1777; August 4, 1777.

RAN away from the subscriber, on the 2d Instant, a Molatto Man named Moses, about 24 years of age, 5 feet 7 inches high, lately lived in Williams Town, much given to running away. Had on when he left the subscirber a brown sailors Jacket, a Hat with a white tape round it, an old pair of Breeches, Stockings without feet, and hath an old sore on his left leg, talks very broken, and but half witted. Whoever takes up said Negro, and confines him so that the owner might have him again, shall have five dollars reward, and
all reasonable charges paid.   JOHN WILLIAMS.
White-Creek, or New Pe[r   ], Charlottee County and State of New York, July 6, 1777.
The Massachusetts Spy Or American Oracle of Liberty, July 24, 1777.

STOLEN from the subscriber of New-Haven, about the 1st instant, 1 light colour'd patch gown, 2 hollands shifts, 1 lawn apron striped round the edges, 1 cambrick ditto plain lawn border, 1 pair speck'd lawn double ruffles, 1 handkerchief of the same, 1 blue sar[sine]t vis[o]r. I pair white stays. The above goods were stolen by a young woman who called herself Polly Barclay, about 17 years of age, red hair, had on a white straw hat, says she belonged to New-York. Whoever takes up the thief and secures her so that she may be brought to justice shall have two dollars reward and reasonable charges paid,
by SAMUEL HOWELL.   New-Haven, July 23, 1777.
The Connecticut Courant, And Hartford Weekly Intelligencer, July 28, 1777; August 4, 1777; August 11, 1777.

Twenty Dollars Reward.
RUN-away on the 26th of March, from Francis Conihane, living at Peck's-Slip, No. 999, a negro fellow named DICK, about 5 feet 6 inches, a baker by trade, and has followed that business with one Naugle, near Kingsbridge, and has waited a while on a gentleman in the Queen's Rangers; speaks thick, has a mark over one of his eyes, and a scar on his breast; was born in St. Kitts, walks sometimes as if he was lame, and is troubled a little with the rheumaticks. Took with him a dark gray coat and jacket, with white and check shirts, sundry strip'd trowsers, and a red and white striped jacket. It is supposed he keeps about Kingsbridge. Whoever brings him to his said master shall be entitled to the above reward.
    N. B. All persons are forewarned not to harbour said fellow, at their peril.
The New-York Gazette; and the Weekly Mercury, July 28, 1777; August 4, 1777; August 11, 1777; September 1, 1777; September 8, 1777; September 15, 1777.

239

RUN-AWAY from the subscriber, a few days ago, living in this city, a mulatto fellow who lately had the small-pox, named JESSEMY, about 25 years of, 5 feet 9 inches high, and pretty well made, but was crooked about the shoulders: Had on when he went away, a black jacket, breeches and stockings, a white cloth coat with plated buttons, a beaver hat, and silver buckles in his shoes. Whoever takes up and secures the said fellow, so that his master may have him again, shall have five dollars reward,
    paid by RICHARD BAYLEY.
The New-York Gazette; and the Weekly Mercury, July 28, 1777; August 4, 1777; August 11, 1777.

RUN-away from the Britannia victualler, at New-York, Thomas Hayman, master, the 23d instant, an apprentice lad named William Tar, about 19 years of age, five feet six inches high, full featur'd, dark complexion, and a heavy countenance, hair lately cut and appears short, sometimes wears a wig; has lost the first joint of the forefinger of his right hand. Whoever apprehends the said apprentice, and brings him on board the said ship, lying at Marston's wharf, or gives such intelligence to his master so as he may be found, shall receive EIGHT DOLLARS reward.
    THOMAS HAYMAN.
The New-York Gazette; and the Weekly Mercury, July 28, 1777; August 4, 1777; August 11, 1777.

    Forty Shillings Reward.
RUN-away from Isaac Valentine, living at West-chester, about the 2d instant, a negro slave named JOE, about 18 years old, a little upon the yellow complexion; his wearing apparel homespun, except a red jacket without sleeves. He was brought up on the West-Farms. Whoever takes up and secures the said negro in any of his Majesty's goals so that his master can have him again, or brings him home, shall receive the above reward.
The New-York Gazette; and the Weekly Mercury, August 11, 1777; August 18, 1777.

LAST sabbath night escaped from Charles Granger, of Suffield in the state of Connecticut, one Stephen Pangman, a prisoner of war taken at Long-Island in May last; he lately belonged to Stamford, and went from there to Long-Island, about six months ago, is about twenty one years old, short of stature, dark hair, his right hand contracted and finger crooked by a burn he received when a child; had on a dark brown coat with white buttons, white woolen vest and breeches, and threat stockings, he stole from said Granger and carried away with him a gun and bayonet, a pair of with stockings, and

twenty four shillings in bills, it is apprehended that he is gone towards New-York, and that he intends to pass for one of our militia on the road. Whoever will take him up and secure him in any goal in this state, and give notice the the subscriber, shall have five Dollars Reward and necessary charges paid, by EZEKIEL WILLIAMS,
Commis. Prisoners.   Hartford, Aug, 11, 1777.

The Connecticut Courant, And Hartford Weekly Intelligencer, August 18, 1777; September 1, 1777; September 8, 1777.

EIGHT DOLLARS Reward.

RUN-AWAY on Thursday last the 14th instant, a negro man named WARE, this country born, of a dark complexion, well made, about 5 feet 7 inches high, 24 years of age, has a large scar in his forehead, and one on his lip: had on when he went off, a white jacket without sleeves, white breeches, and a pair of mixt coloured stockings. Whoever takes up and secures said fellow, or gives any information where he is, so that he may be had, shall receive the above reward from the subscriber, living at Newton, on Long-Island.   ABRAHAM LENT.

The New-York Gazette; and the Weekly Mercury, August 18, 1777.

TEN DOLLARS Reward.

RUN-AWAY from the subscriber, on Wednesday the 6th inst. a negro fellow named FORK, but probably may change it to that of Dick, as he did when he absented at a former time: He is about 25 years of age, of a middling stature, slender made, his right knee bent inwards, a lengthy visage, yellowish complexion, a slender long nose, and has lost many of his fore-teeth.—Had on a pair of osnaburgh trowsers, and spotted flannel jacket. Whoever will take up and secure the said negro, so that his master may have him again, shall receive the above reward.
THOMAS BROOKMAN.

N. B. He was seen last Saturday sen'night in this city, and it is suppos'd he is lurking in or about it at present, all persons are therefore forbid to harbour said negro, and all masters of vessels are forewarned to carry him off.

The New-York Gazette; and the Weekly Mercury, August 18, 1777; September 1, 1777; September 8, 1777; September 15, 1777; September 22, 1777.

EIGHT DOLLARS Reward.

RUN-AWAY on Thursday last the 14th instant, a negro man named WAN, this country born, of a dark complexion, well made, about 5 feet 7 inches

high, 24 years of age, has a large scar in his forehead, and one on his lip: Had on when he went off, a white jacket without sleeves, white breeches, and a pair of mixt coloured stockings. Whoever takes up and secures said fellow, or gives any information where he is, so that he may be had, shall receive the above reward from the subscriber, living at Newton,
on Long-Island. ABRAHAM LENT.
The New-York Gazette; and the Weekly Mercury, August 25, 1777; September 1, 1777; September 15, 1777; September 22, 1777.

RUN-AWAY from the subscriber, on the 26th day of August last, a negro man named BRISTOL, about 5 feet 9 inches high, and upwards of 27 years old: had on when he went off, a reddish coloured jacket, a white waistcoat, and linen trowsers, supposed to be gone to New-York with the regular troops, or on board some vessel. Whoever takes up said negro fellow and secures him in any of his Majesty's goals, or elsewhere, so that his said master can have him again, shall have EIGHT DOLLARS reward, and reasonable charges paid,
by me, PETER HOUSEMAN.
All masters of vessels are forwarned to carry off or harbour said fellow. Staten Island, Sept 3d, 1777.
The New-York Gazette; and the Weekly Mercury, September 8, 1777; September 15, 1777; September 22, 1777.

RUN away on Thursday the 14th instant, a Negro boy named TOM, the property of Doctor Donald M'Lane, at No. 6. six doors west of the Coffee-house; Said Negro is a remarkable well made boy, about 14 years of age; had on a striped jacket, and trowsers, and check shirt, no shoes nor stockings, his jacket tied with pieces of tape in place of buttons. Whoever secures the above deserted Negro, or gives intelligence of him to his said master, shall be entitled to a reasonable reward.
N. B. It is earnestly requested and presumed no gentlemen will harbour the said run away negro.
The New-York Gazette; and the Weekly Mercury, September 22, 1777; September 29, 1777; October 6, 1777.

To the PUBLIC.
THIS is to give notice, that Mary Pontenner, alias Mary Morris, alias Black, alias Mary Sharp, alias Mary Hancock, was to go to Philadelphia to marry one Peter Lynch, after that she was going to be married to one Roberts, who was taken out of her house for horse stealing, committed by Alderman Dyckman to prison, and indented himself as a servant for three years to a New-England man;—at last married one Richard Watkins, and made her

elopement from him the 12th of last May, robbing and plundering of him: This is to inform the publick, that they must not entertain the said Mary Watkins, as he will pay no expence that she may contract.
RICHARD WATKINS.

N. B. Mr. Weston, blacksmith, from New-England, in the King's employ in New-York, with whom the above-mentioned woman lives as a servant, has had proper warning both by word and writing, to discharge her out of his house, but has not as yet done it.

The New-York Gazette; and the Weekly Mercury, September 29, 1777.

TEN DOLLARS Reward.

RUN-away on February last, a negro man named Dick, born in Bermuda, of a yellowish complexion, well made, about 5 feet 9 inches high, 35 years of age, has lost his left eye, was seen at New-York three weeks ago, Whoever takes up and secures the said fellow, or give information where he is, so that he may be had, shall receive the above reward from the subscriber, living at Newtown, on Long-Island.
ABRAHAM LENT.

The New-York Gazette; and the Weekly Mercury, September 29, 1777; October 6, 1777.

TAKEN away by force from the house of Isaac Slover, of Flat Lands, King's County, last Friday, a negro wench named BET, about 17 years of age: She had on a red striped silk handkerchief, a homespun striped gown and petty coat; is of a yellow complexion, and was barefooted. Whoever will secure the said negro girl, so that she may be had again, shall receive Three Pounds reward.

The New-York Gazette; and the Weekly Mercury, September 29, 1777; October 13, 1777.

HALF a JOHANNES Reward.

FOR apprehending ANTHONY, a negro, slender made, about 5 feet 8 inches high, and 28 years of age. He broke open a small chest, and took thereout 11 half johannes's, and 11 dollars: It is suspected he is lurking about this city, and requested by the advertiser that he may be secured, and the above reward will be paid,
By   SANGREY WARREY.

The New-York Gazette; and the Weekly Mercury, October 6, 1777.

NEW-YORK. *October* 9, 1777.

RUN away from the subscriber, the evening of the 7th instant, a negro boy named ALEX, about 4 feet 7 inches high, 15 years old, very black

complexion, smooth face, and speaks tolerable good English. He had on an osnabrug frock and trousers.—whoever apprehends the said boy, and delivers him to the warden of the workhouse, or to me on board the ship Choptank, lying at Bache's wharf, shall receive a reward of three dollars.
              RICHARD WRIGHT.
    Rivington's New-York Gazette, October 11, 1777; *Rivington's New-York Loyal Gazette*, October 18, 1777. See *The Royal Gazette*, January 3, 1778, *The Royal Gazette*, February 7, 1778, and *The Royal Gazette*, May 2, 1778.

RUN away from the subscriber about three months ago, a Negro boy named LUKE, about 18 years of age, a broad round face, with the marks of several cuts about his eyes, slim made, especially about the legs, and is about 5 feet high; had on, when he went away, a green casimir short coat, drill breeches, striped holland trousers, and carried sundry other clothes with him. I am informed he was seen attending on an officer or serjeant in the market, to whom he had hired himself, being a good hair-dresser. It is hoped no Gentleman will harbour him. I will give four pounds reward to any person that will deliver him to me in New-York, who will find me by applying to
           Mr. Rivington. ROBERT GILMOUR.
    Rivington's New-York Gazette, October 11, 1777; *Rivington's New-York Loyal Gazette*, October 18, 1777; November 1, 1777.

              FIFTY DOLLARS Reward.
RUN-away from the subscriber, three negro fellows, viz. PRIMUS, a very likely fellow, about 22 years of age, speaks very civil and mild; went away the first of October, 1776. SYPHAX, about 34 years old; speaks broken English, very lasey and slow; went away some time in November, 1776. SCIPIO, about 18 years old, went away on Wednesday night the 8th inst. he is a very handy fellow, stoops when he walks, and is apt to stammer when he talks quick.—Whoever takes up said negroes, and brings or sends them to their master, shall have the above reward of the three, or separately for Primus 25 dollars, and for Syphax and Scipio, 12 each.
              P. STUYVESANT.
                    Petersfield, near New-York, Octo, 11, 1777.
    The New-York Gazette; and the Weekly Mercury, October 13, 1777; October 20, 1777; October 27, 1777; November 3, 1777.

For KINGSTON, *in Jamaica*,
THE ship Sarah Gonidburn, Nahum Holland, master....RUNAWAY from the above ship, three apprentices, all Welsh boys, speak but indifferent English; had all blue top jackets on, one of them a black complexion, about

23 years of age, slim made, 5 feet 8 inches high: The other two about 5 feet 3 inches high, and about 17 years of age, one of a dark, and the other of a light complexion. Whoever will apprehend all or any of them, by applying as above, shall be handsomely rewarded; and person harbouring or encouraging the said apprentices, shall be prosecuted according to law.

Rivington's New-York Loyal Gazette, October 18, 1777; October 25, 1777; November 1, 1777; November 8, 1777.

DESCRIPTION of three men deserted from his Majesty's ship Centurion, Capt. Richard Brathwaite, Commander, WILIAM LEADBERRY, born at St. Margets, Kent, 22 years of age, 5 feet 6 inches high, wore his own black hair, fresh complexion, had on a pea jacket, and cock'd hat, no trowsers on, slim built.

BENJAMIN BEAMES, born at Albany, in America, 21 years of age, 5 feet 5 inches high, brown hair, fair complexion, had on a brown jacket, and trowsers; snub nose.

JOHN CRAIG, born at North Shields, 20 years of age, about 5 feet 2 inches high, black hair, ruddy complexion, stout built, pitted with the small pox, had on a blue jacket, and trowsers.

N. B. There shall be paid the sum of FORTY SHILLINGS sterling, to the person or persons who shall apprehend each of the above people, or or producing a certificate of their being confined on board any of his Majesty's ship at New-York. October 17, 1777.

Rivington's New-York Loyal Gazette, October 18, 1777; October 25, 1777.

SEVEN DOLLARS Reward.

RUN-away on the 14th inst. a negro wench named BET, born at Flatbush, Long-Island: Had on when she went away, a homespun pettycoat, and callicoe short gown. Whoever will secure the said wench, or give information of any person harbouring her, shall receive the above reward

by me, PHILIP LENZI, Confectioner,

in Hanover-Square, No. 517.

The New-York Gazette; and the Weekly Mercury, October 20, 1777; October 27, 1777; November 3, 1777; November 10, 1777; *Rivington's New-York Loyal Gazette*, October 25 1777. Minor differences between the papers. See *The New-York Gazette; and the Weekly Mercury*, November 17, 1777.

DESERTED from the ship Diana, army victualler, William Brown, master, a boy about 5 feet 3 or 4 inches high, thick set, a little mark'd with the small-pox, brown complexion, straight short dark brown or black hair: Had on when he went away, which was on Saturday the 18th inst. a blue short jacket, a pair of canvas long trowsers, a round bound hat, and square pewter buckles in his shoes; was born in the north of Scotland, went by the name of William Thompson, and is an apprentice to George Brown, Esq; in Stockton, owner of the above ship. A reward of 5 dollars will be paid for securing the said apprentice, by the master of the vessel, who may be found on board, near the ship-yards.

The New-York Gazette; and the Weekly Mercury, October 20, 1777; October 27, 1777; November 3, 1777.

FIVE DOLLARS REWARD.

RUN away, on Thursday the 16th instant, from the subscriber, a negro man named HARR, 16 or 17 years of age, about 5 feet 7 inches high, was formerly the property of Jacob Van Wincle of Acquacanock; had on, when he went off, a check shirt, oznabrug trousers, olive coloured short coat lined with striped homespun; has a smooth face, not very black, his wool lately cut, and his hat remarkable by the letters H H painted on the crown. He pretends to be free, but it is hoped he will find no encouragement from any Gentleman whatever. Any person in whose custody he is found after this notice may depend on being dealt with as they should be. Whoever delivers said negro at his Majesty's naval brewery on Long Island, or gives information so as he may be recovered, shall have the above reward,

        From   ROBERT HARGRAVE.

Rivington's New-York Loyal Gazette, October 25, 1777; November 1, 1777.

FIVE DOLLARS REWARD.

RUN away from this city, some days ago, a Negroe boy, the property of Lieut. Colonel Turnbull, about twelve years old, well looked, and very black, whoever will deliver him to John M'Adam and Co. Will receive the above reward and reasonable charges. All persons are forbid to harbour him on paid of prosecution.

N. B. It is supposed the boy is on Long-Island.

Rivington's New-York Loyal Gazette, October 25, 1777; November 1, 1777.

TEN DOLLARS Reward.

RUN-AWAY last August, an apprentice lad named Gillis M'Gillis: He has light hair, pock marked, with a large scar on the left side of his nose, about 5 feet 5 inches high, slender made, and stoops when he walks, by trade a breeches maker. Any person who will bring the said lad to the subscriber, shall receive the above reward, and reasonable charges,

from WILLIAM BELL.
The New-York Gazette; and the Weekly Mercury, October 27, 1777; November 3, 1777.

Forty Dollars Reward.

RUN away from the subscriber, the 6th of August last, a negro boy named Peter, about 13 or 14 years of age, of a yellowish complexion, lisps, and holds down his head when he speaks to any body. He has been seen a number of times with an officer of one of the new corps, and no doubt impressed himself on the Gentleman as a free negro. If he is still in the possession of that, or any other officer, it is expected he will be given up immediately. When he left my service, he had on, and took with him, a new suit of brown fustian, a suit of claret coloured fine cloth two thirds worn, a round hat, several pair of striped trowsers, &c. Whoever will secure the said negro boy, or bring him to me at No. 21, King-street, shall be paid the above reward immediately.
      HENRY W. PERRY.
Rivington's New-York Loyal Gazette, November 1, 1777; November 8, 1777.

About the 16th Inst. run from his Master's Service a Negro Fellow named FOUNTAIN: He is of slender make, about 25 Years of Age, 5 Feet 6 or 7 Inches high, and has a large Scar on his left Cheek; had on white Linen Jacket and Breeches, and an English Beaver Hat, cocked. He has been seen lately about this City, and is supposed to be yet lurking in some Part thereof, therefore all Persons are forbid to harbour or entertain the said Negro, and Masters of Vessels, from carrying him off. A Reward of Two Dollars will be paid by bringing him to his Master, and if taken out of the City, a reasonable Sum more, with Charges.
      GEORGE WALGROVE.
The New-York Gazette; and the Weekly Mercury, October 27, 1777.

FIVE POUNDS Reward.

RUN-AWAY on the 14th ult. a negro wench named BET: She is about 25 years old, between a negro and mulatto colour, of a smiling disposition, has a mark in her neck nearly resembling the letter C. middle size, and lusty. She formerly belonged to Mr. Vanderveer, of Flatbush, on Long-Island. When she went away she had on a homespun pettycoat, callicoe short gown, red handkerchief, and without either hat or bonnet. Whoever will secure the said wench, or give information of any person harbouring her, shall receive the above reward
    by me, PHILIP LENZI, Confectioner,

No. 517. Hanover-Square.
The New-York Gazette; and the Weekly Mercury, November 17, 1777; November 24, 1777. See *The New-York Gazette; and the Weekly Mercury*, October 20, 1777.

RUN-AWAY from the subscriber, living at New Lots, King's county, the 16th instant, a negro fellow named NAT; has lost his right eye, about 24 years old, pitted with the small-pox, 5 feet 8 inches high, Indian hair, and of a yellow complexion: Had on when he went away, a whitish surtout coat, a homespun coat, and light coloured jacket.—Whoever takes up and secures the said fellow, so that he may be had again, shall receive Five Dollars reward, and all reasonable charges,
                paid by   HENRY WICKOFF.
The New-York Gazette; and the Weekly Mercury, November 24, 1777; December 1, 1777.

Run away from Jordan Holcomb, Esq; on the 11th inst. Dennes Colls, Inhabitant of Long-Island, about 21 years of age, 5 feet 8 inches high. had on an old grey surtout, [claret] coloured coat, white jacket, check'd shirt, old deer-skin breeches, blue stockings, and new shoes. Whoever will up [*sic*] said fellow, and return him to the goal in Hartford, shall have 5 dollars reward, and charges paid, by
        EZEKIEL WILLIAMS, *Com. Prisoners.* Hartford, Dec. 15.
The Connecticut Courant, and Hartford Weekly Intelligencer, December 16, 1777; December 30, 1777.

ESCAPED from Hartford, where they were on parole, two tory prisoners, viz George Hughson, and David White, lately brought from Eusopus prison. Hughes is about 5 feet 8 inches high, fair complexion, brown hair, light gray eyes, broad face, had on an old brown loose coat, the rest of his dress unknown. White is an ugley, gallows-looking fellow a cooper but trade about the said height as Hughson, dress unknown. Whoever takes up and secures either of the above rascals, in any goal upon the Continent, shale be entitled to a reward of Ten Dollars for each of them.
        EZEKIEL WILLIAMS,   D. Commis. of Prisoners.
The Connecticut Courant, and Hartford Weekly Intelligencer, December 23, 1777; December 30, 1777.

RUN away the 15th instant from John Faulkner, Cabinet Maker, an apprentice boy, named
                ROBERT MORRISON,

This is to forwarn all masters of vessels not to carry him off, at it is imagined he may want to go to some part of the West-Indies.

   N. B. All persons are forewarned not to harbour said apprentice at their peril.

   The Royal Gazette, December 20, 1777.

1778

RUN AWAY on the 25th instant, a Negro boy named ALICK, about fifteen years of age. Had on when he went away, a check shirt, reddish coloured jacket, Oznaburg trowers, and a leather cap. He is branded on the breast with the letters R. W. Whoever will secure said boy, or give information of any person or persons harbouring him, shall receive Four Dollars reward
            from Richard Wright, at
         Mr. William Cross's, in George Street, No. 22.

   All Masters of vessels are forbid harbouring or carrying off the said boy on their peril.

   The Royal Gazette, January 3, 1778. See *Rivington's New-York Gazette*, October 11, 1777, *The Royal Gazette*, February 7, 1778, and *The Royal Gazette*, May 2, 1778.

DESERTED the 14th inst. from his Majesty's Brigantine Dunmore, Lieut. John Wright, commander, Patrick Campbell, an able seaman, born in Glasgow, about 25 years of age, sandy hair, fresh complexion, slightly pitted with the small pox, and freckled; has a down look, and speaks broad Scotch, had on when he went away, a blue upper and under jacket, white shirt, long trowsers, and a round hat, with narrow gold binding. Whoever secures the above deserter in the Provost of this city, or gives such information as they he can be secured, shall receive Five Guineas reward, by applying to Mr. Gilchrist at No. 1015 in Water-street, near the bottom of Dover-street. All masters of vessels, and others, are hereby warned not to ship, or harbour the said Campbell, as in so doing they will incur the severest penalties.

   The Royal Gazette, January 17, 1778.

DESERTED from on board the Susannah, Captain Matthew Woodhouse, an apprentice lad named Walter Adam, about 18 years old, about 5 feet 5 inches high, stout built, fresh complexion, and wears his own straight hair: Had on when he deserted, a blue waistcoat, and long trowsers. Whoever will bring the said apprentice on board the Susannah, at the Walebough, or to Mr. Dickinson's, No. 200, Queen-street,
         shall receive FOUR DOLLARS reward.

The New-York Gazette; and the Weekly Mercury, January 19, 1778; January 26, 1778.

TWENTY DOLLARS REWAD. [*sic*]
RUN away from the subscriber about two months past, a negro boy named YORK, about 5 feet 7 inches high, of a very black complexion, had a scar like a burn near one of his eyes; it is supposed he is gone to old Lebanon, to one Mr. Tisdell's the place where he was bought. Whoever shall secure or bring the said Negro to the subscriber, shall receive the above reward and all reasonable charges paid,
    by STEPHEN TUTTLE. Albany, Jan. 13 1778.
The Connecticut Courant, and Hartford Weekly Intelligencer, February 3, 1778.

RUN AWAY, on the 30th of January, 1778, a negro boy named Alick, about fifteen years of age, had on when he went away, a check shirt, reddish coloured jacket, breeches and stockings and hat: He is branded on the breast with the letters R. W. Whoever will secure said boy, or give information of any person or persons harbouring him, shall receive Four Dollars reward
    from RICHARD WRIGHT,
    at Mr. William Cross's, in George Street, No. 22.
 All Masters of vessels are forbid harbouring or carrying off the said boy on their peril.
 The Royal Gazette, February 7, 1778. See *Rivington's New-York Gazette*, October 11, 1777, *The Royal Gazette*, January 3, 1778 and *The Royal Gazette*, May 2, 1778.

Two Dollars Reward.
RUN-AWAY on the 6th of February inst, from the house of the subscriber, in Little Queen Street, No. 20, a bound servant Girl, named
    Mary Barbara Henner,
 She speaks some English, is about 24 years old, of a middle size, black hair, large eyes: had on when she ran-away, a black bonnet, a blue cloth-cloak, the other dress unknown: One the morning she ran-away, she was to give an account of some fine shirts, aprons and other [line intelligible] own'd to have dome, she would give no account; which her running away, instead of clearing up that matter, lays said servant under a strong suspicion, that she must know, that the above articles were not rightly handled by her.
 These are therefore prohibiting all Persons, from harbouring, concealing or carrying off said Mary Barbara Henner, as they would avoid the Prosecution of the Law. But whosoever shall apprehend said servant,

and bring her back to me, the subscriber's Habitation, above mentioned, shall receive the above reward.

     BERNARD MICHAEL HOUSEAL.

The New-York Gazette; and the Weekly Mercury, February 9, 1778. See *The Royal Gazette*, May 30, 1778.

RAN away from the Subscriber, living in Albany, a Negro Man, named POMPEY LARKIN, 19 Years and 10 days old, late the property of Francis Moor, Baker, of Cambridge, an arch, knowing, deceitful Negro. Whoever will take up said Negro, and deliver him to Major John White, Quarter-Master to General Nixon's Brigade, at the American Coffee-House in State-Street, or secure him in any Goal, within 60 Miles of Boston, and give Major White notice thereof, shall be entitled to the sum of Four Pounds, and all necessary Charges,

    paid by NEAL SHAW.

N. B. Twenty Pounds will be paid to any one, that will bring him to said Shaw, in Albany.

The Independent Chronicle and the Universal Advertiser, February 26, 1778; March 5, 1778; March 12, 1778.

A DUMB LAD
Of about 18 Years old, MISSING,

THE above youth about the 17th instant, drove a Sleigh, from Maroneck, to this city, and after stopping, to set down the passengers, immediately strayed away, and has not since been heard of. He is about 5 feet 8 inches high, light complexion, thin visage he can make a noise, but he cannot articulate; he is very deaf, yet on speaking loud, he will answer to his name, which is William Rowe.

Whoever brings him to the Printer shall have FIVE DOLLARS reward.

The Royal Gazette, February 28, 1778.

RUN-away from the subscriber, a negro fellow named POLLY, about 5 feet 3 or 4 inches high: Had on when he went off, a brown jacket, and is well known about the city; he will endeavour to pass for a woman, tho' he wears man's cloathing. Whoever will bring the said negro to the subscriber, at Cruger's wharf, will receive three dollars reward.

     ALEXANDER M'KENZIE.

N. B. I forbid all masters of ship, &c. to employ or conceal the above negro.

The New-York Gazette; and the Weekly Mercury, March 9, 1778; March 16, 1778.

ON Tuesday the 16th inst. at 8 o'clock in the evening deserted from on board the Albion victualling transport; JAMES SINCLAIR, a boy aged 13 years; four feet two inches high, of a fair complexion, light brown hair, curled at the sides; had on when he went away, a green frized jacket lines with white, a white shirt, and round hat, with long cotton trowsers. Whoever apprehends the aforesaid boy, and brings him on board the Albion, in Wallabocht Creek, or to Messrs. Samuel and Levy's store, shall receive TEN DOLLARS reward; and any person harbouring the said boy shall be prosecuted as the law directs.
The Royal Gazette, March 14, 1778.

South-Amboy, March 20, 1778.
NOTICE is hereby given that two Negro men lately came over from Staten-Island, and landed at South-Amboy; the one is a sturdy young fellow named JOE, about 26 years of age, and about five feet ten inches high: the other is also a sturdy fellow named JACK, about sixty years of age, and about six feet high; both of them are supposed to belong to persons in this state. The subscriber has them in charge, and is in fear that they may by chance get away; and therefore desirous that the owner or owners of said Negroes may speedily apply, prove their property, pay charges, and take them away.
    JAMES MORGAN, Capt.
The New-Jersey Gazette, April 15, 1778; May 6, 1778.

FOUR DOLLARS Reward.
RUN away on Tuesday the 7th inst. from the subscriber at Newtown, Long-Island, a negro wench named HESTER, about 34 years of age, short and well set, rather of a yellowish complexion; had on when she went off a striped lindsey short gown and petticoat, has a scar under one of her eyes; she is supposed to be in one of the negro houses in New-York, as she has been seen lurking about the Fly-Market. Whoever will deliver her to the owner, shall have the above reward, with reasonable charges; all persons are requested not to harbour or employ her.
    WATERS SMITH.
The New-York Gazette; and the Weekly Mercury, April 20, 1778; April 27, 1778; May 4, 1778.

RAN-AWAY from the subscriber, on Sunday the 26th inst. the following persons, viz. ISAAC KETCHUM, who was taken from the west end of Long-Island some time ago: He is of middle stature, about 50 years of age, dark complexion, dark hair and eyes, the eyelid of the left eye hanging almost over the same, walks stooping, and has a down look: Had on a greyish coat and vest, leather breeches, and a white felt hat. GEORGE

SNYDER, a German, who was taken prisoner; he is about six feet high, and had on a red coat faced with blue. Whoever secures said persons, shall have Ten Dollars for each.

     JOHN BARNEY, junr. Norwich, April 27, 1778.

The Norwich Packet, April 27, 1778. See *The Norwich Packet*, May 4, 1778.

FORTY DOLLARS REWARD.

RAN-AWAY from Norwich Goal, on Sunday the 26th inst. the following persons, viz. ISAAC KETCHAM, who was taken from the west end of Long-Island some time ago: He is of middle stature, about 50 years of age, dark complexion, dark hair and eyes, the eyelid of the left eye hanging almost over the same, walks stooping, and has a down look: Had on a greyish coat and vest, leather breeches, and a white felt hat. GEORGE SNYDER, a German, who was taken prisoner, at the northward last year by Gen. Arnold's army, and has been on parole in this town for some months past; he is full six feet high, well set, about twenty-five years of age, light complexion, light coloured hair, talks bad English, and is pitted with the small-pox: Had on a red regimental coat faced with blue, the buttons on the same marked 2[ ], a brown jacket, leather breeches, and an old felt hat.—Went off at the same time, PATRICK KELLY, an Irishman, who was brought a prisoner from the State of New-York in October last, and was permitted to stay in this town on his parole for a few months, then to return to the said State:—Said KELLY is about 34 years of age, 5 feet 7 inches high, red face and redish hair, light blue eyes, well made; had on a dark brown coat and vest, buck-skin breeches, white shirt, and two pair of worsted stockings, one pair white the other dark grey, walks remarkable strait, is very fond of snuff, and the produce of the West-Indies. Whoever will take up any of the above persons, and return them to the subscriber, or confine them in any goal in this State, shall have FOUR POUNDS reward for each.

    JOHN BARNEY, junr. Gaoler. Norwich, April 27, 1778.

The Norwich Packet, May 4, 1778; May 11, 1778. See *The Norwich Packet*, April 27, 1778.

TEN DOLLARS REWARD.

RUN away from his Master, JOHN BARTOW, Jun. of the Borough Town of Westchester, a Negro Man named FRANK, about 5 feet high, is a good tempered handy ingenious fellow, has a pleasant look, and a low soft speech, has got a scar on his left leg, which has been lately cut; Had on, when he went off, a brown watch coat and vest, yarn stockings and new shoes. Whoever takes up said fellow, and brings him to his said master, if

upwards of ten miles from home, shall receive the above reward, and all reasonable charges, and in the same proportion for a less distance, paid
        them by the said   JOHN BARTOW, jun.
The Royal Gazette, May 2, 1778; May 9, 1778.

RUN-AWAY from the subscriber, last Saturday, a NEGRO BOY, named ALEX; had on when he went away, a check shirt, a blue jacket, and blue trowsers, with a cap: he is about 15 years of age, five feet high, smooth faced, and branded on the breast R. W. is very artful, and may attempt getting on board some of the shipping. Whoever apprehends the said boy, and will deliver him to me, at Mr. William Cross's, No. 22, at George-Street, shall be handsomely rewarded. All masters of ship, and others, are hereby forwarned at their peril, from harbouring, or carrying him off.
        RICHARD WRIGHT.   New-York, April 30, 1778.
The Royal Gazette, May 2, 1778; May 9, 1778. See *Rivington's New-York Gazette*, October 11, 1777; *The Royal Gazette*, January 3, 1778, and *The Royal Gazette*, February 7, 1778.

RUN-away from the subscriber, last Friday, two black wenches, one an old woman about forty years old, named MOLL; had on when she went away, a striped waistcoat and blue quilted petticoat. The other a young girl of eighteen named DIANA: Had on when she went away, a striped or dark blue waistcoat, a red cloak with ermine on the fore part of it, and a black hat; the girl is very artful, and may attempt getting on board some of the shipping. Whoever apprehends said wenches, and will deliver them to me, at No. 169, Queen-street, shall have FIVE DOLLARS reward for each of them. All masters of vessels and others, are hereby forwarned harbouring or
        carrying them off.   JOSEPH TOTTEN.
The New-York Gazette; and the Weekly Mercury, May 4, 1778; May 11, 1778. See *The Royal Gazette*, May 20, 1778, for Diana/Diona.

RUN-AWAY, yesterday, a likely young negro man named PETER, commonly called Pete, about 5 feet 7 inches high, speaks good English, remarkably sprightly, has a full eye, a great whistler, and had on when he absconded a short brown coat, and long ozenbrig trowsers; formerly belonged to Mr. John Carpender, but lately purchased of Mr. Benjamin Williams.

Whosoever apprehends and brings him to the subscriber, in taken in this city, shall have Five Dollars reward, if in the country, a handsome gratuity proportionate to the distance, and all reasonable charges
        paid by   JOSEPH ALLICOCKE.

The New-York Gazette; and the Weekly Mercury, May 11, 1778; May 18, 1778.

RUN AWAY from the subscriber, a NEGRO LAD, named JEM, about 24 years old, five feet six inches high, had on an hat and a brown coat and trowsers: Whoever will secure the said Negro, that he may be recovered to the proprietor, shall receive FIVE DOLLARS,
    from JOHN PORTEOUS, and Co.
 It is requested that all Masters of vessels with carefully avoid carrying him from this port.
The Royal Gazette, May 20, 1778.

TWENTY SHILLINGS REWARD
FOR apprehending a certain JOHN ———, a Hollander, who came Passenger with Capt. DAVID, in the Schooner JOE, from Philadelphia, who arrived on the 8th Instant, dressed with a red Broad Cloth Coatee with yellow Buttons, a light under Jacket, an old pair Leather Breeches, and a Wool Hat, a smooth Face and fair Countenance, about 5 Feet 6 Inches high. And has on now belonging to the Subscriber, a blue Sagathee Coat, a Linen Jacket, a white Demity pair of Breeches, a white pair of Cotton Stockings, a pair of new Pumps with plated Buckles, a ruffle Shirt, a white Cravat, and a Beaver Hat lined with blue. Any Person apprehending the said JOHN ——— and the Cloaths, shall be entitled to the above Reward,
  by MICHAEL HAUNSEN, in Warren Street,
    or the Printer hereof.
N. B. All Masters of Vessels and Ferries are desired to stop the said Person.
The Royal Gazette, May 20, 1778.

RUN away from the Subscriber, on Friday the first of May, a young black girl, about 18 years of age, named DIONA; had on when she went away, a blue and striped waistcoat, blue petticoat, black hat, short red cloak with ermine of the fore part; she may attempt getting on board some vessel. Whoever apprehends said girl, and will bring her to me, at No. 169, in Queen-street, shall be handsomely rewarded. All masters of vessels and others, are hereby forewarned harbouring or carrying her off.
    JOSEPH TOTTEN.
The Royal Gazette, May 20, 1778. See *The New-York Gazette; and the Weekly Mercury*, May 4, 1778.

FIVE DOLLARS Reward.
WILL be paid by the Printer of this paper to any person who will give information of a Mulatto Man, named James Hulse, who has lately

absconded from his proprietor; he is about five feet nine inches high, straight made, about thirty years of age; was a few weeks hence discharged from his Majesty's service in the forage department, at Turtle Bay; and, as he plays on the violin it is probable he may be skulking in some part of this city.
The Royal Gazette, May 23, 1778; May 30, 1778; June 6, 1778; June 13, 1778. See *The Royal Gazette*, July 1, 1778.

A Notorious Runaway.

MARY BARBARA HENNER, who after having run away from her former mistress, anxiously begged to be bound to the subscriber hereof, but deserted also from him on the 6th February, &c. instead of giving then an account of the shirts, aprons, caps, and other articles, she took at that time out of a glass-closet, against express prohibition, which she has then owned to be guilty of, and who after her return, promising to make amendment, was received with lenity, instead of the punishment she had deserved. But being a very fickle and obstreperous turn of mind, she took a notion to pursue her old scheme, and did run away again twice, on the 25th of this instant May. Said Barbara Henner, speaks some English, is about 24 years of age, of a middle side, large eyes, black hair, was not decently dressed, (designedly by her own fault) when she sneaked away, instead of looking for a cellar-key. These are therefore prohibiting all persons from harbouring, concealing, or carrying off said Mary Barbara Henner, as they would avoid the prosecution of the law. But whoever shall apprehend said servant, and bring her back to the habitation of the subscribe, in Little Queen Street, No. 10, shall receive TWO DOLLARS reward.

BERNARD MICHAEL HOUSEAL.

New-York, May 27, 1778.

The Royal Gazette, May 30, 1778; July 2, 1778. See *The New-York Gazette; and the Weekly Mercury*, February 9, 1778.

TWO GUINEAS REWARD.

RUN away on Thursday the 11th instant from the sloop Endeavour, lying at the New-Crane, a Negro fellow, about twenty one years of age; had on when he went away, a striped jacket and trowsers, and a round tinsel laced hat. Whoever brings the said Negro to the Printer, or Capt. Fordyce, on board the said vessel, shall receive the above reward.
N. B. All masters of vessels and others, are desired not to secret him.
The Royal Gazette, June 13, 1778.

Four Hundred DOLLARS REWARD.

WILL be given to any person that will seize two Common Robbers, now residing in the County of Sussex, a certain Samuel Meeker, noted in said county, for endeavoring several times to murder his father: The other a certain Isaac Morris, a remarkable lusty Indian Mulatto, formerly a resident of Morris-County. Or two Hundred Dollars will be given for either of them when they will get their money immediately, and not is Square Dollars, but in Silver.

N. B. This Advertisement to continue in force during the present month of June; the parties to be lodged in the custody of the Provost of this city.

The Royal Gazette, June 13, 1778.

DESERTED,

FROM the Jenny transport, John Ready, a Frenchman, he is about 21 years of age, 5 feet 4 ½ inches high, dark complexion, and black hair, which he wore tied in a blue and white handkerchief, had on when he went away, a black coarse hat, a white coloured coat bound; also taffeta at the pockets, a white waistcoat on which is several spots of tar, a pair of old long trowsers, much wider than commonly wore, and a pair of new pumps, with a pair of buckles not fellows. Whoever will secure the said deserter, and give notice to William Hamilton, on board, laying near Bedlow's Island, shall receive eight dollars reward.

The Royal Gazette, June 17, 1778; June 20, 1778.

New-York, June 22, 1778.

DESERTED from the Ship Triton, a Victualler, a Seaman, named JOHN SMITH, born in Hull, in the North of England; twenty-two years of age, five feet five inches high, of a light brown complexion, and inclinable to fat; and as it is well known from good information that the said man is secreted in the town of New-York for some other service, whoever will apprehend him, or give information where he is, do that he can be taken into custody, by applying to JOB KEYBURN, Master of said ship, shall have EIGHT DOLLARS reward.

The Royal Gazette, June 24, 1778.

ABSCONDED.

A Dark coloured Mulatto man, named JAMES HULSE, about 30 years of age, 5 feet 9 inches high, and stout made; it is supposed he sailed on the fleet for Philadelphia on the 11th of May, and it is probable may be now returned: Whoever will give information of him to the printer of this paper, so that he may be recovered, shall be rewarded with five Dollars.

The Royal Gazette, July 1, 1778; July 18, 1778; July 25, 1778. See *The Royal Gazette,* May 23, 1778.

LEFT the Ship Nancy, armed Victualler, Stephen Devereux, Master, on Sunday last, an Apprentice, named WILLIAM JONES, about 18 years of age, full-faced, dark brown hair, remarkable small thighs and legs, with a large lump on the fore-part of one of his legs: Had on a blue jacket, a pair of long trowsers, and a round hat.

Left the Nancy, this day, an Apprentice, named WILLIAM HUGHES, about 19 years of age, a thick set lad, with brown hair, pale complexion, hath a very particular mark on one of his legs, occasioned by a scald; had on him a white flannel jacket, a pair of long trowsers, perhaps a frock, and a round hat.—They are both Welch lads, and their first voyage to sea.

Whoever can give information of them to the Printer, so that they may be secured, shall receive TWO GUINEAS reward for each of them.

New-York, July 10, 1778.
The Royal Gazette, July 15, 1778.

King's County, Flat-Bush, July 20, 1778.
RUN AWAY on the 12th instant, from the subscriber, living at New Lotts, on Long-Island, a Negro Man, named HECTOR, about 40 years of age, 5 feet 5 inches high, had on when he went away, a blue camblet jacket, without sleeves, a white shirt and two trowsers; can speak English and Dutch. Whoever takes up and secures said Negro, so that his master may have him again, shall receive FIVE DOLLARS reward, and all necessary charges, paid by   JACOBUS CORNELL.
The Royal Gazette, July 25, 1778.

TWENTY GUINEAS Reward.
WHEREAS WILLIAM WILLMAN, has absconded from this city, on account of defrauding some Merchants, by a forged indorsation of bills: Whoever will apprehend the said William Willman, so as he may be brought to justice, shall receive the above reward, by applying to Messrs. Samuel and Levy, No. 356, Hanover-Square, or at Mr. George Graham's, No. 209, Queen-Street. Said Willman has passed for a considerable time as a cornet of the 17th light dragoons, about five feet five or six inches high, stout made, and dark complexion. He had with him when he went away, and wears frequently a green coat, the uniform of the above regiment; at other times, a scarlet coat of the same uniform, nankeen jacket and trowsers, and slouch'd hat, with a black feather.—He left this city on Saturday the 18th instant, and is reported to have left Red-Hook, on Long-Island, the Monday following. He is supposed to pass at present under the name of Lieut. Greaves.

☞ It is expected he will attempt to make his escape to the rebels, from the East end of Long-Island, or other convenient place there.

The Royal Gazette, July 25, 1778; July 29, 1778; August 1, 1778; August 5, 1778; August 8, 1778; August 12, 1778; August 15, 1778; *The New-York Gazette; and the Weekly Mercury*, July 27, 1778. Minor differences between the papers.

Twelve shillings REWARD.

RUN-AWAY, a negro boy named JOE, about twelve years old, well sett, has a big head, and has one of his big toes cut off. The above reward will be given to any person that will bring him to his Master, night the Albany Pier.
JACOB WILKINS.
The New-York Gazette; and the Weekly Mercury, July 27, 1778.

A RUN-AWAY.

WHEREAS John Henry Nolte, a Hessian by birth, 21 years of age, 5 feet 3 inches high, a servant to the subscriber, run-away on the 23d instant; for fear of the punishment he made himself liable to by his misconduct, whereby he broke his oath of fidelity.—All persons, both civil and military, are requested to apprehend the said John H. Nolte as soon as it may be in their power, and be pleased to send notice thereof to the subscriber, in King-street, No. 38.—Said run-away has in a degree learnt the taylors trade: He commonly wears a whiteish coat with white buttons, blue striped or linen trowsers, a little round hat with a silk ribbon and a steel buckle in the same; he sometimes wears a green striped silk waistcoat. Whoever shall secure the above run-away so that the subscriber may have him again, shall receive Two Dollars reward,
by me   ANTHON GEORGE KYSCH.
Hessian Deputy Commissary.
The New-York Gazette; and the Weekly Mercury, July 27, 1778.

TWO DOLLARS Reward.

RUN-AWAY, a Virginia born Mulatto Girl, named HANNAH, 14 years old, slim made, has lately had the small pox, accustomed to house work; had on when she went away, an ozenbrig petticoat and shift, brown and blue short gown, and an old green bonnet. The above reward will be given to any person that will bring her to her master, in Duke-street, No. 9.
JOHN MYERS.
All Masters of vessels; and others, are forwarned from harbouring or carrying her off.   July 25.
The Royal Gazette, August 1, 1778; August 5, 1778; August 8, 1778.

DESERTED

FROM the William transport, George Stupart, Master, a boy between thirteen and fourteen years of age, named ISAAC TAPPAN; had on when he went away, a red flannel jacket spotted black, canvas trowsers, and a Dutch cap. Short hair and a good deal marked with the small pox. All masters of vessels are particularly requested not to ship said boy, he being an apprentice. Any person who will take up said boy and deliver him to Captain John M'Lean, of the Lord Howe, privateer, shall receive Five Dollars reward.

The Royal Gazette, August 5, 1778; August 8, 1778; August 12, 1778; August 15, 1778.

DESERTERS.

DESERTED from his Majesty's ship LIZARD,

ISAAC COOPER, 5 feet 7 inches high, of a brown complection short dark brown hair.

PHILIP BECKETT, 5 feet 8 inches high, of a fair complection, much freckled, short black hair.

SAMUEL SMITH, 5 feet 6 inches high, of a dark complection, strait black hair.

The above Deserters it is imagined are lurking about New-York.

A reward of FORTY SHILLINGS STERLING, will be given to any person apprehending and securing any one of the before-mentioned deserters, by applying to Mr. RIVINGTON, who is directed to pay ONE GUINEA for each, brought to his house, besides the above allotted sum of Forty Shillings for apprehending Deserters.

The Royal Gazette, August 8, 1778; August 12, 1778; August 15, 1778.

ONE GUINEA REWARD.

SARAH, Mulatto Wench, the Property of Mrs. REID, has absconded from her Mistress, on being accused with Theft, and known to be secreted in this City. Whoever will apprehend her shall have the above Reward, on applying to Mrs. REID in King-street.

The Royal Gazette, August 12, 1778; August 15, 1778.

DESERTED,
From his Majesty's Ship GALATEA,

LOUIS PINARD, five feet seven inches high, stout made, black hair, sallow complexion, and has a cast in one of his eyes. He commonly wears a red and white striped linen jacket and trowsers, and a narrow gold laced hat.

Whoever apprehends the said Deserter, and secures him so that he may returned to his Ship, shall receive the reward offered by act of parliament.
The Royal Gazette, August 12, 1778; August 15, 1778.

TWO DOLLARS REWARD.

RUN or strayed away the 11th instant from the King's Wharf, near the North-River,

A MULATTO BOY,

Named SAM, about eleven years old, strait hair, had on only a shirt and a pair of trowsers. Whoever will deliver said Boy to the subscriber living near Beekman Slip, shall have Two Guineas Reward
    paid by JESSE SMITH.
The Royal Gazette, August 19, 1778; August 22, 1778.

FIVE DOLLARS REWARD.

DESERTED from his Majesty's ship Phoenix's Tender, the third of July, a negro man named GEORGE WATKINS, aged about 21 years, had on when he went away, a blue jacket, check shirt, and long trowsers, with a round hat; about five feet three inches high, smooth faced, with a small cast in one of his eyes; he may attempt getting on board some of the shipping. Whoever apprehends the said man, and will lodge him on board one of his Majesty's ships, and acquaint the Printer, shall receive Five Dollars reward. All Masters of Ships and others are strictly forewarned at their peril from harbouring or carrying him off.
    Wm. FURNIVALL.

 N. B. A certificate must be brought to the Printer from the commanding officer on board the ship to which he may be carried.
The Royal Gazette, August 19, 1778; August 22, 1778.

TWO GUINEAS REWARD.

RUN away from the subscriber the 20th instant, a Mulatto Negro Boy, named PRIAM, 13 years old, about five feet five or six inches high, his hair of a remarkable light coloured woolly kind. Whoever secures said Boy; and will inform, or deliver him to the subscriber at Flatbush, Long-Island, or to Mr. John Taylor, in Queen-Street, No. 15, shall be entitled to the above reward. All masters of vessels and inhabitants are forwarned to carry him off, or conceal him, as they will answer the consequences.
    A. BAINBRIDGE, Surgeon, N. J. V.
The Royal Gazette, August 22, 1778; August 26, 1778.

TAKEN away, from on board the sloop Experiment, on Thursday night last, in Irons, a negro fellow named James Sturrup, and supposed to be

concealed in some house or vessel in the harbour: He is about 6 feet high, of a yellow complexion, and about 45 years old. He is a good seaman, has many grey hairs in his head, and a remarkable white tuft of hair in his forehead, near his face. Five guineas reward will be given to any person that will deliver the said fellow to Messrs. Moore and Neal's.
The New-York Gazette; and the Weekly Mercury, August 24, 1778; August 31, 1778.

RUN AWAY from the ship Cunninghame, lying near Brooklyn-Ferry, an apprentice lad, named JOHN AIKENHEAD: He is about 18 years of age, well grown, and thin visaged; has a small lisp in his speech, and speaks the Scottish dialect.—A reward of TWENTY SHILLINGS will be given to whoever will apprehend and secure the said apprentice, and all masters of privateers and other vessels, are hereby warned against taking him of board their ships.
The Royal Gazette, August 29, 1778; September 2, 1778; September 5, 1778.

New-York, August 28, 1778.
THREE DOLLARS REWARD,
RUN AWAY this morning from the Brig Betsy Ordnance Transport, John Bryson, Master, a Negro Boy named NED, about twelve years of age, this country born; had on when he went away, a checked shirt, almost new, a long pair of canvas duck trowsers, a pea blue duffil jacket pretty much faded, a shackle on his left leg, which may be concealed under his trowsers. Whoever secures said Negro, or brings him on board the said brig, laying in the North River, close to the Old English Church, shall be entitled to the above reward, and all reasonable charges
   paid by JOHN BRYSON.
N. B. As the said Negro has been brought up to the sea from his childhood, all masters of vessels are desired not to employ or harbour said Negro, as they will be prosecuted as the law directs.
The Royal Gazette, August 29, 1778; September 2, 1778.

TEN DOLLARS Reward.
RUN away from the subscriber, a mulatto negro boy named ISAAC, 5 feet 5 inches high, his hair of a dark woolly kind, has lately had the small-pox, had on when he went away, a dark blue coat with short skirts, a small round hat, waistcoat and trowsers. Whoever secures said boy, and will inform or deliver him to the subscribers, at the Queen's Head tavern, in Cherry-street, or to the Printer hereof, shall be entitled to the above reward and reasonable

charges. All masters of vessels and inhabitants are forewarned to carry him off or conceal him, as they will answer the consequences.

JOHN and WILLIAM SMITH.

The Royal Gazette, September 2, 1778; September 5, 1778. See *The Royal Gazette*, September 30, 1778.

To all Masters of Vessels,

A FRENCHMAN, native of Bayonne, in France, six feet high, light hair, remarkably thick, sickly complexion, about 25 years of age; is supposed to be on board some vessel or ship outward bound, as a passenger. He is named BERNARD DU VERDIER. He has been guilty of a robbery, to a considerable amount.—Whoever will secure the said person, shall receive FIVE GUINEAS reward, and all expences, by applying to the Pay-master of the 4th, or King's Own Regiment, at Kingsbridge.

The Royal Gazette, September 5, 1778.

EIGHT DOLLARS Reward.

RUN-AWAY from the subscriber, about five weeks since, a negro boy named DANIEL, about 16 years old, a likely smooth-faced fellow, about five feet high: He formerly lived with Dr. Stewart, and frequently went to Jamaica, on Long-Island, to see his sister. He had on a white ozenbrig trowsers and short, a brown coat with red cuffs, woolen hat with a silver band round it, and silver tossel. Whoever will secure the said boy, and deliver him to the subscriber, in Queen-street, shall be immediately paid the above reward, and all reasonable charges. All masters of vessels and others, are forwarned not to carry him off or conceal him, as they may expect to answer it at their peril.

PHILIP KISSICK.

The New-York Gazette; and the Weekly Mercury, September 7, 1778; September 14, 1778. See *The Royal Gazette*, October 5, 1778.

ONE GUINEA Reward.

RUN away from the Subscriber the second inst. a Negro boy, named WILLIAM, about 18 years of age; had on when he went away, a short dark blue cloth coat, a red waistcoat and brown trowsers, born and bred in the Jersies. Whoever will apprehend secured [*sic*] said negro, or give information to Mr. Gabriel H. Ludlow, in Wall-street, where he may be found, shall be intitled to the above reward and all charges,

by DANIEL LUDLOW.

The Royal Gazette, September 12, 1778; September 16, 1778.

ONE GUINEA Reward.

RUN-AWAY from the subscriber, a negro fellow named YORK, but may call himself George: he is short and well set, speaks broken English, had on when he went away, a blue camblet coat, with a striped lindsey jacket, and striped trowsers. Whoever will secure or give information to the subscriber, shall be entitled to the above reward, and all charges,

by   THOMAS GRESWOLD.

N. B. It is hoped the gentlemen of the army and navy will not give him the least encouragement, as he has been twice inlisted, and cleared by order of the Commandant from the Hessian service.

The New-York Gazette; and the Weekly Mercury, September 14, 1778. See *The Constitutional Gazette*, July 17, 1776, *The New-York Gazette; and the Weekly Mercury*, May 12, 1777, and *The New-York Gazette; and the Weekly Mercury*, June 9, 1777.

TWO GUINEAS Reward.

RUN away from the subscriber, on the 18th inst. a negro boy named POLYDORE, about 13 years of age, slender built, speaks bad English, and very quick, has a scar on his left leg; had on when he went away, an old oznabrig shirt, blue and yellow striped trowsers, an old yellow striped waistcoat, split behind, a black round hat, and a pair of old shoes; all persons are desired not to take away or harbour said negro. Whoever will secure of give information, so the owner may have him again, shall receive the above reward, with thanks, and all reasonable charges,

paid by   JAMES BENNETT,   in Hanover-square.

The Royal Gazette, September 19, 1778.

RUN AWAY from the ship Union, on Sunday last, the following apprentices, viz. PATRICK GREGORY, aged about 19 years, five feet four inches high, pock mark'd: Had on when he went away, a blue jacket, with striped trowsers, and a loop'd hat. JOHN JOHNSON, aged eighteen years, five feet five inches high, with strait black hair, and a cast in his right eye, much bitten by the musketoes in the face and hands, almost similar to the small pox: Had on when he went away, a striped red and white jacket, with brown ribb'd stockings, a round hat, and has served his time to a Taylor.—This is to caution all Masters of ships and house keepers, not to harbour or detain the said Apprentice in their service, as diligent search will be made for them, and if found, will be prosecuted to the rigour of the law. Any person who will bring the said Apprentice to John Sibrell, Master of the ship Union, lying at Bache's Wharf, shall receive for each FORTY SHILLINGS reward.

the ship Union, lying at Bache's Wharf, shall receive for each FORTY SHILLINGS reward.
The Royal Gazette, September 26, 1778.

TEN DOLLARS REWARD.

TO whoever will take up, and bring to the subscriber, or to Richard Williams, near the Fly-Market, a Negro Man servant, who run away about six weeks ago, a short well made fellow, about 5 feet high; had on when he went away, a thickset coat and waistcoat, white breeches, plays well on a violin, is a very good cook, and very handy about a gentleman; besides the above reward, all necessary charges will be
paid by   JOS. GOLDTHWAIT.
The Royal Gazette, September 26, 1778; September 30, 1778.

Forty Shillings Reward.

DESERTED from his Majesty's Ship the Brune, James Syze, a Portugueze, by birth, speaks broken English, of a black swarthy complexion, black eyes, and Raven black long hair, about thirty years of age, five feet ten inches high, an active stout made man to appearance.
The Royal Gazette, September 26, 1778.

RUN-AWAY from Joseph Milford, living in King-street, No. 21, about 14 days ago, a negro boy 11 years old, has a scar in his back, occasioned by a scald: Had on when he went away, a shirt and trowsers. All persons are forbid to harbour or conceal said lad, and whoever secures him and brings him to his said master, shall receive Two Dollars reward.
The New-York Gazette; and the Weekly Mercury, September 28, 1778.

DESERTED

FROM the Dorothy and Catharine transports, Robert Galilee, master, the 17th inst. two apprentice lads, viz. Daniel Forbes, about 5 feet high, smooth face and thick lips: Had on when he deserted, a white flannel under jacket, with a blue upper on lin'd with white, a round hat, long trowsers, and shoes without stockings, wears his own black hair. Robert Hall, about 4 feet 10 inches high, dark thin complexion, much pitted with the small-pox, wears his own short dark-colour'd hair: Had on when he deserted, a blue jacket, Dutch cap, long trowsers, and shoes without stockings. Whoever apprehends the said lads, and delivers them on board the John and Jane, in the North-River, shall have half a Joe reward for each.
The New-York Gazette; and the Weekly Mercury, September 28, 1778.

Three Guineas Reward.

RUN away from the subscriber on Friday morning, the 25th instant, a young Negro Wench named BET, about 16 years old, yellow colour, a little pitted with the small-pox; had on when she went away a green waistcoat and petticoat, and took with her a callico gown. The above reward will be given on the deliver of the girl to the Printer,
or to   ANDREW WALLACE.
The Royal Gazette, September 30, 1778.

TEN DOLLARS REWARD.

RUN AWAY from the subscriber, on Tuesday the 20th of September, a Mulatto man, named ISAAC, 20 years of age, lately had the small-pox, about five feet five inches high, he had on a check shirt, striped trowsers, an old hat, striped under waistcoat, shoes with plated buckles, and pot hooks round his neck, [sic] he is a good cook, and understands no business but house work. Whoever will secure said mulatto, and deliver him to the subscriber in Cherry-street, at the Queen's Head tavern, shall be immediately paid the above reward and all reasonable charges. All masters of vessels and others are forwarned not to carry him off or conceal him, as they may expect to answer it at their peril.
JOHN and WILLIAM SMITH.
The Royal Gazette, September 30, 1778; October 10, 1778. See *The Royal Gazette*, September 2, 1778.

RUN-AWAY on Friday the 25th of September last, from the subscriber, a likely young negro wench, named ——, about 24 years old, and took with her a bundle of cloaths of different sorts: She formerly lived with Mr. Magee, carpenter, was born at Newtown, on Long-Island, speaks good English, and is probably gone that way. All masters of vessels are forbid either to harbour or carry off said wench; but whoever returns her to her master, PHILIP KISSICK, at No. 125, the head of Queen-street, shall receive EIGHT DOLLARS reward.
The New-York Gazette; and the Weekly Mercury, October 5, 1778; October 12, 1778; October 19, 1778; November 9, 1778; November 16, 1778.

EIGHT DOLLARS Reward.

RUN-AWAY from the subscriber, about nine weeks since, a negro boy named DANIEL, about 16 years old, a likely smooth-faced fellow, about five feet high: He was purchased from Mr. Fisher, of this city, merchant. He formerly lived with Dr. Stewart, and frequently went to Jamaica, on Long-Island, to see his sister. He had on a white oznabrig trowsers and shirt, a brown coat with red cuffs, woollen hat with a silver band round it, and silver tossel. Whoever will secure the said boy, and deliver him to the subscriber, in Queen-street, shall immediately be paid the above reward, and all reasonable charges. All masters of vessels and others, are forwarned not to carry him off, or conceal him, as they may expect to answer it at their peril. PHILIP KISSICK.

The Royal Gazette, October 5, 1778; October 12, 1778. See *The New-York Gazette; and the Weekly Mercury*, September 7, 1778.

THREE GUINEAS REWARD.

DESERTED from the ship Grand Duke, army victualler, last Friday, Alexander Lee, an apprentice about 5 feet 3 inches high, of a sallow complexion, wears his own hair, which curled very much, speaks thick; had on when he went away, a blue settee jacket and long trowsers. Whoever apprehends the said apprentice, and brings him on board the above ship, lying near the King's brewery, on Long Island, or lodges him in the provost, shall receive the above reward, and all reasonable charges paid.   RICHARD HARMAN, jun.

N. B. All masters of vessels are desired not to employ or harbour said apprentice.

The Royal Gazette, October 5, 1778; October 12, 1778.

RUN-AWAY from WILLIAM SACKETT, of Newtown, on Long-Island, on Saturday the 26th of September, and was seen at New-York the day following, a negro wench, SUSAN by name, 22 years old, has a scar under her chin on the right side, her right leg is remarkable, being bent very much forwards, with a large scar; is supposed to wear a light callico gown, with a dark blue petticoat. All persons are forbid to harbour or conceal said wench: And whoever secures and brings her to her said master, or to Richard Greaves, at Mr. Isaac Kipp's, in Duke-street, New-York, shall receive FOUR DOLLARS reward,

The Royal Gazette, October 5, 1778; October 12, 1778; October 19, 1778.

STOLEN on the night of the tenth inst. a dark calico striped gown, with spots in the stripes, plain made; a purple and white gown plain made; a red sprigged calico gown, a black flowered satin cloke lined with white, also twenty-two dollars. The thief is a woman who goes by the same of Mary Brian; she is about twenty-four years of age, rather lusty, much tanned and freckled, a cast in her eyes; delights in wearing a coarse black apron; says she came from New York where she was married to a British soldier, but sometimes denies her marriage; also says that her mother, Elizabeth Brian,

lives in Chester. Whoever secures the goods and thief, shall have Twenty Dollars reward, &c. for the goods only Twelve Dollars.
      CATHERINE TODD.
The Pennsylvania Evening Post, October 7, 1778.

      FOUR DOLLARS REWARD
RUN away from the subscriber on Thursday the 1st. instant, A NEGRO BOY named SAM, between 14 and 15 years of age; well made, smooth face, sly look, and of a swarthy complexion. Had on when he went off, a blue jacket with yellow buttons, white and red waistcoat and striped trowsers, new round hat with a silver band about it. It is supposed he is lurking between Bushwick and Flatbush on Long-Island. Whoever brings the said boy to No. 22, Peck-slip, or secures him that he may be apprehended, shall be entitled to the above reward, besides expences,
    from JAMES FRASER,
      corner of Peck-slip, New-York.
  N. B. It is supposed he will enter on board any privateer or other vessel that is going out of this port; all masters of vessels and others are forewarned not to harbour the said negro on board at their peril.
The Royal Gazette, October 10, 1778; October 14, 1778.

ABsented himself Thursday evening, and supposed to be decoyed on board the fleet, a Mulatto Boy named Peter, about twelve years old, speaks remarkable good English, had on when he was missed, a brown thickset suit of cloaths with gilt buttons and round hat. Any person that can give intelligence to the printer where he may be heard of, shall receive a reward of FIVE DOLLARS for their trouble, and any master of a vessel that should harbour him, or attempt to take him off, may depend on being prosecuted by his master. If he should by accident be put on board any of the ships of war, it is hoped he will be sent on shore, he being the property of an officer of his Majesty's hospital.   Oct. 9, 1778.
The Royal Gazette, October 10, 1778.

RUN AWAY from on board the Kitty, Capt. Scales, lying at Wells's Wharf, two apprentices, JAMES DAVIS, and RICHARD DODGSON—James Davis is about 17 or 18 years of age, thick set, and short black hair, dark complexion; had on, when he run away, a red jacket, a round hat, and a pair of dirty striped trowsers.—Richard Dodgson is about 15 or 16 years of age, had on when he went away, a striped jacket, a pair of new oznabrigs trowsers, a checked shirt, and a sharp cocked hat. Whoever brings both or either of the said apprentices on board the Kitty, shall be handsomely rewarded, &c.

The Royal Gazette, October 10, 1778.

RUN away from the ship Sarah, victualler, John Mathews, master, BENJAMIN SIM, apprentice to the above ship, aged 22 years, about five feet 10 inches high, a stout made young fellow, wears his own hair tied, of a fair complexion, has a scar on his left hand; had on when he went away, a blue coatee, check shirt, and long trousers. All masters of vessels are desired not to harbour the above apprentice, as they will be prosecuted as the law directs, and whoever apprehends the above and delivers him on board the said ship, laying a little below Brooklyn Ferry, Long-Island, or secures him in the Main Guard, shall receive TWO DOLLARS reward,
JOHN MATHEWS.
The Royal Gazette, October 10, 1778.

RUN away a Negro Boy, who calls himself Charles Williams, about 18 years of age, had on a brown fustain coat and waistcoat, leather or linen breeches, and a round hat. Any person that will bring him to the 17th regt. of Dragoons at Newtown, shall receive FIVE GUINEAS reward.
The Royal Gazette, October 21, 1778; October 24, 1778.

ABSENTED,
FROM his master's service, a Negro man named ANGUS, about 35 years old, a sawyer by trade, about 5 feet 7 inches high, a likely fellow; had on brown cloaths. Whoever will discover where he is, so that he may be recovered by his master, shall have ONE GUINEA Reward. If on board any of the vessels, it is entreated that he may be sent to his master DAVID THOMSON, late Ship-builder, near Pecks-Slip.
The Royal Gazette, October 21, 1778.

FOUR DOLLARS REWARD.
RUN away from his Master, a Negro Man named Caesar, had on a light blue coat, brown waistcoat, coarse linen trowsers, a stout well made fellow, about 5 feet 6 inches high, three Negro marks on each side of his face, and a little pock-marked. The owner forwarns all masters of vessels not to carry him off, and any person that will apprehend, and bring him to Capt. Taylor, of the ship Good Hope, laying in the North River, or to the Printer hereof, shall have the above reward.
The Royal Gazette, October 21, 1778.

ONE GUINEA Reward.
TO any person that will apprehend and secure a certain negro man, named CHARLES, born in Maryland, but last from Philadelphia; he wears a red

coat with buttons marked I. He is supposed to be on board some vessel, or on Long-Island. He has stole a new check matrass. It is desired that no master of a vessel will carry him off till he is brought to justice.
      ROBERT CAMPBELL.
The Royal Gazette, October 21, 1778; October 24, 1778.

      Twenty Dollars Reward.
RAN-away, a negro boy named Glascow, 25 years of age, 5 feet high, very black and well featured: He wrought some time ago at the press with Messrs. Mills and Hicks, and lately in the King's hay-yard, in this city. Whoever apprehends the said negro and brings him to the Printers hereof, shall have the above reward.
 All masters of vessels and others, are cautioned not to harbour or conceal him, at their peril.
The Royal Gazette, October 21, 1778; October 24, 1778.

RUN away from the ship Munificence transport, Thomas Elding, master, an apprentice named ABRAHAM SPRINGER, a native of New-England; had on when he went away, a large light coloured upper jacket, a pair of long trowsers, a large round hat, his own short light coloured hair, about 16 years of age, 5 feet 2 inches high, smooth faced, and brown complexion. Also run away from the same ship, an apprentice named JAMES YOUNG, about 15 years of age, smooth faced, brown complexion, had on when he went away, an old red jacket, a pair of long trowsers, and an old cock'd hat, about 4 feet 10 or 11 inches high. Whoever will give such information as may enable the master of the above ship to get them back to the ship, shall have ONE GUINEA Reward for each of them.
All persons are cautioned not to harbour them at their peril.
The Royal Gazette, October 24, 1778; October 28, 1778. See *The Royal Gazette,* November 7, 1778, for Springer.

      FIVE POUNDS Reward.
RUN AWAY to the city of New-York from the Subscriber, at Flatlands, in Kings County, on Long-Island, a Black NEGRO MAN, about 24 years of age, 5 feet 1-2 high, uncertain what cloaths he had on; took with him three coats, one blue, one reddish, one homespun, 8 shirts, 4 pair of trowsers, 2 pair of breeches, some stockings, wears in his shoes a large pair of square silver buckles, has also a large over coat. Whoever secures said negro, so that his mistress may get him again, shall have the above reward,
   paid by me HENDERIKIE LOTT, widow.
The Royal Gazette, November 1, 1778; November 7, 1778.

RUN away from the subscriber the tenth of October, a negro man, named Prince, aged about twenty-four years. He is a short well-set fellow, has a large scar on the head in which no hair grows. Had on a brown home made coat and waistcoat, long trowsers, and frock home-spun linen, stockings and shoes. Whoever will take up the said fellow and return him to me, or secure him in any goal in the United States, and send me word, or the Printer hereof, shall have TWENTY DOLLARS reward, and all charges
          paid, by   LEVI ALLEN.
          Dutchess County, State of New-York, Oct. 31.
Thomas's Massachusetts Spy Or, American Oracle of Liberty, November 5, 1778; November 12, 1778; November 19, 1778; November 26, 1778; December 3, 1778. See *The Connecticut Gazette; and the Universal Intelligencer*, December 15, 1778.

ABSENTED himself from his Master's service, William Smith, apprentice unto Thomas Eldding, Master of the Munificence, transport, late in the evening of the 5th of November, had on when he went away, a short double-breasted red jacket, a large blue outside one, long canvas trowsers, silver round womens buckles, and small bound round hat, dark complexion, short hair, long visage, and is a native of South Shields, was late in the watch and clock-making business. It is earnestly requested not Watch-Maker, or other person will employ or harbour him, or they will answer the same at their peril.

    Absented at the same time, Abraham Springer, a native of New-England, about 16 years old, his head lately shaved, had on when he went away, an inside flannel jacket, a soldier's red cap on his head, dark brown stockings, and white cloth officers breeches.
The Royal Gazette, November 7, 1778, November 11, 1778. See *The Royal Gazette*, October 24, 1778, for Springer.

One Guinea Reward.

RUN away yesterday the 10th inst. Joseph Mackenzie, an apprentice boy, by trade a blacksmith, about sixteen years old, had on when he run away, a short brown jacket, with a striped under one, white sheeting trowsers and check'd shirt. Whoever will bring him, or give information to John Jarvis, in Prince-Street, near the new Sugar House, shall receive the above reward.

    N. B. All masters of vessels are desired not to harbour him at their peril.
The Royal Gazette, November 11, 1778; November 14, 1778.

RUN away on Tuesday from the William transport, George Stupart, master, a negro boy named TOM, about 18 or 19 years of age, marked with the

small-pox, with long bushy wool, tied behind; had on when he went away, a blue jacket, grey woollen trowsers, and an old light infantry cap; all masters of vessels, &c. are desired not to ship said negro, he being the property of the above mentioned George Stupart, and whoever will bring him on board the William, lying off the Battery in the North River, or put him in the Main-Guard, till notice is given, shall have EIGHT DOLLARS Reward.
The Royal Gazette, November 14, 1778; November 18, 1778.

TWO SLAVES, both named NED, left the brig BRITANNIA, at Staten-Island, in the night of Monday the 9th inst. One, a black, very sensible and impudent, he pretends being very skilful in keeping race horses, is very talkative when in liquor; about five feet nine inches high, and fifty years of age:

The other, of a yellow complexion, slim made, and speaks slow; he is about five feet eight inches high, and appears to be of the age of one or two and twenty years of age. It is not remembered what cloths they had on when they left the vessel. They are the property of Mr. John Hamilton, late of N. Carolina, and are well known to most of the gentlemen from that province and Virginia, in this city.—A reward of TWENTY DOLLARS will be given to whoever brings them to

Ronald Campbell, No. 12, or to

William Rose, No. 192, Queen-street.

If they return of their own accord before the fleet sails, they shall be forgiven.

N. B. All Persons are forwarned from hireing, harbouring, or carrying them out of the country, as they will answer the same at their peril.
The Royal Gazette, November 18, 1778.

RUN AWAY last Thursday Morning from the Sibelia, George Robinson, Master, a Navy Victualler, at Brownjohn's wharf, Ralph Barton, an apprentice, had on a round hat, his own brown hair, two blue waistcoats, a pair of long canvas trowsers, tall in stature, fresh complexion, aged 20 years, took with him a bundle of cloaths. Whoever is found to harbour the said apprentice in a house or ship, will be prosecuted at the law directs.
The Royal Gazette, December 12, 1778.

Ten Dollars Reward.

RUN AWAY from the subscriber on the first of December inst. a likely Negro Wench named Myrtilla, about 23 years of age, has a large scar on his left wrist. She is a native of Africa, and has lived a long time in the island of Bermuda. Whoever brings the said Negro to the House of Mr. Farrer, No. 27, Duke-street, or to the Printer hereof, shall have the above reward. And I

hereby forewarn all masters of ships and others against harbouring the said Negro, or carrying her off.
J. EILBECK.

The Royal Gazette, December 12, 1778; December 16, 1778; December 19, 1778; December 23, 1778; December 26, 1778; December 30, 1778.

FOUR DOLLARS Reward.
Run away from the Subscriber,
A NEGRO WENCH, named BETT, born in town, is of a middle size, about 18 years of age, marked with the small-pox; she had on a homespun gown and petticoat. Whoever will secure her and bring her to me shall have the above reward. MISPER LEE.

The New-York Gazette; and the Weekly Mercury, December 14, 1778; December 21, 1778; December 28, 1778.

TWENTY DOLLARS REWARD.
RAN-AWAY from the Subscriber, in October last, a Negro Man named PRINCE, twenty-three years old, Guinea born, a remarkable scar on his head: Had on a light brown coat and vest of homespun round felt hat, trowsers and shirt, or rather a frock of homespun linen: A short well set fellow. Whoever will take up and secure said slave, in any gaol, or return him to me, or give information to the Printers, shall have the above reward, and charges paid, by LEVI ALLEN.
Dutchess County, State of New-York, November 3 1778.

The Connecticut Gazette; and the Universal Intelligencer, December 15, 1778; *The Connecticut Courant*, January 5, 1779. See *Thomas's Massachusetts Spy Or, American Oracle of Liberty*, November 5, 1778.

WHEREAS the following Seamen have absented themselves from their duty on board the PERSEUS, for some days, and are seen straggling about this city: FORTY SHILLGS reward will be immediately paid to any person who shall apprehend any of the offenders.

JAMES HARRIS, aged 34 years, 5 feet 5 inches high, dark complexion, has short black hair, born at Malden, in Essex.

WILLIAM ELLIOTT, born in Ireland, 5 feet 11 inches high, thin face, strong made, and black hair.

PATRICK DUFFY, born in Ireland, about 28 years of age, 5 feet 6 inches high, stout made, light hair; the two last were seen on Sunday in the Bowery-Lane, with some of the Irish Volunteers.

SAMUEL HARRIS, aged about 32 years, 5 feet 5 inches high, swarthy complexion, well set, marked with the small-pox, and has received a wound in the left side, which often shews itself.

THOMAS HAYS, born in Dublin, aged about 22 years, 5 feet 5 inches high, fresh complexion, round face, and smooth, black curled hair, and has a little of the Irish pronunciation.

A farther reward of FIVE POUNDS is offered to any person who will inform upon any Masters or Owners of Privateers who have inveigled, concealed, or any ways entertained the above described persons.

PERSEUS, Dec. 15, 1778.

The Royal Gazette, December 16, 1778; December 19, 1778; December 23, 1778; December 26, 1778; December 30, 1778; January 2, 1779.

RUN away from the subscriber a Mulatto servant man named SHADRECK, about 5 feet 7 inches high, well built; when he went away had on a light coloured jacket and breeches. Any person apprehending him and bringing him to his master, near Tea-Water Pump, shall be handsomely rewarded for their trouble.

All masters of vessels and others are forwarned harbouring or carrying off said servant, as they will be prosecuted with the utmost rigour of the law.   GILBERT PUGSLY.

The Royal Gazette, December 19, 1778.

WHEREAS a Person who called himself by the Name of John Gale, (Son of John Gale, of New-York, whose Widow kept the Sign of the Blue-Anchor there; but afterwards married one Mr. Pike, Mariner and with him, 'tis suppos'd removed to Philadelphia,) died at the House of the Subscriber in Middle-Street, Boston, on the 19th ult.—These are therefore to give Notice to all to whom it may concern, That on proper Application to him, they may be informed of the Particulars of the Deceased's Effects.

ALEXr. McLEAD.   Boston, Dec. 19, 1778.

The Boston Gazette, and Country Journal, December 21, 1778; January 4, 1779.

Twenty Shillings, Reward.

INTICED away from the Ship Jane Victualler, lying at Burling's Slip, a Negro Boy, named DICK, about 11 Years of Age, rather short for his Years, but stout made: Had on when he went off, a blue Jacket with a Crimson Plush Colar, striped Waistcoat, blue Breeches, shoes and Stockings. Whoever will take up said Boy, and return him to his Master on board, shall have the above Reward.

CONELLY M''CAUSLAND.
The New-York Gazette; and the Weekly Mercury, December 21, 1778; December 28, 1778.

TEN DOLLARS REWARD.

ABSENTED himself, suspected with a design to run away, on Saturday the 13th inst. a negro fellow named CATO, he is about 21 years of age, of a yellowish complexion, was brought from the Island of Jamaica about six years ago, all which time, until a month past here, he has resided with him master at Rhode-Island. He was born in Guinea, of the Chamba nation, and has his country marks on his cheeks, talks English enough to be well understood, branded on one of his shoulders P. E. and wore a dark coloured surtout coat, the rest of his dress not remembered. Whoever apprehends and brings him to Captain Laird's Office, in Hanover Square, shall receive the above reward, but whoever conceals or harbours him after this public notice shall be prosecuted.
The Royal Gazette, December 23, 1778.

1779

RUN AWAY from the subscriber about the 15th of November last, a likely NEGRO BOY, about 14 years of age, named PRIMUS, had on when he went away, a blue jacket, very long in the sleeves, turn'd up with white, with whitish coloured cloth breeches, brown worsted ribb'd stockings: He lately belonged to the Rev. Mr. Inglis. Whoever brings the said Boy to the subscriber, shall have FOUR DOLLARS reward. All masters of vessels are warned not to take away the said Boy at their peril.
    CATHARINE SPALDIN. Dock-street, No. 332.
The Royal Gazette, January 2, 1779.

DESERTED,

FROM the Horse Department belonging to the Royal Artillery, RICHARD SHEY, about 5 feet 8 inches high, brown complexion, brown hair, stout made, about 46 years of age, had on when he went away a brown short coat.

 JAMES M'MUNNIGAN, about 5 feet 5 inches high, black complexion, black short hair, marked with the small pox, aged about 25 years, had on a short brown jacket with collar and cuffs, and a blanket coat.

 HUGH DAVIES, about 5 feet 7 inches high, well made, of a dark complexion, had on a blue great coat, with a red collars. And

 JAMES JUKE, about 5 feet 8 inches high, fair hair'd and fair complexion, about 20 years of age, had on a claret coloured coat and waistcoat.

A Reward of TWO GUINEAS is hereby offered to any person who will bring any of the said deserters to the Office of Ordnance opposite St. Paul's church. It is imagined they have been enticed to go on board some privateer, or other vessel. This public notice is given to all owners and masters of privateers and other vessels, that they may depend on the most severe and rigourous treatment upon conviction, that the law will admit.
The Royal Gazette, January 19, 1779.

FOUR DOLLARS REWARD.

RUN away from the ship George, transport, Andrew Clunie, Master, January the 25th. inst. a negro man named JACK, Africa born, about 23 years of age, had on when he went away, a light blue jacket, and pair of long white trowsers and round hat. Whoever brings the said negro to the ship, who lays in the Wallabocht bay, or to the Printer, shall have the above reward. I hereby forwarn all masters of vessels not to harbour or carry him off.   ANDREW CLUNIE.
The Royal Gazette, January 30, 1779.

RUN-AWAY from the subscriber, living in Chapel-street, last Tuesday morning, a negro man named YORK, about 5 feet high, of a yellow cast. Had on when he went away, a blue coat with silver twist buttons, blue breeches, with white metal buttons, a new blue duffils great coat, beaver hat, almost new, cocked sharp. Whoever takes up said negro, and brings him to his master, shall receive EIGHT DOLLARS reward.
            SAMUEL PEARCE.
The New-York Gazette; and the Weekly Mercury, February 1, 1779.

TWENTY GUINEAS Reward.

RUN-AWAY from the lively transport, Thomas Hall, Master. JOSEPH STEEL, aged about 20 years, 5 feet 7 inches high, light brown hair. Also, JAMES PETERS, about 20 years of age, 5 feet 8 inches high, black hair. Whoever will secure said deserters, and deliver them on board the Lively, lying on Wallaboght, shall receive the above reward of Ten Guineas for each. All masters of privateers are forbid to harbour them, as they will be prosecuted with the utmost rigour.
The New-York Gazette; and the Weekly Mercury, February 8, 1779; February 15, 1779.

HARTFORD Feb. 6 1779.

MADE their escape from the Goal in this Place, the following Prisoners, viz. NATHANIEL AKERLY, a Tory, belonging to the State of New-York, a stout thick set fellow, light complexion, grey eyes and brown hair....

BLNATHAN BURTS, [sic] a native of Long Island, a slim meagre starv'd looking scoundrel—All the above described fellows are tories.... PETER GANTER, of New-York state, tall stout fellow, black hair and blue eyes...committed for theft. Whoever will apprehend either of the above prisoners, and return them to this, or secure them in any other goal, within this or the neighboring states, and inform the subscriber, shall be entitled to a reward of Twenty Dollars, and all necessary charges paid,
by   BARZ. HUDSON, Goaler.
The Connecticut Courant, and Hartford Weekly Intelligencer, February 9, 1779.

Five Dollars Reward.
RUN AWAY from the subscriber, living at Newtown, Long-Island, on Saturday last, a Negro man named JEFF, about 25 years of age, 5 feet 5 inches high; had on when he went away a light green coat, with a bundle of other cloaths with him. Whoever will secure the said Negro, or bring him to the subscriber, shall receive the above reward.
BERNADES BLOOM.
All masters of vessels and others are desired not to harbour him, but at their peril.
The Royal Gazette, February 17, 1779.

DESERTED *from the Clibbern transport, William Thomas, Master, three seaman, William Rogers, a tall thin man, about six feet high, 25 years of age, John Clemons, a middle sized man, about 5 feet 8 inches high, about same age, and John Craning, a short squat fellow, about 18 years of age, also, an apprentice, named Charles Webmore, a fair boy, about 17 years of age. Whoever will secure said deserters shall have Two Guineas reward for each, by applying to M. Gaine.*
The New-York Gazette; and the Weekly Mercury, February 22, 1779; March 1, 1779.

SIX DOLLARS REWARD,
RUN-AWAY from the subscriber, living at Jamaica, a stout well made negro man named TOM. He is about one and twenty, and about five feet ten inches high. He stutters greatly, had on when he went away a dark grey short coat, belt waistcoat of the same, with yellow metal buttons, buff breeches, white worsted stockings. He was seen in New-York a few days ago. It is thought he will try to go out in some privateer. All masters of vessels are forbid to carry him off at their peril. Whoever secures him so that his master may have him again, shall have the above reward, and all reasonable charges.

BENJAMIN SMITH.
The New-York Gazette; and the Weekly Mercury, March 1, 1779.

DESERTED, *Friday night last, [from] the ship Admiral Keppel, armed Victualler, [   ] Hammond, Commander, PHILEMON ROOK, apprentice, about 18 years of age, fair complexion, light brown hair, a scar upon his right wrist, is supposed to have gone over to Long-Island, is a privateer; had on when he went away a dark brown jacket, and long trowsers. Whoever will give information where the said apprentice is concealed, shall, upon his being apprehended, give Two Guineas reward, or whoever can give information of any person who decoyed the said apprentice away, shall, upon conviction, receive One Guinea reward, from the advertiser. If the said apprentice will return to his master immediately, he shall be forgiven.*
The New-York Gazette; and the Weekly Mercury, March 1, 1779.

ABSENTED from the ship Eagle armed Victualler, at 5 P. M. March the 8th, John Richardson, Chief Mate, aged 30 years, has his own short black hair mixed with white, thin faced, tender eyes, and walks in with his toes. having on a shabby half wide coat.
    William Corbes, Seaman, wearing his own short light coloured hair, has a stoop in his walk, stout made, tender eye, 5 feet 7 inches high, 36 years of age.
    Robert Taylor, 5 feet 7 inches high, marked with the small pox, has his own long sandy hair curled and generally queued, 27 years of age, has on a Dutch cap and long trowsers.
    William Craig, 5 feet 5 inches high, thin faced, his own short brown hair, a Dutch cap, Fearnought trowsers, and about 30 years of age.John Allen, six feet high, of the kingdom of Ireland, has his own fair short hair, a Dutch Cap, with Fearnought trowsers, clumsy made, and stout, 24 years of age. Whoever will apprehend, secure, bring on board, or give notice to said ship now at anchor in the stream, athwart the upper end of the King's wharf, so that the said persons may be got on board, shall receive a reward of Two Guineas for each man so secured and brought on board.
            THOMAS NOBLE.
The Royal Gazette, March 10, 1779.

RUN-away from Captain .Charles Handy, sometime in the month of September last, an active negro man named MOSES, about five feet six inches high, born in Rhode-Island, it is supposed that he is either lurking about this city or gone a privateering. Whoever apprehends the said negro man, and will deliver him to Coupland and Tench, No. 7. Water-street, shall receive Two Half Johannes Reward.

The Royal Gazette, March 10, 1779; March 13, 1779; March 17, 1779; March 20, 1779.

DESERTED,
From His Majesty's Ship ARDENT.

THOMAS PRATT, a Seaman, 5 feet 10 inches high, well made, wears his own dark hair, has a cut in his left cheek, had on when he left the Barge a blue jacket, white shirt, and round hat.

WILLIAM WATSON, a Seaman, 5 feet 6 inches high, well set, wears his own brown hair pretty long, tied behind, pitted with the small pox, and had on when he left the Barge a brown jacket, stripped cotton shirt, and round hat.

Whoever secures the said Deserters do that they may be brought to justice, shall receive TEN GUINEAS for either, about the bounty of Forty Shillings Ster. allowed for apprehending deserters.
S. W. CLAYTON.

The Royal Gazette, March 17, 1779; March 20, 1779; March 24, 1779.

ABSCONDED from his Mistress, the widow of the late Dirck Schuyler of this city, a Negro Man named CATO alias JOSHUA, about 30 years old, strong made, and of a yellowish complexion, and is well known in this city, he is designed to go a privateering, and I do forewarn all Captains of privateers and others from harbouring or concealing him.
ANN MARY SCHUYLER.

The Royal Gazette, March 24, 1779.

TWO HUNDRED DOLLARS Reward.

STOLEN from the subscriber, living in Somerset County, State of New-Jersey, about the 21st of February last, by a certain Henry Rush, the following articles.—

A woman's gold watch and key, the watch has a gold face, chased case, representing Pompey's head shewn to Caesar, maker's name supposed to be Wilsman, London; on the key is represented a hautboy. fiddle, flute, trumpet, &c. lying across each other; also a blue regimental coat, turned up with red, silver epaulet, (made out of knee garters) the coat is lined throughout with white durant, except the skirts which turn up, and about four inches the fore part, which is red shalloon; the buttons are white-flowered, (two or three lost) hooks and eyes, in the fore part, are some of black wire, twisted, some single white white; also a white twilled vest and breeches, the vest lined with white fustian, the breeches not lined, buttons white flowered; all which clothes he went off in;—likewise a full welted hunting saddle, not half worn, the tree has been broke, and is mended by a piece of iron clinched on the inside; the saddle cloth, blue long ells, with a stripe of white cloth, three quarters of an inch wide, sewed round near the edge, and lined with tow linen; a bridle, the reins tied to the bit.—The said fellow was born in Philadelphia, has straight hair, a scar on one side of his face, is very talkative, and speaks both the English and German very well; it is expected he will endeavour to pass for an officer, as he has procured himself a sword, and an old commission. He is now deserted from Capt. Heer's troop of light horse, and it is supposed he is gone to Goshen, in the State of New-York, as he has said his mother lived there, or to Albany, where he is well acquainted.—Whoever will secure the said thief in any of the State's gaols, shall receive one hundred dollars reward, and all reasonable charges, and for the watch, one hundred dollars more,

   paid by JOHN J. SCHENK.
    Somerset County, State of New-Jersey, March 1, 1779.
The Royal Gazette, April 3, 1779.

ONE GUINEA REWARD.

RUN away from the service of Jacobus Lent, of New-Town, on the 3d of April, a mulatto girl named ISABELLA, aged about eighteen Years, she is stout and strong made, long black hair; she is remarkable for having a large scar in her forehead, and another on the left side of her Jaw, also the forefinger on her left hand, off near the middle joint; she is supposed to have gone away in Men's Cloaths. Whoever will take up the said girl, and secure her so that the Owner may have her again, shall have the above reward, and all reasonable charges
   paid by JOHN DEACON.
The New-York Gazette; and the Weekly Mercury, April 12, 1779; April 19, 1779.

FORTY SHILLINGS Reward;
Or FIVE POUNDS on the Prosecution of the
Harbourer.

RUN-AWAY from the subscriber, a NEGRO BOY named JACK, a short thick, full-faced fellow. He formerly lived with Mr. *Christopher Blundle,* now Port-Master of New-York.

 He had on when he went away (on Monday the 5th instant) a fustian coat and waistcoat with sleeves, both have been washed, so that they are almost white, thick-set breeches, rather large, light blue broad ribbed worsted stockings, a pair of short in-grain, one of which is patched in the side, gold washed open worked shoe-buckles, white metal knee buckles, white shirt and cambrick frock, marked B. T. pinchbeck stock buckle, with three prongs, cocked hat, foxy coloured, and generally wearing the right hind cock before, chews Tobacco, speaks very good English, is a shrewd sensible Negro.

All Masters of transports, privateers, and other vessels, are hereby forewarned, by this public notice, not to harbour or employ said Negro, as they may depend on the utmost severity of the Law being put in execution against them, by,

ROBERT THOMPSON, No. 908, Water-street.

The New-York Gazette; and the Weekly Mercury, April 12, 1779; April 19, 1779; May 3, 1779; May 10, 1779.

DESERTED,

FROM the WORSLEY, *Armed Victualler*, JOHN MEADLY, *Commander*, on Thursday the 8th of April Instant, a certain *Williams Gibbs*, [sic] alias *John Smith*, of a middle size, fresh complexion, with his own hair, and had on a blue Jacket. Whoever takes up the said *Gibs*, alias *Smith*, shall receive TWO GUINEAS, *Reward*, from the said Captain on board the VESSEL, lying at the *Crane-Wharff*.

The New-York Gazette; and the Weekly Mercury, April 12, 1779.

The Sloop LADY ERSKINE,
EDWARD DREW, Commander.

Intends sailing on a Cruize on Sunday next, all masters of transports and others, who are in his Majesty's service and have men massing, are requested to come on board and examine the Crew, as he would not wish to carry any men belonging thereto....

Deserted from said sloop, two seamen named RICHARD CLARK and JOHN BARBER, they having signed articles and receive advance. All masters of privateers or merchantmen are cautioned to guard against these impostors, any person that can give information where they can be found, so as they may be detected, shall receive TWO GUINEAS Reward.

The Royal Gazette, April 24, 1779.

Ten Dollars Reward.

RUN AWAY from the subscriber, being near Peck's Slip, a Negro Wench named KATE, about Twenty Years of age, five foot two inches high, pitted with the Small Pox, which she has had a few months ago: she had on a spotted callico short gown, a blue callimanco skirt and check apron, and a black hat. She likewise took with her two purple short gowns. Whoever apprehends the said Wench shall receive the above reward from

JOHN BENNET, Peck's-Slip.

N. B. All masters of vessels are requested not to carry off the above wench, as they may depend on being prosecuted if found out.
The Royal Gazette, April 28, 1779. See *The Royal Gazette*, July 17, 1779.

A Negro Run away.

ON Friday the 23d instant, named Charles, about 23 years old, 5 feet 9 inches high, has a large burn on his leg; of a yellowish cast, plays on the fiddle, had on a blue coat, brown jacket and trowsers. Whoever will deliver him to Cosper Springsteen, at New-Town, Long-Island, shall have Ten Dollars Reward, with reasonable charges. All masters of vessels are hereby cautioned not to carry him off on pain of prosecution.
The Royal Gazette, May 1, 1779.

RUN-AWAY a Negro Wench named Hager, about 18 years of age, born in this town, she is about five feet high, had on a white drilling short gown, and green petticoat. Whoever brings her to the Central Post-Office in Broad-Street, or gives information where she may be found, shall be handsomely rewarded. She is supposed to be gone on board the fleet.
The Royal Gazette, May 1, 1779.

A NEGRO RUN-AWAY.

A LIKELY young Negro fellow of middle Stature, about 19 or 20 years of age, named ROMEO; had on a check shirt, coarse blue cloth upper jacket lined with oznabrigs, and a yellow metal button, with a white cassimir one under it. He had on blue breeches the same with the jacket when he went away, but may probably have put on white cassimire breeches or a pair of blue striped linen trowsers, as he took such things with him. Whoever bring him to his master at No. 278, the corner of Broad-street, and Dock-street, shall receive TEN DOLLARS reward; and all commanders of vessels are desired not to harbour him.
The Royal Gazette, May 1, 1779; May 19, 1779; May 22, 1779.

RUN AWAY from the Gale transport, JOHN BEN, an Englishman, about 20 years old, 5 feet 7 inches high, with black short hair and black eyes. Whoever will bring him or give intelligence where he may be secured, shall receive TWO GUINEAS from his master, Henry Jefferson, on board the Gale, opposite the hay wharf on the North River.
The Royal Gazette, May 5, 1779.

A NEGRO MAN called WILLIAM, belonging to Col. Turnbull, of the New-York Volunteers, let the house of Mrs. Cornelia Clopper, at Turtle

Bay, about a month ago. He is about 20 years old, has lost some of his fore-teeth. Whoever brings him to William M'Adams in Hanover-Square, shall receive Ten Dollars Reward.
The Royal Gazette, May 5, 1779.

FIVE DOLLARS Reward.

RUN-AWAY from Hamilton Young, an Indian boy named DICK, about 5 feet high, well set; had on when he went away, a brown fustian coat, vest and trowsers, and white stockings. Whoever will bring him to the Printer, shall receive the above reward, and all reasonable charges.
The New-York Gazette; and the Weekly Mercury, May 10, 1779; May 17, 1779.

TEN DOLLARS Reward.

RUN-AWAY from the subscriber, on Friday evening last, a negro boy named DICK, had on a brown cloth jacket and waistcoat, with mettle buttons, blue trowsers: He is a tall slender boy, and remarkably knock-knee'd, marked under either his right or left ear, was lately hurt on the right eye, the mark of which is yet distinguishable. Masters of vessels and others, are forewarn'd not to harbour or conceal him. Whoever brings, or gives information where he can be found to the Printer hereof, or the subscriber at No. 46, Maiden Lane, shall receive he above reward.
THOMAS M'KIE.
The New-York Gazette; and the Weekly Mercury, May 17, 1779. See *The New-York Gazette; and the Weekly Mercury,* July 17, 1779.

RUNAWAY, a likely negro wench, named *Jane* or *Gin,* yellow colour, middle stature, about 30 years of age: She stole and took with her, a very large bundle of women's cloathing, so that it is impossible to describe her dress; she is well known in this city, having served in quality of market wench several years. Whoever brings the said wench to her master in Bowry-Lane, shall receive TEN DOLLARS reward, and all reasonable charges paid by me,
JOHN DYCKMAN.

All masters of vessels or others, are strictly forbid carrying off or harbouring the said wench, as they may depend upon being prosecuted for such offence.
The New-York Gazette; and the Weekly Mercury, May 17, 1779; May 24, 1779.

RUN-AWAY,

A NEGRO BOY, named YORK, about 14 Years of Age, likely, but has a remarkable coarse Voice, and has a Cut on one of his Cheeks: He had on when he went away, a green Coat, without Sleeves, new Leather Breeches and Trowsers over them, and a black Velvet Stock—He went with a Negro, named ALEX, who run-away from his Master, on Long-Island, sometime ago.—Whoever takes up said Boy YORK, so that his master may have him again, shall receive a Reward of SIX DOLLARS, besides reasonable Charges, paid by   JOHN LEAKE.
The Royal Gazette, May 19, 1779.

RUN AWAY on Wednesday the 19th inst. an English Boy, aged about 17, named WILLIAM APSLEY, he is about five feet high, of a fair complexion, a little marked with the Small Pox, wears his own short brown hair; had on either a brown coat, or a short pompadour coloured jacket, he is an indented servant.

A Guinea Reward will be given to any person who will bring him, or give intelligence where he may be found, to the Printer.
The Royal Gazette, May 22, 1779.

POUGHKEEPSIE, May 17.

On Saturday the 8th instant, was executed at Albany, pursuant to his sentence, *William Hooghteling,* for sundry robberies whereof he was convicted. This unhappy youth began his evil practices by desertion, from one of the continental regiments raised under the direction of this state, to which he declared he was induced by his step father, and others of the family; this induced him to the necessity of skulking and secreting himself until he was induced to join a banditti of robbers.—Let his fate be a warning to others, not to persuade those who have plighted their faith for the defence of their country, to violate their solemn engagements, lest their latter end should be like his.
Thomas's Massachusetts Spy Or, American Oracle of Liberty, May 27, 1779.

ABSENTED himself from his parents on Wednesday last, a Boy named William Bush, about nine years of age, fair complexion, had on when he went away a scarlet coat, white jacket and breeches. Whoever can give any information of him to his parents living in Chatham Row, near St. Paul's Church, shall be handsomely
    rewarded by   CHARLES BUSH.

N. B. If he should have entered on board any privateers or other vessel, his parents will have no objection to his going to sea, if the master would be so good as to inform them of it.

The Royal Gazette, May 29, 1779.

One Guinea Reward.

RUN AWAY from the subscriber, on Monday the 24th instant, a Negro Wench named Peg, she is about 23 years of age, well built, and has a scar upon her left cheek; she formerly belonged to Mr. John De Lancey, at Corlear's Hook. She had on a Callico short gown of a purple ground, striped and spotted, a black callimanco petticoat, a white straw hat, with black gauze wrapped about the crown, white stockings, and black leather shoes.

Whoever will secure said runaway, so that her owner may have her again, or bring her to his house, No. 25, Queen-street, shall have the above reward.   ANDREW BARCLAY.

The Royal Gazette, May 29, 1779.

Four Guineas Reward.

RAN-AWAY from James Smith, at Herricks, Long-Island, two negro men; one goes by the name of Caesar, is twenty years old, five feet eight inches high, and stout made: the others name is Jack, is 19 years old, and about five feet nine inches high, has rather longer hair than common for negroes. Any person that will take up and secure the said negroes, and give information to their master where they may be found, shall have the above reward; or if one of them, shall have two guineas, and all reasonable charges paid. They are supposed to be with the army, or on board some ship. All masters of vessels and others are not to harbour or conceal the said negroes.

The New-York Gazette; and the Weekly Mercury, June 7, 1779.

RUNAWAY from the ship MARS, the 2d instant, NATHANIEL MURRAY, about 30 years of age, had on when he left the ship, a black coat and waistcoat, his own hair hanging over his shoulders; speaks in the Scotch dialect very much; fresh coloured, full faced, of stupid inactive look; he has embezzeled cash to a considerable amount from Capt. THOMAS KENTISH, Commander of said ship. Whoever will apprehend the said Nathaniel Murray, and bring him on board the said ship Mars, shall receive a handsome reward.

The New-York Gazette; and the Weekly Mercury, June 21, 1779.

RUN away from the Springfield Transport, WILLIAM ARMSTRONG, Commander, an indented servant named JOHN WILLIAMS, about 5 feet 2 inches high, full faced and thick lips; had on when he went away a light blue waistcoat and a round hat. Whoever will deliver him to the Printer, or the master on board said ship at Staten-Island, shall receive TWO GUINEAS Reward.
The Royal Gazette, June 23, 1779; June 26, 1779; June 30, 1779.

New-York, July 12, 1779.
MADE *their escape out of the PROVOST, between the hours of Eleven at Night, and One this Morning, the following persons under sentence of Death viz.*

GEORGE FOGWELL, of the Corps of Pioneers, about Twenty Three years of Age; Five Feet Seven Inches high, dark brown Hair, thin Visage and pitted a little with the Small-Pox, born in England, supposed to have on a Buff coloured Jacket, and a pair of white Corderoy Breeches.

JOHN PURDIE, of the same Corps, about Twenty Years of Age, Five Feet Nine Inches high, black Hair, full faced, born at Bangor in the North of Ireland, supposed to have on a grey Surtout, and a pair of white Cloth Breeches.

JOHN FARREN, an inhabitant, about Twenty Five Years of age, Five Feet Seven Inches high, dark brown Hair, born in Belfast in Ireland supposed to have on a blue linen Jacket, and white linen trowsers. Whoever secures the above FELLOWS, or any of them, shall receive a reward of THREE GUINEAS for each of them, delivered up to any Guard within the Lines, by applying at the Office of the Commandant.
The Royal Gazette, July 14, 1779; July 17, 1779.

A NEGRO BOY, named Dick, RUN-AWAY on Saturday the seventeenth current, is remarkable knock kneed, marked under the right ear, about 5 feet four inches high; had on when he went away, a brown short coat, red waistcoat, and striped trowsers. Commanders of vessels and others are forewarned not to harbour or conceal him. The Printer hereof, or the subscriber, at No. 46, Maiden-lane, will give a reward of TEN DOLLARS to any person who will deliver him, or give intelligence where he may be found.   THOMAS M'KIE.
The New-York Gazette; and the Weekly Mercury, July 17, 1779; July 26, 1779. See *The New-York Gazette; and the Weekly Mercury*, May 17, 1779.

FIVE DOLLARS Reward.
RUN AWAY on Thursday evening the 14th instant, from the Subscriber, a mulatto wench named KATE, has lately had the small pox, had on when she went away, a black callimanco shirt, a red stuff short gown, lined with white flannel, a coarse brown apron, took with her a callico short gown, and a red home-spun petticoat.—Whoever will bring her, or give intelligence where she it, shall receive the above reward
     by JOHN BENNETT, near the new Slip.
The Royal Gazette, July 17, 1779. See *The Royal Gazette*, April 28, 1779.

Forty Shillings **REWARD.**
RUN away from the Subscriber, a NEGRO MAN, named JACK, about 5 feet 8 inches high, aged 18 years, likely and smart: He took with him a brown coat with a red cap, a green ditto, with gilt buttons, and other articles in a knapsack (unknown) It is imagined he intends going on board some privateer. The masters of all vessels are warned not to take him, as they must answer it at their peril. Whoever will bring the said negro to the subscriber, at the North-River, shall receive the above reward.
    RICHARD DEANE.   July 16, 1779.
The Royal Gazette, July 17, 1779; July 24, 1779.

FIVE DOLLARS, Reward.
RUNAWAY on *Thursday Morning* last, from the subscriber living in the bowery at the sign of the *Recruiting Serjeant*, a likely *Negro Wench*, named BINA, [20] years of age, about 5 feet 6 inches high, had on when she went away an osnaburg jacket and pettycoat. I suspect she is lurking about the Virginia negro houses, and hereby forwarn any person, (*white or black*) from harbouring or entertaining her at their peril. Whoever takes her up and brings her to me, shall have five dollars reward.
    JAMES DUN.
The New-York Gazette; and the Weekly Mercury, July 26, 1779.

FIVE DOLLARS, Reward.
RUN-AWAY *this morning*, from the subscriber, living in Water-Street, a negro boy named JACK, about twelve years of age, of a yellowish complexion; he has remarkable thick lips, otherwise likely and well made: Had on when he went away, a ticklenberg shirt and trowsers; his shirt sleeves he may probably wear above his elbows, no hat. It is imagined he is gone on some part of Long-Island, as he was last detected with some man who was returning from market in a waggon. Whoever will bring said boy

to the subscriber, or give information so that he may be found, shall receive the above reward, with reasonable charges.

    JAMES ARDIN.   July 29, 1777.

 N. B. All masters of vessels and others, are hereby forewarned not to harbour, conceal, or carry off the above boy, as they may depend on being prosecuted with the utmost rigour of the law.

The New-York Gazette; and the Weekly Mercury, August 2, 1779; August 9, 1779.

    THREE DOLLARS Reward.

RUN-AWAY from Capt. George Lovie, of the sloop HOPE, a NEGRO MAN, named SAM, he is about 38 years of age, cannot speak English; when he went away, he had on him, an old brown jacket, torn down the back, an old white shirt, and a pair of old dirty trowsers, all over with pitch and tar, and a brown hat on his head. Whoever brings him to the Printer, or to Mr. Hodges, in Hanover-Square, shall receive the above reward.

The New-York Gazette; and the Weekly Mercury, August 2, 1779; August 9, 1779.

    TWO GUINEAS Reward.

RUN away, the 6th instant, from the subscriber, a NEGRO WENCH, named ESTHER, middle stature, tolerably likely, full eyes, talkative, and about 38 years old. Had on when she went away a red striped stuff petticoat, and callico short gown. 'Till lately she was the property of John Folcroft, Esquire. Whoever apprehends her, and will give information by which she may be found, shall have the above reward,

    of JOSEPH ALLICOCKE.

N. B. She has been indisposed, and looks rather thin.

The New-York Gazette; and the Weekly Mercury, August 9, 1779; August 16, 1779.

RUN-AWAY on Sunday the 8th instant, a tall, likely NEGROE WENCH, about 19 years of age, named SYLVIA: Whoever will secure said Wench, and bring her to Charles White, Copper-smith, near Burling-slip, Water-street, shall receive a reward of TEN DOLLARS, and reasonable charges.

    CHARLES WHITE.

The Royal Gazette, August 11, 1779.

RUN away from his Master, a likely negro man, named HARRY, about 25 years of age, 5 feet 9 inches high, speaks both English and Dutch, had one when he went away, a white Osnaburgh trowsers and frock, with a yellow cloth waistcoat. Whoever secures him so that his master can get him again,

shall have a reward of Five Dollars. All masters of vessels are forwarned to harbour or carry him off, on pain of the strictest prosecution.
                   HENRY CUYLER.
The Royal Gazette, August 14, 1779.

RUN away from the armed Transport Ship King George, WILLIAM WILLIAMS, about 5 feet 3 inches high fair complexion, thin face sharp nose, wears his own short brown hair, nineteen years of age: whoever will secure the said Williams, and give information to Captain Kelley, shall receive Five Guineas reward; and if any person employs or harbours the said Willems, they will be prosecuted, he being the apprentice of
                Mr. Thomas Newby, Merchant in London.
The Royal Gazette, August 18, 1779.

Run away from the Barque St. BEES.
TWO apprentices named ROBERT NELSON and LAWRENCE TOMLINSON; the former about 15 years of age, a pale looking boy, wearing short hair; the latter about 13 years old, black eyed, and somewhat pitted with the small pox, wearing short hair likewise: Any person informing Capt. Williamson, at Seaman's wharf, of the place where these boys may be found, shall receive a Guinea reward for each, and any person harbouring them or taking the away will do it at their peril.
The Royal Gazette, August 18, 1779.

RUN AWAY from the Subscriber a likely Molatto Boy named JOE, speaks very good English, about 18 years of age, five feet high, had on when he went away, a Scotch bonnet, brown jacket and ozenbrig trowsers. Whoever secures him, so that the subscriber may get him again, shall have a reward of FIVE DOLLARS; all masters of vessels are forwarned not to harbour or carry him off on peril of the strictest prosecution.
                  JOHN DUNSCOMB.
The Royal Gazette, August 28, 1779.

DESERTED from the Minerva transport, William Dunloss, Master, FRANK, an Indian slave, about 35 years of age, a short squat fellow, remarkable broad face, and short neck, wore his own hair, had on an old blue jacket, check shirt and trowsers; he speaks very bad English, and will endeavour to get on board some of the ships bound to Jamaica. Masters of Ships are forwarned from harbouring or carrying him off.—Four Dollars will be given to any person who shall put him on board the Minerva, lying in the North-River.
The New-York Gazette; and the Weekly Mercury, August 30, 1779.

RUN-AWAY from the ship Nancy, William Marshal, Master, lying at Cruger's dock, HUGH CORNICK, an indented servant, aged 16 years, 4 feet 10 inches high, light brown hair, broad face, much freckled, remarkable well set, had on when he went away, a short blue jacket bound with canvas, long trowsers, and a Dutch cap. Whoever will bring the said boy to said ship, shall receive TEN DOLLARS reward.
The New-York Gazette; and the Weekly Mercury, August 30, 1779.

FIVE POUNDS REWARD.
RUN AWAY from the subscriber living in Smith-Street, on Monday the 23d of August, an apprentice lad, named Joseph Harnet, about 19 years of age, about 5 feet 7 inches high, stout set, short brown hair, by trade a shoemaker, had on when he went away, a short brown coat with metal buttons, claret coloured corderoy waistcoat and breeches, and a castor hat. Whoever will secure the said apprentice, so that his master shall have him again, shall receive the above reward.
FREDERICK WEISNER.
N. B. All Masters of vessels and others are forbid concealing or carrying away said apprentice, as they may depend upon being prosecuted as the law directs.
The Royal Gazette, September 4, 1779.

RUN-AWAY
From the Henry Navy Victualler, Isaac Amory, at London, and supposed to have come here in the last fleet, as they were seen on Friday last, three apprentices, viz. PETER SHERWOOD, GEORGE KNIGHT, and LUKE COATS.

Peter Sherwood, is a lad about 18 years of age, brown complexion, very thick in speech, and has short black hair.

George Knight, is about 16 years of age, thin set, and of a brown complexion.

Luke Coats, is a stout fat lad, about 19 years of age, very full faced, and wears his hair short.—Run away at Portsmouth.

Whoever will apprehend any of the above apprentices, and give information of the same to Captain Amory, on board the said ship, shall receive ONE GUINEA reward for each. If masters of ships have them on board, and will inform Capt. Amory of it, they shall pay no wages due them for their time aboard their vessels.
The Royal Gazette, September 8, 1779; September 11, 1779.

TWO GUINEAS REWARD.

RAN away from the subscriber, on Monday last, a Negro man named SAM, about 20 years of age, 5 feet 4 inches high: He is a well made sprightly fellow, and may probably have been seduced by the crew of some armed vessel or privateer; He had on when he went away, a brown jacket and long trowsers. Whoever will secure said negro, or give information so as his master may get him again, shall have the above reward.

Masters of vessels and others are cautioned against harbour or carrying him off at their peril.

    HENRY DAWSON. No. 200, Queen-street.
       New-York, Sept. 8.

The Royal Gazette, September 11, 1779; *The New-York Gazette; and the Weekly Mercury*, September 13, 1779; September 20, 1779. Minor differences between the papers

RUNAWAY from the corner of Dock-street, a servant girl named *Ann M'Donald*, 17 years of age, has remarkable red hair, walks rather lame, had on when she went away, a black and white calico jacket and petticoat. Whoever will bring her to No. 321, corner of Dock-street, shall receive *Six-Pence* reward.

    THOMAS HARRISON.

The New-York Gazette; and the Weekly Mercury, September 20, 1779.

RUN-AWAY from a Gentleman in the army, a likely NEGRO BOY, named PETER, about 13 years of age, speaks good English, had on an Oznaburg shirt, striped trowsers, and a hat with a gold loop and button. Whoever brings the said boy to Mr. Turner's, the corner of Crown-Street, Broad-Quay, or gives information where he is, so that he may be had again, shall receive ONE GUINEAS reward, and reasonable charges. Whoever conceals or harbours him, will be prosecuted.

The Royal Gazette, September 22, 1779; September 25, 1779; October 2, 1779; October 6, 1779; October 9, 1779.

RUN *AWAY a Negro Boy about* 16 *Years of age, answers by the name of Carolina, had on when he went off a blue lappelled jacket, white cloth waistcoat and breeches, with rose buttons, a white cotton shirt marked* M. H. *at the bottom of the flip of the breast. Whoever apprehends him shall receive One Guinea reward of the printer. He has a small scar on his left temple, and is about 5 feet four inches high.*

The Royal Gazette, September 22, 1779.

Seventeen Guineas Reward.
IN the night between Wednesday and Thursday last, run away from the privateer snow Vengeance, George Dean, Commander, then laying below Governors Island, four men, *viz*, John Murphy, William Finley, Edmund Ryan, and John Collins. and carried with them her Boat, a pinnace, about 26 feet long, rows seven oars, the upper part of her bottom white, the rest lately paid with stuff, her washboards, and gunwales a good deal tore to pieces, rigged with lugsails, and had in her for ballast two 2 pounders and four swivels. Whoever will apprehend with of said villains, shall receive THREE GUINEAS reward for each, and FIVE GUINEAS for the boat and guns, upon their being delivered to
          JOHN PORTEOUS, in Hanover-Square.
                                New-York, Sept. 17.
The Royal Gazette, September 22, 1779.

RUNAWAY about a week ago from the owner, 2 negro men, one of them named BACCHUS, the other LESTER; the former a house carpenter, about 25 years old; the latter was a farmer, and the same age, and are supposed to be lurking about town. FIVE DOLLARS reward will be given to any person who will deliver either of the said slaves, or Ten Dollars for both.
          Enquire of Hugh Gaine.
The New-York Gazette; and the Weekly Mercury, September 27, 1779.

          FIVE DOLLARS Reward.
RUN away the 5th of this month from the Subscriber, living at present in Ann-Street, a Negro Wench named SARAH, about 26 years old, formerly the property of the late deceased George Petterson. Whoever will bring said wench to the subscriber, or give information, so that she may be found, shall receive the above reward, by
          J. MICHAEL KERN.
The Royal Gazette, October 9, 1779.

          ONE GUINEA Reward.
RUN away from the Subscriber on the 10th inst. an apprentice Boy named JAMES GREEN; had on when he went off, a blue jacket turned up with red, blue waistcoat and trowsers; he is well known to all the army that came across the Jersies from Philadelphia; he is supposed to be with the light-infantry or on board some transport; all gentlemen of the navy and army are requested not to harbour or conceal him. Whoever will apprehend or give notice where he may be found shall have the above reward
          paid by JOHN M'KENZIE,
                    tavern-keeper, No. 35, Queen-street.

The Royal Gazette, October 13, 1779.

RUN-AWAY the 11th inst. a NEGRO, named JAMES GALEGO, 19 Years of age, about 5 feet 8 inches high, rather likely, had on a scarlet jacket, flannel cap, and oznabrug trowsers. Whoever apprehends him, shall have *Two Guineas* reward; and whoever harbours or retains him, shall be prosecuted. If he will return to his master *Attained Lansfield*, of the armed sloop *Who'd Have Thought It*, he shall be forgiven. Any information concerning him, will be rewarded and received by the Printer.
The Royal Gazette, October 13, 1779.

RUN AWAY from the Ship Earl of Cornwallis, on Saturday last, Philip Meade, an apprentice boy, aged 15 years, stout made, about 4 [sic] feet 8 inches high, wearing his own brown hair, of a ruddy complexion. Whoever apprehends or gives intelligence of him to Francis Harman, master of said ship, at the Ordnance wharf, North River, shall receive FIVE DOLLARS Reward.   October 22, 1779.
The Royal Gazette, October 23, 1779.

RUN-AWAY from the snow Newcastle Jane, an apprentice boy named RICHARD BREEN, about five feet nine inches high, thin brown complexion, wears a blue jacket and striped trowsers. Whoever secures him shall be paid THREE DOLLARS; whoever harbours him will be prosecuted as the law directs.
The New-York Gazette; and the Weekly Mercury, November 1, 1764; November 8, 1779; November 22, 1779.

RUN-away, from the subscriber, the 6th Instant, a Negro Woman named Isabella, 28 Years of Age, a tall Wench, large full Eyes, talks a little thick, born upon Long-Island, and formerly belonged to Capt. Whitehead, of Jamaica, on Long-Island. Whoever takes up and secures the said Negro Wench so that her Master may have her again, shall be handsomely rewarded for their Trouble
            by   EDWARD BARDEN.
The New-York Gazette; and the Weekly Mercury, November 8, 1779; November 15, 1779.

                    Two Guineas Reward,
RUN away from the Subscriber, on Sunday last, a NEGRO MAN, named STEPHEN, about twenty two years of age, five feet eight inches high, of a yellow complexion, has long wool tied behind: Had on when he went away, a short brown coat, cocked hat with silver tassels. Whoever will apprehend

said fellow, or give such intelligence as he may be brought back shall have the above reward.   OBADIAN WHISTON.

N. B. Masters of vessels and others are forbid to harbour or carry off said negro, at their peril.
The New-York Gazette; and the Weekly Mercury, November 8, 1779; November 15, 1779.

DESERTED from my company in the Hessian Regiment of Losberg, in the night of the 7th instant, a Soldier named JOHN ANSELL, a native Frenchman, 24 years old, five feet one inch high, marked with the small-pox, when he went off he wore his regimentals, a blue coat faced with orange. It is likely the above deserter may be concealed either in this city or Long-Island, whoever should discover him in desired to give notice to the regiment of Losberg.   de ALTENBOCKUM, Captain.
Camp near New-York, Oct. 10, 1779.
The Royal Gazette, November 10, 1779.

FOUR DOLLARS Reward.
RUN away from the Subscriber a negro wench named RAYNER, about 14 years of age, thin made; had on when she went away a brown Bath coating joseph and petticoat, a blue and white check'd cotton handkerchief round her head and neck. Whoever will bring her to me shall receive the above reward.   JOHN MINZIES, N. 8, Dover-street,
New-York, Nov. 11, 1779.
The Royal Gazette, November 13, 1779. See *The Royal Gazette*, February 9, 1780.

Five Guineas Reward.
DESERTED from on board the ship Mary and Charlotte, James Cummings, Master, lying at Well's Wharf, JOSEPH DAY, an apprentice, born in London, aged 19 years, five feet high, dark complexion, smooth face, black hair, dark eyes, wore a blue jacket lined with red, black velvet breeches, a stripped do. waistcoat, dark worsted stockings, large metal buckles in his shoes.

Likewise JOHN MELTON, aged 24 years, five feet six inches high, ruddy complexion, short dark brown hair, a halt in his walk, with one leg very much bent, wore a white jacket inside, and blue outside do. Whoever will apprehend the said deserters, so as they may be returned, shall receive the above reward, or for each Two Guineas and an half, by applying to the Captain on board the said Ship.

Any person harbouring or concealing them after this, shall be prosecuted according to law.   Nov. 12, 1779.

The Royal Gazette, November 13, 1779; November 17, 1779.

RUN-AWAY from the ship Charming Sally, John Rowe, Master, two seamen, one of them named ALEXANDER GAYLOR, the other ALEXANDER ORRACK; two Guineas will be given to any person that will deliver the said seamen on board the ship Charming Sally where she now lies, in the North River.

The New-York Gazette; and the Weekly Mercury, November 15, 1779.

RUN away from the Lion Transport, THOMAS GLOVER, about nineteen years of age, five feet eight inches high, stiff set, dark complexion, pitted with the small-pox, wears his own dark hair, tied behind; had on when he left the ship, a blue upper jacket, and a red under one, a pair of long trowsers, and a round hat.

Likewise JOHN GIBSON, about five feet six inches high, stiff set, smooth faced, light coloured hair tied behind, had on when he left the ship, a blue jacket, long trowsers, and a round hat. Whoever apprehends the said apprentices, shall receive a reward of Ten Guineas, or Five Guineas for either of them. If any person is found to harbour or conceal the above persons will be punished as the law directs. Whoever delivers them on board the Lion in North-River off the Hay-Wharf, or to the Printer shall receive the above reward.

N. B. The above mentioned apprentices deserted the third of November.
    Wm. TOMLINSON.

The Royal Gazette, November 17, 1779; November 20, 1779.

Twelve Guineas Reward.

RUN *away on Thursday night last from on board the Sloop Adrianna, laying at Grifftith's wharf, Three Negroes and a Mulatto sailors; the Mulatto a Lad named Peter, about 20 years old, had on when he went away a white flanel jacket and trowsers, is lame in his left foot which is naturally crooked, Creole born. George, a Negroe lad, has on a blue jacket and blanket trowsers, about 30 years old, Bermuda born. Abraham, a Negro, had on a green jacket and blue trowsers, about 20 years old, Creole born. Lorain, had on a blue jacket and trowsers, about 35 years old, Creole born. The above reward will be given for apprehending the whole of them, or Three Guineas for each by the Subscriber on board, or by Captain Robert Gibb, in Smith street.*   JOSEPH BRIGGS.

All masters of vessels are forwarned carrying them off, or any person harbouring them at their peril.

The Royal Gazette, November 20, 1779.

Five Guineas Reward.

RUN away on the 15th inst. from the ship Mackrel, Capt. Wm. Farrer, Two Apprentices, JOSHUA HUTCHINS, aged 16 years, about 4 feet 6 inches high, black hair and eyes, round face, wears his own hair and a cap. PETER ATKIN, aged 14 years, about 4 feet high, fair complexion, has a scar on his head 5 inches long, wears his own hair, and cap or hat. Any person giving information of them to the Printer, or the Capt. Wm. Farrer, of said ship, shall receive the above reward.

N. B. All masters of vessels, and others, are desired not to harbour them at their peril.

The Royal Gazette, November 24, 1779; November 27, 1779; December 1, 1779; December 4, 1779; December 8, 1779; December 18, 1779.

DESERTED from on board the Henry (Navy Victualler) Isaac Amory, on Friday night the 10th inst. JOHN FOWLE, is a dark complection, dark hair, tied behind, about forty years of age, has a stiff finger on his left hand, was boatswain of the said ship. Whoever will apprehend the said person, or give information of him on board the said ship, lying at the Fly-Market, shall receive Two Guineas reward.

All masters of vessels are forewarned no to employ him, on pain of being prosecuted to the utmost rigour of the law.

The Royal Gazette, November 24, 1779; November 27, 1779.

RUN away on Friday the 19th inst. from the Kingston Transport, in the North-River, JOHN HARDY, a lad about 15 years old, four and a half feet high, wore a green jacket, a Dutch cap, with his short light coloured hair.

A reward of two Guineas will be given to any one who will bring him to the ship as above, or to the printer.

The Royal Gazette, November 27, 1779.

DESERTED from on board his Majesty's ship Robuste, JAMES RUTHERFORD, aged about 21 years, 5 feet 3 inches high, brown complexion, light brown hair, brown jacket; place of abode, Newcastle. Left the ship's long-boat November 21.

WILLIAM WALLER, aged about 21 years, 5 feet 4 inches high, brown complexion, a mole under his left cheek, dark brown hair, blue jacket; place of abode, Whitby. Left the long-boat November 21.++

JOHN RIDLEY, aged about 23 years, 5 feet 7 inches high, brown complexion, pitted with the small-pox, flaxen hair, tied; place of abode Newcastle.

ALEXANDER COWANS, aged about 20 years, 5 feet 2 inches high, fair complexion, white coloured hair; place of abode Newcastle.

☞The two last left the ship about a month ago.

If any of the above men will deliver themselves up to any of his Majesty's ships, within four days of the date hereof, they shall be pardoned;—otherwise, any person who apprehends them, shall receive
FORTY SHILLINGS Sterling for each man.

The Royal Gazette, December 1, 1779.

LOST on Wednesday evening last a Mulatto Boy, named JACK, suppos'd to be trepann'd, had on a dark coloured Coatee, Waistcoat and Trowsers, the Coatee trimmed with a green collar and cuff, between 14 and 15 years of age, about five feet high, a handsome face, with black curl'd hair, American born. Whoever will apprehend the said Boy, or give such intelligence that he may be regained, shall receive Fourteen Dollars Reward.

All Masters of Vessels and others are hereby cautioned against secreting or carrying away the above Lad. Enquire of the Printer.

The Royal Gazette, December 4, 1779; December 8, 1779.

Twenty Dollars Reward.

LOST on Wednesday the first of December, supposed to have been trepanned, A NEGRO BOY. Had on a sky blue cloth jacket, yellow cuff and cape, trimmed with silver lace, and two silver epaulets, red check trowsers, round hat with silver tassels, feathers and cockade. He was born at Ponpon, upon the Ponpon river, in South-Carolina; his name is Abraham, is about 11 or 12 years of age, and very handsome.

Whoever brings his boy to the Printer, or traces him so that he may be recovered by the owner, shall receive the above Reward.

The Royal Gazette, December 4, 1779.

FIVE GUINEAS REWARD,

DESERTED from the King George Transport Ship, Capt. Samuel Kelley, now in the North-River,

NICHOLAS LAURENCE, about 20 years of age, five feet four inches high, very stout made, remarkably round featured, and swarthy; and wears his own dark hair tied or queued with a ribbon, was born in Shetland, North Britain, and is the apprentice of Mr. Thomas Newby, Merchant in London.

THOMAS PROCTOR, Seaman, about 25 years of age, five feet six inches high, fair complexion, wears his own brown curling hair, was born in Northumberland, and served sometime as a Baker.

SIMON GREAVES, about 20 years of age, five feet four inches high, has a smiling countenance, is very lusty, his voice rather effiminate, and wears his own short dark lank hair.

Any person giving information of the said Deserters to Capt. Kelley, on board the said ship, or to Mr. Henry White, in Queen-Street, shall receive in proportion for either of them, and whoever harbours or engages them, will be prosecuted.

The Royal Gazette, December 8, 1779.

TEN DOLLARS REWARD.

RUN-AWAY from Thomas Skinner, the 10th instant, a Mulatto MAN, aged 21 years, about 5 feet 8 inches high, stout, and well made, named Tonay, but may call himself Anthony Frost, has a bushy thick head of hair when comb'd up is very high, and in the shape of a roll; he has a round face, part of one of his fore teeth broke, and a remarkable high breast-bone, is saucy and pert, thinks a good deal of himself, and took with him a blue broad cloth coat, a wilton short coat, a short new blue coat, with white metal buttons, a pale blue jacket and breeches, dark brown trowsers, and sundry shirts.

The Royal Gazette, December 11, 1779. See *The New-York Gazette; and the Weekly Mercury,* December 13, 1779, and *The Royal Gazette,* December 13, 1780.

Ten DOLLARS Reward.

RUN-AWAY from Thomas Skinner, on the 10th of December, a mulatto man, aged 21 years, about 5 feet 8 inches high, a stout well made fellow, named TONY, but may call himself ANTHONY FROST; has a bushy thick head of hair, when comb'd up is very high, and in the shape of a roll; he has a round face, part of one of his fore teeth broke, and a remarkable high breast-bone, is saucy and pert, and thinks a good deal of himself: Took with him a blue broad cloth coat, a wilton short coat, a new blue coat with metal buttons, a pale blue jacket and breeches, dark blue trowsers, and sundry shirts. All masters of vessels are desired not to harbour or carry off said servant, at their peril. Broad-Street, No. 256.

The New-York Gazette; and the Weekly Mercury, December 13, 1779. See *The Royal Gazette,* December 11, 1779, and *The Royal Gazette,* December 13, 1780.

RUN away from the Subscriber, living in Nassau street, opposite the Brick Presbyterian Meeting house, in New-York, a black C[rom]antee Negro Wench named GRACE, smooth face with three scars down her left cheek, her own country mark, about five feet high, well made, and talks broken

English, about 30 years of age, she tells people that she is free; had on when she went away a new purple and white callicoe short gown, an Indian callicoe one under, a new striped homespun petticoat, a coarse brown broad cloth short cloak, with a cap, an old black bonnet, a pair of mens shoes with silver plated buckles, blue stockings with white clocks, a blue and white apron with small checks, a brown Barcelona handkerchief with blue stripes round the edges.

This is to forewarn all masters of vessels and others from carrying away, concealing or harbouring the said negro wench upon any pretence whatsoever as they may expect to answer for it as the law directs; whoever takes up and secures the said wench so that her master may have her again, shall be handsomely rewarded and all reasonable charges
paid, by   ARTHUR M'NEILL.
The Royal Gazette, December 15, 1779.

Innerwick, near Flushing, December 11, 1779.
RAN away yesterday morning from his master, Col. Hamilton, an indented servant man named KENNETH M'KINZIE, a Highlander; whoever will confine him to any guard, and give information to his master, the obligation will be gratefully acknowledges, and all expences cheerfully paid. He had on a red coat with small yellow cuffs and cape, and a blue livery great coat with large red cape and cuffs, stutters in his speech, about 5 feet 10 or 11 inches high, in knee'd, was sometime a driver in the artillery with the British Grenadiers, is a liar and consequently a thief.
The Royal Gazette, December 15, 1779; December 18, 1779; December 22, 1779.

Ten Dollars Reward.
RUN away from LINUS KING, the 13th, inst. A NEGRO FELLOW, aged 26 years, about 5 feet 8 inches high, named Squire, speaks good English, and plays on the violin; had on when he went away an old brown jacket, and blue coating long trowsers. All masters of vessels and others are desired not to harbour or conceal said negro. Whoever will give intelligence to his master, so that he may be found, shall have the above reward.
The Royal Gazette, December 18, 1779.

RAN away on Saturday last (and is supposed to be lurking about the city, or on board one of the vessels in the harbour). a Negro Man named QUASH, but frequently calls himself George. He is a likely middle sized fellow, appears to be about thirty years of age, speaks the Creole French, and English tolerably well, and is very mannerly and civil to all persons. He has taken with him a variety of cloaths; among them two coatees, one a blue, and the other a brown colour, a pair of blue coating trowsers, and a furr'd cap. Whoever will bring him to No. 294, Little-Dock-street, three doors east of the Exchange, or will give information as may discover where he can be found, shall be well rewarded; and any person who conceals him, or shall carry him off from this city, will be liable to heavy damages.

JAMES CREIGHTON. New-York, Dec. 14, 1779.

The Royal Gazette, December 18, 1779.

EIGHT DOLLARS REWARD.

RUN-away, on Thursday the 16th inst. a Negro Boy named SCIP, 14 years old about 4 feet 9 inches high, had on when he went away, a check shirt, white knap jacket, double breasted, with brass buttons, a blue double breasted under jacket, and long white knap trowsers, a pair of boots with square toes. Whoever will give information to Gideon Carstang, at Fresh Water, shall receive the above reward.

N. B. All masters of vessels and others are desired not to harbour him but at their peril.

The Royal Gazette, December 18, 1779.

TEN DOLLARS Reward.

RUN away from the Subscriber on Wednesday the 8th inst. a negro woman known by the name of POLL MOORE, about 18 years of age, tall and slim made; had on when she went away, a striped camblet short gown, and petticoat, garnet colour, a brown cloak and a pair of mens shoes.—Whoever will apprehend the said wench, or give such intelligence to the Printer as she may be brought back, shall have the above Reward.

WALTER FRAZUR, at No. [ ]8, Maiden Lane.

N. B. All masters of vessels and others are forewarned harbouring or concealing the said wench, as they shall answer the same at their peril.

The Royal Gazette, December 18, 1779.

TEN DOLLARS Reward.

RUNAWAY from the subscriber, on the night of Friday the 17th instant, a negro boy named GEORGE, about 14 years old, had on a blue coat and leather breeches; his feet large and flat, and large anckles, was born in Virginia. All persons are cautioned not to harbour or carry off said negro, and requested to send him home and receive the above reward.

HUGH WALLACE.

The New-York Gazette; and the Weekly Mercury, December 20, 1779; December 27, 1779; January 3, 1780; January 10, 1780.

DESERTED from the Horse Department of the Royal Artillery, on command at Staten-Island, MICHAEL FUTCHER, five feet eleven inches high, fair complexion, fair hair, slight made, by trade a Blacksmith; had on when he went away, a short red jacket, round hat and feather in it. Whoever apprehends said deserted, by giving information at the Officer of Ordnance opposite St. Paul's Church, Broad Way, will be handsomely rewarded for their trouble. It is expected he is on board some privateer. Whoever harbours or conceals him will be prosecuted to the utmost rigour of the law.

Likewise THOMAS KEMPTON, about 45 years of age, 5 feet 4 inches high, yellowish cast, sandy hair, had on when he went away a red coat.

The Royal Gazette, December 22, 1779; January 1, 1780; January 5, 1780. Kempton is not listed in the first ad.

Five Guineas Reward.

RAN AWAY from the Ship Andrew Transport, John Geyer, Commander, two apprentice boys, viz. William Clempson, aged about 16 years, with light hair, had on when he went away, a blue frize jacket, a pair of grey duffil trowsers, has an impediment in his speech. Michael Sanders, a native of Ireland, aged about 17 years, slender made, with dark hair, had on a white jacket, a pair of blanket trowsers, carried with him an ash coloured cloth jacket and breeches. Any person apprehending the above described boys, shall receive the above reward or Two Guineas and a half for either of them, by giving information to the Printer of their being properly secured. Whoevr may conceal them will be prosecuted according to law.

The Royal Gazette, December 25, 1779.

1780

RUN-AWAY,

A Negro Wench named RACHAEL, about thirty years of age, of a copper colour, remarkable large nose, and seemingly great with child. Whoever will bring her to No. 919, in Water Street, or the printer shall have a guinea reward, and all charges. All masters of vessels are forewarned not to take her off, as they will answer it at their peril.

The New-York Gazette; and the Weekly Mercury, January 24, 1780.

RUN-AWAY from the subscriber, a negro man named DUKE, about 47 years of age, a yellow cast, bushy head, one leg much thicker than the other, maimed in one foot, limps in his walk, speaks good English, had on when he went away, a whitish great coat, a blue upper jacket, a white under ditto, brown corduroy breeches, yellow buckles, talks much of Rhode-Island and

Philadelphia; he had likewise in his pocket a bunch of keys. Whoever will apprehend the said negro, so that his master may have him again, shall receive a reward of FIVE DOLLARS, by applying to the commanding officer on board the ship Venture, lying at Walter Taylor's wharf, or delivering him to H. Gaine.
    JAMES TWEED.
The New-York Gazette; and the Weekly Mercury, February 7, 1780; February 14, 1780.

    Five Dollars Reward.
RUN AWAY from the Subscriber a Negro Wench named RAYNER, about fifteen years of age, slender made, had on when she went away a brown coloured coating Joseph and Petticoat, a check cotton handkerchief round her head and neck, a pair of white stockings, and shoes tied with twine. Whoever brings her to me, shall receive the above reward.
    JOHN MINZIES, No. 8, Dover-street,
The Royal Gazette, February 9, 1780. See *The Royal Gazette*, November 13, 1779.

    FORTY SHILLINGS Reward.
RUN-AWAY from the subscriber, about the beginning of January last, a negro man named KELSO, he is a stout well made fellow, about 30 years of age, born in the country, and accustomed to all the usual work of a farmer; speaks English only, smooth fac'd, pretty black, and has not had the small pox; had on a new dark brown coarse cloth jacket, lined with old cloth; with buttons of apple tree wood, striped coating breeches with the like Buttons; good shoes and stockings, but probably he might have changed both his name and cloaths: He had from his master a leave of absence for eight days to find out a purchaser, he being to be sold, since which time he has not been heard of. Whoever will give intelligence of the above negro, so as he may be secured, or will secure and deliver him to his said master, or John Kelly, Notary Public, No. 843, Hanover-Square, shall receive the above reward, with all reasonable charges.
The New-York Gazette; and the Weekly Mercury, April 24, 1780; May 1, 1780; May 8, 1780; May 15, 1780; May 22, 1780. The last two ads increase the reward to Five Pounds.

    TEN GUINEAS Reward.
RUN-AWAY on Friday night the 5th instant, from the ship WILLIAMSON, Victualler, John Wray, Master, JONATHAN BOWMAN, about five feet six inches high, wears his own dark brown hair loose, and has a cast in his left eye, about eighteen years old, born in Hull in York-shire. Also, JOHN

CAMP, 16 *years of age, about five feet high, pretty lusty, wears his own light brown hair loose, born in Hull in York-shire, ruddy complexion and black eyes. Said Camp left the Grand Duke, Victualler, Thomas Harman, Master. Whoever apprehends or informs of the said two persons, so that they may be brought back, shall receive the above reward, for both, or Five Guineas for either of them. Likewise this is to caution all masters of vessels and others not to harbour them, as they may depend on being delt with according to law.*

The aforesaid persons were apprentices to the Owners of the said ship Williamson.

The New-York Gazette; and the Weekly Mercury, May 8, 1780; May 15, 1780.

TWENTY DOLLARS Reward.
DESERTED from the armed Sloop Neptune, on Thursday evening the 17th instant, lying at the Kills, at Staten-Island, an apprentice lad, named WILLIAM CARROL, dark complexion, pitted with the small pox, wears his own hair, about 5 feet 7 inches high. Whoever takes up the said lad, and will bring him to Captain Ross, on board the said sloop, or to Captain Laird's Office, in New-York, shall have the above reward
paid by   STEWART ROSS.
The New-York Gazette; and the Weekly Mercury, May 1, 1780.

Extract of a letter from West Point, dated April 23.
In this day's orders, the sentence of death is published against William Burtis, son to the late landlord Burtis, of White-Plains. He is a youth of genteel appearance, good address, and sprightly turn, of a rich and reputable family: he is about 29 years of age, has a mother and sister living near White-Plains: his crime is being a second time detected as a spy. Likewise, one Lakeman, who deserted from Danbury, 1778, and was recruiting as a Lieutenant in the British service. They are to be executed next Wednesday.
The Connecticut Courant, and Hartford Weekly Intelligencer, May 5, 1780.

RAN away from the Subscriber, on the Evening of the 22d Instant, an Apprentice boy, named PAUL SAYRE, a native of Long-Island, by Trade a Goldsmith, about nineteen Years of Age, about five Foot seven or eight Inches high, a thick set Fellow, thick Lips, flat Nose, light Eyes, somewhat pitted with the Small-pox, has short, strait, dark Hair. Had on and carried with him, a broadcloth blue Coat, Jacket and Breeches, a light brown short Coat, with open Sleeves, a Jacket about the same Colour, a blue great Coat, a Pair of brown broad-cloth Breeches, a large castor Hat, almost new, two

Pairs of Shoes, a Pair of pen work Silver Shoe Buckles, and sundry other Articles of Cloathing. Whoever will take up said Apprentice, and return him to his Master, or confine him so that he shall get him again, shall have One Hundred Dollars Continental Money Reward, and all necessary Charges paid by   JAMES TILEY.

N. B. It is supposed that he will endeavour to go on Long-Island. All Masters of Vessels and others, are forbid carrying him off, or harbouring or concealing him at their Peril.   April, 24, 1780.

The Connecticut Gazette; and the Universal Intelligencer, May 5, 1780.

RUN AWAY from the Love and Unity, on Saturday, May 6, Peter Jogie, an apprentice, aged about 17 years, five feet high, stout made, brown complexion, brown hair, sometimes tied, had on a blue jacket, long trowsers and hat. Any one that will bring the said apprentice on board the Grand Duke, under Agent Marr, for victualling his Majesty's Navy, shall receive a Guinea and a Half reward.

The Royal Gazette, May 13, 1780; May 17, 1780.

RUN AWAY from the Subscriber the 5th instant, a Negro boy named JACK, aged about 17 years, pitted with the small-pox, stoops in his walk, talks much a Guinea Negro, very black, about five feet four inches high.

Whoever secures the said Boy, so that his Master may have him again, shall receive Five Dollars Reward from me.
JONATHAN FOWLER.
Living in Chatham Street, at Dr. Betts's.
All Commanders of Vessels are warned against carrying him off, as they will in that case be prosecuted on discovery.

The Royal Gazette, May 13, 1780.

RUN AWAY from the Ship Aurora, Army Victualler, Constable Saunders, Master, on the 7th of May, two indented apprentices, Mark Bushfield, aged about sixteen years, a thick short fat boy, had on when he ran away, a blue jacket and trowsers, wears his own light hair; George Oliver, an indented apprentice, aged 17 years, low stature, pitted with the small pox, thick lips, had on a blue jacket and trowsers, wears his own brown hair.

This is too [sic] warn all persons not to conceal the said apprentices, as they will be prosecuted as the law directs, and a reward of Two Guineas will be paid to any person apprehending the said apprentices.

The Royal Gazette, May 13, 1780; May 17, 1780.

ONE GUINEA REWARD,

RUN away from the Subscriber on Saturday last, a Negro Boy named YORK, about 3 feet 10 inches high, tawny complexion, a scar nearly under his left temple like unto a burn, well made, small bones, speaks pretty good English, is a native of the Island of Jamaica, and came here about 2 years since, has lately been employed in sweeping chimneys, is a smart talkative boy, has been out in the privateer Pollux, Capt. Ross. Had on when he went away, a short brown waistcoat, a check shirt, a kind of woollen trowsers nearly white, a blue cap, his hair wool cut short, and full of foot, is about 12 years old, and is addicted to drinking.—Whoever brings the said boy to the Printer, or to the Subscriber, living in Duke Street, shall receive the above reward. All masters of ship are requested not to carry off the said boy: all other persons are forbid harbouring him at their peril.

PETER CREIGHTON.

The Royal Gazette, May 20, 1780. See *The Royal Gazette*, March 17, 1781, and *The Royal Gazette*, May 22, 1782.

RUN-AWAY from the brigantine John and Mary, Cork victualler, John Sherrard, master, JOHN GILLY, born in Cork, about 18 years of age, 5 feet high, well made, fresh complexion, has brown hair, pitted with the small pox, blue eyes. JOHN KENNEDY, born in Cork, about 18 years of age, 5 feet high, fresh complexion, stout made, has long yellow hair, smooth faced, light eyes, stammers, and speaks bad English. DANIEL DENHANY, nick named on board *Richard Berry*, about 20 years of age, born in Cork, 5 feet 5 inches high, fresh complexion, stout made, pitted with the small pox, has short black hair, black eyes. WILLIAM ROSS, born in Cork, about 20 years of age, 5 feet 4 inches high, dark complexion, slender made, smooth faced, black eyes, short black hair. The above deserters were in sailors habits, with each of them a small bundle. Whoever will secure the above deserters, shall have TWENTY SHILLINGS reward for each.

The New-York Gazette; and the Weekly Mercury, May 22, 1780.

SEVEN DOLLARS REWARD.

RUN AWAY on Tuesday the 20th inst. from the ship Ann Transport, lying near the Hay wharf in the North river, viz. WILLIAM PIGOT, an apprentice, about four feet seven inches high, very round face, a large scar on the back of his neck which is very visible by the shortness of his light hair; had on when he went away a brown waistcoat, light coloured trowsers, and a pair of new shoes. Whoever will give information where he may be found, to James Hill, master of the said ship, shall receive the above reward. N. B. Captains of privateers, &c. are hereby forwarned and desired not to harbour him, as upon discovery they shall answer it at their peril.

The Royal Gazette, June 24, 1780.

DESERTED.

FROM the 64th Regimental Store at Coenties Market; RICHARD HUTCHINSON, private Soldier in the 64th regiment, born in Ireland, about 5 feet 7 inches high, short curly hair, much freckled in the face; had on when he went off, a crimson coloured jacket, a pair of new duck trowsers, (was lately on board the General Pattison privateer.)—Whoever will give information of the said Hutchinson, to Serjeant M'Donald at the said store, so that he may be apprehended, shall receive five Guineas Reward. All Masters of ships are hereby warned not to harbour the above-mentioned Hutchinson, at their peril.

M. WOOD,   Ensign, 64th Regt.

The Royal Gazette, July 5, 1780.

RUN AWAY, on Monday the 26th of June (inst.) from on board the Corsica transport, George Stephenson master, three indented servants, viz.

JOHN M'GAY, about 17 years of age, a tall slender lad, wears his own brown short hair, pitted with the small pox, fresh coloured; had on when he went away, a thin canvas jacket, round hat and long trowsers. By his ship-mates, commonly called LIMERICK, being a native of Ireland.—WESTER PAIN, a short lad, of a dark complexion, has a cut on one eye, wears his own short dark hair, dressed in a blue jacket, and a white round hat, about 15 years of age.—JAMES INGRAM, a short lad, thin faced, sharp nose, very much freckled, wears his own brown hair tied; had on when he went away, a blue jacket and a pair of striped trowsers, he is between 14 and 16 years of age.—A reward of TEN GUINEAS is offered to any person that will give information of the above boys so that they may be apprehended, shall, by applying to Mr. Taylor, near the Coffee-house bridge, receive the above reward, or FOUR GUINEAS for either.

GEORGE STEPHENSON.

☞All masters of vessels are hereby cautioned against concealing or carrying off said servants as they would avoid the penalty of the law.

The Royal Gazette, July 5, 1780; July 8, 1780.

RUN-AWAY,

A *Servant man, about 22 years of age, from the ENDEAVOUR victualler, a stout man, about five feet eight inches high, a brown complexion, with brown streight hair, had on a blue jacket and trowsers, born near Aberdeen: Whoever will secure, or give intelligence of the said Runaway, so that he may be had again, shall receive TEN DOLLARS of Captain Robert Finley, on board the brigt. ENDEAVOUR, near Brooklyn-Ferry.*

The New-York Gazette; and the Weekly Mercury, July 3, 1780.

RUN AWAY from the Endeavour Navy Victualler, Robert Finley, Master, a servant about 22 years of age, named John Emslie, born near Aberdeen, in North Britain, about 5 feet 8 inches high, his own brown strait hair, had on when he went away a blue jacket, and long trowsers. Any person who will apprehend the said run-away, so that he may be had again shall receive Ten Dollars reward of the said Robert Finley, laying near Brooklyn Ferry.

The Royal Gazette, July 5, 1780.

RUN away last Sunday afternoon, the 2d of July instant, a Negro man named CAIN, a stout able young fellow, about five feet 8 inches high, had on when he went away a brown short coat, with white metal buttons, a brown waistcoat and white breeches, a cock'd hat, a black silk handkerchief about his head, and has taken with him sundry other wearing apparel; he is about 26 years of age, is but lately from Charlestown, speaks tolerable good English, has a sore head, and had lately had the small-pox. Whoever will apprehend the said runaway, and give notice thereof to Capt. Norman Tolmey, in Cherry Street, shall have FIVE DOLLARS reward, and be allows all reasonable charges.

The Royal Gazette, July 5, 1780.

Eight Dollars Reward.

RUN AWAY from his master's service, and is now lurking about New-York, a Negro man named Caesar, but calls himself Julius Caesar, he is a stout well built fellow, about 5 feet 7 or 8 inches high, by trade a sail maker; he was in custody on Sunday week last, and made his escape, was then drest in a light blue coat and waistcoat, white shirt, striped trowsers and round hat, but is supposed to wear a sailor's habit on other days, and will attempt to ship himself as a Sailor. Whoever will secure him that the subscriber may have him again, shall receive the above reward.

JAMES HUMPHREYS.

All Masters of vessels and others are cautioned from employing or taking off said Negro.

The Royal Gazette, July 5, 1780.

RUN AWAY from the Subscriber on the 29th day of June last, a Mulatto Boy about 18 years old, about five feet five inches high, yellow complexion, bushy hair; had on when he went away a brown jacket and striped trowsers, a pair of new shoes, a new castor hat with a black band and buckle round the crown, and has taken from the subscriber about One Hundre Pounds in cash. Whoever will secure the said Boy so that the owner may have him again, shall receive Twenty Dollars Reward, and all reasonable charges paid by applying to Thomas Udell, merchant in this town, or to me at Islip on Long-Island.

    GEORGE NORTON. N. B. The Boy's name is Jef.
The Royal Gazette, July 8, 1780.

RUNAWAY,

BETWEEN twelve and one o'clock, on Monday morning, the 3d of July, 1780, from a ship lying in the North-River, a NEGRO MAN, named JAMES DORAS: About five feet seven inches high, a stout made fellow, a little marked with the smallpox, with grey hairs intermixed with black curly on his head, speaks Portuguese, calls himself a Caulker, and says he came from Philadelphia.

Whoever will give information of said negro, so as he may be apprehended, will receive two guineas reward, by applying to Mr. George Moor, at Mrs. Hamilton's in Dock-street. Any person or persons discovered secreting the said negro, will be prosecuted to the utmost rigour.

All boatmen, ferrymen, and others passing to Long-Island, Staten-Island, Powles-Hook, and other ferries, are desired to attend to the above advertisement, as it is thought he means to make his way to Philadelphia.

The New-York Gazette; and the Weekly Mercury, July 10, 1780.

Ten Dollars Reward.

RUN AWAY from the subscriber an apprentice boy named Thomas Brady, about 17 years of age, a little pitted with the small pox, took with him a suit of light blue cloaths, a red waistcoat, two white shirts, one check do. a pair of red striped trowsers. It is supposed he is going to Blue Point, or on board one of the transports. All masters of vessels are forwarned harbouring or carry off said apprentice, as they will be prosecuted with the utmost rigour
    of the law. MARK MULLEN.
The Royal Gazette, July 12, 1780.

RUN-away, a short time ago, from John Carpenter, of Brooklyn Ferry, a negro man named BEN, a likely lusty young fellow, about 25 years of age: Had on when he went away, a rebel uniform; he was lately brought into New-York by the ship Triton. Capt. Lutwy[c]b. This is to forewarn all master of vessels or others, not to harbour or carry him off, and any one that will secure him so that his master may have him again, shall receive TEN DOLLARS, and all reasonable charges
    paid, by JOHN CARPENTER.
The New-York Gazette; and the Weekly Mercury, July 17, 1780.

New-York, July 15, 1780.
Run-away, last Night,
FROM the volunteers that went from the ship Albion, on the present service, JOHN REID, boatswain's mate, a short stout made man, brown complexion, pitted with the small-pox, about thirty years of age, wears his own hair.

ROBERT KELLY about eighteen years of age, fair complexion, wears his own hair, and is sharp visag'd. Whoever apprehends them, or either of them, so that they may be brought to the rendezvous of volunteers, shall receive one guineas reward for each of them, by applying to Peter Lawson, commander of the ship Albion.

The New-York Gazette; and the Weekly Mercury, July 17, 1780.

RUN from his apprenticeship, to the shoe-makers trade, JAMES RIVINGTON, jun. son to the notorious James, the royal, alias, lying printer, in New-York. Those who know the father, need no other description of the son, than to be informed that, allowing for age and experience, he is in low cunning, deceit, lying, and roguery, equal to the sire; and proved, without the marriage knot, that he is the *real* offspring, full blooded. It is thought probable this rogue, on the rumour of the French fleet, is gone, agreeable to tory policy, to join the American army; that by dividing the family, part of the breed may be saved, even should the property be lost. Whoever takes up the above identical son, shall be entitled to the father's privileged gazette, except those which may happen to contain aberrations from the truth.
N. B. The above is not the BAY COLT.

The New-Jersey Journal, July 26, 1780.

TEN DOLLARS REWARD.
RUN-AWAY from LINUS KING, the 13th of December last, a Negro fellow named SQUIRE, aged 26 years, about 5 feet 8 inches high, speaks good English, and plays on the violin. Since his departure he has taken the name of Jack, and been since that time has been in the service of a Captain, of Colonel Delancy's corps of Loyal Refugees, at or near Morrissania. All masters of vessels, and other are cautioned not to secret or entertain said negro, as they will answer it at their peril.

N. B. Said negro was advertised in Mr. Rivington's Paper of the 18th of December last.

The New-York Gazette; and the Weekly Mercury, August 7, 1780; August 14, 1780; August 21, 1780.

RUN away, on Tuesday the first inst. a Negro Boy, named TOM, the property of Dr. M'Lean, No. 6, Water-street; he is a strong thick well made

fellow, about 16 years of age, speaks tolerable good English, had on when he went off, a thickset jacket, and osnaburgh trowsers. Whoever apprehends and restores him to his said master, shall have an adequate reward for their trouble. All masters of vessels are strictly forbid harbouring this negro, who will probably change his name to facilitate his escape.
The New-York Gazette; and the Weekly Mercury, August 7, 1780; August 14, 1780; August 21, 1772.

RUN AWAY from the subscriber a short thick set Negro Boy, named Dick, he belongs to his Majesty's ship the Otter, and took away with him two coats, the one a dark French frock, the other a livery brown, lined, trimmed, and turned up with red; it is supposed he has let himself to some person living in the country, who, if desirous of keeping him, till such time as said sloop arrives at this port, are requested to call on Mrs. M'Fayden, at No. 2, in the Fly-Market, and without such information being given, all persons are hereby desired not to harbour him.
E. M'FAYDEN.
The Royal Gazette, August 9, 1780.

RUN AWAY last Saturday, a Negro Boy named HARRY, about twelve years of age, has had the Small-Pox lately, was born in South Carolina; it is believed the boy is deluded away, as he never was guilty of absenting himself before. I do hereby offer a reward of Four Guineas to any person that will deliver him to me, on board the Ship Charming Sally, laying at Degrushe's Wharf.
ROBERT CARGEY.   August 10, 1780.
The Royal Gazette, August 12, 1780.

RUN AWAY from the ship Father's Desire, lying in the North-River, Richard Morsom, Master, last Saturday morning, an apprentice lad, named JOHN FOLLY, about seventeen years old, five feet high, light brown hair: Had on a check shirt, long trowsers, and a jacket without sleeves. All Masters of vessels are forbid to carry him away. A GUINEA reward will be given to any person who returns him on board his ship
by   RICHARD MORSOM.
The New-York Gazette; and the Weekly Mercury, August 14, 1780; August 21, 1780.

RUN AWAY a NEGRO MAN on Saturday last, went on board a vessel in the harbour his name is JAMES, speaks broken English, he is about five feet 8 or 9 inches high, bandy legged, The master on board whose vessel he

is, may have his services, provided he will pay reasonable wages for his services. Enquire of the Printer,
The Royal Gazette, August 16, 1780.

TEN DOLLARS REWARD.

RUN away from the Subscriber about six weeks ago, a Negro Wench named SAVINAH, she is about 30 Years of Age, slim made, of a very dark Colour, and has a small Scar upon the upper part of her Nose. Also eloped from the Subscriber last Wednesday Evening, a short yellow Wench named Grace, she carried off her Child named Harry, he is nineteen Months old, and is a very yellow Mulatto. It is imagined that the above described Negroes are lurking about this City.—who harbours, or attempts to conceal them may depend upon being treated as they deserve, and any person who will deliver them to their master who resides at the Sign of the Crown, No, 25, Peck's Slip, shall have the above Reward, or Forty Shillings for each of the Women.   JAMES DUN.   August 18, 1780.
The Royal Gazette, August 19, 1780; August 23, 1780.

FOUR GUINEAS REWARD,

RUN AWAY on the evening of the 16th instant, from the Ranger army victualler, laying off the Hay Wharf, in the North-River, two Apprentices, viz.

JAMES B[O]LLINS, about 17 years of age, is near 5 feet high, thin and slender made, has sore eyes, and is much marked with the small pox; had on when he deserted, a green cap, a check shirt, and long trousers.

THOMAS DUKES, about 15 years of age, is near 4 feet 7 inches high, fresh complexion, stout and heavy, and has remarkable white hair; had on when he deserted, a coloured shirt and long trousers.

Whoever will give information of the said apprentices, do as the master may recover them again, shall receive the above reward, by applying on board the said ship, or two guineas reward will be given for each of them separately.   ROBERT NELSON.

N. B. All masters of vessels are forbid to harbour or encourage them at their peril.

The Royal Gazette, August 19, 1780.

ONE GUINEA REWARD.

RUN-away from the Subscriber, the 5th Instant, a Negro Man named JACK, 20 Years of Age, of a yellow Complexion, about 5 Feet 4 Inches high much addicted to hard drinking, and thieving, is branded on the back Part of each Arm & Buttock, & formerly belonged to Capt. Benson. All Captains of Vessels and others are hereby warned from harbouring or

concealing the said Negro, as they will answer the same at their Peril. Whoever takes up and secures said Fellow, so that he may be had again, shall receive the above Reward, and all Charges paid,
    by RICHARD JENKINS, 24 John-street.
The New-York Gazette; and the Weekly Mercury, August 21, 1780; August 28, 1780.

FIVE POUNDS REWARD.
RUN AWAY on Monday last, a likely Negro BOY, named CYRUS, about fifteen years old, he has a great impediment in his speech. Whoever will bring him to the subscriber, at No. 70, near St. Paul's Church, shall receive the above reward. JAMES RICKETTS.
The Royal Gazette, August 23; August 26, 1780.

RUN AWAY from Jamaica, a large fat young WENCH, with three cuts on each cheek, lately from Charlestown. Whoever takes up said Wench, and sends her to Colonel Linsing, or Ray and Fitzsimons merchants in Jamaica, (Long-Island) shall have FIVE DOLLARS Reward, and all reasonable charges paid.
The Royal Gazette, August 23, 1780; August 26, 1780.

RUN AWAY, a Virginia Negro Woman, called PAMELA, the property of the subscriber, aged about 18 years, and came here last summer with her mistress: She is squire built, [*sic*] very lusty and likely, affects to smile when she speaks or is spoken to, and is very deceitful and given to lying. She absconded about a month ago, and says she is a free Negro, tho' born in my family, and often calls herself MIRA, after her sister. As it is imagined some evil disposed persons encourage her in this way, for wicked purposes: All persons, therefore, are hereby forwarned, not to harbour, employ, conceal, or carry off said Negro, by land or water, as they must do the same at their peril: And whoever will secure said Negro or give timely notice who it is that secrets and entertains her, so as I may get her again, shall be handsomely rewarded, by applying to No. 30, in Roosevelt street, to
    J. AGNEW, Chaplain, Queen's Rangers.
The Royal Gazette, August 23, 1780.

THIS is to caution the public from crediting or harbouring my wife, a negro woman named SYLVIA, having dismissed her some time since for her extreme bad behaviour; therefore am determined to pay no debts she may contract after this 26th day of August, 1780.
    GEO. ELLIGER MOORE, *a free Negro.*
The Royal Gazette, August 26, 1780.

FORTY SHILLINGS Reward.

RUNAWAY from his master, Dennis Dennis, [sic] at the Narrows, Long-Island, the 20th instant, a negro boy named Lawrence or Launce: He is about 14 or 15 years of age, had on an osnaburghs pair of trowsers, and shirt; He has been on board the Grand Duke. Whoever will secure the said boy, and deliver him to Mr. James Stewart, No. 955, Burling-Slip, or to his master at the Narrows, shall have the above reward. All masters of vessels are cautioned from carrying him off, as they must answer for it at their peril.

The New-York Gazette; and the Weekly Mercury, August 28, 1780.

EIGHT DOLLARS Reward.

RUN AWAY on Sunday night last, a Negro Girl named JENNY, about 14 years of age, a native of Georgia, from whence she came in the last fleet with her owners; she is of a very black complexion, much marked with the small pox which she had not long since; has remarkable red eyes, short curl'd eye lashes and has lost one of her fore teeth of her under jaw: She had on when she went away a black callimanco coat, a white linen wrapper and cap, and carried all her other cloths with her. The above reward will be given to any person on delivering her to Mr. Dole, No. 128, Great Dock street, or give such information so as she may be taken; She was seen yesterday with some sailors on one of the docks. Captains of vessels and others are cautioned against harbouring her.—She is a remarkable thief and liar.

The Royal Gazette, September 6, 1780.

TWO GUINEAS Reward.

RUN away from the subscriber, the 5th ult. a negro man named JACK, 20 years of age, of a yellow complexion, about 5 feet 4 inches high, is branded on the back part of each arm and buttock, and formerly belonged to Capt. Benson; he has been seen about this city, and on Long-Island. All masters of vessels and others are hereby warned from harbouring or concealing said negro, as they will answer the same at their peril. Whoever takes up and secures said fellow, so that he may be had again, shall receive the above reward, and all charges paid,

by   JOHN CORNELL, Brooklyn Ferry.

The New-York Gazette; and the Weekly Mercury, September 11, 1780; September 18, 1780.

A REWARD,

RUN-AWAY about fifteen days ago, my Negro Man PARIS, about 21 years of age, about five feet nine inches high, he is rather remarkable,

having one bandy leg, so much that one knee knocks against the other when he walks and is much addicted to liquor. Whoever takes up said Negro Man, and will deliver him to me, shall have a reward of Five Dollars, and all reasonable charges paid them.
LAWRENCE KORTWRIGHT.
The Royal Gazette, September 16, 1780; *The New-York Gazette; and the Weekly Mercury*, September 18, 1780. Minor differences. The *Mercury* has "New-York, 9th September, 1780." at the bottom.

RUN AWAY from the Subscriber on the 16th day of September instant, a Negro Wench named ROSE: she is about the middle size, is a handsome black, and has an impediment in her speech; had on when she went away a green stuff petticoat, a red and white callico short gown, a red silk handkerchief, and a black sattin bonnet. Whoever brings her to me the subscriber, or secures her, shall, upon application, at No. 44, Queen street, receive FIVE DOLLARS REWARD, and all charges,
ALEXANDER ZUNTZ.
The Royal Gazette, September 20, 1780.

RUN-away from the subscriber, living in the Bowery-Lane, on the 9th inst. a negro man named MINTO, about 23 years of age, about five feet five inches high, a likely fellow, of a remarkable black complexion, and is much scared [*sic*] on the back. Had on when he went off, an old brown waistcoat, and ozenbrigs shirt and trowsers. Whoever takes up said negro and delivers him to his master, shall have TWO GUINEAS reward, and all reasonable charges paid, by   JOHN DIKEMAN.
N. B. All persons are forbid to harbour, and masters of vessels from carrying off said fellow.
The New-York Gazette; and the Weekly Mercury, September 25, 1780.

ONE GUINEA Reward.
MISSING since Sunday four o'clock in the afternoon the 10th inst. a yellow negro BOY, about 14 years of age, thick set, named BILL, lately belonging to Mr. Watson of Amboy, a few months ago lived with Dr. Bard; it is supposed he is lurking amongst some of the Amboy refugee negroes. This is to caution any person or persons to conceal him or carry him off, at they will be prosecuted as the law directs. The above reward will be given
by   MEDCEF EDEN, Brewer, on Golden-Hill.
The New-York Gazette; and the Weekly Mercury, September 25, 1780; October 2, 1780.

RUN AWAY from the subscriber on Monday evening, a Negro Boy called WILL, about 17 years old, five feet four inches high, remarkably marked with the smallpox and s[ea]med in the face: Had on a blue jacket turned up with red, a canvass pair of breeches and silver plated buckles. Whoever will apprehend or secure the said Negro, shall be handsomely rewarded. All masters of ships and others are desired not to harbour said Negro, as they will be prosecuted according to law.
JOHN SIBRELL.
The Royal Gazette, October 18, 1780.

RUN-away on the 19th inst. a negro boy named JAMES, between 14 and 15 years of age, strong made, has a bruise near one of his eyes, and a scar on his head, occasioned by the kick of a horse. Had on a green jacket, check shirt, oznaburg trowsers; but neither shoes or stockings. Whoever will bring the said boy to Andrew Zimmerman, in Warren street, shall receive 20 shillings, and all charges.
The New-York Gazette; and the Weekly Mercury, October 23, 1780.

Three Hundred Dollars Reward.
RUN-AWAY from the subscriber, living in New-Britain, on the 6th inst. an Apprintice Lad, named SILAS SEARE, a native of Long Island, about 19 years of age, very thick set, 5 feet 8 inches high; had on, or carried with him, a reddish brown coat and vest, 1 pair of light coloured cloth breeches, 1 do. leather, a new large brim'd hat, silver shoe and knee buckles, a brown surtout, with a velvet cape, and sundry other articles too tedious to mention. Whoever will take up said runaway and return him to the subscriber, shall receive the above reward.
ELIJAH HINSDALE. New-Britain, Nov. 10. 1780.
The Connecticut Courant, and Hartford Weekly Intelligencer, November 14, 1780.

RUN-away from the owner, James Baker, Fair-street, No. 181, a negro wench named Rachel, about 30 years of age, big with child, remarkably fat, and very much pitted with the small pox: Had on when she went away, a short gown and black quilted petticoat, and check apron, with large blue beads about her neck. Whoever may find said negro and deliver her to the owner, shall receive ONE GUINEA reward.
All persons are desired not to harbour said wench, on pain of being prosecuted with the rigour of the law.
The New-York Gazette; and the Weekly Mercury, November 27, 1780.

RUN-away from John Hutchinson, on the Night of the 9th Instant, living at the Inn near the four Mile Stone, leading to Fort Knyphausen, a Negro Man about 30 Years of Age, about 5 Feet 6 Inches high, well made, has a Mould under his right Jaw. Whoever will bring him to his said Master, shall receive two Guineas Reward.
JOHN HUTCHINSON. N. B. He answers to the Name of Cuff.
The New-York Gazette; and the Weekly Mercury, December 11, 1780; December 18, 1780.

FIVE DOLLARS REWARD.

RUN AWAY (or impressed) from Thomas Skinner, No. 256, Broad Street, on Saturday evening the 9th inst. a Mulatto Slave, aged 22 years, about 5 feet inches high, [*sic*] a stout well made fellow, named Tony, but may call himself Anthony Frost, has a bushy thick head of hair, which he combs up very high before in the shape of a roll, round faced, has part of one of his fore-teeth broke out, a very remarkable high breast bone, is very saucy and pert, and thinks a great deal of himself; had on a short blue coat, white metal buttons, striped jacket, and a long pair of blue trowsers. Whoever will apprehend or secure said Mulatto so that his master may get him again, shall have the above reward.—All masters of vessels and others are desired not to harbour said Mulatto at their peril, as they will be prosecuted with the utmost rigour.
The Royal Gazette, December 13, 1780. See *The Royal Gazette*, December 11, 1779, and *The New-York Gazette; and the Weekly Mercury*, December 13, 1779.

FIVE DOLLARS Reward.

ABsented from his Master on Friday the 8th inst. a NEGRO BOY, named JACK, about fifteen years of age, rather of a small size, smooth faced, speaks slow, has a simple innocent look. He had on when he went away, a green jacket, with red cuffs and collar, and a pair of blue cloth trowsers, Whoever will give information of said boy to the Printer, or the subscriber his Majesty's Issuing Store, Burling's slip, so that he may be secured will receive the above reward. All masters of vessels and others are forbid to harbour or carry off said boy, as they will answer for the contrary.
LACHLAN MACKINTOSH.
The New-York Gazette; and the Weekly Mercury, December 18, 1780.

ONE GUINEA Reward.
RUN-AWAY,

FROM the brig Britannia, navy victualler, R. Galt, master, on Thursday night the 14th of December, an apprentice named John Chenet, born at

Nancy, in Lotrain, aged about 16 or 17 years, speaks the French, Russian, and English languages fluently, a little German. He is short in stature but very broad, wears his own streight dark brown hair, went off in jacket and trowsers, supposed to be taken by a ship's boat.
The New-York Gazette; and the Weekly Mercury, December 18, 1780.

PHILIP MULLENOR, an apprentice lad, fifteen years of age, has short light coloured hair, left his master's service on the 12th instant: had on a new linsey coat of a lead colour, with pewter buttons, a jacket of the same colour, but much worn, brown cloth breeches, yarn stockings, new shoes with stiffning behind, a fur scollop'd hat, and a flannel shirt. It is supposed he will endeavour to get to New-York, as his mother lives there. Whoever takes up the said apprentice and brings him to the subscriber, shall receive Forty Continental Dollars reward.
               PHILIP GRANDIN.   Lebanon, Dec. 18, 1780.
The New-Jersey Gazette, December 20, 1780; December 27, 1780; January 3,1781.

DESERTED *from the Surprize letter of Marque,* GIDEON DUNCAN, *Commander, four of his apprentice boys, as follow Richard Frankline aged* 1[8] *years, about 4 feet 9 inches swarthy complexion, dark hair: Oliver Stebin aged* 16 *years About 5 feet high, fair complexion, light hair: Henry Gibson, aged* 17 *years,* 4 *feet* 11 *inches high, fair complexion, brown hair: Thomas Adams, aged* 18 *years,* 5 *feet high, fair complexion, dark hair. Any person who will give notice to their master, where they are, so that he may recover them, shall receive half a guinea each as a reward. And any person either in sea or land service, who shall encourage or harbour any of said apprentices after this notice given, may expect to be prosecuted to the utmost rigor of the law, Ship Surprize Hallett's wharf.*
               GIDEON DUNCAN.
    N. B. The ship is in Government's service, which doubles the offence of harbouring them.
The Royal Gazette, December 30, 1780.

1781

THREE GUINEAS REWARD.

RUN-away from the Subscriber, about Fourteen Days ago, (and is supposed to be lurking in and about the City, in order to escape to the Rebels) an Apprentice Lad named John Sacket, 19 Years of Age, 5 Feet and a half high. All Masters of Vessels are forbid to carry him off at their Peril; and all Persons are forbid harbouring him. Whoever takes up and secures the said

Run-away, so that he may be had again, shall receive the above Reward, from   ABEL HARDENBROOK, jun.
The New-York Gazette; and the Weekly Mercury, January 8, 1781.

FIVE POUNDS Reward.
RUN away from her master, a negro wench named Isabella, or Bella, born on Long-Island, at Mr. Van Nostreen's, near the Wallabought, and by him sold to Mr. Skillman, at Bushwick; she is about 22 years of age, well made, rather tall size, her mouth a little of one side, a scar on her left temple which she received from some of her friends by way of a Christmas Box: She had on and took with her a whitish callico gown, black petticoat, and also a long scarlet cloak, and a black cloak, she is now lurking about Brooklyn. Whoever secures said wench so that her master may have her again, by giving information to the Printer, or at No. 1078, Water Street, will receive the above reward, and all reasonable charges paid. All masters of vessels and others are forbid to harbour, conceal or carry off said wench, as they may expect to answer it for the contrary. New-York, 8 Jan. 1780. [*sic*]
The New-York Gazette; and the Weekly Mercury, January 8, 1781; January 15, 1781.

RUN-away from the subscriber, living at Jamaica, Long Island, a negro fellow named DICK, otherwise called MINK, about 5 feet 8 or 9 inches high, formerly the property of one Mr. Boice, of Jersey: Had on when he went away, a brown or snuff coloured coat, waistcoat and breeches, likewise a light coloured old great coat with a red velvet collar. All persons are forewarned not to harbour said negro, and whoever will secure and bring him to the subscriber, shall have ONE GUINEA reward, and all reasonable charges paid.
     JOHN WHEELER.
The New-York Gazette; and the Weekly Mercury, January 22, 1781.

New-York, January 23.
RUN away a NEGRO WENCH, named Sally, aged about 21 Years, smooth faced and low Stature, speaks good English, had on when she went away a short Blue Jacket, and White Petticoat, but may have probably put on a Callicoe Gown.

Whoever will apprehend her or bring account where she is to the Printer hereof shall be rewarded.

All Masters of Ships are warned not to take or harbour such a Wench on Board as they will be answerable for so doing as the Law directs. She is the Property of Mrs. Patterson, No. 71, Queen Street.
The Royal Gazette, January 24, 1781.

WHEREAS on Sunday last, DORCAS WALKER a child of about 14 years of age, in consequence of some difference arising between her and her mother, absconded and has not been heard of since: It is requested that any person, who can give any account of the said Child, will call upon her said mother Elizabeth Walker, living at Whitehall, opposite the sign of the Daphne, by whom the favour will be gratefully acknowledged and a handsome reward paid for their trouble.
The Royal Gazette, January 24, 1781. See *The Royal Gazette*, December 29, 1781.

WHEREAS a transient person being taken at Ripton, for passing counterfeit money, made in imitation of the true bills of credit of this State of Connecticut, of Forty Shillings, dated the 1st day of June, 1780, and taken before authority for examination, and upwards of twenty pounds of counterfeit money found with him; and in the evening of the 29th instant January, in a crowd of persons made his escape; he called himself by the name Joseph Higgins, but his name is Joseph Pine Cable, and is said to belong to the State of New-York; is about 5 ½ feet high, 19 years old, fresh complection, short hair, with a false tail; had on when he went away, a small round hat, a light brown great coat, white metal buttons, a brown coat, a red jacket, black breeches, white stockings, and a pair of boots. Whoever will take up said man, and him convey to me the subscriber, or secure him in any gaol in this State, so that I may have him again, shall receive Five Hard Dollars Reward, and all charges paid by
           NATHANIEL BLACKMAN, Constable of Stratford.
                                  Ripton, January 30. 1781.
The Connecticut Journal, and Weekly Advertiser, February 2, 1781.

Six Dollars Reward.
RUN away from the Subscriber, this morning, a Negro Wench named Belina, about 21 years of age, slender made and short; had on when she went away, a brown jacket, red petticoat, white handkerchief, and a high cap; has a mole on the right side of her nose; she took with her a little hair trunk without a lock, a red and white linen gown, black hat and cloak, and a white dimity petticoat. Whoever secures the said Wench and brings her dome, shall have the above reward.
           HENRY GUEST,   No. 931, Water-street.
                                      February 10, 1780.
N. B. All persons whatever are forbid to harbour her at their peril.
The Royal Gazette, February 12, 1781.

Two Guineas Reward.
RUN away from his master, in Charlestown, a mustee fellow named BRAP, has bushy hair, stout made, a little bandy legg'd, marked with the smallpox, about 25 years of age, and speaks good English. Whoever will secure him, or give information of him to the Printer, & send him to his master, shall have the above reward. All persons are forbid to harbour or carry him off, as they shall answer it at their peril.
The Royal Gazette, February 21, 1781.

MY Negro Wench named Pleasant Queen Anne, ran away on the 18th instant, and had on a red moreen petticoat, a brown short gown, with white lining, a pair of brown rib'd stockings. Whoever will bring her to me shall receive Forty Shillings reward.
        JOHN CURRY, No. 30, William Street.
All Captains of Vessels are warned against carrying her off.
The Royal Gazette, March 3, 1781.

Eight Dollars Reward.
DESERTED from the subscriber's Independence Company, JAMES HARDY, 5 feet 5 inches high, from Ireland, 25 years of age, of a dark complexion, can speak several languages, says he is a peruke maker, and it is supposed will change his name: He had on his regimentals when he left the company. Whoever apprehends the said deserter, and confines him in the main-guard of this city, or brings him to my quarters at the sign of the ship, in the Bowery, shall receive the above reward.
All masters of privateers are desired not to harbour him at their peril.
    ANDREW FORSHNER.   March 10, 1781.
The Royal Gazette, March 14, 1781.

Three Guineas Reward.
RUN AWAY last night from the subscriber living in Crown Street, No. 4. a Negro girl named PRUSSIA, about 21 years of age, tall stout and well made light, complexion, thick lips, speaks good English, has been hears to say she would go on board the first ship that would take her, had a quantity of good cloaths with her. Whoever apprehends the said Negro Girl, or confines her so that her owner may get her again, shall receive the above reward. All persons and masters of vessels are desired not not to harbour or carry said Negro Girl away at their peril.
    ELIZABETH DUNCAN.   March 20, 1781.
The Royal Gazette, March 21, 1781.

Two Guineas Reward

RUN away on Friday the 9th instant, a NEGRO BOY named YORK, who came from the island of Jamaica three years ago, with the subscriber; he is 4 feet 4 inches high, well built, small limbs, round visage, not very black, has a scar on his left temple occasioned by a burn, and a small scar under his right eye. He has, during the last winter, been employed in sweeping chimnies, and has on his sweep cloathes when he went away, viz. two blue kersey waistcoats, breeches of the same, a flannel under waistcoat, a shirt made of Russia sheeting, flannel legings, and a round wool hat. He ran away last May, and went on board the Thames frigate, Capt. Howe, and continued there till the month of August. He is very much addicted to drinking and lying, very talkative, and very subtle for his age. Whoever will secure the said boy, so that his master may have him again, or bring him to No. 20, Princess street, shall have the above reward, and be allowed all reasonable charges.—All masters of vessels are requested not to carry him off, and all other persons are desired not to harbour him, or them must answer it at their peril.

PETER CREIGHTON.

The Royal Gazette, March 17, 1781. See *The Royal Gazette*, May 20, 1780, and *The Royal Gazette*, May 22, 1782.

RAN-away from Mr. James Fuller, in New-York, an apprentice boy, named Benjamin Kiersted; had on when he went away, a green coat, a fustian jacket, a drab coloured velvet breeches, and a round hat. Supposed to be carried away on board the pettiaugre Black-Snake, John Grahams Master, belonging to Hog-Island, on the South-side of Long-Island. Five Dollars reward will be given to any person who apprehends the said boy, and I hereby forewarn all persons not to harbour him, otherwise they will answer to the law for all damages.

The Royal Gazette, March 21, 1781.

ONE GUINEA REWARD.

RUN away from the subscriber, in the Township of Flushing, the 19th instant, a NEGRO MAN formerly called Oliver, but at present calls himself Joe, aged about 28 years, he is about 5 feet 10 inches high, has a thin long face, had on a blue sailors coat, a grey homespun waistcoat and breeches. Whoever takes up said Negro Man, and secures him, so that the subscriber may have him again, shall have the above reward, and all reasonable charges paid by   WILLIAM TALMAN.

Flushing, March 20, 1781.

The Royal Gazette, March 24, 1781.

RUN AWAY a few days ago from the regiment of Brunswick Dragoons, at Flat-Land, on Long Island, a Black named Prince Dermen, Drummer in said regiment, about five feet ten inches high, stout built, had on a suit of light blue cloaths quite new. Whoever will secure him so that he may be brought back, or delivered over to any non-commissioned officer of the said regiment, shall receive a proper reward for so doing; and every one is forbid concealing him at their peril.
The Royal Gazette, April 18, 1781; April 28, 1781.

Staten Island, April 27.
ABSENTED himself from the Subscriber on Sunday last, living on Staten Island, a yellow Negro Man with tied hair, named NED, he is supposed to be in this City; had on when he went away a blue watchcoat, and under coat of grey Forest cloth, white homespun waistcoat, light brown Velvet breeches, white woollen stockings, round Beaver hat more than half worn. Whoever secures the said Negro, so that his master may get him again, shall receive THREE GUINEAS Reward and all reasonable Charges,
         paid by me   LAWRENCE HILLYER.
The Royal Gazette, April 28, 1781.

ABSENTED himself from his Master's service on Saturday the 14th instant, and is lurking about town, a Negro Boy, named Peet or Peter, about 12 years of age, had on when he went away a blue baize waistcoat, tied before with strings, and the legs of blue worsted stockings sewed in for sleeves, osnaburg shirt, and linen trowsers. Whoever apprehends and brings him to the subscriber at No. 56, Water Street between Beekman and Burling Slips, shall receive One Guinea reward. All persons are strictly forbidden harbouring, and masters of vessels carrying him off at their peril.
         BERNARDUS LEGRANGE.
The Royal Gazette, April 28, 1781.

Eight Dollars Reward.
RUN AWAY from the Subscriber, Matthew Daniel, living at No. 14, Duke Street, a Negro Boy, named Duff, and had on when he went away a red waistcoat, check shirt and osnaburgh trowsers, no shoes nor hat. Whoever brings said boy to his master, or gives intelligence where he can be had, shall have the above reward.
    N. B. All masters of vessels and others are forwarned to harbour or conceal the said Negro Boy, as they may expect to answer for the same.
The Royal Gazette, June 30, 1781. See *The Royal Gazette*, April 26, 1783.

FIVE DOLLARS REWARD.

RUN-away from the Aurora victualler, Constable Saunders, master, lying at the commissary's wharf, an apprentice lad named Morris Rowning, about 19 years of age, of a middle size, yellow hair, and paleish complexion: Had on a white flannel Jacket, long trowsers, and a new round hat. The above reward will be paid by Capt. Saunders, (who may be found at Mr. Nutter's,) to any person who will apprehend and bring said lad on board the above named ship.

The New-York Gazette; and the Weekly Mercury, July 9, 1781; July 16, 1781; July 23, 1781.

SIX DOLLARS Reward.

RUN-away on Monday the 2nd of July, from his master John Andrew Simerman, milkman, in Warren-street, New-York, a negro man named Hector, but sometimes passes by that of Henry; he was formerly the property of Capt. Buskirk, of Long-Island, and by information received, has lately crossed the ferry to that Island: He is about forty years of age, very black visage, a little grey headed, and stoops in his walk: Had on a round old hat, a linen stuff colour'd coat, claret colour corderoy breeches, speckled shirt, and pepper and salt colour stockings. All persons are forewarned not to harbour the said negro, and whoever will secure him so that his master may have him again, shall be paid the above reward, and all reasonable charges.

The New-York Gazette; and the Weekly Mercury, July 9, 1781; July 16, 1781; July 23, 1781.

RUN AWAY on Thursday morning last, about 11 o'clock, a negro boy named SAWNEY, about 14 years old, has a scar on his right eye; near 4 feet 9 inches high; had on when he went away a check shirt and osnaburg trowsers (only). Any person that secures the said negro, and will bring him to the printer, shall have six dollars reward. All persons are forbid to harbour him, and masters of ships carrying him off, as they will be prosecuted to the utmost rigour of the law.

The New-York Gazette; and the Weekly Mercury, July 16, 1781.

RUN away from the Ship British Queen, Army Victualler, Captain Hugh Callaway, a three years servant, named Archibald Dickson, about five feet six inches, of a brown complexion, wears his own hair, about Nineteen years of age.

Whoever apprehends the said Servant, shall receive Two Guineas reward.—All Masters of Vessels harbouring him, may depend upon being prosecuted with the utmost rigour of the law.

HUGH CALLAWAY.
The Royal Gazette, July 18, 1781.

RUN away from the Subscriber, a likely Negro Boy named Frank, about 14 years old, having an impediment in his speech, had on when he went away a pair of check trowsers & a check shirt, with a white linen waistcoat.

I do hereby forwarn all masters of vessels from harbouring or carrying him off, or any inhabitant from harbouring him, A reward of One Guinea will be given to any person who shall deliver him to me, or the Printer.
           JOHN MUIRHEAD.
At the Sign of St. George and the Dragon, On Brownjohn's Wharf.
The Royal Gazette, July 21, 1781.

WHEREAS MARY, Wife of JOSEPH BOSS, of Newtown, in Queen's County, on Long-Island, having at different times received a great deal of ill-usage from her said Husband, who has lately turned her out of doors and threatened her life in case she returns to him; she is therefore determined to live separate from him for the future, and is well warranted in this resolution from his cruel and unprovoked behaviour.
And the said Mary Boss hereby forewarns and forbids any person or person whatever from buying or purchasing any part of the property belonging to the said Husband, until such time as he shall have given good and sufficient security for such part thereof as she is entitled to by Law.
           MARY BOSS.
The Royal Gazette, July 21, 1781; *The New-York Gazette; and the Weekly Mercury*, July 23, 1781. Minor differences between the papers.

Five Dollars Reward.

RUN AWAY from the Subscriber, on Tuesday the third instant, A Negro Wench named LUCE, about twenty-eight years old, has a large mark on one of her cheeks which looks like a scar; she had on when she went off, a homespun short gown and petticoat. Whoever takes up the said wench and secures her, or gives information so that her mistress may get her again, shall receive the above reward, from ANN PRICE, on Golden Hill, next door to the corner of Fair-Street.
N. B. If the aforesaid wench will return, she will be forgiven.
The Royal Gazette, July 21, 1781.

RUN-AWAY on Monday night, nine o'clock, from John Obrien, at the Four Alls, near the Ferry-Stairs, a young negro girl named Sarah, about 19 years old, she wore a white short gown and a cotton petticoat. Whoever returns her to her master, or gives information for her recovery, shall

receive eight Dollars reward. All masters of vessels and others are forwarned against harbouring her at their peril.
The Royal Gazette, July 25, 1781.

Ten Dollars Reward.

RUN AWAY from the Subscriber, about six or eight weeks ago, an indented negro man named York Bevers, about one or two and twenty years of age, five feet five inches high; had on when he went away, a brown coat with red cuffs and collar, and osnaburgh trowsers.—Also, on Saturday last a negro boy named Jack, about twelve years of age, had on when he went away, a blue coat faced with red. Whoever will secure the above negroes and bring them to the subscriber, shall receive the above reward, or five dollars for either of them. All masters of vessels and others are hereby strictly charged not to harbour or conceal either of them so that they shall answer the same at their peril.

JOHN GRIFFITHS. No. 193, Water-Street.

The Royal Gazette, July 25, 1781.

Eight Dollars, *Reward.*

RUN-away, Yesterday, from John Obrien at the Sign of the *Four All's*, at the Ferry Stairs, at the Fly-Market, a Negro Wench named Sarah, about 4 [*sic*] Feet high, 18 Years of Age: Had on when she went away, an India Calico Pettycoat, a short white Gown, and a Gauze Cap. She has large Breasts, and is inclinable to Fat. She lived some Time with Mr. Cooper, Merchant, Hanover-Square, and is Virginia born. All Persons are forbid to carry her off, or harbour he at their Peril.

The New-York Gazette; and the Weekly Mercury, July 30, 1781.

EIGHT DOLLARS REWARD,

RUN away from the subscriber, a stout Negro Man named SAM IVY, a carpenter and caulker by trade, marked with the small-pox. I forewarn all Captains of vessels, or others from harbouring or taking him away; also any other person employing him and paying wages without an order from me, shall be answerable for the same after this date. Whoever secures the said negro slave, or delivers him to me at No. 71, Beekman-Street, shall be paid the above reward, with every other expence.

JONATHAN EILBECK. New-York, July 30 1781.

The New-York Gazette; and the Weekly Mercury, July 30, 1781. See *The Royal Gazette*, August 4, 1781.

325

Eight Dollars Reward.
RUN away from the Subscriber, a stout negro Man named SAM. IVEY, a carpenter and caulker by trade, pitted with small pox. I forewarn all Captains of vessels, or others from harbouring or taking him away; also any other person employing him and paying wages without an order from me, shall be answerable for the same after this date. Whoever secures the said Negro Slave, or delivers him to me at No. 71, Beekman-Street, shall be paid the above reward, with every other expence.
JONATHAN EILBECK.   July 30 1781.
The Royal Gazette, August 4, 1781. See *The New-York Gazette; and the Weekly Mercury*, July 30, 1781.

One Guinea Reward.
RUN AWAY from the Provost Marshal, a black man named Richmon, formerly the property of the Rebel Colonel Pattison, at Christeen Bridge, in Pennsylvania: He formerly lives at Mr. Sause's, Merchant at the Flymarket: All masters of vessels are warned against harbouring him at their peril, he being the
Common HANGMAN.
The above reward will be paid to any person who will secure said negro, so as the Provost Marshal may have him again, by
Captain CUNNINGHAM, Provost Martial.
The Royal Gazette, August 4, 1781.

RUN-AWAY on Wednesday Evening 3d August, a negro boy named PRINCE, about eighteen years of age, has a small scar under his left eye, and one on the left side of his neck, remarkable large feet; he is tall, looks well, speaks very good English; he was born in New-York, with Captain Harris, and bred on Long-Island, lived with one Fisher, a tobacco cutter and since with Captain Fletcher. If he returns to his master of his own accord he will be forgiven and no questions asked, and will be used according to his future behavior.
   If carried off in any ship under any pretence whatever, the master will be prosecuted, and the value of the slave being one hundred pounds sterling will be recovered....Two guineas reward will be given to any person who give intelligence so that he may be recovered at New-York. Send a note to the printer.
   The New-York Gazette; and the Weekly Mercury, August 6, 1781.

Five Dollars Reward.
RUN away four days ago, a likely NEGRO BOY, named TONEY, about twelve years of age; had on when he went away a brown Fustian Jacket and

Trowsers. Whoever will apprehend and bring him to his Master at No. 30, Broad-Way, shall receive the above reward; he was last seen in the Bowery.

Any Person or Persons harbouring the said Boy, may expect such punishment as the law directs.

New-York, 10th *August* 1781.
The Royal Gazette, August 11, 1781.

RUN away, on Wednesday morning, at gun-fire, a negro wench and child, had on a striped Holland short gown, and a brown marine petticoat; her name is JANE, and the child's the same. Whoever brings her and the child to No. 22, in St. James's street, shall receive three guineas reward; and all masters of vessels are forewarned not to take them away.

The Royal Gazette, August 18, 1781.

ONE GUINEAS REWARD,

RUN away from the subscriber, a Negro Boy, eleven years of age, small growth, thin face, had on when he went away, a coarse round hat, small strip'd jacket, without sleeves, check shirt, a pair of Russia sheeting trowsers, open at the foot. I forwarn any person to conceal or carry off said Negro Boy, at their peril. Any person bringing him to the Coffee House, shall have the above reward.

JOHN BAIN.

The Royal Gazette, August 25, 1781.

WENT away early on Wednesday morning the 15th of August inst. and has not since returned, a negro lad named MATTIS, he is a good looking well made lad, about 22 years of age but appears rather younger; is about five feet eight or nine inches high, has two scars just under one of his ears: he took with him three check shirts, oznaburg trowsers and frock, a pair of mottled nankeen breeches; a ched on the right knee, a striped jacket, and a round hat. His master is persuaded he did not mean to stay away, but has been seduced, and is still secreted by some one. If the boy will return immediately he has nothing to fear; but should he not, those who detain him after this notice, may depend upon being prosecuted with the utmost rigour. EIGHT DOLLARS Reward will be paid to any one who will bring him home, or FOUR DOLLARS to any person who will give the Printer information where he is.

Sometime about last fall, ran away from his master, a negro lad named SAM, he is a tolerable chunky lad, about 5 feet 7 or eight inches high, about 22 years of age, and has a remarkable scar on one cheek. Also ran away a considerable time since a negro man named CAESAR; he is about 5 feet 7 or eight inches high, by trade a sail-maker, but has employed himself at

times going to sea, and in the wood boating business. Whoever will secure either of the above and give information to the Printer, that they may be had again, shall receive FIVE DOLLARS for each, and reasonable expences. It is pretty certain that both of them are lurking about this town.
The Royal Gazette, August 25, 1781; August 29, 1781.

FIVE DOLLARS REWARD.

RUN away from the Subscriber, Captain Charles Grant, of the 42d, or Royal Highland Regiment of Foot, a negro man named TOM, about 27 years of age, five feet five or six inches high, thick and well made, as a cut in his forehead. Whoever brings the said Negro man TOM, to Captain Grant, or Mr. Hunt, at Newtown, Long-Island, or give information where he can be found, shall have the above reward.

All Masters of vessels and others are forwarned to harbour or conceal the said negro man, as they may expect to answer for the same.
The Royal Gazette, August 29, 1781; September 5, 1781; September 26, 1781.

RUN away from the Ship New Blessing, Transport, Thomas Craven, Master, Robert Cook: He took a Jolly Boat from the Ship, and cut a Skiff adrift, 20 Feet long painted black and yellow above, Chocolate coloured Sides, and white Bottom, with four Oars in her, and 2 coils of small Rope Whoever secures the Boat, and delivers her to Mr. George Fowler, Ship-Chandler at the Crane Wharf, shall receive Two Guineas Reward, will all reasonable Charges.
The New-York Gazette; and the Weekly Mercury, August 27, 1781.

RUN away last Monday night from his Mother in Chapel-street, a Negro Boy named JACOB, near fourteen years old, has a cut on the side of his left eye, had on a red jacket, Osnaburgh trowsers, and check shirt, but without hat or shoes.—Whoever will bring him back to his Mother Jenny, at Mr. Ludlow's, the corner of George's street in Chapel-street, shall receive Three Dollars reward.
The Royal Gazette, September 1, 1781.

ABSCONDED a few days ago, from their owners, from the house of Mr. Robie, at Flat-Bush: two Negro Girls, Slaves, one named Betsey, marked on the right shoulder T A, the other named Polly without any mark, they both speak bad English.

Whoever may apprehend one or both Negroes, and deliver them to Alexander Forteate, No. 53, Burling Slip, shall receive for each Eight

Dollars, if concealed, or harboured by any person, they may depend on being prosecuted.
The Royal Gazette, September 1, 1781.

Twenty-four Dollars **REWARD**

RUN away from on board the Raynham Hall store ship, James Butcher, commander, JOHN PATTISON, of a brown complexion, about 5 feet 4 inches in stature, thin visage and freckled, with short sandy hair; had on when he went away, a blue jacket and long trowsers. Whoever secures and brings him to the Printer, shall have the above reward.
The New-York Gazette; and the Weekly Mercury, September 17, 1781.

RUN-away 8 days ago, a Negro BOY—he had on a coarse check shirt, and oznaburgh trowsers, and a round hat; he has remarkable thick lips, and an awkward sheepish look when spoke to, is about 15 years old. It is supposed he is on board the victualling sloop Betsey lying in the North-River, having reported that his master had given him free—Whoever secures him, or informs the Printer where he may be found, shall receive the reward of five Dollars.   SAMUEL FRAUNCES.
The New-York Gazette; and the Weekly Mercury, October 1, 1781.

RUN-away from his Master, a negro man named CHARLES; he was taken on board the Protector, and sold at Murray's wharff: He is about five feet five or six inches high, had on when he went away, a blue jacket, striped trowsers, and a cocked hat; its likely he may change his dress and name, and attempt to go to sea. All masters of vessels and others are warned not to harbour or carry him off at their peril. TWO GUINEAS reward will be given to any one that takes him up and carries him to James Hallet, coach maker, Broadway, or to Joseph Hallet, at Hallet's Cove Ferry.

N. B. The said negro has attended the ferry from Hallet's Cove to Horns Hook.
The New-York Gazette; and the Weekly Mercury, October 1, 1781.

FIFTEEN GUINEAS REWARD.

RUN-AWAY, DAVID, a Mulatto fellow, about 20 years of age, 5 feet 6 or 7 inches high, thick, well made, lazy, and inclines to be fat, has large nostrils, and takes snuff, thick lips, and very remarkably large scar on the upper part of his right arm; he had on when he went away, a green broad cloth frock coat, the skirts cut short. Likewise JUDE, a yellow mulatto wench, about 30 years of age, thin visage, with a male child, about 4 years old; the wench dressed clean, the child wore a crimson sagathie jacket and petticoat.

Also, YARROW, a new Negro fellow, his teeth filed sharp, and speaks bad English. SYLVIA, a dirty Negro Wench, with a child about two years old.

The above reward of Fifteen Guineas will be paid for the whole, or five for Davy, five for Jude, and five for Yarrow and Sylvia, on delivery at No. 33, Dock-street.
The New-York Gazette; and the Weekly Mercury, November 12, 1781.

RUN AWAY from the subscriber on Thursday last, a Negro Wench named Peg, about 18 years of age, born in Carolina, had on when she went away a blue cloth jacket with long sleeves, made in the form of a riding dress, with bright yellow buttons, this is to forwarn all persons from harbouring her, and all master of vessels in carrying her out of this port, upon the penalty of paying whatever the law directs. Whosoever will take up the said Negro, and bring her to No. 48, Cherry Street, shall receive One Guinea reward.
     WILLIAM WILLSON.
The Royal Gazette, November 17, 1781.

FIVE DOLLARS REWARD.

WENT from her Mistress yesterday, from her house in the Broadway, an Apprentice Girl, about fourteen years of age, fresh complexion, had on when she went away, a Callicoe Jesuit dress, a Scarlet Cloak, and black Bonnet, is lame on the right side. Whoever can give information where she may be found, shall receive the above reward by applying to the Printer.
The Royal Gazette, November 21, 1781.

Ten Guineas Reward.

RUN away from the subscriber, on Sunday last the 16th inst a NEGRO WENCH, named ISABELLA, about five feet six inches high, of a pretty black colour, she lisps in speech. Had on when she went away, a light chintz gown, a light coloured short frize cloke. She was carried off by her husband, a Negro Fellow named Peter Longstriff, about six feet high, a pale black. Had on when he went away, a short coat: has a big nose and a full eye; formerly lived with Col. Lutwich, on Long Island. This is to forewarn all masters of vessels or others, not to harbour her, as they will be prosecuted according to law. The above Reward will be given to any person who will give information, or bring the said Wench to the subscriber, at Jamaica, Long Island, or to Philip Kissick, at the upper end of Queen-Street.   EDWARD BARDLY.
The New-York Gazette; and the Weekly Mercury, November 24, 1781.

One GUINEA Reward.
RUN AWAY on Thursday the 4th instant, a stout Negro Boy, named TOM, of a very black complexion, had on when he went away a long scarlet coat, double lapelled, with gilt buttons, red jacket, double breasted, white breeches, grey worsted ribbed Stockings, strong shoes, and white metal buckles, an old black velvet cap; he probably may change his name and dress. It is presumed that no person whatever, will carry off the said negro; whoever will secure the Run-away, so that his master may get him, will receive the above reward, by applying to the Printer.
December 7, 1781.
The Royal Gazette, December 8, 1781.

RUN AWAY from his master Lieutenant de Bardeleben (formerly in the regiment of Dittfurth) at Charlestown, and supposed to have gone on board a ship, and sailed for New-York, a Negro Man named JOE, of middle size, not very black, but rather a brownish complexion, a Carpenter by trade. Whoever meets or hears of said fellow, or actually is in possession of the same, is desired to secure and brig him, or give notice thereof to Judge Advocate Heymell, quartered at Mrs. Rosevelt's, No. 20, Gold-Street, facing Ferry-Street, where further information about a handsome reward will be given.
The Royal Gazette, December 19, 1781.

ABSENTED herself from her mother, yesterday at 4 o'clock in the afternoon, DORCAS WALKER, she is of a fair complexion, sixteen years of age. Also absented herself at the same time, HANNAH JACOBS, a Girl about the same age. Her Mother should be greatly obliged to any person that would bring them to Elizabeth Walker, opposite the King's Arms, Whitehall Slip, who will pay all expences.
Masters of Vessels are desired not to carry them off.
The Royal Gazette, December 29, 1781. See *The Royal Gazette*, January 24, 1781.

1782

ONE GUINEA REWARD,
RUN away the 6th of December past, from on board of the ship Emanuel and Hercules, Alexander M'Dougal Master, a negro boy named Cudjoe, about five feet six inches high, stout and well made, very black complexion, speaks both English and French; had on when he went away, a blue jacket and trowsers.

Whoever will bring him to Thomas Erskine, at Mrs. Smyth's, No. 5, Hanover-Square, will receive the above reward.
The Royal Gazette, January 5, 1782. See *The New-York Gazette; and the Weekly Mercury,* December 17, 1781.

RUN-away, last Saturday Morning, from the Golden-Lyon Tavern, on Brown-john's Wharff, a Negro Man named Jack: Had on a brown Coat with a green Cape, and came lately from Georgia. A reward of *Six Pounds* will be given to any Person who will secure said Negro. Enquire of the Printer.
The New-York Gazette; and the Weekly Mercury, January 21, 1782.

A NEGRO Deserted.

LEFT his Master's house on the 10th inst, a negro man called ADAM, he is a tall stout made fellow, with a remarkable scar, a mark above his left eyebrow. Whoever will apprehend the said negro, and bring him to Mr. Campbell's Office, near the Coffee-House, shall have a reward of Three Guineas; and the same reward will be given to any person, who may be apprehended. Masters of vessels and others are hereby warned not to employ or protect him, otherwise they may depend upon being prosecuted according to law; concealing a run-away negro being as criminal as receiving stolen goods.
The Royal Gazette, January 23, 1782.

WHEREAS on the 21st instant, a small Black Girl, named SUE, or MARY, was stolen from the Subscriber, (having had on at the time a red cloth frock, a pair of new shoes, with brass buckles, blue stockings with white tops,) by her mother named PENDER a Virginia Wench. Whoever will apprehend either of the said Negroes, shall receive FOUR DOLLARS reward.

All Captains of vessels or others, who shall harbour, conceal, or attempt to carry them off shall, if discovered, by prosecuted with the utmost rigour.

SUSANNAH JUNDINE. *New-York, January 25th,* 1782.
The Royal Gazette, January 26, 1782.

RUN away from her Master on Monday morning last, a NEGRO Wench, named Jane, she had on a pale green callimanco petticoat, a red short gown, a scarlet cloak with a hood on it; about fifteen years of age, very talkative and speaks good English. Whoever takes up said Negro Wench, and brings her to Francis Doyl, No. 63, Chatham-Street, shall have Two Dollars reward. *February,* 7, 1782.
The Royal Gazette, February 9, 1782; February 20, 1782.

TWO GUINEAS Reward.

RUN AWAY, on the 28th instant, a negro wench named LISSA, the property of John Carow, had on when she went away, a brown short gown, and brown serge petticoat, a blue short cloak unbound with a cap to it, and took off with her two striped callico long gowns, and some other cloathing, she has a mark on her breast occasioned by being burnt. She speaks good English, and is rather more yellow than black, aged about 24 years old. Whoever takes up said Wench, and brings her to her master, living in Fair-street, No. 3, shall receive the above reward. All persons are forbid harbouring said wench.

JOHN CAROW.

N. B. The above wench formerly belonged to Parson Burnet, on Long-Island.

The Royal Gazette, February 13, 1782; February 23, 1782; *The New-York Gazette; and the Weekly Mercury*, February 18, 1782. Minor differences between the papers. The *Mercury* spells the parson's last name as Burnett.

EIGHT DOLLARS REWARD.

RUN away from the subscriber, on Sunday evening last, a likely NEGRO WENCH, nineteen years of age, named Charlotte, formerly the property of Captain Salter, she is somewhat pitted with the small pox, had on when she went away, a white gown and petticoat: Whoever takes up said Wench and secures her so as her master can obtain her, shall receive the above reward, and all reasonable charges

paid by me   JOHN VANDERHOVEN.

All masters of vessels and others are strictly forbid to carry off or conceal her at their peril.

The Royal Gazette, March 6, 1782.

One Guinea Reward.

RUN away on Thursday the 12th instant, a stout well made Negro Boy, about five feet four inches, had on when he went away, a black super-fine broad cloth coat and waistcoat, black silk breeches and stockings. and a beaver hat with crape round it. Whoever will secure the said Negro Boy to the Printer, will be entitled to the above reward.

All Masters of vessels and others, are cautioned from harbouring or carrying off the said Negro Boy.

The Royal Gazette, March 13, 1782.

RUN AWAY on Thursday the 12th inst. a stout well made Negro Boy, named Tom, about five feet four inches, has on when he run off, a suit of mourning, he may probably change his name and dress. Whoever will apprehend the said Negro, or give information to the subscriber, so that he may be found, will be handsomely rewarded.
                HENRIETTA M'LEAN.

It is presumed that no masters of vessels or others will harbour of carry off the said Negro Boy, upon any pretext whatever.

The Royal Gazette, March 23, 1782.

RUN or taken away from the subscriber, the 16th of April 1782, a Negro man named Joe, about 5 feet 5 inches high, a slit in the upper part of his left ear, lately from Charles-Town, had on when he went away a blue short jacket, and straw hat. Whoever will secure said Negro, and bring him to No. 10, in John street so that the owner may have him again, shall be handsomely rewarded for their pains.
                JENKINSON JEANES.
All masters of vessels are forbid harbouring said Negro.

The Royal Gazette, April 20, 1782.

RAN-AWAY on the 21st inst. a negro boy named James; had on when he went off, a cap, one part red and the other part light coloured, a short brown coat, white dimity jacket, and homespun linen trowsers. He went off under pretence of searching for some horses that were lost, having a bundle in his hand: He is about sixteen or seventeen years of age.

A reward of two Guineas and all other reasonable expences, will be paid to any person who will deliver him to STEPHEN DAVENPORT, at the New-Slip, in St. James's-Street, No. 27.

The Royal Gazette, April 24, 1782.

DESERTED from the William, Navy victualler's boat, on the 25th inst. Andrew Skulman, about 5 feet 7 or 8 inches high, wears his own hair, and is of a dark complexion, likewise, Frederick Johnson, about the same stature, rather fat and has a fresh complexion; they both speak indifferent English, being Norwegians or Danes: Should be glad if any of the officers of the men of war meet them they would take them into his Majesty's service:—If they will return to the ship to which they belong, they will be received as usual.   Thomas Randall.

The Royal Gazette, April 27, 1782.

Eight Dollars Reward.

RUN AWAY on the 11th instant from the Subscriber a Negro Fellow named George, he is a likely fellow well set, about five feet high, full visaged speaks English middling well, had on when he went away a Pompadour coloured frock, and an old white Cassimir waistcoat, a pair of blue duffil trowsers, a round hat, and a pair of silver buckles in his shoes.

Any person apprehending, or giving information of said Negro to the subscriber at Hodzard and Graham's Hanover-Square, shall be entitled to the above reward.

ALEXANDER M'DONALD.   New-York, May 18, 1782.

N. B. All masters of vessels and others are warned from harbouring or carrying him off, as they may depend on being prosecuted to the utmost rigour of the law.

The Royal Gazette, May 18, 1782.

ONE GUINEA REWARD.

RUN away last Thursday from the subscriber, living at No. 20 Princess-Street, a negro boy named YORK, about thirteen years old, four feet four inches high, a tawny complexion, round visage, has a small scar over his left eye, has remarkable small ears; is well made and when clean dressed is a handsome boy, he has lately been employed in sweeping chimnies, and has on when he went away his old sweep cloths, blanket, &c. is much addicted to getting drunk, and has several times run away before, is supposed to have gone on board one of his Majesty's ships, as he has twice done before; he is, when sober, a smart, active boy, and very artful, he has been on board the Thames and Belisarius Frigates, and a cruise in the private sloop Pollux, Captain Ross; he came to this place four years ago with the subscriber, from the Island of Jamaica, and speaks broken English. All persons are forbid concealing said negro, all masters of vessels are requested not to take him off or harbour him, or they must answer it at their peril. Whoever secures the aforesaid boy, so that his master can get him again, shall be entitled to the above reward.

PETER CREIGHTON.   New-York, May 21st. 1782.

The Royal Gazette, May 22, 1782. See *The Royal Gazette,* May 20, 1780, and *The Royal Gazette,* March 17, 1781.

One Guinea Reward.

RUN AWAY, from the Subscriber, on the 4th of June, a NEGRO-BOY, named BACCHUS, about twelve years old: Had on when he went away, a white jacket, striped trowsers, no shoes nor hat. Whoever takes up the said Negro, and brings him to No. 20, Ann-Street, shall receive the above Reward.

The Royal Gazette, June 8, 1782.

RAN away from the Spanish Polacre St. Joseph, a Negro Boy from the Havana, named Francisco, aged about 15 or 16 years, marked with the small-pox, with small eyes, one less than the other; had on a Chintz Shirt with speckled Trowsers, speaks both English and Spanish; he is a Guinea Negro born in Congo.

Whoever brings him to his owner Captain Antonio Raymond, on board the Polacre, or David Sproat, Esq. Commissary of Prisoners in Maiden-Lane, shall receive a reward of Three Guineas.

The Royal Gazette, June 8, 1782.

Ten Dollars Reward.

RUN AWAY, Friday the 7th of June from the Subscriber, living at No. 7, King's Street, a tall slim yellow NEGRO-WENCH, named DINAH about 28 years of age, speaks good English. All persons are forbid concealing or employing said Negro-Wench, or they must answer it at their peril. Whoever secures the aforesaid Wench, so that her master can get her again, shall be intitled to the above Reward.

JAMES CALLOW.

The Royal Gazette, June 8, 1782; June 15, 1782.

FIVE DOLLARS REWARD.

RUN-AWAY from his master, on Sunday night, the 2d instant, a Negro Boy, named JACK, about 15 years of age, quite black, well set; and speaks broken English.—Had on when he went away, a blue and white striped linen jacket; a pair of parsons grey broad cloth trowsers, white homespun linen shirt, and a small round hat. He was lurking about town for two or three days, and it is imagined he is since got on board some vessel. Whoever brings said boy to his Master, at No. 198, Queen-Street, or secures him and gives information, so that his said master gets him again, shall receive the above reward. And all masters of vessels and others are forbid harbouring, concealing, or carrying off said Negro-Boy, as for so doing they shall be prosecuted with the utmost severity.

WILLIAM RHINELANDER.

The New-York Gazette; and the Weekly Mercury, June 10, 1782; *The Royal Gazette*, June 15, 1782. Minor differences between the papers.

RUN-away last Tuesday, from the subscriber in this city, a negro boy named Cesar Lee, a sweep chimney by trade: He is about 14 years old, and had on when he went away, a brown jacket and trowsers, much be daubed with soot; without any hat, shoes or stockings, and is supposed to be lurking

about town. Whoever takes up said lad, and secures him so that his master may have him again, shall receive five dollars reward from
JOHN POST, Cooper, at Peck's-Slip.
The New-York Gazette; and the Weekly Mercury, June 10, 1782.

DESERTED, Caesar Augustus, black driver to the horse department of the Royal Artillery, about five feet high, very much bandy-leg'd; had on when he went away, a regimental blue coat with a red collar, red waistcoat, linen trowsers and round hat. Whoever apprehends the said deserter, shall receive one Guinea reward, by applying to the office of the horse department, No. 16, Nassau Street. It is suspected that he is gone to Bergen Point, or on board some of the vessels in the harbour. Whoever harbours or conceals the said deserter, shall be prosecuted as the law directs.
The Royal Gazette, June 15, 1782.

Ten Dollars Reward.
RUN AWAY, on Wednesday the 1[2] instant, a NEGRO-BOY, named FRANK, about five feet high; aged 19 years, not very black: He may be known by one of his great toes which has been much bruised: He took with him a pale blue broad cloth Coat and Jacket; a brown Coat; corderoy Jacket and Breeches; a pair of fustain and striped Trowsers; a new castor Hat, and some other articles. It is imagined he intends going on board some privateer. The Masters of all vessels are warned not to take him, as they must answer it at their peril. Whoever will apprehend the said Negro Boy, or give information to the Subscriber, at Jamaica on Long-Island, shall receive the above Reward.
DOUWE DITMARS.
The Royal Gazette, June 15, 1782; June 19, 1782; *The New-York Mercury,* June 17, 1782.

New-York, June 20, 1782.
RAN-away from his master ANDREW VAN HORN, Blacksmith, living in Water-Street, No. 101, an Apprentice Boy named LARREY VAN NURDER; had on when he left his master, a long blue coat, black vest and breeches, white stockings, square buckles, and a round hat.
Whoever will give information of the said Apprentice to the above Andrew Van Horn, shall receive Five Dollars Reward, and all Masters of Vessels are hereby warned against carrying him off.
The Royal Gazette, June 26, 1782.

TWO DOLLARS REWARD.

RUN-AWAY from the subscriber, an apprentice Boy named John Abbot, a Blacksmith by trade, as the above Boy was advertised in Messrs. Robertson, Mills and Hick's paper. This is to caution all Captains and Owners of armed vessels and other inhabitants not to harbour the above run-away as they will answer it at their peril, the above reward will be given by applying to James Pendlebury,
between No. 26, and 27, Gold-Street. 15th June 1782.

The Royal Gazette, June 26, 1782.

WAS taken up in Smith's Clove, last February, a man by the name of Richard M'Donald, on suspicion of being a robber, on whom was found a silver watch, several pair of shoe and knee buckles, several gold rings, one of which is a family one, belonging to the Ross's. Any person interested in any of the above articles, may, on application to Captain Wright, of the Second New-York regiment, or the Printer hereof, be further informed.
June 18, 1782.

The New-Jersey Journal, July 3, 1782.

ONE GUINEA REWARD.

TO any person who will apprehend a certain black fellow of the name of SQUASH, who came from Rhode-Island, he belonged to a vessel called the Supple Jack, burnt at Sandy Hook, the said fellow stole to the value of Forty Pounds from Humphrey Wadey of Sandy Hook, consisting chiefly of womens cloaths, viz. a Green Silk Gown, 1 Brown Silk do. 1 Brocaded Silk, 1 Chrystal Buckle set in Silver, and several other articles, also Seven or Eight Pounds in cash. Enquire of the Printer.

The Royal Gazette, July 6, 1782.

RUN away, Monday the 1st of July, from the subscriber, a Negro Wench named Venus, about 26 years old; this is to warn all masters of vessels and others from harbouring said wench, as they shall answer it as the law directs. Whoever will apprehend the said wench and bring her to No. 27, Rosevelt Street, shall receive three Guineas reward.

Also three Guineas to any person that will inform him of the person that put the Advertisement in Mr. Lewis's paper about her yesterday, for I suppose they are are persons who decoyed the Wench away; if they are not black in colour they are black in action, they may be ashamed of their named, for they dare not sign it to the advertisement.
Charles Beardwine.

The Royal Gazette, July 6, 1782.

Ten Dollars Reward

RUN from the Subscriber, on Friday the 12th Instant, a MULATO BOY, named DAVID, about 13 or 14 Years old, round Visage, and stares much when questioned; had on when he went away, a scarlet Waistcoat and Trowsers. The above Reward will be paid any Person that brings him to No. 39, Dock street. All Persons are forwarned harbouring or employing him at their Peril. JOHN GOODRICH, jun. June 16, 1782.

The Royal Gazette, July 17, 1782.

Ten Guineas Reward.

RUN AWAY from their master's service, and are known to be lurking about this city the four following Negroes, viz. CATO RAMSAY, a stout able bodied man, formerly living with Mr. Willoughby Morgan, in Dover-Street.

DANIEL FISHER, a tall stout man somewhat marked with the Small Pox, and of a yellowish complexion 'tis said he lives on State Island where he has a wife and children.

LUKE WILSON, a short man, has a wife somewhere in town, and is well known among the Blacks.—The above three Negroes were all of them out in the privateer brig Fair America on her last cruize.

SAM, a short chunky man, about twenty-five years of age, and has often been seen at Ellis's Island.—Whoever will secure the above Negroes, and give information to the Printer, that they may be had again shall receive the above reward, or in proportion for either of them.

The Royal Gazette, July 17, 1782; July 20, 1782.

Four Guineas Reward.

RUN AWAY from the subscriber, a Negro Wench, about 24 years of age, middle sized, has a scar over her left eye. Had on when she went off a shift and under petticoat. She is well known in this city, having for several years carried Biscuits through it, she was formerly the property of John White, Baker.

Also, a NEGRO MAN,

Named CAESAR, about five feet four inches high, twenty eight years of age.—he is much addicted to strong liquors, formerly the property of Mrs. Cromeline, of Long-Island, and is well known, by his having carried Bread through the city.

Whoever takes up said Negroes, and delivers them to their master, shall have the above reward or TWO GUINEAS for each.

RICHARD JENKINS, No. 23, John Street.

The Royal Gazette, July 27, 1782. See *The New-York Gazette; and the Weekly Mercury*, January 6, 1783, *The Royal Gazette*, June 11, 1783, and *The Royal Gazette*, June 18, 1783 for Caesar.

TEN DOLLARS REWARD,

Ran away from the Subscriber on Monday the 12th Inst. a Molatta man named YORK, is a stout, well set likely fellow, about 5 feet 7 inches high, 32 years old, has a large corn on the little toe of his right foot which causes him to go lame either with new, or small shoes—had on when he went away, a French flax-coloured home-made coat, a brown corded linen Jacket, and dark brown home spun Breeches. Whoever takes up and secures said Molatta, so that the subscriber may have him again, shall receive the above reward, and all reasonable charges
        paid by   L'VINU[S] LANSING. New-City, August 19, 1782.
The New-York Gazetter or Northern Intelligencer, August 19, 1782.

TWO GUINEAS REWARD.

RUN AWAY on Tuesday morning the 20th ultimo, from Dr. David Brooks, of Cow Neck on Long-Island, a negro boy, named BEN, about five feet 6 inches high, he is tall, round faced, and of a yellow complexion, has a scar under one of his eyes from a burn, and has lost the first joints of three of his small toes on the left foot; he walks limping with one foot turned outward; had on when he went away, a brown homespun coat, with pewter buttons, a black sattin lasting jacket, tow shirt and trowsers, and a round hat.

Whoever will apprehend or secure the said negro slave, so that the owner may get him again, shall receive the above reward.

All masters of vessels and others are desired not to harbour or conceal said slave, as they will answer it at their peril.
The New-York Gazette; and the Weekly Mercury, September 2, 1782.

THIRTY DOLLARS REWARD

DESERTED the service of the subscriber on the 7th instant, one John Allibe, a Refugee from Long-Island, of about 28 or 30 years old, and of a midling stature, dark complexion, dark eyes and black hair, combed back and tied with a string behind; had on a flopt Hat, a white Linnen Coat, Vest and Overhalls, a Shoe maker by Trade, but often tells of a large fortune his Father has upon the Island, it is presumed said Allibe has gone into the Country. Whoever will take him up and confine him in Hartford Goal, or being him to me at Haddam, or give me such information that I may be able to secure him, shall be entitled to the above Reward, and all necessary
        charges paid, by   JOHN WILCOX.
                Haddam August 14th, 1782.

The Connecticut Courant, and Hartford Weekly Intelligencer, September 3, 1782.

ONE GUINEA REWARD,

RUN away from the subscriber, a negro boy named PETT or PETER, about twelve years of age; had on when he went away, a blue and white checked trowsers, coarse white linen shirt, and a white short jean waistcoat without sleeves. Whoever brings him to No. 56, between Beckman and Burling's Slips, Water-street, shall receive the above reward.

All masters of vessels are strictly forbid carrying him off.

The New-York Gazette; and the Weekly Mercury, September 9, 1782.

A GUINEA REWARD.

RAN away, a week since, a Negro MAN, named John Jackson, about twenty-two years of age, an indented servant, (three years of his time unexpired) about five feet five inches high, slight made, shaves and dresses hair, and waits at table well; had on when he went away, a light coloured Fustian Jacket, Waistcoat, and Breeches, and a cock'd Hat; but he has also a Green, and a Red short outside Jacket, and a pair of Black Silk Breeches. if the Master of any Ship or Vessel, or any other person harbours, secrets, or employs him, they may depend on being punished with the utmost rigour.

Whoever will secure and deliver him to Captain Cunningham, at the Provost, in this City, shall receive the above reward.

N. B. If he voluntarily returns to his Master, ask his pardon, and promise never to leave him again, he will be forgiven, and no notice taken of his ungrateful behaviour.

The Royal Gazette, September 25, 1782; September 28, 1782.

Ten Dollars Reward.

RUN-AWAY the 20th instant a Negro Wench named FLORA, about 24 years old, pretty tall long visaged, and has a slow mild way of talking, she was born in South-Carolina, and had a pass at Charles-Town of which she may attempt to avail herself by procuring a passage in the fleet bound to Charles-Town.

This is therefore to warn all masters of transports or other vessels from harbouring or employing her, as they may depend on being prosecuted to the utmost rigour of the law.

Any person who will secure and deliver her to Mr. Charles Keeling, on the New-Dock, or the subscriber at Mr. Stone's, No. 66, Water-Street, shall receive the above reward, and all charges paid.

N. B. If the Wench will come home she shall be forgiven.

WILLIAM O'BRIEN.

The Royal Gazette, September 25, 1782.

One Guinea Reward.
RUN AWAY from his Master a Negro Boy, named PETER, had on when he went away, a white linen shirt, white cloth waistcoat without sleeves, and striped Holland trowsers, Whoever will bring him to No. 56, Water-Street, shall receive the above reward.
B. Legrange.
The Royal Gazette, October 2, 1782.

RUN AWAY from George Powers, Butcher at Brooklyn Ferry, a young Negro Fellow, named CATO, about five feet six inches high, had of a blue short jacket, lined with green, and long linen trowsers. Whoever will bring him home, shall receive Two Guineas reward,
by George Powers.
The Royal Gazette, October 12, 1782.

TEN DOLLARS REWARD.
RUN away from the subscriber the 7th inst. a MOLATTO fellow, named DICK, 22 years of age, about 5 feet 2 or 3 inches high, middling thick, pitted with the small-pox, walks wide with his knees, pretty surly look; had on when he went away a tow shirt and trowsers, took with him an old check'd shirt and leather breeches, which he may have since put on. Whoever will secure said fellow so that I may have him again, shall receive the above reward and all reasonable charges
paid, by JOB MULFORD.
Staatsburgh, (State New-York) Oct. 8, 1782.
N. B. It is likely he will offer to enter on board some vessel to go to sea, or attempt to get within the enemy's lines—All masters of vessels are cautioned against carrying him off; and those who live near the sound, are desired to prevent his going to Long Island.
The Connecticut Journal, October 17, 1782; October 24, 1782; October 31, 1782.

DESERTED *from his Majesty's ship Albacore, John Nucam, aged 22 years, about five feet six inches high, fresh complexion, light brown hair tied, had on when he left the ship, a light coloured coat with white metal buttons, black waistcoat and breeches.*
Whoever will bring the above Deserter on board the Ship, shall receive the usual reward for securing deserters.
The Royal Gazette, October 26, 1782.

DESERTED
From his Majesty's Ship PROTHEE,
ROBERT BLACK, Seaman,
FIVE feet three inches, and three quarters of an inch high, about thirty two years of age, swarthy complexion, stout made, long visaged, grey eyes, short black hair, pitted with the small pox. All masters of merchant ships are hereby warned not to receive him into employ, or entertain him, on pain of being prosecuted according to law. Any person or person upon taking him up and securing him in the main guard at New-York, will be paid Two Guineas, over and above the public reward for taking up Deserters.
The Royal Gazette, October 26, 1782.

One Guinea Reward.
RUN AWAY from the Subscriber, a NEGRO BOY, about Thirteen Years of age; had on when he went away, a check shirt, Oznaburg trowsers, an old red coat with a black collar and cuffs, has a small bare spot on one side of his forehead, a little within the hair. Whoever brings him to the Subscriber, at No. 56, between Beekman's and Burling Slips, Water-Street, shall receive the above reward. All Masters of vessels and others, are strictly forbid harbouring, concealing, or carrying him off, at their peril.
Barnardus Lagrange.
The Royal Gazette, October 26, 1782.

One Guineas Reward,
RUN away some time ago, a stout NEGRO BOY, named TOM, about five feet four inches high; had on when he run off, a long blue coat with a yellow collar, blue jacket, and Linen Trowsers. Whoever will bring him to the Printer, or give information where he may be found, will be entitled to the above reward.
N. B. It is presumed that no person whatsoever will harbour or carry off said Negro Boy.
The Royal Gazette, November 2, 1782.

A NEGRO BOY went off from his Master a few days ago, named JACK, about eleven years old, his cloathing was an olive coloured thickset jacket, with a red cloth collar, a check shirt, and Oznaburg trowsers. Whoever takes said boy up, and brings him to No. 201, water-street, near the Coffee-House, shall be rewarded for their trouble. Should he have gone on board any of the vessels in this harbour, his master will be much obliged if the commander will send him on shore, to the above directions.
The New-York Gazette; and the Weekly Mercury, November 3, 1782.

Four Dollars Reward.
RAN AWAY from the Subscriber, living in Duanesburgh, a MOLATTO WENCH named RACHEL; about 15 years of age, tall and slender made: Had on when she went off, a white short gown, or a white homespun ditto, strip'd homespun petticoat, or a white linen ditto, with small red sprig, blue yarn stockings, high heel'd shoes, and tow cloth shift. Whoever apprehends said Runaway, and commits her to any gaol in this State, or brings her to the subscriber, shall receive FOUR DOLLARS in Specie, and all reasonable charges. ALEXANDER M'DOUGALL.
Duanesburgh, November 11, 1782.
The New-York Gazetteer or Northern Intelligencer, November 18, 1782; November 25, 1782.

Ten Dollars Reward.
RUN AWAY on the 28th ultimo, from the Subscriber, a MOLATTO, named Nicholas (commonly called Claas); He is about five feet eight or ten inches high, slender made, large eyes, much given to liquor: He had on when he went off, a whitish stuff coat, striped linen waistcoat, linen breeches, blue yarn stockings, tow cloth shirt, and large buckles in his shoes. Whoever apprehends said Runaway, and commits him to any Gaol in this State, shall be paid TEN DOLLARS in Specie, and all reasonable charges, by PH. SCHUYLER.
Saratoga, November 4, 1782.
The New-York Gazetteer or Northern Intelligencer, November 18, 1782; November 25, 1782.

RUN-away from Isaac Smith of Dutchess County, State of New-York, on the 8th day of May last, a Negro Man named PETER, about 20 years old, about 5 feet 10 inches high, black but not of the blackest sort, thick lips, he was at Deerfield about the first of June last, and proposed going down Connecticut to look for work. Run-away at the same time a Negro man belonging to Lewis Graham, a middle-size fellow, about 30 years old, some marked with the small pox, very talkative, he was lately in the State of Vermont and very narrowly escaped being taken, and now supposed to be gone to look for the above-mentioned Negro, his name is HARRY. Ten Dollars reward and all reasonable charges shall be paid for either of them, by ISAAC SMITH, and LEWIS GRAHAM.
Dutchess County, November 15, 1782.
The Connecticut Courant, November 26, 1782; December 3, 1782.

RUNAWAY,
From the Subscriber,

On Sunday last, the 17*th Instant,*
A likely young Guinea NEGRO FELLOW, named NERO: He had on when he went away, an ordinary shirt, a blue frized shooting jacket, lined with green baize, had four slack pockets and hair buttons, brown cloth trowsers, and an old flapped hat; he also carried with him a new suit of gray coating, the waistcoat and coat lined with green baize, with plain white metal buttons, and a pair of boots. Whoever will secure the said Negro, and deliver him to the subscriber, at Newtown, Long-Island, or to Mr. Robert Dunbar, No. 37, Maiden-Lane, New-York, shall receive FIVE GUINEAS Reward.   Wm. GARDEN.   *Newtown, Nov.* 22, 1782.
The Royal Gazette, November 30, 1782.

Twenty Dollars Reward.
Ran away from the subscriber, on the 20th instant,
A Negro-Boy,
NAMED BILLY, lately from the Island of Jamaica, about twenty years of age, and he is about 5 feet 6 inches high, he was born in Guinea, and speaks bad English, is of a very black complexion, with a yellow cast in his eyes, he is branded on the breast with a D. S. has a scar over his right eye, which is not quite healed up, and another scar on his chin; he had on when he went off the common dress of a sailor, viz. a blue jacket, a pair of blue trowsers, round hat and a check shirt; as he made some voyages at sea with me, it is probable he may look for employment in some vessel, therefor masters of vessels and others are forewarned not to harbour or carry him off.

The above Reward of 20 Dollars will be paid by Mr. Daniel M'Cormick, to whoever takes up and secures said Negro-Boy.
PATRICK REDMOND.
The Royal Gazette, November 30, 1782. See *The New-York Gazette; and the Weekly Mercury*, January 6, 1783.

One Guinea and a Half Reward.
RUN-AWAY, on the 15th ult. and INDENTED SERVANT-BOY about 17 years of age, named *Samuel Wilkins*, he has fair hair, a little pitted with the small pox, is a smart active boy; had on when he went away, a blue jacket, round hat, and long trowsers, shoes and stockings, plated buckles. The above reward will be given to any person that will secure him or bring him on board of his former ship, *General Friends Transport*, one of of the last fleet from England.

N. B. All Masters of vessels and others, are forwarned not to conceal or carry him off, as they will answer for the same at their peril.
The Royal Gazette, December 18, 1782.

1783

One Guinea Reward.

RUN away from the subscriber, a Negro Man named CAESAR, formerly the property of Mr. Cromeline, of Long-Island. He is about 26 years old, has a very simple look, with a scar over his eye brow, much given to liquor; had on when he went away, a round hat, blue jacket, brown cloth trowsers and a pair of boots.

N. B. He is well known in being used to carry about bread and biscuits. Whoever will bring him to his master, or give information so that he may be found shall receive the above reward.

          RICHARD JENKINS,   No. 23, John-street.

The New-York Gazette; and the Weekly Mercury, January 6, 1783. See *The Royal Gazette*, July 27, 1782, *The Royal Gazette,* June 11, 1783; and *The Royal Gazette*, June 18, 1783.

Five Dollars Reward.

RAN AWAY from the Subscriber, on the 24th of December ultimo, a NEGRO MAN named *CAESAR*, about 40 years of age, about 5 feet 6 or 7 inches high, has had the rheumatism in his right knee, which occasions him to limp a little: Had on when he went away, a light brown homespun coat, a swan-skin jacket something wore, striped trowsers, and an old fashioned cat-skin cap—Talks English and Dutch. Whoever will apprehend said runaway, and return him to his master, or confine him in the City-Hall, in Albany, or otherwise give such information that the subscriber can have him again, shall receive the above reward.

          DIRCJ VAN VEIGHTEN.

          Ramsey's-Bush, in Tryon County, January 4, 1783.

The New-York Gazetteer or Northern Intelligencer, January 6, 1783; January 13, 1783; January 27, 1783.

Twenty Dollars Reward.

RUN away from his master, a negro boy named BILLY, lately from the island of Jamaica, about twenty years of age, and near about 5 feet 6 inches high: He was born in Guinea, and speaks bad English, is of a very black complexion, with a yellow cast in his eyes; he is branded on the breast with a D. S. He had on when he went off the common dress of a sailor, with a blue jacket. a pair of blue trowsers, round hat and check shirt. As he has made some voyages to sea, it is probable he may look for employment in some vessel, therefore masters of vessels and others are forewarn'd not to harbour or carry him off.

          DANIEL M'CORMICK.

The New-York Gazette; and the Weekly Mercury, January 6, 1783. See *The Royal Gazette*, November 30, 1782.

RAN away from the Subscriber, living in Schenectady, on or about the seventh instant, a *MOLATTO WENCH*, named *Sarah* or *Sally*, she is well made, and of a good size; well cloathed—speaks English, High and Low Dutch, well—— pitted a little with the small-pox, wears her hair tied, and generally a high cap—She is a very subtle cunning Wench. Whoever will return said Wench to the subscriber, or give such information that the owner can have her again, shall have *FIVE DOLLARS* reward, and all reasonable charges, paid by
    NICHOLAS WEAVER. *Schenectady, February* 12, 1783.
 The New-York Gazetteer or Northern Intelligencer, February 17, 1783; February 24, 1783; March 3, 1783.

      TEN DOLLARS REWARD,
RUN away from the subscriber, on the 9th instant, a Negro Man named BILL, about 6 feet 9 inches high, [*sic*] well built, about 26 years of age, talks good English, had on when he went away a white Shirt, white Jacket and Breeches and blanket Coat, white yarn Stockings, Silver Shoe and Knee Buckles, but may change his dress, as he took all his cloaths with him, it is supposed he will endeavour to get into New-York, as he was taken at the capture of Cornwallis. Whoever will secure said Negro, or give information so that his Master may get him again, shall receive the above reward and all reasonable charges.
    REUE CROSUIER.   Albany, February 10, 1783.
 The Connecticut Courant and Weekly Intelligencer, February 18, 1783; February 25, 1783; March 4, 1783.

RUN-AWAY from the subscriber on the 2d inst a certain lad named William Crozford, by trade a Shoemaker; had on when he left his master a great coat, a red jacket, and an under one, a new blue jacket, with yellow metal buttons, a pair of blue trowsers, and a pair of half boots; he is about 16 years of age, pitted with the small-pox, of long stature, and was born in England. Whoever secures said lad, so that his master may have him again, shall receive One Guinea reward.
    HENRY SPARING. *New-York, April* 4, 1783.
 The Royal Gazette, April 5, 1783.

TEN GUINEAS REWARD.

RAN-AWAY, from on board the Ship Commerce, David Martindale, Commander, lying in the East-River, about four days ago, *Three Apprentice Boys*, viz. John Curlett, aged 17 years, wears his own hair, of a brown complexion, much pitted with the small pox.— John Murphy, aged 16 years, wears his own hair, of a light complexion.— William Wood, aged 13 years, wears his own hair, of light complexion, has a mark on his left knee.—Whoever will give information of the above Deserters, shall be entitled to Ten Guineas Reward, or in proportion for either of them, by applying to the Master, on board, or to Joshua Mease and Co. No. 191, Water-street.   *New-York, April* 4, 1783.
The Royal Gazette, April 5, 1783.

MADE his escape from the goal in New-Haven, on the night of the fifth of April instant, DENNIES HART, a native of Long-Island, about 25 years of age: Had on a blue great-coat, were his hair: Committed for going over the Long-Island.—Whoever will return said Hart to said goal, or will give information of the person or persons who furnished him with the tools to made his escape, shall receive THREE DOLLARS for either of them, if delivered to the subscriber,
         STEPHEN MUNSON, Goaler.   New-Haven, April 17.
The Connecticut Journal, April 17, 1783; April 24, 1783.

RAN away from the Subscriber, on the Night of the 7th of April inst. a NEGRO MAN, named Richard, about 5 Feet 10 Inches high, 25 Years of Age, is very much pitted with the Small-Pox; he had on a blue Jacket, dark London brown Breeches, is a Native of Virginia, and speaks good English—has followed the Sea for a Number of Years. He has a Wife in New-York, and is supposed to be gone that Way.—Whoever will apprehend the said Negro, and return him to the Subscriber, shall receive the above Reward, and all necessary Charges.
         ALFRED ARNOLD.   *Providence, April* 11, 1783.
The Providence Gazette And Country Journal, April 12, 1783; April 19, 1783; April 26, 1783.

ONE GUINEA REWARD.

RUN AWAY, on Sunday the 6th instant, from his Master, a Negro Boy, eighteen years of age, about five feet six inches high, named EBB. *Had on when he went off, a Brown Coat, made French fashion, Grey Cloth Jacket, Black Breeches, and a large brimed bound Hat. Whoever takes up said Negro, and returns him to Captain Joshua Pell. in the Bowery, shall be*

entitled to the above Reward, and all necessary expences. All masters of vessels are cautioned not to take him away.   New-York, April 9, 1783.
   The Royal Gazette, April 12, 1783.

RUN-AWAY from the Adventure, Joseph Mellanby, Master, JOHN EDMOND, a small boy, about 12 years of age, of a pale complexion, strait black hair.—Also, CANNY EDMOND, his brother, about 16 or 17 years of age, of middling stature, has light brown hair.—Whoever will bring either, or both of them, on board the said vessel, shall be handsomely rewarded.
   The Royal Gazette, April 16, 1783.

ONE GUINEA Reward,
RUN-away from Mathew Daniel, living at No. 34. Duke-street, a negro boy called DUFF: Had on when he went away, a brown jacket, new fustian trowsers, and a new wool hat. Whoever apprehends said boy, or gives information, so that his master may get him again, shall have the above reward. All masters of vessels and others, are fore-warned to harbour or conceal said Negro-Boy, as they must answer for the same.
   The New-York Gazette; and the Weekly Mercury, April 21, 1783; April 28, 1783; *The Royal Gazette*, April 26, 1783; April 30, 1783. Minor differences between the papers. See *The Royal Gazette*, June 30, 1781.

ABSCONDED *about three weeks past a Negro Wench, the property of William Wilson, named PEG, about 5 feet 3 inches high, 20 years of age, a native of South-Carolina. suspected of having a forged freedom pass. Any person or persons that will deliver the said wench to Mr Hugh Miller, Fly-Market, shall receive One Guinea reward. These are therefore to forewarn all persons from harbouring, concealing, or taking away said Negro Wench on their Peril.*
   N. B. The said Negro formerly lived with Mr. Cochran, Sign of Lord Cornwallis, Water-street.
   The Royal Gazette, April 26, 1783.

EIGHT DOLLARS REWARD.
RUN-AWAY from the Subscriber, on the 23d inst. April, a Mulatto Negro Man, named *Sam*, the property of the Subscriber, about 5 feet 9 inches high, well made, and somewhat marked with the small-pox: had on when he went off, a brown short coat and waistcoat, and cloth trowsers, speaks both English and Low Dutch, and formerly lived in Bergen.—Whoever will deliver or secure the said Negro, so that his master may have him again, or

to George and Jeronimus Remsen, shall be entitled to the above reward, by applying to Rem A. Remsen, at the Wallabough, Long-Island.
The Royal Gazette, April 30, 1783; May 7, 1783.

SIX POUNDS Reward.

RUN-away from the subscriber, a negro boy about eighteen years of age, stout and well countenanced, known by the name of Frederick. He was some time waiter upon Col. Weltner of the 33d regt. and is supposed to be about this city or on Long-Island. Whoever takes up said boy, and delivers him to Mr. John Vanderhoven, near White Hall, or secures him in goal so that his owner may get him again, shall have the above reward, and all reasonable charges paid.   ISAAC COTHEAL.
The New-York Gazette; and the Weekly Mercury, May 5, 1783.

FIVE GUINEAS REWARD.

RAN-AWAY from the subscriber, on Monday evening the 6th instant, a negro man named JACK; he had on when he went off a check shirt, blue waistcoat, a blue coatee with a red cape, long white trowsers, white stockings, &c. can speak very little English to be understood, stutters much in his speech, is about 23 years of age, has seven scars on his left arm, and a small scar on his nose.

All house-keepers are forwarned harbouring him at their peril: Masters of vessels are forbid concealing or carrying him off, as they will be prosecuted to the utmost Rigour of the law.
VALENTINE NUTTER.

N. B. Ten Guineas will be given to discover the person that enticed him away.
The New-York Gazette; and the Weekly Mercury, May 12, 1783; May 19, 1783.

WHIGS, TAKE CARE!!!

It is reported, by a person directly from New-York, that the notoriously infamous HOEG declares he will not go to Nova-Scotia, but to Canada, thro' this State, and that he will murder three Persons in Fish-Kill, or its vicinity.—N. B. Might it not answer a valuable purpose to *immediately* offer a proper reward for this daring villain, *dead or alive*, and set a subscription on foot to raise the money? If this is adopted, there will be a propriety in describing his person as accurately as possible, as he will, no doubt, disguise himself, and conceal his [   ]ms. Other precautions that are not eligible to be mentioned at this time, may be taken, to prevent his passing through.
The Salem Gazette, May 22, 1783.

RUN-AWAY from the Subscriber, living at
No. 120, Water-street, near the New Slip,
A Negro Girl, named POLL,
about 13 years of age, very black, marked with the Small-Pox, and had on when she went away a red cloath petticoat, and a light blue short gown, home made. Whoever will take up and secure the said Girl, so that the owner may get her, shall be handsomely reward by
    Thomas Brinckley.   New-York, May 28, 1783.
The Royal Gazette, June 11, 1783; June 14, 1783. See *The Royal Gazette*, July 16, 1783.

ONE GUINEA REWARD.
RUN-AWAY, a *Negro Man*, named *Caesar*, about 26 years old, 5 feet 4 inches high, an honest look, smooth face, a scar over one of his eyes: Had on when he went away, a light coloured cloth waistcoat, without sleeves, white metal hollow buttons, a pair of jean breeches, shoes and stockings, a half worn white hat: He is well known by carrying bread and baskets about the streets. Whoever gives information where he may be found, shall receive the above reward, from the Subscriber, at No. 23, John's Street.
   RICHARD JENKINS.
The Royal Gazette, June 11, 1783; June 14, 1783. See *The Royal Gazette*, July 27, 1782, *The New-York Gazette; and the Weekly Mercury*, January 6, 1783, and *The Royal Gazette*, June 18, 1783.

Twenty Dollars Reward,
RUN away from his Master on the 12th instant, a Negro Boy named Sam, aged about 16 years, five feet high, slim made, is remarkable in turning up the whites of his eyes when spoke to; had on when he went away a white shirt, brown linen trowsers, a blue and white check jacket, shoes, and a white round hat. Any person who will secure said Negro, and bring him back to No. 176, Water Street, shall receive the above reward.

All Masters of vessels and others are hereby forewarned not to harbour or carry off said Negro, as they will answer for the same at their peril.
The Royal Gazette, June 14, 1783.

TWO GUINEAS REWARD.
RUN-AWAY, a *Negro Man*, named *Caesar*, about 26 years old, 5 feet 4 inches high, an honest look, smooth face, a scar over one of his eyes: Had on when he went away, a light coloured cloth waistcoat, without sleeves, white metal hollow buttons, a pair of jean breeches, shoes and stockings, a half worn white hat: He is well known by carrying bread and baskets about

the streets. Whoever gives information where he may be found, shall receive the above reward, from the Subscriber, at No. 23, John's Street.
                    RICHARD JENKINS.
    N. B. He was formerly the property of Mr. Cromelin, on Long-Island, and supposed to be lurking about there.
    The Royal Gazette, June 18, 1783; June 28. 1783; July 2, 1783; July 16, 1783; July 23, 1783. All but the first ad show a reward of ten dollars at the top of the ad. See *The Royal Gazette,* July 27, 1782, *The Royal Gazette,* June 11, 1783, and *The New-York Gazette; and the Weekly Mercury,* January 6, 1783.

                            Ten Dollars Reward.
RUN-AWAY on Monday the 9th of June, from Long Island, a negro man named JACK, formerly belonged to John Acker, of New-York; had on when he went away a brown coat, red jacket, and leather breeches, with a large flopt hat. Whoever secures the above negro, and delivers him at No. 174, Water-street, shall receive the above reward. All masters of vessels, and others, are herby forwarned not to harbour or carry off said negro, as they shall answer the same at their peril.
    The Royal Gazette, June 18, 1783.

STOLEN out of the pasture of the subscriber in the Oblong, Precinct of Little Nine Partners, on the night of the 12th inst. a light sorrel mare, six years old, fourteen hands high, with a blaze in her face, trots single footed, canters well. Likewise stolen a saddle with a plad housing, fringed on the back part, a light coloured great coat with the buttons chiefly off before, a faded green strait bodied coat, and a grey vest, brown overalls, and a castor hat bound with black ferret. The thief is one John Hoffman, of a dark complexion, long black hair, tied behind with a strong, and hangs loose. Whosoever will take up and secure said thief so that he may be brought to justice, shall have ten Dollars reward and all necassary [*sic*] paid.
                URIAH LAWRENCE.   June 13, 1783.
    Vermont Gazette, June 19, 1763; June 16, 1763; July 3, 1783.

                            TEN DOLLARS Reward.
RUN away the 7th inst. from the subscriber, a negro man named RETUS, aged 21 years, a thick-well set fellow, about 5 feet 7 inches high, speaks English well, and plays on a fiddle; took with him a bundle of cloathes, viz. one suit of mixed blue, one suit of dark purple, one pair of brown velvet breeches, with shirts, stockings and trowsers, three pair shoes, one pair boots, and a fiddle.—Whoever take up the said negro and returns or secures him, that his master may have him again, shall receive Two Dollars, and all

reasonable charges paid. All persons are forbid trading with said negro. All masters of vessels are forbid carry off said runaway, or concealing him.
        WILLIAM CLARK. Brookhaven (Long-Island) June 8, 1783.
The Connecticut Gazette; and the Universal Intelligencer, June 23, 1783; July 4, 1783; July 11, 1783.

RUN-AWAY,
From the Subscriber, on Monday the 19*th ult.*
An Apprentice Boy, named
JOHN MULLAN.

    He has carried the *New-York Gazette and Weekly Mercury* to the Customers, in part of this City, for five years, and is well known. He is about 19 years old; his own black hair, and is a well looking lad.—As he has frequently been seen about the Swamp in this city, and supposed to be entertained by some person there, ONE GUINEA will be paid to whoever will give information of the party offending, so that they may be brought to justice; and a handsome reward to any person that brings him to
        HUGH GAINE.
    N. B. Masters of vessels are particularly cautioned not to employ, conceal, or carry off said apprentice.
    The New-York Gazette; and the Weekly Mercury, June 30, 1783.

Fifteen Dollars Reward.

RUN-away on Friday the 13th instant, a negro wench named LUCE, about 30 years of age, middling, or rather low in stature; her right cheek stained with a different colour from her natural black, carries her head remarkably high, and seems to have a difficulty to open her eyes; she is very noisy and quarrelsome in the streets; had on when she went away a green striped stuff gown that has been washed, a dark blue moreen petticoat, a gauze cap and pink ribbons, no hat, she had also with her a dark purple callicoe gown, she commonly goes by the name of Luce Price, from her having formerly lived with Edward Price, the pilot, on Cruger's wharf; she has been seen two or three times since she run away about the streets, the last time at the Fly Market, supposed to be going over the Ferry, where she sometimes used to run, as also to Harlaem and Shrewsbury: It is supposed she is lurking somewhere in this city and afraid to come home. Any person who will discover her to her master, at No. 49, the corner near the Exchange, so that he may apprehend her shall receive the above reward; and if said wench will voluntarily return home, her master will forgive her.—All persons are cautioned not to conceal, harbour, or carry off said wench.
    The New-York Gazette; and the Weekly Mercury, June 30, 1783.

Twelve Pounds Reward,
RANAWAY from the SUBSCRIBER, a very black NEGRO Man named David, he is five feet eight inches high, speaks good English, his left leg much larger than his right, he walks very aukward, has a smiling way and a deceiving tongue; partly lost the sight of one of his eyes, very thick thigh'd, as you will find but few, he is as I think about 42 years of age: Ranaway from his Master the 28th of November last. Whoever apprehends the said NEGRO Man and delivers him to me, shall be paid the above reward.
        PATRICK CLARK   Albany, June [2]6, 1783.
The New-York Gazetteer or Northern Intelligencer, June 30, 1783.

Six Pounds Reward.
RANAWAY from the Subscriber, living in Green-Bush, near Albany, on the 21st instant, a Molatto Fellow, named ROB; 25 years of age, about 5 feet 5 inches high, is very likely, had black hair curling on the back part of his head, but since he ranaway, I am informed, he has purchased himself a cue, and it is probable he will have his hair cued—has two scars near one of his eyes; he speaks good English and Dutch, and pretends to be a great judge of horses; he is remarkably nice, and took with him several suits of cloaths, and a pair of neat boots. Whoever takes up said runaway, and confines him in any jail, and informs the subscriber, so that he may get him again, shall have the above reward, with all reasonable charges, and many   thanks from   JOHN J. VAN RENSSELAER.
   N. B. He has done very little work for the 3 last years, as he was inclined to a consumption, but laterly feigned himself so.
                Green-Bush, near Albany, June 30, 1783.
   The New-York Gazetteer or Northern Intelligencer, June 30, 1783; July 14, 1783.

ONE GUINEA REWARD.
RUN AWAY from Peter Alexander Alaire, on Saturday the 5th instant, a MULLATO BOY, named Jack, between 11 and 12 years of age, full and flat faced; had on when he went away, an Osnaburg shirt and tow trowsers, supposed to be harboured by some free negroes in town. Any person who will apprehend said Negro Boy, and bring him to No. 14, in Wall-street, shall receive the above reward.
All Masters of Vessels are forwarned to carry him off.
                                       New-York, July 9, 1783.
   The Royal Gazette, July 9, 1783.

RUN-AWAY from the Subscriber, a NEGRO GIRL, named POLL, about 11 years of age, pitted with the small-pox; had on when she went away, an

old green callimanco petticoat, and a light blue striped homespun short gown: Whoever shall find and secure her, till her master gets her again, shall be handsomely rewarded.
        THOMAS BRINCKLEY,
          No. 51, Little Dock-Street, at the Corner of the Exchange.
The Royal Gazette, July 16, 1783. See *The Royal Gazette*, June 11, 1783.

           EIGHT DOLLARS REWARD.

RUN-AWAY from the Subscriber, whilst in West-Chester County, New-York State, the 23d of July last, a Negro fellow, named JACK, 26 years old, about five feet high, thick set, he can read and write, and has served as a hostler this some time past to take care of the noted horses, *Pastime* and *Goldfinder*; and it is likely he will make towards Rhode-Island, as he formerly came from thence: He had on when he went away, an old white short brown jacket, and a pair of striped trouser; a wool hat, bound with white and cock'd, no shoes nor stockings on. And I desire all Captains of vessels, to beware not to take on or receive such fellow on board; and whoever will take up and secure him, so that the owner may get him again, shall have the above reward and all reasonable charges, per me,
        DEMAS FORD, or JOSEPH PURDY.
The Royal Gazette, August 2, 1783.

         TWO DOLLARS Reward,

ABSCONDED, on Tuesday last, the 19th ult. an Apprentice Lad, named WILLIAM STERLING; he is twelve years of age, about four feet high, full faced, very much freckled, short red hair: Had on when he went away, a short dark fustain jacket, a check shirt, and a pair of Oznaburg trowsers.— The above reward will be paid to any person or persons that will bring the said Boy to No. 4, Little Dock-street.

    All Masters of Vessels and others, are forbid harbouring or carrying off said Apprentice Boy, as they well be dealt with as the law directs.
The Royal Gazette, August 2, 1783.

WHEREAS Rhuba the wife of me the Subscriber, did on the evening of the 3d day of April last, voluntarily elope from my bed and board, and retire to Pitts-Town; where she has since been criminally familiar with an abandon'd villain [Sylvester Summers.] These are therefore to forbid all persons harbouring her, or transporting her from place to place, as villains have since here elopement done; or trusting her in any respect on my account; for I will never be accountable for any debt contracted by her after this date.
        JONATHAM DUNHAM. Kings District, June 2, 1783.

The New-York Gazetter or Northern Intelligencer, August 4, 1783.

RAN-AWAY from the Subscriber, on the Night of the 25th inst. a NEGRO MAN named QUOM, short stature, well set, has on a brown Cloth Coat with green Basket Buttons, Linen under Cloths, about 20 years old, speaks low Dutch and English,—Also, an apprentice Lad, named Herculus Lent, about 17 years old, had on a brown Worsted Coat, a white Castor Hatt,—each of them wore a pair of large Oval carved block-tin Buckles. Whoever secures the NEGRO, and gives word to THEODOROUS V. W. GRAHAM, Esq: in Albany, shall receive TEN DOLLARS Reward, and all reasonable charges, or on notice given to the Subscriber, the Reward and charges will be paid by THOMAS STORM.

Hopewell, Dutchess County, July 28, 1783.

The New-York Gazetter or Northern Intelligencer, August 4, 1783.
See *Vermont Gazette*, August 21, 1783.

TEN DOLLARS REWARD.

RAN-AWAY from the Subscriber, living in Albany, on the 25th of July, a black NEGRO FELLOW named TOM; 22 years old, about 5 Feet Eight Inches high, has a scar below one of his eyes, his knees bent inwardly,—he speaks good Dutch and English: Had on when he went off, a Tow shirt and Overalls, an old wool Hatt. Whoever takes up said Runaway and confines him in any Goal, and informs the Subscriber, so that he may get him again, shall receive the above reward, with all reasonable charges, and many thanks, from   PETER GANSEVORT.   Albany, August 4, 1783.

The New-York Gazetteer or Northern Intelligencer, August 4, 1783.

DESERTED from the Barrack Master-General's department, the first day of this month, a Driver named THOMAS ALLEN. Whoever will secure the said deserter, and bring him to the Waggon-Yard at the back of the new Bridewell, shall receive three dollars reward.

     A. ROBERTSON, Waggon-Master, B. M Gen. Department.

The Royal Gazette, August 4, 1783.

Eight Dollars Reward.

RUN-away on on Sunday morning the 3d instant, a tall, stout, negro wench and her child; the wench is named LUCY, the child VENUS. The wench is very much pitted with the small pox, and her feet is so large that she is obliged to wair mens shoes. She took with her two short gowns, and two petticoats, one striped bottom short gown and a yellow ground callicoe one; one black petticoat and one other supposed green, either of which she wears. The child had on a tow cloth frock, has a scar on her shoulder, and is about 5 or 6 years old. Her mother is about 28 years. Whoever gives information to the printer so as the owner may have them again, shall receive the above reward.

All persons are forewarned not to conceal, harbour or carry off the said wench and her child, as they will have to answer for it at their peril.

The New-York Gazette; and the Weekly Mercury, August 11, 1783.

RAN-Away a few days ago, a little Negro Boy, had on a blue coat with red cuffs and collar, a pair of Indian trowsers, with buttons all down the sides; he has got marks on the fingers of his left hand like a burn. All Masters of vessels and others are warned against keeping said Negro; any information of said Boy, will be thankfully received, and all reasonable charges paid.

    Enquire of Mr. Rivington. *New-York, August* 15, 1783.

The Royal Gazette, August 16, 1783; August 20, 1783; August 27, 1783.

SANCHO, a Guinea Negro Man, about twenty-four years old, five feet seven inches high, or thereabouts; remarkably black, walks light and straight, on the right hand has the little finger, and the next two contracted, so as he cannot open them; came from Georgia with the Hessian troops. Any one who will bring him to No. 6, in Beekman Street, the Tobacco Manufactory, shall receive Two Guineas Reward.

The Royal Gazette, August 20, 1783.

RAN away from the subscriber, in the night of the twenty fifth instant, a Negro Man named QUOM, of a small stature, well made, about 20 years of age, had on a brown coat with green basket buttons, linen under cloths, speaks low Dutch and English. Also, an apprentice lad, named Hercules Lent, about seventeen years old, light hair, his left knee somewhat stiff, a down look, had on a brown worsted coat & dimity under cloths. Each of them wore away a pair of oval carved block-tin shoe-buckles. Whoever secures the negro, or gives word to Theodorous V. W. Graham, Esq: in Albany, shall there receive TEN DOLLARS Reward, & all reasonable charges, or, if delivered to the subscriber, the said reward and charges shall
    be paid by   THOMAS STORM.

Hopewell, Dutchess County, State of New-York, July 28, 1783.

Vermont Gazette, August 21, 1783. See *The New-York Gazetter or Northern Intelligencer*, August 4, 1783.

Five Dollars Reward a Head,

RUN-away from the subscriber, on Saturday the 16th inst. three negro men, who it is likely will keep together; one of them is named William, a slim

fellow, 27 years of age, about 5 feet 9 inches high, has a remarkable scar across his nose, speaks very good English and Low Dutch: Had on when he went away an old brown coloured coat, and a blue cloth jacket, a pair of new spotted breeches, and linen stockings. Another fellow goes by the name of Harry, about 5 feet 7 inches high, about 30 years of age, had on a linsey woolsey coat coloured grey, a white jacket of ditto, striped overhawls, and new shoes; took with him a short pair of white linen breeches. The third is named John, about 39 years of age, 5 feet 8 inches high, well set, has a remarkable scar on his upper lip: Had on a brown cloth coat, a blue cloth jacket, linen breeches, and black trowsers. Whoever secures the above negroes, so that their masters may have them again, shall have the above reward, and all reasonable charges,
    paid by us,   DAVID HASBROUCK.   NATHANIEL LEFEVER.
    ANDRIES LEFEVER, jun.
New-Paltz, in Ulster County, August 18, 1783.
The New-York Gazette; and the Weekly Mercury, August 25, 1783.

ONE GUINEA Reward.
RUN AWAY, on Thursday the 2d instant, a Negro Man, named CHARLES, about five feet six inches high, with a scar on one side of his Face, of a black complection, resembling an Indian, with a large top before: Had on when he went away, a sailor's blue jacket, leather breeches, worsted stockings, speaks bad English. Whoever will bring said Negro to the Printer, or the Subscriber, will be entitled to the above reward.
    CHARLES M'LEAN.
N. B. It is preseumed that no Captains of Vessels or others, will harbour the said Negro, at they will answer the same at their peril.
The Royal Gazette, September 3, 1783.

RUN AWAY, from the Widow Suydam, at Flushing, a Negro Wench, named PEG, about twenty years of age, very black, thick set.—Whoever will secure the said Wench, shall receive TWO GUINEAS reward, by the Widow Suydam, and all reasonable charges paid.
September 6, 1783.
The Royal Gazette, September 10, 1783.

TO THE PUBLIC.
WHEREAS MARTHA CAFFIELD, the Wife of Thomas Caffield, Lieutenant in the North Carolina Regiment, is secretly conveyed away from him, and kept concealed, supposed to be by her Mother, Mrs. Melleson Carmer, of Hempstead, in Queen's County, on Nassau Island, in the State of New York, on account of having her prohibited from going with her

living Husband, to the Province of Nova-Scotia, or to St. Augustine: Wherefore the said Thomas Caffield, is under the due necessity of cautioning the Public of harbouring, entertaining, or trusting her, the said Martha, as he is determined to pay no debts of her contracting from the date hereof; though at same time doth assure her, that if she will return to her lawful Husband, she will be kindly received, and shall receive, *for the future*, all the indulgence necessary to be allowed by a tender Husband to a virtuous Wife.

  Witness his hand, at the City of New-York, the
    8th Day of September, 1783.
      THOMAS CAFFIELD, *Lieut. N. C. Regt.*
The Royal Gazette, September 10, 1783.

RUN AWAY from the Ship Spring, Capt. Johnson, JOHNSON MORRY, a bound Apprentice, of a brown complexion, about 5 feet 8 inches high.— MORRIS CRIMMING, brown complexion, about 5 feet 9 inches high,— GEORGE HEADS, slender made, about 5 feet 8 inches high, much freckled in the face and hands.— ROBERT LOW, of a low stature, brown complexion.—ROBERT SCARTET, a small boy, with a sore head: They all wear their own hair tied; are lawful found Apprentices.—Whoever harbours, entertains or conceals either of them, will be prosecuted as the law directs.

 The Royal Gazette, September 10, 1783; September 13, 1783; September 17, 1783.

RUN AWAY from the Subscriber, a MULATTO MAN, named SAM, had on when he went away, a striped jacket and trowsers, made out of a bed tick; carried off a bag of cloths, consisting of a red waistcoat, a buckskin pair of breeches, and two pair of white breeches.—Whoever will bring him to the Subscriber, or to William Byron, the Corner of the Fly-Market, by the Forty-Stairs, will be handsomely rewarded.

    EDWARD BARDIN.   Jamaica, Long-Island
The Royal Gazette, September 10, 1783.

    ABSCONDED from his MASTER.
A NEGRO MAN SLAVE, named JEM, belonging to Mr. Anthony Stewart. This Negro is well known in the City, and goes amongst his companions by the name of JAMES BUTLER. He is a likely man, about thirty years of age; and exceeding good House Servant, and understands waiting upon a Gentleman.

Whoever apprehends and secures him so as his Master may have him again, shall receive FIVE GUINEAS Reward, paid by applying to the Printer, or at No. 206, Water-Street.

The Royal Gazette, September 17, 1783.

FIVE DOLLARS Reward.

RUN-away from the Subscriber, on Wednesday last, a negro wench about seventeen years of age. Whoever will apprehend and secure her so her master may get her again, shall be entitled to the above reward, and all reasonable charges paid, by applying to Gilliam Cornell, opposite to the Fly Market, or the subscriber at New-Town, Long-Island.

ISAAC CORNELL.

N. B. All masters of Vessels and others, are hereby warned not to harbour, conceal, or carry off the said wench, as they shall answer it at their peril. Oct. 11, 1783.

The New-York Gazette; and the Weekly Mercury, October 13, 1783; October 20, 1783; October 27, 1783.

Twenty Dollars Reward.

RUNAWAY from the Subscriber, on Thursday the 9th Inst. a NEGRO MAN named SAM, about 24 Years old, but appears by his Countenance to be much old, a tall, stout, well built Fellow, in Colour a dark yellow has a very large Foot, he speaks pretty good English, but with something of the Dutch Accent, which Language he has some little Knowledge of, having been brought up in a Dutch Family on Long-Island; had on an old flap'd Hat, a strip'd blue and white Tow-Cloth Coatee and Vest, a white homespun linen Shirt, a Pair of twill'd Tow-Cloth Trowsers patch'd on the Knees with plain Tow-Cloth, and was bare-foot when he left Home. Whoever will tale up said Negro, and secure him, or return him to the Subscriber, shall be entitled to the above Reward, and all necessary Charges. JOSIAH BURR. New-Haven, October 11th, 1783.

The Connecticut Journal, October 15, 1783; October 22, 1783; October 29, 1783.

FIVE GUINEAS Reward.

RUN AWAY from the Subscriber, on board the Brig Neptune, RICHARD DAVIS, Master, lying at Murray's Wharf, FELIX, a Mulatto Man, of a dark complexion, about 5 feet 8 or 8 inches high, stout built, large head and face, with thick short curled hair, has lost some of his fore teeth, is much inclined to drink, and when so, talks very much; he speaks French and English, and professes to be a Barber, Cook and Sailor; no doubt he will change his name, he being an artful fellow.—Whoever will apprehend the said Felix,

and deliver him on board the said Brig, or to Mr. Bartholomew Anster, No. 24, Water-street, or to Mr. Anthony Van Dam, shall receive the above reward.   JACOB HOWELL.
The Royal Gazette, October 15, 1783.

RUN AWAY, a NEGRO GIRL, about 20 years of age; had on a high cauled cap, and white handkerchief, a short gown of red and white cotton, a blue camblet petticoat.—her name MARY.—Whoever will bring her to No. 44, King-street, shall receive TEN DOLLARS Reward; and all Masters of Vessels and others, are forwarned not to harbour her.
The Royal Gazette, October 15, 1783.

ABSCONDED from her Mistress, a NEGRO GIRL, about 17 years old, named POLLY, and formerly called DYE; had on when she went off a short callicoe gown, and a blue petticoat, speaks tolerable good English, but talks fast.

Whoever will apprehend the said Wench, and return her to her Mistress, at No. 68, Water-street, opposite the Crane Wharf, shall be paid Eight Dollars Reward.

All persons are warned not to harbour the above described Negro Girl; and Commanders of Ships or Vessels not to admit her on board, as they will be prosecuted at the Law directs.
The Royal Gazette, October 18, 1783.

THEATRE, *New-York, October* 17.
WHEREAS a certain ELEANOR MASSEY FITZGERALD, has defrauded the subscriber of the Sum of FORTY-SIX POUNDS SIXTEEN SHILLINGS, by entering into Articles of Indenture, and immediately absconding.—A Reward of TWENTY POUNDS will be paid to any Person, who can inform the Subscriber where she is harboured, so that she may be brought to Justice, previous to the 30th of this Month.
    DENNIS RYAN.
The Royal Gazette, October 18, 1783.

FIVE POUNDS REWARD.
RUN AWAY, on Friday 19th September, a NEGRO WENCH, named KATE, born in the family of Jacob Bennet, on Long-Island, has lived with Mr. George Hunter and Ephraim Smith, of this City: She is very stout made, about 5 feet 9 or 10 inches high, of a light black, and likely face, without any particular marks, generally wears her hair very high and straight up, over a roll, with a great deal of pomatum, a great talker and shrill voice; took with her a variety of clothes, among which there was a

Callico Short Gown, with the figure of horses, carriages, and soldiers, in blue and yellow colours, particularly a row of the latter round the bottom of it; and several caps, all with long ears. Is supposed to feign the name of Boyle, an Ensign in General De Lancey's corps.

Whoever will apprehend and secure her, so that her master may get her, shall have the above reward, and all reasonable charges paid, by applying to the Printer, or No. 19, Crown-street.

All Masters of vessels and others are hereby warned not to harbour, conceal, or carry off said Wench as they shall answer it at their peril.

The Royal Gazette, October 18, 1783; *The New-York Gazette; and the Weekly Mercury*, October 20, 1783; October 27, 1783. Minor differences between the papers.

TWENTY DOLLARS Reward.

ESCAPED last night out of the Main Guard, a mulatto man named THOMAS, a well set thick fellow, long bushy hair; had on a blue sailors jacket, green under waistcoat, whitish woollen, or oznabrig trowsers. Whoever will apprehend, or give information of him to the Printer, or Mr. *David Beekman*, No. 15, Smith Street, so that he may be taken shall receive the above reward. All persons are forbid harbouring him, and all masters of vessels from carrying him off, as they may depend on being prosecuted for the same, as he has been guilty of robbing his Master.

New-York, October 19*th*, 1783.

The New-York Gazette; and the Weekly Mercury, October 20, 1783.

Ten Pounds Reward.

RAN AWAY from the subscriber, on the night of the 15th inst. a Negro Man, named HARRY, aged about 36 or 40 years, is of a very black colour, strong made, and a little above the middle size—had on when he went away a blue waistcoat with sleeves, linen trowsers, white worsted stocking, [*sic*] and a new pair of shoes, with large fashionable pinchbeck buckles—he took with him a brown coat and waistcoat, a large beaver hat, cocked, a good deal worn, and a small old beaver hat, which is very greasy in the crown—he is a great talker, and speaks the German, Low-Dutch and English languages very fluently—he is much addicted to drinking.—Whoever takes him up, and brings him to the subscriber, in the city of Albany, or secures him in the common gaol, in the city of Albany, shall be entitled to receive the above reward

from   LEONARD GANSEVOORT, jun.

The New-York Gazetteer or Northern Intelligencer, October 20, 1783; October 27, 1783; November 3, 1783.

RANAWAY from the Subscriber, the 22d inst, a Negro Man, named ASA or AFRICA, aged between 40 and 50 years, about 5 feet 9 or 10 inches high, knock-knee'd, Guinea born, with scars on each side of his face—had on when he went away, a brown coat, pretty much worn, a blueish mix'd cloth jacket, tow trowsers, and a small round castor Hat—he formerly lived in Stonington, in Connecticut, and has been seen on his way towards Stephentown or little Hoosack—he must be very well known, on account of his having attended the ferry between Albany and Green-Bush during 8 or 9 years—Whoever secures said Negro, so that his master can have him again shall receive EIGHT DOLLARS reward, and all reasonable charges paid,
           by   THOMAS LOTTRIDGE,   Albany, October 13.
The New-York Gazetteer or Northern Intelligencer, October 20, 1783; October 27, 1783.

STOP THIEF!

FIFTEEN Dollars Reward.—Was stolen from the subscriber on the 27th instant, about One Hundred and Twenty Dollars from on board the Schooner Polly, by one Alexander Wilson, a man of about 5 feet 8 inches high, thick set, short blackish hair, had on a white linen coat and vest, black velvet breeches, a Black-smith by trade, he sometimes goes by the name of Sinclair. Whoever will take up said Thief, and bring him to William Dudley, in New-York, Water-street, at the corner of Crane Wharf, No. 151, shall receive the above reward, and all necessary charges,
           by their humble servant.   DANIEL LYON.
The Royal Gazette, October 29, 1783.

RUN away from the subscriber, on the 12th inst. a negro boy named DICK, cock-ey'd, whistles well: Had on when he went away, a green coat with metal buttons, and blue overhawls. It is supposed he sold his master's horse, as he never since returned. The horse is a bright bay, black switch tail and mane, nine years old, trots well. Whoever secures said negro or horse, so that the owner may have them again, shall have four dollars for each, by applying to John Dalton, surgeon, No. 46, Chatham-street. The boy has been some time concealed by the servant man of Lieut. De Ettingeuff, of the Hessian Grenadiers, near said number.
N. B. All masters of vessels are requested not to take said negro off.
The New-York Gazette; and the Weekly Mercury, October 27, 1783.

RUN away from the Subscriber, a Negro Man, named JACK, about 22 years of age, of a yellow complexion, long black hair, speaks good English, and a little Dutch; had on when he went away, a red Jacket and blue Coat, a pair of yellow Breeches, was brought up to the farming business, and is a

good fidler. Whoever takes up said Negro, and returns him to his master, shall have Eight Dollars reward, and all necessary charges
          paid by   EPHRAIM WHEELER,
                   Nine-Partners, (State of N. York) Sept. 16, 1783.
The Connecticut Courant and Weekly Intelligencer, October 28, 1783; November 4, 1783; November 11, 1783.

RUN-AWAY on Tuesday night the 14th instant, from the subscriber at Hampstead, in Queen's county, Long-Island, a negro man slave named ANTHONY, about 35 years old, of a middling stature, a black complexion, very talkative, speaks good English, and pretends to be a preacher, and sometimes officiates in that capacity among the Blacks. Had on when he went away a bearskin great coat, and the rest of the cloaths chiefly of the same kind, and partly worn, and may very likely to have changed his clothes. Any person who will apprehend said negro man, and delivers him to the subscriber, or secures him so that his master may have him again, shall receive a reward of FIVE DOLLARS, if taken in Queen's county; and TEN DOLLARS if taken elsewhere to be paid by me.
N. B. All masters of vessels, and others, are hereby forbid to carry him off,
         &c. S. CLOWES.
The New-York Gazette; and the Weekly Mercury, November 3, 1783.

Reward of Twenty Dollars for each.
RAN away from the Subscriber, two NEGROES, viz. one went away the 4th of October last, a well set Fellow, named Cuffey, a Taylor, speaks pretty good English, had on when he went away a brown Surtout Coat. The other left the Subscriber on the 4th of November inst. called Johannis, speaks but little English; had on when he went away a blue and white striped Linen Jacket, with Shoes and Stockings: They are both from St. Croix. Whoever apprehends the said Negroes, or either, shall be entitled to the above Reward, by bringing them to Mr. TOBIAS STOUTENBURG, just behind the main Guard. or to the Subscriber at the said Mr. Stoutenburg's.   P. H. LOORBURGH.
The Royal Gazette, November 5, 1783.

               FIVE DOLLARS Reward.
RUN-AWAY, on the 3d day of this instant, from his Master, HENRY STANTON, at Brooklyne, Long-Island, a NEGRO BOY, named JESS: Had on when he went away, a brown homespun coat, vest and breeches, and a red fills handkerchief about his neck, has a great turn at whistling.— Whoever takes up said Negro Boy, and brings him to his Master, shall receive the above Reward.

N. B. All Masters of Vessels are strictly forbid harbouring or carrying off said Negro, at their peril. HENRY STANTON.
The Royal Gazette, November 8, 1783.

FIVE DOLLARS REWARD.

RUN away, on the 7th instant, from her master, Colonel Frederick Weissenfels; living in this city, Fair-Street, No. 2, a NEGRO WENCH, named DINA; about fifteen years of age, strong and well built; had on when she ran away, a white short gown, a purple faded moreen petticoat, a white and blue handkerchief, a check apron, a green baize short cloak, a black worsted hat, her hair turned down by her own stratagem, upon the reddish cast. Whoever takes up said Negro Wench, and brings her to her master, shall have the above reward.

N. B. All masters of vessels and other persons are strictly forbid harbouring or carrying off said Negro Wench at their peril.
FRED. WEISSENFELS.
The New-York Gazette; and the Weekly Mercury, November 10, 1783; *The New-York Packet and the American Advertiser,* November 17, 1783; November 20, 1783.

FIVE DOLLARS REWARD,

RUN-AWAY from the Subscriber on Monday the 3d instant, an Apprentice Boy, named JACOB TYLER. All Masters of Vessels, and others, are forwarned from harbouring or carrying off said Apprentice, as they must expect to be dealt with according to law.
CHARLES HORTON.
The Royal Gazette, November 15, 1783. See *The New-York Packet and the American Advertiser,* November 17, 1783, and *The New-York Packet and the American Advertiser,* November 20, 1783.

TWO GUINEAS Reward.

RAN away from the Subscriber, on Sunday the 9th inst. a NEGRO MAN named PETER, about 5 feet 7 inches high, very black, has a down-cast look; had on when he went away a short brown coat lined with striped green baize, double-breasted waistcoat, dark brown, lined with striped linsey woolsey. a pair of red cloth trowsers, quite new, and an old felt hat; and took with him a pair of brown trowsers. Whoever takes up said Negro, and returns him to the subscriber near Brooklyne, on Long-Island, or to Mr. R. SUYDAM, No. 9, Little Dock-street, shall have the above reward and all charges paid.

N. B. All Masters of Vessels, and others are forbid harbouring said Negro, as they may depend on answering for the same at their peril.

November 15, 1783.
The New-York Packet and the American Advertiser, November 17, 1783. See *The New-York Packet and the American Advertiser*, November 17, 1783.

TWO GUINEAS REWARD,

Run away from the Subscriber, on Sunday the 9th inst. a NEGRO MAN named Peter, about five feet seven inches high, very black, has a downcast look; had on when he went away, a short brown coat lined with striped linsey-woolsey, a pair of red cloth trowsers quite new and an old felt hat, he took with him a pair of brown trowsers. Whoever takes up the said Negro, and returns him to the subscriber, near Brooklyn, Long-Island, or to Mr. R. Suydam, No. 9, Little Dock street, shall have the above reward and all charges paid. FERDINANDUS SUYDAM.

N. B. All masters of vessels, and others are forbid harbouring the said Negro, as they may depend on answering for the same at their peril.

November 15, 1783.
The New-York Packet and the American Advertiser, November 17, 1783. See *The New-York Packet and the American Advertiser*, November 17, 1783.

WHEREAS, an advertisement appeared in Rivington's paper, bearing the date the 15th inst. alledging that Jacob Tyler had run away from Charles Horton, with a caution to all masters of vessels not to carry off or harbour said Tyler at their peril.

Now I give the public to understand, that the said Charles Horton, well knew that the said Tyler did not run away, as he falsly inserted, but was obliged to make the best of his way to his parents house, having received a contusion in his head from said Horton's wife with a clothes-stick, and had laboured under said wound from the 3d instant, under the care of a surgeon, and is not yet out of danger, which said Horton well knew. And also, that he the said Horton, had at sundry times prior to this advertisement, treated said Tyler in a barbarous manner.

Brother Horton, did you ever make any concession to a worthy brother, of the ill treatment given to said Tyler? Sometime ago your answers was, that you had whipt him sundry times, could give no account but passion overcame you. If you deny this, I say I'll prove it. This you call brotherhood. *Brother JACOB TYLER.

The New-York Packet and the American Advertiser, November 17, 1783. See *The Royal Gazette*, November 15, 1783, and *The New-York Packet and the American Advertiser*, November 20, 1783.

TEN POUNDS Reward.

RUN-AWAY from the subscriber, on Sunday night the 16th inst. a NEGRO WENCH, named ISABEL, had on when she run-away, a short whitish Cloth Cloak, with a hood, about 5 feet 6 inches high, very black colour, speaks pretty thick. She was taken away by her Husband, a Negro Man named Peter Longster, about 6 feet high, pretty stout, formerly lived with Col. Lutwyche, at Brooklyn-Ferry, Long-Island.—Whoever will secure either of them, or give information to the Subscriber, or to William Bryan, at the Fly-Market Stairs, so that he may get his property again, shall receive the above reward, and all reasonable charges paid.
                  EDWARD BARDIN.

    N. B. All Masters of Vessels and others, are hereby forewarned not to harbour them, but at their peril.

The Royal Gazette, November 19, 1783.

TWO GUINEAS Reward.

RUN AWAY from the Subscriber, on the 14th instant, a NEGRO BOY, named HECTOR, about eighteen years of age, four feet [*sic*] six inches high, speaks tolerable good English. Had on when he went away, a round hat, a short coatee, of a light colour, cloth waistcoat, much the same, a watch-coat, with a velvet cape, a coating pair of trowsers, of a grey colour, a pair of white stockings.—He is a well-set fellow.—Whoever secures the said Negro, and brings him to the Subscriber, living near the Provost, in Great George Street, No. 7, shall be entitled to the above reward, and all reasonable charges paid.

    N. B. All Masters of Vessels, and others, are forbid taking him off, or concealing him, as they shall answer it at their peril.
                  PHILIP RUCKEL.

The Royal Gazette, November 19, 1783.

TEN POUNDS Reward.

RAN away from the Subscriber, some time ago, a stout young NEGRO MAN, aged 22 years, about 5 feet 10 inches high, his name formerly was NEPTUNE, but now goes by the Name of JOHN NEPTUNE. Any persons delivering him at No. 12, in Crown-street, shall be entitled to the above reward.

    All Masters of Vessels are forbid carrying his away, as they may depend on being prosecuted,
            by   THOMAS GUION.   *New-York, Nov.* 17, 1783.

The Royal Gazette, November 19, 1783.

FIVE DOLLARS REWARD,

RUN-AWAY from the Subscriber on Monday the third instant, an Apprentice Boy, named JACOB TYLER, Jun.—All masters of vessels and others are forewarned from harbouring or carrying off said Apprentice, as they must expect to be dealt with according to law.

CHARLES HORTON.

And, whereas on Monday the 17th instant, an Advertisement was inserted in the New-York Packet, by one well known by the name of Bumfogger, formerly a man before the mast, endeavouring to smother my former advertisement, and cloke the crimes of drunkenness and other bad vices, instilled into the said Apprentice, by reason of having good paterns set before him: I now inform the public that the said Apprentice came home on Monday the third instant, and was drunk, and abused his mistress, in a scurrilous manner, with bad language, to an insufferable degree: There is sufficient evidence to be produced upon oath of the badness of his behaviour, and that this is not the first nor second time that his parents have encouraged him in it, until they were obliged to deliver him up, by order of the magistrates of this city; and in a short time the public will be convinced of the certainty of it.   CHARLES HORTON.

The New-York Packet and the American Advertiser, November 20, 1783. See *The Royal Gazette*, November 15, 1783, and *The New-York Packet and the American Advertiser*, November 17, 1783.

Ran away from the subscriber, a NEGRO MAN named Cuff, belonging to John Van Rensselaer, he is about twenty three or twenty four years old, a short thick set fellow, very black. A reward of five dollars will be given to any person who will deliver said fellow at the New City, or four dollars if delivered at St. Croix, and necessary charges
paid, by   PETTER VAN RENSSELAER.

Vermont Gazette, November 20, 1783; November 27, 1783.

RUN-AWAY from the Subscriber this morning about nine o'clock, Two Negro Lads called STEPNEY and PRINCE: The first 20 years of age, about 5 feet 8 inches high, well made genteel fellow, has a small impediment in his speech, red eyes, from an inflamation in them, and has taken clothes with him of a various kinds, but generally wears a green short coat, a blue under waist-coat, and buck-skin breeches, with a blue surtout coat and and been used to wait on a Gentleman's family.—PRINCE is about 5 feet 5 inches high, 17 years of age, has thick lips, and a remarkable large mouth; he is talkative and impudent; had on a pair of blue cloth trowsers, a reddish sailors jacket, and dark brown great coat, he has been used to work at the

Ship-Carpenters Business, and understands caulking and mast-making pretty well. It is supposed they have gone on board some vessel immediately bound to sea.

All Masters of vessels are requested not to harbour or take them off. Any person delivering them to Capt. Nicholson, No. 93, William-street, shall have Five Guineas Reward for each.

New-York, Dec. 2, 1783.

Rivington's New-York Gazette, and Universal Advertiser, December 3, 1783.

TWO GUINEAS REWARD.

RUN-Away from the Subscriber, the 14th day of November last, a likely Negro Woman, named Sarah, brought up in the family of Mr. Deycay, deceased, where she went by the name of Clarender, about thirty years of age; she is pretty tall and slender made, her complexion being very black, has a remarkable wart on her right eye-lash. Had on when she went away, a callicoe short gown, black skirt, and a black hat trimmed with edging, but as she has a great number of good cloaths, which she carried away with her, it is impossible to describer the dress that she may now be in. It is suspected, that she is kept concealed somewhere in this city, she having a great many relations and acquaintances here. This is to forewarn all persons from harbouring her, as they will answer it at their peril. Any person who will apprehend the said Negro Woman, and secure her so that her master may have her again, shall receive the above reward, paid them by me, living at No. 385, Murray-street.

ELIZABETH MILLER.

N. B. All Masters of vessels are forewarned not to harbour or carry off the said Negro Woman.

Rivington's New-York Gazette, and Universal Advertiser, December 17, 1783.

TWENTY DOLLARS REWARD.

RUN AWAY from the Subscriber, at Yongkers, near Kingsbridge, about two months since, a negro man named YAFF, but generally goes by the nickname of MINK, about 20 years of age, 5 feet 6 inches high, thick set, yellow complexion, a scar upon his cheek and another upon his forehead, given very much to drink; had on when he went away a blue coat, with white lining, a clouded velvet waistcoat, and white plush breeches. The above reward will be paid to any person who can give such information that he may be found again, by applying to Edward Huestus, Shoe-maker, the upper end of Queen-street, near the Tea-Water Pumps, or to the Subscriber.

JESSE HUESTIS. *December* 16, 1783.

Rivington's New-York Gazette, and Universal Advertiser, December 17, 1783; December 24, 1783.

WHEREAS I the Subscriber did the middle of October last a year ago, leave my late wife HAPPY, then residing in the Town of Plainfield, county of Windham, on consideration of her uneasy, fractious, and quarrelsome disposition, which I considered as a duty Incumbent on me when our mutual happiness could no longer exist, together with her wasting or otherwise parting in an unwarrantable manner with the necessaries provided for the family, which has given me the greatest uneasiness, and as no other remedy could be provided, I must leave it to the consideration of the public and those concerned, forbidding them at the same time to harbour or otherwise trust her on my account after this date, as I am unable and will not pay any debts she may contract after this date.

JOHN-THO'S TRANTUM. County of Albany, Nov. 30, 1783.

The Connecticut Gazette; And The Universal Intelligencer, December 19, 1783.

ABSCONDED from his Master, since Sunday morning, an INDIAN BOY, of a yellow colour, about 13 years of age, had on a blue short jacket, and breeches of the same cloth. It is imagined he was inticed away by a white boy, who went about the city offering some gold rings for sale, and said he run away from a ship of war. Whoever will apprehend said Negro Boy, [sic] and bring him to his Master, at Mr. Stoutenberg's shall have Four Dollars Reward. All Masters of Vessels are requested to search for him on board their vessels, and also forbid carrying him off, under penalty of the law.

Rivington's New-York Gazette, and Universal Advertiser, December 24, 1783.

INDEX

Abbot, John, 9, 337
Acker, Jack, 351
Ackland, Captain, 168
Adam, Walter, 248
Adams, Nathaniel, 29
Adams, Thomas, 316
Addington, John, 41
Agan, Joshua, 112
Agnew, J., 311
Aikenhead, John, 261
Airy, Mrs., 217
Aitken, Robert, 150
Aitkin, Charles, 137
Akerly, Nathaniel, 275
Alaire, Peter Alexander, 353
Alberson, Thomas, 112
Albertson, Joseph, 37
Alexander, Mr., 1, 21, 28
Allen, Elizabeth, 48
Allen, Heman, 199
Allen, Henry, 31
Allen, Jeremiah, 31
Allen, John, 277
Allen, Levi, 270, 272
Allen, Thomas, 141, 355
Allen, Zimrie, 94
Allibe, John, 339
Allicocke, Joseph, 237, 253, 287
Allin, Ebenezer, 157
Altenbockum, de, Mr. 293
Amory, Isaac, 289, 295
Anderson, Abraham, 221
Anderson, Andrew, 158
Anderson, John, 111
Andress, John, 17
Angele, Christopher, 13
Angle, Mrs., 31
Annan, Robert, 165
Ansell, John, 293
Anster, Bartholomew, 360
Anthony, John, 37
Anthony, Nicholas, 28
Apsley, William, 283
Arden, Thomas, 141
Arding, Charles, 215
Arell, Peter, 103
Armstrong, John, 166
Armstrong, William, 285
Arnold, Alfred, 347
Arnold, Benedict, 252
Arnold, Mary, 173, 175
Arthur, William, 152
Ash, Gilbert, 41
Ashley, John, 44
Atkin, Peter, 295
Auchmuty, Samuel, 107
Augustus, Caesar, 336
Ayscough, Capt., 155
Bacher, John J., 134
Bachman, Jacob, 9
Badgely, Joseph, 187
Badgely, Moses, 187
Bailer, John, 195
Bailey, William, 131, 136, 150
Bain, John, 326
Bainbridge, A., 260
Bainbridge, John, 92
Baker, James, 314
Baker, Remember, 94
Baldhead, John Sullivan, 91
Balding, Jacob, 41
Bales, James, 115
Ballantine, Hamilton, 9
Banker, Mr., 159
Banks, Alexander, 231
Banks, James, 138, 139
Banks, Samuel, 63
Baptist, John, 61
Barber, John, 280
Barberie, Mr., 160

Barclay, Andrew, 284
Barclay, David, 52
Barclay, Mr., 141
Barclay, Polly, 238
Bard, Dr., 313
Bard, Samuel, 207
Barden, Edward, 292
Barden, Jacob, 56
Bardin, Edward, 358, 366
Bardin, Mr., 25
Bardly, Edward, 329
Barew, Abraham, 64
Barnes, John, 26, 158
Barnes, William, 59
Barney, John, Jr., 252
Barnhardt, Samuel, 125
Barres, John, 23
Barrow, James, 78, 174
Barrow, John, 230
Barrow, Thomas, 78
Barton, Ralph, 271
Bartow, John, Jr., 252
Bartow, Thomas, 235
Bartram, George, 142
Bass, Samuel, 228
Bateman, William, 158
Bates, Stephen, 68
Baxter, John, 109
Bayard, Samuel, Jr., 27
Bayard, William, 48, 51, 86
Bayley, Richard, 239
Baylis, Richard, 113
Beames, Benjamin, 244
Beard, Victor, 126
Beardwine, Charles, 337
Beasley, Catherine, 60
Beck, James, 115
Beck, John, 115, 117, 199
Beckett, Philip, 259
Beech, Gersham, 106
Beekman, David, 361
Beekman, Gerard B., 201

Bell, William, 7, 246
Ben, John, 281
Benedict, Elisha, 66
Benjamin, Theodorus/Dorus, 55, 56
Bennet, Jacob, 360
Bennet, Jacob, Jr., 226
Bennet, John, 280
Bennet, Mr., 25
Bennett, James, 263
Bennett, John, 286
Bennit, Justice, 99
Benson, Capt., 310, 312
Benson, Sampson/Samson, 80, 82
Benson, Samson, Jr., 59, 76
Bergett, William, 45
Berkins, David, 68
Berry, Richard, 304
Berton, Peter, 159
Bessonet, John, 13, 15
Betts, Benjamin, 20
Betts, Dr., 303
Bevers, York, 324
Bevoise, George, 197, 224, 237
Bickle, John, 218
Biles, Samuel, 154
Bill, Ambrose, 167
Birmingham, James, 112
Bixton, James, 195
Black, James, 156
Black, John, 108
Black, Mary, 241
Black, Robert, 106, 342
Blackman, Nathaniel, 318
Blackwell, Jacob, 170
Blackwell. Jacob, 167
Blockley, Thomas, 166
Bloom, Bernades, 276
Blundle, Christopher, 279
Blunt, Samuel, 8
Bodfield, A., 231

Bog, Capt., 132
Bogart, Mr., 174
Bogie, Andrew, 203
Bogie, Thomas, 203
Boice, Jeremiah, 112
Boice, Mr., 317
Bollins, James, 310
Bolton, Joseph, 41
Bolton, Richard, 34
Bolton, Sarah, 74
Bolton, William, 74
Bond, Abraham, 177
Bonfield, John, 133
Bortle, John, 203
Boss, Joseph, 323
Boss, Mary, 323
Bourne, Melatiah, 133
Bowman, Jonathan, 301
Boyle, Ensign, 361
Boyle, John, 136, 150
Boyle, Mr., 131
Brace, Robert, 175
Bradey, Mary, 74
Bradstreet, Colonel/Col., 20, 24
Brady, Thomas, 307
Braithwaite, Richard, 244
Brasier, Henry, 3
Bratt, Mr., 25
Breen, Richard, 292
Brewer, Col., 229
Brian, Elizabeth, 266
Brian, Mary, 266
Brideam, Frederick, 130
Bridgewater, John, 64
Briggs, Gabriel, 39
Briggs, Joseph, 294
Brinckerhoff, Dirck, 5
Brinckley, Thomas, 350, 354
Broadhead, Charles, 70
Brooke, Richard, 179
Brookman, Fortune, 220

Brookman, Thomas, 182, 220, 240
Brooks, David, 339
Brophill, John, 174
Brower, Jeremiah, 58, 64
Brower, Jeremiah, Jr., 58
Brown, George, 245
Brown, John, 169
Brown, M., 55
Brown, William, 3, 244
Brownejohn, Wm., Jr., 46
Bruff, Charles Oliver, 158
Brush, Mr., 191
Bryan, John, 91
Bryan, Josiah, 215
Bryan, Patt., 124
Bryan, William, 366
Bryson, John, 219, 261
Buchanan, T., 104
Buchanan, Thomas, 79
Buchanan, Walter, 79, 104
Buckman, John, 194
Buell, Nathaniel, 95
Bumfogger, Mr., 367
Burch, Ann, 210
Burke, Captain, 152
Burke, John, 130
Burks, George, 179
Burling, Samuel, 234
Burling, Thomas, 157
Burn, John, 80, 81
Burnet/Burnett, Parson, 332
Burnham, Robert, 172
Burns, David, 180
Burr, Josiah, 359
Burtis, William, 302
Burton, Thomas, 155
Burts, Blnathan, 276
Bush, Charles, 283
Bush, William, 283
Bushfield, Mark, 303
Buskirk, Capt., 322

Butcher, James, 328
Butler, James, 113, 358
Butler, Parnel, 29
Butler, Thomas, 98
Butler, William, 65
Byron, William, 358
Cable, Joseph Pine, 318
Caffield, Martha, 357
Caffield, Thomas, 357
Cain, Anne, 164
Callaway, Hugh, 322
Callow, James, 335
Camp, John, 301
Campbell, Archibald, 172
Campbell, George, 61, 88
Campbell, Mr., 331
Campbell, Patrick, 248
Campbell, Robert, 269
Campbell, Ronald, 271
Candull, William, 228
Canfield, John, 177, 179
Carener, Andrew, 160
Cargey, Robert, 309
Cargill, James, 49
Carman, Joshua, Jr., 94
Carmer, Melleson, 357
Carmichael, Thomas, 194
Carnes, John, 10
Carow, John, 332
Carpender, John, 253
Carpenter, John, 199, 307
Carpenter, Samuel, 19
Carrol, William, 302
Carstang, Gideon, 299
Cartay, Mary, 64
Carthy, James, 107
Carton, Mr., 154
Case, Jonas, 63
Catherwood, Robert, 151
Chace, Henry, 218
Chadwick, Capt., 229
Chapman, Abel, 138

Cheevers, Captain/Capt., 124, 157, 159
Chenet, John, 315
Child, Ann, 210
Child, Francis, 165
Child, Jonathan Friend, 53
Child, Joseph, 210
Chilman, Thomas, 226
Chisholm, Alexander, 142
Chovet, Doctor, 46
Christey, Daniel, 51
Christey, John, 51
Christie, Robert, 133
Clark, Abijah, 212
Clark, Elizabeth, 103
Clark, James, 8, 139
Clark, Patrick, 353
Clark, Richard, 280
Clark, William, 352
Clarke, Thomas, 172
Clarkson, David, 47
Clayton, S. W., 278
Clemons, John, 276
Clempson, William, 300
Clopper, Cornelia, 281
Close, Jabez, 108, 109
Clowes, S., 363
Clunie, Andrew, 275
Coats, Luke, 289
Cochran, Mr., 348
Coleman, Daniel, 59
Coleman, Hannah, 75
Coleman, Patrick, 152
Collard, Capt., 35
Collings, Joseph, 179
Collins, Daniel, 16
Collins, John, 291
Colls, Dennes, 247
Colman, Jeremiah, 6, 99
Colvil, Patrick, 114
Conary/Conray/Conroy, William, Jr., 207, 211

Concking, Tim., 9
Concklin, John, 183
Conihane, Francis, 238
Conklin, John, 200
Conklin, Lewis, Jr., 166
Connell, Daniel, 107, 174
Conner, Barry, 50
Conner, James, 202
Conyn, Casparus, 199
Cook, Daniel, 32
Cook, Robert, 327
Cooley/Coley, William, 120
Cooper, Anne, 169
Cooper, Isaac, 259
Cooper, Mr., 324
Cooper, Obadiah, 197
Corbes, William, 277
Corey, Elizabeth, 156
Cornell, Gilliam, 359
Cornell, Isaac, 359
Cornell, Jacobus, 257
Cornell, John, 312
Cornick, Hugh, 289
Cornwall, John, 192
Cornwell, Joseph, 24
Cortlandt, Col., 22, 24
Cory, Braddock, 68
Costekin, Anthony, 69
Cotheal, Isaac, 349
Cotton, William, 185
Coupland, Mr., 278
Couwenhoven, Rem, 223
Cowan, Alexander, 296
Cox, David, 22, 153
Coxetter, Bartholomew, 4
Cozine, Garret, 12
Crabb, Thomas, 191
Crage, Benjamin, 9
Cragg, Capt., 137
Craig, John, 244
Craig, William, 277
Craige, Robert, 68

Crane, John, 228
Craning, John, 276
Craven, Thomas, 327
Crawford, Capt., 154
Crawford, Gideon, 154
Crawford, James, 16
Creddie, Jane, 153
Creighton, James, 299
Creighton, Peter, 304, 320, 334
Crimming, Morris, 358
Cromelin, Mr., 351
Cromeline, Mrs., 338
Cronk, Timothy, 120
Crook, William, 25
Cross, William, 248, 249, 253
Crosuier, Reue, 346
Crozford, William, 346
Cruger, John Harris, 17, 105
Cruger, Mr., 43
Cullem, James, 145
Cullen, Bryan, 218
Cummings, James, 293
Cunningham, Captain, 325, 340
Cunningham, James, 26
Cunningham, Mr., 11, 102, 152, 153
Curlett, John, 347
Currie, Elizabeth, 84
Curry, Elizabeth, 71
Curry, John, 319
Curson, Mr., 133, 138
Cushing, Nathaniel, 224
Cutler, William, 224
Cuyler, Henry, 288
Cuyler, Mr., 22, 24
Dakins, Joshua, 229
Dalton, John, 362
Daniel, Matthew, 321, 348
Darby, Arnold, 224
Darby, William, 113
Darling, Amleton, 216
Darlington, William, 61

Davenport, Stephen, 333
David, Capt., 254
Davies, Hugh, 274
Davis, Benjamin, 32
Davis, Evan, 8
Davis, James, 267
Davis, John, 18
Davis, Richard, 359
Davis, Robert, 104
Davison, John, 235
Dawson, Henry, 290
Day, Isaac, 171
Day, Joseph, 293
Day, Thomas, 229
Dayton, Jonathan I., 166
De Bardeleben, Lieutenant, 330
De Ettingeuff, Lieut., 362
De Lancey, General, 237, 361
De Lancey, James, 58, 70, 126
De Lancey, James, Jr., 94
De Lancey, John, 284
De Peyster, John, 90
De Peyster, John, Jr., 77, 87
Deacon, John, 279
Deal, Capt., 234
Deal, Jonathan, 234
Dean, George, 291
Dean, Issachar, 140
Deane, Nesbitt, 136
Deane, Richard, 286
Deas, James, 113
Debevoise, George, 224, 237
DeCamp, Mary, 155
DeCamp, Morris, 155
Degraw, Cohus, 197
Degrout, Garret, 234
DeHuff, Jacob, 143
Delamator, Isaac, 44
Delametter, Jon, 60
DeLancey, John, 21, 23, 186
Delancy, Colonel, 308
Denhany, Daniel, 304

Denison, Daniel, 103
Dennis, Dennis, 312
Dennison, James, 196
Denton, Henry, 229
Denyse, Jaques, Jr., 67
Depeyster, John, 169
Depeyster, Mr., 25
DeReade, Lumbertus, 29
Dermen, Prince, 321
Derwin, William, 98
Devereux, Stephen, 257
DeWit, John, 203
Deycay, Mr., 368
Dickinson, Mr., 248
Dickson, Archibald, 322
Dickson, James, 60
Digman, George, 218
Dikeman, John, 313
Disko, John, 224
Ditmars, Douwe, 336
Divikin, Matthew, 111
Dobbs, William, 1
Dobs, Mr., 17
Dodgson, Richard, 267
Dole, Mr., 312
Doras, James, 307
Dorchester, Abraham, 194
Dougel, Robert, 230
Douglas, Col., 234
Douglas, James, 88
Douglass, James, 146
Douglass, Robert, Jr., 72
Doutherts, George, 227
Doyl, Francis, 331
Doyle, Darby, 160
Doyle, Thomas, 224
Drake, Joseph, 38, 46, 68
Drake, Joshua, 18
Drew, Edward, 280
Drewry, Capt., 235
Du Verdier, Bernard, 262
Dudley, William, 362

Duffy, Patrick, 272
Dukes, Thomas, 310
Dun, James, 286, 310
Dunbar, Robert, 344
Duncan, Elizabeth, 319
Duncan, Gideon, 316
Dunham, Jonathan, 354
Dunham, Rhuba, 354
Dunlap, Thomas, 17
Dunloss, William, 288
Dunscomb, John, 288
Durant, Benjamin, 172
Durham, Thomas, 86
Dyckman, Alderman, 241
Dyckman, John, 282
Earle, Mr., 185
Eberly, George, 18
Eden, M., 112
Eden, Medcef, 313
Edmond, Canny, 348
Edmond, John, 348
Edwards, Benajah, 32
Edwards, Charles, 229
Edwards, John, 86
Edwards, William, 168, 224
Eilbeck, J., 272
Eilbeck, Jonathan, 324, 325
Elding/Eldding, Thomas, 269, 270
Elliott, Robert, 216
Elliott, William, 272
Ely, Capt., 234
Emery, James, 147
Emigh, Jurry, 15
Emons, Hendrick, 89
Emslie, John, 306
Enger, Elizabeth, 14
Enger, George, 14
English, John, 8
Enslee/Ensly, Daniel, 148, 202, 203, 204, 205, 206
Erskine, Thomas, 331

Ettredge, James, 8
Euins, Thomas, 83
Evens, Isaac, 203
Evens, Samuel, 113
Everson, Jacob, 199
Everson, Thomas, 107
Fairchild, Jesse, 77
Fairfield, David, 230
Fallen, Hugh, 148, 174, 175
Fallon, Hugh, 107
Farren, John, 285
Farrer, Mr., 271
Farrer, Wm., 295
Farrington, Daniel, 47
Farrington, Thomas, 47
Faulkner, John, 247
Fay, Silas, 229
Ferris, Joshua, 218
Field, John, 202
Field, Joseph, 205
Field, Nathan, 72
Field, William, 67
Finley, Robert, 305, 306
Finley, William, 291
Fisher, Abraham, 95, 97, 114, 144
Fisher, Christopher, 51
Fisher, Daniel, 338
Fisher, Mr., 155, 265, 325
Fisk, Bezaleel, 225
Fitched/Fitchet, Abraham, 95, 97, 114, 144
Fitz Gibbons, Gilbert, 181
Fitz Randolph, Hartshorne, 168
Fitzgerald, Catharine, 148, 174
Fitzgerald, Eleanor Massey, 360
Fitzgerald, Nicholas, 33
Fitzgerald, Peggy, 174
Fitzsimons, Mr., 311
Flaglor, Simon, 122
Flaningham, Alexander, 99
Fleet, Gilbert, 82

Fletcher, Captain, 325
Fletcher, Mr., 84, 85
Fletcher, Nicholas, 32
Flories, Antonio, 227
Floyd, Richard, 134, 137
Fogwell, George, 285
Folly, John, 309
Folton, Thomas, 159
Forbes, Daniel, 264
Forbes, William, 197, 224
Ford, Anthony, 201
Ford, Demans, 354
Forester, Joseph, 102
Forman, William, 183
Forshner, Andrew, 319
Forteate, Alexander, 327
Foshy, John, 60
Foster, David, 127
Foster, Jacob, 201
Foster, John, 93, 95, 96, 97, 98, 120, 200
Foster, Joseph, 224
Fowle, John, 295
Fowler, George, 327
Fowler, Jonathan, 303
Francis, Basil, 118
Franklin, Matthew, 47
Frankline, Richard, 316
Fraser, James, 267
Frasier, Sarah, 10
Fraunces, Samuel, 121, 328
Frazer, John G., 224
Frazur, Walter, 299
Frederick, Hannah, 75
Frederick, Mr., 75
Freeman, Simeon, 35
French, Benjamin, 178
French, Christopher, 218
French, Jeremiah, 34, 36
Frost, Anthony, 297, 315
Fullanton, John, 121
Fuller, James, 320

Fuller, Mr., 155
Furnivall, Wm., 260
Futcher, Michael, 300
Gage, Thomas, 169
Gaine, Hugh/H., 72, 74, 75, 76, 106, 129, 141, 190, 291, 301, 352
Gaine, M., 276
Gaine, Mr., 165
Gale, John, 273
Galego, James, 292
Galilee, Robert, 264
Galt, R., 315
Gamble, Samuel, 130
Gannon, Barney, 21
Gansevoort, Leonard, Jr., 361
Gansevort, Peter, 355
Ganter, Michael, 69
Ganter, Peter, 276
Garden, Wm., 344
Gardner, Thomas, 140
Garnsey, John, 100
Garson, Peter, 135
Gaylerd, Benjamin, 190, 191
Gaylor, Alexander, 294
Getfield, Rachel, 196
Geyer, John, 300
Gibb, Robert, 294
Gibbbs/Gibs, William, 280
Gibbons, John, 56
Gibbs, John, 12
Gibson, Henry, 316
Gibson, James, 133
Gibson, John, 294
Gilbert, Samuel, 101
Gilbert, Samuel, Jr., 102
Gilchrist, Adam, 70
Gilchrist, Mr., 248
Giles, Captain, 17
Gill, J., 208
Gilley, John, 185
Gilliland, William, 173

Gillon, Alexander, 178, 180
Gilly, John, 304
Gilmour, Robert, 243
Glasford, Rosamond, 48
Gleason, Caleb, 51
Gleason, Thomas, 218
Glen, Mr., 131
Glover, Samuel, 224
Glover, Thomas, 294
Gojion, Lawrence, 79
Goldsmith, Ephraim, 27
Goldthwait, Jos., 264
Goling, Joseph, 161
Goodrich, John, Jr., 338
Goodridge, Capt., 32
Goodwin, William, 200
Gordon, Capt. A., 53
Gordon, Duchess of, 86
Gordon, George, 73
Gordon, James, 54, 56
Gorman, Hugh, 79
Gorman, John, 18
Gossling, John, 119
Graham, Daniel, 2, 6
Graham, Doctor, 236
Graham, Ennis, 13
Graham, George, 257
Graham, Lewis, 343
Graham, Mr., 334
Graham, Robert, 2, 6
Graham, Theodorus V. W., 355, 356
Grahams, John, 320
Grandin, Philip, 316
Granger, Charles, 239
Grant, Charles, 327
Grant, John, 77
Grant, Rosey, 20
Gray, Mr., 84, 85
Greaves, Lieut., 257
Greaves, Richard, 266
Greaves, Simon, 297

Green, Daniel, 214
Green, James, 291
Green, John, 60
Greene, Mr., 140
Greenfield, Michael, 30
Greg/Gregg, Mr., 102, 152, 153
Gregory, Patrick, 263
Greswold, Joseph, 48
Griffiths, Anthony, 37, 53
Griffiths, John, 324
Griffiths, Mrs., 227
Griswold/Greswold, Thomas, 210, 230, 233, 263
Grove, William, 99
Guelet, Peter, 231
Guest, Henry, 318
Guffen, Andrew, 78
Guion, Abraham, 212
Guion, Isaac, 49
Guion, Peter, 211
Guion, Thomas, 366
Gustan, Catherine Araway, 61
Gustine, Lemuel, Jr., 16, 26
Guyer, Nathan, 215
Hadden, Phebe, 19
Hait, Abraham, 217
Haley, Peter, 180
Hall, George, 88
Hall, Peter, 127
Hall, Robert, 264
Hall, Thomas, 275
Hallet, James, 328
Hallet, Joseph, 167, 328
Halstead, John, 8
Hamill, Daniel, 122
Hamilton, Archibald, 223
Hamilton, Col., 298
Hamilton, John, 218, 271
Hamilton, Mrs., 307
Hamilton, William, 221, 256
Hamlinton, George, 73
Hammond, Mr., 277

Hampton, Jonathan, 183
Hams, Ezekiel, 76
Hancock, John, 187
Hancock, Mary, 241
Handy, Charles, 277
Hanns, Christopher, 10, 11
Hardenbrook, Abel, Jr., 317
Hardy, James, 319
Hardy, John, 295
Hargrave, Robert, 245
Haring, Frederick, 52
Haring, John, 44
Harman, Francis, 292
Harman, Richard, Jr., 266
Harman, Thomas, 302
Harmes, Henry, 170
Harnet, Joseph, 289
Harriman, John, 170
Harriot, Thomas, 232
Harris, Captain, 325
Harris, James, 272
Harris, Richard, 30, 222
Harris, Samuel, 273
Harrison, Thomas, 290
Hart, Dennies, 347
Hart, John, 57
Hart, Samuel, 49
Hasbrouck, David, 357
Hasenclever, Francis Casper/Gasper, 177, 180
Haunsen, Michael, 254
Hayman, Thomas, 239
Hays, Thomas, 273
Heads, George, 358
Heagan, James, 100
Hease, John, 174
Heer, Capt., 279
Hefferman, Edward, 98
Hellers, Simon, 166
Henderson, Capt., 104
Henderson, Richard, 104
Henderson, William, 78

Henner, Mary Barbara, 249, 255
Henry, Mrs., 10
Henry, Samuel, 33
Herrenton, Jabez, 36
Herron, Peter, 218
Hewett, Thomas, 66
Heymell, Judge Advocate, 330
Hicking, William, 111
Hicklen, John, 26
Hicks, Edward, 103
Hicks, Jacob, 233, 234
Hicks, Mr., 269, 337
Higgins, Joseph, 318
Hill, Ann, 174
Hill, Arthur, 158
Hill, James, 304
Hill, Samuel, 141
Hill, William, 118
Hillyer, Lawrence, 321
Hilton, William, 224
Hinsdale, Elijah, 314
Hitchin, John, 232
Hix, Charles, 151
Hodges, Abraham, 192, 195
Hodges, Israel, 34
Hodges, Joseph, 34
Hodges, Mr., 287
Hodzard, Mr., 334
Hoeg, Mr., 349
Hoffman, Hermon, 30
Hoffman, John, 351
Hoffman, Nicholas, 178, 180
Hogstrasser, Paul, 102
Hoit, Nathan, 179
Holcomb, Jechaniah, 63
Holcomb, Jordan, 247
Holland, Frances, 176
Holland, Nahum, 243
Holly, Joseph, 118
Holme, Donald, 109
Holmes, Thomas, 171
Holyoake, John, 8

Honce, John, 134, 137
Hooghteling, William, 283
Hopkins, Benjamin, 93
Hopkins, Thomas, 224
Horneffer, Henry, 14
Horsmanden, Mrs., 2
Horton, Charles, 364, 365, 367
Horton, Gill Budd, 117
Horton, James, Jr., 198
Horton, Silas, 73
Houseal, Bernard Michael, 250, 255
Houseal/Hershal, Michael, 143, 144
Houseman, Peter, 241
Houston, James, 215
Howard, Ann, 174
Howard, William, 174
Howe, Capt., 320
Howe, Estes, 83
Howe, William, 224
Howell, Jacob, 360
Howell, Samuel, 238
Hoyt, Nathan, 177
Hubbard, Daniel, 208
Hubbs/Hubs, Zephaniah, 94, 186
Hubert, Serjeant, 219
Hudson, Abraham, 75
Hudson, Barz., 276
Hudson, Mr., 225
Huestis, Edward, 368
Huestis, Jesse, 368
Huggeford, Peter, 38
Hughes, Daniel, 29
Hughes, William, 257
Hughson, George, 247
Hulet, John, 46
Hull, Joseph, Jr., 202
Hull, Tiddeman, 139
Hulse, James, 254, 256
Humphrevil, David, 29
Humphrevil, Parnel, 29

Humphreys, James, 306
Humphreys, Thomas, 109
Humphry, Thomas, 148
Hunt, Abraham, 226
Hunt, James, 136
Hunt, Josiah, 90, 92
Hunt, Mr., 327
Hunt, Stephen, 8
Hunt, Ward, 196
Hunter, Capt., 21
Hunter, Elijah, 81, 82
Hunter, George, 360
Hunter, Richard, 84, 85
Hurd, James, 226
Hurlbut, William, 77
Hutcheson, Hannah, 135
Hutchins, Joshua, 295
Hutchinson, Benjamin, 184, 187
Hutchinson, John, 315
Hutchinson, Richard, 305
Hyatt, Mr., 166
Hyer, Matthias, 50
Indians, Abraham, 14, 235; Andress, John, 17; Charles, 67; Dick, 135, 282; Frank, 288; Honce, John, 134, 137; Jack, 46, 104; James, 41; January, Peter, 134, 137; Jeffery, 40; Joe, 135; Morris, Isaac, 256; Peter, 82; Robin, 162; Syme/Symon, 43; unnamed, 119, 369; Wooly, Jacob, 19
Inglis, Charles, 89
Inglis, Mr., 274
Ingram, James, 305
Inslee, Daniel, 148, 202, 203, 204, 205, 206
Isaac, Solomon, 168
Ivers, Thomas, 80
Ivy/Ivey, Sam, 324, 325
Iwins, Thomas, 194

Jackson, John, 340
Jackson, Joseph, 225
Jackson, Josiah, 179
Jackson, Thomas, 211
Jacob, Joseph, 19
Jacobs, Hannah, 330
Jacobs, Maximilian, 42
Jameison, Neil, 180
January, Peter, 134, 137
Jarvis, John, 270
Jarvis, Munson, 22, 25
Jay, Mr., 141
Jeanes, Jenkinson, 333
Jefferson, Henry, 281
Jenkins, Richard, 311, 338, 345, 350, 351
Jogie, Peter, 303
Johnson, Capt., 91, 180, 358
Johnson, Frederick, 333
Johnson, George, 35
Johnson, James, 1
Johnson, Jeffery, 223
Johnson, John, 51, 218, 263
Johnson, Parson, 74
Johnson, Richard, 194
Johnson, Samuel, 196
Johnson, William, 115
Johnston, Ezekiel, 37
Johnston, John, 79
Johnston, Mr., 160
Johnston, Samuel, 49
Jones, Capt., 17
Jones, Isaac, 168
Jones, James, 103
Jones, John, 108
Jones, Joseph, 106
Jones, Mr., 185
Jones, Thomas, 57, 235
Jones, William, 257
Joseph, John, 12
Juke, James, 274
Jundine, Susannah, 331

Kearsley, Dr., 181
Keating, John, 153
Keeling, Charles, 340
Keer, Henry, 100
Keith, Timothy, 148
Kelley, Captain, 288
Kelley, Dennis, 236
Kelley, Samuel, 296
Kellog, Eliphelet, 36, 45
Kelly, John, 301
Kelly, Lawrence, 88
Kelly, Patrick, 252
Kelly, Robert, 308
Kelly, Thomas, 33
Kempton, Samuel, 147
Kempton, Thomas, 300
Kennedy, Hugh, 59
Kennedy, John, 131, 136, 150, 180, 304
Kennedy, Mr., 89, 178
Kennedy, William, 39
Kentish, Thomas, 284
Kerin, Terrence, 235
Kern, J. Michael, 291
Ketchum/Ketcham, Isaac, 9, 251, 252
Keteltas, Peter, 89
Kettey, Thomas, 110
Keyborn, Job, 256
Kidd, Alexander, 43
Kiersted, Benjamin, 320
Killock, Oliver, 69
Kilty, Timothy, 148, 174
King, John, 78, 168
King, Linus, 298, 308
Kingston, Francis, 234
Kip, Mr., 58
Kipp, Isaac, 266
Kirk, John, 119
Kissick, Philip, 262, 265, 266, 329
Knap, Samuel, 115

383

Knapp, Grover, 117
Knapp, John C., 126
Knecht, John, 200
Knight, George, 289
Kortwright, Lawrence, 137, 313
Kysch, Anthon George, 258
Laboyteaux, John, 13
Lacey, Joseph, 100
Lagrange, Barnardus, 342
Laird, Captain, 274, 302
Lakeman, Mr., 302
Langden, John, 214
Lansfield, Attained, 292
Lansing, L'Vinus, 339
Larkin, Pompey, 250
Lashel/Lasher, Mr., 221
Laurence, Nicholas, 296
Lawrence, Abraham, 1, 127, 128, 165
Lawrence, Jacob, 79
Lawrence, John, 178, 180
Lawrence, John, Jr., 158, 160
Lawrence, Stephen, 176
Lawrence, Uriah, 351
Lawrence, William, 121
Lawson, James, 1
Lawson, John, 222
Lawson, Peter, 308
Lawson, William, 44
Lawton, Capt., 27
Lawton, John, 26
Lawyer, Johannis, Jr., 137
Lay, Asa, 234
Leadbeater, Peter, 227
Leadberry, William, 244
Leake, John, 283
Leathermount, Peter, 194
Lee, Alexander, 266
Lee, Cesar, 335
Lee, Col., 35
Lee, Mary, 197
Lee, Misper, 272

Lee, Mr., 35
Lee, Seth, 197
Lee, William, 99, 147
Leely, Ebenezer, 212
Lefever, Andries, Jr., 357
Lefever, Nathaniel, 357
Legrange, B./Bernardus, 321, 341
Lent, Abraham, 240, 241, 242
Lent, Henry, 221
Lent, Herculus/Hercules, 355, 356
Lent, Jacobus, 279
Lenzi, Philip, 244, 246
Leonard, William, 101
Leslie, Alexander, 23, 71, 84
Leverage, John, 191, 197
Levisan, Catherine, 204
Levy, Mr., 251, 257
Lewis, Daniel, 50
Lewis, Israel, 50
Lewis, Jacob, 58
Lewis, Joseph, 65
Lewis, Mr., 337
Lidle, John, 10
Liggett, Isaac, 79
Lindsey, Mr., 174
Linsing, Colonel, 311
Lising, Samuel Pese, 37
Little, Deodat, 231
Lloyd, Henry, 171
Longster, Isabel, 366
Longster, Peter, 366
Longstriff, Isabella, 329
Longstriff, Peter, 329
Loorburgh, P. H., 363
Lord, Lynde, 215, 225
Lot, Mr., 215
Lott, Henderikie, 269
Lottridge, Thomas, 362
Loudon, William, 157
Lovell, John, 54, 56

Lovie, George, 287
Low, Peter, 43
Low, Robert, 358
Lowden, Richard, 213
Lowe, Joseph, 62
Loxford, William Newman, 193
Ludlow, Daniel, 262
Ludlow, Gabriel H., 231, 262
Ludlow, George, 14
Ludlow, Mr., 327
Lupton, William, 174
Luttridge, Thomas, 208
Lutwich, Col., 329
Lutwycb, Capt., 307
Lutwyche, Col., 366
Lynch, Catharine, 110
Lynch, Mrs., 108
Lynch, Peter, 241
Lynch, Thomas, 148, 174, 175, 235
Lyon, Daniel, 362
Lyon, Samuel, 186
Lyon, Thomas, 120
Mabbit, Samuel, 26
Mabee, Simon, 93
Mackenzie, Joseph, 270
MacKintosh, Lachlan, 315
Magee, Mr., 265
Mahony, John, 110, 140, 148, 174
Main, William, 129
Malcom, W., 206
Manley, John, 151
Mansfield, Theophilus, 229
Markland, John, 72, 73, 75, 76
Marr, Agent, 303
Marshal, William, 289
Marshall, George, 147
Marshall, Robert, 176
Martin, William, 183
Martindale, David, 347
Marven, Elihu, 213

Maslin Mr., 114
Mason, James, 231
Mathers, Obadiah, 63
Matheson, Robert, 175
Mathews, John, 268
Mathews, Robert, 31
Matthews, David, 219
Mattin, Thomas, 228
Maxwell, George, 165
Maxwell, William, 177, 216
Mayfield, Thomas, 110
McAdam, John, 245
McAdams, William, 282
McArthur, Duncan, 149
McArthur, Isabel, 142
McArthur, John, 43
McCalay, Daniel, 163
McCann, Hugh, 123
McCausland, Conelly, 274
McCleane, John, 198
McClughery, James, 215
McCormick, Daniel, 157, 344, 345
McCormick, John, 179
McCoy, Daniel, 18
McCoy, James, 106
McCready, John, 137
McCreddie, Jane, 154
McCue/McCuw, James, 105, 154
McCurdy, Archibald, 90
McCurdy, Daniel, 88
McDaniel, Lewis, 123
McDavitt, F. M., 224
McDavitt, Patrick, 87
McDiarmed, Hugh, 161
McDonald, Alexander, 17, 334
McDonald, Ann, 290
McDonald, Capt., 4
McDonald, Collin/Colin, 84, 85
McDonald, Lewis, 122
McDonald, Richard, 337
McDonald, Serjeant, 305

McDonald, Susanna/Susanah, 4
McDougal/McDougall, Alexander, 330, 343
McDougall, William, 137
McDurcan, Patrick, 125
McElvey, Patrick, 21
McEwen, William, 227
McFadzean, Capt., 217
McFall, Robert, 87
McFarlong, John, 194
McFayden, E., 309
McFayden, Mrs., 309
McGay, John, 305
McGillis, Gillis, 245
McGoun, Jeremiah, 129
McGuire, Patrick, 65
McIntoch/Mcintosh, John, 33, 143
McKelson, Michael, 162
McKenney, James, 101
McKenzie, Alexander, 250
McKenzie, Donald, 43
McKenzie, John, 291
McKie, Thomas, 282, 285
McKim, William, 89
McKinsey, James, 9
McKinzie, Kenneth, 298
McLane, Donald, 241
McLarman/McLarnan, John, 119, 126
McLauglin, James, 165
McLead, Alexr., 273
McLean, Charles, 357
McLean, Donald, 195
McLean, Dr., 308
McLean, Henrietta, 333
McLean, John, 259
McLeod, Alexander, 202
McLintock, John, 143
McLister, John, 42
McLoud, Martha, 142
McMahan, John, 140

McMiking, Patrick, 137
McMunnigan, James, 274
McNeill, Arthur, 298
McPherson, James, 4
McVicker/McVickers, Archibald, 29, 39, 231
Meade, Philip, 292
Meadly, John, 280
Mease, Joshua, 347
Meeker, Samuel, 256
Meharg, Alexander, 179
Mehelm, Hannah, 124
Mehelm, John, 124
Meigs, Col., 236
Mellanby, Joseph, 348
Melton, John, 293
Men, Limerick, 305
Men, unnamed, 12, 45, 105, 117, 132, 162, 164, 177, 181, 217, 243, 254, 305
Mendenhall, Thomas, 143, 144
Mercer, Doctor, 193
Meredith, Johnathan, 111
Merrit/Merritt, Abraham, 162, 164
Mesier, Abraham, 142
Messel, John, 69
Meulin, John, 201
Miford, John, 64
Mildolar, John, 200
Milford, Joseph, 264
Milldollar, John, 185
Miller, Abraham, Jr., 94
Miller, Ann, 71
Miller, Charles, 2, 5
Miller, Elizabeth, 368
Miller, Garret, 28
Miller, Hugh, 348
Miller, William, 228
Mills, James, 27
Mills, Joshua, 65
Mills, Mr., 269, 337

Milner, William, 16, 26, 35
Miner, Ephraim, 224
Miner, Isaac, 236
Minzies, John, 293, 301
Mitchel, Andrew, 208
Mitchel, George, 196
Mitchel, John, 164, 210
Mitchell, Jecamiah, 37
Montgomery, Alexander, 63
Montgomery, Hugh, 181
Moor, Francis, 250
Moor, George, 307
Moore, Andrew, 181
Moore, Blaze, 91
Moore, Geo. Elliger, 311
Moore, Jacob, 91
Moore, James, 161
Moore, Mr., 106, 190, 191, 261
Moore, Poll, 299
Moore, Sylvia, 311
Moore, Thomas, 112
Moore, William, 149
Morgan, Caleb, 82, 83
Morgan, James, 251
Morgan, Mr., 88
Morgan, Willoughby, 338
Morril/Morrill, Benjamin, 222
Morris, Isaac, 256
Morris, John, 77
Morris, Lewis, 85, 196
Morris, Mary, 241
Morrison, Alexander, 142
Morrison, Capt., 156
Morrison, Robert, 247
Morry, Johnson, 358
Morsom, Richard, 309
Moses, Jacob, 62
Moses, Levy, 55, 56
Moss, Daniel, 219
Moulton, Jonathan, 193
Mowatt, John, 232
Moyland, Joseph, 218

Moynihan, Andrew, 127
Muirhead, John, 323
Mulford, Job, 341
Mulford, John, 104
Mullan, John, 352
Mullen, Mark, 307
Mullenor, Philip, 316
Mulligan, Hercules, 147
Munson, Stephen, 347
Mure, John, 128
Murphy, John, 291, 347
Murphy, Thomas, 5
Murray, Nathaniel, 284
Murrison, George, 32
Murry/Murray, James, 188, 189
Murry/Murray, James Jeffry/ James Jeffray, 188, 189
Mustees unnamed, 120; Brap, 319; Lucey, 19
Myers, John, 171, 258
Myford, John, 153, 155
Naugle, Mr., 238
Neal, Mr., 261
Neer, Zachariah, 31
Negroes, Abel, 69; Negroes, Abraham, 38, 235, 294, 296; Adam, 331; Africa, 362; Alex, 283; Alex/Alick, 242; Alick/Alex, 248, 249, 253; America, 172; Andrew, 234; Angus, 268; Ann, 233; Anthony, 242, 363; Asa, 362; Aser, 47; Augustus, Caesar, 336; Bacchus, 291, 334; Baptist, John, 61; Bartlet, Elijah, 194; Belina, 318; Bella, 317; Bellow/Bella, 29; Ben, 21, 24, 58, 65, 182, 199, 307, 339; Bet/Bett, 242, 244, 246, 265, 272; Betsey, 327; Betty, 221; Bevers, York, 324; Bill, 313, 346; Billy, 344,

Negroes, 345; Bina, 286; Bon/Bond, 21; Bram, 134; Bristol, 241; Brookman, Fortune, 220; Brutus, 46; Butler, James, 358; Caesar, 122, 123, 158, 197, 220, 268, 284, 306, 326, 338, 345, 350; Caesar, Julius, 306; Cain, 306; Cambridge, 184; Carolina, 290; Caster, 213; Cato, 32, 34, 56, 69, 77, 87, 90, 176, 193, 208, 211, 274, 278, 341; Charity, 236; Charles, 51, 268, 281, 328, 357; Charlotte, 332; Chess, 232; Claas, 343; Clarender, 368; Claus, 79; Closs, 145; Cudjoe, 330; Cuff, 15, 122, 123, 315, 367; Cuffey, 363; Cuffy, 223; Cush, 93, 95, 96, 97, 98; Cyrus, 223, 311; Daniel, 210, 222, 262, 265; David, 328, 338, 353; Dermen, Prince, 321; Diamond, 148; Diana/Diona, 253, 254; Dick, 3, 4, 38, 68, 89, 115, 135, 182, 237, 238, 240, 242, 273, 282, 285, 309, 317, 341, 362; Dido, 2; Dina, 364; Dinah, 335; Doras, James, 307; Dorcas, 178; Duff, 321, 348; Duke, 237, 300; Dye, 360; Ebb, 347; Esther, 287; Exeter, 173; Felix, 359; Feonce, 216; Fil, 52; Fisher, Daniel, 338; Flora, 173, 340; Fork, 182, 240; Fountain, 246; Francisco, 335; Frank, 58, 64, 188, 224, 237, 252, 323, 336; Frederick, 349; Frost, Anthony, 297, 315; Fufu, 3; Gaffee, 149; Galego, James, 292; George, 14, 62, 127, 128, 263, 294, 298, 299, 334; Gin, 282; Glascow, 269; Grace, 297, 310; Hack, 131; Hager, 281; Hannah, 258; Hannibal, 19; Harman, 237; Harr, 245; Harry, 44, 51, 66, 192, 195, 287, 309, 310, 343, 357, 361; Hector, 257, 322, 366; Henry, 322; Hester, 251; Hix, Charles, 151; Hix, Mrs. Charles, 151; Hulse, James, 254, 256; Ireland, 173; Isaac, 50, 213, 261, 265; Isabella, 279, 292, 317; Ishmael, 36, 45; Ivy/Ivey, Sam, 324, 325; Jack, 9, 46, 85, 89, 125, 206, 208, 221, 251, 275, 279, 284, 286, 296, 303, 308, 310, 312, 315, 324, 331, 335, 342, 349, 351, 353, 354, 362; Jackson, John, 340; Jackson, Thomas, 211; Jacob, 3, 200, 209, 327; Jaff, 223; James, 33, 41, 94, 207, 309, 314, 333; Jane, 282, 326, 331; Jef, 306; Jeff, 276; Jem, 254, 358; Jenny, 171, 312, 327; Jerry, 165; Jess, 363; Jessemy, 239; Jim, 29, 223; Joe, 219, 228, 239, 251, 258, 288, 320, 330, 333; John, 13, 357; Johnson, Jeffery, 223; Joshua, 278; Jude, 328; Kane, 39; Kate, 280, 286, 360; Kelso, 301; Larkin, Pompey, 250; Lawrence/Launce, 312; Lee, Cesar, 335; Lester, 291; 98; Lill, 37; Lissa, 332; Liverpool, 229; Longster, Isabel, 366; Longster, Peter, 366; Longstriff, Isabella, 329; Longstriff, Peter, 329; Lorain, 294; Negroes, Loui, 225;

Negroes, Luce, 323, 352; Lucy, 355; Luke, 243; Manley, John, 151; Manuel, 79; Mark, 171; Mary, 331, 360; Mattis, 326; Michael, 188; Mingo, 86, 184, 187; Mink, 192, 317, 368; Minto, 313; Mira, 311; Moll, 235, 253; Money-Digger, 3; Moore, Geo. Elliger, 311; Moore, Poll, 299; Moore, Sylvia, 311; Moses, 238, 277; Myrtilla, 271; Nan, 23; Nat, 247; Nathaniel, 209; Ned, 93, 106, 217, 219, 261, 271, 321; Neptune, John, 366; Nero, 150, 344; Newport, 54; Nicholas, 343; Nick, 196; Oliver, 165, 320; Osborn, 227; Pamela, 201, 311; Paris, 312; Peet/Peter, 321; Peg, 284, 329, 348, 357; Pender, 331; Peter, 31, 103, 233, 234, 236, 246, 267, 290, 294, 341, 343, 364, 365; Peter/Pete, 253; Pett/Peter, 340; Phoebe, 220; Pierot, 137; Plato, 72; Pleasant Queen Anne, 319; Plymouth, 234; Poleet, John, 42; Poll, 350, 353; Polly, 250, 327, 360; Polydore, 263; Pomp, 191; Pompey, 105; Pompy, 232; Priam, 260; Price, Luce, 352; Primus, 243, 274; Prince, 103, 136, 145, 146, 181, 206, 207, 209, 211, 221, 270, 272, 325, 367; Prussia, 319; Quash, 298; Quom, 355, 356; Rachael, 300; Rachel, 314, 343; Ramsay, Cato, 338; Rattan, John, 151; Rayner, 293, 301; Redding, 190; Retus, 351; Richard, 347; Richards/Richardson, James, 233; Richmon, 325; Rob, 353; Robbins, Harry, 233; Robin, 162; Roger, 13; Romeo, 281; Rose, 313; Sally, 317; Sam, 82, 91, 152, 193, 197, 215, 230, 260, 267, 287, 290, 326, 338, 348, 350, 358, 359; Sambo, 83, 100; Sancho, 356; Sarah, 200, 259, 291, 323, 324, 368; Saunders, Tom, 116; Savinah, 310; Sawney, 322; Scip, 299; Scipio, 243; Scotland, 93; Shadreck, 273; Sim, 196; Simeon, 152; Simon, 201; Singo, 90; Smart, 183; Spier, 40; Squash, 337; Squire, 70, 298, 308; Steph/Steve, 81; Stephen, 73, 151, 292; Stepney, 367; Sturrup, James, 260; Sue, 331; Susan, 266; Sylvia, 287, 329; Syme/Symon, 43; Syphax, 243; Thom, 47; Thomas, 361; Thompson, Joseph, 226; Tim, 86; Timbo, 70; Titus, 182; Tom, 27, 37, 44, 52, 59, 60, 70, 76, 199, 202, 203, 204, 205, 206, 214, 241, 270, 276, 308, 327, 330, 333, 342, 355; Tonay/Tony, 297; Toney, 101, 325; Tony, 315; Truddle, James, 216; Negroes, unnamed, 8, 21, 23, 32, 42, 46, 86, 88, 128, 155, 158, 183, 186, 214, 219, 255, 264, 265, 269, 311, 326, 328, 332,

Negroes, unnamed, 338, 342, 346, 356, 359, 369; Venus, 337; Violet, 116; Wan, 240; Ware, 240; Watkins, George, 260; Waverage, 24; Waybridge, 48; Wilkes, 232; Will, 36, 42, 63, 138, 198, 314; William, 187, 207, 262, 281, 356; Williams, Charles, 268; Wilson, Luke, 338; Yaff, 368; Yarrow, 329; York, 112, 210, 215, 216, 230, 233, 249, 263, 275, 283, 304, 320, 334, 339

Neilson, William, 22, 124
Nellson, John, 7
Nelson, Robert, 288, 310
Neptune, John, 366
Nestell, Jasper, 126
Nestell, Martinus, 126
Newbergh, Mary, 175
Newby, Thomas, 288, 296
Newcomb, Zacheus, 40
Newman, Thomas, 5
Nicholls, Capt., 129
Nichols, William, 128
Nicholson, Capt., 368
Nicholson, Mr., 178
Nicol, James, 231
Nicoll, Mr., 220
Nixon, General, 250
Noble, Abel, 98
Noble, Thomas, 277
Nolte, John Henry, 258
Noonan, Robert, 157
Norris, John, 83, 88
Norton, George, 307
Nucam, John, 341
Nutter, Mr., 322
Nutter, Valentine, 349

O'Brien, John, 323, 324
O'Brien, William, 340
O'Bryan, Patt., 124
O'Niel, Michael, 54
Odell, James, 212
Odgen, Samuel, 74
Ogden, Nicholas, 237
Ogden, Samuel, 86
Oliver, George, 303
Onderdonk, Henry, 141
Oram, William, 53
Orrack, Alexander, 294
Overpaw, Peter, 42
Owen, Hugh, 110
Owens, Moses, 28
Owens, William, 212
Page, Samuel, 100
Pain, Wester, 305
Pall, James, 33
Palmer, Fenner, 73
Palmer, Mr., 17
Palmer, Thomas, 202
Pangman, Stephen, 239
Parmele, Alexander, 156
Paterson, Garrit, 132
Patterson, George, 131
Patterson, Mrs., 317
Patterson, Peter, 229
Patterson, Robert, 218
Pattison, Colonel, 325
Pattison, John, 328
Paxson, William, 114
Pearce, Samuel, 236, 275
Peck, William Augustus, 59
Pell, Joshua, 347
Pell, Thomas, 235
Pendergast, Richard, 39
Pendlebury, James, 337
Penn, Governor, 86
Perkins, Abijah, 157
Perry, Henry W., 246
Perry, Ruth, 130

Peters, James, 275
Peterson, Garret, 140
Petterson George, 291
Philips, Samuel, 152
Phillips/Phillya, William, 167
Phoenix, Daniel, 97
Pickering, John, 217
Pickett, John, 224
Pigot, William, 304
Pike, Mr., 273
Pilcher, William, 15
Pinard, Louis, 259
Pine, Amos, 150
Pine, Mrs., 155
Pinkney, Philip, 69
Platt, Zepheniah, 69
Plumsted, Nathaniel, 57
Poleet, John, 42
Polleman, John W., 2
Pontenner, Mary, 241
Porteous, John, 254, 291
Porter, Andrew, 127
Post, John, 336
Powell, Morgan, 118
Powers, George, 119, 341
Pratt, Thomas, 278
Preston, Belcher, 34
Prevost, Major, 171
Price, Ann, 323
Price, Edward, 352
Price, Luce, 352
Prince, James, 17
Proctor, Thomas, 296
Provost, Captain, 14
Provost, Peter, 60
Pruym, John F., 133
Pryor, Matthew, 113
Pryor, William, 78
Pugsly, Gilbert, 273
Pulby, John David, 126
Pulver, Andrew, 187
Purdie, David, 229

Purdie, John, 285
Purdie, Nathan, 69
Purdy, Joseph, 354
Pyer, Jacob, 178
Quakenbos, Walter, 52
Queen Anne, Pleasant, 319
Quit, Toby, 21, 24
Raline, Jacob, 6
Ramsay, Cato, 338
Randall, Thomas, 333
Rankin, George, 231
Rapalje, Garret, 129
Rapalje, John, 216
Rapalje, Stephen, 145, 146
Rattan, John, 151
Ray, Mr., 311
Raymond, Antonio, 335
Raynolds, Broughton, 34
Reade, Mr., 118
Ready, John, 256
Reagan, Jeremiah, 119
Redmond, Patrick, 344
Reed, James, 6
Reedy, James, 203
Reese, John Hendrick, 173, 175
Reid Mrs., 259
Reid, John, 193, 308
Reily, Jeremiah, 127
Remsen, Aris, 54
Remsen, George, 349
Remsen, Henry, 141
Remsen, Jeromus, 209
Remsen, Jeronimus, 349
Remsen, Rem A., 349
Renaudet, Adrian, 155
Reuter, Valatine, 2
Reyer, Michael, 162
Reynolds, Broughton, 34
Rhinelander, William, 335
Richards, Nathaniel, 20
Richards, Samuel, 36, 45
Richards/Richarson, James, 233

Richardson, Aweray/
   Awbray, 186
Richardson, John, 277
Richey, James, 18
Ricket, John, 170
Ricket, William, 170
Ricketts, James, 311
Riddle, James, 117
Ridley, John, 295
Ring, Nancy, 135
Ritter, Jacob, 204
Rivington, James, 308
Rivington, James, Jr., 308
Rivington, Mr., 243, 259, 356
Roach, Elenor, 148
Roara, Jacob, 18
Robbins, Harry, 233
Roberts, Ebner, 31
Roberts, John, 27
Roberts, Jonathan, 8
Roberts, Mr., 241
Roberts, Zachariah, 167
Robertson, A., 355
Robertson, Alexander, 147
Robertson, James, 3
Robertson, Mr., 337
Robie, Mr., 327
Robinson John, 143
Robinson, George, 271
Robinson, John, 143
Robinson, Samuel, 185
Robinson, Thomas, Jr., 32
Robson, George, 118
Rodgers, Joseph, 22
Rodman, Joseph, 207
Rogers, James, 213
Rogers, William, 276
Rollins, Philip, 132
Rook, Philemon, 277
Rooker, William, 99
Rosbottom, James, 115
Rose, William, 271
Roseboom, Barent, 116
Rosekrans, Henry, Jr., 59
Rosevelt, Mrs., 330
Ross, Alexander, 138
Ross, Captain/Capt., 302, 304
Ross, Stewart, 302
Ross, William, 304
Ross, Zebulon, 190, 191
Rossboutom, James, 117
Rowan, Daniel, 121
Rowan, William, 121
Rowe, John, 133, 294
Rowe, William, 250
Rowning, Morris, 322
Ruckel, Philip, 366
Rush, Henry, 278
Russel, Capt., 105
Russel, James, 155
Russel, John, 124
Russell, Matthew, 104, 106
Rutherford, James, 295
Rutter, John, 196
Ryan, Cornelius, 111, 158, 200,
   204
Ryan, Dennis, 360
Ryan, Edmund, 291
Ryder, Jacob, 100
Ryder, Mrs., 220
Ryenson, Martin, 236
Sacket, John, 316
Sackett, Samuel, 219
Sackett, William, 266
Sagers, Benjamin, 185
Salter, Captain, 332
Samond, William, 156
Sample, John, 22
Samuel, Mr., 251, 257
Sanders, Michael, 300
Sands, Ambrose, 167, 170
Sandwich, James, 227

Sanford, David, 44
Saunders, Capt., 322
Saunders, Constable, 303, 322
Saunders, Parnel, 29
Saunders, Tom, 116
Saunders, William, 29
Sause, Mr., 325
Sawyer, Moses, 119
Sayre, Paul, 302
Scales, Capt., 267
Scartet, Robert, 358
Schenck, Abraham, 135
Schenck, P., 163
Schenk, Abraham, 134
Schenk, John I., 279
Schermerhorn, Jacob, 39
Schick, Catharina Margarita/ Lilith, 66
Schick, Christian, 66
Schutz, Christian, 119
Schuyler, Ann Mary, 278
Schuyler, Dirck, 278
Schuyler, Mr., 22, 24
Schuyler, Ph., 343
Scot, Archibald, 146
Scott, John M., 192
Seabury, David, 173
Seabury, Samuel, 173
Seare, Silas, 314
Sebring, John, 172
Seger, John, 52, 62
Semple, Robert, 100
Sergeant, Capt., 228
Seton, Mr., 133, 138, 154
Seymour, Moses, 220
Sharp, Mary, 241
Shaw, George, 229, 233
Shaw, John, 131, 136, 150
Shaw, Neal, 250
Shepherd, Joseph, 165
Sherrard, John, 304

Sherren, Capt., 74
Sherwood, Peter, 289
Shey, Richard, 274
Shonnard, Frederick, 96
Short, William, 165
Sibrell, John, 314
Sickelles, Daniel, 174
Sickles, Daniel, 185, 191, 198
Sickles, Garrat, 184
Siegler, Goodheart, 209, 210
Sim, Benjamin, 268
Simerman, John Andrew, 322
Simm, William, 141
Simons, John, 102
Simons, Maurice/Morice, 145, 146
Sinclair, Alexander, 362
Sinclair, James, 251
Skene, Andrew P., 106
Skene, Major, 129
Skene, Philip, 217
Skilman, Mr., 317
Skinner, Stephen, 232
Skinner, Thomas, 297, 315
Skulman, Andrew, 333
Slack, William, 222
Slack, Wm., 222
Slidell, John, 40
Sline, Enos, 108
Slinlang, Abraham, 151
Slough, Matthias, 144
Slover, Isaac, 242
Smith, Abner, 184
Smith, Benjamin, 277
Smith, Capt., 35
Smith, Charles, 202
Smith, Claudius, 6
Smith, Ephraim, 360
Smith, Henry, 53
Smith, Ichabud, 9
Smith, Isaac, 343

Smith, J., 220
Smith, Jacob, 218
Smith, James, 100, 158, 284
Smith, Jesse, 260
Smith, John, 63, 92, 114, 121, 211, 224, 256, 262, 265, 280
Smith, Mrs., 145
Smith, Nehemiah, 164
Smith, Paschal N., 37, 53
Smith, Richard, 49
Smith, Samuel, 165, 192, 259
Smith, Thomas, 94, 138
Smith, Waters, 221, 251
Smith, William, 110, 132, 136, 180, 262, 265, 270
Smyth, Mrs., 331
Snyder, George, 252
Soper, Allen, 218
Southerland, John, 16, 25
Spaldin, Catharine, 274
Sparing, Henry, 346
Sparling, Philip, 2, 5
Spence, James, 134
Spicer, John George, 204
Spragge, Joseph, 59
Springer, Abraham, 269, 270
Springsteen, Cosper, 281
Sproat, David, 335
St. Croix, Capt., 91
Stacy, Joseph, 222, 223
Stagg, John, 33, 107
Stanton, Henry, 363
Stanton, William, 132
Starkey, George, 64
Starn, Jacob, 5
Stebbins, Thomas, 217, 218
Stebin, Oliver, 316
Steel, Joseph, 275
Steele, Thomas, 170
Stephenson, George, 305
Stephenson, John, 105, 154

Sterling, William, 354
Stevenson, Benjamin, 33
Stewart, Alexander, 54, 79
Stewart, Anthony, 358
Stewart, Dr., 262, 265
Stewart, James, 158, 160, 312
Stewart, Mr., 145
Stiles, Jonathan, 88
Stoddard, Israel, 169
Stone, Mr., 340
Storm, Thomas, 355, 356
Stout, Abraham, 117
Stout, Seemer, 116
Stoutenberg, Mr., 369
Stoutenburg, Tobias, 363
Stover, John, 226
Strickland, Capt., 72
Strickland, John, 57
Strong, John, 224
Stupart, George, 259, 270
Sturrup, James, 260
Stuyvesant, Peter/P., 87, 243
Summers, Sylvester, 354
Sutten, John, 199
Suydam, Ferdinandus, 365
Suydam, Mrs., 357
Suydam, R., 364, 365
Swan, George, 203
Swaney, John, 63
Sweedland, Christopher, 181
Swinburn, Hannah, 135
Sydelman, John, 91
Syllia, Lewis, 226
Syze, James, 264
Taggart, Robert, 20
Talmadge, James, 164
Talman, William, 320
Tankard, James, 153
Tanner, John, 135
Tappan, isaac, 259
Tar, William, 239

Tarbitt, Robert, 12
Tate, George, 228
Taylor, Benjamin, 7
Taylor, Capt., 268
Taylor, James, 1, 23, 140
Taylor, John, 260
Taylor, Jonathan, 163
Taylor, Mr., 29, 305
Taylor, Robert, 277
Taylor, Walter, 301
Templeton, Mr., 145
Ten Eyck, Anthony, 25
Ten Eyck, Harmanus, 25
Ten Eyck, Jacob H., 25
Ten Eyck, Richard, 88
Tench, Mr., 278
Tetard, L. G., 125
Thirsby, Richard, 227
Thomas, John, 14, 224
Thomas, William, 7, 276
Thompson Hugh, 124
Thompson, Humfrey, 166
Thompson, Humphrey, 125
Thompson, James, 96, 130
Thompson, Joseph, 226
Thompson, Mr., 1, 21
Thompson, Robert, 280
Thompson, Thomas, 124
Thompson, William, 80, 82, 245
Thomson, David, 268
Thorp, Joseph, 132, 154
Thorp, Stephen, 171
Thorpe/Thorpp, Joseph, 141
Thropp, Joseph, 142
Thurman, Ralph, 142
Tice, Gilbert, 112
Tiley, James, 303
Tillford, William, 165
Tilton, Elisha, 219
Tisdell, Mr., 249
Titus, Samuel, 9, 118

Tod, William, 11
Todd, Catherine, 267
Tolmey, Norman, 306
Tomlinson, Lawrence, 288
Tompkins, Jonathan Griffing/
  Griffin, 178
Ton, John, 86
Tongue, Wm., 221
Tooker, Charles, 77
Totten, Joseph, 253, 254
Townsend, William, 28
Traesey, Eliazer, 194
Traill, George, 206
Trantum, Happy, 369
Trantum, John-Tho's, 369
Tredwell, Samuel, 52
Trimingham, John, 105
Trindle, John, 100
Tripp, James, 93
Truddle, James, 216
Truman, Thomas, 99
Trumbull, Governor, 231
Trumbull, Lieut. Colonel, 245
Tryon, George, 63
Tubbs, Benajah, 205
Tucker, Mrs., 65
Tucker, Thomas, 65
Turnbull, Col., 281
Turner, Mr., 290
Turner, Samuel, 103
Turvey, Nathaniel, 228
Tuthill, Daniel, 107
Tuttle, Stephen, 249
Tweed, James, 301
Tyler, Jacob, 364, 365
Tyler, Jacob, Jr., 367
Udell, Thomas, 307
Ulmer, Philip, 226
Underhill, John, 19, 205
Underhill, Nathaniel, 150
Upham, John, 44

Ure, Andrew, 149
Ustick, Henry, 31, 188, 189
Usticks, Henry, 71
Vail, John, 214
Valantine/Valintine, Isaac, 104
Valentine, Isaac, 239
Valentine, John, 162
Van Brunt, Rutgert, 67
Van Bunschoten, John, 191
Van Buskirk, Lawrence, 131
Van Cortlandt, James, 143
Van Cortlandt, John, 171
Van Dam, Anthony, 360
Van Der Veer, Belirje, 30
Van Der Veer, Cornelius, Jr,, 221
Van Der Veer, John, 30
Van Dervoort, Jacob, 67
Van Dyck, Henry, 182
Van Etten, John, 95, 97, 114, 144
Van Eyck, Anthony, 89
Van Gelder, Abraham, 201
Van Gelder, Collin, 58
Van Horn, Andrew, 336
Van Nostreen, Mr., 317
Van Nurder, Larrey, 336
Van Petta, Philip, 69
Van Phull, Christian, 173, 175
Van Rensselaer, John, 367
Van Rensselaer, John J., 353
Van Rosen, Ryner, 218
Van Schaick, Jacob, 137
Van Schaick, Wessel, 58
Van Veighten, Dircj, 345
Van Vienck, Mr., 58
Van Vlack, Abraham, 103
Van Wincle, Jacob, 245
Van Zant, J. Wynant, 70
Van, Rensselaer, Petter, 367
Vander Velden, Isaac, 102
Vanderhoven, John, 332, 349

Vanderveer, Mr., 246
Vanlieu, John, 42
Vardill, Capt., 217
Varian, Isaac, 205
Varian, James, 6
Varian, Michael, 116
Varian, Richard, 140
Veal, Samson, 26
Vernon, Martha, 54
Verwy, Lawrence, 58
Vicetur, Adam, 126
Vinderburg, John, 73
Vinton, John Harrison, 35
Vredenburg, John W., 116
Wadey, Humphrey, 337
Waldon, Phipps, 161
Waldron, Adolph, 202
Walgrove, George, 246
Walker, Dorcas, 318, 330
Walker, Elizabeth, 318, 330
Walker, James, 118
Walker, John, 13, 15, 167
Walkins, Isaac, 86
Wall, Edward, 153
Wallace, Alexander, 106, 151
Wallace, Andrew, 265
Wallace, Hugh, 106, 151, 165, 299
Wallace, James, 123
Waller, William, 295
Walsh, Edward, 217
Ward, Isaac, 162
Wardrope, John, 146
Warey, Sangrey, 242
Warner, Ely, 77
Washington, George, 218
Waters, Robert, 226
Watkins, George, 260
Watkins, Mary, 241
Watkins, Richard, 242
Watson, Isaac, 226

Watson, John, 123
Watson, Mr., 313
Watson, Ralph, 31
Watson, Rebeccah, 89
Watson, William, 278
Watts, John, 86
Wayman, Moses, 111
Wear, David, 127
Wear, William,, 163
Weaver, Nicholas, 346
Webb, John, 41, 194
Webb, Samuel, 121
Webmore, Charles, 276
Webster, Capt., 91
Weekes, George, 47
Weeks, Gilbert, 184
Weeks, James, 189
Weisner, Frederick, 289
Weissenfels, Frederick, 364
Weldon, Robert, 203
Well, Samuel, 145
Weltner, Col., 349
Wendell, Henry, 116
Weston, Mr., 242
Weston, William, 149
Wetzel, John, 159
Weyman, Hester, 230
Wharton, Joseph, Jr., 133
Wheeler, Ephraim, 363
Wheeler, John, 317
Wheeler, Solomon, 204
Wherton, Jacob, 224
While, Charles, 287
Whiston, Obadiah, 293
White, Alexander, 112
White, Charles, 172, 287
White, David, 247
White, Edward, 229
White, Henry, 297
White, James, 1
White, John, 40, 250, 338

White, Mrs., 227
Whitehead, Capt., 292
Whitman, Jacob, 90, 92
Wickhoff, Nicholas, 34
Wickoff, Henry, 247
Wilcox, John, 339
Wilkins, Jacob, 209, 258
Wilkins, Samuel, 344
Wilkinson, Captain, 18
Wilkinson, Thomas, 73
Willett, Thomas, 55, 56
William, Benjamin, 253
William, Mr., 29
Williams, Charles, 268
Williams, Ezekiel, 63, 218, 236, 240, 247
Williams, Henry, 92
Williams, John, 160, 166, 231, 238, 285
Williams, Richard, 264
Williams, Robert, 55
Williams, William, 288
Williamson, Capt., 288
Willis, John, 92
Willis, Zachariah, 224
Willman, William, 257
Willson, William, 329
Wilmington, John, 20
Wilmot, George, 119
Wilson, Alexander, 362
Wilson, Archibald, 227
Wilson, Luke, 338
Wilson, Samuel, 161, 218
Wilson, William, 348
Winekoop, Lucas, 189
Winten, William, 129
Winterbottom, James, 156, 159
Women, unnamed, 55, 201, 329
Wood, John, 232
Wood, M., 305
Wood, Samuel, 213

Wood, William, 220, 347
Woodhouse, Matthew, 248
Woodhull, Jesse, 6
Woodhull, Nathaniel, 135
Wool, Jeremiah, 129
Wooley, Henry, 188
Wooley, John, 188
Wooly, Jacob, 19
Wooster, David, 174
Wray, John, 301
Wright, Anthony, 236
Wright, Captain, 337
Wright, James, 166
Wright, John, 6, 28, 248
Wright, Richard, 243, 248, 249, 253
Wright, Robert, 193
Wyatt, Lemuel, 91
Wyckhoff, Henry, 209
Yates, Mr., 118
Yates, Mrs., 232
Young, Hamilton, 282
Young, James, 269
Young, John, 138
Young, Zoessennah, 83
Zedtwitz, Herman/H., 151, 156, 159
Zedwitz, Mr., 159
Zeigler, Jacob, 143, 144
Zell, John, 142
Zimmerman, Andrew, 314
Zuntz, Alexander, 313

www.ingramcontent.com/pod-product-compliance
Lightning Source LLC
Chambersburg PA
CBHW071230290426
44108CB00013B/1357